BUSINESS

CAROL CARYSFORTH
MAUREEN RAWLINSON
MIKE NEILD

LEVEL 2

HEINEMANN

Heinemann Educational,
a division of Heinemann Publishers (Oxford) Ltd
Halley Court, Jordan Hill, Oxford OX2 8EJ

OXFORD LONDON EDINBURGH
MADRID ATHENS BOLOGNA PARIS
MELBOURNE SYDNEY AUCKLAND SINGAPORE
TOKYO IBADAN NAIROBI HARARE
GABORONE PORTSMOUTH NH (USA)

First Published 1993

97 96 95 94 93
10 9 8 7 6 5 4 3 2

A catalogue record for this book is available from the
British Library on request

ISBN 0 435 45238X

Designed by Taurus Graphics, Oxon
Printed in Great Britain by Bath Press Ltd, Bath

CONTENTS

ACKNOWLEDGEMENTS

The authors would like to acknowledge personally the co-operation, assistance and support of all those who helped in the writing of this book.

Especial thanks for specialist help and advice are due to Kay Kelly and the Officers of NCVQ, Mervyn Pierson of Artefex, Margaret Berriman for her everlasting support and encouragement and Sheri Hill for her dogged determination to see everything through. We would also like to thank Val Warrilow for allowing us to use copyright material.

A final acknowledgement must go to our collective children - without whom this book would probably have been published several weeks earlier!

The authors and publishers would also like to thank the following individuals and organisations for permission to reproduce photographs and other copyright material:

Alfred Marks, an Adia Company; Alton Towers; ASDA Stores Limited; The Association of British Travel Agents Limited; The Body Shop International plc; British Telecom; British Railways Board; British Heart Foundation; Celltech plc; Citizen Charter Unit; The Creative Company; Forte Hotels (UK) Limited; The Guardian; Heart of England Training & Enterprise Council Limited; Homepride Foods, Michael Manni Photographic; The International Co-operative College; J Sainsbury plc; Ken Randall; MG Owners Club and Rover Cars External Affairs; Morgan Motor Co Limited; Morphy Richards; National Westminster Bank; Nissan, Sunderland; The Office of the Building Societies Ombudsman; Oxfordshire County Council; P & O European Ferries; Peter Hill; Philip Parkhouse; Plain English Campaign; Prudential; Renault; Williams Renault FW15C Cars; Rover 800 series final assembly at Cowley; Rover Learning Business; Saga Holidays; Trades Union Congress Library; Vauxhall; William Grant & Sons Limited, Glenfiddich Distillery; Wyeth Laboratories.

Front cover acknowledgements
Designed by: Tadeusz Kasa
Photogragh by: Image Bank

INTRODUCTION

This book has been written to help you to achieve your GNVQ level 2 award in Business. To be successful you will have to:

- produce a portfolio of evidence which proves you have covered and understand the full range of topics specified for each unit of the award. Four of the units are **mandatory**. This means they are compulsory. Two units are **optional**. You also have to cover three **core skills**
- pass an external test for each unit which is set and marked by your awarding body. The pass mark for this test is 80 per cent.

You have the opportunity of achieving a merit or distinction providing that at least one third of the work in your portfolio meets the criteria for that grade (see under Grading in the Student Guide).

You are strongly advised to read the Student Guide very carefully. This explains

- the layout of the book and how this has been designed to help you
- the methods you can use to collect evidence (and some ideas for practising these)

- how you can achieve a merit or a distinction.
- Core Skills and Personal Skills

Your tutor will give you the remaining information you need, which will include

- the name of your awarding body
- the course content you have to cover - including your option units
- how you must record and store your evidence.

You may find some of the information overwhelming at first - or even confusing. Remember that your tutor is there to help and advise you on any particular points. As you get used to the scheme you will soon find that everything starts to fit into place.

We hope that you will enjoy your GNVQ course and learn much which is interesting and will be of help to you in the future.

Carol Carysforth
Maureen Rawlinson
Mike Neild
July 1993

· THE LAYOUT OF THIS BOOK ·

The four main sections in this book relate to the four mandatory units in the award. The chapters within each section relate to the individual elements you need to cover.

Within each chapter you will find

- **the main text** – which covers all the topics you need to know about

- **activities** – designed to help you to *think* for yourself and work with your fellow students

- **Evidence Collection Points** – opportunities for you to collect evidence for your portfolio. These are numbered consecutively through each chapter. Therefore ECP 10.2 is the second Evidence Collection Point in Chapter 10.

- **Evidence Assignments** – case studies which give you the chance to collect additional evidence as well as prepare you for the type of mini case studies you may find in the external tests. These are numbered as before, but this time the actual assignment is shown as a letter. Therefore Evidence Assignment 3A is in the third chapter and is the first assignment in that chapter.

- **Evidence Checkpoint** – at this stage you should *stop* and check that your work for this element is complete – and of the required standard. Make sure that your tutor agrees with you!

Check that you have entered the details on the recording sheets or log book you are using in your course.

If you have any items still outstanding these should be recorded on your Action Plan with agreed target dates for their completion.

- **Evidence Project** – this is a final piece of work, at the end of each chapter, which covers a wide range of topics within the element you have just studied.

- **Revision Test** – preparation for your external test.

If you work through each chapter, and undertake the activities shown, then you will have enough evidence to prove that you have successfully covered that particular element.

· COLLECTING EVIDENCE ·

There are very many ways in which you can collect evidence. The following is therefore only a guide to the main methods used in this book. If you have never used some of these methods before then you may be uncertain as to what some of the terms mean. Read the explanations below carefully – and return to this section to refresh your memory whenever you wish.

If you wish to practise any of these methods then you can try the 'trial run' exercise(s) mentioned after some of these explanations. This will help you to understand the method described before you try it 'for real'.

Brainstorming

This is a good way of generating new ideas within a group.

- Nominate a group leader.

- For a limited period (about 10 minutes) the group leader should ask for as many ideas as possible.

- Write *all* these down – no matter how wild some of them may seem to be! Don't criticise anyone's ideas at this stage.

- Group ideas together where they overlap – see if there are any 'themes'.

- Rate them in one of three ways: S (sensible); P (possible); F (far-fetched).

- Look at your themes and see how many sensible (or possible) ideas would fit. You should find that as you do this

  – there are ways in which some of the ideas could be adapted

  – you realise that some of the more far-fetched suggestions may be able to be linked to the more sensible ones to give usable suggestions.

Trial run

1 Your group wishes to raise money for a charity. In 15 minutes write down as many ideas for fund raising as you can for the group's nominated charity.

2 In 10 minutes, how many uses can your group find for a paperclip?

Debating

If you have been involved in a debating society at school then you will know that, in a debate, there are two 'sides'. One side is 'for' the issue being debated, the other side is 'against'. A chairperson is in charge of the session. He or she should be impartial (i.e. not take sides) and in the early days this role may be taken by your tutor.

- Prepare your case well – this will mean researching additional information to support your arguments and making sure these are up-to-date.

- Nominate your speaker(s). These should be people who can present the argument well – but during your course everyone should have a turn at this.

- The main speaker for each side should present the team's case, without interruption, for an agreed, limited time. The speaker should stick to the facts but use these to try to persuade the audience that his or her argument

is right. The chairperson will bring the speech to a close if the speaker overruns. Because this may mean important points being omitted, it is important the speaker times his or her speech well.

- After the two main speakers have finished then each side has the right of reply. This may be the main speaker again, or someone else in the team who can think on his or her feet and respond to the arguments which have been given by the opposing team.

- The debate is then thrown open for everyone to discuss – with the chairperson saying who should speak when.

- After a limited time a vote is taken – either for or against the issue (or 'motion' as it is often called).

- You should record yourself the vote taken by the group, and whether this agreed with your own vote. You should note whether the group was persuaded more by the arguments than the facts – and note down the main points which were raised.

Trial run

1 At present you can only vote in local or national government elections if you are over 18. Debate the topic 'People over the age of 16 should have the right to vote'.

2 Debate the topic 'Women are safer drivers than men'.

Interviewing

Interviewing means talking to people to find out information. A good interviewer

- starts by thinking about all the information which he or she would like to find out

- prepares the questions thoroughly and makes sure each point is covered

- asks 'open' questions (which require an explanation), rather than 'closed' questions (which only need a yes/no answer). (See also Core Skills, page 418.)

- asks the questions and *listens* to the answers!

- asks extra questions to clarify certain points or to find out more about an interesting topic

- makes a careful note of the answers

- thanks the people interviewed for their help.

In the early stages you may wish to check your draft list of questions with your tutor. It is also helpful to divide your notepad into two columns for interviews – one side for your questions and the other side for the answers.

Be careful: don't stick rigidly to your prepared questions if the interviewee obviously can give far more useful information in another area. Try to think on your feet! And remember – a good interviewer always lets the person being interviewed do most of the talking.

Trial run

1 Interview one of your fellow students. Find out all you can about what he or she watches on television.

2 Interview a parent or older relative. Find out how this person spent leisure time when your age.

Presentations

Usually you will be asked to do a presentation as a member of a team. If the whole team works together, and supports each other, then this is far less of an ordeal than it may seem! Don't be surprised or worried if you are nervous – this is perfectly normal and, providing you are not too badly affected, it can actually improve your performance!

- Divide up the work of researching for the presentation fairly between the team.

- Work out how long each person must speak so that you don't 'overrun' – either individually or as a group.

- It can be useful to nominate a 'leader' who will co-ordinate the actual presentation and introduce individual members. Everyone should have their turn at this role at some stage.

- Prepare some good visual aids: acetates for an overhead projector; or a model; or booklet; or even a handout. Anything is preferable to nothing!

- Dress smartly in a business like way. No jeans, trainers or T-shirts!

- Be prepared to answer questions on your particular topic from those who are watching you.

- Be prepared to help someone else who is asked a question and is having difficulty thinking of an answer!

Trial run

As a class hold a 'What the Papers Say' session.

Each group chooses a separate newspaper published on the same day. The topic of the presentation is the content of the paper. You could include

- a summary of the main three stories

- an overview of the different type of information and how much there is on different subjects, eg home news, foreign news, business, sport etc

- the type of diagrams, charts and other graphics which are used

- the type of people who might buy or read that paper.

Researching

The first time you do this you may wonder where to start. Guidance is given in this book early in each section as to where you should look. The basic rules are

- get to know your library well – both the one at school or college and the central one in your area. Find out how it works, how the information is stored and methods for finding out about topics other than looking at books. This may, for instance, include searching through a CD-ROM on computer. (See Core Skills Information Technology chapter, page 437.)

- Always be polite and friendly to the library staff. They can be an invaluable source of help if you don't know where to start.

- Remember that some reference material can only be used when you are in the library – so take a paper and pen with you! And beware of becoming so engrossed in other items of interest you take twice as long as you need to find anything out!

- Other sources for research include: your friends, relatives and other people you know, plus local organisations in your area (eg banks, town hall, Citizen's Advice Bureau etc).

- If you have to write for information then make sure your letter is correctly worded, set out in a professional way and prepared on a word processor or typewriter. Remember to enclose a stamped, addressed envelope.

- If you go on a work experience placement then this gives you an ideal opportunity to gain valuable information on the company for which you are working. Remember that you should never take any documents or quote any company information without permission.

Further information on researching is given in the Core Skills Communication chapter, page 371.

Trial run

Choose a famous personality and find out as much as you can about him or her. Ask a librarian which books would be useful. Talk to five people to find out what they know about the person you have chosen. Write a short report and show this to your tutor.

Surveys

How to design a questionnaire and carry out a survey is covered in Core Skills, Application of Number, page 416.

Remember that *analysing* your responses carefully is very important – as this will affect your results.

Writing a letter or a report

This is covered in Core Skills, Communication, pages 362 and 366.

Writing a project

The project at the end of each chapter is the most substantial piece of work you will do for that particular element. It both tests your ability to find out information across the whole range of that element on your own and also gives you the opportunity to work towards achieveing a distinction grade for your portfolio.

You should make sure that your project is well researched, presented properly using proper sections and headings (use the way the questions are grouped or worded as a guide), prepared on a word processor or typewriter and bound properly. The front cover should give the project title, your name and group and the date. A back cover should be added (preferably in card).

If you are including videos or audio cassettes or things you have made (such as promotional materials) make sure these too are clearly labelled and included with your written submission.

Your tutor may give you a special submission date for each project. You must make a careful note of this and make sure you hand the project in on time. It's a good idea to buy a diary – and use it!

Further information on project writing is given in the Core Skills Communication chapter on page 371.

Assessed activities

Your tutor may assess you during other activities. For instance, by observing you during a role play exercise or when you are doing 'real' work, eg dealing with visitors to your school or college. You may be shown a video and asked to prepare a summary. You may be questioned orally from time to time, especially after a presentation.

Assessing yourself

On other occasions you may have to assess yourself *before* your tutor makes a final assessment. For instance, you may be asked to make a tape recording of a conversation and then assess your own performance. Try to do this objectively by listening to yourself as a stranger would. Start by commenting on your performance, then say what you would change, and why, if you repeated the exercise.

· GRADING ·

One of the important features of a GNVQ course is that *you* have to take responsibility for collecting your own evidence and keeping track of this. The more you can prove you are capable of working independently, the more likely you are to achieve a good grade.

To achieve a high grade then you have to show that you can do the following things.

- Draw up a plan of action on your own which shows the tasks you need to carry out, and the order in which you are going to do these.

- Monitor your plan regularly to see whether you need to change your ideas (for instance, if you were relying on information from a company which then refuses to help you).

 If you need your tutor's help to do this then you can only achieve a merit grade. If you can do this on your own then you may achieve a distinction.

- Identify the information you need to fulfil the evidence requirements.

- Identify the sources of suitable evidence and collect this information on your own. If you need your tutor's help to suggest additional sources then you can only achieve a merit grade. If you can choose these on your own – and say why you selected each one – then you may be able to achieve a distinction.

You should also be aware that your tutor will be expecting you to show an increasing depth of knowledge and understanding as you progress on the course. Therefore, you may find that you are producing 'distinction' level work only after the first few months. This is acceptable, providing that in your final portfolio at least one third of the work is at this level.

Joint projects and assignments

You should note that if you are asked to undertake a project or an assignment as a member of a group, then it must be absolutely clear which parts of the final work are your contribution. Many tutors will ask you to include a special page with such a piece of work, which clearly states the contribution of each member and is signed by everyone in the group. This is important so that your work can be assessed accurately for grading.

. CORE SKILLS AND . PERSONAL SKILLS

There are three core skill areas – Communication, Application of Number and Information Technology.

These topics are covered in three special chapters – and there are exercises to help you in these areas.

It is very important that you cover all these areas thoroughly. Some of these can be assessed in the Evidence Collection Points, the Evidence Assignments and the Evidence Projects in the main part of the book. In the case of IT, it may be that you have almost continuous access to a computer, for example in a workshop. If this is the case, make sure you use a computer whenever possible. If your opportunities to use one are more limited you and your tutor may agree that some of the work must be done in a different way. This is acceptable provided that you acquire sufficient evidence of your ability to use a computer as your course continues.

Personal skills refers to your ability to

- take responsibility for yourself and your own self-development, and

- work with others as a co-operative member of the group.

Your tutor will be monitoring your development in these areas and will discuss these with you when you meet for counselling or tutorial sessions.

You may like to note that your ability to prepare a sensible Action Plan, to use this as a guide, revise it when necessary and keep it up to date are good examples of personal responsibility. So too is the ability to complete work before a deadline!

You may also be assessed on your problem solving abilities. In practical terms this means thinking of something different when your first ideas don't work. For instance, if you have difficulties finding a particular item of information or if someone you know will not agree to be interviewed, don't give up at the first hurdle – there are always several other options if you think about solutions positively.

GNVQ courses do expect you to take a considerable amount of responsibility yourself – both for acquiring evidence and storing it neatly – and for keeping track of where you are and what still needs to be done. If you do this properly, you will find that, at the end of the course, you have a portfolio of work of which you can be justly proud. And because of your personal involvement with it, you will easily be able to remember most of the information in it – which will be invaluable for your external tests.

chapter **1** THE PURPOSES AND TYPES OF BUSINESS ORGANISATIONS

Learning Objectives

This chapter is concerned with the purposes of different types of business organisations, the industrial sectors in which they operate and the type of business activities with which they are involved.

After studying this chapter you should be able to:

- explain the types and purposes of different business organisations
- describe and give examples of industrial sectors
- identify local and national business activities.

▪ BUSINESS ORGANISATIONS ▪

In every industrialised country in the world the vast majority of the population go out to work to earn their living. As you travel to school or college you pass people on their way to work, in cars, buses and on trains. It may be that your parents or your sisters and brothers work, or are studying for a qualification – like you – so that they can earn their living in the future.

Virtually everyone you see is employed by one type of organisation or another, although the reasons for the existence of these organisations may vary. The jobs people do are likely to be just as varied – and some even may work for no financial reward.

Activity

1 Below are statements made by six people who work in different organisations. From these, try to identify which person works for:

a a large electronics company

b the Samaritans
c local government
d a hospital
e Marks & Spencer plc
f a solicitor's office.

2 Before you read any further, write down what you consider is the main purpose of each organisation. Keep your sheet carefully for future use.

i 'I've worked in the store for nearly five years but always part-time. At present I'm mainly on the Customer Service Desk but we do move around. The food section is very busy – and if you're on too long it can be hard to concentrate. The pay's quite good and there are lots of facilities for staff, e.g. a hairdresser and chiropodist and subsidised meals.'

ii 'I joined because I wanted to help other people and I work one evening a week. We are only known by our first names and aren't allowed to discuss our calls with anyone. Sometimes some of the calls can be upsetting but if you feel at least one person has benefited it makes it all worthwhile.'

iii 'I started training four years ago and qualified last year.

I now specialise in working with children, which I always wanted to do. Although I don't earn a fortune and sometimes have to work unsocial hours or at Christmas, I do quite enjoy working alternate weekends with free time during the week. I enjoy my job very much – which isn't something everyone can claim to do!'

iv *'I work in a very competitive industry. We try to keep one step ahead of our competitors but it's not easy. I work in the production office and it can be hectic – life seems full of deadlines. If we fall behind our schedules then some of our customers will be disappointed. If people can't buy our goods then I could be out of a job. My security depends on our sales, when all is said and done.'*

v *'I like working for a small organisation though it's sometimes hectic. There are four senior partners and five junior partners in the practice and they all specialise in one way or another. Our clients come for a variety of reasons – because they are buying a house, making a will or need specialist advice.'*

vi *'I work in our local tourist information office. I enjoy this as we get many enquiries every day both from visitors and over the telephone. I've been here for the past year. Before that I worked in the business rates section. That department is responsible for collecting rates from all business premises in this area and sending the total amount collected to the government.'*

THE PURPOSES OF BUSINESS ORGANISATIONS

Businesses can exist for a variety of purposes. Your list above may have included such reasons as:

- **to make a profit**
- **to provide a service to the public**
- **to help others**
- **to promote a special cause.**

You may have listed other reasons, such as to provide good working conditions for employees or to sell as many goods as possible. Indeed, most businesses have several **aims** or **goals**, although there may only be one *main* purpose for their existence.

Making a profit

This is usually the main purpose of businesses that are owned privately – and is essential for the owner(s) to be able to make a living. Someone who starts a small business and invests his or her own money (and takes the risk of losing this if the business doesn't do well) is called an **entrepreneur**. However, many people set up a business not so much to make a fortune, but because they want to be their own boss or because they have redundancy money to invest. Often it may be because they have a good idea and feel that, if they can supply consumers with something they need, and keep their customers happy, then they will have the opportunity to do well.

Business organisations may therefore have other aims besides making a profit. Examples are:

- To provide excellent **customer service**. Unless this is good the business is unlikely to do well.
- To increase their **market share**. This is the number of sales made by a company compared with its competitors (see also Section 4). Many companies aim to increase their market share year by year.
- To **expand and grow** as much as possible. This may mean expansion by selling more goods (see above), or by opening new offices and selling to new markets (e.g. abroad) or by diversifying. Diversifying means making different goods or providing new services.

MAKING A PROFIT

- To be at the forefront of **technological development** – either selling the most up-to-date products or using the latest technology when manufacturing products.

All these are *strategies* a company can use to try to increase its profits. Usually the aim is to increase the number of customers it supplies. However, in a recession some companies may just have to concentrate on survival – doing the best they can to stay in business when times are difficult and demand for their product or service is low.

Evidence Collection Point 1.1

You have just gone into business with a friend, Marsha Yarrow, selling various types of office stationery to the general public. The venture has taken all your savings and you obviously hope to make a profit.

If there is a recession and few people are buying your goods, what can you do to improve your sales?

1 *As a group*, hold a brainstorming session to see how many ideas you can think of. Make an individual copy of the final list the group devises.

2 Go around your town and see if you can find any examples of shops and stores in your area where they have put into practice some of the ideas you have on your list. Make a note of these. See if you can find any other examples to add to the list.

3 Prepare a memo to Marsha, using a word-processor, giving the best three ideas you think would work and justifying your choice in each case. Attach your list so that she can refer to this if she wishes.

Providing a public service

A public service is provided by organisations such as schools and hospitals as well as by the police, fire and prison services, army, navy and so on. In all these cases we, as the public, do not pay directly for the service we receive. Because these services are provided for the good of society as a whole, the money to finance them is collected by the government through taxes. The service is then available free to everyone. This is totally different from the provision of private services (such as those provided by an estate agent or bank) which are charged for as they are used.

Activity

1 How many services can you think of which are provided both publicly and privately?

2 Discuss as a group what you think would happen if people had to pay on delivery for services such as police assistance or calling out the fire brigade – and whether you think this would be a good idea or not. Be prepared to present your arguments to the rest of your class.

The mixed economy

The fact that Britain has organisations which are owned privately and those which are run by the government on behalf of the public means that it has a **mixed** economy. The arguments for having both types of ownership are mainly that:

1 **Private ownership** encourages people to start up in business and work hard. Their aim is to supply what their customers want so that they will make a profit. Unless they sell their goods at a competitive price customers will not buy from them. Therefore private ownership encourages people to work hard *and* means that the price of goods is usually competitive, which benefits the consumer.

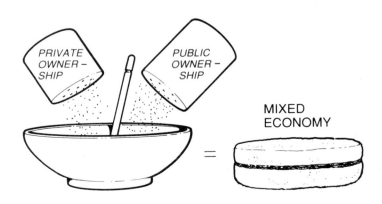

2 Public ownership is needed to provide those services which:

- people would find unprofitable to provide privately (e.g. education on a national scale)
- are considered essential for the well-being of the community (e.g. health care)
- it would be impossible to deliver to only those who pay (e.g. street lighting or defence).

In all these cases there is a social, rather than a profit-making purpose for their existence.

DID YOU KNOW?

Privatisation is the term used when an organisation that has been owned wholly or partly by the government on behalf of the public is transferred into private ownership. Examples include British Telecom, British Gas and British Airways (see page 21).

Helping others and promoting causes

Helping other people and promoting special causes is the role of *charities* – sometimes known as the **voluntary sector**. Charitable organisations do not exist to make a profit in the true sense of the word. Their aim is to raise money for their own particular causes. From this is deducted their own expenditure on administration. Traditionally money was raised by a variety of fund-raising activities, including:

- selling goods
- finding sponsors or people willing to make regular gifts
- holding special events.

Today, however, many charities are run on a more sophisticated basis with professional public-relations staff and fund-raising directors. They advertise in the national press, become involved with Telethon appeals, operate computer mailing lists, and send regular direct mail shots to try to persuade people to support them.

There are over 170 000 charities in Britain, all of which have **trust status**. A 'trust' is a relationship in which a person called a *trustee* is responsible for holding funds or other assets which have been given for the benefit of other people. A charitable or public trust can be set up for one of four reasons:

- for the relief of poverty (e.g. Oxfam)
- for the advancement of education (e.g. an examinations board or a public school)
- for the advancement of religion (e.g. maintenance of a church or other place of worship)
- for other purposes (e.g. conservation or environmental charities such as Nature Conservancy Trusts and Greenpeace).

Most charities have to be *registered* with the Charity Commissioners who, under the Charities Act 1992, have general powers of supervision over their administration and the power to investigate if there is any suspicion about fraud or 'bogus' fundraising.

The structure of a large charity may be as shown in Figure 1.1.

It is important to remember that voluntary organisations must be properly governed and regulated, and keep accurate records, just like companies. If a charity went bankrupt because of incompetence, or if funds were used for non-charitable purposes, the trustees would find that they were both legally and financially liable.

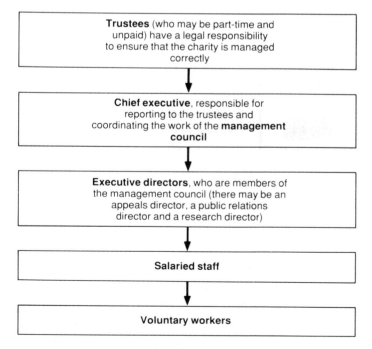

Figure 1.1 *Organisational structure of a large charity*

DID YOU KNOW?

1 Voluntary organisations handled more than £17 billion during 1992.
2 A manager in a large charity may have a budget of more than £50 million each year.
3 Under the Give As You Earn scheme employees can donate a percentage of their salary to a nominated charity. The giver pays only the net amount of his/her donation *after tax* but the charity receives the gross amount.
4 There are more than 5500 charity shops in Britain and over £200 million a year is spent in them. In many cases a local authority or landlord would rather let a charity have an empty shop for nothing (or at a reduced rent) than leave it empty.
5 Working for a charity is a professional career with salaries paid at similar levels to those paid by the civil service or local government.

Evidence Collection Point 1.2

Working in groups of two or three, investigate the work of *either* a local *or* a national charity. Find out:

- how it is organised and the job titles of its senior personnel
- the amount of money it has raised in the last few years
- the ways in which the money was raised.

1 Prepare a short report using a word-processor. Use clear headings to order your information logically.

2 Create a bar chart or line graph (see pages 385–386) to show how donations have changed over the last few years, preferably using a spreadsheet package.

3 Illustrate by means of a pie chart the ways in which money was raised, again preferably using a spreadsheet package.

4 Prepare and deliver a short presentation on your findings to the rest of the class. Your presentation should include a brief numerical analysis of the *percentage differences* in funds raised from year to year.

Note: You will learn more if each group investigates a different type of charity in terms of both purpose and size.

Voluntary workers

Voluntary workers are people who are willing to work without payment. They are not only to be found working for charities, many also work in the public sector. Your local hospital will have voluntary workers who may run a hospital radio station, take round library books or run a coffee shop for visitors. The WRVS is well-known for its work with meals on wheels to help social services departments care for elderly people. Your local school may have people who help on a voluntary basis (e.g. to listen to children reading).

Evidence Collection Point 1.3

By asking either amongst your family and friends or within your school or college, find someone who is (or has been) a voluntary worker. Interview them about their work and then draft a short report on the work they do, the hours they work and why they decided to become a voluntary worker. Prepare your final document on a word-processor.

Evidence Collection Point 1.4

Go back to the sheet you prepared on the purposes of different organisations in the Activity at the beginning of this chapter (see page 1).

1 Use the information you have read since then to update your sheet and amend any information which was wrong. Write it up neatly.

2 Add a short paragraph explaining *why*:

   a the main purpose of private organisation is usually to make a profit, and

   b the main purpose of many public services is often that they are for the good of society as a whole.

• TYPES OF BUSINESS ORGANISATION •

If you walk around your own town or local area you will see many types of business organisation. Some are large and some are small, some provide a service and others manufacture goods, some are one-person businesses and others are more complex. Sorting them out is not as difficult as it may seem.

Some people consider that there are three groups of business organisations in the British economy:

1 private enterprises (which comprise the private sector)
2 public enterprises (which comprise the public sector)
3 those which are either non-profit making or do not distribute their profits in the usual way (and therefore don't really fit either sector).

Figure 1.2 shows the main types of organisation which operate in Britain today.

• SMALL BUSINESSES •

Small businesses are usually **non-corporate organisations**. This basically means that:

● If anything happens to the owner(s) of the business then the business ceases to exist
● The owner can decide, at any time, to stop trading.

There are two types of non-corporate organisations – **sole traders** and **partnerships**.

Sole traders

A sole trader is a person who enters business working for him/herself. He/she puts in the capital to start the

---

PRIVATE ENTERPRISES

1 **Sole traders** – a person is in business on his or her own behalf. The business is usually small, although the sole trader may employ other people as well.

2 **Partnerships** – two or more people own the business between them. Again they may employ other people.

3 **Private limited companies** – have the letters 'Ltd' after the name of the company. Private companies are often family businesses.

4 **Public limited companies** – have the letters 'plc' after their name. These are the largest type of company and the company shares are quoted on the Stock Exchange.

Note: A **franchise** is a small business run with the permission of a larger organisation – see page 14.

PUBLIC ENTERPRISES

1 **Local authorities** – enterprises organised and operated through the local town hall or council offices.

2 **Central government departments** - public enterprises run by the government and administered by government departments (e.g. Department of Health and the National Health Service, Department of Employment and Job Centres).

3 **Public corporations** – run in the same way as large private firms but owned and controlled by the government (e.g. the Post Office, British Rail, British Coal). Remember that in recent years many public corporations have been privatised (i.e. moved into the private sector).

OTHER ORGANISATIONS

1 **Clubs** of many types – usually run by volunteers for the benefit of all members (e.g. your local squash or golf club).

2 **Voluntary organisations and charities** – where the money raised, less administration costs, is spent on a particular cause (e.g. Greenpeace, NSPCC, RSPCA, Oxfam, etc.).

3 **Co-operatives** – some of these are organised for the benefit of the consumer and some (called producer co-operatives) are run for the benefit of the workers. Profits are shared equally among the members.

Note: Building societies used to be run on a non-profit making basis – as Friendly Societies – but now some have become public limited companies and exist primarily to make a profit.

Figure 1.2 *Main types of business organisations*

enterprise, works either on his/her own or with employees and, as a reward, receives the profits.

Sole traders are mainly found in those areas of business where a personal service is desirable (e.g. some retail shops such as newsagents or grocers, window cleaners, hairdressers, decorators, etc.).

Evidence Assignment 1A

*Read the following case study and, **as a group**, discuss the questions which follow. Type out your own set of answers on your word-processor.*

When he left school, Tony Sinclair trained to be a hairdresser. He has worked in three salons since, the latest being the most prestigious and expensive hairdresser's in the town. He has built up his own list of clients who refuse to have their hair done by anyone else and he is now chief stylist where he works. He earns a good salary and excellent tips and gets on well both with his boss and the other employees.

Last month Tony's aunt died and left him £50 000. At the same time he found out that suitable premises for a hairdressing business are for sale on a prime town centre site. He is very tempted to leave his job and start up on his own, especially as he knows many of his customers will follow him.

Tony's friend, Neil, is in favour of this idea and they have talked nearly every night of the advantages of Tony setting up on his own. However, his sister, Paula, who is two years older, is more wary. She has told Tony to think carefully about the scheme. She has pointed out to Tony several disadvantages which could occur if he 'goes it alone'.

Questions to consider

1 What advantages do you think Tony has put forward in favour of the change?

2 What disadvantages do you think Paula has put forward?

3 If you were Tony what would you do – and why?

Compare your answers with Figure 1.3, which shows the advantages and disadvantages of being a sole trader. Note that your answer to question 3 will very much depend on whether you are prepared to be a gambler – and risk your inheritance – or play safe and invest it. If you would be prepared to gamble then perhaps you would be good as an entrepreneur – someone who is prepared to risk his or her own money in the expectation of making a profit.

ADVANTAGES

- Easy to set up – no formal procedures if he/she is using his/her own name (apart from informing the Inland Revenue).
- Can make quick decisions and put plans into effect rapidly.
- Is independent.
- Can keep all the profit.
- Has no-one telling him/her what to do.
- Can provide a personal service to customers.
- Can avoid bad debts (unpaid debts) because he/she knows the customers well.
- Minimum of paperwork (but more if registered for VAT).

DISADVANTAGES

- Long working hours – little time off.
- Earns no money if business closed (e.g. if on holiday or off sick).
- Difficult to raise capital – borrowing is expensive and many banks don't like lending money to sole traders because of the risk involved.
- May be no room for expansion – or part of the house may have to be used for equipment or storage.
- The business may have to be sold on the death of the sole trader and the heirs may be liable for inheritance tax.
- Small-scale enterprises usually have high costs – no economies of scale (compare the amount a small grocer will pay for his stock in comparison with Sainsburys!).
- The flair of the owner may be for the job he did. He may have little, if any, financial expertise or management skills.
- **UNLIMITED LIABILITY**.
  The biggest disadvantage for sole traders is the fact that they have **unlimited liability**. This means that if they lose a substantial amount of money and are declared bankrupt, then they may have to sell off their personal possessions (e.g. house, car, furniture and jewellery) to pay off their debts. In other words, their liability for their debts is not limited to a specific amount.

Figure 1.3 *Advantages and disadvantages of sole traders*

Evidence Collection Point 1.5

1 Visit your local neighbourhood shops and make a list of those that are owned by sole traders.

Remember that a sole trader *may* employ other staff, so don't be put off if your local butcher has two assistants. It is very likely that he is the sole owner of the business.

2 Interview one of the traders you or your family know well, and ask him/her about the advantages and disadvantages of being an own boss.

Compare your interviewee's comments with the chart in Figure 1.3. Make a note of any main differences you found between the advantages and disadvantages listed on the chart and the content of the interview. Say *why* you think these differences occurred.

Type out a report of the interview and your assessment. Don't forget to state who you interviewed, the name and type of business being run, the questions you asked and the answers that were given.

Partnerships

Most partnerships in Britain are **ordinary partnerships**. This means that they also have unlimited liability. An ordinary partnership is easy to set up. Each partner signs a Deed of Partnership which sets out the important details of the future business relationship. This is likely to include:

● the salary of each partner
● the share of the profits of each partner
● the name of the firm.

There are usually between 2 and 20 partners in most firms. You will usually find partnerships amongst the *professions* (e.g. accountants, solicitors, estate agents, doctors, dentists). In some cases more partners are allowed.

DID YOU KNOW?

The term 'firm' is usually used for partnerships whereas the term 'company' or 'organisation' refers only to corporate organisations (see below).

Activity

Imagine that you and a friend go into business as partners. You each invest £10 000. Ten years later you are doing well and your investment in the company has risen to £45 000 each. Your partner, who has recently married, dies and you find that he has left all his money to his wife. She claims his share – £45 000.

As a group, decide your answers to the following:

1 What would be the effect on you, and your business, when you paid the money you owe?

2 Is there any action either you or your partner(s) could have taken to prevent this happening?

See if you can decide what happens before you read it later!

Advantages of partnerships

1 Because each partner is expected to bring some money into the business, the partnership as a whole has more capital with which to operate.
2 Problems can be shared and discussed by everyone, and a variety of solutions may then be put forward.
3 New ideas and skills can be introduced.
4 The business affairs are still private.
5 The responsibility no longer rests with one person. It is therefore possible for the partners to take holidays and have free weekends – or even be ill – without worrying about the business.
6 Partners can specialise in their own fields. For example, solicitors can have someone specialising in conveyancing (buying and selling houses), divorce, criminal law, business law etc.

DID YOU KNOW?

The term **specialisation** is used when a person concentrates on a particular aspect of their job. Another term you may see is **division of labour**. This is when each person is responsible for a particular job, process or even a part of a process. The aim is to develop and use a person's skill and talent to the full to increase both quality and volume of production.

Activity

Imagine you work in a factory doing a very repetitive job. *As a group*, discuss what you consider are the *disadvantages* of division of labour for the employees.

Evidence Assignment 1B - Part 1

Read the following case study. Then, as a group, discuss the questions which follow.

Jane, David and Saika became partners six months ago when they opened an employment agency. Each of them knew personnel officers in various companies in the area and felt sure that they could use these contacts to get to know about job vacancies in the area. They advertised in the local paper so that people who wanted jobs would also contact them. In the early months everything went well – several people were found permanent jobs and a register of temporary staff was set up. These were people willing to work for companies at short notice for a few days or weeks.

Lately, however, there have been problems. The business has been struggling as many companies have been making employees redundant, rather than taking them on, and both the number of vacancies and the number of callers into the office have dwindled. At the weekly meeting there have been more and more disagreements.

- Jane and Saika wanted to spend more money on advertising their business, both by sending leaflets to companies and putting adverts in the local paper. David said they couldn't afford this.
- Saika had recently purchased a fax machine without consulting either of the others. While the cost of this was not great, and the fax would be invaluable, Jane objected, on principle, to the fact that she was not consulted beforehand.
- David, who was learning how to drive, had started arranging his lessons during office hours. Both of the others objected to this.

At the last meeting they agreed that the business was desperately short of capital. Jane had said that her father was prepared to invest £5000 in the business – but only if he could be a sleeping partner. Neither of the others knew what this meant.

As a group, discuss:

1 Whether or not the partners should spend more on advertising. Think of *both* the advantages *and* the disadvantages of doing this.

2 Your views on Saika's action in buying the fax machine.

3 Whether David should be allowed to take his driving lessons during office hours.

On a more general level, consider:

1 What partners could do if they began to disagree about how to run the business.

2 What they could do if a partner became unreliable, or took actions without consulting the others.

3 What they should do if a partner was lazy or incompetent.

4 If you know the difference between an active partner and a sleeping partner (if not, see page 10).

Type your answers on your word-processor and save them on disk. You will be asked to retrieve them later to edit them before printing out.

Partnership agreements

Because partners are all jointly responsible for the business, the actions of each of them affects the others. Therefore acting irresponsibly could jeopardise the business and bring the other partners into debt (remember they all have unlimited liability). Other problems can include disagreements, death of a partner or bankruptcy. Any of these may mean the termination of the partnership.

To prevent problems in case this happens, many partners draw up a **partnership agreement** to clarify matters which may cause a disagreement later. Although this document is not legally necessary, its existence may prevent problems occurring during difficult times. It is likely to include such points as:

- how the profits (or losses) should be shared
- what will happen to any assets if the partnership is dissolved
- the circumstances under which a partner could be asked to leave (e.g. what would be considered to be professional misconduct).

DID YOU KNOW?

The reason most partnerships are to be found in the professions is that, in many cases, the rules of the professional association may demand that the partners have unlimited liability. This is because it is believed that certain professional people (e.g. doctors, solicitors and accountants), should be seen to be fully committed to their clients (even including their own personal finances) – usually because the results of negligence could be very severe. However, professionals take out insurance to cover the most risks.

Death or retirement of a partner

The death or retirement of a partner can cause severe financial problems for the continuing partner(s) as they may have to find the money to 'buy out' the other partner or anyone who would receive his or her share on death. It is therefore usual for the partnership to make sure that each partner has taken out life assurance which can then be used to pay the family of a deceased partner. Some policies will pay out an amount when the holder has reached a certain age, and this money can be used to buy out a partner who is retiring.

DID YOU KNOW?

Most partners in a business are **active** partners – that is, they take an active part in the running of the business. A different type of partner is a **sleeping** partner. This partner invests money in the business but does *not* take an active part. Usually he or she will therefore receive a smaller share of the profits than the active partner(s).

Limited partnerships

These are quite rare in Britain. In this case, as well as ordinary partners (who have unlimited liability) there is one or more partner who has limited liability. This means that their liability for the debts is limited to the amount they have invested in the business.

Having this option can be useful for people who want to participate in a partnership but are unwilling to risk their personal possessions. However:

- there *must* be at least one ordinary partner with unlimited liablity
- the limited partner *must* be a sleeping partner.

Evidence Assignment 1B – Part 2

Recall the answers you saved on disk for the first part of this assignment on page 9. Amend any that were wrong and add any information that was missing. Print out a final version of your work.

· BIGGER BUSINESSES ·

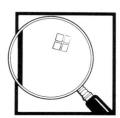

Evidence Assignment 1C

Read the case study which follows and prepare your answers to the questions in Section 1. Then read the information given on private limited companies on page 11 before attempting Section 2.

Paul Makin and Andrea Wright have worked together for several years as computer consultants. They are both employed by a large national computer company and are based in Bristol. However, over the last twelve months they have both been concerned that their career prospects are very limited and they can see several opportunities for their services in the area which they feel their present employer is ignoring.

After much consideration they have decided to go into business together. They have each saved £6000. They think this may be enough capital for them to rent a small office and start up on a small scale. They now have to decide what form of business would be the most appropriate; i.e. whether to be a partnership or to form a private limited company.

Section 1

1 What other expenses do you think Paul and Andrea will have to meet besides their rent? Write down what you consider would be a realistic figure for each expense for a year. (You may need to interview one or two people who regularly pay bills before you can do this!) Add the figures to find the total amount required.

2 Do you think £12 000 capital will be enough? If not, where do you think they can go for additional money and how much do you think they will need?

3 What will be the main disadvantages to them if they go into business as a partnership?

4 Do you think there would be any advantages to them if they formed a private limited company?

DID YOU KNOW?

The term **capital** is used for the money the owner(s) put into the business. This can then be divided into:

- **fixed capital** (used for assets which last a long time, e.g. office furniture and equipment)
- **working capital** (the money used for day to day expenditure and buying stock).

If a company spends too much on fixed assets and leaves itself short of working capital, it is rather like buying an expensive car and not being able to afford any petrol, or buying an expensive house and having nothing left to pay for food!

Section 2

5 If you were Paul and Andrea, what name would you give the company?

6 Why will they not be allowed to choose the same name as another organisation?

7 Who do you think will be the directors of their company?

8 If their authorised (allowed) capital, with their savings and the money they borrow, is £15 000, and they each hold 50 per cent of the shares, what is the maximum amount each of them could lose if the company went into liquidation?

9 What would happen to their company if a major disaster occurred in six months' time and both Paul and Andrea were killed in a car crash?

10 If Paul had saved more than Andrea, and owned 60 per cent of the shares, what difference, if any, would this make?

Private limited companies

A company differs from a partnership or a sole trader in two ways:

1 All shareholders in companies are protected by **limited liability**. A shareholder is someone who invests money in a company – he or she buys a 'share' in it. The company can be sued for its debts but the amount the shareholders owe is limited to the amount they spent when they bought their shares.

2 A company is known as a **corporate body**. This means that it has a separate legal identity. It can:

- employ staff
- sue people and be sued (if you hurt yourself in your local newsagent's you would sue the shopkeeper; if you hurt yourself in Debenhams you would sue the *company*, not the manager!)
- own property.

In addition, if all the shareholders died the company would still exist until it was formally wound up.

A company is run by the **directors**, who are also usually the major shareholders. There is no limit to the number of shareholders, but in a small organisation these may be just the members of a family. At a meeting, each shareholder has **one vote per share** – large shareholders can therefore out-vote those with fewer shares. For that reason, the balance of shares (and the balance of power) in a small company can be important.

In a private company, shareholders must remember that:

- shares can only be transferred to someone else by agreement of *all* the shareholders
- shares cannot be sold to the general public.

DID YOU KNOW?

A new business is not allowed to trade under the same name as an existing company if there is likely to be any confusion to suppliers or customers. This is to stop a rogue organisation trading under false pretences by using the name of a reputable organisation.

Activity

Companies always give their registered office address on their company letter headed paper (often at the foot of the page). You should note that no matter how many regional branches an organisation may have, *one* address will be its registered address – i.e. the one listed on its Memorandum of Association.

Look at documents you or your parents have received at home from companies. Try to obtain at least two examples of letter headings which show a registered office address, and preferably a branch office address as well.

DID YOU KNOW?

The letters 'Ltd', which are found at the end of the name of a private limited company, stand for the word 'Limited'. Originally they were intended to be a warning to **creditors** (people to whom the company owes money). Because liability is limited, creditors are being warned that if the company goes into liquidation they may not get their money back!

· LARGE BUSINESSES ·

Evidence Assignment 1D

Read the case study below before discussing the questions which follow. Then type your answers on a word-processor.

Five years later Paul and Andrea are doing very well indeed. They have four offices and employ 52 staff. There are six directors. Paul and Andrea still retain control with 35 per cent of the shares each. The other three directors each own 10 per cent of the shares.

Over the years they have ploughed back the profits into the business and borrowed money from the bank to finance their growth. Their total capital is now £120 000. All of the directors have ambitious plans to expand the organisation even further – and preferably quite quickly. However, to do this they would need to borrow even more money. At this week's board meeting they are discussing the advantages of asking the bank for a further loan or 'going public'. In this case they would apply to become a public limited company so that they could sell shares to the general public, and raise a lot more capital.

Paul is worried about the idea of becoming a public company as this will mean issuing and selling shares outside the company and therefore, to some extent, losing control. Large investment companies could buy many shares in their company and therefore have votes on how it is run. The company will have to publish its accounts every year, there will be more formal procedures to be followed, and the shares will be quoted on the Stock Exchange.

Andrea is against the idea of borrowing from a bank. She thinks that interest rates may go up, so that they would have to pay a lot of money to the bank on top of the money they have borrowed. She also knows that the bank won't lend them more than £20 000 – and this is not enough to finance the planned expansion programme. She gives the meeting several examples of small, successful companies which have become public companies to attract the capital they need to expand (e.g. Body Shop and Richard Branson's organisation, Virgin).

The meeting adjourns for one week, during which time all the directors must consider how they will vote on the issue.

As a group:

1 Draw up a list of advantages and disadvantages of 'going public'. Read other books besides this one to help you to compile your list!

2 Why do you think large institutions (e.g. banks and investment companies) and members of the public might be willing to buy shares in the company?

3 Look on the financial pages of a daily newspaper. Prepare a line graph charting the share movements of four large organisations for a week (preferably using a spreadsheet package).

   ● Are the share values going up or down?
   ● Are they all moving in the same direction? If so, discuss with your tutor why this is the case.
   ● How many reasons can you think of why shares fluctuate in value?

4 If Paul and Andrea go public, what letters will their company have after its name?

5 Assume your group is the board of directors. Debate the issue of whether to go public or not. Summarise both the conclusion of the debate and your own views.

DID YOU KNOW?

1 Not every company can 'go public'. There are certain requirements of companies which must be met before their shares can be traded on the Stock Exchange. For instance, they must have a minimum of £50 000 in capital.

2 **Flotation** is the term used to describe a private company becoming a public limited company.

▪ WHO OWNS A COMPANY? ▪

Limited companies are owned by their shareholders – those people (individuals and institutions) who invest their money in shares issued by the company. The total amount of those investments provides the capital to finance the different business activities which the company undertakes – although additional capital may be borrowed.

A proportion of the profits is distributed to shareholders in the form of a **dividend**, usually paid every six months (see Figure 1.4).

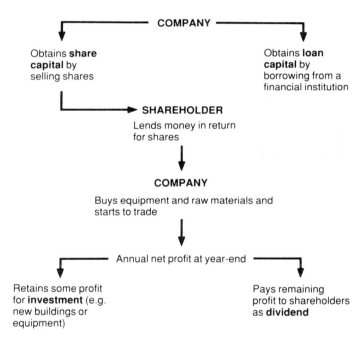

Figure 1.4 *The capital of public limited companies*

Shareholders buy shares:

● in the hope that they will increase in value
● to receive the dividend.

Each shareholder has one vote for each ordinary share he or she owns. This right to vote may be used at the Annual General Meeting but, in reality, unless a great number of shares are owned there is little hope of a shareholder influencing the activities of the directors – those salaried employees who actually control the company on a day-to-day basis (see Figure 1.5).

Type of organisation	Number of owners	Capital	Control	Transfer of ownership	Profits	Debts
Sole trader	1	Little required to start. Obtaining more for expansion may be difficult	Owner has full control	By sale of business	Kept by the owner	Unlimited liability means owner personally responsible for debts up to limits of personal wealth
Partnership	2–20	Provided by all partners	Shared by partners	By consent of all partners	Shared according to partnership agreement	Joint unlimited liability to limits of personal wealth
Limited partnership	2–20	Provided by all partners	Only general partner(s) can manage	By consent of all partners	Shared according to partnership agreement	General partner has unlimited liability. Limited partner only liable to amount of capital invested
Private limited company	2 or more	Provided by shareholders	Directors have control. Directors also often shareholders	By consent of all shareholders	Shared by shareholders	Limited liability means shareholders only liable to amount invested
Public limited company	2 or more	Must have minimum £50 000 on formation provided by shareholders	Directors, appointed by shareholders, control day-to-day running of business	Shares freely tranferable	Profits paid as dividends to shareholders	Limited liability for all shareholders

Figure 1.5 *Comparison chart of business organisations*

DID YOU KNOW?

In private limited companies, which are often family businesses, the directors are usually members of the family. They are *also* the shareholders. In contrast, in a public limited company the shareholders are normally large institutional investors with large amounts of money to invest (e.g. pension funds and insurance companies). Even after privatisation, shareholders who are ordinary members of the public are still in a minority in Britain.

MIXING SMALL AND LARGE BUSINESSES – FRANCHISES

DID YOU KNOW?

The Body Shop, Benetton, Spar, Kentucky Fried Chicken, BSM, Wimpy and Pizza Hut have something in common. They are all retail *franchise* operations – operated by individual owners who are allowed to use the trade name and business appearance of a larger organisation.

Franchise operations

Franchises are a relatively new form of business and have grown enormously in Britain over the last ten years. The aim is to enable a person to run his or her own small business and yet have the security and expertise of a large, national (or international) organisation behind them.

The person who operates the business is the **franchisee**. He or she has to organise and carry out the business in the way determined by the **franchisor** – the organisation which controls the product or service being sold. Most of the capital has to be raised by the franchisee who will then be keen to work hard and make a success of the business. He or she has to pay an initial licensing fee plus a share of the profits to the franchisor for the use of the trade name. In return the franchisee often has exclusive rights to a specified area (e.g. only one shop per town) as well as expert advice and help from the franchisor.

In some operations franchisees may sell direct to the public (e.g. Tupperware reps) *or* be allocated the franchise by an organisation which provides its own service to the public (e.g. a hospital, hotel or leisure centre). In this case the franchisee is given permission to run a shop on the site of the main organisation. For example a hotel may have a florist's, hairdresser's, newsagent's and chemist in its main foyer – the hotel will be the franchisor and will charge the franchisees for the right to operate their businesses on its premises.

Franchises in Britain are overseen by the British Franchise Association (BFA) which operates a code of conduct for its members.

In 1992 there were nearly 19 000 retail franchise outlets employing nearly 190 000 people. Their annual sales were more than £5 billion, and are expected to be nearer £20 billion by the year 2000.

DID YOU KNOW?

Franchise operations are not restricted to the retail trade. Others are operated by manufacturers. The most well known example is in the soft drinks trade. Coca Cola, Pepsi Cola and Seven-Up all franchise the bottling and canning of their drinks to independent companies.

International franchises

With the growth of the Single Market many European companies are setting up franchise operations in Britain. An example is Delifrance, which specialises in French pastries and bread. The pastries are prepared and frozen in France and transported to franchisee outlets for baking. Foreign franchisor organisations are nothing new – the Spar operation is based in the Netherlands yet there are nearly 2500 retail Spar shops in the UK, and have been for many years.

Evidence Collection Point 1.6

1 The failure rate for franchise operations is less than half that for ordinary small businesses. Why do you think this is the case?

2 Your friend Dominic is thinking of starting up in business. You think a franchise would be a good idea. He thinks not – he says he would only be a 'manager' as he would not have the freedom to run his business his own way, but would have to follow the instructions laid down by the franchisor.

In a brief letter to him, produced on a word-processor, give your comments on his views and state why you are in favour of a franchise operation.

3 Discuss as a group and then list the advantages to:
   a a hospital,
   b a large organisation (e.g. Prontoprint or Tie Rack) of operating as a franchisor.

WORKING TOGETHER – CO-OPERATIVES

All co-operatives exist to provide mutual benefits for their members. There are several different types of co-operatives, including:

1 **Retail co-operatives** – which are owned by the consumer
2 **Producer co-operatives** – which are owned and controlled by the people who work there. The enterprise provides them with employment.

Retail co-operatives

The co-operative movement was founded in the mid-1840s by a group of textile workers in Rochdale. Their aim was to be able to buy foods and other necessities and sell these more cheaply. At that time mill owners could operate a shop in or near the mill and charge high prices on the basis that the workers had no choice but to buy from them. The Rochdale Pioneers (as they were called) had the idea of joining together, buying goods and then selling them to members of their movement without adding on any profit. At the end of the year any surplus was to be distributed amongst the members (i.e. those who had bought from them all year).

Activity

Before you read any further, answer this question – if you had been one of the Rochdale Pioneers how would you have distributed the surplus? Equal shares to everyone or a different system? Discuss your ideas with the rest of your group before you read on.

The principles of co-operation

The International Co-operative College

The principles of co-operation are the same for all co-operative institutions:

- Anyone can be a member.
- Each member has only one vote (compare this with the shareholder of a public limited company).
- A fixed interest rate is paid on capital invested.
- The members decide how any profits are distributed. Distribution should be fair and reasonable, for the benefit of the business, for the members or for the community.
- The organisation should also be concerned with educational and social issues (e.g. members' personal development).
- All co-operatives should work and co-operate with each other.

DID YOU KNOW?

The Rochdale Pioneers decided to distribute any end-of-year surplus to the members *in proportion to the amount they had spent on goods that year.*

In this way, those who spent the most money would receive the largest return.

The retail co-operative movement today

The retail co-operative movement went from strength to strength until the late 1960s. Goods were supplied by the Co-operative Wholesale Society (CWS) to the retail shops which ensured a constant supply at a reasonable price.

Problems were encountered because:

- Resale price maintenance ended. This meant that instead of goods having to be sold at a price specified by the manufacturer, there could be 'price wars' between supermarkets. The co-ops found it difficult to compete *and* pay their members a dividend.
- Most retail co-operatives were corner shops, so managing dozens of these from an area office proved difficult – especially for managers who had received little professional training.
- Because the profits were given back to the members at the end of each year there was insufficient money to finance expansion or change.
- Social changes occurred which altered people's life styles and shopping habits.

Evidence Assignment 1E

*Read the two stories below. Then, **as a group**, list all the social changes you can find which are illustrated in the stories. Prepare an individual summary of these on a word-processor. Finally, indicate which of these may have contributed to the demise of the small, corner co-ops, and in what way.*

March 1952

Sarah rushed out of the house holding the ten shilling note carefully. She chanted the list of things she needed to herself as she ran to the co-op on the corner. Her mother bought all their groceries from the local co-op so that they could benefit from the dividend. Because prices were the same in every shop the co-op actually worked out cheaper because all the customers received some money back at the end of every six months. It was also essential that they shopped locally as they couldn't afford a car. Sarah's mother also shopped very frequently as otherwise perishable food would go off.

Sarah knew their dividend number off by heart – 54381. When she bought the things her mother wanted and said the number it was written on a special form, with the amount she had spent. She took a copy of this form home and the 'master copy' went to the main Emporium in town so they could calculate how much dividend was due for the goods her mother had bought. Normally the money was used for special things – this year Sarah was 11 and the money had gone to help to buy her uniform for her new school. Really it was her mother's way of saving. This was important as her mother didn't go out to work and they only had her father's wage to live on.

Sarah opened the door of the co-op and was immediately greeted by Mr Skinner, the friendly manager. He had been with the co-op since he left school and knew all his customers well. He took pride in the fact that all his customers regularly left their weekly orders with him and that he made them up personally and had the delivery boy get them out the same day. He lifted the cheese from the special cheese slicer and carefully put it under cover – then he turned to Sarah to see how he could help her.

March 1992

Sarah rushed out of work at 5 p.m. aware that she had very little food in the house and six people coming for supper. She had searched both the fridge and the freezer in vain that morning, but without any luck. Usually she only shopped in bulk, once a month, as like many other mothers she also worked full-time so had little time to spare for shopping.

She drove as quickly as she could to the supermarket she used regularly. Although it was about three miles out of her way she liked the range of goods they stocked, thought their prices were competitive, and knew where everything was – which saved precious time.

She grabbed a trolley and quickly collected the things she needed. Virtually everything was prepacked and easy to find. She had to queue for a while at the check-out as the girl was new and rather slow. Sarah's turn eventually came and she decided to pay by Access, as her bank account was running rather low that month.

At the supper party, later that evening, the conversation turned to shopping. One person, Mark, was quite keen on the co-op supermarket in another part of town, though he remarked that it was a pity they didn't offer dividends any more – but agreed people had more sophisticated ways of saving their money these days.

Producer co-operatives

Imagine a situation where you and a group of your friends want to set up in business together. You all want to work hard and make money but no-one wants to take charge. You all want to be equals, with an equal share of any profits you make. What do you do?

One answer would be to start a producer or worker's co-operative with the same principles of co-operation as shown on page 16. When you investigate you find that:

1 There are several producer co-operatives in existence, and some very successful ones indeed in Europe.
2 You can form a limited company and so have the protection of limited liability.
3 All the workers can be involved in decision-making.
4 Jobs can be rotated. Everyone can take turn at work that is pleasant and at work that is dirty or boring.
5 It does not matter if not all the workers are members – it is up to you to decide.

You therefore think it rather puzzling when you find out that in Britain worker co-operatives have never been as successful as those abroad. You decide that you need to find out more.

DID YOU KNOW?

Some worker co-operatives are the result of a **worker buyout**. This is when the owner of a business wants to sell and the enterprise is bought by the employees. In some cases, if a business is in difficulties, the employees may buy it to save their jobs – especially if they think they can run it better. They may decide to run this as a co-operative, or as an ordinary private limited company.

Even more common are **management buyouts**. In this case the *managers* of a business which is under threat of closure buy it from the existing owner. This may happen if a large company decides to sell or close down small subsidiary companies which have not been particularly successful. The managers may feel that they know enough to turn the business around and make it successful, if they can run it in their own way.

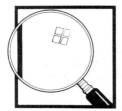

Evidence Assignment 1F

Imagine you work for the producer co-operative described below. Read the questions and then prepare your answers as a report on producer co-operatives. If possible, use a word-processor.

WORKERS UNITED – A PRODUCER CO-OPERATIVE

Workers United was formed in 1988 by a group of ten women who had either been made redundant in the last two years or who were trying to find a job after being at home with their children. They had decided to form a producer co-operative with no-one in overall charge so that the profits could be shared by them all. They decided this would make everyone work harder, as they all had an interest in how much money was made. The co-operative had been quite successful, despite a few setbacks, and now 16 people worked there.

In the beginning the co-operative had struggled for recognition. The local banks hadn't wanted to lend them any money and all their suppliers had wanted to be paid before they would make a delivery – mainly because they distrusted the set-up of a co-operative and didn't want to deal with a company which didn't have a manager. Eventually they had obtained a loan from a special fund after obtaining help and advice from their local authority (see page 24) – but knew they may have serious problems raising additional finance in the future.

Actually the co-op seemed to work quite well apart from one or two internal disputes. A system of job rotation was in operation, so that everyone had the chance to do both the boring and the interesting jobs. The problem was that some people were better at some things than others, especially in relation to the office work and book-keeping. The same difficulties arose when a decision had to be made. Some members were forceful, intelligent and decisive and were apt to dominate the others at the regular weekly meetings. In some cases it had taken several weeks before everyone was roughly in agreement, and even then there were often complaints afterwards by those who felt that their views had not been considered.

Another problem was that no-one felt they had the right to tell other people what to do. When someone was thought to be slacking or was persistently late, there were no formal disciplinary procedures to be followed.

However, last week a serious problem had arisen. A group of workers had been investigating the idea of buying a new type of machine which would produce goods more cheaply and more quickly. The enterprise could benefit from technological development and stay competitive. However, others feared that this machine might put some members out of work, as there was a limited market for their goods. There seemed to be a clear split between those who thought the machine should be bought and those who wanted to protect jobs.

1 What advantages and disadvantages do you feel there are in being a member of a worker co-operative as opposed to being an employee in an ordinary company?

2 List all the reasons you can think of why worker co-operatives may fail.

3 If you were a member of Workers United, what would you suggest to help them overcome each of their problems and yet still retain the principles of co-operative membership?

4 Divide into two groups. Group A should prepare arguments to defend the purchase of the new machine. Group B should prepare arguments to defend jobs. Debate the issue and reach a conclusion. Write up both arguments and the conclusion neatly.

• THE PUBLIC SECTOR •

The public sector refers to those organisations which provide goods or services and are owned by the government. These may be:

● run by central government departments (e.g. hospitals which are run by the Department of Health or Job Centres which are run by the Department of Employment)
● owned by local government and administered through your local town hall or county hall (e.g. leisure centres and libraries)
● public corporations or nationalised organisations which are owned by central government but run like private organisations to make a profit (e.g. British Coal, British Rail and the Post Office).

The cost of the goods and services provided by the public sector varies. They may be:

- free (e.g. borrowing library books, asking for advice in the Job Centre)
- offered at a reduced price (e.g. the entrance fee to a swimming pool may be subsidised by the local authority)
- offered at the market price (e.g. coal, train tickets and postal services).

Services provided by the state

Probably the most famous state service is the National Health Service which provides medical care for the people of Britain through hospitals, health centres and family doctors. However, this is not the only service provided by the government. Indeed the state has a wide range of responsibilities and provides a great number of services to both private citizens and businesses. Some of these are provided by **central government** (administered by Whitehall) and others by **local government** (administered by your town hall).

▪ CENTRAL GOVERNMENT SERVICES ▪

The policies of central government are determined by the political party currently elected to run the country. Since 1979 Britain has had a Conservative government, firstly with Margaret Thatcher as Prime Minister, followed by John Major.

The **Cabinet** consists of the Prime Minister and his or her chosen ministers and usually has about 21 members. Many of the cabinet ministers are responsible for the activities which take place within their own departments. For example the Home Secretary is responsible for the Home Office, the Secretary of State for Trade and Industry is responsible for that department, and so on.

Each department has its own budget and has to submit its spending plans to the **Treasury** each year. Each department is responsible for providing a range of services.

Through their policies and activities some departments have a direct influence on business organisations, others concentrate mainly on providing services to the general public.

DEPARTMENT	RESPONSIBILITIES
HM Treasury	Plans and supervises the spending of all government departments, local authorities and public corporations. Advises the government on economic policy and puts this into effect.
Ministry of Defence	Administers the armed forces and the implementation of defence policy.
Department for Education	Coordinates full-time education up to the age of 16, plus further and higher education for those over that age.
Department of the Environment	Links with local authorities on local planning and inner cities. Responsible for conservation and environmental protection, including energy efficiency.
Export Credits Guarantee Department	Assists UK exports by providing export credit insurance to British exporters as well as guaranteeing repayment to British banks which provide finance for exports.
Employment Department Group	Employee rights, Health and Safety (by liaison with the Health and Safety Commission), pay and equal opportunities, Training and Enterprise Councils, local and regional employment policies.
Department of Transport	Airports, coastguards, motorways and trunk roads, road safety legislation, and licensing of vehicles.
Department of Trade and Industry	Promotes UK exports, gives information and advice to small firms, responsible for company legislation, consumer safety and protection and competition policy. Promotes the use of new technology.
Foreign and Commonwealth Office	Operates diplomatic missions and embassies worldwide to promote British interests and protect British citizens abroad.
Department of Health	Responsible for the operation of the National Health Service and the supervision of social services provided by local authorities.
Department of Social Security	Responsible for the operation of the social security and benefits system (e.g. child benefit, family credit, income support and the social fund).
Home Office	Responsible for the police, probation and prison services and immigration policy.
Ministry of Agriculture, Fisheries and Food (MAFF)	Responsible for policies on agriculture (including EC policies), plants, fisheries and forestry as well as food regulations.
HM Customs and Excise	The collection and administration of customs and excise duties and Value Added Tax.
Board of Inland Revenue	Administers and collects direct taxes – mainly income tax and corporation tax (paid by companies).
Department of National Heritage	Responsible for broadcasting, films, libraries, sport and tourism. Will oversee the national lottery when introduced.

Figure 1.6 *Government departments*

Evidence Collection Point 1.7

1 Examine the table in Figure 1.6 and state, for each department, whether the services are mainly provided for the government itself, businesses, the general public – or a mixture of these.

2 Try to find out the name of the current Minister of each department and type these as a list. Bear in mind that the Chancellor of the Exchequer is the head of HM Treasury.

DID YOU KNOW?

1 The letters HM stand for Her Majesty.

2 The First Lord of the Treasury is the Prime Minister – although he or she does not take part in the day-to-day activities of that department.

Raising the money and spending the money

The money to provide government services is raised in two ways:

- by taxation - both **direct** taxes (e.g. income tax or corporation tax) and **indirect** tax (e.g. VAT)
- by government borrowing – from the general public (e.g. the sale of National Savings certificates and Premium Bonds) and from financial institutions.

The way in which the government raises and spends its money affects *you* – firstly as a *taxpayer* when you go to work, and secondly as a *user* of government services.

Evidence Collection Point 1.8

1 The pie chart in Figure 1.7 shows how the government raises its money.

a List these sources of revenue in order, with the highest one at the top of your list.

b What is the difference between corporation tax and income tax?

c What is the total income of the government for the year in question?

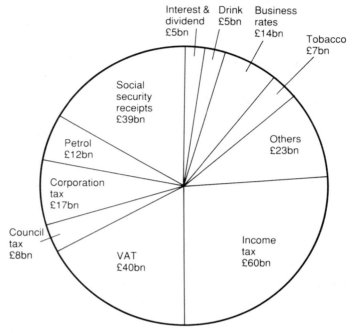

Figure 1.7 *Sources of government finance*

2 During the same year assume that the government plans to spend its money as follows:

Social security £65bn (billion = one thousand million)
Health £30bn
Defence £24bn
Scotland, Wales and Northern Ireland £27bn
Education £10bn
The Home Office £7bn
Employment £4bn
Transport £6bn
Agriculture £3bn
Trade and industry £3bn
Environment £39bn
Other £29bn

a Prepare a pie chart (similar to the one in Figure 1.7) to show how the money was spent, preferably using a spreadsheet package.

b How much is the government spending in total?

c How will the government raise the difference between the amount you calculated in (1) above and the amount it plans to spend?

d Look back to the chart on government departments

(Figure 1.6) and find out what the Home Office will spend its money on.

e If you were the government would you spend your money this way? *As a group*, discuss any changes you would wish to make and be prepared to say why you would like to make them. Type out your conclusions.

· THE PRIVATISATION ISSUE ·

Since 1979/80 the government has had a policy of selling off industries which were publicly owned, to private shareholders. Over 20 companies have now been sold, including British Telecom, British Aerospace, British Gas, British Steel, British Airways and Rolls Royce. The money raised has meant that the government has been able to reduce its own borrowing to finance its expenditure. Over £30 billion has been raised so far from privatisations.

Plans for further privatisations include British Coal, British Rail and the Post Office. This will leave only the nuclear industries, the Civil Aviation Authority and London Transport as 'nationalised industries'.

Why privatise?

The belief of the government was that public sector companies were frequently inefficient because they were 'protected' in two ways:

1 They could not go bankrupt (if they made losses the government gave them more money).
2 They were frequently **monopolies** (i.e. the only supplier), so they could dictate supply and price.

The idea was that if the companies were in the private sector they would have to become more efficient to cope with the increased competition.

A typical example was *transport*. If buses were privatised then competition would mean there were increased services and lower fares. Reducing the restrictions on taxis has had a similar result.

Advantages

Those in favour of privatisation claim that:

- Industries must lower their costs to remain competitive – which is better for consumers.

- The consumers will be able to choose from a wider variety of goods sold at cheaper prices – again because of competition. For instance, the choice of telephones on the market has increased dramatically since British Telecom was privatised.
- Privatisation will make managers and staff more efficient and give better service. If customers are lost because of inefficiency then the company may go out of business and both managers and staff would lose their jobs. This fear will encourage them to give good service.
- Government finance in supporting loss-making industries is reduced, so there is less burden on taxpayers.
- Private individuals are encouraged to buy shares.

Disadvantages

Those who disagree with privatisation claim that:

- In many cases there are no 'real' competitors so the customer is worse off. In this case the company which was a public monopoly is now just a private monopoly. For instance, who will supply you with gas if you fall out with British Gas?
- Standards of service do not always improve. One survey carried out about British Telecom revealed that customers thought that standards of service were worse after privatisation than before.
- Unprofitable parts of an industry cannot be subsidised by profitable parts. For instance, the *real* cost of delivering a letter in the Scottish Highlands is much greater than in Inner London. What will happen to remote services if the Post Office is privatised?
- The government is at present using the money it raises to reduce its own borrowing. But when everything has been sold off there will be nothing else left.

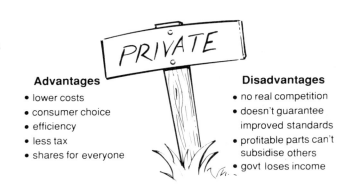

Advantages
- lower costs
- consumer choice
- efficiency
- less tax
- shares for everyone

Disadvantages
- no real competition
- doesn't guarantee improved standards
- profitable parts can't subsidise others
- govt loses income

Activity

Major job losses have occurred in many privatised industries, especially British Airways, British Steel and British Telecom as they have 'slimmed down' to reduce their operating costs and become more efficient. Critics blame the privatisation programme. Others argue that many other companies have had to reduce their staff levels to stay competitive during the recession, and the privatised companies have only done the same thing. Another opinion is that many jobs have been lost because of new technology. This issue is covered in Chapter 3, on page 88.

1 Decide *as a group* how you would define a **recession**. Check your answer with your tutor.

2 Work out how a company can improve its profits if it decides to reduce the number of staff. Translink is a delivery company which employs 50 staff. Last year its total revenue was £3 000 000 and its costs were £1 750 000. Last year the average pay for each employee was £20 000.

    a What was the total wage bill for the year?
    b How much profit did Translink make?
    c What is the total wage bill as a percentage of the total costs?
    d How much would the company save, on average, if 20 staff were made redundant?
    e If revenue remained the same next year, what would be the new profit figure?

3 *As a group*, decide why a company would be more likely to reduce staff in a recession, rather than increase the price of its products.

Watchdogs

Because many privatised industries do *not* have many (or any) competitors and are therefore virtually monopoly suppliers, the government has set up watchdog or regulatory bodies who will pursue customer complaints and oversee the profits (to make sure these have not risen too much).

Activity

Below are given the titles of three watchdog bodies and the industries they represent. Can you decide which belongs to which?

● Oftel ● Ofgas ● Ofwat

a British Gas
b The water industry
c British Telecom

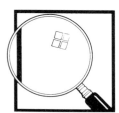

Evidence Assignment 1G

At the time that it was planned to privatise British Rail there was opposition from many people (including the Chairman of British Rail). Below is given a summary of the arguments for and against this issue. Read them carefully and then supplement them with any current information you can find in any quality newspapers. Think how privatisation could have affected fares or train services in your own area.

Divide into two groups, one representing the government and one representing the pressure group Transport 2000, who are campaigners against the move. Prepare your case and debate the issues.

Finally, write down the arguments for both sides and the conclusion that was reached.

The case for privatisation

1 The plan would separate the ownership of Railtrack (responsible for tracks, stations and maintenance) from the running of trains. Only the latter would be privatised.
2 BR had losses of about £250 million in 1992 and received grants (paid for by taxpayers) of £1 billion. Privatisation would save the taxpayer money.

3 Greater investment to replace old track and modernise the system is required – up to £1.6 billion a year for the next ten years. Taxpayers could not be expected to provide this amount of money.

4 Services on the railways were very poor, yet prices on many commuter routes were high. The consumer would get better value for money from private operators who need to provide a good service to attract customers, especially if they are in competition with each other.

5 Profits during the 1980s for InterCity were about £50 million a year. This would tempt private operators to take part.

6 Trains and stations could be *leased* from Railtrack. Therefore, for example, airline operators could carry their own passengers to airports such as Heathrow and Gatwick.

The case against privatisation

1 If Railtrack is inefficient then private operators would not be interested in running trains, as maintenance, signalling etc. are vital to an efficient train service.

2 Unprofitable 'local' lines would be forced to close as they could no longer be subsidised by profitable InterCity routes.

3 Freight costs would rise sharply. More companies would use road transport, thereby increasing pollution.

4 Fares would increase as private operators must make a profit. More people would choose to travel by road, which would increase congestion and pollution.

5 Job losses would result. More than 5000 people at BR had lost their jobs by mid-1993. Up to 30 000 job losses could follow.

6 Private operators may not be willing to finance track maintenance and development. This would still have to come from public funds.

Deregulation

You may often see the word **deregulation** used in connection with both privatised and other industries. At the same time as the government started to introduce its privatisation programme in the early 1980s, it was also involved in removing regulations which protected many organisations from competition. Examples of deregulation include:

1 Changing the regulations which protected British Telecom by preventing any other company providing a telephone service.

2 Changing the regulations which prevented anyone other than solicitors from undertaking the legal work connected with buying and selling houses (called conveyancing). Today this type of work can be done by estate agents, banks, building societies or even the buyer. The price of conveyancing has therefore fallen.

3 Changing the regulations which protected opticians from competition and kept the price of spectacles and contact lenses high. Today there are hundreds of shops selling spectacles at competitive prices.

4 Changing the regulations which protected public sector transport services and opening these routes to private operators.

Evidence Assignment 1H

This assignment brings together the formation, expansion and growth of an actual company with the opportunities which can be created by privatisation.

Read the information carefully and prepare short answers to the questions which follow, on your word-processor. Look back at previous sections if you need to revise any points.

In 1980, Brian Souter and his sister Ann Gloag set up their own small coach business. They bought two second-hand coaches with money from their father, who backed their enterprise with his £25 000 redundancy money, and by borrowing from the bank. They called their company Stagecoach and initially operated just one route – between London and Dundee – taking advantage of the Transport Act 1980 which deregulated long distance bus and coach services. In 1993 Stagecoach had 5 per cent of the UK bus market, employed about 5400 staff and operated about 2300 buses. In 1992 it made a pre-tax profit of £8.2 million. The 1993 profit was forecast to be at least £12.8 million.

Throughout the 1980s Stagecoach expanded. Luxury double-deck coaches were bought and new express services introduced. In 1985, when the National Bus Company was broken up and privatised, Stagecoach purchased five smaller bus companies in England and Scotland. By 1988 Brian Souter and his sister had to decide whether to remain as a private family company or to look outside for additional finance. To continue expanding they needed more capital to buy municipal and London bus companies coming on to the market after privatisation. They therefore decided take steps to become a public limited company. The company flotation took place in April 1993 – it is now listed on the Stock Exchange and shares are traded daily.

The flotation made Brian Souter and his sister multi-millionaires – between them they own about 90 per cent of the company, now valued in total at £100 million. However, their staff benefited from the flotation as well. In 1992, 7 per cent of the family shares were put into an employee share ownership plan which over 1200 members of staff belong to. The senior executives also have their own share option scheme.

However, success did not come to Stagecoach's owners without a lot of hard work. Brian Souter worked full time as both a bus driver and a conductor to pay his way through university and took a part-time job with Strathclyde buses when he was training to become a chartered accountant. His sister, for her part, was voted 1990 Businesswoman of the Year.

In the future they hope to benefit from the privatisation of British Rail. They plan to buy franchises on certain rail routes which will enable them to offer linked coach/rail/coach journeys, enabling people to travel on one ticket by both forms of transport. In 1993 Stagecoach was still expanding.

1 For how many years was Stagecoach a private limited company?

2 How did it obtain its initial finance?

3 What are the advantages to Stagecoach of becoming a public limited company?

4 List three ways in which privatisation has helped Stagecoach.

5 What was the *percentage* increase in Stagecoach's profit between 1992 and 1993?

6 Why do you think Stagecoach's owners decided to make some shares available for their employees and managers to buy?

7 The owners will receive approximately 80 per cent of the total value of the flotation. How much will they *each* be worth?

8 They hope to buy a franchise on some British Rail routes. What does this mean?

9 Chart the progress of Stagecoach's shares over a 10-day period. Prepare a line graph to show how they change, on your computer.

10 Give three reasons why you think the company has been so successful.

· LOCAL AUTHORITIES ·

Local authorities are responsible for providing a wide range of services on a local basis. This is because it would be both impossible and impractical for the government to administer these services on a central basis, because:

1 Areas in the country vary in what they need. For instance, the type of services required in an inner city will be different from those needed in a country area. The way in which money is spent locally can therefore reflect the needs of the area.
2 Local politicians are more aware of the needs of the local people.
3 The size of England and Wales is too great (over 94 000 square miles) for it to be administered properly from London.

Local government structure

In most of *England and Wales* there are two tiers of local government:

● **county councils** – which provide services that need either considerable resources or need planning and administration over a wide area
● **district councils** – which provide local services to their area (in some cases these are known as borough councils).

In *Scotland*, county councils are known as **regional councils**.

In London and some heavily populated areas the situation is slightly different. London is administered by the **London boroughs**, which provide nearly all the services.

The fire service is an exception – this is run by joint authorities to serve the whole of the area.

The six heavily populated areas of West Midlands, Greater Manchester, Merseyside, South Yorkshire, West Yorkshire and Tyne & Wear are known as **metropolitan areas**. In these cases, services (apart from transport, police and fire) are run by district councils. The three other services are again run by joint authorities which consist of representatives of all authorities using the services.

DID YOU KNOW?

The government is planning to change the structure of local authorities in England and Wales and to change some of the names. One plan involves splitting up the metropolitan areas.

Look in the newspapers and check with your tutor if the situation has changed either nationally or for your own area.

Evidence Collection Point 1.9

1 Find out the name of the council(s) which are responsible for the area in which you live. Unless you live in a city area, *two* councils will be involved – a county council and a district (or borough) council.

2 Below is given a list of services provided by local authorities. Decide which you think will be provided on a local basis (e.g. by a district council) and which on a wider basis (e.g. by a county council). If possible, refer to your local council's literature on how it spends its money.

Strategic planning	Fire service
Housing	Police
Education	Social services
Environmental health	Leisure services
Consumer protection	Local planning
Transport	Tourism
Libraries	Refuse collection
Economic development	and disposal

Organisation and control

Local people elect their own council representatives in elections every four years. Each representative (called a **councillor**) usually represents a political party, so that the town or county may have an overall majority of councillors from one party (which may or may not be the same as the political party in power in central government). If there is no overall majority then this is called a 'hung' council – and the balance of power may be held by a minority party (e.g. independents). The mayor is a councillor who has had long service on the council. The major parties usually take it in turns to nominate a mayor.

Local policy is decided by councillors during council meetings (e.g. of the Transport Committee, the Education Committee, etc.). Their decisions, and the day-to-day running of the council offices are carried out by paid employees, known as **local government officers**.

Theoretically, local people can have a say in the actions of their council. If they do not agree with what their council is doing then they can show their disapproval when they vote in the next local elections.

DID YOU KNOW?

The organisation of local government is similar to that of central government. Both MPs and local councillors are:

● elected by the people
● responsible for making decisions on behalf of the people.

In the same way, both civil servants and local government officers are:

● paid employees
● responsible for carrying out policy and the day-to-day running of central or local government offices.

Local government finance

In order to spend money on the services it provides, a local authority must raise money. The amount required varies from one area to another depending on:

- the services offered
- the number of employees
- the efficiency of the council.

The government provides the largest amount to councils (an estimated £68 billion in 1992/3) and is therefore very concerned with the efficiency of local authorities and the way in which they spend the money. In some cases (e.g. refuse collection) the government has made councils 'buy in' the service from outside providers if this would reduce the cost.

The councils raise money in six ways. The first two are the most important and raise the most money:

1 the Government Revenue Support grant
2 council tax
3 loans
4 rents from council houses
5 sale of services (e.g. swimming pools, leisure centres, etc.)
6 sale of council houses to tenants.

DID YOU KNOW?

All council spending can be divided into two types – capital expenditure (on items such as schools or roads which last a long time) and revenue spending (on running council services, e.g. wages, cleaning and fuel). Each council is issued with a Standard Spending Assessment which states how much the government has calculated it should spend to provide a standard level of service.

The council tax

The **council tax** was introduced on 1 April 1993 and replaced the community charge (or poll tax). The council tax is a local tax, set by local councils, and each household receives one bill based on the value of their property relative to others in the area. Discounts or benefits are available for some home owners. For instance, if there is only one adult living in the property then the bill is reduced by 25 per cent. If people are on low incomes or are disabled then they can claim a reduction.

Each house has been placed in one of eight council tax valuation bands according to its value. Changes in house prices will not affect the value, but if the state of a local area changes for the worse (e.g. if a motorway is built

nearby) then houses in that area may be revalued and put into a lower band.

The amount of the council tax is set by the local council. The amount to be paid will depend on the valuation band each home is in.

DID YOU KNOW?

1 Businesses do not pay council tax – they pay **business rates**. These are collected by the local council and paid into a national pool. They are then *redistributed* to each area on the basis of the size of the local population.
2 The valuation bands vary between England, Scotland and Wales, as shown by Figure 1.8.

Band	Range of house values ENGLAND	Range of house values WALES	Range of house values SCOTLAND	Tax proportion to be paid
A	Up to £40 000	Up to £30 000	Up to £27 000	6/9 or 67%
B	£40 001 to £52 000	£30 001 to £39 000	£27 001 to £35 000	7/9 or 78%
C	£52 001 to £68 000	£39 001 to £51 000	£35 001 to £45 000	8/9 or 89%
D	£68 001 to £88 000	£51 001 to £66 000	£45 001 to £58 000	9/9 or 100%
E	£88 001 to £120 000	£66 001 to £90 000	£58 001 to £80 000	11/9 or 122%
F	£120 001 to £160 000	£90 001 to £120 000	£80 001 to £106 000	13/9 or 144%
G	£160 001 to £320 000	£120 001 to £240 000	£106 001 to £212 000	15/9 or 167%
H	Over £320 000	Over £240 000	Over £212 000	18/9 or 200%

Figure 1.8 *Valuation bands for council tax*

Evidence Collection Point 1.10

Imagine that you have recently started work for your local council. You are currently involved in answering queries about the council tax and helping to prepare information on the council's income and expenditure for the year. This information will go into a leaflet which is sent to all homeowners with the council tax bill.

1 Your council has set a council tax of £500 for the current year. From the valuation bands given in Figure 1.8, calculate what each of the following callers will pay in tax this year. Write a brief memo to your assistant, Hanif Ahmed, setting out this information clearly. If possible, use a word-processor.

a Mrs A, who lives in a house valued at £72 000.
b Miss B, who lives in a house valued at £28 000.
c Mr C, who lives on his own in a house valued at £350 000.

2 Below is a list of the services which will be provided by the council next year and the amount it is proposed to spend on each. Prepare a bar chart on your computer which shows this expenditure clearly and which can be included in the new leaflet.

Education	£560m
Social services	£150m
Police	£65m
Highways and public transport	£75m
Fire service	£32m
Recreation and tourism	£20m
Waste disposal	£10m
Planning	£4m
Other services	£21m

• INDUSTRIAL SECTORS •

Traditionally, it is usual to divide all business organisations into three sectors of production (see Figure 1.9):

● **primary**

● **secondary**

● **tertiary**.

The **primary** sector is concerned with extracting natural resources from the environment. A farmer, a miner, a fisherman, a forester, an oil driller – all work in primary industries.

The **secondary** sector is concerned with manufacturing, processing and assembling finished goods as well as construction work. A car production worker, a furniture maker and a motorway construction worker are all found in secondary industries.

TYPES OF PRODUCTION

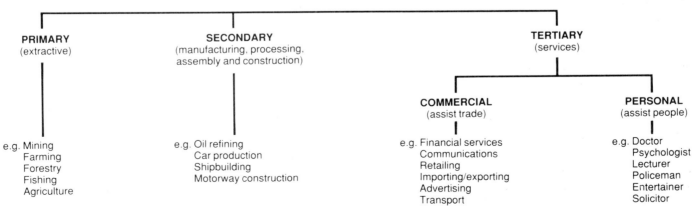

Figure 1.9 *Types of production*

The **tertiary** sector is concerned with the provision of services either to members of the public (e.g. tourism and health) or to other industries (e.g. transport, banking and insurance).

Evidence Collection Point 1.11

1 Draw a simple chart with the headings of *Primary*, *Secondary* and *Tertiary* production, using the same sub-divisions as in Figure 1.9. Enter the following people in the correct category according to the job they do:

Carpenter	Stockbroker	Nurse
Oil driller	Priest	Musician
Engineer	Journalist	Bank clerk
Builder	Fisherman	Teacher

2 Now identify *at least* 12 more occupations and categorise these. Try to make these as varied as you can (from a Mafia boss to a baby minder!). Make sure you add at least two under each heading on your chart.

3 The following table shows the percentage of organisations in Britain in each sector of production. Study the table and the text below, then write your answers to the questions which follow.

	Primary	Secondary	Tertiary
1989	9%	30%	61%
1990	7%	30%	63%
1991	7%	28%	65%

The long term trend in Britain is towards the production of **services** – i.e. the growth of the tertiary businesses. Today a large number of people are employed in what are termed as 'the professions' – e.g. as solicitors, accountants, doctors, teachers, etc.

However, employment in primary and secondary industries has fallen considerably. Oil production in the North Sea helped the primary industries until 1985, but output has since fallen. There has been a substantial decline in the number of manufacturing industries in Britain over a number of years, particularly in metals, mechanical engineering, motor vehicles and construction. Growth industries in the secondary industries have included electrical engineering and chemicals. However, this has not stopped Britain's overall decline as a world trading nation. In 1950 Britain produced 25.5 per cent of the world's manufactured goods. In 1960 this had fallen to 16.5 per cent and in 1970 to 10.8 per cent. By 1979 this had shrunk still further to 9.1 per cent. In 1992, the UK was responsible for 8.4 per cent of manufactured goods, with the USA producing 16.4 per cent, Germany 10 per cent, Japan 17.1 per cent, France 9.9 per cent and other nations 28.2 per cent.

In the service sector there has been a major growth in financial services, distribution and hotels and catering. Technological developments have meant the growth of some new industries. The information/communications industry is a typical example with the advent of satellites and cable television networks and the growth of the computer industry.

a What reason is given for the decline in the primary sector?

b Which industries have declined in the secondary sector?

c Which industries have grown in the secondary sector?

d What reasons can you give for the increase in the tertiary sector?

e If the total amount produced by *all* the industries was worth £497 billion in 1991, calculate how much was produced by *each sector* during that year.

f Produce a line graph, preferably using a spreadsheet package, which shows Britain's decline in producing world manufactured goods between 1950 and 1992.

g Produce a pie chart, again preferably using a spreadsheet package, which shows the percentage shares of each nation listed for 1992.

h Discuss, *as a group and/or with your tutor*, the implications for the British economy if the trends shown continue into the twenty-first century. Note down your conclusions.

i Produce a short report summarising all your answers, using a word-processing package. Attach your line graph and pie chart.

• TYPES OF BUSINESS ACTIVITY •

Most businesses can also be categorised as being involved in one of the following activities:

- **manufacturing**
- **transport and distribution**
- **retail and wholesale**
- **service industries**.

However, no business operates in isolation – all are dependent on other sectors to operate efficiently. For instance, a furniture maker will need transportation for his goods either to a wholesaler or direct to a retailer. He will also use the services of several other organisations in doing so. He will require finance from a bank and will want to insure his goods in transit.

Activity

Look back at Figure 1.9 and Evidence Collection Point 1.11.

1 In which sector will you find manufacturing industries?

2 In which sector will you find retailers?

3 How many *different* service industries can you identify?

Manufacturing industry

A manufacturer is usually considered to be someone who uses raw materials and changes them into a finished product.

Manufacturers are not just involved in producing the **consumer goods** you buy in the shops. You buy a range of consumer goods, probably every week, from which you derive a certain amount of satisfaction (otherwise you wouldn't spend money on them). These are mainly **consumables** (e.g. food, drink, cigarettes, etc.), which you buy and use immediately. Less frequently you will buy **consumer durables** which have a longer life (e.g. radios, domestic appliances, televisions and cars).

However, many companies produce goods that are sold to other organisations, either for their own use (e.g. barrels sold to a brewery) or which are components of another finished product (e.g. headlamps that are sold to car manufacturers).

The last category are goods that are needed to make possible the production of *another* good. These are called **producer goods** and include machinery, raw materials, commercial vehicles, cranes etc.

Some companies manufacture just for the British market, others *export* many of their goods either to other countries in the European Community or worldwide.

Manufacturers are usually concerned with their **product mix**. This is the *range* of products and brands they produce. Often these are linked to a theme. For instance, sportswear manufacturers may make trainers, shorts, vests and other clothes as part of their range. Others also make equipment for various sporting activities. In this case all the goods will be sold through the same type of outlet – retail sportswear shops.

Diverse products from one manufacturer

Manufacturers who have **diversified** make a range of goods which may be sold to *different* markets. As an example, Dalgety plc makes a wide range of snackfoods (e.g. the Golden Wonder brand range), petfoods (Prime, Winalot and Bonio) and grocery products (Homepride flour). All these will be sold through the same type of outlets – retail shops and supermarkets. However, Dalgety are also involved in making food ingredients for commercial bakers and agricultural supplies (such as dairy feed) for farmers. These are obviously sold to a different market and through different outlets.

Most manufacturers will have their own research and development section to investigate new technology and develop new products (or redesign old ones).

They will also have an active marketing department, responsible for selling and promoting their goods. Part of the responsibility of the marketing department may be to arrange transport and distribution of the manufactured goods so that they are in the right place at the right time to be sold to customers. However, most organisations use specialist companies to help them achieve this.

Evidence Collection Point 1.12

Interview someone (a friend or relative) who works for a manufacturing company in your area. Find out as much as you can about the product that is made and that person's own job. If the interviewee agrees, record your interview on tape.

1 Type up the interview neatly as a report to your tutor, preferably on a word-processor.

2 Attach an assessment of the interview, with notes on how you consider you could improve your own performance next time. If you have taped the interview then listen to this a few times before you prepare your assessment. Give the tape to your tutor so that he or she can also assess the interview and discuss your performance with you.

Transport

Every manufacturer has to decide on the best method of transporting goods. This will depend on:

- the *distance* involved
- the *type of goods* (size, weight, value, whether they are perishable)
- the *urgency* with which they are required
- the *cost* of alternative forms of transport
- the wishes of *the customer*.

There are three basic choices – **air**, **sea** and **land**. A large machine, for example, being sent halfway across the world would be sent by sea.

It is usual for goods travelling by sea to be packed in special **containers** which are labelled and then loaded on a ship. A container is like a large packing case and will be filled with a variety of goods. The main advantage is that containers stack neatly on board ship and can be delivered to the port *intact* on a lorry from a packing company and, upon arrival, loaded on to another lorry to be transported to the final destination. For this reason, container ships are often known as 'freight ro-ros' (roll-on, roll-off ships) in a similar way to ferries which people drive on and off, which are known as 'passenger ro-ros'. Other types of ships used to carry freight include cargo liners, tramp steamers (which are specially hired to carry particular cargoes), and specialised ships (e.g. oil tankers and bulk carriers). Coastal steamers move from port to port around Britain carrying heavy goods, such as coal and very heavy equipment.

Air cargo is used for goods that are required urgently. A small component, needed immediately for a machine abroad, would be sent by air. Insurance for goods travelling by air is cheaper than for sea, because there is less handling and therefore less chance of damage. Obviously, however, the cost of transporting the goods is greater than by sea. As cost is calculated by weight, usually only relatively lightweight or perishable goods are sent by air.

The specialised packing and documentation required for sending goods abroad means that many organisations will use the services of a **shipping** or **freight agent** to transport their goods overseas.

Goods travelling within Britain are usually sent by road or by rail. Road transport is popular because it is door-to-door whereas goods transported by rail can only be sent to the nearest freight depot – unless a company has its own sidings. Again containers may be used which can be filled and then lifted on to goods trains. Rail transport is cheap for bulky goods and more environmentally friendly (trains don't cause the pollution that lorries do).

Road transport is more flexible. The company can decide its own delivery schedule, especially if it uses its own vans or lorries. These can also be used as moving advertisements as they travel up and down motorways. However, road transport can be subject to delays through bad weather, traffic congestion, delays and accidents. By law, a driver can only work a specified maximum number of hours each day. It is also costly if a driver has to drive a long distance with a full load and then return empty. For this reason many organisations use the services of specialised **haulage companies** who can either plan a circular route or 'match' loads in two directions which reduces the cost.

Special vehicles are used for perishable goods. For instance, refrigerated lorries are used for many food products and for fresh flowers. In some cases, a mix of transport methods may be used. For example, fresh flowers from Holland will travel to Britain in a refrigerated lorry which crosses the North Sea by ferry and then travels to its main distributors in Britain.

DID YOU KNOW?

Pipelines and cables can also be included as methods of transporting goods (e.g. oil in pipelines and electricity through cables). The main expenditure is in constructing the system in the first place and then maintaining it.

Gas pipelines are marked with orange topped posts, so that if there are leaks or other problems the pipeline can be identified from the air. Can you find any in your area?

DID YOU KNOW?

The canal network in Britain owes much of its existence to the entrepreneurial spirit of Josiah Wedgewood. Having established a porcelain factory in the Midlands he then had two problems. He needed china clay (from Cornwall) to make his porcelain and then needed to send the finished goods to London (his main market). The clay was heavy and the finished goods were very fragile – and in the eighteenth century the roads were uneven and rutted, delays were common and transport was unreliable. He solved the problem by financing the building of part of the canal network, which both brought his china clay to his factory and sent his porcelain smoothly on its way to London.

Today the Wedgewood factory still operates at Burslem in Staffordshire, though their methods of transportation are rather different!

Evidence Assignment 1I

Many companies are often faced with what are known as 'conflicting objectives'. A typical one may be cost versus concern for the environment. Imagine you are the Transport Manager for a large cement company in the North of England. You have read the following article this morning in your daily paper. Type a short memo to your Managing Director which:

- *summarises the article,*
- *gives him your proposed plans for transporting your company's cement in the future – with your reasons.*

Rail or road – that is the question

Trainload Freight – the freight 'arm' of British Rail – has problems. At present it is forced by the government to make a minimum 4.5 per cent profit on its freight contracts. As a result its charges have risen steadily, so that companies which transported over 2 million tonnes of freight have changed from rail to road transport in the last few months. Famous names who have made the switch include Blue Circle and Castle Cement, Pedigree Petfoods, and Taunton Cider. Goods such as china clay, stone, petroleum and limestone are likely to be moving by road in future rather than by rail.

The result? Over 100 000 additional lorry journeys a year – through national parks, rural beauty spots and small towns and villages. Environmentalists are furious and are pressing for more grants to subsidise rail freight. They accuse Transport Secretary John MacGregor – who has encouraged companies to use rail as a less polluting and safer form of transport – of ignoring the problem now faced

Activity

Visit your local supermarket and list the items you can find which have been transported by air-freight. As a clue, look for perishable items (fruit, flowers, vegetables, fish, etc.). Compare your list with those prepared by your fellow students and see how many items you can find altogether.

by many companies. 'Who will pay the cost,' they ask, 'of the greater wear and tear on roads, the hospital costs of people injured in lorry accidents and the additional environmental pollution?'

A spokeswoman for Trainload Freight pointed out that 8 million tonnes of freight contracts had been saved by negotiating with companies to cut costs. A government spokesman said that over £6.6 million was given in grants last year for rail freight. In the meantime companies need to consider their costs – and road hauliers are quoting rock bottom rates. Not only that – but if British Rail is privatised the costs of rail freight could increase even more.

Distribution

All producers (of primary and manufactured goods) have to decide how to distribute their goods – in other words what process should they use to bring their goods to the final consumer. There are four main methods (see Figure 1.10):

1 Direct from the producer to the customer is the system used by most mail-order companies. You may also see 'mill' shops next to some factories which sell goods or 'seconds' direct to the public. Some manufacturers or mail-order companies also have their own retail outlets.

2 The traditional method is via a wholesaler to a retailer and then to the customer. This method is used when the manufacturer produces goods in bulk and this bulk has to be 'broken down' into smaller quantities for retailers. Some wholesalers provide credit and transport facilities, others operate on a 'cash and carry' basis. Your local grocer, for instance, is likely to buy his supplies from a cash and carry wholesaler who deals only with retailers and not the general public.

3 Many companies deal direct with retailers – particularly large retail chains such as Dixons and Currys or larger supermarkets such as Tesco and Sainsbury. In these cases it is in the interests of both parties to deal direct as special prices for bulk orders can be agreed. In some cases large retailers will then use their *own* transport for onward distribution to their stores.

4 Manufacturers that produce goods for tradesmen usually distribute them via a specialist merchant. This is the case, for instance, with builders and plumbers, who will buy from builders' merchants or plumbers' merchants.

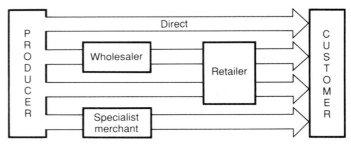

Figure 1.10 *Channels of distribution*

DID YOU KNOW?

Many imported goods are firstly handled, or distributed, via **special markets**. Examples include:

- the London Commodity Exchange (which deals in cocoa, coffee, sugar, jute, spices etc.)
- the Corn Exchange (wheat, barley, oats, fertilisers, flour etc.)
- the Metal Exchange (copper, tin, lead, silver and zinc)
- the London Diamond Market at Hatton Garden
- Nine Elms fruit and vegetable market
- the London Provisions Exchange (bacon, butter, cheese, hams and lard).

Importers and distributors in all these products will therefore deal in these specialist markets before the goods are sold more widely throughout Britain.

Activity

Find out for what products Billingsgate and Smithfield markets are famous.

Evidence Collection Point 1.13

Look in your local *Yellow Pages* and find *two* examples of each of the following:

- a specialist merchant
- a road haulage company
- a shipping and forwarding agent

- a cash and carry wholesaler
- an import/export merchant (or agent).

In pairs, contact *one* organisation and obtain information on the service it provides and how it operates. Present your findings to the rest of your class.

After the presentation, prepare brief notes on the work of *each* type of organisation, on your word-processor.

The retail trade

Retailing is concerned with selling goods. Therefore the door-to-door salesman and a large department store are *both* retailers. The retailer is the final link in the chain of distribution and can operate as the 'middleman' between a customer and a wholesaler or manufacturer – providing goods to one and information to the other about changing tastes and preferences.

In Britain there are five main types of retailer:

- Small, independent retailers who are usually sole traders (see page 6).
- Multiple traders, such as Burtons and Currys who deal with one type of good (known as single-trade multiples) and variety multiples, such as Bhs and Marks & Spencer. These usually have a standard 'national' appearance and are easily recognisable by consumers wherever they are.
- Retail co-operatives (see page 15).
- Department stores which deal in a wide variety of goods

in (mainly) one location (e.g. Harrods, Selfridges, and Kendal Milne in Manchester).
- Shopping centres and hypermarkets. The trend is for 'out-of-town' sites with easy parking, low rates and a variety of large retailers in a 'mega centre'. Examples include the Meadowhall centre (Sheffield), Merryhill (Birmingham), Brent Cross (London), and the MetroCentre (Gateshead).

However, there are other outlets – retail markets, mobile shops, mail-order companies. Even automatic vending machines can be classed as relating to the 'retail trade'.

Each type of outlet has its own advantages and disadvantages, as are shown in Figure 1.11. In addition certain outlets are increasing in popularity (e.g. mega shopping centres) whilst others are declining (e.g. mail-order companies). The reasons for this are discussed in Chapter 9 – Consumer Demand.

Outlet	Advantages	Disadvantages
Independent retailer	• Local, so convenient • Personal attention to customers • Flexible opening hours • Wide range of goods	• Higher prices • Limited choice (often only small sizes/ limited brands available)
Multiple trader	• Easily recognisable nationwide • Same quality throughout • Competitive prices through bulk buying	• Impersonal service • Mass production sometimes unpopular (e.g. in clothing) • Pre-packaging = less variety of size/choice
Department stores	• Variety of goods in one place • Pleasant premises – carpets, restaurants etc. • In-store demonstrations/offers • Specialist knowledge of staff • Delivery service/ credit facilities	• Some goods expensive • Temptation to spend more than intended • Credit terms expensive • Impersonal/slow service
Supermarkets/hypermarkets	• Bulk buying means low-cost goods • Late opening/Sunday trading • Special/bargain offers (e.g. 3 for the price of 2)	• No delivery service • Own transport essential • Impulse buying can mean higher bills than intended • Queues at busy periods

Figure 1.11 *Retail outlets: advantages and disadvantages*

Wholesalers

The wholesaler acts as the link between the producer (or manufacturer) and the retailer. Other terms you may see used include **distributor**, **merchant**, **dealer** or **agent**. In many cases, their functions are very similar. When goods are *imported* they are frequently handled by an import merchant or agent. Often this is essential, particularly when rare goods are involved which require specialist knowledge and contacts. The job of the **buyer** is essential – in terms of type of goods, quantity and price. If he or she buys the wrong goods or too many of them at too high a price, the wholesaler is unlikely to stay in business for very long.

Basically, a wholesaler undertakes the following functions:

- buys in bulk and sells onwards in smaller quantities
- plans for demand and stores the goods as required
- offers a specialist service
- assists producers/manufacturers to reach small traders/gain new customers
- offers credit facilities to retailers
- may grade/blend or brand goods before selling (e.g. grain, tea, coffee, fruit and vegetables)
- acts as a communications link between seller and producer.

The rise of high-volume retailers like supermarkets and hypermarkets, and the growth of cash-and-carry warehouses, have all led to the decline of the 'traditional' wholesaler. Many large retailers now deal with their suppliers direct and negotiate their own terms. However, in the case of many imported goods the role of the wholesaler or merchant is essential or even protected. For instance, on the London Metal Exchange only privileged 'Ring' members may become involved in deals. Anyone else wishing to buy metals must become involved with someone in the 'Ring' – or do without.

Evidence Collection Point 1.14

1 Identify one retail organisation in your area in *each* of the categories listed in Figure 1.11. List the main features of each one.

2 Try to find out more about the work of a local wholesaler, for instance by visiting a local fruit and vegetable wholesale market or cash-and-carry wholesaler and interviewing someone who works there.

Type out your findings neatly.

Service industries

On page 29 you were asked to identify as many service industries as possible. How many did you find? Check your list with ours below.

- Retailing
- Wholesaling
- Importers
- Exporters
- Communications
- Insurance
- Finance
- Advertising.

In many cases, these industries have already been covered previously.

The role of service industries is to provide *assistance* for business. An obvious example is banking. Companies not only need a safe place to deposit their money but may also need to borrow money from time to time. They may also need financial advice and assistance, for instance in obtaining a credit reference on a new customer at home or abroad. Importers will require currency exchanged so that they can pay for goods they have bought. Exporters may need help with providing special credit terms for foreign buyers.

Insurance is necessary to *reduce the risks of trading*. Cover for standard risks (e.g. theft, fire, goods in transit, etc.) may be obtained through an insurance company (or broker, who will give advice on what several companies have to offer). All companies must, by law, take out Employers' Liability Insurance which protects their employees in the case of injury. Exporters can obtain insurance from the government's Export Credit Guarantee Department (ECGD). This department covers risks such as political coups, riots and other problems which may result in an exporter not being paid for the goods he has supplied. (Imagine the problems faced by a company which had supplied Saddam Hussein with a large quantity of goods just before the Gulf War!) Britain houses the most famous insurance organisation in the world – Lloyd's of London – which is renowned for taking on risks which other insurance companies could not afford (e.g. insuring a jumbo jet).

Both the communications and advertising industry are relatively new. Good communications are essential for all companies in an age when up-to-the minute information is essential. This is possible via computers, satellite links, and fax machines (see also the Technology Core Skill chapter, page 431). Advertising today is a sophisticated industry covering a variety of media – the press, television, posters and hoardings, the cinema and commercial radio (see Chapter 11).

All these organisations employ *specialists*, not only in terms of their own trade but in relation to specific businesses. For instance, **advertising agencies** can be hired by companies to plan a campaign, design the artwork and select and cost the probable outlets. The staff who would deal with a campaign to sell a new brand of coffee would not be those who would be employed on promoting agricultural tractors. In the same way, banks employ 'small business advisers' (the size relates to the businesses, not the advisers!) who are specialists in the problems faced by people running small businesses. A large company, wishing to plan a takeover bid of another large company, would employ the specialist services of a **merchant banker** for advice and expertise.

Evidence Collection Point 1.15

For this task your tutor will divide you into small groups. Visit either a local bank or insurance company *or* write to an advertising agency or communications company (e.g. BT or Mercury) to find out the range of services they offer to businesses. Prepare a short report on the service industry you have investigated and exchange your report with others from your group.

Remember that, if possible, your work should be prepared on a word-processor and you should use clear headings.

1 Identify *at least* three businesses or companies in *each* of the following categories. You should select a mixture of both local and national organisations.

- Sole trader
- Partnership
- Private limited company
- Public limited company
- Charity.

Using these categories as headings, write a short paragraph on each, giving information on the businesses you have identified. This must include:

a a brief explanation of the characteristics of that type of business (e.g. legal status, control, advantages and disadvantages etc.)
b details of each business you have identified; i.e.
– its name
– the type of business activity it carries out
– its main purpose
– the industrial sector in which it operates.

2 Identify in your area:

a a franchise operation, *and*
b a consumer or producer co-operative.

Write a short paragraph on each, stating clearly how each differs from any of the organisations you discussed in question 1. Again, state clearly the purpose, activity and sector in which each business operates.

3 Choose *one* government department and find out as much as you can about the services it provides. Use the chart on page 19 as your starting point. You can then find out further information by visiting your school, college or local library *or*, if you choose a department which has offices near to you, you will be able to obtain leaflets and other information to help you.

Write a paragraph explaining its purpose and the services it provides and stating how you obtained this information.

4 *Either*

a Visit the information office of your local town hall or council offices and find out how tourism is promoted in your area. Obtain relevant literature and information.

Or

b Refer to the literature you obtained on economic development and grants in your area offered by your local authority.

Write out a summarised version of the services or financial assistance available neatly and clearly.

5 Make a front cover for your project. Title this 'Private and Public Sector Business Organisations'. Don't forget to add your name. If possible, bind your project (and add a sturdy back cover made of card) so that it looks professional and business-like.

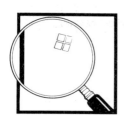

Evidence Checkpoint

If you cannot remember what you should do here, refer back to the Student Guide on page vi!

Revision Test

True or false?

1 The main purpose of most public sector organisations is to make a profit.

2 Local authorities obtain some of the money they need by means of the council tax.

3 A person who runs a franchise operation on a day-to-day basis is called a franchisor.

4 A member of a co-operative organisation has one vote per share.

5 The maximum number of members in a partnership is 50.

Complete the blanks

6 The type of business organisation whose shares are quoted on the Stock Exchange is called a ....

7 A .... is someone who relies on his/her own capital to run a business.

8 The business organisation where those who invest have limited liability and yet shares are not publicly available is called a ....

9 Three services provided by local authorities are ...., ... and ....

10 The name of the person who is legally responsible for the management of a charity is a ....

Short answer questions

11 Name two government departments and explain briefly the work of each.

12 State what transport methods would be used for:

a diamonds from Amsterdam to London

b oil from Kuwait to Rotterdam

c fresh flowers from Holland to Manchester.

13 State two advantages and two disadvantages of forming a partnership.

14 Give three occupations in *each* of the primary, secondary and tertiary sectors of industry.

15 Name four service industries and in each case give a brief explanation of how each assists business.

Write a short paragraph to show you clearly understand each of the following terms:

16 Unlimited liability.

17 Privatisation.

18 Franchising.

19 Wholesaling.

20 Public sector.

chapter **2** BUSINESS ORGANISATIONS AND PRODUCTS

Learning Objectives

This chapter is concerned with the size and scale of business organisations, their location and the way in which they can be compared in terms of their scale, scope, markets and products. It also examines the potential for introducing new products to meet market demand.

After studying this chapter you should be able to:

- explain reasons for the location of business organisations
- describe the scale and scope of business organisations
- identify the product of business organisations
- identify different markets
- propose new products which meet identified needs.

THE LOCATION OF BUSINESS ORGANISATIONS

No matter where you live in Britain it is extremely probable that the type of industries in your area have changed considerably over the last 50 years. Traditionally, the North of England was renowned for the heavy industries – steel, shipbuilding, coal mining – and for cotton and wool manufacture. The Midlands were famous for car production, pottery and engineering. The South East had a range of manufacturing companies plus canneries, refineries, tobacco companies and warehouses near the docks (e.g. in 'old' London docklands). Cornwall and South Wales were mining communities – the first for tin and the second for coal.

Today few of these industries survive, for the following reasons:

- The cotton industry failed to cope with newer, synthetic textiles and cheap imported cotton from abroad.
- Newer forms of energy production have reduced the demand for coal. Again, when it is required it is usually cheaper to import it.
- Too much capacity worldwide – or declining demand – saw the end of the shipbuilding industry and the decline of steel.
- Japanese imports of cars threatened British car production. The UK motorbike industry has now virtually gone out of existence for the same reason.

The trend today is for newer industries to emerge (e.g. in computers and electronics, light engineering and telecommunications), together with a growth in the service sector (see also page 28). Automation has reduced the numbers of people employed and the size of factories and in virtually all areas industries have moved out of towns and inner city areas to new industrial areas and parks on the outskirts – away from residential areas.

What causes industries to set up in certain areas? To what extent are some of them 'footloose' and able to operate anywhere? What can the government do to help areas which have been badly affected by industry closing?

. REASONS FOR INDUSTRIAL .
LOCATIONS

Traditionally, industries chose their location because of natural factors and resources.

- **Geographical reasons and natural resources.** Steel companies were sited near to iron ore *mineral deposits*. The wine industry of France and the bulb industry of Holland were located on the basis of *climate* and *soil*. Paper-making, chemicals, cotton and wool production all require *running water*.
- **Nearness to raw materials** – especially when these are heavy. Sheffield became a steel centre because it was near to coal, iron ore and limestone deposits (all required for the making of iron). Cement companies are found near chalk deposits (e.g. in the South East).
- **Nearness to fuel.** The introduction of coal as the main fuel to power factory production during the Industrial Revolution was the main reason for the siting of the iron and steel industries.

Climate is still important for some industries. Whisky production is sited because of the type of water to be found in certain areas of Scotland. Lincolnshire and other agricultural regions are still dependent on natural factors – although greenhouses can be used on a large scale (e.g. for tomatoes and freesias in the Channel Islands) to *simulate* natural conditions.

Many mineral deposits (e.g. iron ore) are now either too expensive to be extracted in Britain (and cheaper to buy from abroad) or have been virtually exhausted. In this case heavy goods being imported arrive by sea, which is why the steel industry has *relocated* from inland sites to those near ports.

Additional factors

In many cases none of the reasons given above explain either the siting of new industries – or the continuance of old industries in their old locations. There are various reasons for this:

1 **Labour supply and skills.** A pool of 'expert' labour in a particular area will attract industry. The most famous example is Silicon Valley in California, where so many computer firms are located because of the specialist programmers and operators who live there. In Britain the M4 corridor has often been called England's silicon Valley and Scotland has its own Silicon Glen.

Firms will also be tempted to start up where there is a ready supply of labour (often part-time assembly workers). This is the case in many new towns where light engineering factories are to be found, and in 'old' industrial areas where there is large-scale unemployment and a labour force which is ready to adapt quickly. Generally, the greater the supply of labour the less likely it is that the organisation will have to offer high wages to attract workers.

2 **Industrial inertia.** This is the name given to a firm's preference to stay in the same place rather than bear the costs of relocation when the situation changes. In Sheffield, there is still a skilled labour force and many companies have preferred to stay in the region and adapt skills rather than reduce the costs of bringing in raw materials.

The urban to rural shift. Between 1959 and 1975 employment in London in manufacturing industries fell by 37.8 per cent and by 15.9 per cent in other large cities. This was mainly because of the closure or relocation of large factories. Many companies were forced to find cheaper factory space as they either increased in size or as automation meant more space was needed for production. Rural areas meant cheaper sites, so there was a migration of both employment and people from inner city areas.

3 **EC restrictions.** The European Community has tariff restrictions on goods imported to the community from outside the EC. This means that imported foreign goods

will have an additional amount (the tariff) added to the selling price. This has prompted some foreign companies (e.g. Japanese car producers) to set up factories in Britain, so that goods can be produced and sold in the EC *without* the tariff.

4 **Financial and Government incentives.** In the case of the Japanese car producers, such as Nissan, they were able to obtain financial incentives from the government to locate in regions with high unemployment. Sometimes this was caused by the closure of traditional industries such as shipbuilding and mining. In these cases the areas are also attractive to new companies because there is likely to be strong competition for jobs. They can therefore hire the best people more cheaply than they could if labour was scarce.

Both local and national government may offer incentives to companies to tempt them to locate in particular areas (e.g. a region where there is a high level of unemployment). These incentives may range from special grants to reducing the amount of money companies have to pay in business rates in a particular area.

Full details of the type of incentives on offer at present are given in Chapter 3, page 82, under regional investment.

The proximity of other businesses

Companies are usually 'grouped' together in regions. For instance, the area around Stoke-on-Trent is still famous for its pottery industry, the area around Leicester is renowned for the boot and shoe trade, and so on. Why are organisations attracted to an area where *similar* companies are to be found nearby? The answer is that they will benefit from **external economies of scale**. These are advantages to all firms from the growth of an industry in a particular area:

- There will be a skilled local labour force.
- There will be relevant courses at local colleges (e.g. catering courses in Blackpool).
- A range of small *supplier* companies are attracted to the region as they can serve many larger organisations.
- There can be co-operation between companies (e.g. in research facilities which are established as joint ventures to share the cost).
- There can be formal contact at business meetings and informal contact locally (e.g. at the golf club).
- Local service industries develop a good knowledge of the needs of the industry and can therefore offer specialist advice (e.g. special insurance cover).

Transport services

Many 'new towns' in Britain have been developed since the 1950s. These have been most successful when situated where there is access to rapid motorway links, so that goods can be brought in to the area and distributed from the area quickly and easily. Examples are Milton Keynes and Warrington New Town.

Good transport links reduce the costs companies have to bear, especially when they are involved in a **bulk increasing** industry. This means that they receive small components and assemble them into a larger product (e.g. refrigerators, computers, furniture). In this case it is cheaper for the company to be located near to its markets than to its sources of supply. In Britain the largest market for goods is the South East – which is why most furniture companies are to be found in that area.

This contrasts with industries that are **bulk reducing**, where large heavy materials are received and broken down before being distributed (e.g. cement, slate and coal). In this case the industry will be situated near to where its raw materials are to be found as it is cheaper to transport the goods after processing, rather than before.

Proximity to raw materials or fuel is less important in an age of modern motorways and transport. However, the importance of a good distribution centre, and nearness to markets, has always been important – especially for goods that are imported or exported. Probably the best example of this is Rotterdam in Holland – this has giant terminals for the storage of imported grain, oil, iron ore and sulphur, which are then distributed (sometimes by river and canal) to the vast markets of West Germany.

DID YOU KNOW?

In Britain many companies who intend exporting to Europe have located their factories in the South of England to be near the Channel ports and the Channel tunnel.

Evidence
Assignment 2A

Alton Towers is a famous theme park situated near Alton in Staffordshire. Initially this may seem to be a remote rural area with poor transport links – which would obviously affect the number of visitors who could obtain easy access to the park. However, the reality is that its situation is ideal for attracting people from all over Britain, rather than from just one area. In addition, there is no immediate competition in the area from *other* theme parks.

The only disadvantage of setting up in a remote location may be shortage of labour but, in the same way as staff are 'bussed in' to motorway service areas, a large organisation will make its own arrangements to transport staff to and from large towns nearby. However, the rural area will also benefit as the needs of the organisation itself will attract smaller satellite industries to set up nearby. For example, a laundry, an electrical contractor, a bakery and a dairy may operate successfully by becoming suppliers to a theme park such as Alton Towers. However, rural residents may be less pleased with the increase in traffic, noise and litter in the area!

Other theme parks have been set up because of natural resources – nearness to water for an 'Aquapark' or nearness to a large market and labour supply (e.g. Blackpool Pleasure Beach). In many cases, these are clear examples of businesses in the leisure industry choosing their location on a similar basis to businesses in other types of industry.

1 a Find Alton Towers on a map. Calculate its distance from both the M6 and M1 motorways.
   b Look at a large-scale map of England. Roughly calculate the distance of Alton Towers from a northern town (e.g. Carlisle) and a southern town (e.g. Brighton).
   c Identify *four* towns in the area where Alton Towers may recruit staff and offer transport provision.
   d Write a brief conclusion of your opinion of the location of Alton Towers, bearing in mind the type of business it is.

2 Choose one other theme park in Britain, either small or large. Find out about the attractions it offers and draw a map showing its location. Summarise why you think this location has been chosen and its advantages and disadvantages.

3 *As a group*, you have been approached by a foreign business person who wishes to invest in a new theme park somewhere in Britain.

   a Select a suitable location.
   b Draw this on a map, showing its proximity to transport links, its market for customers and any natural resources which will be important.
   c Prepare a ten-minute presentation which you can give to your investor, stating why you have chosen that particular location, the effect you think this will have on the local community, any disadvantages you can identify and how you propose to overcome these.

THE SCALE AND SCOPE OF BUSINESS ORGANISATIONS

The **scale** of business organisations relates to their size. In Britain there are many business organisations ranging from sole traders to massive enterprises employing thousands of people.

The **scope** of business organisations relates to whether they sell their goods or services on a local, national or international basis.

Why do some businesses grow large and others stay small? Why do some operate only locally and others sell their products all over the world? Is it because of the nature of the industry itself and the products they make, or simply because some owners and managers are more ambitious than others? And is size relevant to success? Are large organisations more likely to be successful because they can spend more money on advertising to dominate the market? Or are small businesses better because they can be more flexible and respond to changing consumer demands more quickly? By the time you have completed this chapter you will be able to answer these questions.

Activity

From what you read in the previous chapter, can you say whether each of the following types of organisation is likely to be small, medium or large – or a mixture of these? Which do you think are likely to operate on a local, national or international basis?

1 A sole trader.
2 A partnership.
3 A private limited company.
4 A public limited company.

The very largest organisations are known as **multinationals**, so called because they own or control production facilities in more than one country in the world. Examples include the oil companies, drug companies, car producers and computer giants (e.g. IBM) which both produce and sell their goods on a worldwide basis.

If they are based in Britain they will be public limited companies (plc). If they are based abroad then they will have a different name; for example, in America you would see Corp or Inc after a company's name, in Australia you would see the letters Pty and on the Continent the letters SA.

Activity

As a group, decide which soft drinks multinational you consider to be the largest in the world. Why did you reach this conclusion?

Calculating the scale of organisations

You probably said 'Coca Cola' (or 'Coke') to the question above – but why? Was it because you have seen many of its advertisements, or because you think it sells more – worldwide – than any other firm? If you made your judgement because you think that more Cokes were sold than any other soft drink (e.g. Pepsi) then you have judged the company on its **market share**. In other words, you have assumed that more people drink Coke than any other drink, so Coca Cola has the largest share of the soft drink market.

Alternatively, you may have made your decision on the basis of the actual size of the organisation in terms of the **number of people it employs**. You may have thought that, because Coke is bottled, canned and distributed worldwide, Coca Cola is the largest employer in the soft drinks industry.

However, you must remember that these measures – market share and number of employees – only tell you about *size*. None of them tells you whether Coke made more profit than any other soft drink manufacturer! Not only that, but there are dangers in using both of these measures, as you will soon see.

DID YOU KNOW?

A company's sales are known as its **turnover**. This is the total amount of sales revenue a company receives in a year. The company with the largest market share will usually have the highest turnover of all organisations operating in a particular industry.

Evidence Collection Point 2.1

If you are wondering whether Coca Cola really is the largest soft drink manufacturer then check it yourself! Ring their Freephone Consumer Information line on 0800-227711 and find out – but consider first what questions you are going to ask and what measures you will use! If you ask, Coke will also send you booklets on their organisation, market share, etc. You should also find out what British company merged with Coke in 1987 – as this is referred to again later in the chapter.

Summarise the information you obtain, preferably on a word-processor; keep it safely with any literature you receive.

You may at some time have heard the expression 'lies, damn lies and statistics'. All this means, quite simply, is that figures can often be used to give inaccurate information because important factors have been left out (either deliberately or accidentally). Therefore, when you are collecting information on anything you must be careful to consider other factors which could influence your final conclusion. For instance:

- A town has two paper mills. Company A employs 550 people and Company B employs 720 people. Which is the larger organisation?

The answer is that you do not know – unless you find out how many employees work part-time and how many work full-time! It could be that 600 people in Company B work there on a part-time basis and the total hours worked by the labour force as a whole is greater at Company A – even though, at first sight, this would seem to be the smaller company of the two.

Comparing like with like

It is very important that you do not attempt to compare two organisations in different industries. For instance, a highly automated industry will employ fewer people than one which relies heavily on manual skills.

Similarly, you cannot compare the market share of organisations in different industries. Not only is the actual

market different but the *size* of the total market can vary enormously. For instance, the British market for sweets and chocolate is measured in billions (approximately £4 billion in 1992) but for computer games the market is only £650 million – because not everyone has a computer but nearly everyone eats sweets and chocolate!

In addition, you need to be careful which 'market' you are using. The market for sweets alone is only £1 billion, whereas chocolate accounts for £3 billion worth of sales a year. If you were assessing the market for cars then it would be one thing to look at cars as a whole, and quite another to find out details of the 'sub' markets – diesel cars, sports cars, estate cars, etc.

DID YOU KNOW?

Some organisations quote their market share internationally, others quote it in relation to the UK alone. For instance, Coca Cola may give you information which refers to their operations *worldwide* as they operate on an international basis.

Activity

Again, see if you can answer this question before you read on! Bearing in mind what you learned about companies in Chapter 1, on which *type* of organisation would you find it easiest to obtain information, and why?

DID YOU KNOW?

All organisations, apart from public limited companies, have the right to refuse to disclose any details about their operations – so remember this when you are trying to find out information. A **public** limited company has, by law, to disclose information on its operations and financial situation each year. A **private** company has the right to keep this information private, just as its name implies.

For this reason you would be more sensible to confine your investigations of sole traders, partnerships and private companies to finding out facts such as the numbers of employees. They will probably consider any type of financial information to be confidential, unless you know one of the owners or managers very well indeed!

A similar restriction operates in terms of finding out market share. Your local grocer will not have a clue as to his market share because no-one has measured the total market for groceries in the town or area! Therefore this measure is only of any use if you are looking at large companies in an industry where the total market has been calculated – for instance if you were investigating the market share of large supermarkets such as Tesco, Asda and Sainsbury.

Evidence Collection Point 2.2

From the information you have just read, prepare a brief list of things you must be careful about when collecting evidence on the scale of companies. Do this on a word-processor under two separate headings:

1 *Number of employees*
2 *Market share.*

Check with your tutor that your information is correct before you continue.

· PRODUCTS AND THE SCALE AND · SCOPE OF OPERATIONS

Over the last 40 years there has been a growth in the number of very large organisations operating worldwide. Indeed, it is predicted that by the year 2000, the world's largest 250 multinationals will produce about half the world's output of goods.

In many industries the trend has been towards a small number of large-scale businesses operating on a worldwide basis rather than a large number of smaller

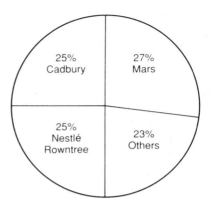

Figure 2.1a *Market shares in the chocolate industry*

organisations selling on a national basis. A typical example is car production. In the 1950s there were many UK car producers – Rootes, Triumph, Rover, Morris, Austin, etc. Today there is only one left – Rover – which currently has 14 per cent of the UK car market. More popular are Ford, with 22 per cent of the market and Vauxhall with 17 per cent – both American-owned companies. With a few exceptions, the day of the small car company has gone.

In cases like this, a few firms share most of the market between them. For example, in the UK the chocolate industry is dominated by Cadbury, Mars and Nestlé/Rowntree, while in the brewing industry the UK market is dominated by Bass, Courage and Carlsberg/Tetley (see Figures 2.1). In both these industries the larger companies may choose to export their goods *or* to concentrate on selling purely in the UK. In the same way, foreign producers may decide to operate internationally and sell their products in Britain (e.g. Swiss chocolate and Australian lager).

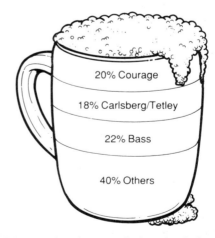

Figure 2.1b *Market shares in the brewing industry*

Evidence Collection Point 2.3

In both of the industries shown in Figure 2.1 a proportion of the market is taken up by other, smaller producers.

1 Name at least three of the other producers in both of the markets shown. If necessary, visit a supermarket to get some ideas!

2 Why do you think there is still room for small companies to operate if the market has been dominated by the giants?

Brainstorm these questions *as a group* and write down your answers. If you don't know how to do this then refer to the Student Guide on page vi. Keep your answers safely – you will need them again later.

DID YOU KNOW?

If a market is dominated by *one* firm it is said to be a **monopoly**. If it is dominated by a *few* large firms (e.g. banking and oil production) it is called an **oligopoly**. If you continue your studies to higher level you will meet this term again.

How companies grow

Companies which operate in an expanding market have the best chance of achieving internal growth and extending the scope of their operations. The computer industry is an obvious example – companies such as IBM, Apple and Microsoft grew rapidly as more and more computers were sold. In addition, because computers are bought worldwide, most of these companies operate on an international basis.

Other companies grow by adding to the number of goods they produce. In many cases these can be made from the same raw material used for the basic product. For example, oil refineries have grown larger not just because more vehicles are owned, so more fuel is bought, but because of developments in petrochemicals and other byproducts.

However, if a company wants to grow larger *quickly* then the most usual method is by merger or takeover. Mergers are usually friendly – this is when two companies join together for mutual benefit. A takeover is when one company buys out another – and this may not be friendly at all if the current management do not wish to see the company run by someone else.

Evidence Collection Point 2.4

1 Write down the name of the British company the Coca Cola Company merged with in 1987 (you should have found this out as part of Evidence Collection Point 2.1).

2 The number of building societies in Britain has declined dramatically because many have merged together. Find out how many were in existence in your area about 20 years ago. You can do this by visiting the library and looking in an old street directory or *Yellow Pages*. Now list those in existence today.

What benefits do you think there were to these organisations of 'joining together' or merging? Note down your suggestions before you read further.

Market movements

Markets vary in whether they are expanding, stagnant (not moving very much) or contracting. If a market is contracting then companies have *either* to reduce the scale or scope of their operations (e.g. by closing down factories) *or* diversify and make different products. This is easier for some companies than others.

For instance, the demand for whisky has declined both in Britain and abroad by about 10 per cent, to the extent that more whisky was being produced than was needed. One of the main whisky producers in Scotland, United Distillers (owned by Guinness), therefore announced job losses and the closure of several distilleries and bottling plants. Because these are specialised plants and in remote locations (see Figure 2.2) there is little chance that they can be used for anything else.

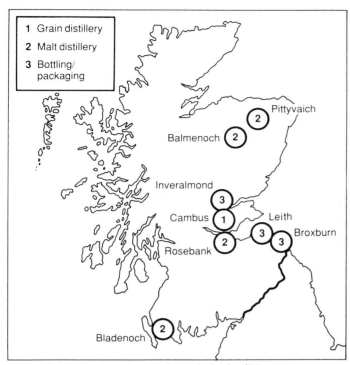

Figure 2.2 *Locations of redundant whisky facilities*

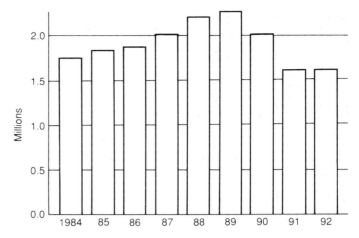

Figure 2.3 *New car sales in Britain*

Evidence Collection Point 2.5

Figure 2.3 gives the numbers of new cars sold in Britain between 1984 and 1992.

1 Which was the best year for car sales?

2 Is the market growing, contracting or stagnant?

3 *As a group*, discuss why you think the pattern of car sales was as shown between 1989 and 1992 and summarise your ideas.

4 Calculate the approximate *total* size of the car market in Britain in terms of unit sales.

Figure 2.4 gives the sales of cars in the UK in 1992 per manufacturer.

5 Calculate which ten companies had the largest market share and put these in order with the highest sales at the top of your list.

6 On a computer, create a pie chart which displays this information.

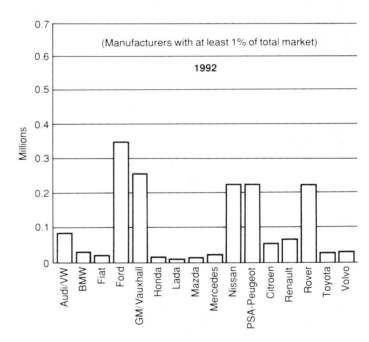

Figure 2.4 *Car manufacturers' unit sales*

DID YOU KNOW?

Some markets are more volatile (i.e. changeable) than others, depending on whether the products are considered as necessities or luxuries. If you hadn't very much money you might not buy a magazine but you would still need to buy basic items such as food.

Evidence Assignment 2B

Reckitt & Colman is a large multinational company. Its products include Windolene, Brasso, Steradent, Dettol, Robinson's Barley Water and Colman's mustard. The products are made in 35 countries of the world and sold in 80. The company aim over the years has been to develop brands that consumers know and trust and therefore build up its market share. It employs 23 000 people and its sales amounted to £1904 million in 1992/3, with profits of £182 million.

Sales around the world amount to 20 per cent in the UK, 30 per cent in Africa, 20 per cent in the Pacific, 15 per cent in Latin America, 8 per cent in North America and 14 per cent in other European countries. Its current aims are to invest in new product development and marketing, and increase markets in the USA and Europe.

1 Enter the information on Reckitt's world sales on to a spreadsheet.

  a Produce a pie chart which shows the current position.

  b From the total value of sales in 1992/3 (given above), calculate the value of sales in each region listed.

  c If sales increased in the USA and Europe by 4 per cent each year, and in the other regions by 2 per cent a year, what would the total value of sales be in 1995/6?

2 Three other large-scale producers of household products are Colgate Palmolive, Proctor & Gamble and Unilever.

  a Find out at least six of the products made by *one* of these companies. You may like to start by looking around your own kitchen and bathroom, or your local supermarket.

  b Either by contacting the company itself, or by researching in your library, find out details of the scale and scope of the company you have chosen, i.e. the number of employees, market share, where abouts in the world it operates, and so on. Write a summary of your findings similar to the details given on Reckitt & Colman in this assignment.

  c Compose a paragraph which you consider explains *why* food and household products can be produced and marketed on an international basis. (You may want to do this when you have finished this chapter and have read more about this topic.)

· INTERNAL ECONOMIES OF SCALE ·

One reason why many companies aim to grow large is because they gain **internal economies of scale**. This means that they can increase their profits because operating on a large scale means they can reduce their costs and do more to attract customers. For example:

- They can afford to advertise nationally, and employ specialists to plan their campaigns (i.e. advertising agents).
- They can hold special promotions – free gifts, competitions and special offers.
- They can buy in bulk, so reducing the cost of their raw materials.
- They can afford to invest in new technology and specialist machinery so that the goods can be mass produced very quickly using the latest techniques (probably with reduced labour costs, see page 88).
- They can afford to spend money on research and development so that they can stay ahead of their competitors.
- They can raise additional capital relatively easily, either from shareholders or from a bank.

In the case of the building society mergers mentioned on page 44, the *costs* of operating their town centre offices would, in many cases, be virtually halved in terms of staff and running costs (electricity, telephones etc.), as one might be closed down. Marketing would also work out cheaper in terms of cost per client.

· LARGE-SCALE INDUSTRIES ·

The type of industries in which large-scale organisations are to be found are those:

1 where heavy investment in equipment or ongoing research is required

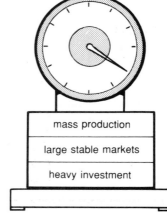

2 where there is a large total and relatively stable market
3 where internal economies of scale can be achieved (e.g. through mass production techniques).

Manufacturing industries

When a product can be sold worldwide with few changes the market can be classed as 'global'. As an example, soft drinks can be sold worldwide without *any* changes. Cars, on the other hand, may have to be slightly modified – for countries with different regulations on emissions, right hand or left hand drive, etc. The *fewer* changes which have to be made for overseas markets the better, which is why Ford have designed the Mondeo to need the minimum of changes and have called it the 'global car'.

Therefore the overall size of the market is critical for a company in determining the eventual scope of its operations (e.g. whether this should be local, national or international).

Evidence Collection Point 2.6

Examine the chart below and find out in which industry each company is involved (i.e. the type of products they make). Then establish which industries are the most common and which explanation – 1, 2 or 3 (above) – applies in each case.

Summarise your answer before you read any further.

Top ten European companies

Name of company	Country	Turnover 1991 (£bn)
Royal Dutch/Shell	Holland/GB	58.0
British Petroleum	GB	32.6
Daimler-Benz	Germany	32.4
Fiat	Italian	25.8
Unilever	Holland/GB	23.1
Elf	France	20.1
Nestlé	Switzerland	19.9
RWE	Germany	17.0
BAT Industries	GB	16.4
Hoechst	Germany	16.1

DID YOU KNOW?

In Britain, a billion *used to be* a million million. In America it is thousand million – and this version is now widely used in Britain too.

Activity

To check you can tell the difference, convert all the figures given above into millions. Check with your tutor you have done this correctly.

Large-scale manufacturing industries

Drug companies need to spend millions of pounds on research and development to stay ahead of their competitors. The chart below shows the turnover of the top ten drug companies in 1991. A high level of sales is essential to repay the amount of money which has been spent on research.

Company	1991 sales ($ million)
Merck & Co	6167
Glaxo	5388
Bristol Myers Squibb	5065
SmithKline Beecham	4182
Ciba-Geigy	4031
Johnson & Johnson	3861
American Home	3872
Hoechst	3751
Lilly	3382
Pfizer	3296

Similarly, oil companies are very large scale because of the amount of money required for exploration.

The food and drink industry is worth billions of pounds each year, both to producers and retailers – as you should have discovered when you did Evidence Assignment 2B. However, as you already know from Chapter 1, retailers are a *service* industry (see page 27).

Other industries that require millions of pounds in investment in plant and machinery are likely to be large scale (e.g. car producers, chemical refineries, steel plants and airlines). ICI employs about 114 000 people and sold 12.1 billion worth of goods in 1992. It was so large it was split to form two companies ICI and Zeneca. British Steel employs 41 800 people and made sales of £2206 billion in the last six months of 1992.

Activity

1 The sales figures for the drug companies in the table on page 47 were given in dollars. Using today's rate (check in a newspaper), convert all these figures to sterling and write them out accurately.

2 Now convert all the figures to billions.

3 If the companies listed were the *only* companies in the world making drugs then what would be the total value of the market?

4 Based on this figure, what would be the market share of each company listed? Work these out in percentages.

Evidence Assignment 2C

The problem with gaining economies of scale is that this *can* mean that large operators – who can produce goods much more cheaply – 'push out' smaller companies who cannot compete with them on prices. This is good news for the consumer in terms of price. For example, a computer which cost £5000 a few years ago would now retail for only £1100. However, it is less good in terms of variety and there is always the danger that, in the future, with only a few companies left in the industry they could manipulate prices between them.

A typical example is the computer industry. Many smaller companies have closed as the 'giants' such as IBM, Compaq, Apple and Dell have cut their prices drastically to increase their sales volumes. At present price reductions have been running at about 40 per cent a year, and have boosted sales by about 10 per cent – though experts now think that even large producers can only stand a further 25 per cent cut, probably in two stages.

Large operators have the advantage in several ways. They can buy microchips at bargain prices because they buy in bulk. A high-performance chip, which would cost a large manufacturer $60, would cost between $100 and $500 on the open market – and if demand was large the small producer probably wouldn't be able to get one at any price. In addition, large manufacturers can tie up deals with software companies so that expensive software, such as Lotus, which would cost about £700, can be included for nothing.

1 What term is used when only a few large companies dominate an industry? Is this the case with the computer industry today?

2 In your own words, explain why the large computer companies are gaining from economies of scale, and the ensuing advantages/disadvantages to the consumer.

3 a Find out the cost of six *comparable* computers. Enter these into a spreadsheet. Work out what their price will be in two years' time if the further cuts predicted by experts occur.
   b Note any 'special offers' (e.g. free software) being included by large companies.
   c If you were buying a computer, which one would you choose, and why?

4 In your own words, explain why it is possible for large-scale production to take place in the computer industry and why these goods can be sold on an international basis.

· DISECONOMIES OF SCALE ·

Being large scale is not always a recipe for success – sometimes the higher you climb the further there is to fall! The most spectacular fall in 1992 was that of IBM, the American computer giant which made sales worldwide of $64.5 billion and a loss of $5 billion! In the UK, IBM's sales were £3751 million with a loss of £616 million! ICI was another firm which had a disastrous year in 1992 – with a turnover of £12.1 billion in 1992 it made a loss of £384 million.

As a result ICI has restructured the company and reduced its size by splitting itself in two – a process called a **de-merger**. IBM has followed a similar route, closing down parts of the business and going through a period of reorganisation.

What went wrong in both these cases? So far as ICI was concerned one of the problems was termed 'the dead weight of being a huge organisation'. IBM was called 'slow-moving, bureaucratic and ineffectual'. In neither case could such a large organisation respond quickly to changes in its markets. In other words:

- The firm has increased beyond its best operating size and become inefficient.
- It is difficult to control or manage.
- Communications may be poor.
- There may be many 'layers' of employees between the bottom and the top, so that top managers who make the decisions have only a vague idea of what is happening lower down (see Chapter 4).
- The aim of the staff may be to 'please the boss' rather than to 'tell the truth'. In this case it would be difficult for an employee to disagree with what he or she thought was a bad management decision.
- Employees may be dissatisfied especially if there is large-scale division of labour (so that jobs are routine and monotonous). This can lead to absenteeism and high staff turnover.

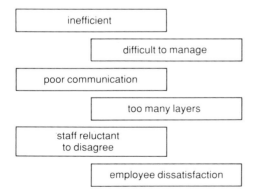

The problems of being big

These are all called **diseconomies of scale** – i.e. the problems associated with being big. In this situation many companies have to face the task of restructuring and reorganising themselves, or going out of business. In ICI's case the company was divided into two, ICI retaining the chemicals side of the company (including Dulux paints) and Zeneca, the drug and agrochemical part of the organisation, now operating as a separate entity .

Because of the problems of diseconomies of scale, some writers disagree with the idea that the computer industry will eventually be controlled by the giants – as mentioned in Evidence Assignment 2C. Instead, they consider that smaller companies will have the benefits of being able to be flexible, to develop and market new products more quickly and stay in touch with what their customers really need.

DID YOU KNOW?

The nickname of IBM is Big Blue. If you wonder why then take a moment to look at its logo. Many press articles called the company Big Red after its financial problems last year. If you don't know why, then ask your tutor!

· SERVICE INDUSTRIES ·

In Chapter 1, you learned that under 'tertiary production' there are two types of service industries – direct services and personal services. British Telecom provides a direct service, that of telecommunications. Other large organisations which provide a direct service include retailers, banks and insurance companies. Again the trend in many cases has been for larger organisations, rather than small ones, especially where vast amounts of capital are required. One exception is retailing, which can be on a large or small scale. Sainsbury – one of Britain's largest supermarkets – employs about 113 000 people and, between June and December 1992, had sales of £5.2 billion. Compare this with your local grocer.

Chain stores and multiples, which sell a variety of goods throughout the country, can benefit from internal economies of scale, especially in terms of their purchasing and marketing. W. H. Smith, the retailer, employs about 29 000 people and between June and December 1992 made sales worth £1 074 000.   `

Another exception in services are those organisations involved in the travel trade. British Airways employs

48 453 people around the world and owns 227 aircraft. In contrast, Virgin employs 2400 people worldwide and owns only eight aircraft. In the same way you can find large travel agencies (e.g. Thomas Cook) and small local operators – who may be successful because they are flexible, helpful and build up a number of 'regular' customers over the years, even if they cannot offer all the services of a large operator.

DID YOU KNOW?

Many supermarkets increased their profits during 1993, and consider that the reason is because they are now open on Sundays. Two-thirds of the money spent would have been spent on other days but, it is estimated, *one-third* of the money taken each Sunday would not have been spent at all if the supermarket had been closed.

Assessing the scale of service industries

It can sometimes be difficult to assess the scale of organisations that operate in service industries. For instance, you may find it difficult to assess a bank in terms of the number of employees as this, as you have seen, can depend on the number of part-time employees and the degree of automation. You *could* find out the market share of each bank, but one measure often used to assess size is to find the number of assets owned by each organisation. This can also be used as a measure of security, in that a bank with a great number of assets is more 'safe' than one with a lot less. However, none of these measures will give you any indication of profitability, only of size.

Evidence Collection Point 2.7

In 1992 the assets of the top UK banks were given as follows:

Barclays	£138.1bn
National Westminster	£122.6bn
Midland	£59.4bn
Lloyds	£51.3bn
Royal Bank of Scotland	£32.2bn
TSB	£25.8bn

1 Find out the current market share of each bank and draw a pie chart on your computer to show this.

2 How do your results compare with the asset list shown above?

3 Find out with which bank the Royal Bank of Scotland merged in the 1980s. State clearly why you think the merger took place and the advantages of this strategy.

4 Barclays Bank made a loss of £2.42 billion in 1992. This was blamed on bad debts and bad management decisions. As part of its recovery strategy Barclays intends to invest more in banking technology and increasing fees for services.

   a What are 'bad debts' and why did they cause the bank to lose money?

   b How do you think the company will save money by investing in banking technology? (You may like to wait until you have read Chapter 3 before you answer this question.)

   c What could be the result of charging customers higher fees?

   d Many industrial companies made losses from falling demand for their products, either because of fashion changes or because of the recession. Do you think the same problems affect banks? If not, is there any excuse for a large bank making such a loss?

Evidence Collection Point 2.8

Another way of checking the size of an organisation operating in a large-scale service industry can be to find out the number of branches of each one.

Figure 2.5 opposite shows the number of branches owned by the top ten estate agents in 1991 and 1992.

1 Enter the figures on a spreadsheet.

   a What was the *trend*, in terms of scale, between 1991 and 1992?

   b If the trend continues for the next three years, how many branches will the Halifax and General Accident have in 1995? How many branches will there be in total?

   c Produce a bar chart which displays your information, clearly labelled.

	Branches at end 1992	Branches at end 1991
Halifax	550	565
Royal	517	584
Hambro Countrywide	453	486
Black Horse	393	397
General Accident	390	434
Nationwide	361	378
Cornerstone	355	373
Legal & General	264	270
Woolwich	257	294
Connells	172	171

Source: OCEA

Figure 2.5 *Top ten estate agencies*

2 *As a group*, discuss *why* this trend has occurred and the extent to which you think it is likely to continue. Summarise your views on a word-processor.

3 Identify two other service industries where size of organisations could be assessed in terms of number of branches. State two disadvantages of using this type of measure rather than market share or number of employees.

Medium and small-scale organisations

In contrast with those organisations offering a direct service, many which offer a personal service are much smaller in scale (e.g. hairdressers, window cleaners, plumbers). This also applies to some manufacturing companies which produce specialist goods. Indeed, Britain has a very large number of small enterprises which either:

- offer a specialist service, or
- have identified a 'niche' in a larger market, or
- operate only on a local scale.

When you were looking at the chocolate and brewing industries earlier you were asked to identify 'other' producers. For chocolate, you may have identified companies such as Terrys of York or Thorntons. These are typical examples of 'niche' producers. A **niche** is a segment of an established branded market which can be filled by a specialist product. Terrys, for instance, does not openly compete with Cadbury, Mars or Rowntree. Instead it produces its own specialised types of chocolates, as does Thorntons. Niche producers operate in many large markets; for example TVR and Morgan sports cars are bought

because they are different and quite rare. Therefore small producers can operate in what is, essentially, a large mass production market. In addition they are likely to supply a much smaller market and may not export their goods.

Here are some other reasons why small organisations continue to exist:

- Many entrepreneurs prefer to be independent and avoid the involved legislation and restrictions of operating a large organisation. In 1988, out of nearly 800 000 organisations interviewed, nearly 55 per cent said they had no plans to grow beyond their present size, 35 per cent expected to grow slowly and only 10 per cent expected to grow rapidly.
- The government usually looks to encourage small enterprises because of the economic benefits. In Britain there are actually twice as many large companies for the size of the country than in any other European country. There is a definite lack of small and medium-sized companies. Economic evidence shows that these enterprises are more likely to provide new ideas, future leaders and greater job opportunities than large organisations. For that reason, in successive budgets, various organisations have lobbied the government to assist the formation and growth of small businesses – especially in relation to the problems they have in obtaining finance.
- Consumers like variety, so there are limits to mass production. Few of us like to spend money on new clothes, for example, and to see everyone else in the same outfit! Jewellery and furniture are other markets where people will pay more for something that is individual or hand-crafted.

- Some geographical areas are too remote for bulk production. For instance, a small village may have its own bakery which serves the local population, whereas it would be uneconomic for a national bakery to try to supply the area because of transport costs.
- Large organisations often require the services of many small companies. For instance, in the textile industry, the dyeing and finishing of cloth is often done by small, specialist companies who serve the market as a whole. Japanese car producers who have set up business in the North East of England have attracted around them a whole host of small suppliers of specialist components.
- Small firms can join together to gain internal economies of scale. A typical example is a grocer combine (e.g. Spar, VG and Mace). In this case small grocers can gain from their association with a larger organisation which bulk buys and markets the goods on their behalf.
- Luxury goods cannot be mass produced. People want to pay for the 'name' and acquire status by owning something which is expensive and exclusive. Therefore the organisations which have a reputation for making prestigious goods will be small-scale and may even be choosy about their customers!

DID YOU KNOW?

A few years ago Porsche stopped manufacturing the model which was the bottom of its range. Even though the car cost many thousands of pounds it was selling too well! Porsche was worried that if too many of their cars were seen on the road, and thought to be commonplace, they would lose their customers to Lambourghini or Ferrari.

Activity

How many luxury goods can you think of with famous names, which you would want to own if you were very rich? As a group, see if you can think of five items to buy with your first million!

Evidence Collection Point 2.9

In 1992, 32 000 people went bankrupt in England and Wales and nearly 24 000 companies went into liquidation - often because they hadn't enough money to repay the bank for loans and overdrafts they had taken out. This was a record number of business closures in Britain and led to many organisations, such as the Smaller Firms Council and the Forum of Private Businesses, lobbying the government to do more to help small and medium-sized businesses.

1 What kind of traders 'go bankrupt' and what kind of organisations 'go into liquidation'?

2 How does the close of all these small businesses affect Britain's economy?

3 Follow the government's Budget with your tutor in the November of your year of study and note all the measures which would help small businesses. If it is after November when you read this, then look up the information in your library. Prepare a summary of the main points which affected small businesses.

4 Interview a local business person who operates on a small scale. Note down the type of business, product (or service) offered, scale and scope of operation. Find out:

a if he or she considers there are opportunities for expansion in the future
b if there are any limitations on growth
c how the owner sees his or her business in five or ten years' time.

Evidence Collection Point 2.10

Figure 2.6 shows the market share of record producers in 1990. The company with the largest market share, Polygram, employs 11 000 people and in 1992 had sales of £2.51 billion – mostly earned by the sale of pop records. Its labels include Decca, A & M, Polydor, Island, Mercury, London and Deutsche Grammophon.

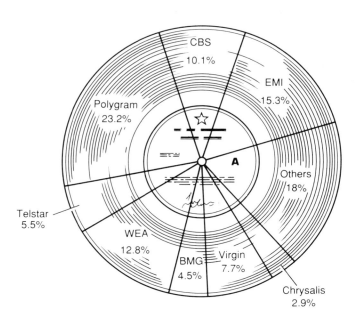

Figure 2.6 *Market share of record producers in 1990*

The entertainment business is a typical example of a global industry. Most of the large organisations involved in producing records or films operate on an international basis.

1 Investigate and find out the number of employees or the turnover of at least two of the other companies shown with a specific market share. Comment on whether this information supports the ranking in terms of market share, or not.

2 'Others' – with a market share of 25.4 per cent – refers to the small independent record producers, known as 'Indys' in the trade. Find out the names of at least two independent companies and obtain more information on the scale and scope of their operations.

3 Write at least two paragraphs stating, in your view:

   a the advantages of large-scale operation in the record industry
   b why small companies still exist in the same market.

4 The film industry is given as an example of a global industry. Why do you think film companies operate on such a large scale? What limitations do you think there are to marketing films worldwide, and how can these be overcome?

· MARKET NEEDS AND WANTS ·

In business, the successful company does not just stay in touch with the market but should be one step ahead. If it then identifies a 'gap' in the market which it can fill it becomes a **market leader**. Sir Clive Sinclair revolutionised the home computer market with his Spectrum ZX – he was the first to invent a cheap, mass produced games computer. However, when he tried to repeat this success with his single-seat, battery and pedal-powered tricycle – the C5 – it was a disastrous flop. Sir Clive had lost touch with what the consumers wanted.

What consumers want and what they need are two different things. You need to eat every day, and basic items such as bread, potatoes, meat and vegetables would keep you healthy. However, tonight you may *want* to eat a pizza, tomorrow you may like the idea of fish and chips. Again, you need to be clean and fresh if you want to stay healthy (and have any friends!). However, the idea of only a bar of soap may be less appealing than shower gel or bubble bath.

To a large extent, your wants have been developed by producers of goods who persuade you that life is far more interesting, pleasurable or easy if you buy their goods.

On a different level, when you are buying a particular product you can sub-divide your requirements into needs and wants. You may *need* a new sweater to keep you warm. You may *want* a green one with a round neck and long sleeves – but these are 'extras' rather than essentials.

Organisations that want to be successful will spend a considerable amount of time and money trying to assess the needs and wants of their consumers, and often undertake market research to establish these (see Chapter 9). To a great extent, much may depend on the type of market in which they operate.

Types of market

Markets can be sub-divided into two types, the consumer market and the industrial market.

The **consumer market** refers to individuals and households who buy goods and services for their own personal use. These may be:

- **durable goods** – which last a long time and are only purchased infrequently (e.g. cars, furniture, electrical goods)
- **non-durables or consumables** – bought frequently and used quite soon afterwards (e.g. food and toiletries)
- **services** – bought because the consumer will benefit in some way (e.g. hairdressing, car repairs, entertainment).

The **industrial market** refers to organisations (and a few individuals) who buy products or services that will be used in manufacturing other goods, be used in running their own business, or be resold to other customers. These may be:

- **capital goods** – which are purchased infrequently and used over a long period of time (e.g. machinery, computers, vehicles)
- **consumable products** – bought frequently and used almost immediately (e.g. oils and lubricants, raw materials, office stationery)
- **services** – provided by specialists to carry out specific tasks for the organisation (e.g. road haulage and distribution companies, advertising agencies and accountants).

Evidence Collection Point 2.11

1 Can you identify two products and two services which are sold in *both* the consumer and the industrial markets?

2 Into which category would you place each of the following products?

paint	excavators
toothpaste	vending machines
hairdriers	paper clips

3 Selling techniques in the industrial market are different from those used in the consumer market. One reason is that industrial buyers are less likely to be persuaded to buy goods they don't really need (i.e. 'impulse buy') than consumers.

   a Why do you think this is the case?

   b What methods do manufacturers use to tempt you to 'impulse buy' their products?

   c Can you identify three products you have been tempted to buy in the past year which you didn't think you wanted until you saw them advertised?

4 You are buying your first car. List five features which you *need* and five features which you would *want*. Upon which type of features do you think car producers concentrate in trying to sell their product, and why?

Needs, wants and innovation

There are dozens of products on the market today which did not exist ten or twenty years ago. They have probably been introduced as:

- they were developed because of technological breakthrough (e.g. silicon chips, lasers and videos)
- they have evolved from other products (e.g. personal stereos, laptop computers and car phones).

In some cases, this can mean that existing products become obsolete. Slide-rules are no longer used because the pocket calculator has taken over. Typewriters were first of all manual, then electric, finally electronic and are now being replaced by word-processors.

These products have catered for the need of individuals and businesses to make calculations and process documents more quickly and easily. As standards of living rise (so consumers have more money to spend) and the pace of living gets even quicker, people are likely to spend more money on items which save them work, time or both.

DID YOU KNOW?

Many companies operate suggestion schemes so that staff can contribute ideas for new products or new ways of doing things. In many cases employees can win monetary prizes if an idea is implemented. Hewlett Packard, the computer company, is reputed to think up ideas for eight new products a week – even though they may not be used.

In some cases ideas need not be radical but can be developed from an existing product. 3M designed the Post-It note, which is simply a development from ordinary small pads of paper but with a sticky top part for keeping the note firmly on a vertical or horizontal surface. The idea was simple, but the organisation saw its profits increase rapidly after the idea caught on.

Innovation and change

It is no use a company developing a new product and then assuming it will meet the needs and wants of consumers forever more! Our needs and wants change because of various factors – social trends, fashion and new legal requirements to name but a few.

Changing social trends have included the following:

- More women work and have less time to shop (and therefore buy instant meals or take-aways).
- People work fewer hours and have more time for leisure.
- Fewer people go to church on Sunday or belong to an organised religion which stops them from shopping on that day.
- More people are becoming health conscious, and therefore buy diet meals and low calorie drinks, visit exercise salons and try to stop smoking (hence the success of non-smoking patches).

Fashion trends also affect our needs and wants. Clothes in particular change from one year to the next, so although, for instance, many people wear jeans, the colour of these and the style will vary from one year to another. Other trends can become 'crazes' which just last for a short time (e.g. skateboards and BMX bicycles).

Finally, legal requirements can affect our needs and wants. Seat belts were seen by the government as essential to reduce the scale of injuries received in vehicle collisions. Many people did not want them but were forced to wear them when the law made this compulsory. The current concern with the environment has led to most cars being fitted with catalytic converters, which convert toxic gases from the engine exhausts into less harmful emissions.

Note: Consumer wants and needs and how these change are dealt with more fully in Chapter 9.

DID YOU KNOW?

Innovation need not be confined just to products but can also be applied to services. In Britain, you would check in at an airport by queuing up with your heavy luggage at a check-in desk, sometimes for up to an hour. You would then be handed your boarding card, go to the departure lounge and finally proceed to the departure gate. In America the system is different. Your luggage is taken away from you immediately upon arrival at the airport (on the pavement outside!) and weighed in. You receive your boarding card near to the gate itself. In the meantime you can wander around the airport, visit the shops and have something to eat.

Evidence Collection Point 2.12

1 All the following items are relatively recent innovations. Can you identify the needs and wants fulfilled by each one?

kitchen paper towels	Sellotape
non-stick pans	vegetarian ready meals
non-drip paint	automatic teller machines (cash machines)

2 Add four products of your own to the list above, again stating the needs and wants that are catered for in each case.

3 Some products are successful because of change – in consumer taste and fashion and legal changes. Identify at least three products (other than those mentioned above) which have been introduced because of these factors.

4 a What do you think are the advantages of the American method of checking in travellers over the British system?

 b Identify one service which is provided in your own school or college where you may have to wait or queue (e.g. the refectory?) and make suggestions to improve this.

5 *As a group* hold a brainstorming session to see how many new products you can think of which would fulfil the needs or wants of a member of your family or group. For instance, your mother may want clothes to be made out of a fabric which never needs ironing, your father may want grass which doesn't grow, an unstealable car and a cure for baldness, and you may like the idea of a computer which teaches you to keyboard perfectly in an hour! Your tutor may prefer a computer which automatically scans, marks and corrects all your work!

555555555555555

Choose the best idea and refine this so that you can 'sell' your product verbally to the other groups at the end of the session.

Then write a summary of the session and your final conclusion to add to your portfolio.

Evidence Project

This project is designed to be carried out in small groups of three or four. The group is responsible for dividing up the work so that everyone is equally involved. Make sure that your project contains a final sheet which states clearly the contribution of each person and which has been signed by each member of the group.

1 Draw up a survey sheet which you can complete after visiting local business organisations. The sheet should enable you to record the scale and product of each business and the reasons (if any) for their location. You should also be able to identify those which operate on a local, national and international basis.

2 Compile a list of 20 different business organisations in your area which you plan to survey. Make sure that there is, in your opinion, a mixture of size, type of ownership and service or product offered.

3 Visit each organisation and interview either the manager or a supervisor to obtain the information you need to complete your survey sheet.

4 Produce a summary of your findings. Include a paragraph which identifies the type of industries which predominate in your area and any particular reasons for this.

5 Write a paragraph assessing the number of organisations in your area which operate on a national or international basis and those which operate only on a local basis. Analyse the difference in the *products or services* of each, and how these have affected the scale of operations.

6 Identify two *new* products which you consider either one or two of your organisations could make which would satisfy market wants and needs. These may be completely new or be a development from an existing

product. State why you think the product would be successful in each case.

7 Make a front cover for your project. Title this 'The Scale and Product of Business Organisations'. Include your name and, if possible, bind your project so that it looks professional.

Evidence Checkpoint

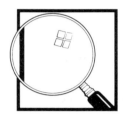

Check that all your assignments and Evidence Collection materials are complete and to the correct standard. Can you improve anything to achieve a higher grade?

Revision Test

True or false?

1 The majority of small businesses would prefer to operate on a large scale.

2 Market needs and wants are constantly changing.

3 Calculating the number of employees will always give an accurate measure of the scale of an organisation.

4 A small business would not know its market share.

5 A footloose industry is one where companies move around a lot.

Complete the blanks

6 A .... is a large organisation which owns or controls production in more than one country.

7 The worst effect of the closure or moving of large-scale industry from an area is ....

8 The difference between consumable durables and non-durables is ....
....

9 Three geographical reasons for the traditional siting of industry are ...., ... and ....

10 The type of organisation which has to publicise its annual results is a ....
....

Short answer questions

11 State four products usually made by large-scale organisations.

12 State two internal and two external economies of scale.

13 Give two measures which can be used in assessing the scale of business organisations.

14 Give two service industries in which small-scale businesses predominate.

15 State four products which have been introduced in recent years to fulfil a market want or need.

Write a short paragraph to show you clearly understand each of the following terms:

16 Market share.

17 Merger.

18 Labour supply.

19 Service industry.

20 Diseconomies of scale.

chapter **3** THE UK EMPLOYMENT MARKET

Learning Objectives

This chapter is concerned with different types of employment and their features, and the training and qualifications required to gain employment in the business world. It examines the regional differences in employment and the effects of changing technology.

After studying this chapter you should be able to:

- describe different types of employment

- describe the main features of employment

- identify and explain the levels of employment in your own region and another region in the UK

- describe the effects of changing technology on physical conditions and levels of employment

- present your findings on regional employment.

· TYPES OF EMPLOYMENT ·

At one time it was standard practice for many people to leave school, obtain a full-time job – firstly at trainee or apprentice level – and then, once fully skilled, stay in the same type of job until they retired. Those who had the capital to invest (and the courage to go it alone) may have decided to start a business and become self-employed, or they might have worked in a family business and inherited it at some stage in their lives.

Today the pattern of employment is far more varied and unemployment is far more widespread. No longer are jobs 'for life' – many people have two or more careers during their working life. No longer are all jobs full-time. No longer is it the case that once in a job you will be secure forever more, or only required by your employer to do the job for which you specifically trained. No longer is it the case that few people either have the opportunity or the finances to start in business for themselves.

This chapter examines the different types of employment you may encounter. The next chapter also looks at different trends which have affected the patterns of employment and how these have changed.

DID YOU KNOW?

 It is estimated that only one in three people now works the standard 9 a.m. to 5 p.m. day – the rest work shifts, flexitime, part-time or regular overtime.

Employed or self-employed?

It seems easy to say that you are employed if you work for somebody else and you are self-employed if you work for yourself! But life isn't quite so simple. What would be your status, for instance, if you applied for and accepted one of the jobs advertised in Figure 3.1?

KEYBOARD OPERATORS
required **urgently**

Must be capable of inputting data at minimum of 40 keystrokes per minute.

Only freelance operators should apply.

Ring Claire Southern for details on 0891-930849

**Data Processing Services Ltd
Marsh Lane
HIGHTOWN**

Figure 3.1

In this case you would actually be classified as self-employed, and your rights, responsibilities and obligations so far as tax and National Insurance are concerned would be different from someone with employee status. Your rights and responsibilities as an employee are covered in Chapter 5.

Self-employment

Being self-employed is not restricted to people who run their own business, in the physical sense of owning property and stock and perhaps employing their own staff. A great number of people work from home in a wide range of occupations and many of them are classed as self-employed. Examples are the hairdresser who has set up shop in one room of the house, the freelance book-keeper who does the accounts for other small businesses, the woman who holds clothing or Tupperware parties, and the artist who takes on freelance work from various publishing companies.

People who work on a freelance basis 'hire out' their skills to anyone who will pay them. A freelance photographer, for instance, may either be contracted to do a specific job for a newspaper or may even take photographs of events on the chance that he/she can sell them.

The number of people in Britain who are classed as self-employed rose by 52 per cent between 1981 and 1991 –

from 2.2 million to 3.3 million people – and most of them work on their own (i.e. they do not employ other people). In many cases these are people who have been faced with redundancy and who have used their savings or their redundancy payments, or taken advantage of one of the government schemes (see pages 83–85) to set up on their own. More men than women are self-employed (76 per cent men, 24 per cent women) – although this type of work is also popular amongst mothers of young children. Self-employment becomes more popular as people grow older – young people under the age of 25 are the least likely to be self-employed. It is very popular with those above retirement age who, usually, work 12 hours a week or less.

Evidence Collection Point 3.1

Figure 3.2 gives the main characteristics of being self-employed and employed as they apply, say, to someone running a small business.

1 Read the chart carefully and write a brief summary of the *differences* between being employed and self-employed.

2 Note down all the points which would probably not apply to the freelance keyboard operators in the advertisement.

3 List all the advantages and disadvantages you consider there would be to working from home on a freelance basis.

4 What reasons can you give for

● self-employment being popular with young mothers
● self-employment being rare for people under 25?

5 Hold a brainstorming session *with the rest of your group* to list as many work opportunities you can for someone wishing to become self-employed. Don't forget to think about those people you or your family know who work for themselves. Remember market traders, door-to-door salesmen and franchise operations (see page 14). Look in your local paper for other ideas.

Self-employed	Employed
Risks own money and is personally responsible for debts	Is paid a wage or salary on an hourly, weekly or monthly basis
Is own employer *or* works for several employers	Has to work specific hours
May choose the hours and days to work	is responsible for doing the job for which he/she is employed
May hire other people to help	Uses the employer's equipment and/or works at the employer's premises
Provides own equipment	Has to carry out instructions as they are given
Must correct inferior work in own time – or risk not being paid	Can claim benefit if unemployed
Cannot usually claim unemployment benefit if out of work	Can claim statutory sick pay if absent through illness (if paying National Insurance)
Is not eligible for statutory sick pay when ill	Has income tax and National Insurance deducted by employer
Is responsible personally for own income tax and National Insurance	Is normally protected under the EPCA. Rights vary depending on the length of employment
Has no protection (e.g. against dismissal) under the Employment Protection (Consolidation) Act	

Figure 3.2 *Features of employment and self-employment*

Full-time or part-time?

The number of people working part-time has increased dramatically over the last ten years, not just in Britain but also throughout the European Community. This is one of the consequences of the growth in the service industries discussed in Chapter 1 – in retailing, catering, hotel work, health centres, banking and education many jobs are now part-time. In many cases companies are converting full-time jobs to part-time positions. For example, in late 1992 Burtons announced that 1000 full-time shop jobs were to be replaced by up to 3000 part-time posts. Not only is retailing affected – many British companies employ far greater numbers of production, administrative and clerical staff on a part-time basis than ever before.

The main *difference*, of course, between working part-time and working full-time is in the number of hours worked. A part-time employee will work less than the standard opening hours of the company. In some cases, two part-time employees might **job share** one full-time job – i.e. they do the work between them.

Employers may prefer part-time staff because:

1 The company's wage bill is reduced. If part-time staff are employed for evening work or weekend work they are not eligible for the overtime rates which would be paid to full-time staff. The employer also saves on National Insurance payments if part-time staff earn less than the lower earnings limit and, in many cases, staff benefits and training.
2 Part-time staff are more flexible. They can be used to cover for absent staff and work extra hours when the company is busy or wants to open longer hours. This is especially useful for organisations which operate outside the 'normal' 9-5 pattern.
3 They do not have the same legal rights in employment law as full-time staff unless they work more than 16 hours a week. If they work between eight and 16 hours a week, they will need to work for five years before becoming eligible for the same rights. Those working fewer than eight hours a week can never gain protection. This means they cannot claim for unfair dismissal and do not receive other benefits, such as maternity rights or pension rights – unless the employer is prepared to give more than the statutory minimum.
4 There may be more people willing to work part-time in areas where there is a skills shortage. Therefore a company prepared to offer part-time jobs can recruit the people it needs.

DID YOU KNOW?

Only in the UK and the Irish Republic do part-time workers not gain the same employment rights as in other European countries. However, many companies do give some benefits (e.g. holiday pay) to part-time staff but this often depends on length of service and number of hours worked.

Employees may prefer to work part-time because:

1 They can have a greater say in the days and hours they work. This is often important for those with school children.
2 Part-time work enables a person to earn some money and yet have more time for leisure.
3 Most companies pay part-time workers at the same hourly rate as full-time staff.
4 It is better than being unemployed.
5 It is a useful way of earning some income for those who cannot work full-time (e.g. students, those who are

disabled or ill and/or pensioners who want to supplement their pension).

Evidence Collection Point 3.2

1 Look in your local paper and local Job Centre and note down the number of full-time and part-time jobs on offer in offices and retail stores. Work out the ratio between these.

2 Carry out a survey of:
  ● your fellow students
  ● your friends and relatives
  ● at least 20 other people

to find out whether they have part-time jobs and, if so, their reason for working part-time. For instance, is this because they did not want a full-time job or could not find one, because they are still at school, disabled or for some other reason?

Analyse your findings. Then sub-divide your findings into male and female and see if this makes any difference. Summarise your findings neatly in a short report.

Note: If you are unsure how to calculate ratios or how to carry out a survey refer to the Application of Number chapter.

Permanent or temporary?

Temporary staff are used by many companies to cope with very busy times or to cover for absent staff. In most industries there is always some temporary working; in others (e.g. construction), temporary or **casual work** is normal.

The main difference between a permanent member of staff and a temporary worker is that the latter is hired for a limited period of time, usually for a specific reason. Examples include:

● seasonal workers, who may be employed over a holiday season in a tourist centre or hired just for the Christmas period (e.g. additional Post Office delivery staff)

● 'temps', provided by employment agencies to fill staff 'gaps' caused by holidays or sickness or to deal with emergency workloads

● casual workers, whose days and times of working may be subject to day-to-day demand

● fixed-term contract workers, who are employed for a specified period of time

● temporary workers, employed for an unspecified period of time.

Temporary workers may be employed on a full-time or part-time basis. They may even be eligible for overtime. Needless to say, they can be laid off at any time or, automatically, at the end of their contract. There is no difference in British employment law between temporary and permanent employees – everything depends on the number of hours worked and the length of service (see also page 60).

AN ADIA COMPANY

Temporary workers who are provided by employment agencies are paid an hourly rate *by the agency*. The agency receives a higher rate from the employer and deducts an amount for administration. Many clerical workers in large cities start out 'temping' to gain experience. In addition to their wage they can also claim travelling expenses. Some employment agencies pay their regular 'temps' sick pay, holiday pay and even give them specialised training (e.g. on word-processors and computers).

Evidence Collection Point 3.3

1 Try to arrange an interview with someone who works for a local employment agency. Obtain as many details as possible on their 'temp' scheme; for example:

● whether holiday or sick pay is paid
● what training is given
● whether 'temps' can arrange time off (e.g. for hospital appointments)
● whether there are any other benefits.

2 Try to interview at least one person who has worked as a temp. List the advantages and disadvantages of this method of working.

3 Do you think temporary working is more suitable for some people than others? Think about the type of person who would most prefer it and the type of person who would not (e.g. in terms of age, qualifications, marital and family status etc.).

4 Look in your local newspaper and/or Job Centre and collect three examples of temporary jobs. In each case state why you think the job is not a permanent one.

Evidence Assignment 3A

Karen Mitchell is 19 years of age and has worked in the Administration section of Taylor Electronics for the past six months. She is employed full-time as a wages clerk. Two other women work in the same section – Betty, the section supervisor and Kathleen, the second wages clerk. Kathleen is 26, has two young children and has worked in the wages office for nearly a year.

Taylor Electronics have just introduced a computerised payroll system. All the employees are now paid directly into their bank accounts at the end of each month. This has resulted in a reduction in the work load of the wages office. Last Friday, the Chief Accountant interviewed all the wages staff and informed them that, as of the beginning of next month, only Betty would be able to remain as a member of the full-time staff.

He points out that neither Karen nor Kathleen has employment protection as they have not worked for the company for two years. However, in good faith, the company is prepared to give them the following options:

a they could each work part-time independently
b they could job-share
c they could offer their services freelance and charge their own fee to the company (and use their spare hours to hire their services to other organisations).

Kathleen prefers the idea of job sharing but Karen doesn't agree. She likes the idea of working freelance as this will give her more flexibility and may enable her to earn more money.

The two of them have until Monday morning to make a decision.

1 If you were Karen, what would you suggest to Kathleen and why? (Use the advantages and disadvantages of each method of work to each person to support your argument.)

2 Find out yourself how the situation might have been different if the two women had both worked for the company for more than two years. To do this, you will have to research how a full-time employee is protected by the Employment Protection (Consolidation) Act 1978.

· FEATURES OF EMPLOYMENT ·

No matter how well qualified you are, how much experience you gain, or how many jobs you have in your working life, one fact soon becomes clear – all jobs are different. For this reason, whenever you start work in a new job, a different company, or even a different department in the *same* company, there will be new things to learn. If you have a radical career change then you will probably have to start from scratch all over again.

As well as types of employment and qualifications required, jobs can vary in terms of their physical working conditions, the technology used and the wages that are paid.

Physical working conditions

There is a vast difference between the physical working conditions experienced by a bank clerk and a farmer. The first works in a clean, heated and probably attractively decorated and carpeted building. He or she deals with other members of staff and customers – so there is a 'social' aspect to the work. The hours are probably relatively predictable and fairly standard e.g. 9 a.m. to 5.30 p.m. Holidays can be planned in advance and can be arranged, within reason, to suit the person concerned. The work is clean and safe, and employees will therefore wear quite formal, 'good' clothes.

Contrast this with the farmer who works outdoors in all weathers, may have little or no contact with other people for much of the day, has to work a long day – especially if there is a dairy herd which needs to be milked – and at certain times (e.g. harvesting) may work almost around the clock. Holidays are difficult if not impossible to organise. The work may be dirty and sometimes involve the use of dangerous chemicals. Old clothes are standard wear, with special protective clothing worn when necessary.

Whilst these are obviously two extreme cases, if you look back at page 27, where jobs in the **primary industries** are listed, you will see that in many cases the situation is similar.

Evidence Collection Point 3.4

1 Select any three jobs in the primary sector and evaluate the physical working conditions which apply.

Think in terms of:

- place of work (hot/cold, inside/outside, pleasant/ unpleasant, etc.)
- contact with others
- hours and holidays
- cleanliness
- safety
- clothing required.

2 List the common aspects you can identify which would apply to jobs in this sector in terms of their physical conditions.

Secondary industries

Physical working conditions in secondary industries can vary tremendously, between industries, within industries, and within one organisation!

Between industries

For a moment, think about the difference in physical working conditions experienced by a motorway construction worker and an electronics engineer. You might know very little about electronics companies or electronic engineering – but you should realise, at the very least, that one worker will be working outside, exposed to the elements, and the other will not! The

motorway worker is involved in doing a job which is basically dirty, and will wear clothes which reflect this fact. In contrast, in parts of the electronics industry people work in a 'clean' room where dust is kept to a minimum. The operators wear special nylon suits to prevent dust from their clothes contaminating the components and have to pass through a changing room to get to their work.

In some industries the work is particularly arduous. Conditions may be hot and dangerous (e.g. in an iron foundry or steel mill).

DID YOU KNOW?

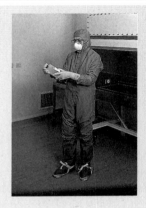

1 Protective clothing is widespread in all types of industries, and is not just restricted to safety hats or safety shoes. Male workers in drug companies involved in producing the contraceptive pill have to wear special overalls to prevent them being adversely affected by the female hormones in the pill itself.

2 People who work in very hot conditions, or who operate welding equipment or work near high-temperature gas-fired ovens, sometimes have special 'relaxation periods' built into their job so that they can cool down at regular intervals.

Within industries

In manufacturing, probably more than in any other sector, physical conditions between different organisations may vary. One factory may be modern and airy and situated on a new industrial estate, another may be in a run-down area – possibly an old converted mill with several storeys.

DID YOU KNOW?

The Health and Safety Executive (HSE) is responsible for standards of safety in factories and for appointing inspectors to check that *all* organisations comply with safety legislation, such as the Health and Safety at Work Act 1974 and the Control of Substances Hazardous to Health (1988).

Health and Safety legislation is covered in more detail on pages 164–168.

Within organisations

If you have never been in a factory then you may have only a very hazy idea of what it is like. The first thing you would probably notice is that either different buildings, or different areas of the same building, are used for different purposes.

Production is carried out in large rooms usually called the 'shop floor'. The size of the shop floor will depend on the product being made and the scale of operations. A large car factory may have an enormous assembly area; a small plastics factory – which makes items such as the outer casing for ballpoint pens – may have a much smaller area. Some assembly areas are noisy, others are quiet and streamlined. Some have individual workers operating different machines, others have a continuous or automated process.

In contrast, the administration work will almost certainly be carried out in offices which may be situated in a different block, away from the production areas. These may be small and cramped or large, spacious and airy. They may be purely functional, with a basic desk and filing cabinet, or designed to impress important clients, with carpets, executive furniture and paintings on the walls.

Some jobs require people to move around both within the same building and between different buildings. A maintenance engineer will go to different departments whenever machine breakdowns occur. A salesperson may travel 200 miles or more in a day visiting customers.

Evidence Collection Point 3.7

During your course try to arrange to go on two visits to factories. If possible, these should be in totally different industries.

Whilst you are there make a note of the areas you visit, the work carried out and the physical conditions in each case.

Use a word-processor to produce a report which compares and contrasts the different areas in each factory and also compares both organisations. Try to link your findings to the type of product made by each company and the stages required in its manufacture.

Service industries

Service industries, you may remember, are divided into two types – commercial services and personal services.

If you look back at Figure 1.9 on page 27, you will see that this sector contains a wide variety of occupations, and therefore incorporates very different physical conditions. Transport drivers, postmen and policemen often work outdoors, insurance workers, teachers and those in the medical profession usually work indoors. Retail work is probably the most varied – from a market stall to a department store.

Evidence Collection Point 3.8

Select *either* two contrasting occupations in commercial services *or* two contrasting occupations in personal services.

1 Evaluate the physical working conditions which apply for each occupation.

2 *Either*

   a State how these may change if a job holder gains promotion (e.g. from police constable to inspector or from student nurse to nurse manager)

   or

   b state how these can vary *within* the occupation you

have chosen (e.g. the various jobs within the postal or telecommunications industry).

· GETTING PAID ·

Unless you are undertaking voluntary work, no matter where you are employed you will have one thing in common with everyone else – you will want to receive payment for your work! In different organisations you will find that:

- Some people are paid hourly, others weekly and others monthly.
- Some people are paid more than others.
- The 'perks' or additional benefits vary from one place (and one job) to another.
- Everyone has to pay National Insurance and income tax out of their salary (unless they earn a very small amount each week).

Unless you understand how these systems operate you cannot check your own pay or know what to do if something is wrong. It is therefore in your own interests that you understand how both the National Insurance and PAYE income tax systems operate.

· WAGES AND SALARIES ·

The terms 'wages' and 'salaries' are sometimes used to mean the same thing. The most common way of distinguishing between them is as follows:

- **wage** is the term usually used for the money paid to manual workers who are paid every week, possibly on a Friday. Wages can vary from week to week if manual workers are paid according to how hard or long they work. Manual workers can also be asked to work on Saturdays and/or Sundays and be paid overtime. Wages consist of a basic rate or flat rate with additions for overtime or bonus payments.
- **salary** is the term usually used for the money paid to clerical and managerial staff who are paid once a month. Some companies pay every four weeks (13 times a year), whereas others pay every calendar month (12 times a year). It is often the case that salaried staff may be expected to work late *without* being paid overtime especially those at management level.

Today, the distinction between wages and salaries is becoming more blurred. For instance, a part-time worker may be employed on a temporary basis and yet be paid monthly. And how would you define a clerk in the administration section who receives a weekly wage/salary?

Additional payments

Usually, the higher up the organisational ladder you climb the more likely it is that your salary will be fixed. However, additional payments which may be made to employees include the following:

- **Commission** may be paid on top of a basic salary. This method is often used to pay sales staff – the more they sell, the higher their commission. Alternatively, commission may be paid at a high rate *instead* of a wage or salary. Such earnings can obviously not be relied upon, as in a bad week nothing will be earned.
- **Bonus payments** may be paid to staff as a reward for higher productivity or extra effort at a busy time of year.
- **Profit sharing** schemes are organised by some companies. Employees receive a share in any profits made and announced at the end of the year.
- **Expenses**, strictly speaking, are not really an additional payment as the employee might only be being reimbursed for money he or she has already spent (e.g. on petrol or taking a customer out for a meal).

The total amount an employee earns, from all sources, is known as **gross pay**.

Deductions

Unfortunately for the recipient, the total wage or salary a business agrees to pay an employee has to have various

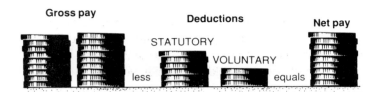

Gross pay — Deductions — Net pay — STATUTORY — VOLUNTARY — less — equals

amounts taken out. These are known as **deductions**. The pay which is then taken home (i.e. gross pay minus deductions) is known as **net pay**.

There are two types of deductions:

- **statutory** – required by law
- **voluntary** – agreed or requested by the employee (e.g. union contributions and charitable contributions).

Statutory deductions

The main statutory deductions are income tax and National Insurance.

Most employed people have income tax deducted from their wage or salary by their employer, who then sends the money to the Inland Revenue. The amount due is calculated in relation to how much an employee earns in each **tax year** (from 6 April one year to 5 April the next). This is known as **PAYE** (the Pay As You Earn system).

Self-employed people or those who run small businesses pay their tax in a completely different way. Their accountants send their end-of-year accounts to the Inland Revenue, which calculates the amount of tax due. Payment is then made in two instalments during the following year – usually one in January and a second in July.

DID YOU KNOW?

Most self-employed people have an accountant who will help them to arrange their affairs to keep the tax they pay to a minimum each year. This is quite legal and is known as **tax avoidance**. It is totally different from **tax evasion** (trying to get out of paying by making a false statement), which is illegal.

National Insurance (NI) is paid by both employed and self-employed people. In the case of employees, the company will calculate and deduct National Insurance on a weekly or monthly basis. Those who are self-employed

will receive a quarterly bill from the DSS for the amount due (or may choose to pay by direct debit from their bank account).

National Insurance contributions pay for a number of cash benefits, including:

- unemployment benefit
- statutory sick pay
- statutory maternity pay
- the basic state retirement pension
- industrial disablement benefit
- child benefit
- widow's benefit
- death grant.

NI contributions are payable by *both* employees *and* employers though obviously under the deductions column of the pay slip only the *employee's* contribution is listed.

DID YOU KNOW?

Just before their sixteenth birthday everyone receives notification of their National Insurance number. This stays the same all their working life.

Voluntary deductions

These can include:

- trade union subscriptions (if you have requested your employer in writing to make this deduction)
- charity donations
- social club subscriptions.

In all these cases the employee has a choice – whether to pay or not. However, in some cases (e.g. charity payments) the amount paid may be 'tax deductible' up to a specified amount each year.

Evidence Collection Point 3.9

Some employees have money deducted from their pay for food and board provided by their employee. Others *receive* an allowance for a uniform. *As a group,* can you think of jobs where either of these might apply? Write a list of jobs and allowances and put this in your portfolio.

Pension contributions

You may think you are far too young to be thinking about a pension. However, decisions in this area will come sooner than you think, as when you start work you will be asked if you are going to contribute towards the government pension scheme (called SERPS – State Earnings Related Pension Scheme) or join a private or company pension scheme. Those who pay towards SERPS pay a higher rate of National Insurance than those who are in a private scheme.

DID YOU KNOW?

1 You are not allowed to opt out of SERPS *without* joining a private or company pension scheme. Whilst you should take advice on this for your own personal circumstances, it is usually true that if you are young and starting work you will be much better off – eventually – if you join a private or company scheme.

2 Even if you opt out of SERPS and join a company or private pension scheme, your payslip will still show National Insurance deductions at the full rate. This is because the DSS still receives the full payments and then *they* pay it into any personal scheme you have. You can check that the correct amount has been paid in at the end of the year by asking your pension scheme manager for a list of all the contributions made by the DSS during the year.

· TAXATION ·

The first thing to note about tax is that no-one likes paying it! The second is that if you earn or receive more than a certain amount in a tax year then, by law, you must pay income tax. The third is that the more you earn the more you will have to pay.

However, income tax does not have to be paid on *all* your earnings. Everyone is eligible for certain **allowances**, which vary according to personal circumstances. Therefore, if you are working and then your circumstances change, you must inform your tax office immediately. You should also find out exactly what allowances you can claim.

DID YOU KNOW?

If you are a student and have any savings then you can register with your bank or building society to receive interest on your savings *without tax being deducted*. If you registered before you were 16 then you must *re-register* after that date if you want this to continue. When you start work, however, you will no longer be eligible and *must* inform your bank or building society immediately so that they deduct tax from any interest you are paid.

Evidence Collection Point 3.10

This chapter is only a general *guide* to the tax system and allowances. It is therefore in your own interest to get as much information as you can which might help you.

1 Look in the telephone directory to find the address of the nearest tax office and obtain from them their booklets on:

- PAYE (IR34)
- Income Tax and School Leavers (IR33)
- Income Tax and Students (IR60)
- Independent Taxation – a Guide to Tax Allowances and Reliefs (IR90)
- Tax Relief for Vocational Training (IR119).

In addition, your tutor might wish to contact the Inland Revenue Education Service, PO Box 10, Wetherby, West Yorkshire, LS23 7EH, on your behalf. They provide a useful student pack with examples of all the main tax forms.

2 From the information provided, find answers to the following questions:

a What is PAYE?
b What is a PAYE code?

c What is form P45?

d What is the emergency code?

e Will you have to pay tax on holiday earnings while you are a full-time student?

f If you are over 18 and pay for your own training, for what type of courses can you claim tax relief?

g What is the personal allowance?

h How much is the personal allowance at the moment?

i What are the current rates of income tax?

Produce your answers on a word-processor, using a simple report format and the main wording of the questions as a heading in each case.

Evidence Collection Point 3.11

Your brother, Matthew, is about to start up in business on his own. At the moment he is very busy trying to sort everything out and has asked you to help him by giving him advice on what he should do about paying tax.

1 Obtain for him the following booklets:

- Tax and Your Business – Starting in Business (IR28)
- Your Tax Office – Why It Is Where It Is (IR52)
- Thinking of Working for Yourself? (IR57)
- Tax and Your Business – How Your Profits are Taxed (IR105)
- You and the Inland Revenue (IR120).

2 Your brother is concerned that at his last place of employment he paid too much tax during the last 12 months and is due a rebate. Write him a letter, explaining the procedure he should follow if he wants to take up this matter with his tax office. Don't forget to tell him about the Taxpayer's Charter and what this means. Assume he still lives with you and give him the address of his nearest tax office.

Activity

The government changes the rate of income tax or the value of the allowances people can claim. Discuss *as a group*, and with your tutor, why

these may be sometimes increased and sometimes reduced.

Note: From Chapter 1, can you remember why the government raises money through the tax system, and what it does with it?

• TRAINING AND QUALIFICATIONS •

The type of training and level of qualifications required obviously vary tremendously from one job to another. Even in 1990, about 30 per cent of the population of working age had *no* formal qualifications at all. This does *not* mean they all had jobs and, as you may realise, without any qualifications the type of work for which people can apply is very limited.

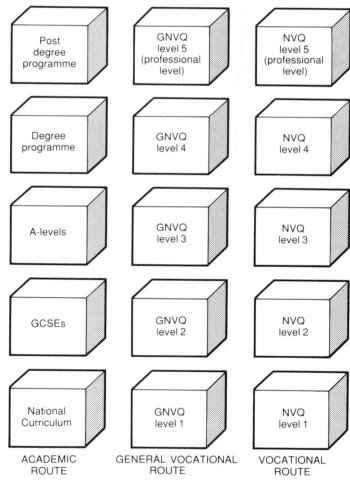

Various paths and combinations are available to higher qualifications

Figure 3.3 *Paths to higher qualifications*

There are various levels of qualifications through which people can progress (see Figure 3.3). At certain ages (e.g. 16 and 18) major decisions have to be made. The first is whether to *continue* in education or try to find a job. The second is whether to take an academic or a vocational route. Both GNVQ and NVQ qualifications are known as **vocational** routes – this means they are job-related. GNVQ courses are usually taken by full-time students who do not know yet whether they will continue to study or get a job after the age of 18. NVQ courses are usually taken by people who are working, whether they are full-time employees or on a training scheme. *Do remember that you can change from one route to another as you progress – or even, in some cases, take a 'mixture' of qualifications (e.g. GNVQ plus A-levels).*

As you are currently taking a GNVQ course in Business, you have already made certain decisions. You have decided to continue your education, which is wise, and you want to work in the business world. However, as yet you may have little idea of what you want to be eventually. For that reason it is wise to be obtaining a *general* vocational qualification in Business at this stage; i.e. one which is applicable to a wide range of jobs. As you get older, and become more aware of the opportunities available, you may start to specialise and obtain a particular *professional* qualification (e.g. in personnel, purchasing, accountancy or general management).

For that reason, this section concentrates on skills and qualifications required for the business world – so that you can use it for careers guidance as well as for recognising and understanding some of the requirements of employers for different types of jobs.

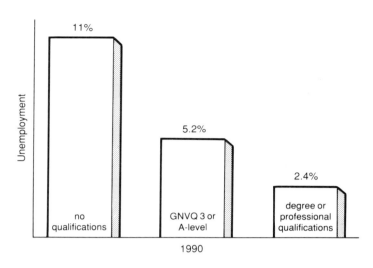

1990

DID YOU KNOW?

The higher level your qualifications are, the less likely you are to be unemployed. Unemployment rates in 1990 were 11 per cent for those without qualifications, 5.2 per cent for those with qualifications equivalent to GNVQ 3 or A-level and 2.4 per cent for those with degrees or professional qualifications. So keep going – it's worth it!

Types of training

As well as being available on a part-time or full-time basis, training can be **on-the-job** or **off-the-job**. The first refers to skills you can learn whilst you are at work, and the second to skills and knowledge you learn when you are away from work. Some skills are better taught on the job – for instance, a switchboard operator will learn how to operate the actual equipment he or she will be using. A word-processor operator may also learn how to operate a new software package at work.

An alternative is to attend a formal course or to join a 'drop-in skills centre'. The latter are operated on a system whereby people who want to gain specific skills or qualifications can attend, at the hours that are most convenient to them, until they have achieved the level of competency (or qualification) they desire.

Formal courses, such as the GNVQ course you are attending, are often run on a part-time or full-time basis. Part-time courses are usually for people who work every day who may be given **day release** by their employers to attend a course which runs during their normal working hours. Otherwise they could only attend in an evening. The higher you go in trying to attain professional qualifications, the more likely it is that the course in which you are interested is offered on a part-time basis, possibly evenings only.

Organisations may arrange for their employees to attend special courses either on the premises (e.g. on health and safety) or at a different location (e.g. supervisory management courses). This is usually best if people need to concentrate and work together as a group away from the pressures of the working environment.

Evidence Collection Point 3.12

People can study NVQs and GNVQs in certain **occupational areas**. You have chosen to study in Business. Alternatively you could have selected Art and Design or Leisure and Tourism. You could decide to change areas at higher level – to progress to a Management qualification at level 4, for instance.

1 Find out the different occupational routes which offer *both* NVQ and GNVQ qualifications. List these neatly.

2 Select two occupational routes in which you may be personally interested and find out the qualifications which are available at *each level*, the length of study for each of these, and whether they are available on a full-time or part-time basis, or both. Design a chart on which you can show this information.

3 Make out for yourself two proposed career routes:

   a assuming you leave full-time education at 18 or 19 and obtain a job

   b assuming you remain in full-time education until your early 20s.

Skills required in business

All courses will enable you to gain both knowledge and skills. The skills required in business change constantly with technological developments. For example, most people in business now use computers, so this is the most obvious skill required. A range of software can be used, from word-processing to desktop publishing, from payroll packages to computerised accounts. The better your IT skills the more jobs for which you can apply!

The other main skills you need are the ability to communicate (both verbally and in writing) and the ability to work with numbers and do business calculations. All these three areas – IT, communications and working with numbers – are covered in the Core Skills sections of this book. If you particularly enjoy – and are good at – one of

these skills then you can consider specialising in this area. For instance, you could specialise in computer work or go on to study finance or accounts.

Many people, however, would argue that additional 'personal skills' are just as important. At work you must have the ability to work with other people, to get on with them, to negotiate (rather than argue!) and to cope with people who hold views different from your own. You must be able to cope when you are faced with problems or are under pressure to produce something quickly. You must also have the skills to research information and present it effectively.

This book should help to give you a start in many of these areas, provided you are willing to learn. Personal development is something which never ends, and the degree to which you 'grow' and mature as a person is mainly up to you.

DID YOU KNOW?

Your ability to key in data quickly and accurately makes all the difference to your effectiveness on a computer. So, if your course includes keyboarding, *don't* think that you can afford to ignore this element. A *professional* worker – in any field – is always recognisable by his or her ability to work rapidly and accurately with the minimum of effort. Fumbling around the keyboard or keying in on a 'hunt and peck' basis simply makes you look incompetent.

Evidence Collection Point 3.13

1 Find out the range of qualifications you can gain in IT *plus* any other skill area which particularly interests you.

2 Use the quiz on page 71 to give yourself some idea of your own strengths and weaknesses. Don't pause too long on a question – often your 'gut reaction' is the most accurate. If you are in doubt on an area think about occasions when this has been tested. Can you offer any evidence to back up your answers?

Finally, go through the quiz with a good friend. See if he or she can 'second-guess' the answers you gave. Bear in mind that your friend will give you an idea of how *other people* see you.

QUIZ – ASSESS YOUR PERSONAL SKILLS

Achievement profile

- Are you competitive or laid back?
- Are you willing to accept responsibility for your own actions – or do you expect someone else to 'rescue' you when you encounter problems?
- Are you always looking for new challenges or are you prepared to rest on past glories?
- Are the targets and goals you set yourself realistic and well thought out?
- How do you react to failure?
- Do you stay with a job until it is finished – or give up if the going gets tough?
- Do you ever put the blame on someone else when you have made a mistake?
- Would you cheat to get what you want?

Emotional profile

- Do you get upset easily?
- Are you easily bored – if so, do you show it?
- Are you easily depressed?
- Do you enjoy arguing or are you nervous when you are with someone in authority (e.g. a boss or your tutor?)
- Are you ever aggressive?
- Do you jump onto the defensive if someone comments on something you have done?
- Do you think you are tactful?
- Can you compromise with other people when necessary?
- Do you sulk or bear grudges?
- Have you got a temper – if so, can you control it?
- Do you think before you speak?
- Are you a good listener?
- Can you express yourself clearly and fluently?

Work profile

- Do you like work which calls for accuracy and detail?
- Do you think and plan out a job carefully?
- Are you well organised and do you find what you put away?
- Do you like a known routine or do you like new things to happen on a regular basis?
- Are you observant?
- Do you have a good memory?
- Are you sometimes 'difficult' to work with – and in what way?
- Are you always punctual?
- Do you write neatly?
- Do you take great care when you do a job or are you rather slapdash?

Social profile

- Do you make friends easily?
- Do you like a busy social life?
- Do you like being 'in' with the crowd?
- Do you like being on your own?
- Are you always friendly?
- Can you keep a secret easily?
- How do you react if you find out someone doesn't like you?
- Are you easily impressed?
- Do you respect other people's opinions – even if they differ from your own?

Life profile

- Are you always in a rush?
- Do you burn the candle at both ends?
- Do you like to keep fit?
- Do you work quickly?
- Can you cope with – and meet – deadlines?
- Are you a worrier – or does nothing bother you?
- Do you quickly grasp what to do or need it spelled out for you?
- Do you find it difficult to relax – or very hard to get going?

3 Talk to your tutor about your own personal skills. Use your answers to the quiz as a starting point.

Identify with him or her any areas of personal development you particularly need to work on. Make out an action plan to show how you intend to develop these areas.

You should note that this information can be used in your Record of Achievement.

Qualifications and careers in business

The best way of finding out about careers is to see what other people do, and how they have 'moved up' within an organisation. When they first start work, most people start at the bottom of the career ladder, work hard and carry on to gain additional qualifications. As they gain qualifications and experience they apply for more senior jobs, either in the same organisation or in a different one. Slowly they move up, usually one level at a time, undertaking progressively more senior job roles. Needless to say, some people are more ambitious than others – they try to get to the very top, whilst others are content to stay in an easier job lower down in the organisation.

Evidence Assignment 3B

Imagine that you have obtained a temporary job in the local Job Centre for the summer. Inside the main reception area is a noticeboard on which are given job titles with cards underneath telling people about the experience and qualifications required in each case. Recently the reception area was redecorated. The painters removed the board, and when they returned it this morning you noticed they had taken off all the cards. Only the headings had been left on the board.

1 Match up the cards with the headings below so that they can be replaced accurately on the board.

Computer Applications Programmer	Public Relations Officer
Company Secretary	Purchasing Officer/Buyer
Distribution Manager	Quality Control Inspector
Draughtsman/woman	Receptionist
Market Research Executive	Sales Manager
Payroll (or Wages) Clerk	Security Officer
Personal Secretary	Telephonist
Product Designer	Telephone Order Clerk
Production Manager	Training Officer
Production Worker	Works Study/O&M Officer

Running short training courses in a variety of subjects. Supervising other forms of training – part-time day-release courses at local colleges/apprenticeship schemes etc. Qualifications required are normally minimum of 2 'A' levels or a degree. The Institute of Training and Development offers a Certificate in Training and Development. The Institute of Personnel Management also offers relevant qualifications.

REF 1

Buying materials, manufactured goods and services for the organisation. Liaison with suppliers, monitoring of progress, checking of delivery. Obtaining quotations and making out contracts. Qualifications vary. Advisable to have the Institute of Purchasing Certificate or Diploma.

REF 2

Analysing, interpreting and presenting information about an organisation's existing and potential customers. Degree normally required and there are short courses run by the Market Research Society or Industrial Marketing Research Association.

REF 3

Making manufactured goods, involving working alone at a bench or on an assembly line. No formal qualifications required.

REF 4

Maintaining and preparing documents such as share registers, reports and accounts. Preparing the documentation relating to Board meetings. Writing the company annual report. Normally a degree or professional qualification required such as that awarded by the Institute of Company Secretaries Association.

REF 5

Keyboarding, taking minutes of meetings, arranging events, running an office, undertaking some research duties. Qualifications normally good GCSEs, 'A' levels or degree plus secretarial skills.

REF6

Responsibility for the movement and storage of goods and materials, co-ordination of warehousing, transport, materials handling, inventory control, order processing and packing. Qualifications normally HNC/D (GNVQ/NVQ level 4) in Distribution or Business Studies plus Institute of Logistics and Distribution Management's Diploma in Distribution Studies.

REF 7

Producing plans and drawings from which a range of products can be manufactured. Normally a minimum of 4 GCSEs required including Maths, English and a science or technology subject. An engineering qualification may be taken on a part-time basis.

REF 8

Taking orders from customers over the telephone and giving information about various products before an order is taken. Normally no formal qualifications required.

REF 9

Writing computer programs to perform specific tasks; e.g. stock control, payroll. GCSEs including English and Maths normally required although nowadays degree important. British Computer Society and Institute of Data Processing Management offer professional qualifications.

REF 10

Making sure that the customers receive the goods or services they want, when and where they want them, at a price that suits both the customers and the company. Dealing with the planning and co-ordination of all stages of marketing, market research, product development, promotion, pricing, sales and distribution. Normally a degree required or HNC/D (GNVQ/NVQ level 4) in Business and Finance. Institute of Marketing run part-time courses at various levels.

REF 11

Applying logical and analytical methods to the solution of problems, advising on how to improve productivity and use of resources. Degree or relevant experience normally required. Institute of Management Services offers a number of relevant qualifications. City and Guilds offer a Certificate in Work Study (742).

REF 12

Organising and arranging trade fairs, writing press releases, making use of market research, countering bad publicity, promoting positive view of the company. GCSEs or 'A' levels required preferably followed by the Communication Advertising and Marketing Education Foundation Diploma covering Management and Strategy and Public Relations Practice.

REF 13

Working at switchboards and handling incoming and outgoing telephone calls. No formal qualifications normally required.

REF 14

Protecting property, goods, money and people. Preventing theft and vandalism, minimising the danger of fire, flood etc. No formal qualifications normally required.

REF 15

Translating the objectives of the marketing plan into sales targets for individual representatives. Reporting back to management on how well the goods or services are received and on the activities of competitor firms. Normally a degree is required and/or an Institute of Marketing or Institute of Sales and Marketing Management qualification.

REF 16

Overseeing activities associated with production. Ensuring production targets are met. Planning and controlling resources. An engineering qualification required. A supervisory management qualification such as NEBSM (National Examination Board in Supervisory Management) or GNVQ/NVQ level 3 is also useful.

REF 17

Dealing with members of the public, answering enquiries, organising appointment systems, using the telephone, handling petty cash. No formal qualifications required but GNVQ Level 2 in Business useful.

REF 18

Ensuring that everything entering and leaving a factory is tested and meets precise specifications. Qualifications normally 4 GCSEs including English, Maths and a science qualification. Qualifications also offered by Institute of Quality Assurance.

REF 19

Keeping accurate and up-to-date records of employee wages. Calculating pay. Operating a computerised system. GNVQ Level 2 in Business useful.

REF 20

2 Your boss is considering adding a section on personal qualities under each job. From the list given below, which qualities would you attach to each job? *(Note that you can use any quality more than once.)*

Accuracy	Numeracy skills
Creativity	Organised and methodical
Discretion	Patience
Flexibility	Persistence
Good judgement	Persuasiveness
Honesty	Speaking skills
Imagination	Tact
Leadership skills	Writing skills
Logic	

Career opportunities

Once you have a fair idea of what makes you 'tick', and the type of work you *think* would suit you best, you need to find out what jobs there are in these areas – and to analyse whether these may be 'dead end' jobs or lead to a career. Before you do this in detail, you first need to think about the *type* of organisation which would suit you best, and this is closely related to the working environment of the organisation as a whole and the departments within it.

Evidence Collection Point 3.14

1 Look at the list of the addresses of the various professional institutes given at the end of this chapter. Discuss *as a group* the type of employment each organisation represents and list these.

2 Choose two jobs which interest you and write to the relevant institute to ask for details about both the employment prospects and the qualifications required.

· EMPLOYMENT AND UNEMPLOYMENT ·

In February 1993 unemployment in the United Kingdom passed 3 000 000 for the second time this century. This figure left out several categories of people who are not counted in the unemployment statistics, even though they may not have a job (see Figure 3.4). If they are included then the figure is over 4 000 000. When you read the newspapers or listen to the news you will find that many people either blame the government or expect the government to do something about it – or both.

You are NOT classed as unemployed if you

- register for work at a Job Centre but do not claim unemployment benefit

- are on an employment or training programme

- are a housewife or married woman looking for work

- are a man over 60 without a job (because you would receive income support *not* unemployment benefit)

- are aged 16 or 17 (because you are not entitled to unemployment benefit)

- are not available for work or actively seeking work (e.g. because you are currently on a full-time course)

Figure 3.4 *People not counted in unemployment statistics*

Activity

If you were the Prime Minister, what would you do to promote employment and reduce unemployment? Discuss your ideas *as a group* before you read on.

The problems of unemployment

High levels of unemployment are unpopular with *all* governments because:

- People who are unemployed no longer pay income tax. Instead they claim unemployment benefit.
- The unemployed can no longer afford to buy many consumer goods.
- Demand for goods falls, businesses sell even less.
- More businesses have to close – making even more people unemployed.
- Businesses which have closed down no longer pay corporation tax to the government.
- The country makes fewer goods for export so loses money on the 'world' market.
- People who are unemployed might vote for an alternative government at the next General Election!

Employment levels

The total number of people who work in Britain is called the **working population**. This does not include everyone – some people are too old, too young or too infirm to work. In other cases people want to stay at home (e.g. some mothers of young children). In 1991, 49.1 per cent of the total population was classified as the 'working population' – 28 293 000 people.

If you subtract from this number all the people who are employed then you end up with the total number of unemployed people. As you should have realised at the beginning of this section, the actual number will depend on the method of counting (and this changed regularly in Britain during the 1980s).

The level of unemployment will increase if firms are laying off people faster than the unemployed can find new

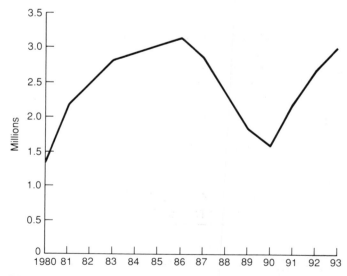

Figure 3.5 *The upward trend of UK unemployment*

jobs. The level of unemployment will 'stick' if there are not enough unfilled vacancies for those who want jobs. In February 1993 there were only 105 000 vacancies in the whole of Britain. If the level increases beyond a figure which is politically acceptable then the government has to take action to try to reduce the numbers unemployed – or risk losing the next election.

As you will see from Figure 3.5, unemployment peaked in July 1986 – and again in February 1993.

Activity

The ratio of the working population to those who do not work is important because the government can only raise taxes from people in work. As this money goes towards paying unemployment benefit, family allowance and pensions, those in work are responsible, through their taxes, for keeping those who do not work. This is known as **the burden of dependency**.

It is forecast that, because more people are living longer, the burden of dependency will increase considerably in the twenty-first century.

1 How do you think this situation will affect the taxes *you* might be asked to pay in the future?

2 *As a group*, can you think of any solutions to the problem which would be politically and socially acceptable?

DID YOU KNOW?

Moonlighting is the term used for people who claim benefit but are working for cash (which they don't declare for tax). This is also known as the **black economy**. At present it is estimated that if there were no black economy then income tax rates could be reduced by up to 5p in the pound.

Evidence Collection Point 3.15

One way of reducing the numbers of unemployed is to reduce the retirement age (e.g. to 60 for men) as this would increase job opportunities for young people. The problem is that it would also increase the total cost of pensions to the government.

In Britain the government *must* review the pensions rules because the European Courts have ruled that it is discriminatory that women can retire at 60 but men must work until they are 65.

1 What do you think would be the result if the government made all women work until they were 65? Consider both the effect on government finances *and* the views of British women (who are also voters!).

2 Carry out a survey of at least 15 women who would be affected and obtain their views. Summarise these.

3 If you were an adviser to the government what would you suggest that they do, and why?

4 Cut out any newspaper articles you can find on this topic to see what the government eventually decides to do.

Government measures to increase employment

During the 1980s these included the following:

● Reducing benefits (or making them more difficult to obtain) to try to reduce the number of people who might prefer to remain unemployed rather than find work.

● Reducing trade union power as it was claimed that trade union activities resulted in higher wages. If a company has to meet a high pay settlement for its workers then it may lay some workers off to reduce its total wage bill (or not take on additional workers).

● Providing incentives for companies to move to Assisted Areas (see page 83) or inner cities with severe unemployment levels.

● Introducing schemes such as the Enterprise Allowance Scheme to encourage unemployed people to start in business themselves.

● Introducing training schemes such as Youth Training (YT).

· REGIONAL EMPLOYMENT ·

Employment patterns vary from one region to another. In the early 1980s Britain experienced a recession which severely affected employment levels in the northern counties. The recession in the early 1990s has affected the south east badly, yet unemployment has fallen slightly in the north.

Activity

The EC currently has 12 members. Find out the names of each of the member countries.

Regional differences

How often are you asked to give your address – and how often do you give it without any real thought as to the importance of the place where you live? You may have many reasons for liking or disliking the place where you live. You may live in the country and feel cut off from some of the entertainments your town-based friends enjoy. You may live in a town or city and envy your friends who live in the country because they can take part more easily in outdoor or other leisure activities.

Where you live may be of even greater significance, however, when you start to look either for your first job or for a change of job. You may, for instance, live in an area where, for a variety of reasons, the level of unemployment is particularly high so that your job opportunities are more limited. You may also find that, although many jobs will be open to you they may not always be available. If, therefore, you have set your heart on one particular job, you may have to move to certain specific areas of the country to find it.

Activity

Look at the list of occupations given below.

Accountant	Oil rig worker
Bank clerk	Crofter
Teacher	Shipyard worker
Forestry worker	Taxi driver
Miner	Doctor
Zoo attendant	Secretary
Hotel manager	Lifeguard
Librarian	

Draw up a table with headings Column A and Column B. In Column A list the occupations that can be found in almost any part of the country. In Column B list those that are more likely to be found in certain specific areas only.

Add further examples to each column as you think of them.

The map in Figure 3.6 shows the regions of the UK and you should find it easy to pinpoint your own particular

Figure 3.6 *The regions*

region. If you live in England you will probably be more used to identifying your *county* than your region. Wherever you live you should know both your own region or county and those that are nearby.

Activity

The government is planning to change the names of the regions of Wales and (later) some of the counties in England. Check with your tutor that the names given on the map are still correct. If they are not, trace the map and insert the correct names.

Evidence Collection Point 3.16

In the last chapter you learned why industries locate in certain areas. Now it is time for you to consider why industries came to your own region – and to others in the UK.

To do this, you will be asked to read different sets of information and to compile an information sheet on your own region and *one other* – which you can choose for yourself.

You are advised to collect your information by doing one section at a time and taking care over what you are doing. You will then have the basis of much of the information you will need for the Evidence Project in this chapter.

. SECTION 1 – REGIONS AND THE . PRIMARY SECTOR

In Table 1 is given an account of the natural resources to be found in different areas of the UK. These affect employment in the **primary sector**. (If you have forgotten what this is, refer back to page 27.)

1 Read the account carefully and undertake each of the activities given.

2 Identify the natural resources that relate to your own region and list these.

3 Select one more region in which you are interested and identify the natural resources which relate to that area.

4 List the industries in the primary sector which would be found in each region, bearing in mind this information.

TABLE 1 – THE PRIMARY SECTOR

NATURAL RESOURCES IN THE UK

You will probably know quite a lot already about the region in which you live. It may be by the sea or inland, in the north or the south, in the town or the country, flat or hilly etc. As you know, these factors affect the type of industry (and therefore the type of employment) which there is in your locality. If you live by the sea there may be a thriving fishing industry in your area, there may be a dockyard or a port – or there may be a number of leisure industries. If you live in the south you may be aware of the number of market gardens which exist because of the milder climate there. In addition to climate, the **natural resources** of an area – gas, oil, coal, water, woodland – affect the type of industry that has grown up there.

Coal

Coalmining has been going on in various areas of the country since Roman times. Although at first mines were owned privately, in 1947 they were taken into public ownership by the National Coal Board (now the British Coal Corporation). More recently, however, the government has introduced legislation to privatise the industry. In March 1992, 50 British collieries were in operation together with 58 British Coal opencast sites.

Activity

The map on page 78 shows British coalfields. Draw a chart listing in Column A the major coalfields and in Column B the region in which each field can be found. Look back at your regional map for any information you need.

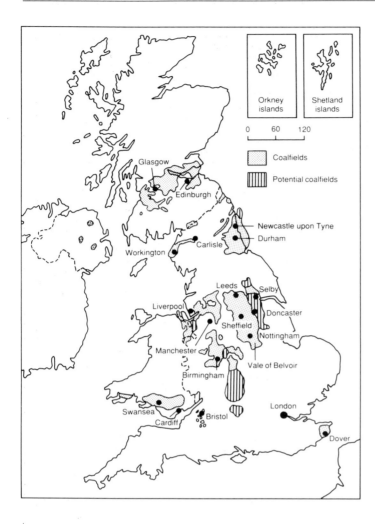

- sand and gravel
- chalk
- limestone and dolomite
- sandstone
- common clay and shale
- salt

About 47 700 people are employed in the 'extractive' industries (i.e. those engaged in mining and processing these minerals). In addition some tin and zinc ore is still being mined in Cornwall.

DID YOU KNOW?

Exploration for gold continues, especially in Scotland, Northern Ireland and South West England. A little gold has already been obtained from a mine in South Wales.

Water

Britain's water supplies are obtained either from surface sources such as lakes, streams and rivers or from underground sources by means of wells or springs. The Water Act 1989 privatised the ten Water Authorities in England and Wales and these authorities are now responsible for the water supply and sewage treatment in their own region.

The water supply in Scotland is regulated by nine regional and three 'island' councils and is plentiful both in supply and in the amount of unpolluted water from upland sources. In Northern Ireland, the Department of the Environment is responsible for the public water supply and sewerage.

DID YOU KNOW?

- About 99 per cent of the population of Britain and 97 per cent in Northern Ireland live in houses connected to a public water supply system.
- Water put into the public supply system in England and Wales amounts to about 17 379 megalitres a day and the average daily consumption per head is about 140 litres.
- Electricity generating companies and other undertakings take some 16 400 megalitres a day. Agriculture takes just over 500 megalitres a day.

DID YOU KNOW?

The coal industry is at present in decline. In 1955, for instance, there were 850 mines in operation (as compared with the 50 now remaining) and the government has announced plans to close a further 10 fields. Since 1984, however, British Coal, through its job creation activity, British Coal Enterprise, has helped to create job opportunities for 76 500 people in areas where mining was previously the main source of employment.

Non-fuel minerals

Britain's output of non-fuel minerals totalled over 318 million tonnes in 1990 valued at £1993 million. The major non-fuel minerals are:

Oil

Britain no longer has to rely purely on coal for its energy now that oil has been discovered offshore on the UKCS (UK Continental Shelf).

DID YOU KNOW?

- Since 1964 the government has granted exploration and production licences as a result of 12 offshore licensing rounds and there are now 4864 wells being drilled in the UKCS – 2198 development wells, 1660 exploration wells and 988 appraisal wells.
- 1202 miles of major submarine pipeline bring oil ashore from the North Sea oilfields. These are offshore pipelines. Onshore pipelines are in operation from harbours, land terminals or offshore moorings to oil refineries.

Activity

Go to your school or college library and see what you can find out about North Sea oil. Write down the names of all the oil fields. There are also some oil wells in Southern England. Try to find out where these are (see map opposite) and which company is drilling them.

Gas

Natural gas from the seven largest of the 35 gasfields now accounts for about one-third of the total gas produced in the UKCS. Gas from the South Morecambe field in the Irish Sea and from the twin North Sea and South Sea fields is used to supplement supplies to meet peak demand in winter. The British Gas national and regional high pressure pipeline system transports the gas around Great Britain and is supplied from four North Sea shore terminals and from a terminal in Barrow-in-Furness. There are also two newly-built natural gas pipelines not operated by British Gas.

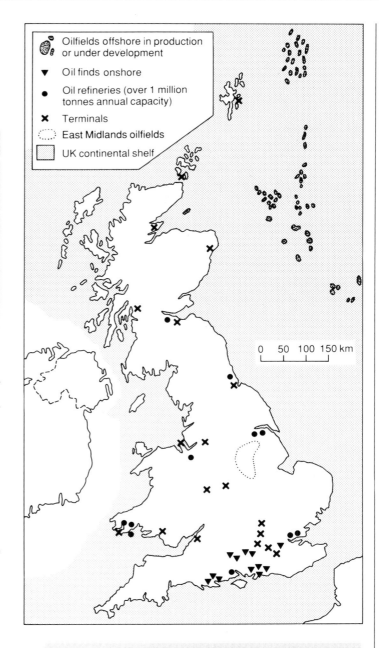

Legend:
- Oilfields offshore in production or under development
- ▼ Oil finds onshore
- ● Oil refineries (over 1 million tonnes annual capacity)
- ✕ Terminals
- ⬭ East Midlands oilfields
- ▢ UK continental shelf

0   50 100 150 km

DID YOU KNOW?

The gas industry in Britain was privatised in 1986 under the Gas Act 1986. It is currently the only public supplier, but has an obligation to act as a 'common carrier' for other companies. There are currently eight independent companies which supply gas in competition with British Gas under the company's transport network.

Activity

The discovery of oil and gas off the coast of Britain led to changes for many people — the people who worked on the rigs and those who lived in towns nearby (e.g. Aberdeen in Scotland).

a *As a group*, discuss how the discovery of oil off a coastal town would affect local industries in that area. Summarise your discussion afterwards.

b What do you think are the advantages and disadavantages of working offshore on an oil or gas rig? Try to find out more about this before you write out your findings.

Timber

There are 53 million acres of productive forest in Great Britain, 40 per cent of which is managed by the Forestry Commission. Wood production has nearly doubled since 1970 and there are plans to create 12 new forests on the outskirts of major English cities such as the Great North Forest in Tyne & Wear, the Forest of Mercia in Staffordshire and Thames Chase, east of London.

Farming

Sheep and cattle farming is carried out in the main in Scotland, Wales, Northern Ireland and South West England.

Pig and poultry farming is carried out in eastern and northern England.

Arable crops are grown in eastern and central England and eastern Scotland. Vegetable cultivation takes place in Cambridgeshire and South Lincolnshire, areas around the Thames and Humber and South Lancashire. Potato growing is carried out in Kent, Cornwall, Scotland and Northern Ireland.

Fishing

Britain is one of the EC's leading fishing nations and the fishing industry provides 59 per cent of British fish supplies. Among the main ports from which fishing fleets operate are Aberdeen, Peterhead, Fraserburgh (Grampian), Lerwick (Shetland), Kinlochbervie, Ullapool (Highlands), North Shields (Tyne and Wear), Grimsby (Humberside), Lowestoft (Suffolk), Brixham (Devon), Newlyn (Cornwall) and Kilkeel, Ardglass and Portavogie (Northern Ireland). Fish and shellfish farming industries are found in the Highlands and Islands of Scotland.

. SECTION 2 – REGIONS AND THE . SECONDARY SECTOR

The secondary sector refers to manufacturing and production industries. A summary account of these is given in Table 2.

1 Read this carefully. Identify which parts relate to the two regions you are investigating.

2 List all the relevant information you have found, including the names of major companies in your regions.

3 For at least three industries you have listed, find out the names of major organisations that operate in that region.

TABLE 2 – THE SECONDARY SECTOR

MAJOR MANUFACTURING AND PRODUCTION INDUSTRIES IN BRITAIN

1 Britain is the world's tenth largest **steel** producing nation and has operated a balance of payments surplus since 1983. The major areas of steel production are in Wales, and northern and eastern England. British Steel is the fourth largest steel company in the Western world.

2 Britain is a major producer of specialised **metal manufacture** for high technology requirements. Nearly half of the industry is situated in the Midlands and Wales.

3 The **ceramics** industry manufactures clay products, such as domestic pottery, sanitaryware and tiles and clay pipes for the building trade. Domestic pottery, which includes the manufacture of china, earthenware and stoneware, accounted for 22 per cent of the industry's output in 1990. Tableware is

produced in Stoke on Trent and Britain is the world's leading manufacturer and major exporter of fine bone china.

4 **Glass** is manufactured in the main by Pilkington Brothers, St Helens.

5 Britain is the world's biggest exporter of **china clay** (kaolin) and the main production is carried out in Cornwall and the South West.

6 Britain's **chemical** industry is at the forefront of modern technology and is the third largest chemical industry in Western Europe and the fifth largest in the Western world. The most rapid growth in recent years has been in speciality chemicals, particularly pharmaceuticals, pesticides and cosmetics. Imperial Chemical Industries (ICI) accounts for a substantial part of the industry's production. It is the fourth largest chemicals company in the world, has a range of 15 000 products and is one of Britain's biggest exporting companies. It is also one of the world's largest **paint** manufacturers. Major areas of production are in the North, the North West and the South East.

7 Exports of **mechanical machinery** amounted to 13 per cent of visible exports in 1991. Britain is among the Western world's major producers of **tractors** which make up over three-quarters of the country's total output of agricultural equipment. Amost all of Britain's **machine tools** are purchased by the engineering, vehicles and metal goods industries. Britain is the world's seventh largest producer of machine tools. The West Midlands and Yorkshire and Humberside are major producing areas.

8 Amstrad is Britain's biggest personal **computer** manufacturer, whose products are aimed at the mass market. It has almost one-third of the domestic market in portable personal computers. Many of the high technology industries are based in the South East and in Scotland's silicon glen.

9 Britain's **aerospace** industry is the second largest in the Western world, after the USA. Short Brothers in Belfast manufactures civil and military aircraft and Westland manufactures military helicopters and hovercraft.

Rolls Royce is one of the three major manufacturers of aeroengines in the Western world.

Over 400 companies in Britain are involved in space activities, particularly in the manufacture of satellites. British Aerospace Space Communications Systems is Europe's leading – and the world's third largest – producer of communications satellites. Many of them are concentrated in the South West, South East and North West.

10 Britain has a considerable **food processing** and **drinks manufacturing** industry which accounts for a growing proportion of the total domestic food supply. Convenience foods have formed the fastest growing sector of the food market in recent years. The market in health and slimming foods also continues to expand. The South East, East Anglia and the North West are major production areas. Yorkshire and Humberside specialise in cocoa, chocolate and confectionery products.

Of major significance among the alcoholic drinks produced in Britain is Scotch whisky, which is one of Britain's top five export earners. There are 114 distilleries in Scotland.

The brewing industry has five major brewery groups whose products are sold nationally, and 160 local brewers.

The British **tobacco** industry manufactures 99 per cent of cigarettes and tobacco goods sold in Britain.

11 There is a high degree of regional concentration in the **textiles** industry. Particularly important areas are the North West, West Yorkshire, the East Midlands, Scotland and Northern Ireland. West Yorkshire is the main producing area of the **wool** industry, although Scotland is also a specialised producer of high quality yarn and cloth. The **linen** industry is centred in Northern Ireland.

Most of the **clothing** industry is widely scattered throughout the country although there are a significant number of such firms in Manchester, Leicester, Leeds and London. **Hosiery** and **knitwear** industries are concentrated mainly in the East Midlands and Scotland.

12 **Printing** and **publishing** is concentrated in firms based in South East England.

DID YOU KNOW?

The small area between Slough and Silverstone is known as the motoring equivalent of Silicon Valley with racing car companies such as Ferrari and Williams. So if you know an aspiring racing car engineer tell him or her to move there for the best job opportunities!

SECTION 3 – REGIONS AND THE TERTIARY SECTOR

1 Read the information about service industries in Table 3. Write to the tourist boards as suggested.

2 Then compile a brief paragraph on the service industries in your two regions of interest.

TABLE 3 – THE SERVICE SECTOR

SERVICE INDUSTRIES IN THE UK

Many people want to find a job which does not involve manufacturing but which instead provides a service. They may want to open a shop or work in a hotel, hospital or bank. In most cases they should be able to find a job in almost any part of the country. However, even in the case of service industries some jobs are concentrated in certain areas of the country. One example is the media – jobs in television, newpapers, advertising etc. are more likely to be found in the South East. Another example is that of the tourism and leisure industries, which now found one of Britain's major sources of employment, employing 1.5 million people.

Although most regions of the country are interested in attracting tourists some have more natural advantages than others – it is probably easier to attract people to visit London than it is to attract them to visit Manchester. Nevertheless the British Tourist Authority (BTA) and the tourist boards try to promote the activities of every region. The English Tourist Board, for example, works closely with 12 Regional Tourist Boards.

Activity

1 Visit the library to find out the addresses of the Regional Tourist Boards in either your own region or your region of interest. Write to at least three Boards to ask them for information about the various tourist attractions in their particular areas.

2 Visit your local tourist information centre (usually situated in your town hall) and obtain as much information as you can on your own region.

3 Analyse the attractions each region has to offer and write a short report on your findings. Include a section on the sort of jobs you think might be available in those areas.

· SECTION 4 – FINAL CHECK ·

1 Check your notes. Make sure that you have no major industries omitted – particularly in the service sector.

2 Add any that you have not already included and *then* check if this industry is actually operating in your own particular region today. If so, give two examples of organisations that produce these goods.

(Note: A good source of reference for organisational names may be your local Business Pages telephone directory.)

· REGIONAL INVESTMENT ·

Some regions of the country are more prosperous than others and can therefore create more employment opportunities for those who live there. There may be more job opportunities in London than in Inverness, for example, because London is bigger, is the centre of many major industries and businesses, is within easy reach of ports and airports and has a good communications network. Some regions are more attractive than others and can therefore attract more people, particularly if they are highly qualified and might be able to create job opportunities for others. A computer systems expert, for instance, might prefer to live in a pleasant country town rather than an industrial city and may therefore set up his or her company in that town.

Obviously, therefore, there can be problems for anyone who is looking for work in areas of the country which are neither very prosperous nor popular. What can help, however, is the fact that the government does try to improve job prospects in some areas. Although the **Department of Trade and Industry** has reduced the number of grants it gives, it still provides grants to companies to encourage them to set up or continue in business in certain specified or **'assisted'** areas or in **'urban programme'** areas.

In addition the **Department of the Environment** offers grants, particularly in the inner city areas through the City Challenge and City Grant schemes (see Figure 3.7). In some inner city areas there are Industrial Improvement Areas and companies which move to these areas can obtain additional assistance.

To assist in the co-ordination of these grants, the government has set up **urban development agencies** in England, Wales and Scotland. Non- urban areas also have development agencies such as the Welsh Development Agency and the Highlands and Islands Development Agency in Scotland. In addition most towns now have their own development schemes which concentrate on the getting and giving of funds to help create employment opportunities.

Grants are also available through the **European Regional Development Fund**, which is designed to reduce regional imbalances, and the **European Social Fund**, which concentrates on training and the problems of young people in areas of high unemployment (see Figure 3.8).

Figure 3.7 *Urban priority areas in England*

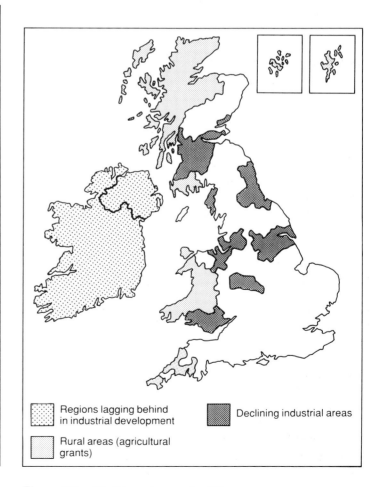

Figure 3.8 *Eligible regions under EC grants*

DID YOU KNOW?

Virtually all councils are involved in economic development of their areas. This is particularly true in areas of high unemployment. Part of the council's role will be to attract industry (and jobs) to the area. Many councils produce glossy brochures and literature on suitable sites for the relocation of industry, grants available and so on.

Evidence Collection Point 3.17

Find out if your local town hall or council offices have an economic development office. Obtain a copy of their literature and find out the type of grants available for:

- companies moving into the area
- worker co-operatives
- people wishing to start a small business.

Summarise your findings in a short paragraph.

Training and Enterprise Councils

In December 1989 a network of Training and Enterprise Councils (TECs) was set up in England and Wales and Local Enterprise Companies (LECs) established in Scotland. What they are required to do is:

- promote more effective training
- provide practical help to employers to improve their training
- deliver and develop youth training and 'Training for Work'
- stimulate enterprise and economic growth through the **Enterprise Allowance Scheme** – by which help is given to those setting up in business
- stimulate business/education partnerships.

Urban investment in towns and cities

One major initiative has been concerned with the 'inner cities' which in the past few years have been experiencing all sorts of employment problems.

DID YOU KNOW?

In England the initiative is called 'Action for Cities', in Scotland it is known as 'Partnerships,' in Wales the 'Programme for the Valleys' and in Northern Ireland 'Belfast Action Team'.

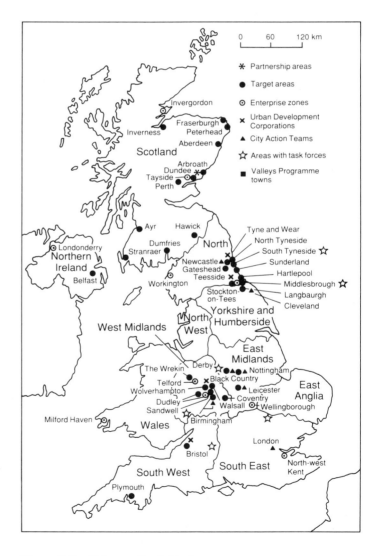

Figure 3.9 *Urban policy initiatives*

DID YOU KNOW?

Only in Greater London and the North West is there an increase in small business start-ups according to a report by the small business unit at Barclays Bank. In Greater London just under 55 000 new ventures were set up in the first half of 1992, an 8.8 per cent rise over the corresponding six months of 1991.

One reason for this increase has been the general recovery in the services sector which is heavily concentrated in the London area. The North West managed a 2.9 per cent increase to about 20 500 start-ups. The figures compare with a 2.6 per cent decline in new small businesses nationwide.

Evidence Collection Point 3.18

Find out the address of your nearest TEC. If you do not know it write to PAI Section, Department of Employment, Moorfoot, Sheffield SI 4PQ. Then write to your local TEC and ask for details of the financial assistance you might be able to get if you are thinking of setting up your own business.

Rural investment

Not all investment is centred on urban areas. Indeed there has been concern expressed over the past few years about the move of people (particularly young people) from the country to the towns, simply because there is no work for them to do in the country.

The **Rural Development Commission** has therefore been set up by the government to encourage enterprise and provide a broad range of job opportunities for rural communities. It works closely with many partners including the TECs, and there is now a consortium of rural TECs (CORT) which has recently introduced a Training and Enterprise Fund (TEF) designed to promote employment opportunities. CORT will finance projects to a maximum of £250 000 provided they:

- contribute to the enterprise and/or training needs of rural firms and aim to attract continued funding from TECs and other bodies
- involve networking and collaboration with other organisations
- address the particular needs of people and businesses in rural areas.

So far projects have included:

- helping unwaged women back into employment, education or training
- a 'Focus on Rural Enterprise' project to research rural business trends, issues and training needs in an area vulnerable to job losses from agricultural decline
- a mobile telecottage to provide on-site computer training in such areas
- an 'executive link' to utilise the skills of unemployed executives and women returners in rural businesses.

DID YOU KNOW?

Telecottages are a computerised access point to a range of services available to those living and working in rural areas. Examples include:

- the Ribble Telebusiness Trust based at Whalley and Clitheroe in East Lancashire which provides on-line commercial company information down-loaded from a series of remote databases and delivered to the customer's fax or computer
- the Shetland-based 'Isles Telecraft' which involves four homeworkers updating computer records for the Shetland museum.

Activity

1 Write to CORT, Enterprise Centre, James Street, Carlisle CA2 5BB, for further information on the Consortium of Rural TECs.

2 Write to ACRE Teleworking Advisor, Somerford Court, Somerford Road, Cirencester GL7 1TW, to ask for more information on the benefits of the network of telecottages.

A part-time job pulling pints in a Scottish pub launched Stewart Graham as a manufacturer of lobster pots when he was just 19 years old. It all started with some of the pub's customers who, knowing that he had some engineering skills, asked him to mend their lobster creels. Then they asked if he could make some. He completed his HND in mechanical and production engineering and then set up in business. He had £1000 of his own money, plus a bank loan of £2000 and another £3000 in grants and loans from the Highlands and Islands Development Board (HLDB). He soon had three workers and a 500 square foot industrial unit. He then won one of the Livewire's trophies – an organisation sponsored by Shell UK which encourages business start-ups among people aged between 16 and 25 – and was judged Scotland's most promising young entrepreneur. At 27 he has a turnover approaching £1 million and controls nearly half the creel market in Scotland plus much of the Scandinavian market.

Evidence Collection Point 3.19

As a group, either

1 Find out the name and address of your local Development Agency.

2 Contact the Department of the Environment *or* the DTI *or* your local Development Agency. Find out what grants are available for companies moving to your area. Prepare a short presentation to inform the rest of your class of the current situation. The presentation should include a brief report which summarises your information and which can be included in your portfolio.

or

1 Assume you are the board of directors of a company wishing to locate to a different area. Contact a Development Agency or Local Authority in your area of interest and obtain details of their incentives for new businesses and local economic development plans.

2 Prepare a presentation to the rest of your class (the shareholders) reviewing the advantages and disadvantages of each area and finishing with your recommendations for relocation.

Overseas investment

The creation of new jobs in certain areas has been helped by grants from the **European Regional Development Fund**. In addition some regions are now attracting **private investment** from overseas firms. Recent examples include:

- the sale, for £80 million, of Felixstowe, Britain's largest and busiest container port to Hutchison Whampoa, the Hong Kong Group
- the investment of over £600 million by the Ford Company of America in its engine plant at Bridgend, Mid Glamorgan.

Evidence Assignment 3C

Read the following passage and then write down your answers to the questions given below.

According to figures from the Invest in Britain Bureau (IBB), a trade and industry department organisation which works with all the various regional development and investment agencies, Britain still attracts more inward investment than any other country in Europe. In world terms, Britain is second only to the United States.

Between 1951 and the end of 1990, Britain took no less than 38 per cent of all American direct investment in the EC. The nearest competitor was Germany, with 16 per cent. In the same period, 39 per cent of total Japanese investment in the EC came to Britain, with Holland attracting 22 per cent. The Germans have also been investing money in Britain. In 1990, 19 per cent of all German investment abroad came here while 12 per cent went to the States. This has meant the creation of 22 714 new jobs and the safeguarding of a further 28 643.

Wales has been the most successful in terms of foreign investment and has secured 71 projects in 1991/2, more than a fifth of all those in the UK. Another area that has seen considerable Japanese investment in recent years is the North East. More than 28 Japanese companies are located in the Tyne & Wear region. Nissan, which started up in 1986 with 400 jobs, now employs about 4600. Fujitsu has recently invested £400 million in a new manufacturing facility which will create jobs for about 1500 people by 1995.

Scotland has also attracted Japanese and American investment. The Japanese company, Semiconductors, has been based in Livingstone for ten years and the American firm, Motorola, now has three plants in Scotland carrying out manufacturing and research and development.

However, despite the marketing efforts of the IBB and the regional agencies, the task of attracting investment is becoming increasingly difficult, particularly since America is in recession and the Japanese government is now adopting a policy of containing the outflow of funds.

One major factor for funding to be continued overseas investors have made it clear is that the UK must be part of Europe, with completely free access to the whole Single European market.

1 Which countries are the major investors in Britain?
2 Which are the most popular regions for investment?
3 Give at least one reason for the importance of overseas investment in the country.
4 Why do you think the USA in particular likes to invest in Britain?
5 Write a short paragraph about ways in which foreign investors might be attracted to invest in your own particular region. Think, for instance, of the efforts made by the North East to create good relations between the people of that region and the Japanese investors by setting up Anglo-Japanese societies. Think also of the different amenities each area can offer – Scotland can rely on unspoilt countryside, quiet roads etc. Other regions have different things to offer. Remember also the type of UK investment which may exist in your area – is it part of an enterprise zone etc?

DID YOU KNOW?

One major factor for funding to be continued overseas is that investors have made it clean the UK

Nissan, Toyota and Honda are the 'new' British car producers. In 1990 they produced 106 000 cars. They aim to produce around 900 000 by the year 2000.

By the year 2000 it is estimated that *at least* one in five UK manufacturing jobs will be in foreign-owned companies.

• LABOUR AND SKILLS SUPPLY •

If you are hoping to set up a business in a particular region, you will be very interested not only in the number of people who live in that area but also the number who are available to form part of your workforce. The number of people employed in each region differs greatly, as you can see from the table below (which refers to 1992 – the numbers are in thousands):

	Male	Female
South East	3562	3333
East Anglia	412	360
South West	862	828
West Midlands	1015	878
East Midlands	798	718
Yorkshire & Humberside	936	880
North West	1172	1126
North	549	506
Wales	488	456
Scotland	1008	948
Northern Ireland	265	254

Evidence Collection Point 3.20

1 Draw a bar chart, preferably using a computer, to illustrate the difference between the regions and between the employment of males and females in the workforce.

2 Write down the answers to the following questions:

a Which are the two regions with the highest number of employees in employment?

b Which is the region with the lowest number of employees in employment?

c In which region is there the lowest difference between males and females in the numbers employed?

d In which region is there the highest difference?

3 Write a short paragraph suggesting reasons for these differences.

Future trends

Regional figures are constantly changing. You therefore have to be careful to check not only on the present situation, but also on possible future trends so that you do not, for instance, set up a business in an area in which the number of people is declining, or one from which the young people in particular are moving.

However, the labour force of working age in Britain is projected to grow by 694 000 in the next ten years. This growth is illustrated region by region on the bar chart in Figure 3.10.

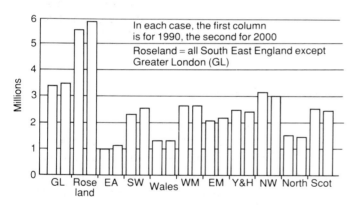

Figure 3.10 *The government's regional labour force projections, 1990 and 2000*

DID YOU KNOW?

Much of the growth in the labour force during the next ten years will be brought about by an increase in the number of working women, which by the year 2000 is expected to have increased by 44 per cent. This is the case in all regions except Scotland. The increases will be largest in the South, East Anglia, the South West and Wales.

Evidence Collection Point 3.21

1 Look in your local newspaper and cut out at least two articles about local firms that have either closed or announced redundancies.

2 Find out from the Job Centre the unemployment figures for your region for each of the past five years. Plot a graph (preferably using a spreadsheet) and identify the trends. Can you find reasons to explain any changes?

3 If possible find a friend or someone you know who has in the past been unemployed and is now working. Ask them what steps they took to find their present job and how long it took them to find it.

Write a short report on your findings.

Regional pay rates

Although you might expect to be paid the same rate for the same job no matter in which part of the country you work, this is not always the case. The biggest difference is between those who work in Greater London and the South East and those who work in the rest of the country. In 1992 earnings for employees in the South East were estimated to be 14.4 per cent higher than the average for Britain. In Greater London earnings were estimated to be over 26 per cent higher. Some employers pay extra as a 'London allowance'.

Outside the South East the variations are much smaller. The average weekly earnings of a worker ranged from £288.40 in East Anglia to £270.90 in Wales (as compared with an average £385.30 in Greater London and £315.60 in the South East).

· TECHNOLOGY AND EMPLOYMENT ·

Many jobs have changed dramatically over the last 20 years or so because of technological developments. Technology can affect jobs in one of four ways:

● it can create them
● it can destroy them

- it can change their content
- it can change their location.

All these changes are *ongoing*, so that the information you read about today may be obsolete in another five or ten years! However, opinions vary on whether the *total* effect of technology is a net increase or a net decrease in the number of jobs. The majority of experts consider that the overall picture is one of neither gain nor loss, but *change* in the type of jobs and the type of skills required.

Robotics

In many industries robots are used to perform dangerous, dirty, monotonous or intricate jobs more efficiently than human beings. Many industrial robots are simply 'arms' which may be programmed for tasks such as welding, paint spraying, machine loading and basic assembly work (see Figure 3.11). Multi-arm robots with up to four arms have been developed and used successfully. The main problem with industrial robots is their cost, which is anything from £15 000 to over £50 000 each, depending on their capability.

However, robots are not limited to manufacturing industry. In 1992, BT launched a trial of a robotic telephone exchange to answer calls and deal with many of the routine tasks and enquiries now handled by human operators. In medicine, robots are being developed to help to move patients who are immobilised or paralysed and who need frequent manipulation. They are also being developed to be able to carry out delicate operations, such as brain surgery, as the robot's movements can be precisely programmed and repeated whenever required.

DID YOU KNOW?

1 Whereas 'blue collar' has traditionally been the term used for manual workers and 'white collar' the term for clerical workers, **steel collar** is the term now being used to describe robots!

2 The trend is towards miniaturisation. The smallest robot is just 1 cubic centimetre, shaped like a bug, and weighs 4.3 grams. Today it is an executive toy – tomorrow it could be programmed to crawl around the human body to carry out intricate operations that surgeons cannot do at present.

Telecommunications

Whether you realise it or not, you are using telecommunication equipment every time you turn on your radio or TV set. Both receive *analogue* signals; i.e. radio or television waves that are transmitted at different frequencies. Until recently, telephones used the same type of technology. All these common household objects are telecommunication devices – because they receive *communications from a distance*.

Modern telecommunication devices differ in two ways. Firstly, most of them use *digital* technology. Secondly, in many cases they can transmit information as well as receive it. Digital signals are transmitted as pulses, rather than as waves, and these pulses are understood by computers.

Two computers can be linked over a telephone line by using *modems*. These devices convert the analogue signal to the digital signal required by the computer (see Figure 3.12).

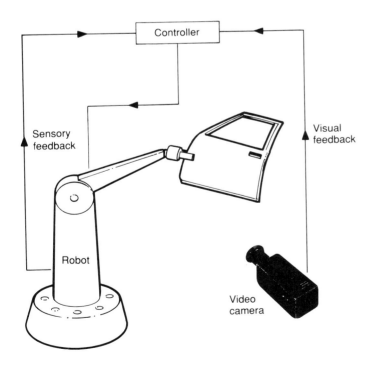

Figure 3.11 *Basic components of a robot*

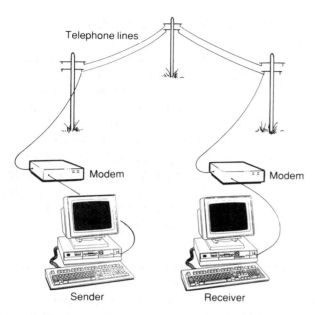

Figure 3.12 *Connecting two computers at a distance*

DID YOU KNOW?

When all the telephone systems have become digital, modems will not longer be required. Instead a special feature will be incorporated into the computer to link to the digital network. ISDN is the name of the new **integrated services digital network** which about 160 countries, including Britain, aim to support.

Activity

Find out whether your local telephone network is digital. If it is you will be able to set a telephone to 'pulse' setting, rather than 'tone'. You will then find that the number you require is ringing almost as soon as you have finished pressing the keys. You willl also have access to BT's Star Services. Find out what these are and the charges for each.

Telecommunications services and equipment

A wide range of telecommunications equipment is used by businesses all over the world. In most cases this has the benefit of enabling companies to send and receive information far more quickly than if they used the traditional postal services. Here are some examples:

- Digital telephone switchboards not only handle calls but also remember what they are doing and keep the operator informed by means of a small VDU screen. Extension users have a variety of facilities they can use, including making their own calls, which frees the operator to concentrate on incoming calls and enquiries.
- Answering machines can now not only take and play back messages but can be activated from a remote location if a business person is travelling away from the office.
- Bleepers and pagers enable those working away from the office to stay in touch with their base.
- Mobile or 'car' phones may include an answering machine.
- Videophones are the latest development. They need digital telephone networks on which to operate.
- Fax machines transmit images of text and graphics quickly and easily to other fax machines. Many can call other machines automatically and 'collect' any messages left in store for them.
- Telex machines (which today usually look like computers) send *text* (not graphics) to other telex machines. They are still used in situations where fax is either not suitable or not available.
- Electronic mail (or Email) is a messaging system whereby documents prepared on a computer are then transmitted to other computers via a 'mailbox' system. The mailbox stores messages until the user is ready to access them. Companies with a computer network (see below) will have their own internal electronic mail system. External electronic mail systems are Telecom Gold or the Prestel Mailbox service.
- Videoconferencing gives business people the opportunity to hold meetings without travelling very far from their office. British Telecom provides a service called Confravision which links videoconferencing studios in several major cities in Britain.
- On-line databases or databanks are electronic libraries to which companies can subscribe to receive information they need. The most basic are Ceefax and Oracle, which give a one-way flow of information. Prestel is two-way – the user can interact with the system (e.g. to order a holiday brochure). Other databanks have a more specialised use; e.g. TOXLINE/MEDLINE gives information on medical matters and LEXIS gives legal information.

Evidence Collection Point 3.22

Select *one* of the telecommunications services mentioned above and research it in more detail. You will be able to get information from up-to-date business and IT textbooks as well as from equipment manufacturers and suppliers.

Prepare a talk which includes the advantages and disadvantages of the system you have chosen, its present cost and main features. Your presentation should last about five minutes and include some visual aids.

Give your presentation to the rest of your group and, when they make theirs, take notes of the main points that are made. Type up your notes on a word-processor as soon as possible afterwards, and check anything you are not sure about with the individual speakers.

Mainframe computers

A **mainframe** is a computer with a large memory capacity used to undertake large-scale data processing operations. It will usually be found in a central computer services section, and used by specialist computer operators. Computer programmers may be employed to write special customised programs for the organisation. Information will be keyed in by data processing operators and may be processed immediately or later.

Because mainframe computers are very expensive they usually run 24 hours a day – so that routine functions can be undertaken overnight.

A typical mainframe installation might be in a mail order company. Orders are received and keyed in by data processing operators. The computer checks the orders against existing stock levels and transmits them to the warehouse. 'Pickers' then assemble the orders from racks, laid out in a predetermined sequence. The computer automatically issues an invoice to customers based on goods supplied, and reorders any outstanding stock. At the same time as these main functions are being carried out, other staff in the organisation can use the mainframe terminals for word-processing, database listings (e.g. of customers and suppliers), spreadsheet calculations, payroll and so on. In addition, the mainframe may be linked to other branches and offices throughout the country or even overseas, through telecommunication networks.

The advent of the mainframe resulted in more *specialised* employment to manage, program and operate the computer, with job titles such as Systems Analyst, Computer Programmer and Computer Operator. The computer department would virtually dictate the way in which other departments operated – so that all the systems in the organisation were linked to the computer.

Microcomputers

The first **microcomputers** were developed in the early 1960s following the invention of the silicon chip, a tiny wafer which functions as an electronic processor (microprocessor).

Development has become more and more rapid over the years. Miniaturisation is the name of the game, with laptop computers, notebook and even 'palm' computers. The latest computers are a fraction of the size of the earlier ones, with far more memory and improved processing speed. The latest microcomputers are faster and more powerful than the original mainframe computers were years ago!

Computers in the future will be more powerful, smaller and cheaper, and with an even greater range of

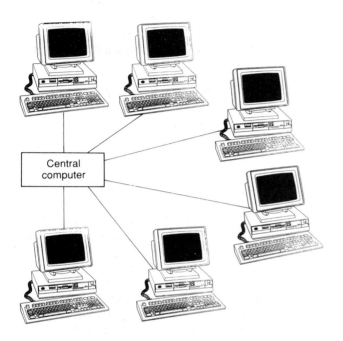

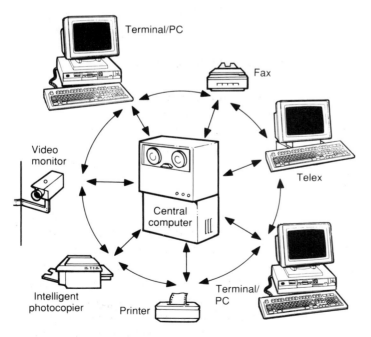

Figure 3.13 *Networks*

applications. The first 'pen' computers, with touch-sensitive screens that recognise handwriting, are already on the market. Those which will recognise spoken commands are predicted to follow shortly.

The increasing memory size and power of the microcomputer has meant that more organisations have installed a series of micros, rather than a mainframe computer, and linked these together via a **network**. Software can now be bought 'off-the-shelf' with less need for specialist programmers.

DID YOU KNOW?

A computer network consists of cables which link personal computers so that they can exchange information. Other equipment can be included on the network (e.g. fax machines and photocopiers). Networks can operate over a small or large geographical area, and can be used to transmit information long distances by satellite.

Evidence Collection Point 3.23

You now need to consider the ways in which modern developments in technology may affect employment, both now and in the future. You should remember that robotics, telecommunications and computers have changed not only the way people do their jobs but also the *speed* at which they are done.

Divide into three groups. Each group should brainstorm one of the following, bearing in mind the information given above. Suggest as many changes to employment as you can think of for each area.

a The effect on traditional occupations (e.g. postmen or welders).
b The effect on office work.
c The effect on numbers of staff required.

Store your completed lists on computer. When you have completed this chapter, retrieve your lists and add any other points you have read about which weren't included.

• THE EFFECTS OF NEW TECHNOLOGY • ON EMPLOYMENT

Job creation

The most obvious jobs to have been created are in the electronics and computer industries. This does not mean just the people who manufacture and assemble consumer electronics (e.g. videos), telecommunications equipment (e.g. fax machines) and computers, but also those who are involved in research and development, marketing, distribution and retailing. Most companies now employ computer specialists – operators, programmers or computer service staff who maintain and develop the company's network and microcomputers. Software engineering and development is another spin-off from the rapid growth of the computer industry.

People who work in 'peripheral' jobs include those in the leisure industry (e.g. in theme parks and virtual reality studios) which not only utilise the new technology but have more customers as people work fewer hours and therefore have more time for leisure activities. Designers who work in computer graphics, text creators for teletext and commercial databanks, and editorial staff and journalists who work for IT journals and computer magazines are people who work in other growth areas.

DID YOU KNOW?

Scotland has its own version of Silicon Valley – called Silicon Glen. In 1992, a new microchip was invented there by Digital. Called Alpha, it contains nearly 2 million transistors and can handle 400 million instructions per second. Yet in Silicon Glen, during 1992, over 1000 jobs were lost, despite the fact that over 40 per cent of all Europe's desktop computers are made there.

Job losses

Firstly, it is important to distinguish between jobs that have been lost as a result of technological developments, and those that have been changed (see page 95). Jobs may be lost altogether because:

- The work can be done by robot or by a computerised or automated process.

- Productivity has increased, so that only one worker is required, say, instead of two.
- Fewer supervisors or managers are required to supervise machines.
- There are too many companies competing in one sector of the market (e.g. making computers) so that if there is a fall in demand for their products the smaller firms (or the most inefficient) go out of business.
- Computer manufacturers may relocate overseas where labour is cheaper so the cost of producing the goods is less.

The problem for computer companies trying to survive in a highly competitive market was dealt with in the last chapter. This section concentrates on the type of jobs that have been computerised or automated.

DID YOU KNOW?

In 1991 over 35 000 jobs were lost in the banking industry – and a similar number in 1992 – many because of developments in banking technology. This included the introduction of ATMs (automatic teller machines) which are now used for over 60 per cent of personal cash withdrawals, centralised cheque processing, telephone and computer banking and the increased use of debit cards (see page 210) rather than cheques.

Computerisation and automation

Even without the use of robots it is possible to link a variety of equipment, via computer, so that a manufacturing or assembly process is completely automated. If necessary, robots can be used at various points throughout the process to undertake specific operations.

It is envisaged that, in the future, flexible manufacturing system (FMS) technology could result in factories where the design and drawing of the components will be produced in the office by a CAD package, programmed directly into a computer which oversees the operation of the entire machinery and robots in the plant. A completely automated factory would need far fewer people doing supervisory, planning, maintenance or loading/unloading operations.

The advantages to the company are lower labour costs, greater reliability and accuracy and the ability to operate 24 hours a day, seven days a week (as machines and robots don't get tired, nor do they need paying for overtime).

It is not only in industry that jobs have been lost. Traditionally newspapers were produced by skilled typesetters who literally 'set the type' in metal. Today text for newspapers is keyed in by journalists to computers linked to presses which produce the papers. The craft of the typesetter has been overtaken by technology.

DID YOU KNOW?

 Early in 1993 *The Guardian* became the first newspaper to be delivered electronically to blind and partially-sighted people via PCs in their home or at the local college or library (see Figure 3.14).

Evidence Collection Point 3.24

1 Visit your local bank and find out about both telephone banking and computer banking *or* contact a 'specialist' telephone bank such as First Direct. List the type of transactions which can be carried out in this way.

2 Interview at least one person who can tell you about banking roughly 15 years ago – the number of branches in your area, the hours the bank opened, the range of services etc. Write a brief report on the interview which includes the questions you asked and the answers you received.

3 Summarise how technology has changed banking and the implications for bank employees.

Increased productivity

This can be achieved not only in industry, by the use of robots, but also in offices by the use of computers. Today computers can perform calculations and produce documents in a fraction of the time it would have taken people with conventional calculators or typewriters. As office systems such as accounts and payroll become computerised there is obviously a need for fewer clerks.

However, the industry which has probably felt the greatest impact is retailing. Self-service has been greatly facilitated by electronic devices such as tagging (to prevent shop-lifting) and automated tills where a checkout operator can deal quickly and accurately with a range of purchases. Bar-codes on products are read automatically by a reader attached to a cash register which also automatically prints cheques and checks and processes debit and credit cards.

Both in industry and retailing, computers are used for automated stock control procedures. Each sale in a supermarket, for instance, is logged by the cash register and used to adjust automatically the number of goods in stock. When the number falls below a pre-set figure, an order is automatically produced to the supplier.

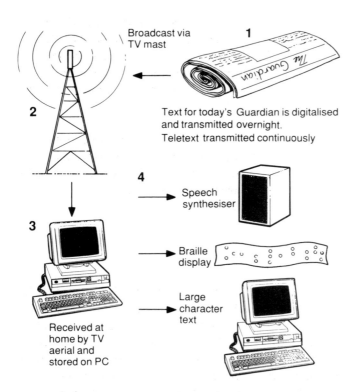

Broadcast via TV mast

1

Text for today's Guardian is digitalised and transmitted overnight. Teletext transmitted continuously

2

4 Speech synthesiser

3 Braille display

Large character text

Received at home by TV aerial and stored on PC

Figure 3.14 *How the electronic Guardian works*

Job content

There are three possible changes to job content, known as:

- de -skilling
- multi-skilling
- up-skilling

De-skilling

This term is used when technology has led to traditional craft skills no longer being required. Imagine if all computers had speech input: the days of the keyboard operator would rapidly be drawing to a close – he or she would be required merely to switch on the machine, monitor its progress, load the printer and distribute the printouts. That is a typical example of de-skilling.

De-skilling has affected a wide range of occupations. The traditional 'television engineer' needed to know exactly what could go wrong with your television – and where, in the workings inside it, to find the fault and repair it. Today it is simply a case of replacing printed circuit boards. A television repair person will spend more time travelling from call to call than he or she will spend on mending television sets! In industry, maintenance workers may be similarly affected. Indeed in some cases, computers are not only used to operate machinery but also to diagnose faults.

A final example can be taken from the retail trade. If you ask your parents or an elderly relative about the skills required to run a retail shop 30 years ago, they would probably say 'a good memory' (to remember prices) and 'numeracy' (to total the goods). Neither of these skills is required today – the automated cash register does both. However, others may argue that this frees staff to look after customers and find out more about the product range they have in stock.

Multi-skilling

If the traditional craft, or skill, possessed by a worker is either no longer required or required to a lesser extent, then it is usual for him or her to be asked to undertake other jobs as well. This may mean acquiring new or different skills. It also implies flexibility – people have to undertake a variety of tasks.

Generally multi-skilling is popular as it means a more varied and interesting job. It can, however, come as a shock to workers who have been in a job for many years to suddenly find they have to learn new skills and new procedures.

Up-skilling

This means that the level of skills required is increased. A typical example would be the machine operator who is now responsible for a range of computerised equipment and is therefore trained to supervisory level. In an office, an example would be the former invoice typist who, with a microcomputer, can produce documents much more quickly and is therefore trained as a word-processor operator and made responsible for a wider range of jobs.

Evidence Collection Point 3.25

Interview *either* someone who worked in retailing *or* someone who has worked in an office for several years. Find out about *one* of the following:

- The range of manual operations that are now done by computer, and list these.
- The number and type of jobs that were formerly carried out by typists and are now done using a word-processor.
- The way in which computers have affected the role of managers and the information available to them.

Write a short report on how you think jobs have altered because of these changes and the advantages and disadvantages for employees.

Job location

It is no longer the case that anyone located away from the organisation cannot be in touch with what is going on. Travelling executives can contact their organisations even when in mid-air by the use of an 'airphone', or link with the company's computer to leave messages on an electronic mail system. They can do this simply by dialling the computer and linking their telephone with the laptop computer they take with them on their travels.

However, probably the biggest revolution in the future could be in **teleworking**. This term is used for people who work at home and are linked to their organisation by means of computer. In July 1992, British Telecom set up a teleworking project in Scotland. Ten operators now work from home to operate the Inverness directory enquiries exchange. In many cases teleworkers are sales people – Texaco UK links its salespeople to head office via home-based computers by which they can 'report in' and 'discuss' their queries.

It has been forecast that by the middle of the 1990s, over 4 000 000 people could become teleworkers, as companies look at cheaper options than paying for expensive office space, and as employees come to prefer the idea of working from home to commuting to work through heavy traffic in all weathers.

Evidence Assignment 3D

Your friend, Anita, is lively and vivacious and has been working as a word-processor operator for the last two years in a large company situated two miles away. Because of increasing costs the company is relocating to a more remote area approximately ten miles away. Anita has three choices. She can:

- travel every day (she has no car), or
- resign, and get a job nearer home, or
- become a teleworker – as the company has offered to provide her with the equipment to work from home if she wishes.

She has two weeks to make a decision. At the moment she is quite tempted with the idea of teleworking. You don't know if this would be such a good idea.

Summarise the advantages and disadvantages of each option and come to a conclusion about the action you think she should take.

Evidence Collection Point 3.26

1 The chart below is only partially finished. The facts given in the text should enable you to complete it.

Occupation	Technological changes
Typesetter	
Welders	
Draughtsmen	CAD/CAM
Typists	
Sales staff	
Telephone staff	Automated exchanges
Bank employees	
Despatch workers	Automated packaging and checking
Postal workers	Electronic mail

Mineworkers

Assembly workers

Computer controlled machinery

2 Select any two occupations listed above. Write a brief summary of the changes that have occurred that have affected the job, and their severity (i.e. whether the job has disappeared altogether or merely been altered, and in what way).

3 Write a final paragraph as you envisage the future for office workers in the twenty-first century. Research current information on technological developments to help you.

Evidence Assignment 3E

Read the information below and prepare your answers using a word-processor.

British Telecom was privatised in 1984. At the time of its privatisation there were 20 million lines in Britain and about 137 countries could be dialled direct. Out of 77 000 payphones many were not working at any given time. There had been little investment in new technology and initially more staff had to be employed to improve service and install a digital network.

Before privatisation BT had the monopoly on selling telephones and related equipment, line installation and connections. The range of telephones which could be bought was limited and the cost was considered by many people to be excessive. After privatisation other manufacturers were allowed to sell telephones and other equipment in competition with BT, and Mercury Telecommunications was allowed to compete by offering an alternative telephone network.

Today BT is far more efficient. By 1990 there were 25 million lines in service and 197 countries could be dialled direct. There were over 90 600 payphones, most of them in working order. All trunk lines and over half of local switching is digital, giving a better service with fewer staff. BT's profits in 1991 were £3.1 million and expected to continue increasing over the next five years. Under Operation Sovereign, announced in 1990, 19 000 jobs were shed in the first year with a total of 80 000 scheduled

to go in five years. Redundancies will be mainly among white collar workers – especially managers earning up to £30 000 a year. The aim is that the workforce will have been cut by a third by 1996, and the wage bill of BT dramatically reduced.

1 List the advantages and disadvantages of the operation of British Telecom since privatisation from the customer's point of view.

2 Now do the same exercise, this time from the point of view of a BT clerical worker.

3 To what extent has modern technology enabled BT to make staff cuts? What other factors do you think have created redundancies?

4 If unemployment continues to rise, to what extent do you think the government should intervene if a company is still announcing job losses and even higher profits?

Evidence project

1 Investigate two different regions in the United Kingdom. One can obviously be your own. In each case find out:

a the *main* types of industry which exist in each region

b specific regional information on investment, natural resources and labour and skills supply and the ways in which these affect employment in each region

c the current level of employment and unemployment in each region.

Note: Much of the evidence you collected during this chapter should help you for this part of the project.

2 Find out at least *one* major industry which used to exist in your region.

a List the factors that caused it to be located in your region.

b State why it has now ceased to operate.

c Give a brief account of the effect of its closure on your local area and community.

3 Check with your local TEC, your Job Centre, the local papers and the reference library to see which organisations have been relocated in your area during the past five years. Make a list of them and give a brief description of:

   a what they do
   b how many people they employ
   c whether they are part of a nationwide chain
   d if possible, the reasons for their coming to your particular region.

4 Investigate a business organisation in your own region which operates in the retail, manufacturing or service sector. It may be a national or a local company.

Find out the following information. It will help if you can arrange an interview with a senior member of staff or visit the company at some stage.

- The types of employment offered by the company (i.e. how many part-time/full-time workers there are, whether they hire temporary staff and so on).
- The skills and qualifications they require of their clerical or administrative staff.
- As much as you can about the physical working conditions in which the staff operate.
- The amount and type of technology used and how this has changed over the past few years.
- The way in which technology has affected employment within the company.
- The number of people employed – and whether this has grown or declined in the past few years, and why.

If possible, produce your finished document on a word-processor with a suitable title page. Bind your project to give it a professional appearance.

Evidence Checkpoint

At this point you have completed the first section of this book and should have sufficient evidence to have completed the first unit of your GNVQ award. Check that you have nothing missing and nothing could be done again to improve your grade. Make sure everything is filed neatly and labelled clearly.

Revision Test

True or False?

1 A teleworker is someone who works from home and has telecommunications links with his or her company.

2 Income tax is paid by people who are self-employed.

3 The more qualifications you have the less chance there is that you will be unemployed.

4 The longer you have been unemployed the more difficult it is to get a job.

5 Unemployment in Britain in early 1993 was just under two million people.

Complete the blanks

6 The type of telecommunications equipment which can transmit both text and graphics to another machine is called a .....

7 A person who uses technology to work at home is known as a ....

8 A ...... is a device used to convert digital signals from a computer into analogue signals for transmission along a telephone network.

9 Temporary staff who are hired as they are needed, often on a daily basis, are known as ....

10 Trying to defraud the Inland Revenue is a criminal offence and is known as ....

Short answer questions

11 Give two measures the government can take to try to reduce unemployment.

12 State three disadvantages of unemployment.

13 Give four benefits which people can claim as a result of paying National Insurance contributions.

14 Give four examples of jobs which have been created as a result of technology.

15 State three ways in which you could assess the working environment in an organisation.

Write a short paragraph to show you clearly understand each of the following terms:

16 Telecommunications.

17 Physical working conditions.

18 National Insurance.

19 Robotics.

20 Regional differences.

. ADDRESSES FOR EVIDENCE . COLLECTION POINT 3.14

Association of Accounting Technicians, 154 Clerkenwell Road, London EC1R 5AD

Chartered Institute of Certified Accountants, 29 Lincoln's Inn Fields, London WC2A 3EE

Chartered Institute of Management Accountants, 63 Portland Place, London WIN 4AB

CAM Foundation Ltd, Abford House, 15 Wilton Road, London SW1V 1NJ

Chartered Institute of Marketing (CIM), Moor Hall, Cookham, Maidenhead, Berkshire SL6 9QH

Computing Services Industry Training Council (COSIT), 16 South Molton Street, London W1Y 1DE

Engineering Training Authority (EnTra), Vector House, 41 Clarendon Road, Watford, Hertfordshire WD1 1HS

Institute of Chartered Secretaries and Administrators, The Careers Department, 16 Park Crescent, London W1N 4AH

Institute of Logistics and Distribution Management, Douglas House, Queens Square, Corby, Nottinghamshire NN17 1PL

Institute of Management, Management House, Cottingham Road, Corby, Northants NN17 1TT

Institute of Management Services, 1 Cecil Court, London Road, Enfield, Middlesex EN2 6DP

Institute of Market Research Association (IMRA), 11 Bird Street, Lichfield, Staffordshire WS13 6PW

Education Office, Market Research Society, 15 Northburgh Street, London EC1V 0AH

Institute of Personnel Management, IPM House, Camp Road, Wimbledon, London SW19 4UW

Institute of Public Relations, The Old Trading Houses, 15 Northburgh Street, London EC1V OPR

Institute of Practitioners in Advertising, 44 Belgrave Square, London SW1X 8QS

Institute of Purchasing and Supply, and the Association of Supervisors in Purchasing and Supply, Easton House, Easton on the Hill, Stamford, Lincolnshire PE9 3NZ

Institute of Quality Assurance, PO Box 712, 61 Southwark Street, London SE1 1SB

Institute of Sales and Marketing Management, 31 Upper George Street, Luton, Bedfordshire LU1 2RD

Trades Union Congress, Congress House, Great Russell Street, London WC1B 3ES1

chapter **4** # STRUCTURES AND FUNCTIONS IN BUSINESS ORGANISATIONS

Learning Objectives

This chapter is concerned with the way in which business organisations are structured, the way in which this affects decision-making and the main functions to be found in different types of organisations.

After studying this chapter you should be able to:

● describe different types of organisational structure

● describe the influence of different structures on decision-making

● describe and explain the functions within organisations

● identify the different structures and functions of business organisations.

. WHAT IS ORGANISATIONAL . STRUCTURE?

The structure of an organisation refers to the way in which its activities are grouped or arranged. In any organisation it is sensible for people who do similar types of work to be grouped together, so that they can communicate more easily and the work can be divided between them effectively.

In a small organisation this happens quite informally. In a business with only two or three staff the work is divided between everyone, depending on their skills, qualifications and experience. If there is a manager then he or she is responsible for making the decisions about allocating the work. In a crisis, everyone would be expected to help out.

As an organisation grows in size it becomes unmanageable unless it is more formally structured. If you work in a business which employs 30 people, you need to know which jobs are carried out by which members of staff – otherwise you could waste hours looking for the right person to contact about a particular item. Equally, the managers of the enterprise need to know who is responsible for each aspect of the work, so that they can check everything is being done properly – and know who to blame if it isn't! In an organisation with a large number of employees, a proper structure is crucial to its efficiency.

Variations in structure

The structure of an organisation will not depend only on its size and number of employees. It will also depend on other factors such as:

- whether it is in the manufacturing or service sector
- whether it is a local, national or international organisation
- the type of work with which it is involved.

Therefore all companies are different! There is no right or wrong structure – provided that the way in which the company is organised helps people to do their work more efficiently and communicate with each other easily, and assists the business to achieve its objectives.

DID YOU KNOW?

In a large organisation there will be more **specialisation**; i.e. each person will concentrate on his or her own specific job. For instance, accounts staff will only deal with financial matters. In a small organisation, finance may be simply a part of a manager's job.

The organisation chart

The structure of an organisation is shown on an **organisation chart**. This usually gives the job titles of employees and their relationships with each other. Sometimes the job-holder's name is shown. Those at the top of the chart have more responsibility (and are paid more) than those lower down. They can also give instructions to those below them, who have a duty to carry these out.

As an example, DPTS is a small computer consultancy. There are two partners, David and Paul, and they employ two consultants, Jane and Martin, and an administrator, Sajida. On an organisation chart the structure of DPTS would be shown as in Figure 4.1. This shows that David and Paul are of equal status (they are on the same level on the chart) and they are *equally* responsible for the

consultants and for Sajida. At the same time, all the staff are on the same level.

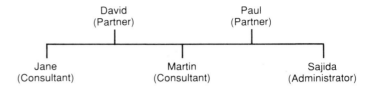

Figure 4.1 *A flat organisation chart (two levels)*

If David was responsible for Jane and Martin, and Paul was responsible for Sajida, then the chart would be drawn differently. If Sajida was less senior than the two consultants this would also be shown by her position on the chart (see Figure 4.2).

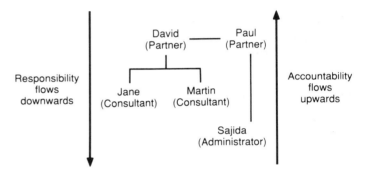

Figure 4.2 *A flat organisation chart (three levels)*

The arrowed lines on the chart show that a manager or supervisor is *responsible* for staff who report to him or her, and that, in return these staff are *accountable* to the manager for their actions.

DID YOU KNOW?

The phrase 'passing it down the line' can refer to jobs and information passed down an organisation from one level to another – as shown by the lines on the organisation chart.

Flat structures

An organisation with only two or three levels is known as a **flat** structure. The business is likely to be run relatively informally, as everyone will know everyone else. There will probably be good communications between bosses and employees. This should mean that they can respond quickly to changing situations and specific customer requests.

Evidence Assignment 4A

1 Draw an organisation chart for a doctors' practice with three partners, Dr Gilbert, Dr Ahmed and Dr Ashe. They employ four receptionists, Anne, Pat, Marion and Lorraine, for whom they are jointly responsible.

2 Now draw the chart again, showing how it would look if they employed a nurse, Bridget, who was at a higher level than the four receptionists.

3 Bearing in mind the type of work carried out, why do you think it is important that a doctors' practice has a flat organisational structure? Discuss the reasons as a group and make a list of as many advantages as possible.

Changing the structure

As an organisation grows, keeping a 'flat' structure becomes very difficult. If DPTS employed another ten consultants then David and Paul would be in charge of 13 people altogether. They would also need office staff. If five more office staff were employed then the directors would be in charge of 18 people. They would then spend more time supervising the work done by other people than they would on doing their own jobs.

A special term for the number of people each manager can oversee is **span of control**. If David and Paul divided the staff into two halves, they would each have a span of control of nine people (Figure 4.3). Whilst this may be possible if employees are undertaking very routine or similar work (e.g. assemblers on a production line) it is almost impossible to supervise a large number of staff properly if they are involved in complicated work or very different types of jobs.

There would also be another problem. Officially David cannot give instructions to Paul's staff, nor can Paul give orders to those who report to David. In a small office this would be unworkable and would reduce flexibility dramatically.

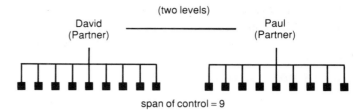

Figure 4.3 *Illustrating span of control*

The obvious solution is to introduce another 'level' into DPTS. Let us assume that 12 months later DPTS is a limited company and David and Paul are now the two directors – and have reorganised the company.

Stage 1

David and Paul again take joint responsibility for Martin, Jane and Sajida. They promote Martin and Sarah to the position of Senior Consultant. Each is responsible for the work of five other consultants. All the office staff report to Sajida, who has been promoted to Administration Manager. The organisation chart of the company now looks like Figure 4.4.

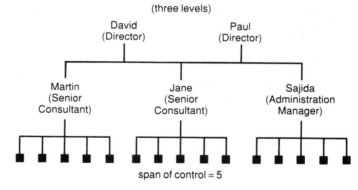

Figure 4.4 *Span of control after reorganisation*

Activity

As a group, can you give at least two reasons why this structure is far more practical than the structure shown before they reorganised?

Stage 2

As time goes by, DPTS Ltd continues to expand. Four consultants have left and David and Paul decide that they now want to recruit *trainee* consultants who they can train in their own ways of working. They also appoint a Financial Manager, Gerry, and a Sales and Marketing Manager, Brian. These managers are at the same level as the Senior Consultants.

At the same time they reorganise the office staff, who now number six. In addition Paul appoints his own Secretary/PA, Vivien. Because she does not report to anyone but him, she is shown as linked to him by a dotted line. The organisation chart now looks like Figure 4.5.

Evidence Assignment 4B

1 Examine the chart in Figure 4.5 carefully and answer the following questions:

a How many levels are there in DPTS now?

b Who is responsible for the trainee accountant?

c If Damien has a problem with the trainee consultants for whom is he responsible, who should he go to?

d Can Susan, the WP operator, give instructions to the receptionist/telephonist?

e To whom is Viyja responsible on a day-to-day basis? Who should she see if her immediate boss is absent through illness and a serious problem arises?

f At what level is Sui in relation to (i) Bernadette, (ii) Sandra, (iii) Sahida?

2 Re-draw the chart, assuming the following changes are made:

- Jimmy is promoted to consultant and reports direct to Martin.
- Another trainee consultant, Yvonne, is appointed in his place.
- Paula gains a clerical assistant, Michaela.
- A second WP operator is appointed, Naomi.
- An office junior, Ben, is appointed. Although he reports to Sahida he is at a lower level than anyone else in the organisation.
- David also appoints his own PA/Secretary, Cathie.

3 *As a group*, discuss the differences there will be for the directors working in an organisation of this size, rather than the original DPTS structure. Summarise your answers on disk and be prepared to update them later.

4 What differences do you think there will be for 'old' employees, such as Sahida?

5 An organisation chart only shows the 'formal' structure of an organisation, not the informal relationships. What difference do you think it would make to Martin if David played golf with Guy every Sunday morning?

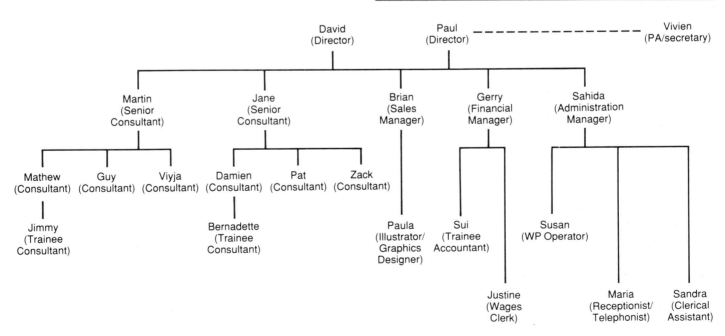

Figure 4.5 *DPTS Ltd after expansion*

DID YOU KNOW?

A deputy is higher than an assistant, and therefore has a different position on the organisation chart.

Examine Figure 4.6. The deputy is directly below the manager – which means that if the manager leaves the deputy could move 'up the line' and take her place. He would certainly be eligible to apply for the job.

The assistant, on the other hand, is to one side. This means he is literally 'not in line for the job'.

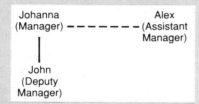

Figure 4.6

Hierarchical structures

A **hierarchical** structure is one in which there are many levels, so it looks 'tall'. Each person has a narrower span of control. Jobs are now far more specialised. As an example, since the appointment of the Financial Manager, neither of the Directors of DPTS will expect to be involved in this type of work – except to be kept informed as to how the company is doing.

Usually, the more hierarchical an organisation the more 'formal' it is. There will be more official procedures which have to be followed and a greater number of written rules and regulations. There will be, for example:

- official job titles and a specified salary scale for each 'level' of job
- a formal health and safety policy
- standard procedures laid down on hours of work, holidays, personal days off, punctuality, disciplinary procedures and so on
- an official interview procedure
- guidelines (or rules) on dress, customer service, layout of documents, methods of working, etc.

Why is all this necessary? There are two main reasons:

1 To ensure that the standards throughout the organisation will be the same – for customers and for employees.
2 To ensure that there is fairness to all employees – because they are all treated the same.

With a large number of employees these would be impossible unless some standards were laid down. Different managers would respond to situations in different ways, and this would lead to problems.

DID YOU KNOW?

Hierarchical structures are often called **pyramid** structures. This is because the shape is like a pyramid if you take into account the fact that at each level downwards in the organisation there will be more employees. The more hierarchical, the steeper the pyramid (Figure 4.7).

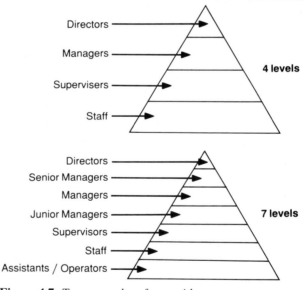

Figure 4.7 *Two examples of pyramid structures*

Evidence Assignment 4C

Read the assignment below and then answer the questions which follow.

When DPTS was formed relationships with staff were very informal – a situation both David and Paul, the founders, enjoyed. Regularly staff would get together either at lunchtime or in the evenings for a meal. Information was readily exchanged and everyone knew who did what.

As the company grew, and new members of staff were appointed, it became more difficult for the old relationships to continue. The office needed to be covered at lunchtime, so someone was always left out if everyone else went off together, and this caused problems. In addition, both David and Paul were becoming inundated with requests from staff for days off, decisions on how to solve problems, and for salary increases.

Over time, things have become even worse. In the past week four problems have arisen and all have jeopardised good working relationships:

- The two word-processor operators of the same age and with the same qualifications discovered there is over £500 a year difference in their salaries.
- A new receptionist arrived for work in a pair of jeans two days running. This was accepted by one of the managers on the first day but on the second day another member of staff sent her home to get changed. She was annoyed because she claimed no-one had told her how she should dress.
- Two consultants have compared notes on their days off. One had asked Paul for two days personal leave which had been agreed with full pay. The other had asked David for a day off, for personal reasons, and had been informed this would have to be without pay. The second consultant was annoyed as he had never asked for time off before, and had been employed by the company for the same length of time as his colleague.
- David's PA is annoyed. She had asked David for information on how to set out a special report which she and Paul had written between them. She had followed his instructions faithfully. When Paul saw it he complained he didn't like the layout and asked her to change it.

All the original members of staff were of the opinion that the place was disorganised and no one seemed to know what they were doing any more.

1 Why are the informal systems which used to work no longer effective?

2 What solutions can you offer for each of the problems that have occurred this week?

3 What can David and Paul do to prevent problems such as these occurring in the future?

4 Briefly summarise the differences between working for a 'flat' organisation and a 'hierarchical' organisation.

DID YOU KNOW?

Hierarchical organisations are often called 'bureaucracies' – a name given to them by Max Weber, a German sociologist, who was one of the first people to look at the advantages and disadvantages of this type of organisational structure. Typical bureaucracies are the civil service and local government, as well as large-scale public companies.

One problem with bureaucracies can be that, because everyone has to follow rules and procedures, decision-making can be slow. In addition there might be a desire to impress the boss – and tell him what he wants to hear, rather than the truth!

. ORGANISATIONAL STRUCTURE . AND DECISION-MAKING

The differences between working for a small or a large organisation are not seen only by the more junior employees. Managers, too, find there are considerable differences – the main one being in the number and type of decisions they make.

In a small organisation, with a flat structure (such as a sole trader or partnership), the owner(s) will be responsible for most of the decisions which involve both the current operations and the future plans of the enterprise. These decisions will range from those that are fairly basic (e.g. how to set out the goods in a shop) to those that are more important (e.g. which bank offers the best service and loan facilities). In a large organisation, many of these decisions will be taken by other people. This will then free senior management from having to make day-to-day operational decisions and allow them to concentrate on decisions which affect the long-term prospects of the organisation.

Evidence Assignment 4D

1 Bill Jones owns a shoe shop. He employs two assistants. Below are ten decisions which were made yesterday. Identify those that *only* Bill could make, as the owner, and those that could be made by the assistants.

a New opening times for the shop.
b The style of the new window display.
c The style of the new uniforms for the assistants.
d Which customer to serve first.
e When to unpack some new stock.
f Whether to hold a sale next month.
g Whether to buy a new computerised cash register.
h Whether to start to accept credit cards.
i Whether to ask a mother to control an unruly child.
j Whether to tidy up a messy area of the shop.

2 If Bill employed an additional member of staff, as a supervisor, which decisions could he or she now make *instead of* Bill?

3 The two assistants have been arguing recently about who should take early lunch and who should take late lunch. What advantages are there in Bill telling them to make up their minds themselves, rather than dictate the times to them?

DID YOU KNOW?

The term **delegation** is used when responsibility for undertaking a task is passed down from a manager to a subordinate. This helps to develop staff, makes their work more interesting and enables the manager to concentrate more on the type of work only he or she can do.

Managerial decisions

In the early years of DPTS, David and Paul made virtually all the decisions about the company (see page 101). They had to decide:

- how much capital they needed
- how much they should spend on office premises, equipment and stationery
- how many staff to employ and how much to pay them

- how to 'sell' their company to potential customers
- which other companies would be interested in their services
- which services they should offer
- how much they should charge for these services
- which of them should be responsible for different types of work (e.g. sales, finance etc.)
- when to order new stock
- what quality of work they should insist on.

All these are *management* decisions which can only be made by the owners of the enterprise. When the company is operational, the managers will still retain the powers of making the final decision on areas such as:

- staffing and overall salary levels
- raising additional finance
- plans for the future
- company organisation and structure
- overall expenditure levels
- company policy and ethics.

DID YOU KNOW?

The word **ethics** refers to the *standards* that are allowed or encouraged by the company. For instance an ethical organisation will promote honesty and fair dealing with its customers, staff and suppliers and will only produce or sell quality products. It will never use high-pressure sales tactics or deliberately mislead its customers.

Operational decisions

These are the day-to-day decisions which are made by staff in the organisation. The type of decisions will depend upon the area of responsibility of each member of staff. For instance, DPTS now has a Finance Manager, a Sales and Marketing Manager and an Administration Manager. They would be responsible for making decisions in their own areas, as follows:

Finance
- the authorisation level for petty cash expenditure
- whether to extend a customer's credit
- whether the organisation can afford to take on an additional member of staff

Sales & Marketing
- where to advertise the company's products
- how to run a sales campaign
- which printing firm would be the best to produce a new leaflet

Administration
- whether a new photocopier is required
- who should cover for the switchboard operator at lunchtime
- how the filing system should be organised.

Equally, the staff for whom they are responsible would also be making their own day-to-day decisions.

DID YOU KNOW?

The larger the organisation, and the more specialised it becomes, the more decision-making will be 'spread' amongst staff and not concentrated in one particular area.

Activity

In relation to your GNVQ work, your portfolio and your evidence collection, some decisions are made by you and some by your tutor. Think of three examples of decisions which you would make and three examples of decisions which your tutor would make.

As a group, try to analyse the differences between the *types* of decision being made. Can you find any pattern? Ask your tutor for his or her comments.

Evidence Collection Point 4.1

1 Find out the structure of your own school or college. Draw an organisation chart which shows the *main* job titles (there is no need to include the names of the job-holders) and who is responsible for whom.

2 Compose a short paragraph stating whether you consider this to be a flat or a hierarchical structure and the reasons for your decision.

3 Write a second paragraph which summarises the advantages and disadvantages of this particular structure for an educational establishment.

4 Interview at least two members of staff – one of whom is at management level. (Note that your tutor may prefer you to do this as a group during a visit from his or her colleagues.) Prepare a list of questions so that you find out the type of decisions made daily by each person. Summarise the type of decisions being made at each level and how these vary.

Save your work on a word-processor. You will need to recall it (and add to it) later.

· FUNCTIONS WITHIN ORGANISATIONS ·

Our fictional company DPTS Ltd has created three functional areas so far – Finance, Sales & Marketing and Administration. This is normal. As a company increases in size, the most obvious way in which to group people is according to their **function** – i.e. the job they carry out. It is likely that:

- some people are involved in producing the goods
- some people are responsible for selling the goods
- other people provide support services – in general administration, finance or personnel.

The company may then be structured into departments as shown in Figure 4.8.

Figure 4.8 *Functional departments of an organisation*

Obviously, an organisation that is concerned with providing a *service* will not have a production department. For instance, a mail-order company which buys goods from elsewhere, and stores and distributes these to its customers, may have a large distribution department (which includes warehousing) but no production department. Therefore the titles of the departments, and their number, will depend very much on the work carried out by the organisation.

Departments in the public sector

In the public sector, virtually all organisations provide a service. However, these services may not be suitable for sub-dividing in the same way as in the private sector. Therefore the names of the departments, or the way in which they have been selected, may be very different:

- A local authority has departments such as Housing, Finance, Operations, Economic Development, Leisure Services and Development.
- A hospital is likely to be divided into specialist areas (e.g. Paediatric, Orthopaedic, Maternity, Psychiatric, etc.).
- A university has departments based on subject specialisms; e.g.
  - Engineering, Computing and Mathematics
  - Physics and Material Sciences
  - Biology
  - Performing Arts
  - Information Technology
  - Humanities.

Organisations that are structured on specialist lines, such as hospitals and universities, usually have general support services which are used by every department:

- A borough council or hospital may have a personnel department, a legal department and an administration department.
- A university may have a finance department, a buildings department, a personnel department and a student services department.

To differentiate these support services from the main departments they may be called by another name (e.g. a unit or section).

DID YOU KNOW?

If a department offers a support service to the rest of the organisation then this is known as a **centralised** service. For instance, a council may have its own centralised printing section which will do the printing work for everyone. This is cheaper than having individual machines in each department and enables specialist staff to be trained.

Evidence Collection Point 4.2

1 *As a group, either*:
   a Find out the departments at your local council offices. Write a brief paragraph on the work done by each one and make sure you clearly distinguish those which provide a support service, *or*
   b Find out the structure of your local hospital, the names of each department and the types of work carried out there. List separately those departments (or sections) which provide a support service.

2 Obtain a prospectus from a university and list the different departments described. Under each department, list at least three subjects you could study.

Make a separate note of those departments which provide a service – to students, to staff or to other departments.

DID YOU KNOW?

1 What is called a department in one organisation may be titled something entirely different in another. Educational establishments, for instance, may call their departments either **schools** or **faculties**. In any case, if a department is very large, this itself may be sub-divided into sections. For instance, a student services department may be divided into sections or units on:
   - student enquiries
   - careers advice and counselling
   - student records
   - loans and grants.

2 You can't go far wrong in trying to work out how a company is structured if you forget the titles (at the start) and concentrate on the size of each unit. Then see how each unit has been sub-divided. It then doesn't matter if the largest unit is called a division, a department, a school or a faculty, and if the next unit down is a called a section, a unit, a department or a division! So long as you keep it clear in your mind which is the largest unit and which is the smallest you should have few problems.

Evidence Collection Point 4.3

Recall the work you did on your own school or college for Evidence Collection Point 4.1.

a List any departments (or sections) which provide a support service for the rest of the organisation. State clearly what each one does.

b Note down the *titles* of each (i.e. whether they are called departments or sections, etc.). Make it clear which are the largest units and which are the smallest.

c Compose at least two paragraphs explaining *how* the organisation is divided (e.g. which subjects are taught in which department).

d State why you think the organisation has been structured in this way and whether or not you think it could be improved, and why.

Functional structures

You have already seen that in the private sector the majority of organisations are sub-divided according to functions. The advantages of doing this are:

- Specialists can work together.
- Staff can become more experienced.
- There are opportunities for promotion and career development.
- The manager will be an expert in a particular area.

There are, however, disadvantages. For example, departments can become competitive, rather than having the aims of the organisation as a whole in mind. If, for instance, staff cuts have to be made, every manager will try to defend his or her own department.

It is quite common for employees to stay in a particular type of department for most, if not all, of their working life – although they may move from one organisation to another. Before you can make any decisions about which area you would prefer to work in, it is important that you understand functions carried out by the main departments.

DID YOU KNOW?

The *scope* of each department, and the type of work it carries out, will *not* be identical in any two organisations. There will be similarities, but you should also expect to find differences. You are therefore not wrong if you find that in an organisation you are investigating there are several functions for a department which you didn't expect – or several missing which you *did* expect.

To help you, the descriptions below contain virtually everything you may find during your investigations. But don't be surprised if your eventual list is rather different!

DESIGN AND PRODUCTION

Typical job titles	Departmental functions
Works Manager	Production of goods
Chief Engineer	Maintenance of equipment
Chief Designer	Quality control
Factory Operatives	Stock control
Production Control Clerks	Work study
Quality Controllers	Production planning and control
Production Planners	Design and product development
Buyers	Purchasing
Order Clerks	Stores control
Storemen	Despatch
Draughtsmen	
Foremen	
Despatch Clerks	
Designers	
Engineers	

In some organisations you will find that design and production are part of the same department, in others that they are separate. In this case, the design function may be called **research and development** – more commonly known as R & D – or **design and development**.

Types of design

There are basically two types of design:

- **Industrial design** – concerned with appearance and product use.
- **Engineering design** – concerned with performance.

For instance, when a car is being developed the industrial designers will be concerned with the shape and features of the car whereas the engineering designers will be concerned with engine size, fuel consumption and acceleration.

New products are being developed all the time, and existing ones re-designed. Today, for instance, we use lightweight plastic jug kettles which can boil one cup of water at a time, rather than the traditional heavy metal kettles which had to be half full before they could be used. Video recorders, camcorders, televisions and computers are changing all the time – in many cases getting smaller or, in the case of televisions, thinner. In the fashion trade, new designs for clothes are a main feature. The packaging industry is another area where design is important – although you may think not if you have ever struggled to open a packet of sandwiches quickly during your lunch hour! The design of a can, tin or box (and the colours used) can influence us as consumers whether to buy or not to buy.

DID YOU KNOW?

The cost of designing and developing a product can mean a major investment by a company. For instance, the Ford Mondeo took five years to develop at an estimated cost of £3 billion! To protect the investment, and stop anyone copying the design, in many industries new designs are shrouded in secrecy and no photographs or literature are available until the official launch.

The job of the designers

The job of the design department is to create a design which:

- will appeal to consumers
- reflects the image of the product
- costs as little as possible to manufacture
- fulfils safety standards and regulations
- is as easy as possible for production to manufacture

- is constructed so that it will last over the life of the product
- will enable product maintenance to be carried out easily.

DID YOU KNOW?

Being the first with a new design can make a fortune for a company – even if the design is simple. The makers of the Post-It note, 3M, saw their profits increase rapidly after it caught on.

Re-designing an old product can bring an industry back from the brink of disaster. Swiss watch manufacturers saw their sales of watches fall dramatically after the introduction of digital watches. One company gave its old style watches new bold colours and designs, called them Swatches (for Swiss watches), and took the market by storm.

Evidence Collection Point 4.4

1 Investigate one of the articles shown below and decide which features are part of the industrial design and which are part of engineering design:

- an electric razor
- a hairdrier
- a portable CD player
- a computer printer
- a camera
- a calculator.

2 Visit a shop which sells the article you have selected and survey at least five different makes in relation to their design and performance. State which you think is the best, and why. Include any improvements you think could be made.

3 Cars have changed radically over the last 20 years in terms of both design and performance. The latest models feature airbags for use in an emergency. Obtain a leaflet on the car of your choice and analyse the design. List any features which you consider are new or revolutionary, and state why you think the designers have included them.

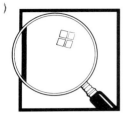

Evidence Assignment 4E

Working as a member of a small group, decide a new design for a T-shirt which would be readily saleable to your fellow students. Factors you should consider include

- shape
- size (one size or many?)
- material (washability, cost, etc.)
- graphic design (front or back, both or none – and type of design)
- colours
- projected selling price.

Test your early ideas by surveying other students (see Core Skills: Application of Number – page 416 for how to design a questionnaire and carry out a survey).

Then carry out a prediction of costs and different levels of sales at different selling prices using a spreadsheet package.

Prepare a report on a word-processor which gives details of how you eventually decided on the design. Include a sketch of your T-shirt, and give the reactions of your fellow students to your final product.

DID YOU KNOW?

Many products are designed using a computer. A **CAD (computer-aided design)** package enables a designer to sketch a basic shape and then vary the dimensions, angles and sizes of certain parts. The product can even undergo stress testing by computer.

In some industries CAD packages are linked to **CAM (computer-aided manufacturing)**. In the carpet industry, a new design can be planned on computer and the tufting machine which actually makes the carpet (and looks something like a giant knitting machine!) can be pre-set and controlled to produce the design by computer.

PRODUCTION

The method of production you will see in an organisation will depend upon the type of product being made and the size of the average order. Therefore aeroplanes are not manufactured in the same way as ballpoint pens!

There are basically four types of production process:

- **Job production** is concerned with orders for small numbers or luxury goods. Examples are designer fashions, designer jewellery, shipbuilding and the aerospace industry.
- **Batch production** is where whole batches of products are made. A typical example is a small bakery where the baker makes batches of meat pies, loaves, fruit tarts etc. before the shop opens.
- **Mass production** is where large quantities of identical products are made on a production line. This is the case with cars, many household appliances and consumer electronics.
- **Flow production** – where the product is produced continuously using a technological process, e.g. gas or oil.

DID YOU KNOW?

Japanese car manufacturers use a system known as **lean production**. This is a variation on the traditional mass production system. Workers are arranged in groups and take responsibility for *all* aspects of the process they are undertaking, including quality control checks. A car passes from one bay of workers to another, rather than on a continuous production line. This enables changes to be made to certain cars – or different models to be made – so the system is far more flexible than the traditional production line.

The production function can be divided into two areas: **planning** and **control**. Although these obviously overlap, it is easier to understand them if you think of each area separately at the beginning.

Production planning

After a product has been designed then its manufacture must be carefully planned:

- What raw materials will be needed and in what quantities?
- How much of these should be stored and how much bought as required?

- What machines will be required?
- What personnel will be needed?
- Do existing personnel have the necessary skills?
- How will the product be assembled?
- What will be the average time needed to manufacture each item?
- What packaging materials will be required?

Many of these factors will influence the final price of the product (e.g. the cost of the raw materials and the time and skills needed to make the product). For this reason there will be close liaison between the production planners and the cost accountant (see page 119). There will also be close links with sales and marketing departments because there is no point in producing something that cannot be sold.

DID YOU KNOW?

Many companies today use what is known as the **JIT** system of purchasing supplies. (JIT stands for 'just-in-time'). This means that they do not have to hold large stocks of materials (which saves both money and storage space) but instead they expect suppliers to deliver the raw materials as they are needed. The system is obviously most suitable for large organisations who, because of the size of their orders, have more control over their suppliers.

Working out how many machines or operators are required for a process is a key part of production planning. It is no use having ten people working on the first part and only five on the second if this would create a bottleneck (or hold-up) between the two stages. The same applies to machines, as some work faster than others.

Activity

Test your numeracy skills on the following problem. You are about to go into production making chocolate Easter eggs. For this imagine you need four machines:

A	B	C	D
mixes the chocolate	cooks the chocolate	moulds the eggs	wraps the eggs

The problem is that they all work at different speeds. In one hour machine A will mix the chocolate for 400 eggs, machine B will cook the chocolate for 1200 eggs, machine C will mould 800 eggs and machine D will wrap 600 eggs. If, therefore, you buy one of each machine then not only can you only produce 400 eggs every hour (i.e. the speed of the slowest machine) but you have idle capacity on all the other machines.

Assuming money is no problem, how many of each machine must you buy to ensure you have no bottlenecks or spare capacity? And how many eggs will you be making every hour?

DID YOU KNOW?

The layout of the production area is carefully planned to minimise time being wasted by people having to walk backwards and forwards. Normally the product will start to be assembled at one end and finish at the other.

Production control

Once the plans have been made and the manufacturing process started, then it is obviously vital that controls are in place to make sure that what was planned really happens. Otherwise production targets may not be met – and nobody will know why.

For this reason a variety of controls exist:

- **Progress control.** Progress chasing means checking that planned output is as scheduled. If it is not then the cause of the problem has to be found (e.g. machine breakdown, substandard materials or labour problems). Not only does the problem need to be solved but production schedules have to be readjusted to try to make up for lost time.
- **Quality control.** Quality controllers check the standard of the finished product. They may do this by examining each article or by random sampling (selecting certain items for inspection on a random basis).
- **Stock control.** This ensures that supplies of raw materials and components are always available so that production schedules are not interrupted.

- **Machine utilisation control**. This controls the use of the machines, to ensure none is overloaded or overused without being checked and maintained. Because machine breakdowns can be critical, many organisations have a maintenance plan which shows the dates on which machines will be out of operation for inspection and servicing.

DID YOU KNOW?

Automation and computers have changed many of the functions of production workers. Not only can the products themselves now be made by a completely automated process and controlled by computer (known as **CIM** – computer integrated manufacturing), but traditional jobs may now been done very differently. Here are two examples:

- Quality control may be done automatically by machine. For instance, a machine which makes hacksaw blades of a certain length will have a computerised checkpoint at the end, so that the length and thickness of each blade is automatically checked. The machine will stop if faults are detected.
- Progress chasers may now receive much of their information on either computer VDU or computer printout. They do not need, therefore, to run around a large factory checking on progress. In days gone by, some chasers in large factories (e.g. at British Aerospace) used a bicycle to get round the area they needed to cover!

Progress chasing today

Evidence Collection Point 4.5

During your course you should arrange to visit *at least* one manufacturing organisation. Revise the section you have just read before your visit. Whilst you are there make notes on what you see when you visit their production section. Then prepare a report on a word-processor which gives information on:

- the type of product(s) being made
- the scale of production (e.g. small, medium or large)
- the type of production process being used
- the degree to which the process was automated or computerised
- the layout of the production area
- the way in which production was scheduled and controlled
- the way in which quality control checks were made or quality assurance measures are being taken (see below).

DID YOU KNOW?

Many companies today are more interested in **quality assurance** than quality control. They can apply to the British Standards Institute to be awarded to BS5750 – the official quality standard in this country. A company will only gain this award if it can prove that its manufacturing and administrative systems are such that they can consistently guarantee the quality of the goods they produce (or service they offer). In this case quality is 'built-in' at every stage, rather than simply checked at the end of the process.

PERSONNEL

Typical job titles	Departmental functions
Personnel Manager	Recruitment and employment of staff
Training Officer	Keeping staff records
Welfare Officer	Education and training
Employment Officer	Industrial relations and trade union
Personnel assistants	negotiations
Record Clerks	Staff welfare
Canteen Staff	Health and safety
Welfare/Nursing Staff	Wages and salary administration
Security Staff	Manpower planning
	Security

Your first contact with an organisation is likely to be with the Personnel Department – as, amongst other things, they are involved with recruitment and selection. Therefore if you apply for a job you will be in touch with this department. However, this is only one part of their work.

All organisations regularly need new staff, to replace those who are leaving or to fill new vacancies if the company is expanding. When a vacancy occurs in any department, the Personnel Department is required to:

- Obtain a full job description. This is a summary of the job which lists the duties to be carried out and the areas for which the job-holder is responsible.
- Look at various ways of filling the vacancy.
- Send out application forms and other details to those who apply.
- Look at all the job applications received.
- Draw up, in consultation with the manager of the department affected, a shortlist of people to be interviewed.
- Arrange the interviews, either on a one-to-one basis, with a panel of interviewers or by means of a series of interviews.

Activity

Discuss *as a group* how many methods of recruitment you think may be used. A list of these is given after the Revision Test.

DID YOU KNOW?

Sometimes candidates are given a test. This may be either an aptitude test (generally to test speed of reaction, etc.), an intelligence test, a personality test or a practical test (e.g. a keyboarding exercise). If you are going for an interview, it is worth remembering this!

The selection process

After all that care has been taken, the right candidate *should* be selected (although that is not always the case). Nevertheless there are certain guidelines interviewers normally follow to cut down the chances of their making a wrong choice:

- They will check carefully that the job applicant has the right qualifications and experience.
- They will also want to check on the candidate's personal qualities, which are more difficult to identify. Someone who is good at an interview may not necessarily be good at the job.

Experience is more difficult to identify – particularly *relevant* experience. Someone who has had a lot of experience in making and serving sandwiches in a sandwich bar might have a suitable catering qualification and 'experience' in catering, but might be hopeless at making and serving canteen meals for 150 people!

Evidence Assignment 4F

Imagine you work as a Personnel Assistant in a Personnel Department. You are asked to check on the experience of the following job applicants. Why do you think they may *not* be suitable for the jobs for which they have applied?

1 *For a job as an HGV driver:*

   'I've had a full driving licence since I was 17 – and I've driven my boss all over the place – he hates driving.'

2 *For a job as a private secretary:*

   'I'm an excellent typist – I spend at least 3 days a week typing out orders and invoices.'

3 *For a job as a sales representative:*

   'Everyone says I can be very persuasive – I'm always the one who's sent round to collect for Children in Need.'

4 *For a job as a security guard:*

   'I don't stand any nonsense – any cheek from anyone and they're out. I learned that when I was a bouncer at a nightclub.'

The interview

No matter how confident you are, you aren't likely to look forward to an interview – very few people do. It is annoying – but a fact of life – that some people are naturally very good at interviews even though they might not be quite as good at doing the job. Unless you are one of these people, take comfort from the fact that most interviewers are trained to ask the right questions and to assess the personality and ability of each candidate. In addition, you can *improve* your own interviewing skills.

The main rule is to *be prepared*. Even if you are noted for your witty, off-the-cuff remarks at college, you might not be able to use that approach so easily when the interviewer asks you to give him two good reasons why he should offer you the job. Nor is it a good idea to arrive 30 minutes before, or worse, 30 minutes after the stated time of the interview having had to run all the way from the car park or bus stop. It goes without saying that you will have found out as much information as possible about what the organisation actually does.

Take your Record of Achievement to the interview. Not only will it tell the interviewer something about you but it can be used as the focus of several questions. As this means you will be asked about things you know and have done, this sort of 'warm up' will help you relax at the start of an interview when you are the most nervous.

Activity

1 Discuss with your tutor how you would go about finding out information on an organisation in your area.

2 Ask your tutor for the name of a well-known company in the area and then find out as much as you can about it. Prepare two questions you could sensibly ask at an interview, based on your research, and check these with your tutor.

10 golden rules for the interview

1 Make sure you know where the firm is situated and the best way of getting there. Have a trial run if necessary.

2 Check on your appearance. What goes down well at the local disco might not impress an interviewer. *Wear what you think you would be expected to wear if you had been offered the job and were actually working in the organisation (apart from a uniform).* Ask your parents what they think – the chances are that the interviewer will be nearer their age than yours, and hold similar opinions.

3 Make sure you know the interviewer's name. Ask him or her to repeat it if you haven't heard it the first time. Don't snigger if it's an unusual name.

4 *Smile* when you are first introduced and then follow the interviewer's lead. Sit down when asked, shake hands if the interviewer wants you to do so. Remain *pleasant* and try to look interested and enthusiastic. Look at the interviewer, not at the floor.

5 *Expect* to be nervous at the beginning of the interview. The interviewer will take this into account and should try to put you at your ease. If he or she doesn't then that's a sign of a poor interviewer and you just have to cope.

6 Try to answer each question as fully as possible. Again the interviewer should help you by asking questions which require more than a 'yes' or 'no' answer. If he or she does not, you have to try to find a way round. If, for instance, the interviewer asks you whether you have enjoyed being at college don't just answer yes or no. Say instead something like: 'Yes, I have. I didn't realise that computer studies was so interesting. I've got one at home now ...' The interviewer should be able to pick up that lead and that will give you the opportunity of talking about something you're good at.

7 If you don't know the answer to a question, say so. Don't bluster.

8 At the end of the interview the interviewer may ask you whether you have any questions. If your mind goes blank at this point, don't worry. But it may be as well if you have a list of possible questions at the back of your mind in case you are asked. It is a good idea to have them written down, so you can't forget them.

9 When the interviewer indicates that the interview is over, thank him or her and remember to gather up all your belongings before you leave the room.

10 If you are offered the job there and then, accept it if that is what you want. If you are not sure, however, ask for a day in which to think it over and discuss it with your parents or someone else. You take the risk that the job will be offered to someone else but that's better than accepting a job you are unhappy about.

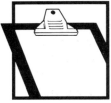

Activity

You are asked the following questions at an interview. Give an answer which is more than just 'yes' or 'no'.

'Have you had this part-time job since you left school?'

'Did you like your course at college?'

'Do you like working with people?'

'Are you good at figures?'

'I see that you like swimming. Are you interested in all sports?'

'Have you a full driving licence?'

DID YOU KNOW?

It may be helpful to attempt to 'second guess' your interviewer; to try to think *how* he or she is judging you. Most interviewers have a check list which they use to judge whether or not someone is suitable for a particular job. Such lists include:

- Your appearance – the way you dress and the way you speak.
- Your qualifications and previous experience – have you actually done what you claim on the application form to have done, can you explain some points in more detail, etc.?
- Your general intelligence – do you answer the questions correctly, do you understand what is being said, can you follow an argument?
- Any special skills – are you bilingual, etc.?
- Your personality – are you friendly or quiet, confident or nervous, quick or slow on the uptake?
- Your background – where do you live, how do you propose to get to work, have you a car, could you 'relocate'?

Activity

Attempt this exercise only if you know that afterwards you can remain on speaking terms with your partner. If you both think you can cope and give

positive feedback about your skills as an interviewee, then:

1 Look in the local newspaper for two suitable job vacancies.
2 Get together about the possible questions to ask.
3 Interview each other for the jobs advertised.
4 Assess each other using the checklist given above.
5 Give feedback – but don't let it develop into a fist-fight!

Where possible ask your tutor to observe what you are doing. He or she may be able to give you some additional feedback. Make an audio or video recording and analyse your performance yourself.

Activity

Your best friend, Nicki, just can't seem to get a job. She is fed up, so you suggest that you try out the exercise given above and give her a mock interview. You look in the local newspaper and spot the following advertisement:

> **Clerical assistant** required for the sales department of a small engineering firm. Candidates should be able to use a keyboard and input information at about 50 wpm. They should also have a sound knowledge of English and be able to cope with basic business calculations. A pleasant personality is essential as is the ability to use initiative. A good telephone manner is desirable.

You prepare a list of questions and decide to record the interview on cassette so that you can play it back if necessary. After the interview you go home, replay the cassette and decide how best you are going to break the bad news to her.

Read a transcript of the interview given below and write down what you will say to Nicki about where you think she is going wrong. If you wish, record what you will say to Nicki on a cassette. Compare your answers with those of the rest of your group.

Nicki   I've come about the job you advertised.
You   Let me go through your application form for some details. Why did you apply for this job?
Nicki   I were out of work.

You   Anything which appealed to you about it?

Nicki   (shrugs) Nothing special.

You   You've just left college haven't you? What did you like best about college life?

Nicki   (long pause)

You   Well you've done quite a bit of work with computers haven't you? How did you get on?

Nicki   Well I didn't like the teacher for a start. If it hadn't been for him I'd have done all right. He has favourites you know – and I wasn't one of them.

You   Well let's get down to hard facts – what examinations did you pass?

Nicki   Well I did the assignment for the CLAIT certificate.

You   Did you pass?

Nicki   No – but I'm very good on a computer really – I just panic when I have to have a test.

You   What about English?

Nicki   What about it?

You   Did you like it?

Nicki   Not much – I did English at school – I don't know why we had to waste our time at college. It were called communications anyway.

You   What does that mean exactly?

Nicki   I never found out.

You   Have you passed any examinations in it?

Nicki   No.

You   Well have you any business qualifications at all?

Nicki   No.

You   Shall I tell you a bit about the job?

Nicki   (leans back in the chair) If you like.

You   You'll be expected to do a number of clerical duties – answering the telephone, dealing with customers, keeping the petty cash, using the electronic filing system. How do you feel about that sort of work?

Nicki   It's a job I suppose.

You   Are you used to speaking on the telephone?

Nicki   Never off it at home.

You   No, that's not quite what I meant – did you learn telephone techniques at college.

Nicki   They never taught us anything there – it were a right waste of time.

You   Well I don't think there's much point in going further. You don't seem to know too much about this job do you?

Nicki   I've read the ad.

You   Have you any questions to ask me?

Nicki   (pause) How much do I get?

You   (passing her a paper) Here are the details.

Nicki   Is that all?

You   Are there any other questions?

Nicki   No.

You   Well, thank you very much. I think that's it for the moment.

Nicki   Have I got the job then?

        You don't give any reply – you're speechless.

chapter **5** # THE RIGHTS AND RESPONSIBILITIES OF EMPLOYEES AND EMPLOYERS

Learning Objectives

This chapter is concerned with the rights and responsibilities of both employees and employers, the means by which these are exercised, and the legislation which relates to them.

After studying this chapter you should be able to:

- explain the rights and responsibilities of employees and the means by which these can be exercised

- explain the rights and responsibilities of employers and the means by which these can be exercised

- describe the legislation governing employee and employer rights.

WHAT ARE RIGHTS AND RESPONSIBILITIES?

When you start work you have several expectations. For one thing, you expect to be paid, unless you have agreed to become a voluntary worker. You also expect to be paid a fair wage in relation to other people in similar jobs, and to receive your money at specified times. You expect to be treated fairly and reasonably both by your boss and by others who work in the organisation. You expect to work in a clean and safe environment and not be asked to undertake dirty or dangerous jobs for which you have received no training or protective clothing. You expect to have holidays and to work a reasonable number of hours each week.

Equally, your employer will have expectations of *you*. He or she will expect you to arrive on time, be a willing and co-operative worker, be prepared to learn new skills or tasks, be sociable with other employees and relate well to customers. You will be expected to obey company rules and regulations and to follow standard procedures (e.g. notifying your boss if you are off sick).

In many of these areas both you and your employer are affected by **legislation**. This means that in some of these areas you have a legal right to have your expectations met. And so does your employer! The two main areas of legislation which affect employee and employer rights and responsibilities are:

- employment law, and
- health and safety legislation.

In these areas the law imposes certain obligations on both of you which must be followed. In addition, legislation has also set up procedures for settling disputes.

The employee

As an employee you have a right:

- to be given a written statement of the terms and conditions of your employment

- to be allowed to choose whether or not to join a trade union
- not to be discriminated against on grounds of race or sex
- to be paid (unless you are a voluntary worker)
- to work in an environment which conforms to the Health and Safety at Work Act.

You have the responsibility to:

- comply with the terms of your contract of employment
- comply with any health and safety regulations and co-operate with your employer in his or her attempts to provide a safe working environment.

The employer

An employer's responsibilities include:

- to pay you fairly (e.g. at the standard rate for the job) in relation to other employees in the organisation
- to consult you over important matters which will affect changes to your terms and conditions of employment
- to treat you reasonably
- to ensure that you are not discriminated against on the grounds of race or sex
- to provide you with a safe and healthy place of work.

Your employer also has the right:

- to expect you to work to the terms of your contract
- to take disciplinary action against you if you do not
- to expect your co-operation with his or her attempts to comply with the Health and Safety at Work Act.

· EXPRESS AND IMPLIED RIGHTS · AND OBLIGATIONS

When you start a new job most of your rights and obligations will be made clear to you during your interview or period of induction, and many of them will be *expressly* stated in your contract of employment (see page 137).

However, there are other rights and obligations which may not be written down or even expressly stated. These are known as *implied* conditions and are called that simply because they are regarded as being so obvious that nothing more need be said – 'it goes without saying' that you have agreed to accept these obligations.

Therefore, when you agree to work for an employer you are agreeing to five conditions. You must:

- be ready and willing to work
- use reasonable care and skill
- obey reasonable orders
- take care of your employer's property
- act in good faith.

DID YOU KNOW?

When an employer employs someone, he or she accepts the responsibility for actions carried out by that employee during the course of employment. If, therefore, you accidentally injure another employee, your employer must pay damages to that employee. However, your employer may be able to claim compensation from you because you have broken the term in your contract to use reasonable care and skill.

Obey reasonable orders

If your employer asks you to carry out a particular job you must be prepared to do it, provided that it is within the scope of your contract. Remember, it may be wise to be flexible in your approach.

When can you refuse to work?

You can, of course, refuse to obey an order that:

- is unlawful (e.g. if you are asked to falsify some accounts)
- may place you in a position of danger (e.g. if your employer asks you to drive a car which has faulty brakes).

DID YOU KNOW?

Employers are entitled to expect employees to conform to the company image especially when they are going to come into contact with the general public or when the way they dress affects hygiene or safety standards. Even if no rule is laid down about this there is an implied duty that employees should wear suitable and acceptable clothes.

Evidence Assignment 5A

Daniel, Winston and Patrick have been at college together. Daniel finds a job in the food department of a large retail establishment and takes his turn stacking shelves and operating the POS cash register. Winston finds employment as a production assistant at the local radio station and is expected to carry out a number of routine jobs including making the tea and clearing up after the studio technicians. Everyone dresses casually and he is laughed at when he turns up on the first morning wearing a tie. Patrick starts work as a trainee solicitor. His job is concerned mainly with routine paperwork. All three think of themselves as sharp dressers – long hair, jeans, earrings, etc. After a few days Daniel and Patrick find they are in trouble with their immediate bosses about the way they dress. Winston has followed everyone else's lead and has turned up every day wearing jeans – which is fine until he is transferred to the front desk, when his new supervisor starts complaining about the way he looks, even though he, the supervisor, is very casually dressed himself.

Discuss *as a group* and then write your *own* answers to the following questions.

1 What possible reasons would each employer have for objecting to each new employee's appearance?

2 What arguments do you think the employees could have, if any, if they were disciplined for refusing to obey a reasonable order?

Secret profits

Do not be tempted to accept a bribe (or even a 'gift') to put in a word for someone who wants to obtain some work or a contract from your employer. Don't start selling the office furniture at discount prices, and don't use your employer's equipment to work on private jobs!

Disclosure of certain information about yourself

Although you are not forced to tell your employers all your dark secrets (and the Rehabilitation of Offenders Act 1974 allows you to 'forget' about certain criminal convictions after a certain period of time), it is wise for you to let them know any *relevant* facts. If, for instance, you suffer from an illness which may affect the work you should do, you should not keep that secret. One employee who did not tell his employer that he suffered from epilepsy was killed when he fell while working at some height above ground level. His widow claimed compensation but the amount of the compensation was reduced because he had not told his employers of his condition.

Disclosure of confidential information

What you must be very careful *not* to do is to reveal any confidential (i.e. private) information. The more senior you are, the more likely it is that you will get to know all sorts of company secrets, and the more important it is that you keep these to yourself. Even a junior shop assistant in a jeweller's shop was found to be in breach of contract when she told someone how much a customer had paid for an engagement ring!

Beware of being tricked into giving confidential information. The office gossip (and there's always at least one in every organisation) will be skilled at pretending to know something about a confidential matter in order to check your reaction and to see if you agree or disagree. Beware also of 'hinting' – 'If you'd heard what was said at this morning's meeting about the new pay rises ...' Such comments can be dangerous!

DID YOU KNOW?

Most contracts of employment end when you leave or are dismissed. In some cases, however, there may be a clause in your contract which limits your right to work where and for whom you choose when you do leave. This is generally known as a **restraint of trade** clause. If, for instance, you work in the sales department of your organisation, there may be a clause in your contract which prevents you from working as a sales representative for another organisation either within a certain period of time (say two years) or within a certain distance (say 20 miles). The courts normally allow such a clause to be included *provided it is reasonable*. If you were banned for a period of 50 years or for a distance of 500 miles, the courts may not be willing to support such a clause.

Activity

Discuss *as a group* why you think some organisations make use of such a clause. Which organisations do you think are the most likely to use it?

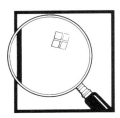

Evidence Assignment 5B

Read the following case study and then answer the questions which follow, in each case giving a reason for your answer. Prepare your final answers on a word-processor.

Naomi and Kirti have started work in different departments of the same company and have met during the company's induction training programme. They agree to have lunch each week to discuss how they are getting on. After a few weeks it is apparent that they are both having some problems.

Naomi works as a clerical assistant in the personnel department. Her job description says that she will be expected to prepare and update personnel records of all members of staff, send out letters asking job applicants to attend for interview and make all the interviewing arrangements.

However, in the course of her work, she has had to deal with certain situations, some of which she feels she hasn't dealt with very well.

- She is not 'computer minded' and when the personnel record system became computerised she felt she would not be able to cope and refused to do the work.
- She mentioned to one of the other clerical assistants in the accounts department that one of the members of staff in his department would be off for at least six months with a nervous breakdown.
- She went for lunch one day and left unlocked a filing cabinet containing confidential papers. When she returned she found that some papers had disappeared.
- A desperate job applicant telephoned her and promised her two Cup Final tickets if she could get him an interview. She agreed to see what she could do.

Kirti has a different problem. He works in the accounts department but feels he is being asked to carry out jobs he doesn't think he is obliged to do. In the past week he has been asked to do several tasks he considers are beneath him.

- On Monday he was asked to collect his boss's suit from the dry cleaners.
- Later that day he was asked to clean the boss's car.
- On Tuesday he had to answer the telephone and re-direct calls when the switchboard operator was at lunch or on a break.
- On Wednesday and Thursday he had to make tea for the other members of the department.

1 Consider Naomi's problems carefully. For each situation compose a short paragraph about:

    a where you think she may have made a mistake and why, and

    b what you would have done in the same circumstances.

2 State which duties you think Kirti is obliged to carry out and which he is not. In cases where you think he is not obliged to do what he is asked to, suggest what he should do to avoid annoying his boss too much by an outright refusal.

3 With a colleague role-play the meeting between Kirti and his boss. As Kirti can you assertively and politely refuse your boss's requests?

• CONTRACTS OF EMPLOYMENT •

In the past, whatever agreement you and your employer reached was up to you. If you agreed to a contract which later caused you some hardship, that was your misfortune.

However, the law has now made it clear that both employer and employee have certain *specified* legal rights and responsibilities whatever else they may agree to. These rights and obligations are contained in the **Employment Protection (Consolidation) Act 1978 (EPCA)** (now amended) which covers (among other things):

- the right to be given a written statement of terms and conditions of employment
- the right to an itemised pay statement
- the right to a statutory period of notice

- the right to choose whether or not to be a member of a trade union
- the right to maternity pay and to return to work after a pregnancy
- the right not to be unfairly dismissed
- the right to a redundancy payment.

In addition the **Equal Pay Act 1970,** the **Sex Discrimination Act 1975** and the **Race Relations Act 1976** all try to ensure that everyone, no matter what sex or race, is treated fairly over employment matters.

One of the terms covered by the EPCA is the **contract of employment** and what it *must* contain.

DID YOU KNOW?

If an employer wants to give *more* information than that required by the Act he or she can do so. Some companies, for instance, take the opportunity of giving their employees a complete handbook of information about the company in addition to the bare details of their contract.

Statutory contractual terms

When you are offered a job by a company it will be subject to certain terms and conditions which will be specified at the interview and may also be repeated in the letter which offers you the job. When you agree to accept the job then you are also considered to have agreed to those terms and conditions. Within 13 weeks of starting work you will then receive your contract of employment which sets these out in writing. As with all contracts, both parties (i.e. you and your employer) then have a legal obligation to comply with the terms laid down.

In any contract there must be three basic elements:

- **the offer** – your employer offers you the job

- **the acceptance** – you accept it

- **payment** – you agree to do some work in return for some pay.

You should also *intend* to enter into the agreement. If you misheard what the interviewer said and thought you were only being offered a work experience placement then you would not be held to the agreement.

Under the EPCA the major terms and conditions which must be put in writing are as follows:

1 **Your name and the name of your employer.** 'To whom it may concern' is not enough.
2 **The date you began work.** This is important because many of your rights under the EPCA depend on how long you have worked for a particular organisation. (See Figure 5.1, page 139.)
3 **Your pay.** This can be the actual amount or the relevant point on a pay scale (see page 149).
4 **When you are paid.** Every week, every month etc.
5 **Your hours of work.**
6 **Your holiday entitlement (if any).** Your employer is normally not *obliged* to give you any holiday unless you work in an industry covered by a Wages Council or the Agricultural Wages Board, both of which bodies have the power to fix holidays and holiday pay. Note: at the time of writing the government is drawing up legislation to abolish Wages Councils.
7 **Your entitlement to holiday pay.**
8 **Your entitlement to time off** because of sickness or injury, and any provisions regarding sick pay.
9 **Your pension rights.**
10 **The length of notice** you or your employer must give when either of you wants to end the contract. There's a *minimum* entitlement, although your employers may give you a longer entitlement if they wish.
11 **Your job title.**

DID YOU KNOW?

Employers are not obliged to give a full job description, so potential employees should be careful. One woman agreed to a contract in which her job title was stated to be 'cleaner'. She thought she was going to be an office cleaner when in fact she was expected to do heavy industrial cleaning in the loading bays of a factory.

Additional items

Your statement must also include a reference to:

- **disciplinary rules** and

- **grievance procedures.**

If something goes wrong at work it is difficult for either you or your employer to know what to do unless there are certain procedures to follow. Most organisations therefore have introduced procedures to cover:

- what should be done if you break one of the rules of the organisation – these are called disciplinary procedures
- what should be done if you want to make a formal complaint about something – these are called grievance procedures.

Because the documents outlining the disciplinary and grievance procedures tend to be very long, your contract need not contain everything they cover, provided it tells you where you can obtain a copy of them.

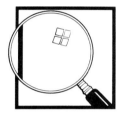

Evidence Assignment 5C

Read the following letter containing a job offer.

Dear Ahmed

Thank you for agreeing to come to work for us as an Assistant Purchasing Officer in the Purchasing Department.

Your hours of work are from 9 am to 5 pm, Monday to Friday. You will be paid on the Purchasing Officers' Grade 1 salary scale. You will be entitled to 35 days paid holiday. Details of company policy on sick pay and pension rights are enclosed.

Please take this to be your formal contract of employment.

Best wishes

Yours sincerely

Frank Chappell

Frank Chappell

Personnel Officer

Do you think Mr Chappell has given Ahmed *all* the information to which he is entitled? If not, decide what has been missed out.

Continuous employment

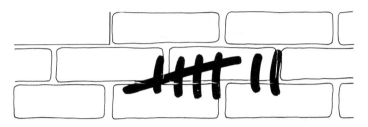

Your contract of employment must give the date when you first start work. This is important because many of your employment rights under the EPCA (and other Acts) depend upon the length of time you have worked with one particular organisation. From Figure 5.1 you will see that, although you have some rights immediately you start work, for other rights you need to have been working for the organisation for some time.

Claim	Qualifiying period		
	Nil	13 weeks	2 years
Equal pay	✔		
The right not to be discriminated against	✔		
Unfair dismissal for TU reasons	✔		
Action short of dismissal for TU reasons	✔		
Time off for antenatal care	✔		
Contract of employment		✔	
Unfair dismissal			✔
Maternity pay			✔
Right to return to work after pregnancy			✔
Redundancy payment*			✔

* Starting on the 18th birthday if the employee began work before that date

Figure 5.1 *The length of employment needed to be eligible for certain employee rights*

DID YOU KNOW?

Your period of employment is counted in *weeks* not in *years* – therefore two years' employment is counted as 104 weeks. In order to qualify as a week's employment, a week has to be 16 hours in length. Normally this doesn't matter, as most working weeks are over 35 hours. However, if you can only find a part-time job or want to work part-time for some other reason you might find that you do not qualify for certain rights even if you have worked for an organisation for two years.

If, however, you work between 8 hours and 16 hours for five years you will eventually gain those rights. The European Court of Justice is concerned about the treatment of part-time workers in the UK and is trying to put pressure on the UK government to change the law.

depending on how long he or she has worked for the organisation (see Figure 5.2).

Length of continuous employment	Period of notice
Less than 1 month	No period necessary
1 month but less than 2 years	1 week
2 years or more	1 week for each completed year up to a maximum of 12 weeks

Figure 5.2 *Statutory periods of notice*

Evidence Assignment 5D

Your friends know that you have been studying some basic employment law. They have asked for your help with several queries. Refer to the table in Figure 5.1 and then, on a word-processor, write up your answers to their problems.

1 Sam has been working for the same firm for nine months. He wants to know the legal rights she has acquired.

2 Your elder sister is pregnant. After what period of time is she eligible for time off for antenatal care – and for the right to return after pregnancy?

3 Mark is working four mornings a week from 9 a.m. to 1 p.m. His employer wants to change these hours to five mornings a week from 9 a.m. to 12 noon. He will give Mark extra pay. What should Mark do?

4 Ahmed has worked in an organisation for only one month but thinks he has been racially discriminated against in several ways. Can he do anything about it?

Statutory period of notice

Under the EPCA an employer must give an employee a certain period of what is known as 'statutory' notice

Activity

1 You have just started work for EC Electronics plc. You like your job and intend to stay with the company for some time. What will be the statutory period of notice to which you will be entitled if you work for them for

a one year
b 18 months
c 2 years
d 8 years
e 15 years?

2 Under the EPCA an employee also now has to give a *minimum* period of one week's notice – but some do not! What do you think an employer would offer you if he or she wanted you to leave immediately, instead of allowing you to work your notice period?

Evidence Collection Point 5.1

Although the EPCA gives the statutory minimum amount of notice you should be given, it does not prevent an employer from giving you a *longer* period of notice.

Interview at least five people you know who are working at present and ask them to what period of notice they are entitled. Write a short report on your findings indicating how long they have worked, what position they hold and whether or not they are entitled to a longer period of notice than the statutory minimum.

Use a spreadsheet to display a table showing notice periods.

Normally the more senior a person is in an organisation the longer will be the period of notice. See whether your findings support this.

Grievance procedures

Your contract of employment should make reference to what you can do if you feel you have been treated unfairly.

If you feel that this is the case, your first step should normally be to talk to your immediate supervisor to see if some solution can be reached. If a solution cannot be found *or* if it is your relationship with your supervisor that is the problem, you may decide instead to talk to someone in the personnel department (possibly someone who is appointed specifically to look after staff welfare) or even to your supervisor's manager. You can also discuss the matter with your union representative. If your problem cannot be sorted out informally you may have to use a more formal procedure known as a **grievance procedure**.

Most grievance procedures cover two broad areas:

- **money** – for example, mistakes in the calculation of payments, loss of pay because of a change in the basis of payment (payment by results, performance related pay, etc.)
- **work issues** – the way in which different jobs are allocated, the transfer of employees from one type of job to another, changes as a result of job grading schemes, physical conditions, allocation of overtime, time off, holidays, etc.

Activity

Discuss *as a group*, and *with your tutor*, the advantages and disadvantages of making a complaint to your supervisor's own manager.

DID YOU KNOW?

If a particular problem concerns not only you but also a number of other people in the organisation, the union might bring what is known as a **collective grievance** on the group's behalf.

Activity

Many organisations have a **grievance policy** such as that illustrated in Figure 5.3. Discuss as a group what is meant by the terms 'duress', 'status quo' and 'precedent'.

1 Management accepts the rights of employees, individually or collectively through their recognised unions, to present complaints to it.

2 It is in the interests of all concerned to establish and maintain formal procedures for dealing with such complaints.

3 Any differences which may arise should, wherever possible, be resolved quickly and without the use of industrial action.

4 Management is not prepared to discuss or consider any complaint under duress whether actual or threatened.

5 Whenever there is a difference in respect of a change in terms and conditions of employment, the status quo will apply until the matter is resolved.

6 Management will ensure that even though a decision is reached in one particular case, it will not necessarily set a precedent which might subsequently be claimed to apply throughout the organisation.

Figure 5.3 *A typical grievance policy*

Evidence Collection Point 5.2

1 Divide into small groups of three or four. Select two or three of the unions listed in in Figure 5.4 and find out their addresses from the library.

a Draft out a letter asking each union for some information on any guidelines it gives to its union representatives about what they should do if asked to help a member with a grievance procedure.

b Collect together your findings in a short report and then present these to the rest of your class.

2 Find out the grievance procedures, if any, which exist in your school or college for students who have a complaint. See how these compare with the information you obtained from the unions.

Association of Clerical, Technical and Supervisory Staffs (ACTTS)

Confederation of Health Service Employees (COHSE)

Electrical, Electronic, Plumbing and Telecommunications Union (EEPTU)

General, Municipal, Boilermakers and Allied Trades Union (GMB)

National and Local Government Officers' Association (NALGO)

National Union of Civil and Public Servants (NUCAPS)

National Communications Union (NCU)

National Union of Public Employees (NUPE)

Manufacturing, Science and Finance Union (MSF)

Transport and General Workers Union (T&GWU)

Figure 5.4 *Major unions*

DID YOU KNOW?

Over 95 per cent of establishments with more than 200 employees and 70 per cent of those with between 25 and 49 employees have individual grievance procedures.

Stages in an individual grievance procedure

There are normally three stages in a grievance procedure:

1 **Within the department**. The department manager should first of all check the facts and, if necessary, alter the decision of the supervisor or other member of the management team. If he or she does so the grievance procedure will usually come to an end. If not, it goes on to stage 2.
2 **Outside the department**. The dispute is taken to the next level of management who have to check the facts, listen to the evidence and reach a decision. Sometimes a joint committee of both union and management representatives is involved at this stage. (See page 154 for details of *joint consultative committees*.)
3 **Outside the organisation**. In some organisations the grievance procedure may allow for a 'third party' such as ACAS (see page 156 for further details) to judge whether the management's decision is fair.

The grievance interview

1 The manager must establish what the grievance procedure is all about and must decide whether or not to make an immediate response or whether time is needed to gather more information or to consult with other members of management.
2 The manager must then explain the organisation's position.
3 He or she should try to identify alternative courses of action to arrive at a joint agreement.
4 The final stage is the decision, details of which should be given in a letter of confirmation to the employee.

Evidence Assignment 5E

Tracey has worked for the organisation as a telephone sales representative for the past four years. She is expected to sell the company's products over the telephone to customers, some of whom have bought goods before and some of whom have not. She has met the targets set in relation to goods sold to existing customers but not in relation to those sold to new customers. She thinks this is because of increased competition from two new firms in the area. She also feels that she has not had sufficient training in modern selling techniques. She was hoping to get a performance related pay increment this year but has just found out that she has not received one. She protests but her supervisor remains firm.

At the interview with the departmental manager she outlines her case. The manager, having talked to the supervisor, says that the other telephone sales representatives have met their targets. He also says that Tracey's number of sales has decreased steadily over the past six months. Tracey says that she has been under pressure because she has just had to move house and has also had to nurse her mother through a serious illness.

1 The manager has now to come to a decision. Discuss *as a group* what you think he should do. Remember that it is better for him (and Tracey) at this stage to think of a compromise.

2 Prepare a summary of your discussion on a word-processor.

▪ TRADE UNIONS ▪

TUC, Congress House

There have been several statutes covering trade union matters, the most important of which are the EPCA and the **Trades Union and Labour Relations (Consolidation) Act 1992**. Under this legislation you have the right:

- to choose whether or not to be a member of a trade union
- to take part in trade union activities
- to take time off for trade union duties or activities.

You must also be allowed to take part in trade union activities 'at an appropriate time'.

If you become a trade union representative or official, your employer must also allow you reasonable time off – with pay – during working hours to let you carry out your duties (e.g. attend meetings, training courses).

Your employer must not harass or victimise you because you are or are not a trade union member (e.g. by refusing to promote you or by not giving you the same fringe benefits as other employees).

Activity

As a group, decide which of the following times would be regarded as 'appropriate' for trade union activities:

- before work starts in the morning
- at the end of the working day
- during the lunch period
- during the break
- during a time when there is no work to do.

Union officials

If a union is operational where you work, you will probably be approached to join soon after you start your

Steve Dean was elected shop steward and represents 34 workers in a factory in Croydon. He is not paid for the work he does which includes the following:

Pay and conditions
Every December he negotiates, with the owners of the company, rates of pay for the workers. Last year they were granted a 2.5% pay rise, roughly in line with inflation.

Training
He makes sure that all the forklift truck drivers have the correct licences and are properly trained. Accidents have declined since a training package was introduced.

Health and safety
Mr Dean ensures that health and safety regulations are followed. He checks all chemicals and materials to make sure they are safe. He ensures all dangerous materials are clearly marked, and that everyone knows how to deal with them safely.

Figure 5.5 *The duties of a shop steward*

start your job. A **shop steward** is the elected worker representative who voluntarily represents the members of the union to management and tells you about the benefits of being a member (Figure 5.5). In a large company there may be several shop stewards with a **convenor** – the chief shop steward who arranges the meetings.

Union membership

Joining a union will help to protect an employee in relation to:

- security of employment
- unfair practices and discrimination in areas such as recruitment, training, discipline, redundancy and dismissals
- conditions of employment (e.g. hours, holidays)
- rights under the Health and Safety at Work Act and other safety regulations.

In addition the union will continually negotiate for improvements in pay and working conditions. If the union wants its members to take any type of industrial action then it must **ballot** them first (i.e. allow them to vote in secret). This is because the union is, in effect, asking employees to break their contract of employment and they risk dismissal by their employer – provided that the employer treats everyone the same. If some employees decide not to take part in the action then the union has to respect their wishes.

TGWU
- Transport and General Workers' Union.
- 1,270,000 members
- General union mainly covering transport and manufacturing

AEU
- Amalgamated Engineering Union
- 740,000 members
- Any aspect of engineering including ships, power stations, oil rigs

GMB
- General, Municipal, Boilermakers Union
- 820,000 members
- General union mainly covering unskilled workers in almost every industry

NALGO
- National and Local Government Officers Association
- 750,000 members
- Union for anyone in public services, eg housing, water, some health service

USDAW
- Union of Shop, Distributive and Allied Workers
- 375,000 members
- From check-out operators to managers of superstores

MSF
- Manufacturing, Science and Finance
- 650,000 members
- NHS, universities, car production electronics, banking

NUPE
- National Union of Public Employees
- 600,000 members
- Local government workers, NHS nurses, water workers

UCW
- Union of Communication Workers
- 200,000 members
- Represents Post Office and BT workers

UCATT
- Union of Construction, Allied Trades and Technicians
- 260,000 members
- Carpenters, joiners, stone masons, bricklayers etc

COHSE
- Confederation of Health Service Employees
- 210,000 members
- Members are from all grades of the health service

Figure 5.6 *Britain's ten biggest unions*

DID YOU KNOW?

1 There are various types of industrial action. A **work to rule** means that you only do what is expressly required of you under your contract of employment. Other forms of action include an **overtime ban** or a **go slow** – where workers do the work properly, but deliberately under their normal speed.

2 There has been a steady decline in union membership since the late 1970s. This has come about partly because of a fall in the number of people employed in manufacturing (members of **blue collar** unions) and a rise in part-time employment.

Evidence Collection Point 5.3

1 The ten biggest unions in Britain are shown in Figure 5.6. Choose one of these and investigate their work in more detail. Produce a brief report on your findings.

2 Interview two people who are members of a union. Find out why they joined, the benefits of membership, how much they pay to be a member and any disadvantages they have experienced.

3 Interview a shop steward or a staff representative (or ask him or her to address your group) and find out his or her duties, and how much time this takes each week.

· THE RIGHT NOT TO BE · DISCRIMINATED AGAINST

The law states that you have the right not to be discriminated against on the grounds of sex or race. However, many employers go further than the law and publish their 'equal opportunity statements'. This may say something like – 'This organisation will not discriminate against anyone on grounds of sex, race, age, creed, colour, religion or disability.'

Activity

Many schools and colleges have their own equal opportunities policies. Does yours? Make sure you have a copy and keep it in your folder.

DID YOU KNOW?

The law does take some measures to try to help the disabled worker.

- The **Disabled Persons (Employment) Acts 1944/58** place a statutory duty on all employers employing 20 or more full-time workers to employ a quota of registered disabled people based on a percentage of the total workforce.
- The **Companies (Directors' Report) Employment of Disabled Persons Regulations 1980** require that every annual company report to which the regulations apply should contain a statement outlining what the company has done to give fair consideration to applications for employment by disabled persons and to arrange for appropriate training for them.

Evidence Collection Point 5.4

1 The Department of Employment has Disablement Resettlement Officers whose job it is to look after the interests of disabled workers. Try to arrange an interview with one of them to gather some information about:

a the number of disabled workers in your area
b the types of employment they undertake
c any special measures (such as sheltered workshops) which have been set up for them in the area
d the difficulties placed in their way when looking for employment.

2 Discuss *as a group* why you think:

a disabled people might find difficulty getting work even though there is legislation to assist them (you might have gained some useful information from your visit to the Disablement Resettlement Officer)

b why it is helpful to insist that companies state what their policy is towards disabled workers.

Using a word-processor, summarise your discussion in a short paragraph.

Activity

Some job advertisements state: 'Applicants should be under 35 years of age...'. Many people consider age limits unfair and think this is a form of discrimination. What do you think? *As a group* discuss whether younger workers are better workers. Try to find out what the policy is of the DIY chain, B&Q, for recruiting older people.

Equal pay

Under EC law 'men and women should receive equal pay for equal work'. The **Equal Pay Act 1970**, amended by the **Equal Pay (Amendment) Regulations 1983**, also provides for equal pay for men and women. A woman must get the same pay as a man (or vice versa):

1 If a woman is employed on the same work as a man (minor differences don't count). If she works next to a man in a packing department, she must get the same rate of pay. It won't matter if she is packing chocolate biscuits and he is packing plain biscuits.

2 If a woman's job is rated as the same as that of a man's under a job grading scheme.

3 If a woman's work is regarded as being of 'equal value'. In one case, a woman who worked as a cook in a shipyard canteen claimed that her work was of equal value to the organisation as that of a man who was a shipyard worker.

there is no man doing the same work, the women have no-one with whom they can compare themselves. Their only solution therefore is to take the same route as the shipyard cook and to try to compare themselves with a man doing a *different* job but one which they can claim is of no greater value than theirs.

Employer defences

However, an employer may be able to use one of two defences:

1 That there is an *important* difference between the two jobs. In one case some female cleaners claimed equal pay with male cleaners. However, the work involved cleaning newly built houses. The men did the heavy work such as removing the plaster: the women did the lighter cleaning jobs. The men were held entitled to their higher rate of pay.

2 That there is an important difference between the man and the woman (e.g. the man is better qualified, older, more experienced, takes more responsibility etc.). Again this must be a real difference. If, for instance, the man has only had a couple more years' experience than the woman he would not be entitled to be paid very much more than her.

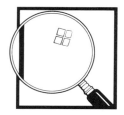

Evidence Assignment 5F

Salma works as an assembler alongside John but does not get the same pay. John has been working in the factory for many years. Marian works as an office supervisor but thinks her job is just as important as that of Frank, who is the safety officer and who gets more money than she does.

Alison and Michael work together in the payroll section but Michael is responsible for checking the work.

1 Do you think Salma should receive the same pay as John, Marian the same pay as Frank, and Alison the same pay as Michael? Give reasons in each case for your decision.

2 Salma decides she has a grievance. From what you have read, what steps do you think she should take?

Sex discrimination

The **Sex Discrimination Act 1975** (as amended by the **Sex Discrimination Act 1980**) forbids discrimination in areas such as employment. It also specifically forbids discrimination against married women. Amongst other things it covers:

- selection for jobs
- promotion
- job training
- dismissal
- fringe benefits.

DID YOU KNOW?

Although the majority of sex discrimination cases are brought by women, men can also claim that they have been discriminated against. In one case it was the custom at a factory to allow women to leave five minutes earlier than the men to avoid congestion at the factory gates. A male employee claimed this was unfair. An industrial tribunal dismissed his claim saying that it was too trivial. The Equal Opportunities Commission (see page 148) disagreed. What do you think?

Types of discrimination

There are two types of discrimination:

- **direct discrimination** (e.g. 'I am never going to employ a woman' or 'I don't want a male secretary')
- **indirect discrimination** (i.e. where it is far more difficult for members of one sex than the other to meet the requirements – e.g. 'I am only going to employ someone who is over 6 feet tall and who has a beard').

DID YOU KNOW?

Industrial Tribunals deal with most employment law cases. They consist of a legally qualified chairperson appointed by the Lord Chancellor, and two people representing both sides of industry who are selected from a panel consisting of nominations from the Trades Union Congress and management organisations. An appeal against an Industrial Tribunal decision can be made to the **Employment Appeal Tribunal**.

DID YOU KNOW?

An employer may be allowed to employ a person of one particular sex if he can justify it on other grounds. For example:

- It might be too expensive to do otherwise (although this defence is not very popular with the court).
- There may be a 'genuine occupational qualification' (GOQ) where the nature of the job requires a man or woman (e.g. modelling or acting).
- The work may be carried out in a private home or require the employee to 'live in'.
- The job may be outside the UK and in a country whose laws and customs prevent the work being undertaken by a woman.
- The job may be one of two to be held by a married couple.
- Personal services may be required which are most effectively provided by a man (e.g. work in a boys' hostel).

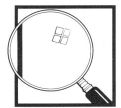

Evidence Assignment 5G

Imagine you are working in the advertising section of your local paper, accepting and checking text for job vacancies. Several advertisements you have received today are worrying you. Write a memo to your supervisor giving your comments to the following:

1 Two advertisements, one of which asks for a 'barman' and one for a 'Girl Friday'.

2 One advert which asks for a building site worker who is willing to work topless in the summer.

3 The copy of a job advertisement received earlier by another member of staff:

> WORD PROCESSOR OPERATORS
> **urgently required**
>
> Only white females under the age of 35 need apply.
>
> Ring 0389 3879198 for details

4 An advert which asks for a local girl to play Cinderella in the Christmas pantomime.

Racial discrimination

The **Race Relations Act 1976** forbids discrimination on grounds of 'colour, race, nationality or ethnic or racial origin'.

It contains much the same provisions as the Sex Discrimination Act. It forbids both direct and indirect discrimination unless there is a need for a GOQ or if the employer can justify it on grounds other than race. Therefore, one employer who told a Job Centre he didn't want to be sent any more black job applicants because of customer complaints, was held to be guilty of *direct* discrimination.

A condition placed on applicants for management training that they should have had certain previous managerial experience was held to be a more difficult requirement for overseas applicants to meet and was therefore regarded as *indirect* discrimination.

Activity

Can you remember what the letters GOQ mean? If not, look back to page 147 and check the answer.

Victimisation

The law tries to protect people who have claimed racial or sexual discrimination from being victimised when they return to work. If, for instance, they are made redundant or are transferred to a less well paid or unpleasant job, they can complain to an Industrial Tribunal.

DID YOU KNOW?

A special body known as the Equal Opportunities Commission (EOC) has been set up to check that the Sex Discrimination and Equal Pay Acts are working. The Commission for Racial Equality (CRE) does the same in respect of the Race Relations Act.

Evidence Collection Point 5.5

1 Write to both the EOC (Overseas House, Quay Street, Manchester M3 3HN) and the CRE (Elliot House, 10/12 Allington Street, London SW1E 5EU) to ask for information about the way in which they operate.

2 Obtain at least one example of an equal opportunities statement by a leading employer in your area.

Evidence Assignment 5H

Read the following extracts from some conversations between work colleagues and write a short paragraph stating whether or not you think each woman is entitled to equal pay – and if so, why.

Conversation 1

Norman What's the problem?

Katie I've just found out that I'm getting less pay than Peter and I don't think it's fair.

Norman Why isn't it fair? You're getting a better rate of pay than most other admin assistants you know. Go down to the Job Centre and look at all the job vacancies on display if you don't believe me.

Katie I'm not arguing about that. All I'm saying is that my work is just as important as Peter's but he gets more money than me.

Norman Well, you'll just have to apply to be an accounts clerk like him then.

Katie But I don't want to be an accounts clerk ....

Norman Well, that's the only way you'll get the same pay as he does.

Conversation 2

Farouk You don't do the same work as I do you know. It's a very different job. I have to sort through a mass of information, key it into a computer terminal, index it, update it and recall it when required. It takes a lot of time and effort.

Brenda I agree – but I collect together information, I word-process it, I store it and update it, retrieve it when it's wanted. You use a computer. I use a filing cabinet. Where's the difference? I should be paid the same as you.

Conversation 3

Manager It's like speaking to the wall – how often do I have to tell you that you can't have any more pay?

Robina Why not?

Manager Because although you and Jack work together he has to work in the outside office. Workpeople are coming in and out all day long and it's very difficult to keep the place warm. You work in a very much more comfortable place.

Robina It isn't all that comfortable. People are pushing past me all day long to get to the drinks machine.

Manager Well, I know where I'd rather work.

· REMUNERATION ·

One of the main reasons you work is to get paid. The word 'remuneration' is merely a term used to describe the amount you are paid.

It is hardly surprising, therefore, that a large part of your contract of employment is concerned with how much you will be paid and how often. (Look at page 137 to remind yourself about contracts of employment.)

DID YOU KNOW?

1 If you are not paid anything at all, there is no contract of employment between you and your employer. However, provided you are paid *some* money the law will not generally concern itself about how much! That is normally a matter for you or your trade union to negotiate.

2 If your employer pays you, generally speaking he need not give you any work to do. Although that might sound wonderful, you may find that in reality if that happens to you for some reason, you will either be worried about your career prospects or about being made redundant. Your employer *must*, however, provide you with work if you work on a piecework or on a commission-only basis. The same is true where your future career prospects depend on your reputation. If, for instance, you are a well-known journalist, whose work appears regularly under your own name in a paper or magazine, your prospects of any future work will be harmed if you are not allowed to write anything, even though you are still being paid.

Activity

Why do you think an employer must provide work for someone being paid on a piecework or a commission-only basis?

Salary scales

Many large organisations operate salary scales which ensure that people are treated fairly. If you accept a job as a bank clerk, for instance, you may find there is a salary scale which ranges from a starting point of £7851 to a finishing point of £11 197, with various stages or **increments** in between.

In a salary scale each 'rise' is known as a **point in the scale** and is also referred to as an increment. If you are given one increment at the end of the year that is normal. If you receive more than one this usually means you have worked exceptionally well.

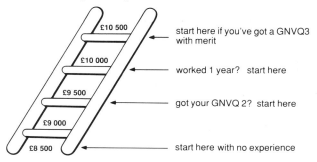

In some cases you will begin right at the bottom of the salary scale 'ladder'. In other cases your employer might take into account factors such as:

● your age
● your qualifications
● your past experience

and start you at a higher point on the scale.

Young workers' pay

Young workers are normally paid at lower rates than the adult workforce. In most cases this will be a percentage of the adult rate. For instance, the Automobile Association pays its 16-year-olds 80 per cent of the adult rate and its 19-year-olds 90 per cent.

However, the actual amount of pay normally depends on the type of work and the area in which it will be undertaken. An apprentice may only receive 30-50 per cent of the adult rate. If you are a junior worker in another area the percentage might be higher.

Additional payments

You can increase your basic pay by working overtime or by being on some type of bonus scheme.

Overtime

The higher up the organisation you climb the less likely it is that you will receive overtime for any additional time you work. However, at the beginning of your career, you will probably find that you will be paid for overtime.

The time counted as overtime varies. Although the 'normal' working week is usually defined as Monday to Friday, in some organisations Saturday (or at least Saturday morning) is also included in the normal working week so that you would only be paid the basic rate during that period. Most organisations, however, treat Sundays as outside the normal working week.

In some organisations 'time and a half' is the usual overtime rate (one and a half hour's pay for one hour's work). Others are prepared to pay only 'time and a third' or even 'time and a quarter'.

In some cases, however, you may be expected to work a certain number of hours of overtime before you become entitled to the extra pay. For example, if your normal working day is from 9 a.m. to 5 p.m., you may be expected to work an extra half hour or hour for the basic rate of pay before you can start being paid the overtime rate.

You may be *obliged* to work overtime whether you want to or not. Read your contract of employment carefully – if overtime *is* compulsory this must be made clear.

Bonus schemes

You may receive a bonus if you:

● are paid on a piecework basis
● receive commission for sales
● are paid a productivity bonus

- receive performance related pay
- are employed in a company which operates a profit sharing scheme.

All these schemes are designed to reward people who work hard. Obviously it is in the company's interests for its employees to be hard working as, normally, higher profits will be made at the end of the year.

Evidence Collection Point 5.6

1 Visit your local Careers Office or Job Centre. Select three jobs in business and write down the current rates of pay.

2 Collect advertisements from your local newspaper which advertise similar jobs. Note down the rates of pay and any salary scales given.

3 Interview at least three people who you know go to work and find out what bonus systems (if any) operate within their organisation. *Don't* ask them how much they are paid!

DID YOU KNOW?

Some organisations will encourage you to become a member of a **Save As You Earn (SAYE)** scheme under which you invest a certain sum of money regularly into the scheme for five years. At the end of this time you will have accumulated some savings plus the bonus paid by the financial institution which is administering the scheme.

Fringe benefits

Many organisations offer their employees what are known as 'fringe' benefits. Here are some examples:

- **An occupational pension scheme**, which is paid in addition to any state pension
- **An occupational sick pay scheme**. All employees who pay sufficient National Insurance contributions are entitled to **statutory sick pay** if they are ill (see Figure

5.7). In some cases, employers will also pay the difference between SSP and the normal weekly wage or even offer a **private health insurance scheme** – so that their employees can obtain treatment privately if they are ill.

- **Holiday pay**. Most employers allow employees some paid time off for holidays. The number of days normally depends on length of service and the seniority of the employee.

Eligibility
To be eligible your average total pay in the eight weeks before the start of sickness must be above a certain limit (if you earn below a certain sum you will not pay NI contributions but neither will you get SSP).

Payment
There are two rates of SSP. One rate is paid to lower-earning employees and one to higher-earning employees.

Qualifying days
SSP is paid only for periods of sickness for four days or more. These days must be days when an employee is supposed to work (e.g. a Sunday will not count if you do not normally work on a Sunday).

Waiting days
The first three qualifying days of sickness are unpaid. If, however, you are ill again less than eight weeks after the first period of sickness, you will not need to serve any further waiting days.

Maximum entitlement
SSP is payable for a maximum of 28 weeks in any period of sickness.

Notification procedure
If you are ill for at least four days but no more than seven, your employer can ask you to fill in a **self certification form**. If you are ill for longer than seven days then you must get a medical certificate from your doctor.

Figure 5.7 *Current statutory sick pay provisions*

DID YOU KNOW?

Some organisations go much further in providing benefits for their employees. Staff who work in Marks & Spencer stores can have their hair done, visit a chiropodist and eat a good meal – all subsidised by their employer!

Evidence Collection Point 5.7

As a group, hold a brainstorming session to see how many fringe benefits you can think of in ten minutes. Then make a fair copy of your ideas.

Visit your library and research this topic in business administration books. Interview people you know who go to work. Your final list should include at least ten items.

Write a brief description under each item saying exactly what it is that the employee receives.

Company vehicle!

DID YOU KNOW?

It could be quite easy to lose track of all the payments to which you are entitled. For that reason, the law says that you must be given an **itemised pay statement** which provides most of that information. (For details of what it should contain see page 215.) If you are refused such a statement, then you are entitled to complain to an Industrial Tribunal.

Evidence Assignment 5I

Imagine that you are offered a job as a market research assistant. You have to carry out some clerical duties involving preparation of reports on the results of various market research surveys. You also have to take part in market research, interviewing of the general public. You

are saving to get married and to buy a new house and you are therefore very interested in how much money you are going to get.

1 The salary scale for market research assistants is:

£	£
9 000	10 500
9 500	11 000
10 000	11 500

and you can expect to get one increment each year. When you telephone the personnel manager before the interview to find out exactly how much you will be paid, she tells you that you will normally start on the lowest point of the scale but that you will be given one increment in each of the following circumstances:

- if you are 21 or over
- if you have a GNVQ level 3 qualification or two A-levels
- if you have two years *relevant* experience.

You left college two years ago at the age of 18 and have worked in an advertising agency since then. You have a GNVQ level 3 in Business. At what point in the scale do you think you should start, and why?

2 Your employer is trying a new American scheme of offering a package of benefits to each employee. You are offered the choice of two benefits from the following list:

- pension rights
- private medical insurance
- a company car
- participating in a profit sharing scheme
- additional holiday entitlement.

a Which two would you choose *at present*, and why?
b Do you think you would choose any differently if you were older? Can you say why?

3 After working for the company for six months you become ill and have to have some time off work. You think that you are entitled to some statutory sick pay (SSP) and try to work out how much:

a You are only off for three days and come back on the fourth. Are you entitled to any SSP? Would your answer be different if you had also been away ill three weeks ago?
b What if you fell ill on the Friday and returned to work on the Tuesday? Would you be eligible for SSP?

c Your cold develops into chronic bronchitis and you are away from work from the first week in January to the first week in July. Will you be paid SSP throughout your entire period of sickness?

Note that the salary you are paid is above the minimum level to be eligible for SSP.

· OTHER EMPLOYER · RESPONSIBILITIES

Your employer owes you certain obligations. (Check back on page 135 to see what they are.) Some of them – the right to be paid, to choose whether or not to be a member of a trade union and the right not to be discriminated against – have already been dealt with. However, you are also entitled to expect your employer to:

- treat you reasonably
- give you the opportunity (although not necessarily the right) to participate in and be consulted on certain company matters
- provide you with a safe and healthy place of work.

Reasonable treatment

Legally, if your employer treats you so unreasonably that the court considers it to be a breach of your contract, you may be able to leave and yet still claim that you have been dismissed. This is known as **constructive dismissal**. Remember, however, that the treatment must be serious – minor changes to your contract or personal irritations don't count!

Suppose, for instance, your employer is in some financial difficulty. In order to save your job he asks you to continue doing the same work but for a lower rate of pay. If you agree to this because you want to keep your job – fine! If you don't, however, and your employer insists on paying you less, you could leave and claim that you have been constructively dismissed. You would not *actually* have been dismissed but your employer's action would probably be regarded as a breach of the contract under which you were to be paid a certain sum. The same situation might arise if you were moved from one job to another with fewer promotion prospects or if you were expected to work in a different physical working

environment – outside rather than inside, standing up rather than sitting down, etc.

In some cases, too, if your employer is so unreasonable that you feel he or she is making your life a misery and possibly affecting your health, this might be regarded as a breach of contract. But remember, just being told off for coming back late from lunch is not likely to be considered a sufficient reason for claiming constructive dismissal, even if you think everyone else is getting away with it. The courts don't usually interfere in such cases.

DID YOU KNOW?

Normally it doesn't matter whether or not you resent any changes *unless* you can show that your efficiency or health is being affected.

Remember, however, that you also have a duty to behave reasonably. If, therefore, your employer asks you to accept a minor change in your job description or to co-operate with him or her in another way, the Industrial Tribunal isn't going to be too sympathetic if you leave and then try to claim constructive dismissal.

Evidence Assignment 5J

Look at the facts of the cases given below. *As a group* decide – giving reasons – whether or not you think the employee could claim constructive dismissal. Type up your answers, preferably on a word-processor.

1 Your employer moves Mildred from a day job to a night job which makes it difficult for her to deal with her domestic commitments.

2 Paul really enjoyed his job working at the counter of the bank. He has been moved to a 'backroom' job and neither likes it nor feels that he is any good at it.

3 Audrey has been moved from the main office to a branch office where there are only two other employees who have been there for years and are not likely to leave until they retire.

4 Your employer seems to pick on you all the time. You are constantly criticised, although the rest of the

employees are not. You are not sleeping very well and have been to see the doctor because you are so depressed.

5 Frank's employer asks him to have his holidays in July rather than August.

6 His employer then asks him to postpone his holidays until next year.

Employee participation and consultation

In the past your employer was expected to make *all* the decisions relating to what went on at work. All you had to do was to obey his or her instructions. Nowadays, however, many managements recognise that their employees might have some very good ideas which could be used to the benefit of the company. They also realise that employees who are consulted about major changes to company practices, procedures or working conditions are more likely to co-operate than those who are not. This has led to an increase in what is known as **employee participation**. There are two forms of participation, direct and indirect:

Direct	*Indirect*
● Regular team briefings between employees and supervisors	● Worker councils
	● Worker directors
● Redesign of work to focus on employee needs and opinions	
● Transfer of some work-related decisions from management to employees	

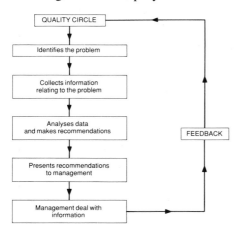

How a quality circle works

Worker councils

These are principally consultative (i.e. they give advice and assistance rather than make decisions) and consist of worker representatives. They tend to run in parallel with any union/management bodies set up for the purpose of negotiating terms and conditions of employment. (See below for details of **joint consultative committees**.)

Much depends on the organisation as to their terms of reference. Most concentrate on staff welfare issues, although Cadbury Schweppes and Bulmers have both established what they call 'Employee Councils' which act as the centre point for all their communication and consultation arrangements.

Worker directors

The idea of having an employee as a director who sits on the board and attends board meetings is well established in many European countries – and is a legal requirement. In the UK, however, not many organisations have adopted this idea, two exceptions being the British Steel Corporation and the Post Office. The advantages of having such directors are that they should be able to:

● improve the quality of board-level decisions and discussion by giving the workers' views first hand
● secure greater employee commitment to board decisions
● reduce conflict by making employees aware of the problems management have to face.

Employee consultation

Many organisations now have **joint consultative committees**. In most cases these are union-based and tend to consist of a number of trade union and management representatives. Normally at such meetings:

● management decisions are notified and discussed
● negotiations take place on all major industrial relations issues (e.g. pay, working conditions, grievance and disciplinary matters, redundancy issues).

However, much again depends on whether the committee is merely an *advisory* or *consultative* body or whether it has *negotiating* powers. If this is the case, then the decisions made there are normally binding on the company.

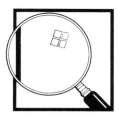

Evidence Assignment 5K

You have been appointed to be a member of the Workers' Council and eagerly look forward to attending the first meeting. You then return to the office to tell your colleagues about the issues discussed, which weren't confidential.

You attend the meetings each week, and are flattered to think that you are highly thought of both by management and by your work colleagues. However, after six weeks your supervisor is complaining because of your continued absences from your desk and your colleagues have started to claim that you only tell them what you want them to know and don't really represent their interests. You don't feel they understand the problems of trying to tell senior management how you all feel.

Things came to a head yesterday. Several workers were indignant about changes to the canteen opening hours. They think you should have told management how they feel, and now won't include you in any of their discussions.

1 From the above passage, list the advantages and disadvantages there are to being a member of a Workers' Council.

2 *As a group*, decide how you think these could be overcome. Summarise your findings.

One specific type of consultation required by law is when an employer is proposing to make some employees redundant. In such cases the employer must give the union a **minimum statutory period of notice** before the redundancies are scheduled to occur, to allow the union time to consult about any alternative courses of action which might be considered.

Activity

Discuss *as a group* what types of alternatives unions may suggest to avoid redundancies.

Evidence Collection Point 5.8

Arrange for each member of your group to write to at least two organisations in your area to ask them whether or not they have a joint consultative committee and, if they do, whether they will provide you with some information about it.

Together, write a short report on your findings.

· DISCIPLINARY ACTION ·

Your employer has the right to expect that you will carry out your side of the contract of employment and that you will behave reasonably. If you do not, he or she may be entitled to take some action against you.

Most organisations have a clearly stated **disciplinary policy** which sets down guidelines on the ways in which they are going to handle any disciplinary problems (see Figure 5.8 for an example).

---

1 It is the employee's responsibility to follow all the company's rules and working procedures

2 If an employee is performing or behaving badly, the first step management will take will be **informal** counselling.

3 **Formal** disciplinary procedures will be put into operation only when informal counselling has been unsuccessful or where the actions of the employee show that informal counselling is inappropriate.

4 No employee will be formally disciplined without a fair hearing and an opportunity to put his or her case.

5 Management will seek to act fairly and consistently when carrying out any disciplinary action.

Figure 5.8 *A typical disciplinary policy*

Activity

As a group discuss:

a   the difference between 'informal' and 'formal' procedures

b   the occasions on which you might suggest that informal counselling would not be appropriate.

Disciplinary procedures

As well as a disciplinary policy, organisations should also have a set of **disciplinary procedures** details of which should be made available to all employees (see below). If an organisation wishes to draw up its own procedures it can do so, but most organisations follow a common set of procedures recommended by the **Advisory, Conciliation and Arbitration Service (ACAS)** in its Code of Practice, *Disciplinary Practice and Procedures in Employment.*

In 1974 the government set up the Advisory, Conciliation and Arbitration Service (ACAS) to:

1   Set up inquiries to investigate the facts and underlying causes of various industrial disputes.
2   Act as a 'peacemaker' or middleman in disputes between two parties – normally employer and union.
3   Act in the same role where the two parties are employer and employee.
4   Advise management and unions on industrial relations, in respect of pay, collective bargaining arrangements, etc.
5   Hold investigations into matters of general concern.

The Code of Practice is not legally binding on employers but, if not followed, employers may find that they have difficulty in winning a case at an Industrial Tribunal.

The Code of Practice recommends that the disciplinary procedure should:

● be formal and in writing
● state to whom it applies
● state what disciplinary action may be taken and which level of management has the authority to take such action.

If a complaint is made, the employee concerned is notified of the complaint and is given the opportunity to state his or her case, and is represented, if he or she wishes, by a union representative or fellow employee.

An employee should not be dismissed for a single incident *unless* it is gross (i.e. very serious) misconduct. The employee should be provided with a right of appeal against any disciplinary action.

Activity

From what you have already read in relation to the implied terms in a contract of employment, suggest what types of behaviour could be included in a list of disciplinary offences. See how many you can think of before you read any further.

Types of misconduct

Each organisation must decide what offences are going to result in disciplinary measures being taken. Normally, provided the same rules are applied to everyone, an Industrial Tribunal will not rule them unfair. Common examples of what are regarded as disciplinary offences include:

● frequent absence
● frequent lateness
● fighting
● swearing
● drunkenness
● giving out confidential information
● sexual harassment
● stealing
● clocking or signing in or out for someone else
● using company equipment/tools for a private job.

Evidence Collection Point 5.9

1   Obtain a copy of the Code of Practice on disciplinary practice and procedures in employment (sold by the HMSO). Ask also for details of other codes of practice which are available. (You can get the address of your local ACAS from the Yellow Pages Directory.)

ADVISORY
CONCILIATION
AND
ARBITRATION
SERVICE

2 Obtain a copy of the disciplinary policy and procedure of your college or school.

a Discuss *as a group* how these affect you as students. Write down your comments plus any items you think should be changed, and why.

b Read carefully the type of offences for which you can be disciplined. Do you think everything important has been included – or can you add anything extra?

c Read carefully the way in which you can be disciplined and the system used. How does this compare with the system used in industry, which is discussed below?

Types of sanction (punishment)

As you can see from Figure 5.9, there are normally at least five stages in any disciplinary procedure. Each stage is progressively more severe so that an employer has the opportunity merely to warn an employee who has been guilty of a minor offence (e.g. by means of a verbal warning) before any more serious action need be taken. Very serious offences, however, might be dealt with more severely even though it is the first offence the employee has committed.

Activity

Look at the list of offences given on page 156 and try to decide which might be regarded as minor unless repeated frequently and which might be regarded as more serious even if only committed once.

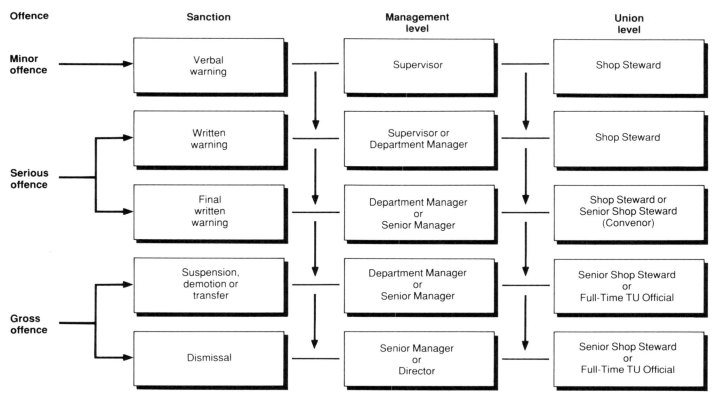

In some organisations the Personnel Department will be involved at a very early stage and the Personnel Manager may take the place of or act with the Department Manager.

Figure 5.9 *Stages in the disciplinary procedure*

Verbal warning

This is the most frequent and least severe penalty. Quite often an employee will be 'told off' by a supervisor on a very informal basis which will normally be the end of the matter. You therefore need to distinguish between those verbal warnings which are *not* part of the formal procedure and those which are. An employee should be left in no doubt as to whether or not the warning is formal.

Evidence Assignment 5L

Decide in which of the following situations you would suggest that the warning should form part of the formal disciplinary procedure. Give reasons. You may like to discuss these in a group first.

1 You miss the bus two days running and come in late. Your supervisor asks you why you are late and, when you explain, asks you to be a bit more careful about your time-keeping in future.

2 You pretend to feel ill one afternoon so that you can go to the Job Centre to look for another job. Unfortunately someone sees you and tells your supervisor. He calls you into his office and tells you that that sort of behaviour is unacceptable.

3 Your supervisor asks you to change your lunch hour from 12 to 1. You don't like this idea and say that you prefer to lunch at 12. He insists and you have a slight argument about it. He tells you to be careful about your attitude.

4 You find out that your company is interested in buying some property owned by the local brewery where your friend works. You tell him and he tells his boss. Word gets back to your company and your supervisor tells you that you have committed a serious offence.

DID YOU KNOW?

Even though a formal verbal warning is *verbal* (i.e. spoken), an employee should be given *written* confirmation of it – and a note to this effect will be put on his or her file – in case, at a later date, there are any disagreements about what was really said.

Written warning

If you repeat an offence despite being given a warning, *or* if your misconduct is more serious, you may be given a written warning. In it you will be told:

- the offence for which you have been disciplined
- where relevant, any previous warnings you have been given
- what your future conduct is expected to be.

You may also be asked to sign that you have received and understood it.

Depending on the nature of the offence, you may be given a 'first' or a 'final' written warning.

DID YOU KNOW?

If you have been given a formal warning you may be concerned at the effect it may have on your future prospects. Most organisations, however, will give you a fresh start after a certain time. Depending on how serious your misconduct has been you may find that a record of it will be removed from your file at any time between a period of three months to two years.

Suspension

There are two types of suspension:

- suspension *with pay* pending a disciplinary investigation
- suspension *without pay* as a punishment within the formal disciplinary procedure.

Transfer or demotion

Sometimes employees may be transferred to another job or even moved to a more junior position (i.e. demoted) as an alternative to being dismissed.

DID YOU KNOW?

In the nineteenth century it was common for an employer to fine an employee for any breach of company rules. The problem there, however, was that if the fine was too small it had no effect.

If it was too large it could be regarded as what is known as a 'penalty' and thus be considered illegal. Nowadays the **Wages Act 1986** restricts the right to impose fines to cases where it is actually stated in the contract of employment and the employee agrees in writing to such an arrangement.

Dismissal

In most cases dismissal takes place only where all other options have been exhausted. If an employee is dismissed he or she normally has the right of appeal to a top level of management. The procedure should specify the period of time within which the appeal must be lodged and a further period of time within which it must be heard. If the appeal is dismissed the employee is left with the alternative of accepting the dismissal or of taking his or her case to an Industrial Tribunal (see page 147) on the grounds that the dismissal was unfair.

Activity

An appeal must be heard by a level of management not previously involved in, and of a higher level than, the level of management involved in the initial procedures. Suggest why this should be the case.

The disciplinary interview

A manager who is asked to conduct a disciplinary interview generally has to:

- hold it within a reasonable period of time of the offence having been committed
- make sure that the employee knows that it is a disciplinary interview
- establish the facts
- impose a sanction (if justified).

He or she therefore needs to be satisfied that the employee has been guilty of some misconduct by:

- checking on what rule has been broken
- looking at the evidence
- deciding whether or not there is a case to answer.

It is also advisable that the interview is held in a suitable place (e.g. away from the open office or shopfloor and in private) and that sufficient time, free from any interruption, is allowed for it.

During the interview the manager should:

- allow the employee to state his or her case
- behave calmly and not get angry, sarcastic or rude
- suggest ways in which the employee could improve and listen also to the employee's suggestions
- summarise the facts and make sure the employee knows he or she has been disciplined (if this is the case) and that he or she knows about the right of appeal
- send written confirmation to the employee after the interview with a copy to the trade union representative.

Evidence Assignment 5M

Faisal and Robert have been discovered having a fight on the shop floor. Both of them know it is against the rules to fight in an area in which there is heavy machinery and equipment because of the obvious health and safety risks. However, neither of them has been involved in any trouble before. Faisal is particularly annoyed because he feels he was provoked by Robert and was acting in self defence. A supervisor who happened to be passing at the time broke up the fight but didn't see how it started and wouldn't listen to any explanations. He merely says he will report the incident.

Ten days later both Faisal and Robert are called into the manager's office. He asks them why they were fighting. They both give him their version – although there are slight differences in their accounts as Robert now says *he* was the one who was provoked. The manager asks them if they *really* expect him to believe their story – he's heard it all before, only told more convincingly. Both Faisal and Robert insist that they are telling the truth. The manager leaves the office for ten minutes to chat to the foreman. He returns and says that the foreman does not confirm their story. He tells them that they are therefore both going to be given a written warning and that they had better get out of the office before anything worse happens to them. They hear nothing more.

1 *As a group*, discuss what mistakes the manager has

made. Write down what preparations you think he should have made, the questions he should have asked, the way the interview should have been conducted and the attitude he should have adopted.

2 If you had been the manager, what action would you have taken?

3 Have Faisal and Robert any defence against fighting?

· FAIR AND UNFAIR DISMISSAL ·

Ultimately your employer does have the right to dismiss you if all other disciplinary procedures have failed or because your misconduct has been so serious that it warrants dismissal without the need for any other disciplinary action.

You may in turn, however, claim that you have been unfairly dismissed and take your claim to an Industrial Tribunal.

Proof of dismissal

It is up to you to prove that you have been dismissed. In most cases this is quite easy to do! In some cases, however, particularly if there has been an argument or series of arguments, it is difficult for a tribunal to decide whether your employer has actually dismissed you or whether he has merely lost his temper (e.g. if, in the course of an argument, your manager tells you to leave, does he mean leave his office or leave the company?).

Activity

Look at the following statements:

- From a sales manager to a sales representative – 'If you don't like the way we work, there's the door.'
- From a manager to a cleaner – 'It looks as though we might have to part company.'

In what ways could you argue that a dismissal has occurred in both these cases, and in what ways that it has not?

Discuss *as a group* what other factors a tribunal may take into account when reaching such a decision. Consider, for

instance, the status of the two people concerned and whether or not the incident was a one-off or part of a series of arguments.

Unfair dismissal

Once the fact of dismissal has been proved, an employer then has the right to defend his or her decision by using one of the following defences:

- you were incapable of carrying out the work
- you were guilty of some type of misconduct
- you were redundant
- an Act of Parliament prevented you from continuing to be employed
- there was 'some other substantial reason' (SOSR) to justify the dismissal.

Capability

Remember the implied duty in your contract of employment that you have the skills needed to do your job. If you don't have these skills, theoretically your employer can dismiss you and claim that he or she has done so fairly. However, nowadays, the tribunals are more sympathetic to incompetent employees. They will expect the employer to have made it clear to you that you are not reaching the required standard – it mustn't come as a surprise to you to be called into your manager's office and be dismissed. They will also expect an employer to arrange extra training sessions for example.

Two *actual* cases show the right and the wrong way to deal with such a situation. In one case an employee who had worked for the same garage for many years was, as the result of a reorganisation, asked to undertake some clerical duties in addition to his other work. He found it difficult to cope and the firm dismissed him. The tribunal was not pleased to discover that although he had been told that he wasn't doing his job properly, no attempt had been made to help him. By contrast the manager of a dress shop, who was dismissed for inefficiency, was held to have been fairly dismissed because the company could show that they had tried to help her in many ways – by giving her training in window display, book-keeping, staff relationships etc.

DID YOU KNOW?

If you are ill for a long period, this could eventually justify your employer in dismissing you on the grounds that you are incapable of work. As you might expect, however, a tribunal is normally reluctant to hold that such a dismissal is fair unless the employer has taken measures to find an alternative solution. It will want to know, for instance:

- that all reasonable efforts have been taken to check on your state of health – including consulting a doctor – and that you have been made aware that further or continued absence could result in dismissal
- that the dismissal was reasonable because of the nature of your work and the effect your ill-health has had on the organisation.

Factors to be taken into account include

- the nature of your illness
- your age
- the length of time you have been employed
- your nearness to retirement
- the need for your job to be done and the need for a replacement to do it.

Activity

Discuss *as a group* what factors the tribunal will consider in the case of each of the following people who have been dismissed on ill-health grounds:

a a 63-year-old man with chronic bronchitis
b a 20-year-old drummer with a pop group which is currently touring the UK, who has had a nervous breakdown
c a 40-year-old production manager responsible for meeting the company's production targets who has had a minor heart attack.

Misconduct

In most cases an employee is dismissed for misconduct only after all other disciplinary measures have been taken. If an employer cannot prove that these procedures have been followed, a tribunal will not usually hold the dismissal to be fair.

DID YOU KNOW?

The most common *criminal* act carried out in the workplace is stealing. In such cases the employer can only dismiss if he or she has good reason for believing that an employee is guilty of theft – at the time of dismissal. If he or she merely suspects the employee of theft, dismisses him or her and then finds out afterwards (e.g. because of a police investigation) that theft has been proved, this might not necessarily make the dismissal fair. Note, however, that if an employer has carried out a thorough investigation he or she need only have 'good reason to believe' that an employee has been stealing and not proof 'beyond reasonable doubt'. Note too that in one case in which it was almost certain that one of two employees had stolen some cash from their employer's safe, the employer was held entitled to dismiss both of them.

Conduct outside working hours

Normally what you do in your own time is your own concern. If, therefore, an employee gets very drunk one evening and ends up in the police cells charged with drunk and disorderly conduct, his employer, even though he or she disapproves of the behaviour, will not normally be able to dismiss the person because of it – although his chances of any promotion might have vanished!

However, if your conduct outside work is such that it could have an effect on what you do at work, then the situation changes.

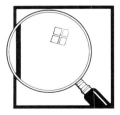

Evidence Assignment 5N

Consider the following cases and decide in each whether or not you think the employee's conduct will affect his or her work. Give reasons for your decisions.

1 A sales representative is found guilty of a drink-driving offence and his driving licence is revoked.

Fair or unfair?

2 A company accountant is found guilty of embezzling funds from the social club of which she is the treasurer.

3 A teacher, who is also a football fan, is involved in a riot and found guilty of assault and battery.

4 An RSPCA officer is found guilty of ill-treating his dog.

5 A clerk is convicted of shop-lifting.

6 A personnel manager is found guilty of obstructing the police at a trade union rally.

Redundancy

If a company closes down altogether and all the employees are made redundant because there is no work for them to do, then they are regarded as being *dismissed because of redundancy*. In most cases, of course, this dismissal will be regarded as fair because the employer has little other choice. Again, if some only of the employees are dismissed because of redundancy this is normally regarded as fair (if the proper consultation has taken place) unless they can show that the employer has ignored a redundancy selection agreement negotiated with the union (e.g. that those with the shortest amount of service have to be made redundant first).

Evidence Collection Point 5.10

The most common criteria contained in redundancy selection agreements are:

- volunteers
- sub-contractors
- last in first out (LIFO)
- men over 60
- women over 55.

However, some organisations also have a set of 'efficiency' criteria by which employees are judged on absence, timekeeping, work performance, disciplinary record, etc.

Discuss as a group the advantages and disadvantages of each criterion. For instance, the advantage of asking for volunteers first is that no-one is *forced* out of work. The disadvantage, however, may be that the employer loses a very good employee who will find a job elsewhere and therefore doesn't mind taking voluntary redundancy. Write a paragraph on your conclusions.

Statutory restrictions

Not many employees are dismissed under this heading. On some occasions, however, employees are dismissed because a Statute or Act of Parliament forbids the employer to employ them. Suppose, for instance, you have been employed to work on a night shift in a factory and then your employer discovers that by law you are not old enough to do so. Unless he can find you another job, he has no choice but to dismiss you.

Some other substantial reason

This is a 'catch all' phrase which allows an employer to claim that a dismissal is fair even though the reason for it doesn't fit in to any of the other categories. In one case, for example, an employee who was already working in an organisation refused to sign a 'restraint of trade' clause which the company wanted to include in his existing contract of employment (see page 137). He was good at his job and it would have been difficult for the employer to claim that he was guilty of any misconduct – given that he had initially been employed on different terms. However, because of the genuine fear that the company had that they would lose customers to other rival firms if their ex-employees left them to work for these firms, the tribunal held the dismissal fair.

Evidence Collection Point 5.13

1 Obtain a copy of the health and safety at work policy in the college or school where you are studying or at your work experience placement. Make a note of how it covers the points listed on page 166.

2 Write to the Health and Safety Commission, Baynards House, 2 Chepstow Place, London W2 4TS (which is a body responsible for the administration of the Health and Safety at Work Act) and ask for a copy of the Code of Practice for Safety Representatives.

Employee obligations

Although your employer cannot delegate his or her responsibility for health, safety and welfare, you must remember that under the Health and Safety at Work Act you also have an obligation to make sure that you:

- take care of your *own* health and safety
- take reasonable care of the health and safety of other people who may be injured by your careless actions
- co-operate with your employer or any other person carrying out duties under the Act.

DID YOU KNOW?

In some circumstances, if you are injured, your employer may be able to claim one of the following:

- You *voluntarily* took the risk of being injured (if, for instance, you knew you were undertaking some dangerous work) – although the courts are not very impressed with this argument.
- You 'contributed' towards the injury, by not wearing safety goggles, by not following set safety procedures etc. If this is the case then the amount of damages you can claim if an accident does occur will be reduced.

A safe working environment

Whilst it is up to the employer to make sure that working areas are cleaned regularly, that there are adequate storage areas and safe equipment, there is a duty on employees as well. If you have a desk like a bombsite and never put anything away then you are hardly 'co-operating with your employer'. Safe working practices can be divided into:

- good housekeeping
- the provision of suitable equipment and training in use of it
- the provision of suitable furniture and proper care and use of it
- suitable accommodation
- reduction in noise
- safe working habits
- provision of information.

Evidence Assignment 5Q

Read the following suggestions as to the sort of safe working practices which should be carried out by both employer and employee. Divide the information into what you think an employer should do and what an employee should do and include it in a table containing two columns – one headed 'Employer responsibility' and one 'Employee responsibility'. Add any other suggestions you can think of in relation to each of the items.

- **Good housekeeping** – tidiness and cleanliness of working areas and safe storage of dangerous or inflammable substances.
- **Equipment** – no electrical hazards through trailing leads or broken sockets. Any equipment which can give out dangerous fumes (e.g. a photocopier) should be kept in a well ventilated, preferably separate, room. Safety filing cabinets should be installed where only one drawer can open at a time to prevent tilting. Equipment should only be used in accordance with correct operating procedures.
- **Furniture** – safety stools provided for reaching items stored on high shelves, adjustable chairs for keyboard operators to reduce backache.
- **Accommodation** – no overcrowding, offices above 61°F (16°C) but not too hot, good ventilation and blinds for windows in direct sunlight. Good lighting, safe floor surfaces (not worn or slippery) and adequate toilet facilities.

- **Noise** – kept to reasonable limits (e.g. acoustic hoods on computer printers).
- **Safe work habits** – e.g. not running down corridors, not carrying heavy objects, not carrying so many items that vision is obscured.
- **Provision of information** – all employees to know the correct procedure in case of fire, where extinguishers are situated, who are first-aiders and safety representatives, how to report an accident, etc.

Evidence Collection Point 5.14

1 Look at each of the statements below and identify the part of the Act under which each action would be categorised.

a An employee ignores the usual procedure and uses the lift after the fire bell has sounded.

b Inflammable liquids are stored in a busy area.

c A pile of rubbish is left near the entrance to a works.

d An employee empties the sand out of the fire buckets as a joke.

e The filing clerk leaves the bottom drawer of the cabinet open after use.

2 Add five more employee actions of your own which you consider would contravene the Act. In each case state why you think the employee is failing to comply with the regulations.

3 Whilst no-one should ever attempt to lift heavy equipment, even relatively lightweight items can be lifted correctly or incorrectly. Lifting things wrongly is a major cause of back problems. Find out the correct method to use and make out an attractive information sheet to be put on the notice board in your organisation.

4 Find out the different colours of fire extinguishers in your building and the differences between them. List all the other types of fire-fighting equipment supplied and why it is used, as well as the number of alarms and how these should be activated.

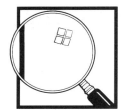

Evidence Assignment 5R

1 You are asked to operate some printing equipment with an automatic guillotine. You are not given much training and are therefore a bit nervous about using it. You also think – but don't know – that it should have a safety guard on it but you don't want to be thought of as a nuisance or as stupid by persisting in asking about it. Your supervisor has told you that your long hair could get caught in the equipment and asks you to have it cut or to tie your hair back. You don't want to do this.

If an accident occurs discuss whether your employer would be considered negligent in any way. How far could you be held responsible? (Look back to page 167 for details of *your* responsibilities in this respect.)

List what you think *should* have happened.

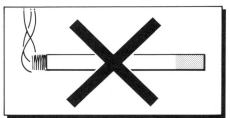

2 There is an increasing awareness of the dangers of smoking at work both for the smokers themselves and for those who work with them. Your employers wish to introduce a no-smoking policy. Decide how they should go about this. Bear in mind factors such as:

- the need for consultation with staff
- the imposition of a *total* ban or a partial ban (i.e. to have designated smoking areas)
- the offer of professional advice to smokers to encourage them to give up smoking
- the involvement of the trade unions
- the means of dealing with those employees who won't follow the no-smoking rules.

As a group decide the course of action you think they should take.

If a total smoking ban is implemented, what sort of behaviour do you think would mean that a smoker in the office is failing in his or her personal or social obligations to the employer?

Evidence Project

1 Select *two* organisations and ask them if they will provide you with a copy of the standard contract of employment they issue to their employees. Otherwise ask some of your friends who are working to provide you with this information. Check each contract to see what, if any, additional information is included in the contract and make a list of what it is.

2 Interview two people who are working and two who are still at school or college and ask them:

a if they know what a contract of employment *should* contain

b what their rights are in respect of equal pay

c what their obligations are in relation to health and safety at work.

Compare their answers and write a short report outlining your findings.

3 Below are given two situations which have taken place recently. One involves an employee with a grievance, and in the other case the employer is considering disciplinary action.

Grievance procedure

Damien has been working in a bank for some years now and is hoping to be promoted shortly. He knows, however, that Head Office has asked all managers to try to reduce staff costs. Even so, he is very concerned when he is asked to move to a smaller branch to replace one of the employees there who has just retired. The work is very routine and gives him little opportunity to develop his interest in overseas financial transactions. He protests but his manager tells him that as his salary is going to remain the same, he has no cause for complaint. Damien points out that because this branch office is 20 miles away he will have to spend more money on travelling and he will not be able to continue attending the local college to finish his course. More importantly – for him at least – he will have to get up an hour earlier each morning and will not arrive home until 7 p.m. every night. His social life will be in ruins.

Disciplinary action

Jennifer has just started work after leaving college. At the interview she was so keen to get the job that she 'exaggerated' slightly what she could do and led the interviewer to believe that she was a more competent keyboard operator than she actually is. During her second week at work her supervisor tells her that she is not performing well enough and that she is going to monitor her work the following day. Jennifer is very nervous. During the morning she completes two memos and starts one letter. She is, however, interrupted on a number of occasions and, because she is new, has difficulty in answering the queries. This wastes some time. She thinks she might be able to catch up on some work during her lunch hour but when her friend calls in she decides to have the full lunch hour and to discuss her difficulties at work. Unfortunately she is five minutes late getting back and her supervisor spots this. During the afternoon Jennifer completes the letter and manages to type a three-page document. At 4 p.m. her supervisor has another word with her, tells her that her work that day has been well below standard and issues a verbal warning.

a Select one of these scenarios and develop it into a script which accurately illustrates the rights and responsibilities of the employee/employer.

b Make sure that your script includes a suitable ending, bearing in mind the legislation covered in this chapter.

c With a colleague act out your script and if possible video it. Ask for comments from your fellow students!

Type your project on a word-processor, using suitable headings. Include a copy of your script. Make a front cover for your project which gives your name, the date and the title – 'The Rights and Responsibilties of Employers and Employees'. Add a back cover and bind it so that it looks professional.

Evidence Checkpoint

Check that all your assignments and Evidence Collection materials are complete and to the correct standard. Can you improve anything to achieve a higher grade?

Revision Test

True or false?

1 An employee has the right to be given some work to do.

2 Health and safety is the sole responsibility of the employer.

3 An employee must be given a written statement of the terms and conditions of employment within 13 weeks of starting work.

4 An employee can insist on being paid in cash.

5 Statutory sick pay is paid only for periods of sickness of four days or more.

Complete the blanks

6 For a first offence an employee is normally given a ...... warning.

7 If you are told you cannot have the job because you are a woman this is an example of ....

8 An elected union representative who represents the members of a union is called a ....

9 If you accept a bribe or disclose confidential information about your company you may be in breach of your obligation to act ....

10 Advice to employers and unions about how to resolve a dispute can be obtained from the ....,
.... Service.

Short answer questions

11 List the five main defences an employer can use if an employee claims unfair dismissal.

12 State how long a statutory period of notice should be given by an employee.

13 List the major health and safety responsibilities of an employer.

14 List three ways in which you might earn a bonus payment.

15 List four of the main items covered by the Sex Discrimination Act.

Write a short paragraph to show you clearly understand each of the following terms.

16 Disciplinary procedures.

17 Equal opportunities.

18 Contract of employment.

19 Employee consultation.

20 Remuneration.

chapter **6** # JOB ROLES IN BUSINESS ORGANISATIONS

Learning Objectives

This chapter is concerned with the main job roles to be found in business organisations and the tasks which different role holders undertake. It identifies how these may vary depending upon the functional area in which the role holder is employed.

After studying this chapter you should be able to:

- describe the main job roles in business organisations
- identify the functions of different job roles
- identify the tasks undertaken by different role holders.

• ROLES IN DIFFERENT TYPES • OF ORGANISATIONS

When you start work in a particular job you want to know not only what *you* are expected to do (i.e. your own job role) but also what others around you are expected to do.

Unless you are working in a small business with a very flat structure (see Chapter 4), you will probably find that job *roles* are attached to job *levels* and are graded from junior to senior level. The managing director normally occupies the most senior job role in a private sector organisation. The chief executive might occupy a similar role in a public sector organisation.

Within the private sector the roles of those in charge differ, depending on the size of the organisation. In a large organisation there will be more **specialisation** so a person will carry out a more specific role, while in a small organisation or one-man business the roles are less defined. The manager may be doing virtually everything!

Evidence Collection Point 6.1

As a group, discuss how the role of a manager may differ in each of the following types of organisation. Think in terms of how much freedom each of them has to operate, the variety of their work and the number of people above them (to whom they are responsible) and the number below them (for whom they are responsible). From what you learned in Chapter 1 you should also be able to identify how the type and range of decisions they make would vary.

From notes of the discussion, prepare a final version of your work, preferably using a word-processor.

a A sole trader who runs a retail business and employs two part-time staff.

b A junior partner in a firm of solicitors which has four senior partners, six junior partners, six section heads/legal executives and 12 clerical staff.

c A director in a small, family-run motor vehicle repair garage which is a private limited company. The two directors are brothers, there is one foreman, four mechanics and two part-time office staff.

d The personnel manager in a large retail store which is a public limited company – reports directly to the personnel director at head office and is responsible for the branch's recruitment of full-time and part-time staff.

e The training officer at the local town hall – responsible for organising and planning training for all staff and operating within a specified budget.

f A nurse manager in a large hospital, responsible for six wards and the staff on each.

· GENERAL JOB ROLES ·

In *general* terms, the major roles in an organisation are those of directors, managers and team members (see Figure 6.1).

Figure 6.1

Activity

Why do you think these roles are shown as a pyramid – bearing in mind the *shape* of a pyramid? Discuss your answer with your tutor.

DID YOU KNOW?

The above roles can be undertaken by people in *all* parts of the organisation, whether they work in production, finance, personnel etc.

Directors

In the private sector the chief executive would normally be called the **managing director** and be assisted by a team of other executives who would normally be on the **board of directors**. In the public sector you may find that the equivalent structure is for the principal of a college, the head teacher of a school or the general manager of a hospital to be the 'chief' and to be assisted by a board of governors.

The **chairman** of the board of directors is elected by the other directors. In some companies this job is also undertaken by the managing director.

The board of directors may consist of two types of directors. **Executive directors** work for the organisation on a full-time basis. **Non-executive directors** do not work for the organisation but are asked to take a seat on the board because of their knowledge, experience and ability to take a 'wider view' than the executive directors.

DID YOU KNOW?

Many Members of Parliament, leading industrialists and financial experts hold seats on the boards of several companies at once.

Evidence Collection Point 6.2

Visit your library and find a reference book which lists the directors of large organisations.

1 Select three large companies and note down the number of executive and non-executive directors. (If the book in which you are looking for the information doesn't sub-divide them in this way, then write down a complete list.)

2 Look up information on two famous personalities (e.g. MPs past or present or well-known people in the business world) and find out for which companies they are non-executive directors.

Duties of the board of directors

- To set appropriate targets.
- To establish the policies and strategies of the organisation.
- To decide long-term plans.
- To make important financial decisions (e.g. regarding future investment and large-scale capital expenditure).
- To ensure the organisation always acts within the law.
- To control all the organisation's activities.
- To look after major personnel functions – the recruitment and promotion of senior managers and the dismissal and redundancy of any staff.

Duties of individual executive directors

The duties of the individual directors will be of two types. They have an overall responsibility for the development of the organisation as a whole, which relates to the board meetings which they attend. Each executive director will also be in charge of a particular functional area (e.g. personnel or sales). Therefore he or she will have responsibilities in relation to that area which will include:

- deciding the long-term plans of the department
- setting targets for the department and checking that these are being met
- telling the departmental managers of any policy decisions made by the board of directors (if these are not confidential)

- reporting back to the managing director or board of directors when necessary
- overseeing the activities of the managers, keeping them informed of all developments and receiving information from them
- delegating duties to the management teams.

Activity

Directors and managers are often expected by their organisations to undertake activities outside that organisation and to become JPs, governors of schools or colleges, advisory members of local government committees, etc. Why do you think they are encouraged to do so?

Discuss your ideas with your tutor.

Managers

The role of manager can be undertaken by many people in an organisation. Senior managers may be heads of departments and be assisted by 'middle' or 'junior' managers who each run their own section or unit. Some managers look after people, others look after tasks.

Duties of managers

- Carrying out the instructions of the director to whom they are responsible.

- Scheduling and allocating work between the people they manage.
- Ensuring that the staff do the work effectively.
- Making operational decisions which relate to the work of the department.
- Checking that staff are meeting pre-agreed targets.
- Solving day-to-day problems.
- Carrying out the administrative and personnel duties relating to their area of work, including identifying training needs.
- Informing their director of developments, progress or problems.
- Keeping their own staff informed of non-confidential organisational developments.

DID YOU KNOW?

The term 'first-line manager' is sometimes used for junior managers who are at the first level above team members. This is because they have day-to-day contact with the team members in their work and so operate at the 'first line' above them.

Team members

Although team members need not always be at the most junior level in the organisation, it is likely that when you start work your first role will be that of team member. If you are a clerk in the wages section you will be a member of that team, if you are an administrative assistant in a solicitor's office you will be a member of that team, and so on.

Duties of team members

- To carry out the duties as specified on the job description and as required by the manager or supervisor.
- To obey reasonable instructions (remember your legal obligations – see Chapter 5).
- To co-operate with other team members.

· TEAMWORK ·

The ability of a team to work together well, help one another and be sensitive to the needs of each other is critical, for two reasons:

1 People who work in a good atmosphere will work harder, and produce better work.
2 A team which works co-operatively together can achieve far more in a short space of time than a team which does not.

The qualities of a good team member include:

- listening to other people and not interrupting or criticising their ideas
- taking account of other people's views and beliefs
- thinking before you speak
- offering help, support and suggestions when they are needed
- being prepared to accept *constructive* criticism from other people gracefully
- putting your own views in a calm manner
- acting as a peacemaker if necessary.

Work teams

Different departments have different types of 'work teams'. The sales department, for instance, may have a sales team which will be brought together for sales training days, to exchange information on customers and so on. However, for the most part each member may work alone, perhaps being responsible for a specific geographical area.

Other teams may work more closely together in the same area. For instance, many people who work in production are involved in *assembly* work. This involves putting together the parts of a machine or article to make the final product. As an example, a car travels along a production line with each assembly worker adding his or her 'part' to the final product until the car is complete. Today more and more assembly workers operate as members of a team. They will be concerned with the output of the team as a whole as well as the quality of their part of the production process. They may even undertake *job rotation* (i.e. members of the team switch jobs, which gives them more variety and helps them to understand the work of other people).

An important team in a manufacturing company is the *maintenance team*. When machines are used to produce goods, output will fall if machines break down. The work of the maintenance staff is therefore critical, both in undertaking routine servicing and in repairing machines which have broken down for some reason. The faster the machine is repaired, the quicker normal production levels can be resumed.

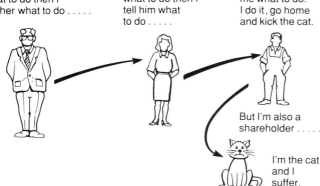

I'm a director. My shareholders tell me what to do then I tell her what to do . . . . .

I'm a manager. My director tells me what to do then I tell him what to do . . . . .

I'm a worker. My manager tells me what to do. I do it, go home and kick the cat.

But I'm also a shareholder . . . . .

I'm the cat and I suffer.

Evidence Collection Point 6.3

Your tutor will divide you into teams of four and provide you with white A4 paper, red and black sticky paper and scissors. As a team you are going into production making paper aeroplanes, and competing with other teams to see how many saleable aeroplanes you can produce. Much will depend on the quality of your planning and how well you organise yourselves and co-operate as a team.

At the end of the exercise you should prepare an account of the process which includes:

- how well you consider the team operated together
- the value of your own contribution (in your opinion!)
- what improvements or adjustments you would make if you did the exercise again
- what you consider the role of a team member was in this exercise.

Details for aeroplane construction
Your organisation makes four kinds of aeroplanes:

- black stripe – with a black stripe on each wing – worth 10 points
- red stripe – with a 3 cm long red stripe on each wing – worth 15 points
- multi-stripe – with a 3 cm black and 4 cm red stripe on each wing – worth 25 points
- star series – with a black star on one wing and a red star on the other – worth 50 points.

Your task is to plan your production schedule and divide up your team (think of division of labour!) to achieve this. You have *20 minutes* for planning, during which time you can practise making aeroplanes, but these cannot be counted towards the final score and must be thrown away at the end of the planning time. You then have *15 minutes to produce and display* as many high quality aeroplanes as you can. The team which achieves the highest number of points wins. Bear in mind that:

1 There should be some quality control built in to your production line, as any 'faulty' aeroplanes will be rejected by the final consumer (your tutor!).

2 Your final aeroplanes must be displayed in a tidy area. This means that you have to clear up your production debris at some stage. Any team which has a poor 'sales area' will have its two highest value aeroplanes discounted.

▪ ROLES AND TASKS ▪

Everyone who goes to work carries out a range of tasks in their day-to-day work, but the scope of these varies. Some people will be involved in thinking about problems, considering alternatives and making decisions. Others will be concerned with operating a machine, filing some documents or inputting information to a computer. The tasks with which people are involved will vary considerably depending on their role in the organisation.

There have been many famous studies to find out how directors and managers spend their time, and to see if people's activities change as they move up into higher positions in an organisation. Certain activities are common to both directors and managers:

- **Planning**. This involves deciding what must be done in the future and how it is to be done – and what will be needed to do it in terms of staff and other resources.
- **Decision-making**. This is choosing between different alternative courses of action. It is often closely linked to planning.
- **Communicating**. This involves talking to their staff, both above and below them, and those *outside* the organisation on a 'one-to-one' basis as well as attending meetings at which they may act as a representative of their organisation.

- **Supervising**. This refers to the way in which they relate to the staff they manage. The aim of all managers should be to motivate their staff so that they do a better job and are happy to work hard. To do this managers need to be **supportive** – *you* would want to feel that your boss was on your side and understood your problems and difficulties. At the same time, however, a manager has a **disciplinary** role – if a member of staff is not working hard enough or is creating problems for someone else by their actions. Finally, a manager needs to organise the **training** of staff, especially if he or she wants them to work in a new area or to learn a new skill.

- **Setting targets and monitoring performance**. All organisations today set targets in relation to what they want to achieve. It is important that managers *check* whether these are being achieved. Targets are dealt with in more detail on page 178.

- **Problem-solving**. Problems may be simple or complex, involve people or tasks, and require immediate solutions or a considerable amount of thought. One theory says that people respond to problems on a priority basis (i.e. the most urgent, not the most important) and that those which involve other people are more difficult than those which involve tasks.

Team members may also be involved in some of these tasks, but they will be specifically related to their own particular job. For instance, an operator working a machine will have to check that the settings are correct, that safety precautions are being taken and that the goods produced are of the right quality. A clerk in an administration department may have to plan his or her work for the day, making sure that urgent jobs are done first. This will obviously involve a certain amount of **decision-making.** If anything goes wrong (e.g. the machine develops a fault, or a crisis occurs in administration because three people are away with 'flu) then these problems will have to be solved before work can continue.

Evidence Assignment 6A

There is a considerable difference between the work of a director, a manager and a team member. Below are given three extracts from interviews with people in each of these roles.

Read these carefully and then answer the questions which follow.

A 'We have a large centralised reprographics section in our company, and my job is to do the photocopying for all the departments. I need to sort this into urgent and non-urgent jobs. Often I have to explain to people why there might be a delay – for instance, if the machine breaks down. My supervisor is very good, though, and supports me if there are any problems with other staff. Minor problems I can sort out myself, but sometimes I have to send for the technician. I need to decide what to do in these situations. I like my job – I can plan my own day, though sometimes it does get very busy and I have to bear in mind the pressures on the other staff I work with in this section.'

B 'I sometimes regret not having more contact with my staff on a day-to-day basis. Sometimes I seem to go from one meeting to another all day. A lot of my time is spent planning for the future of the organisation – often over the next five years. This involves looking at both the opportunities available to us as an organisation, and the type of problems we may encounter. I also deal with people from outside the organisation quite frequently, and have to represent the company in an official capacity. Although I trained to be an accountant I do very little of that type of work now – most of my job is looking at the company as a whole to see which would be the best course of action to take in the future.'

C 'Although I have a considerable number of staff for whom I am responsible, and like to see most of them regularly, I don't have time to see them all every day. I would expect to be told if there were problems on which I need to take action. These may involve difficulties with people – either staff in my own department or elsewhere in the organisation – or with work scheduling and how our sales targets can be achieved. Customers, too, can be a problem if they want something quickly that we cannot supply. No matter what problems we face, I think it's my responsibility to create a good working atmosphere, otherwise I wouldn't get to know what was going on. A major aspect of my job is representing the staff to my own boss, and making sure those at the top understand how we operate and what we need.

1 One extract was said by a director, one by a manager and one by an team member. From the descriptions, can you say who said which?

2 From the extracts can you say:

- Who spends the most time planning?
- Who spends the most time supervising?
- What activities are common to all?

3 The type of problems faced by each person are different. Under the headings of 'Director', 'Manager' and 'Team member' write a brief account of the type of problems they encounter.

4 From what you read in Chapter 4, can you say in which functional area the speaker of extract C works? Give reasons for your choice.

Decision-making

One activity which is common to all roles is that of **decision-making**, although the *type* of decision you make may differ according to your job role.

You make decisions every day of your life – what you want to eat for breakfast, where you want to go in the evening – even though there may be some obstacles placed in your way. You may decide not to hand in an assignment but your tutor might decide to insist that you do so.

Many of the decisions that you make are simple and do not carry much risk. If you choose to buy a cup of tea rather than a cup of coffee and the tea is cold you haven't made a major error–you either drink it cold or ask for another cup. Some decisions, however, are much more important. At 16 you normally have to decide to try to find a job or to remain in full-time education. That's a crucial decision for you to make. So too is whether or not you are going to get married to a particular person.

In the business world the decisions you are called upon to make can be classified in a similar way. They may be low, medium or high risk, major or minor.

Activity

Look at the following decisions which have to be taken. Discuss as a group which you think are low, which medium and which high risk.

1 A manager has to decide which of two members of staff to promote to a senior post.
2 A supervisor has to decide on a weekly work rota for his or her staff.
3 A managing director has to decide whether or not to finance the production of a new product.
4 The staff welfare committee has to decide where to hold the office Christmas party.

Decision-making and problem-solving

Obviously these are closely related. If you think carefully before you make a decision, you have often solved a problem at the same time.

When you are at work you are being *paid* to make decisions, whatever role you have. It is therefore important for you to know what guidelines to use when you are making decisions. Remember, of course, that the higher you climb in any organisation, the more decisions you will have to make and the more likely it is that they will be important.

1 Think carefully about the situation. If you are worried, write it down (e.g. I can't understand the new ordering system).

2 Analyse the problem more carefully. What exactly can't you understand? Is it the procedure to be followed, is it the information on the order itself, is it inputting it to the new computer system?

3 Consider as many solutions to the problem as possible. Read through the instruction manual again (if there is one), ask a friend to help you, ask your supervisor to help you.

4 Select the solution which you think is most likely to work.

5 If this doesn't help, try the second one on your list. Keep trying until you succeed, and don't be afraid to ask for help.

DID YOU KNOW?

Group decisions can often be helpful. A good manager or team leader will include all members of the team in most of the decisions. In that way they should feel 'ownership' of any decision made and may be more willing to stick by it.

The following guidelines are intended to help you to avoid too many mistakes in making decisions:

● Try not to make a decision under stress or on the spur of the moment (although this isn't always possible to avoid).

● Remember, however, that generally speaking you will feel better when you do make a decision. If you keep delaying a decision, you will feel worse and worse about it.

● Accept the fact that sometimes you will make the wrong decision. Everyone does.

● Once a decision is made, it's made – don't keep changing your mind (although there are occasions when you can be persuaded to change your mind, and that's not always a bad thing).

Problems with tasks and problems with people

It is often said that problems involving people are always more difficult to solve than those involving tasks. You can test this for yourself. If you buy a new gadget and have a problem getting it to work, the answer is relatively straightforward. You read the instruction leaflet carefully

and, if it still doesn't work, you take it back to the shop where you bought it. People are more problematical, because they all have *views* of their own. If you try to organise where you should go with six friends next Saturday night you may find that getting total agreement is near impossible. If some people are particularly difficult you could end up never making a decision at all.

Evidence Assignment 6B

The administration manager in a large organisation has decided to dispense with all the electronic typewriters and to replace these with word-processors. He has two basic problems:

a which computers to buy and which word-processing software to purchase

b how to convince the typists that the change will be for the best.

1 Which, in your opinion, could be the more difficult problem area – (a) or (b) – and why?

2 What information will he need before he can make the best decision in part (a)? Make a list of everything you can think of.

3 *As a group*, discuss all the objections which might be raised by staff who are having to change from typewriters to word-processors. For each objection, try to think of something positive the manager could do or suggest to help to solve the problem.

Summarise your ideas.

Setting targets

Imagine you are going on a car journey of 200 miles to catch a cross-channel ferry at the start of your holidays. If you miss the ferry then it is doubtful you will be able to catch one later, as during the summer the ferries are booked up several months in advance. It is therefore important that you arrive at the ferryport at the correct time for check-in or earlier.

You cannot, therefore, set off aimlessly at whatever time you want. You will need to have a plan or schedule to follow so that you can achieve your objective of arriving

P & O European Ferries new £68 million superferry Pride of Burgundy

on time. You need to decide at what time to leave, and this will depend on various factors – weather, traffic, speed of your car etc. This will be your first target – to ensure everyone meets at the specified time, with everything done, so that you leave punctually.

However, during the journey things can go wrong. Unexpected road works, a puncture, queues at the service station – all these can disrupt your plan. You would then have to make adjustments to ensure that you can still arrive on time. If you were sensible, you would have plotted **target** times throughout the journey. If you found that you were falling behind at any particular stage, then you could try to put things right. You would also be able to recognise if your plan was disintegrating completely! For instance, if a *real* emergency developed, and you had no hope of arriving on time, then you might have to abandon your plan altogether, telephone the ferryport and see if an alternative could be arranged.

In business, plans are made and targets are set to ensure that progress towards the final objective can be achieved. If the final objective is to make a profit at the end of the year, then the steps towards this need to be worked out and set down. They can then be monitored regularly, and adjustments made if the plan is falling behind. Achieving the targets needs everyone's co-operation (in the same way that you would be reliant on other people going with you on holiday to be able to leave on time).

Costs and budgets

All organisations compile a budget for the year. This gives details of the planned revenue and the expected costs. The difference will be the projected profit for the year. Obviously, if revenue falls and costs increase then the profit could be zero, or the company might even make a loss. It is therefore important that the budget plan is followed.

To do this, the budget is broken down into **departmental budgets**. Each department then knows its own contribution (e.g. the sales department knows how much to sell to achieve the revenue required, and the production department knows how many goods will have to be made). All departments are told the maximum amount of money they are allowed to spend.

A manager may then divide the targets up between his or her staff (e.g. each sales representative is given an individual sales target). The manager's job would then be to check, at regular intervals, that the target is being achieved. If it is not, it is the manager's job to find out why, and see if something can be done to remedy the situation.

Many organisations offer financial incentives to help people achieve targets. Production workers may receive a productivity bonus or sales people may receive commission. The employees as a whole may participate in a profit-sharing scheme. Types of bonus payments were dealt with in Chapter 5.

How targets are set

A manager has two roles in relation to targets. As well as monitoring progress he or she is normally involved in setting these in the first place, and will often consult his or her staff beforehand.

Setting realistic targets is important. Targets that are too high will depress everybody, targets that are too low will mean the organisation is not as profitable as it could be. It will be the manager's job to obtain accurate information on the current situation and other details which may affect the future. For instance, a sales manager setting sales targets for the year will need to know:

● the level of current sales
● the sales made by competitors

- whether the market is increasing or decreasing
- how much can be spent on advertising and promotion
- what customers think of current products
- what new products are being developed.

The manager will consult the sales representatives as they will have a better idea of what customers think and what can be achieved. If the sales representatives are actively involved in setting the targets then they will be more motivated to try to achieve them. Therefore, both the setting and achieving of targets is undertaken by people in a variety of job roles, from senior management to team members.

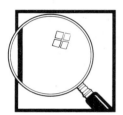

Evidence Assignment 6C

The type of target varies from one department to another. In addition, some targets are *positive* (e.g. to meet or increase the number of sales), whilst some will be *negative* (e.g. to reduce the number of customer complaints).

The chart in Figure 6.2 shows the targets which normally operate in different departments.

1 In each case, identify which would be positive and which would be negative targets.

2 From what you learned in Chapter 4 about the functions of each department, add one target of your own in each case.

3 *As a group*, discuss the information a manager would need to set realistic targets in each of the following areas:

- projected staff turnover for the year
- speed of delivery service
- quality control on goods produced.

Summarise your answers.

4 You have recently been employed as a clerk in the administration department. Your manager wants you to improve your performance in three areas and has given you your own targets below. What action would you take to achieve each of these?

- improved quality of photocopying
- better telephone manner with customers
- more accurate keying-in of data on computer.

Department	Type of target
Sales and Marketing	Number of sales Number of new customers Number of complaints
Production	Number of goods produced Number of faulty goods Amount of time machines being repaired
Personnel	Speed of filling vacancies Rate of staff turnover
Finance	Total of outstanding debts by customers Speed of processing accounts
Administration	Speed of mail distribution Speed of answering by switchboard operator
Distribution	Speed of deliveries Damage to goods

Figure 6.2 *Typical departmental targets*

JOB HOLDERS AND THEIR FUNCTIONS

Although the *general* title of director, manager, or team member can be given to many people in an organisation, those people will carry out specific functions depending upon:

- their job title
- their job description
- the department in which they work
- the type of organisation in which they are employed.

Evidence Collection Point 6.4

For the rest of this chapter we are going to follow seven people who work in different departments of a typical manufacturing organisation through a fairly average day to find out what functions they carry out by looking at the key events in their day. You should be able to link these fairly easily with the work of each department you studied in Chapter 4 of this section.

As you read about the work each person carries out you will be asked various questions. When you have finished, then you should assemble all your answers and produce a final version, on a word-processor, which clearly shows the type of tasks carried out:

a by job holder

b by function.

Activity

What is the job role of each of the people listed below?

Design and production

- Zakar Malik,
  Maintenance Manager

- Shabbir Adam,
  Quality Controller

Personnel

- Paul Evans, Personnel Director

Finance

- Barbara Woodhead,
  Financial Manager

Administration

- Cheryl Wright, Administration Clerk

Sales and Marketing

- Martin Gold,
  Advertising Manager

Distribution

- Malcolm Obindi, Shipping Clerk

Design and production

Zakar Malik, Maintenance Manager

Zakar is on the night shift this week. This is usually quieter than the day shift and he hopes therefore to be able to think about some long-term issues. He manages to catch the Production Director before he starts his shift and outlines the problems of some of the equipment he and his team are expected to maintain – much of it is old and keeps breaking down. Zakar's team are skilled maintenance engineers, but because of the age of some of the equipment they have difficulty in repairing it. In some cases they have to take the machine out of action and wait for a new part to be sent from the suppliers. In recent months even this has not been possible in all cases because the parts required are now obsolete and Zakar estimates that at best only about 80 per cent of the equipment is in operation at any one time, whereas the target for the organisation is over 90 per cent.

As a result some of Zakar's team have become demoralised. They feel that they are always the ones who are blamed every time a machine breaks down – particularly by those operators who are keen to earn a production bonus and who are prevented from doing so. On one occasion the previous week a fight broke out between one of the operatives and one of Zakar's team and both men had to be disciplined.

Zakar and the Production Director discuss the possibility of a replacement programme for equipment. This would involve a certain sum of capital expenditure being set aside each year to replace a proportion of the equipment. The Production Director feels that this has to be a board of directors' decision. He asks Zakar to give him some detailed information about the type of programme he has in mind, together with the estimated costs. He will then prepare a report to present to the board of directors.

At 10 p.m. Zakar checks that all his team have arrived in on time. He checks the weekly roster of duties to see that everything is covered. One of his team phones in to say that he is ill. Zakar re-allocates his work as far as possible and notifies the absence to the Personnel Department by electronic mail.

At midnight Zakar makes a tour of the Production Department to check that everything is operating smoothly. He then spends some time getting together the figures he needs for the Production Director.

Evidence Collection Point 6.5

Zakar's role is that of a manager. From what you have just read, see if you can find examples where he was involved in each of the following:

a   plans for staffing his section
b   checking his staff
c   decision-making
d   problem-solving
e   disciplining staff
f   achieving targets.

List one example for each category.

Shabbir Adam, Quality Controller

Shabbir works as a quality controller. He has worked for the company for several years and started in the assembly line in Production. There are two main sections in the Production Department. In the first section the operators use the machines which make some of the parts of the cameras and camcorders made by the company. The remainder of the parts are bought in from outside suppliers. In the second section the parts are assembled into finished products. Shabbir works at the end of the production line, checking the work of the assemblers. It is his job to ensure that all the cameras are assembled correctly. He does this by random sampling (i.e. selecting a number of cameras at random and checking these carefully).

This morning there is a crisis – three cameras in sequence have not been assembled properly. Shabbir decides this is a serious problem and tells the supervisor immediately. He knows the supervisor may decide to halt production whilst the faults are investigated as the reputation of the company is too important to lose.

During his lunchtime Shabbir has an informal discussion with two other members of the quality control staff. They are being sent on a health and safety training course next week and have decided to share a car to save expenses.

During the afternoon, Shabbir is approached by a member of his production team. Several of the new camera cases

are blemished and the assembler isn't sure whether to continue using them or not. Shabbir examines the cases carefully and sees that they are well within the limits allowed. However, he thanks the assembler for bringing the matter to his attention.

Evidence Collection Point 6.6

As a quality controller Shabbir is a member of two teams, the quality control team and his own production team.

1   Find examples in the extract above where he:

a   makes a decision
b   is involved in problem-solving
c   is supporting other members of his team
d   is involved in achieving targets.

List one example for each category.

2   If the problem with the cases had been more serious, and Shabbir wasn't sure whether to continue using them or not, what should he have done and why?

Personnel

Paul Evans, Personnel Director

Paul begins the day with a meeting with the Personnel Manager and his deputy. It is held every week and involves a discussion on routine matters such as:

● number of vacancies
● a check on interview schedules organised
● a check on staff absences.

This week the group are concerned with the results of a recent survey which shows that in the Administration Department staff are leaving the company after an average of only ten months, whereas the retention target for the organisation as a whole is two years per employee. Paul argues that it is expensive to recruit and train staff and then to lose them quickly as all this money is wasted. He authorises the Personnel Manager to carry out a further investigation and to check the figures carefully before they discuss the matter further. He also informs him that from now on it will be company policy for anyone leaving the company to attend a short interview with personnel staff so that their reason for leaving can be assessed and recorded. The Personnel Manager agrees to put the necessary procedures into operation immediately.

Paul then attends the first interview for the replacement Purchasing Manager. It is part of the recruitment policy of the company that he attends all interviews for both manager and director positions.

Paul then has a discussion with the Personnel Manager and the Training Manager about their plans for putting on in-house training courses for all staff in stress management, assertiveness and personal effectiveness. He asks the Personnel Manager to find out details of how much this will cost before he agrees to put the plans into operation.

After lunch Paul is faced with a rather awkward situation. A cleaner has been caught twice trying to smuggle out some cleaning materials. On the first occasion she was given a verbal warning and on the second a written warning. She is protesting that her supervisor told her that she could have the cleaning materials and is threatening to go to the Press about what she says is harassment by the firm. Paul and the Personnel Manager meet her and her trade union representative to try to sort matters out. Paul refuses to make any decision until he speaks to the supervisor.

Mid-afternoon Paul attends a meeting of the board of directors and outlines a proposed new scheme for employees wanting to take early retirement. His paper is accepted and he is asked to put the plan into operation.

Evidence Collection Point 6.7

Paul is a director of the organisation. From the information you have just read, give one example in each case in which Paul has:

a made a policy decision
b been involved in recruitment
c been involved in disciplining a member of staff
d been involved in problem-solving
e been involved in monitoring targets.

Look back at page 173 to remind yourself of the duties a director carries out. How many of these was Paul involved in?

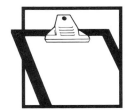

Activity

How many reasons can you think of for the high turnover of staff in the Administration Department, and what solutions can you offer? Discuss your ideas with your tutor.

Finance

Barbara Woodhead, Financial Manager

Barbara has a feeling that she has a hard day ahead. One of the wages clerks has been persistently late over the past few weeks. The Chief Cashier has spoken to him on several occasions but this has not solved the problem. The Chief Cashier has now reported the matter to Barbara. She calls the clerk into her room to find out if there are any special reasons she should know about. There are not. She tells the clerk that disciplinary action will be taken if his lateness continues.

Barbara then has a meeting with her Finance Director to talk about the suggested change from a manual to a computerised payroll system. She has prepared a report for him outlining the advantages that such a system will bring and emphasises in particular the amount of time the computerised system will save because it will produce figures accurately and quickly and enable any updating of the figures to be done quickly and easily.

She is concerned, however, about possible staff reaction. They have already said that they are worried about coping with the new skills involved, and are even more worried about the possibility of losing their jobs.

She wants, therefore, to arrange for a meeting at which all staff can be given full information about the plans and reassured that their jobs will not be affected. She also decides to meet her team leaders first, to discuss how and when the new system could be installed and the training which would be required.

After lunch Barbara has a difficult decision to make. She has been anxious for some time about the unpaid bills situation, particularly as the Finance Director has been under pressure from the Managing Director to do something about it. She spends some time looking at the sales ledgers which record customers' paid accounts and finds her suspicions confirmed that too many customers are being allowed too high levels of credit. She has a meeting with the Credit Controller and discusses the existing policy with him. At present all customers are allowed to run up bills to a maximum of £3000 before any stop is placed on their purchases.

Barbara feels that customers fall into different categories; i.e.:

- new and existing customers
- 'good' and 'slow' payers.

She also wants new cash limits to be imposed. She therefore prepares a report to the Finance Director proposing that:

- New customers should be allowed to run up bills of no more than £500.
- Existing customers of at least six months should be allowed a higher credit limit of up to £1500 if their past record shows them to be good payers. 'Slow' payers would be held to the £500 limit.

Evidence Collection Point 6.8

Barbara's role is that of a manager. From what you have just read, give at least one example where she:

a reported a decision she had made to her own boss
b was supporting a member of her staff
c was involved in problem-solving
d was disciplining a member of staff
e was setting targets.

Now look back at pages 173–174 to remind yourself of the duties a manager carries out. How many of these was Barbara involved with that day?

Activity

Why would staff be worried about losing their jobs if a computerised payroll system was installed? What

advantages would there be in Barbara giving them full information about the proposed changes, both from *her* point of view and that of the staff? Discuss your ideas with your tutor.

Administration

Cheryl Wright, Administration Clerk

Cheryl started work in the Administration Department two weeks ago after leaving college. She finds the directors rather frightening, but the rest of the staff are very friendly and her own supervisor, Joan Glover, very helpful and understanding. Joan Glover is the Office Manager.

Cheryl's first job every morning is to see to the incoming mail for the Administration Department. She follows Joan's instructions and:

- opens all correspondence with a letter opening machine (other than those marked 'personal' or 'private and confidential')
- date stamps it
- checks the enclosures and staples or pins them to the main document
- sorts out the mail marked 'urgent', 'private and confidential', 'personal'
- checks the envelopes to make sure they are empty
- delivers the mail to the right people.

She has been instructed that all the mail has to be delivered no later than 10.30 a.m. each day. Cheryl is also responsible for doing most of the photocopying for the department. She has learned most of the functions, and how to correct a paper jam. In case she forgets what to do there is a manual in a side pocket of the machine. Sometimes she finds some of the instructions written by the staff almost impossible to read. She knows it is important to check what they want first, rather than waste dozens of copies.

Cheryl then sees that one of her colleagues, Mark, is overwhelmed with a tremendous amount of filing to do. Mark was off sick earlier in the week and is trying to catch up a backlog of work. Because Cheryl hasn't as much photocopying to do as usual, she decides to help Mark. The files are stored in filing cabinets and are in alphabetical order. There is a folder in which to record the dates when any files are borrowed and also the dates when they are returned. Cheryl copes quite well until the Marketing Director's secretary arrives in a hurry and demands a file quickly. When Cheryl looks in the cabinets the file is missing! She checks the book and soon discovers that it was borrowed this morning by the Marketing Director himself. She tells his secretary who goes off to track it down herself.

After lunch Cheryl undertakes some routine tasks. On several occasions the telephone rings. Cheryl knows how to answer correctly and how to pass calls on promptly or take a message if the person isn't available. She knows this is important to give a good impression of the company. She also knows how important it is to follow up messages. Last week a junior member of staff had placed an important message on the desk of the Office Manager, telling her that a meeting that evening was cancelled. The junior never checked before he went home that the Office Manager had seen the message. The following day he was in serious trouble. Joan Glover had gone straight from a meeting in the Managing Director's office to the second meeting – 26 miles away – only to find out that it had been cancelled.

Evidence Collection Point 6.9

Cheryl's role is that of a team member. From what you have read, find one example in each case where Cheryl has:

a made a decision
b solved a problem
c supported a colleague
d checked before taking action
e been involved in customer service.

Activity

1 Do you think Cheryl was right to volunteer to help Mark when she found she had some spare time, or should she have checked with her supervisor first? Discuss with your tutor occasions when *each* type of action would be suitable and when it would not.

2 If you made a serious error, such as not checking that an important message had been received, how would you feel about being reprimanded by your supervisor or manager? How would you respond? Discuss your answers *as a group* and with your tutor. What action should the junior employee have taken in this situation?

Sales and Marketing

Martin Gold, Advertising Manager

At 12 noon Martin arrives in the office having just got back from attending a conference in London on the latest developments in video presentations. He has dictated some notes on to his cassette on his way back from the conference and gives them to his secretary to sort out into a report for the Marketing Director.

He has to deal with a crisis almost immediately. The Quality Assurance officer has just discovered that a batch of 500 cameras despatched a month ago is faulty. Some of these will be in retailers' shops and some will have been sold. Martin decides to place adverts in the local press and the trade press to recall as many as possible. Anyone who returns a camera is to be given a replacement plus free film for six months to compensate them for the inconvenience.

Martin then has a working lunch with his advertising assistant plus the Public Relations officers from two large stores to discuss arrangements for in-store promotions of the company's new camcorder and camera range. After lunch, Martin asks his assistant to check the current advertisement rates being charged by the national newspapers and the relevant trade journals. He is worried that the department will overspend on advertising this quarter.

Early in the afternoon Martin discusses with his team some quotations he has received from a new firm of printers. Their prices are far lower than those of the printers normally used by the department. The team discuss whether or not to try out the new firm, although some anxiety is expressed about possible reduction in quality and reliability. Martin suggests that a representative from the printers be asked to come to one of the team meetings to make a presentation to them.

Martin then checks through some draft advertisements prepared by members of his team. He also reads a report prepared by the market research officer who has been asked to investigate customer reaction to the television commercial advertising the organisation's new range of cameras. First reaction is favourable and Martin therefore lets his advertising team know the good news.

Finally Martin has to spend some time with a member of his team who is upset because her son is ill in hospital. The woman is a very hard worker and Martin realises that she is under stress. He tells her he will lighten her workload so that she can cope more easily, and to take the next two days off to get her personal life more in order.

Evidence Collection Point 6.10

Martin is also a manager. From what you have read, find at least one example in each case of where he:

a made a decision
b solved a problem
c gave information to his staff
d was involved in achieving targets
e was involved in dealing with people from outside the organisation.

Distribution

Malcolm Obindi, Shipping Clerk

Malcolm has worked for the organisation for the past five years. He started in the administration section and moved to distribution two years ago. His job is complex and only now does he feel confident of all the procedures he has to follow. Basically, because the company exports many of its goods, Malcolm has to arrange the transport for these to their overseas destinations. Most go by sea, but some urgent items are sent by air. There are complicated documents to complete, to satisfy the customs authorities, and Malcolm also has to insure all the items so that the company will receive payment if they are damaged in transit.

If a large consignment is due to leave then Malcolm may even work on Sundays – when the lorries leave for the docks – to ensure that everything is in order and the paperwork is correct. He knows that if a delivery is late this can cause severe problems for the company.

The morning's work is fairly routine. However, near lunchtime a crisis occurs. A film company have agreed to purchase a large number of specialist cameras provided that they can be shipped to North Africa, where they are filming, no later than next Wednesday. A large order is at stake and Malcolm sets to work to try all his contacts to see what can be done. He rings around his contacts. His cheapest shipping agent cannot help until Wednesday morning – which is cutting it too fine. By 2 p.m. he has solved the problem and arranged for the order to be air-freighted to its destination on Tuesday afternoon. Even though the cost is rather more, at least the goods will arrive on time.

However, when he rings one of the production staff he is told that as the goods won't be packed until Tuesday lunchtime they won't be ready in time. Desperate, he refers the problem to the Distribution Manager. Just before he leaves, he is told that the problem is solved. The Distribution Manager talked to the Production Manager and, because of the importance of this consignment, the goods will be ready for collection on Monday afternoon.

Evidence Collection Point 6.11

Malcolm is a team member in that he is a member of the Distribution staff but mainly works on his own as he operates in a specialised area.

1 Give one example in each case where he:

- was involved in problem-solving
- was involved in decision-making
- helped to achieve targets.

2 Can you say why Malcolm did not try to solve the production problem himself but decided to refer it to his boss instead?

3 Add two more examples of where it would be unwise for a junior employee to try to solve a problem on his or her own.

Evidence Assignment 6D

All the people whose working day has just been described have faced certain problems. Some of them were solved immediately. Others were not. Practise your own decision-making skills by deciding what steps you think should now be taken to solve the particular problems outlined below.

1 Paul receives a phone call from a reporter on the local newspaper who says that he has heard that one of the female cleaning staff is being victimised. How do you think Paul should deal with him?

2 Barbara receives a phone call from an irate customer who is protesting very strongly about not being allowed a higher limit of credit. He has not dealt with the firm before but – according to him – he was prepared to give a very large order. He gives the names of several other firms with whom he has done business in the past and asks Barbara to check with them whether or not he is a good payer. However, if Barbara allows him the higher limit she realises she may be opening the door to similar requests from other new customers who might not be such good payers. What should she do?

3 Zakar is continuing to have trouble with ill-feeling between his maintenance staff and the production staff over the breakdown in the machinery. What can he do to improve the situation?

4 Martin and his team listen to a presentation made by the firm of printers anxious to be given some business. They are quite impressed with what they hear as their prices are lower but are a bit reluctant to stop dealing with their existing firm of printers who have given them good service in the past. What should Martin do?

5 Cheryl's biggest problem is when she is involved with the filing system. She knows that no-one should be allowed to borrow a file without having it recorded but one or two senior members of the staff insist on doing so and she is too nervous to stop them. Is there anything she can do?

6 Shabbir's departmental manager is obviously concerned about the faults found in the cameras. He discusses the matter with Shabbir and questions his method of random sampling. He asks him why all goods should not be checked. If Shabbir agrees, the cost will be immense; if he does not, and more faults are found, he might be in trouble. What should he do?

7 Malcolm is used to claiming overtime at double time when he has to work on a Sunday for one or two hours to supervise a shipment. However, the company is now trying to cut costs and a memo has been received from the Financial Manager to say that all weekend working has been suspended for the time being. An important shipment is due to leave next Sunday. What should he do?

Evidence Project

Arrange to interview two people who work in different job roles and undertake different functions in a commercial organisation. These may be people you know personally, or are known by your family – or you could undertake this project whilst you are on work experience. You can either make notes during the interview or record them on audio-cassette.

Prepare a list of questions which will enable you to:

1 Write a description of the key tasks they carry out in an average day.

2 State clearly how they are involved in:

  a decision-making
  b problem-solving
  c setting targets
  d achieving targets

3 Identify which decisions they can make alone and which they must refer to other people.

4 State the type of targets which affect their work and how progress towards these is monitored.

5 Highlight two recent problems with which they have been involved and the way in which these have been solved.

Prepare a report on your interview on your word-processor, with clear headings. Prepare a suitable front and back cover and bind your finished report so that it looks professional. You may also wish to keep your audio recording with your portfolio of work.

Evidence Checkpoint

When you have carried out all the tasks in this chapter you will have sufficient evidence for Element 2.3. Are you sure it is complete, filed neatly and cannot be done to a higher standard?

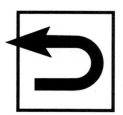

Revision Test

True or false?

1 All directors have a seat on the board of directors.

2 Managers are more senior than directors.

3 All staff, no matter what their role, have to make decisions.

4 A good manager will involve his staff in setting targets which affect them.

5 Non-executive directors are employed full-time by the organisation.

Complete the blanks

6 Two targets which could be set for the sales and marketing department are .... and ....

7 The most senior role in a private organisation is usually occupied by the ....

8 Two differences between managers and directors are .... and ....

9 An advantage of group decision-making is that . ...

10 Two functions of the board of directors are ....and ....

Short answer questions

11 You work in the sales and marketing department processing orders. Give two examples of problems you might face – one of which you would need to refer to your manager.

12 Give three ways in which you could improve your performance as a team member.

13 State three decisions a personnel manager may make in the course of a day.

14 Why do you think it is important for a manager to be supportive of his or her staff? Give two examples of occasions when this might be necessary.

15 State three targets which might have to be achieved by a production manager and his staff.

Write a short paragraph to show you clearly understand each of the following terms:

16 Job role.

17 Targets.

18 Director.

19 Team member.

20 Manager.

chapter **7** FINANCIAL TRANSACTIONS AND DOCUMENTS

Learning Objectives

This chapter explains the various types of financial transactions that occur in business. It also describes the documents needed to record the transactions and explains how these should be completed.

After studying this chapter you should be able to:

* explain the reasons for financial recording in business organisations, and why documents must be completed correctly

* describe purchases transactions and how to fill in purchases documents

* describe sales transactions and how to fill in sales documents

* describe payment transactions and how to fill in payments documents

* describe receipts transactions and how to fill in receipts documents

* explain security checks for payment documents.

The first thing to realise is that you are involved in **transactions** every day! If you buy a can of Coke from a shop you complete a transaction because you *pay* some money and you *receive* the can. When you go to the cinema you *pay* the admission fee and are then *allowed to watch* the film. So a transaction occurs when a person pays some money in return for goods or services.

∙ REASONS FOR RECORDING ∙ FINANCIAL TRANSACTIONS

When a transaction takes place in business a **record** will nearly always be made. This can be either on paper, on computer or both. The main reasons for this are so that:

* there is evidence of the transaction
* annual accounts can be produced
* security measures can be taken
* business performance can be monitored.

Keeping financial records

All businesses, whether large or small, have to keep accurate and up-to-date financial records. The reasons for this are as follows:

* To provide a permanent record which can be referred to in the future if anything needs to be checked. You cannot rely on people's memories!
* To ensure that bills are paid and debts are collected.
* So that the profit or loss figure can be worked out. This shows how well (or badly) the business is doing. Public limited companies have a legal duty to inform their shareholders about the performance of the business.

- To provide the Inland Revenue with information. This enables them to assess the **income tax** for the owner(s) of small businesses (sole traders and partnerships) and **corporation tax** for limited companies.
- To enable the Customs and Excise office to assess the **VAT** owed – with the exception of businesses who deal only in exempt goods or whose turnover is under the limit required for VAT registration.

This chapter describes and explains the use of all the main types of financial transaction records.

DID YOU KNOW?

Most people don't know how they spend their money. There is a constant cry of 'I had £10 yesterday but don't know where it's gone!'

Could you write down now how much spending money you received last month? The answer is probably 'yes'. Could you also write down exactly what you spent it on and on which day? Probably not! If you were a business you would *have* to record this type of information. The only way to do this is to record things *as they happen*.

Evidence Collection Point 7.1

Keep a record of all the money you receive and pay out during a week. Include:

- how much
- when
- who gave you the money *or* who you paid it to
- why the transactions took place.

In addition, keep all the receipts you obtain. This will help you to understand the process of record-keeping in business transactions.

Write the information out as a list with the following headings:

Date   Reason   Received from/   Amount
                  paid to

You will need to record the information at least once a day. Even then you may struggle to remember details. (We

think this is one of the hardest ECPs in this book– and challenge you to be able to do it purely because you need to persevere and be methodical!)

Producing annual accounts

All businesses have to produce annual accounts so that tax can be assessed. Large businesses have accounts departments to look after all their financial records and reports. People in small businesses either do their own accounts or employ the services of professional accountants. All annual accounts have to be approved by a qualified registered accountant. However, limited companies have a legal requirement to have their accounts **audited**. This means that all transactions are checked in detail by an auditor.

Activity

Financial accountants use several special words which you will need to know. Look at Figure 7.1 to see how many you know already. How many of the terms refer to annual accounts? Try to decide before you read any further.

Types of annual accounts

The balance sheet and the profit and loss accounts together are known as the **annual accounts**. All businesses have to produce their accounts so that their tax can be assessed. Sole traders and partners in a partnership are assessed for income tax, which is paid twice a year. Private and public limited companies have to pay corporation tax. In both cases the amount of tax due will depend on the net profit, which is the profit minus any expenses the business has incurred.

Financial records are used to produce the annual accounts as shown in Figure 7.2. Once the profit (or loss) is known, then this is transferred to the balance sheet.

Financial year	Businesses summarise their financial situation on the same date each year. The date is known as the **end of the financial year**.		its customers is an asset. Customers who owe money are called **debtors**.
Turnover	The total amount of sales income for a financial year.	**Liability**	This is the money which the business owes to its suppliers or other organisations. These are called **creditors**. Credit is used to describe a situation where goods have been received, or a service given, and there is a delay before the account is paid. If the company has borrowed money from a financial institution then this organisation is also a creditor until the money has been repaid.
Transaction	Every time a product or service is bought or sold a **transaction** takes place.		
Purchases	Businesses buy goods and services and must pay for these. Some goods will be for their own use and some for resale.		
Profit and loss account	A summary of all the transactions which take place during a financial year, for both income and expenditure. The difference between income and expenditure is known as **profit** or **loss.**		
		Balance sheet	A summary of all the assets and liabilities of a business at the end of a financial year.
Gross profit	The difference between the cost price of stock and the selling price.	**Value Added Tax**	VAT is one way in which the government raises money. When most goods or services are sold VAT is paid at a fixed percentage of the selling price. This includes transactions between one business and another. Some goods and services have no VAT levied on them. These are either **exempt** from VAT (e.g. a dentist's treatment) or are **zero-rated** because they are considered to be essential goods (e.g. food).
Net profit	The amount left out of the gross profit after all the expenses have been deducted (heating, rent, wages etc.).		
Asset	This can be money held as cash or in the bank. The term is also used for anything of value such as stock, buildings or equipment. Finally, any money owed to the business by		

Figure 7.1 *Terms used in finance*

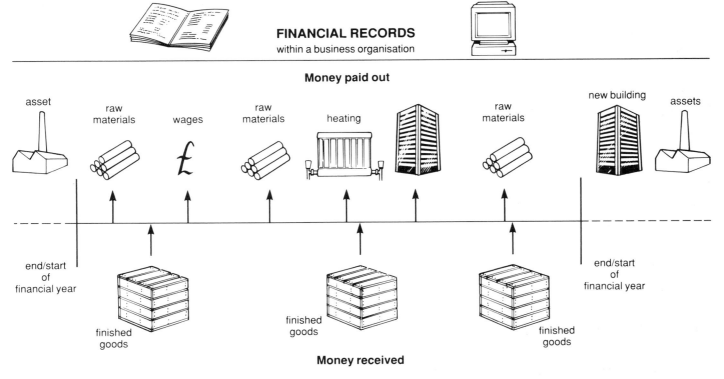

Figure 7.2 *Financial records must be kept for annual financial events*

Activity

If Tesco had not kept a record of *all* the expenses it incurred the company would have paid *more* corporation tax than necessary.

1 Why is this the case?

2 Suggest ten types of expenses Tesco would have listed.

Evidence Collection Point 7.2

1 Write a short paragraph *in your own words* which explains what is meant by the following terms. Do this *without* referring back to earlier pages in this chapter!

a transaction
b financial year
c turnover
d profit and loss account
e balance sheet
f annual accounts.

2 A company loses a file which records the purchases and sales transactions for a week. What effect would this have on the annual accounts if the information was not found?

3 A sole trader has a gross profit at the end of the year of £32 000. He has spent £4000 on rent, £3500 on a van, £500 on electricity, gas and rates and £350 on his telephone, advertising and stationery. What is his net profit for the year?

Security

Another important reason for recording transactions is **security**. When money or goods change hands mistakes can be made and, unfortunately, there may be opportunities for unscrupulous people to steal. In addition, businesses may attempt to cheat the Inland Revenue or other authorities out of money which ought to be paid.

The main reasons for security measures are:

- to have information available for inspection by officials
- to ensure that people with authority carry out or authorise the transaction (this is particularly important when cash is involved)
- to enable errors to be traced.

If any problems occur the records will be examined to discover exactly what happened. When cash is being handled then this can be vital, as money cannot easily be traced. With cheques and credit cards it is usually easy to find out where the money has come from and where it has gone to.

Activity

As a group, decide your answers to the following questions:

1 If you return faulty goods to a shop you will be asked to show your receipt. Why do you think this is so?

2 How would you check back to see if a cheque transaction really did take place? What steps do you think you would have to take?

Fraud and theft

Fraud is a sophisticated form of theft. As different methods of payment, such as credit cards, have become available, so opportunities for fraud and theft have increased. A person using a stolen credit card is an obvious example. All major banks have special departments which try to minimise this type of problem. For example, it is now possible to monitor all credit card transactions immediately they take place and look for any unusual patterns of spending (see page 210). This can help to catch a thief red-handed.

Evidence Assignment 7A

Tom Field is a plumber who works as a sole trader. He is often paid in cash by customers, not all of whom ask for a receipt. Also, when Tom buys materials from the plumbers' merchant, he pays in cash and sometimes loses the receipt.

Tom's wife is worried that at the end of the year there may be a problem as he may be unable to persuade the tax authorities that his annual accounts are accurate.

You know Tom well. Write him a letter to his home address – 24 Sutton Road, Hightown, HG4 9TG – on a word-processor and explain the importance of keeping records of all his transactions.

Monitoring business performance

You already know that the profit and loss accounts and balance sheets are produced at the end of the financial year. They are important for the tax authorities but are not much use in helping to run the business on a day-to-day basis. This is because both documents are *historic*, which means that they deal only with transactions that took place in the past. There is not much point in knowing that the business made a loss for four months last year if this information was only discovered last week! It is therefore important that information from financial transactions is examined regularly to find out how well the business is doing.

The most common way of doing this is to have a **budget**. A budget is a financial plan. Forecasts are made for income and expenditure on a weekly or monthly basis. Actual income and expenditure are checked against the budget. Budgets are normally split between **revenue** items and **capital** items. For example, a catering manager may be allowed to spend £12 000 on food in a year and £5000 in the same year on capital items. These could include a new microwave oven or a chilled food display rack.

The catering manager will almost certainly divide the food budget into a monthly or weekly amount. A record will then be kept for each period, by adding up all the amounts from the orders that have been placed. If the total for one week exceeds the budgeted amount then less may have to be ordered the following week. If your refectory serves beans on toast all next week, this may be the reason!

Evidence Collection Point 7.3

Copy out the form in Figure 7.3 and use it to work out a budget for yourself for the next week.

Name				
Date	Income		Expenditure	
	Plan	Actual	Plan	Actual
Mon				
Tues				
Wed				
Thurs				
Fri				
Sat				
Sun				
TOTAL				

Figure 7.3 *Form for a personal budget*

Write in the date for each day you are going to keep a record in the left-hand column. Then write in any income you expect to receive in the days on which you expect to receive it. Finally, write down how much you plan to spend each day in the planned expenditure column.

Now for the hard part! On each day of the week write down how much you receive and spend in the appropriate spaces. Then compare your *planned* income and expenditure with your *actual* income and expenditure at the end of the week.

Finally, write a short report on how well your plans matched with reality! Include a paragraph on how easy or otherwise you found this exercise. Did you struggle at the end of each day to remember how much you had spent? Think how much easier it would have been if you had kept a record for each transaction *at the time you made it*. Or did you simply have problems 'keeping to your budget' – and spending *only* the amount you planned to spend?

· COMPLETING DOCUMENTS ·

Later in this chapter, and during the project which follows, you will be completing several types of document yourself. When you do so you must make sure that the information is *complete*, *accurate* and written as *neatly as possible*.

Ensuring documents are complete

It is no use half-completing a document, as someone else has to go back to do the rest of the work for you – in which case that person might as well have done it in the first place! Most financial documents that are incomplete are useless – a cheque without a signature or date, an invoice without all the items included, a paying-in slip with the cheques omitted. You may think these are obvious. What are less obvious are such items as delivery charges and discounts, yet without these the document is both incomplete and inaccurate.

To help you, most financial documents have headings and spaces where information must be inserted. Do check carefully that nothing relevant has been missed out.

Accuracy

When you fill in financial documents accuracy is vital. One incorrect figure or even a decimal point in the wrong place can cause a major problem. Think what would happen if a clerk processing an order for ready-mixed concrete added an extra nought to the quantity ordered – there is a lot of difference between 10 cubic metres of concrete and 100 cubic metres! Or, if he or she filled in the wrong address of a customer, the results could be very embarrassing.

Sometimes, documents are designed to provide duplicate information so that errors can be spotted. For example, when you write a cheque you have to write the amount of money in words *and* figures, and they must match. If they do not, the bank will not accept it. On orders there is often space for a description of the goods required *and* a catalogue or serial number. Even though these safeguards exist, it does not mean that people who complete the documents can be any less careful.

Writing neatly

This may seem to be so basic you wonder why it is included now. After all, you have done your GCSEs and are taking a qualification which will lead to either higher education or employment, so why are we telling you to write clearly? The answer is simple: if you don't, people will not be able to read the information – and whilst they may be able to guess at the words *it is impossible to guess at figures as there are no clues to help!*

If you write unclearly, and someone copies this information on to another document, a disaster could occur. Imagine the situation where you are asked to pass on a message about the balance in a friend's account. *You* write down £17.80 but it looks more like £77.80. Your friend happily writes out a cheque for £60 and then finds the account is overdrawn at the end of the month and the bank has charged £15 because of this!

Checking

When a document has been completed, it is important that the information which has been inserted is *checked*. Go back over each item carefully and check it for accuracy. Some people find it difficult to check their own work because they are likely to assume that they did it properly the first time. A useful tip is to check the form in a different sequence from the way it was filled in – or check it out loud with someone else.

In some business situations where large amounts of money are involved one or more people may have to check that a document is correct. When you start work or are on work experience, people may ask you to complete a document and take it to them for checking. Also, if you are nervous or uncertain, it is much better to ask someone to check your work rather than risk an embarrassing error. People will respect you for this provided that you build up confidence to do things on your own eventually.

Evidence Collection Point 7.4

What do you think would happen if the following errors were made when documents were completed? Start by discussing the possibilities *as a group*, then with your tutor. Finally summarise your answers on a word-processor.

1 An order form is sent out with two items missing.

2 An invoice requesting payment is sent to the wrong customer.

3 A pay slip shows the wrong amount for overtime – £8 instead of £80.

4 A cheque is sent without being signed.

5 A receipt has the wrong year in the date.

Reliability of data

One particular financial record can be used for many purposes. An order form, for example, may have several copies:

● one for the supplier
● one for the customer
● one for retention in the purchasing department
● one to check goods received against the order
● one for the finance department to authorise payment.

Documents may therefore be used by several people at different times for different reasons. An error made when the original document is completed can lead to a whole series of problems which would be very hard to put right later.

QUALPRINT

Most of the transactions and documents described in this chapter will be related to a *fictitious* business called Qualprint, a printing company which was set up four years ago by Chris Gaston. As well as printing posters, invitations, brochures etc. in response to customers' orders, Qualprint also has a retail counter which sells stationery and similar items.

This chapter explains all the financial transactions with which Qualprint is involved. You will also be referred to blank examples of the documents used. These are located at the end of this book. *Please don't write on them!* Your tutor will help you to take photocopies so that you can practise completing them later. Most of the opportunities you will have for completing documents for your portfolio are given in the project in the next chapter.

• PURCHASE TRANSACTIONS •

All businesses must buy goods and services in the following categories.

Materials

These can take the form of items which go into a manufacturing process to be converted into products – known as **raw materials**. They can also be items such as stationery and cleaning products which are used in the running of the business. Such items are called **consumables.** All these goods are ordered using an **order form**.

Another type of item which a business can purchase is capital equipment. This category includes production equipment, buildings, office furniture, etc. These are known as **capital items** and special purchasing systems are used.

This chapter is concerned with materials which are purchased and used on a regular basis.

Services

Businesses ask other businesses to provide specific services. Examples of services include window cleaning, machine maintenance and decorating. Services are normally 'ordered' by means of a **contract**. This is a legal agreement in which details of the service are written down (e.g. how many windows should be cleaned and how often) as well as the amount to be paid. Normally both supplier and customer sign the contract.

Further information on contracts is to be found in Chapter 5 (contracts of employment) and Chapter 12 (contracts of sale).

DID YOU KNOW?

If companies are buying an expensive item then they may ask for several **quotations** from different suppliers which state the price at which the goods can be purchased and any discounts offered. Instead of a quotation a supplier *may* issue an **estimate**. This is less precise than a quotation.

A buyer may advertise that certain goods or a particular service are wanted and ask people to submit **tenders** (offers) stating at which price they are prepared to provide the service (or supply the goods). The buyer will have a closing date for tenders to be received and, on that day, will open them and choose the best one.

DID YOU KNOW?

Very expensive purchases of capital equipment may also be agreed in a contract. A contract may contain a **penalty clause**. This is a statement which normally says that if the goods are not delivered or the service is not performed by a certain date then the buyer has the right to pay less than the agreed sum. If a company is paying a building contractor to erect a new warehouse, for instance, it may be critical that the agreed completion date is met – in which case a penalty clause would put pressure on the builder to keep to schedule.

Wages

Employees of a business can also be considered to provide a service. In return they are paid wages. (See Chapter 5, for employer and employee rights and responsibilities.) In this case the document involved is the **contract of employment**. When an employer agrees to pay someone a wage, they also commit themselves to paying National Insurance contributions (if these apply) and probably pension contributions. National Insurance and pensions are covered in Chapter 3.

Activity

1 Make a note of what you see written on ten large vans or lorries you spot on the road. Write down what type of goods they are or may be carrying. Can you guess the type of businesses to which they will be delivering (e.g. a supermarket, wholesaler, factory etc.)?

2 Look in your local newspaper and see if you can find any examples of requests for tenders. These are usually placed in or near the classified advertisement section.

Remember that when goods are delivered this is part of a transaction. Each stage of the transaction will be recorded.

Evidence Collection Point 7.5

1 *As a group*, compile two lists of materials which Qualprint *could* purchase. In the first list include as

many items as possible which might be bought for use in production. The second list is for consumable items. Use brainstorming for this exercise.

2 *On your own*, write down as many types of services as you can which a business might purchase. Compare your list with your fellow students' lists and see if they have thought of anything you have not.

3 *As a group*, discuss why businesses might wish to buy in a service rather than do the work themselves. For instance, should Chris Gaston decorate his office or should he pay a decorator to do it? How many reasons can you think of?

Make a good copy of all your lists and your answers to question 3 on a word-processor.

DID YOU KNOW?

Many companies offer discounts to businesses to persuade them to place an order.

- **Trade discount** is given either as an allowance to people in the same type of business or because the buyer is placing a large order.
- **Prompt payment cash discount** is a percentage off the price given for paying on time. The term 5% *one month* means that a buyer can deduct 5 per cent from the price if he pays within one month.
- **Cash discount** is a percentage off the price for immediate payment. The term *3 per cent cash discount* means that he can deduct 3 per cent from the price of the goods if he pays cash or cheque there and then.

The buyer can calculate how much he will have to pay by:

1 taking the total price (excluding VAT) and subtracting any discounts
2 adding on VAT at the current rate to the *discounted* price
3 adding on VAT to the quoted delivery charge
4 adding together the totals obtained in stages 2 and 3.

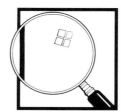

Evidence Assignment 7B

Chris Gaston is thinking of buying two new computers. He has obtained catalogues from major office equipment suppliers he knows about and has compared:

- the type and range of goods offered by each supplier
- the prices and discounts available
- delivery times and charges
- length of warranty or guarantee
- servicing or maintenance offered.

He has now decided on the model of computer he wishes to buy and has narrowed his search down to three companies.

- Computalk, situated locally, is a new company. They want payment in full with order. The price of each computer from them will be £1450 + VAT. They do not offer a discount but there are no delivery charges. Chris has heard mixed reports about this company.
- Data Supplies is situated 200 miles away but has been in business for many years. They are quoting £1550 + VAT. They offer 6% discount on all orders over £3000. Delivery charges are £20. Chris will have one month to pay if he orders from them. Chris has no information on this company's reputation at all.
- Rainbow Computers is a large company situated 20 miles away. It has been in business for the past three years but has an excellent reputation. Their quote is £1600 + VAT less 5% cash discount. Delivery charges are £10. If Chris buys from them he must pay immediately if he wants to gain the discount. Otherwise he can pay the full price at any time in the next 3 months.

1 What are the advantages to Chris of buying from a local company?

2 Why do you think Chris is concerned about how long each company has been in business and its reputation?

3 Calculate the price Chris would have to pay if he bought from each supplier.

4 Decide which supplier you would use and give reasons for your decision.

PURCHASING DOCUMENTS

There are three main documents involved in the purchasing process.

1 First of all, an order is placed by completing an **order form**. This is sent to the supplier, normally through the post.
2 When the materials are received, a **goods received note** (GRN), is completed and passed to the accounts department.
3 Finally an **invoice** is received from the supplier requesting payment for the goods.

DID YOU KNOW?

When goods are delivered by the supplier they are usually accompanied by a **delivery note**. If the goods are sent by another form of transport, (e.g. by rail or by haulage company) the supplier will send the buyer an **advice note** so that the buyer knows that the goods are on their way.

The order form

Qualprint wants to buy a special type of card on which to print wedding invitations. They have dealt with the supplier – Business Supplies Ltd – for some time and therefore know exactly what and how to order. The buyer completes a Qualprint order form and includes details of exactly what type of card is required. The price is checked with the catalogue. Although no money will change hands at this stage, the buyer needs to be sure of the cost of the materials being ordered.

All Qualprint's order forms are completed with a unique serial number for easy reference. The order is sent to the supplier and a copy kept by Qualprint, in case there are any queries later.

When order forms are sent, this is taken as a firm commitment that the goods are required. Occasionally people send order forms to suppliers and then change their mind, but this is rare. Goods may also be ordered by telephone in an emergency but an order form is then sent as soon as possible as confirmation. If a fax is used, orders can be sent immediately.

The latest system of ordering goods is by computer using **electronic data interchange** (EDI). This is discussed in Chapter 3. Private individuals may use their credit cards to order goods by telephone and give the supplier their name, address, card number and expiry date. This is a reasonably secure system, especially if the goods are sent to the address associated with the card. Credit cards are described in more detail on page 210.

DID YOU KNOW?

Many businesses issue printed price lists *separately* from their catalogues. This means that a new catalogue will not have to be produced every time there are price changes, as this would be too expensive.

Most price lists are shown in page order to match the catalogue, but the buyer must be very careful to:

● check the correct catalogue number in the price list against the one shown in the catalogue, as the numbers will vary for different colours and sizes
● write the number accurately when completing the order, because transposing the numbers will mean the wrong goods arrive.

Evidence Collection Point 7.6

Figure 7.4 shows an illustration of Qualprint's order form.

1 List the sections completed at Qualprint. Explain in each case why the information is needed.

2 If the unit price is £10, calculate how much the order is worth in total.

3 Obtain a computer supplies catalogue and price list *and* a blank Qualprint order form. Order the following goods for Chris Gaston on order number 122/934:

● 1 disk box to hold at least twenty 3 1/2 inch disks
● 6 boxes of 3 1/2 inch high-density disks
● 2 mouse mats.

QUALPRINT LTD.
22 CARNEI WAY
GLENDALE
NEWSHIRE
FE1 8CA

Tel: 032 745612   **ORDER**   VAT Reg. No. 680/73842/88

To: Business Supplies Ltd   Date: 15 October 199–
     14 Docklands Parade
     GLENDALE   Order No.: 121/934
     FE2 8DJ

Please supply:

QUANTITY	DESCRIPTION	REF. NO.	UNIT PRICE
2 packs	A4 Superlux Card, White	SL/7	£10

Delivery: AS SOON AS POSSIBLE

Signed: *L. Gaston*

Figure 7.4

Goods received note (GRN)

This is completed by the person who receives the goods when they are delivered. He or she checks the description of the goods given on the packages or containers. The quantity delivered is also noted. If there is any doubt then the items may have to be counted. All the items are checked against the delivery note as the GRN is completed.

The GRN is a record of what has *actually* been delivered. The person receiving it may not know what was on the original order. The GRN will be checked by the accounts staff against the order before payment is authorised.

Today many large businesses produce their GRNs on computers. The GRNs can then either be printed out and sent to the accounts department *or* the information can be accessed direct by the accounts department on their own computer screens. The accounts department check the GRN against the invoice when this is received.

An illustration of a GRN produced on computer is shown in Figure 7.5 (on page 200).

Problems with deliveries

Problems arise if goods are damaged or missing, or if the wrong goods have been sent in error. This is why it is important that the goods are unpacked, counted and carefully checked.

Missing goods

Goods may be omitted because they were out of stock when ordered or because the firm forgot to send them. Out-of-stock goods will either be marked as 'to follow' on the delivery note (i.e. they will be delivered later) or noted as 'discontinued'. Sometimes a firm will substitute another similar item for a discontinued line.

If the omission is because of a mistake on the part of the supplier then there will be a discrepancy between the number listed on the delivery note (which will match the order) and the actual number received.

The fact that the GRN will show a difference between the order and the number delivered will enable the accounts department to ensure nothing is paid for which wasn't received. It will also mean that substitute items can be inspected to see if these are suitable. The supplier should be contacted to find out what has happened to any goods that are missing if they are not marked as 'to follow'.

Additional goods

A mistake by a packer may mean goods are received which were not ordered. These should be returned to the supplier. They will show up on the GRN but *not* on the original order.

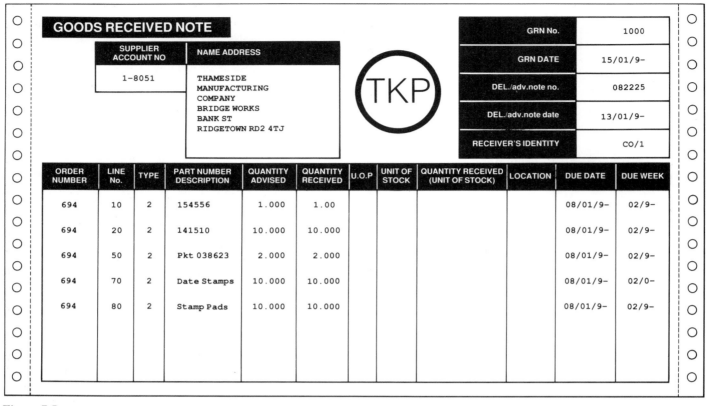

GOODS RECEIVED NOTE

SUPPLIER ACCOUNT NO	NAME ADDRESS
1-8051	THAMESIDE MANUFACTURING COMPANY BRIDGE WORKS BANK ST RIDGETOWN RD2 4TJ

TKP

GRN No.	1000
GRN DATE	15/01/9-
DEL./adv.note no.	082225
DEL./adv.note date	13/01/9-
RECEIVER'S IDENTITY	CO/1

ORDER NUMBER	LINE No.	TYPE	PART NUMBER DESCRIPTION	QUANTITY ADVISED	QUANTITY RECEIVED	U.O.P	UNIT OF STOCK	QUANTITY RECEIVED (UNIT OF STOCK)	LOCATION	DUE DATE	DUE WEEK
694	10	2	154556	1.000	1.00					08/01/9-	02/9-
694	20	2	141510	10.000	10.000					08/01/9-	02/9-
694	50	2	Pkt 038623	2.000	2.000					08/01/9-	02/9-
694	70	2	Date Stamps	10.000	10.000					08/01/9-	02/0-
694	80	2	Stamp Pads	10.000	10.000					08/01/9-	02/9-

Figure 7.5

Incorrect goods

If the wrong goods are received then these too must be returned unused. Again these will be easy to identify because the description on the GRN will not match that on the order.

Damaged or faulty goods

The supplier should be notified immediately and there will normally be no problem exchanging these. On some GRN forms there is a space for the goods inwards clerk to note any damage found.

Goods ordered in error

These are the biggest problem as the supplier is under no legal obligation to take them back! Much will depend on the relationship between the two companies – in many cases a supplier will exchange them rather than risk losing a customer.

Evidence Collection Point 7.7

Figure 7.6 shows the GRN form completed at Qualprint.

1 List the sections which have been completed by the person receiving the goods.

2 Why do you consider that all GRNs must be signed?

3 Check the GRN against the order on page 199. List any differences you find. How could these have occurred and what should Chris Gaston do?

4 Your friend works for a company where nobody bothers to complete GRNs – he says there is no point. You disagree. Give four advantages of using GRNs rather than simply checking the delivery note against the order.

5 The goods you received from the computer supplies company are complete and undamaged. On a blank Qualprint GRN form, record the goods inwards against GRN number 1073.

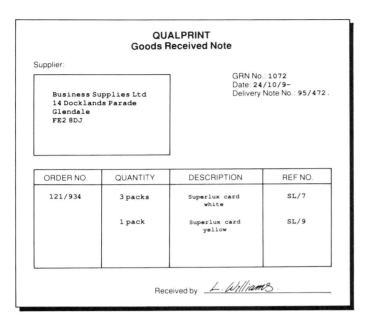

Figure 7.6

Purchase invoice

After the goods have been delivered an invoice is sent to the buyer, usually by post. The invoice will describe the goods sent and give the total amount of payment due. This should be checked by the buyer against the information on the order form and the GRN. The invoice is, in effect, a bill saying how much money must be paid. It may also state a time period (e.g. 28 days) within which payment should be made. A copy of the invoice is always kept by the supplier for his own records.

DID YOU KNOW?

All invoices are printed with the letters E & O E at the bottom. This stands for 'errors and omissions excepted'. It ensures that the supplier can send a further invoice if a mistake is made and the buyer is undercharged.

Checking an invoice

All invoices received are carefully checked before they are passed for payment. The invoice shown as Figure 7.7 has been received by Qualprint from Business Supplies. The accounts staff must check that:

BUSINESS SUPPLIES LTD
14 DOCKLANDS PARADE
GLENDALE
FE2 8DJ

Tel: 032 782943   VAT Reg. No.: 483/28372/75
Fax: 032 212314

INVOICE

To: Qualprint Ltd   Deliver to:
    22 Carnei Way
    GLENDALE
    Newshire
    FE1 8CA

Your order no.	Invoice date/tax point	Invoice no.	Despatch date
121/934	24.10.9–	1274	23.10.9–

Quantity	Description	Cat. no	Unit price	Total price	VAT rate	VAT amount
2 packs	A4 Superlux Card, White	SL/7	£10	£20	17.5%	£3.50
	Delivery charges		£1		17.5%	£0.17
	Sub-total			£21.00		
	VAT			£3.67		
	Total amount due			£24.67		

Terms: **28 days**
E & O E

Figure 7.7

- the invoice is meant for them (i.e. it has been sent to the correct address)
- the order number quoted is correct
- the goods listed match those listed on the GRN both in terms of description and quantity
- the price is the same as on the quotation or as shown in the catalogue (this can be checked by looking at the order)
- the calculations are accurate
- any discounts are as agreed.

If there are any discrepancies then the accounts staff (or the owner of a small business) must be notified. If there is no record of delivery then it is usual to telephone the supplier and ask for proof of delivery.

Evidence Collection Point 7.8

Study carefully the invoice Qualprint has received and then answer the following questions:

1 Identify the entries that are *different* from those shown on the order.

2 Has Qualprint received any discount from the supplier?

3 Is the amount Qualprint owes the same as the total you calculated for the order in ECP 7.6. If not, why not?

4 What do you think would happen if Qualprint did not pay the supplier in 28 days?

5 Check all the calculations on the invoice. If they are correct then write a short memo to Chris Gaston advising him that the invoice can be paid. If they are incorrect then notify Chris of any discrepancies.

▪ SALES DOCUMENTS ▪

Businesses must have customers to be able to survive. When a customer makes a purchase, this is the end point of all the marketing and promotional activities described elsewhere in this book. Customers buy goods or services

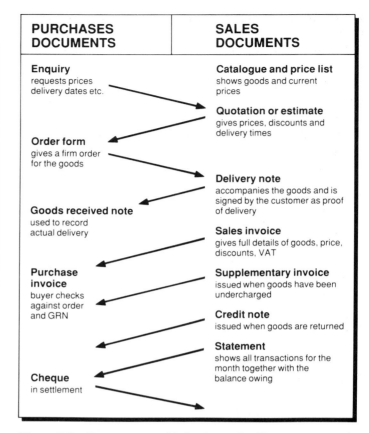

Figure 7.8 *Documents used in buying and selling*

and, in some cases, both. For example, someone buying a photocopier may buy a *service contract* as well as the machine itself. These transactions need to be recorded by the supplier so that the appropriate action can be taken.

Sales documents are closely linked to purchasing documents, as you will see from Figure 7.8. Remember that every written order sent by a purchaser is a sale to the supplier and all orders received are recorded and processed to ensure that customers receive the correct goods.

Sales take place from one business to another and also to members of the public. The documents used may vary depending on the circumstances but the principles involved are the same.

Orders received

You should already know quite a lot about orders. The order which Qualprint placed with Business Supplies Ltd was described on page 198. Orders can take other forms; for example, computers are increasingly used to transmit orders electronically using EDI. When you walk into a shop and ask for a magazine, in effect you are placing an order. In business, however, orders are usually received in written form and anyone placing an order by telephone is asked to confirm it in writing immediately *or* give their official order number. This protects the supplier from sending goods which have not been officially requested and which are therefore returned.

When an order is received it must first be checked to ensure that the information is complete and correct. For example:

- Does the description of the goods match the catalogue or serial number?
- Is the price given correct? If there has been a recent price change the customer may not know.
- Is the customer allowed credit (i.e. extended time to pay)? Most business to business transactions are done on a credit basis – see next page.
- Is the customer allowed discount? If so, then how much?
- Are there any special conditions which must be met (e.g. delivery by a certain date)?

If there are any problems with the order then these must be resolved before any further action is taken.

If the order is acceptable then the supplier will take the necessary steps to meet the customer's requirements. This may mean that the production department has to be informed so that the goods can be manufactured. It may be, however, that the items are already in stock, in which case the goods can be supplied reasonably quickly. Alternatively, they may have to be ordered from another supplier before being resold to the customer.

- Another item, some clipboards, can be supplied but not by the required date.
- The organisation concerned has not paid its account for some time and is near its credit limit.

Assume that credit will be allowed but that a gentle reminder about payment is needed. Write a tactful letter to the buyer at J & J Briggs – Mrs T Hanson – explaining the problems listed above.

Delivery Note

Goods sent to a customer are often accompanied by a **delivery note**. When the customer is satisfied that the quantity and type of goods are correct he or she signs the delivery note. One copy is kept by the supplier and one by the customer. Therefore a delivery note is a formal record that the goods have been received. In effect, once the delivery note is signed, the goods belong to the customer.

Activity

Business Supplies delivered another order to Qualprint. The order was for 200 black ballpoint pens and 20 staplers. Each came in a box correctly labelled and so the delivery note was signed. When the boxes were opened later, however, it was discovered that the ballpoint pens were red and one of the staplers was damaged. What should Qualprint do? Discuss your answers *as a group*.

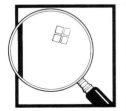

Evidence Assignment 7C

Qualprint receives an order from a regular customer – J & J Briggs Ltd, 15 Castle Way, Hightown, HG4 9TM. However, there are some problems with it:

- Qualprint no longer stocks blotting paper as there is very little demand for it.

DID YOU KNOW?

If you receive goods yourself and are asked to sign a delivery note to acknowledge receipt, it is possible that you won't have time to check the goods. You should therefore sign the delivery note but mark it 'goods received but not examined'.

Evidence Collection Point 7.9

A copy of the delivery note sent to Qualprint is shown in Figure 7.9.

BUSINESS SUPPLIES LTD.
14 DOCKLANDS PARADE
GLENDALE
FE2 8DJ

DELIVERY NOTE

To: Qualprint Ltd
22 Carnei Way
Glendale
Newshire
FE1 8CA

VAT Reg. No: 483/28372/75

YOUR ORDER NO.	INVOICE DATE/tax point	invoice no.	DISPATCH DATE
121/934	24.10.9-	1274	23.10.9-

QUANTITY	DESCRIPTION	CAT NO.
2 packs	A4 Superlux card, white	SL/7

Received by *L. Williams*   Date 24/10/9-

Figure 7.9

1 For each entry on the delivery note say *why* you think it should be included.

2 When the cards are unpacked some of them are found to be damaged. Write a letter to Business Supplies explaining the situation. Decide what you want Business Supplies to do to rectify the situation and advise them accordingly.

3 On a blank delivery note form, insert the details for the computer supplies you ordered earlier. Your invoice number will be 19083, date of despatch is tomorrow.

DID YOU KNOW?

Delivery notes and invoices are sometimes almost identical and are printed at the same time. The two main differences are usually that:

- delivery notes do not include prices
- there is space for the signature of the person who receives the goods.

Sales documents can be handwritten or typed but today it is more usual for them to be produced by computer. Special stationery, which makes copies without having to use carbon paper, is used to produce up to six copies of the documents – each for a different purpose (Figure 7.10).

Sales invoices

You have already seen what a purchases invoice is like on page 201 when you saw the invoice Qualprint had received from Business Supplies Ltd.

In the same way, when Qualprint sells goods it will issue a **sales invoice** to its customers. However, invoices are not always used in sales. When people call in to Qualprint to buy stationery for cash they are not given an invoice because they are paying for the goods immediately. Invoices are a formal record that money needs to be paid and are therefore issued when the goods have been sold on credit. In other words, payment is made some time after the goods are delivered or the service has been performed.

It is important that invoices are *accurate* and sent *promptly*. Most customers don't pay immediately the invoice is received and if the invoice is delayed or is incorrect then payment will be made even later.

DID YOU KNOW?

One of the biggest problems for small businesses is having to wait a long time to receive money they are owed. This obviously affects the amount of cash the company has to work with (known as its **working capital**). If the business also has to pay its own bills on time because it is pressurised from its own suppliers, then the consequences can be disastrous – and include bankruptcy.

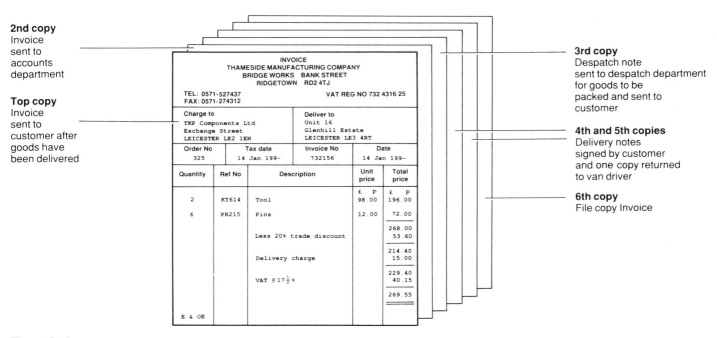

2nd copy
Invoice sent to accounts department

Top copy
Invoice sent to customer after goods have been delivered

3rd copy
Despatch note sent to despatch department for goods to be packed and sent to customer

4th and 5th copies
Delivery notes signed by customer and one copy returned to van driver

6th copy
File copy Invoice

Figure 7.10

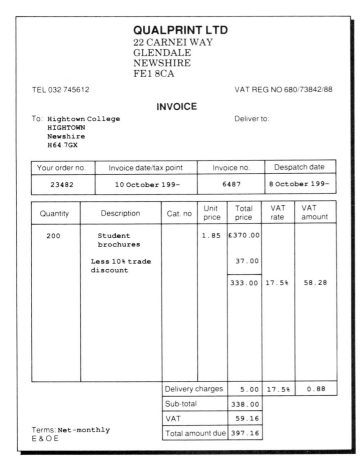

Figure 7.11

Figure 7.12

Activity

1 What is the difference between trade discount and cash discount?

2 Look at the invoices illustrated in Figures 7.11 and 7.12. What is the difference between them? See if you can decide before you read further.

Calculating invoices

The difference between Figures 7.11 and 7.12 (trade discount and cash discount) is in the terms offered and therefore the amount of VAT. It is important that you remember that the total amount shown on an invoice will vary, depending on whether cash discount is allowed or not.

- VAT is levied on both the goods and any delivery charge.
- If the goods are supplied with cash discount available it is assumed that the buyer will want to take advantage of this. In the second invoice (Figure 7.12), if the buyer paid within ten days he would pay £333 minus £16.65 (5%) = £316.35 for the goods. The VAT is calculated on *this* figure – 17.5% of £316.35 = £55.36.
- The VAT for the delivery charge must then be added to the VAT for the goods to calculate the total amount of VAT.

You must remember that if the invoice is settled within ten days then the amount owing is:

- the discounted price of £316.35
- plus VAT of £55.36
- plus £5.87 for delivery and VAT.

Therefore the total due is £377.58.

If the invoice is settled *after* ten days then the full amount for the goods is due but the VAT figure *does not* change. The buyer therefore pays the total amount shown on the invoice of £394.23.

Evidence Collection Point 7.10

Qualprint has undertaken the job of printing 2000 leaflets for the college at a price of 35p per leaflet. Chris always offers the college 10 per cent trade discount because it is a good customer. Again he is offering 5 per cent cash discount if the invoice is settled within ten days. This time delivery is £8 extra.

1 Carry out the following calculations:

   a What is the total price of the leaflets?
   b How much VAT is due on the *goods*?
   c How much VAT is due on the *delivery charge*?
   d What is the total amount due if the college pays within ten days?
   e How much is payable after this time?

2 Make out an invoice to the college on a copy of the blank Qualprint invoice form at the back of this book. Make sure it is neat and accurate.

3 Bearing in mind the problems a small business may experience in getting paid (see page 204), write a short paragraph explaining why some owners, such as Chris Gaston, are prepared to offer cash discount.

Statements of account

At the end of each month, the supplier will usually send a **statement** to each customer. Chris will therefore receive one from Business Supplies Ltd and also send one to Hightown College.

Statements are summaries of transactions between two businesses or between a business and its bank. (Bank statements are dealt with on page 224.)

For example, a business sells a customer several items at different times during a month. At the end of the month a statement is sent to the customer listing the totals shown on all the invoices. If any payments have been received this is also noted. The balance shown at the end of the statement is the amount of money still to be paid. This figure will be carried forward as a running total to the next statement – and printed at the top.

Statements allow businesses to check that each knows what the other owes them. They can also act as a tactful reminder that bills have not been paid.

Evidence Collection Point 7.11

1 The statement in Figure 7.13 has been received by Qualprint from Business Supplies. Study this carefully.

BUSINESS SUPPLIES LTD.
14 DOCKLANDS PARADE
GLENDALE
FE2 8DJ

Tel: 032 782943
Fax: 032 212314

VAT Reg. No.: 483/28372/75

STATEMENT

To: Qualprint Ltd
22 Carnei Way
GLENDALE
Newshire FE1 8CA

Date: 31 October 199-   Account no. 4872

Date	Details	Debit	Credit	Balance
1 Oct	Balance			£00.00
21 Oct	Invoice 1274	£24.67		£24.67
26 Oct	Invoice 1289	£41.92		£66.95

Figure 7.13

a Does Qualprint owe them any money from last month?

b Check the information which has been entered from the invoice shown on page 201. Is it correct?

c Chris Gaston had just confirmed with you that the second entry for 26 October is correct. You can now check the calculations. Write a short memo to him either confirming these are correct or notifying him of any errors you find.

2 On a blank Qualprint statement form make out a statement to Hightown College. At the beginning of the month Hightown College owed £163.20. Then enter the total for the invoice *which included cash discount* (Figure 7.12). Finally add the details from the invoice you produced yourself for Hightown College in Evidence Collection Point 7.10. Check your final balance carefully.

3 A new member of staff has recently started work in the accounts office. List for her all the details which must be checked when a statement is received.

· PAYMENT METHODS ·

Basically, there are five main ways in which a customer can pay for an item he or she has purchased:

- in cash
- by cheque
- by credit card
- by debit card
- by hire purchase (or credit sale agreement).

Customers who pay in cash, by cheque or by debit card are paying *immediately* for the goods they purchase (these are generally termed as 'cash' payments). When customers pay by credit card the *organisation* receives the money quickly, but it is up to the customer whether or not he or she settles the account from the credit card company promptly, or over several months. If a customer is buying an expensive item, and wants to pay over a period of time, then he or she may choose to take out a hire purchase (or credit sale) agreement. What does each method entail and why would a customer choose one, rather than another?

CASH SALES

Today very few people carry large sums of cash, for obvious reasons. Quite apart from the bulk, there is the worry of it being lost or stolen.

DID YOU KNOW?

No business – legally – *has* to give change if the customer cannot offer the exact amount. However, it is unlikely any business would survive for long if it insisted on all its customers offering an exact amount! Where restrictions can occur, however, is in terms of **legal tender** (i.e.

the type of money which is legally acceptable in payment). A business has the right to refuse to accept, say, 100 × 2p coins in payment of a £2 account. Technically, too large a quantity of coins can be refused as not being legal tender:

- more than 20p worth of bronze coins
- more than £5 of 5p and 10p coins
- more than £10 worth of 20p and 50p coins.

You should note that Scottish banknotes and Northern Ireland notes are both legal tender in England, just as Bank of England notes are acceptable in those countries.

Evidence Collection Point 7.12

1 You have been saving your small change and have now decided to buy a new sweater. You have a jar full of bronze and small value silver coins. You know you can't take the jar to the shop as they may refuse to accept it. What would you do to change your savings into a more acceptable form?

2 Find out the largest denomination bank note issued by:

- the Bank of England
- the Bank of Scotland.

3 In reality, how strict do you think shops are about the type of coinage they will accept? Do you know any other services (e.g. bus transport) where only the exact amount is accepted? How do you think customers (or travellers) feel about this? Discuss your answer *as a group* and write down your conclusions.

DID YOU KNOW?

Businesses are now so concerned about the number of fraudulent bank notes in use that most ask sales assistants to hold them to the light to check the metal strip is present. An alternative is to buy a small machine which automatically scans the note to check it.

PAYMENT BY CHEQUE

Cheques are probably the most common method used to pay suppliers. When a company sends a cheque for the amount shown on an invoice or statement it is, in effect, instructing its bank to take the amount from its own account and pay this into the supplier's account. The way that this happens is quite complicated but is very efficient and rarely goes wrong.

Paying by cheque is better than paying by cash because:

- Cash can easily be lost or stolen and used by anyone who has it. A cheque is normally only of any use to the receiver. Therefore cheques are a more secure way of transferring money.
- The system of processing cheques means that a **receipt** is not needed. Confirmation that the transaction has taken place is shown on both companies' **bank statements**. However, some businesses still send receipts when they get a cheque to inform the sender that it has been received.
- Cheques can be sent through the post because, unlike cash, they are of no use to anyone stealing them – provided they are **crossed**.

A cheque book is supplied by a bank when a **current bank account** is opened. As an extra record, there is a counterfoil attached to each cheque where information is recorded about:

- the name of the person or business to whom it is made out
- the date
- the amount
- the reason for payment.

All cheques have a unique serial number and this number is also printed on the counterfoil.

DID YOU KNOW?

A crossed cheque is one which has two lines printed down the centre. All cheques are printed like this automatically today and most have the words 'Account Payee' written in this space for added security. The crossing means that the person receiving it *must* pay it into a bank or building society account – it cannot be exchanged for cash or passed on to someone else.

Cheque guarantee card

When someone opens a current account the bank often issues them with a **cheque guarantee card**. If a cheque is presented to a retailer for less than the amount on the card, the recipient must write the number from the card on the back of the cheque. This *guarantees* that the bank will transfer the money even if the cheque and card are stolen or if the purchaser has not enough money in the bank. A cheque which is guaranteed cannot be 'stopped' for any reason (e.g. if the buyer later changes his or her mind).

Figure 7.14

Evidence Collection Point 7.13

Visit one of the main bank branches in your town and get one of their leaflets which tells you about current accounts. Note the range of services offered by the bank and the information given about cheque books, cheque guarantee cards and bank statements. Summarise this in a brief report on a word-processor.

Items on a cheque

There are three parties to any cheque:

- The **payee** – the person or company named on the cheque to receive the money
- The **drawee** – the bank from which the money is drawn
- The **drawer** – the person making out the cheque who will be drawing the money out of their account.

Activity

Study the example of a cheque in Figure 7.14 and find the name of the drawee and the drawer and where the payee's name would be written. Identify the vertical lines which mean the cheque is crossed. Note the different numbers printed on the cheque and why they are used.

Why do you think the amount of money has to be written in words *and* in figures?

Writing a cheque

Needless to say, all the details on a cheque must be written clearly and accurately. In addition, most banks prefer them to be written in blue or black ink.

- Write the date in full; i.e. 30 January 199- rather than 30.1.199-.
- Write the payee's name clearly on the top line. If it is a long name then keep your writing small to fit it in! If the cheque is made out to a person rather than an organisation, most banks prefer the name to be written in full and do not require the title. Therefore 'Peter Stevens' is better than 'Mr P. Stevens'.
- Start writing the amount to the left of the lines to make alterations or additions difficult if not impossible.
- Some people add the word 'only' after writing the amount (e.g. 'Three hundred pounds only').
- Note that you can write the amount of pence in figures throughout.
- Cancel any blank spaces remaining by drawing a line through them.
- Remember that you will not usually be authorised to *sign* a business cheque!

Evidence Collection Point 7.14

Using the blank cheques at the end of this book, make out four cheques for Chris Gaston and pass them to him for signing. Date them all with today's date.

Data Services Ltd – £247.25
Glendale Property Services – £600
Newshire County Council – £750
British Telecom – £154.70

DEBIT CARDS

Debit cards are a relatively new method of paying for goods and are like an 'electronic cheque'. The system saves the customer the trouble of writing out a cheque and the funds are transferred immediately from the customer's account to the supplier's account. Debit cards are marked as such and are issued under the Connect or Switch system. When the card is swiped through an electronic cash register linked to the system the customer's bank account is automatically checked (to make sure there are sufficient funds in the account) and the money is then transferred.

Because there will be no record of the transaction in the customer's cheque book (e.g. like a counterfoil), when a customer pays by debit card a voucher is printed (similar to a credit card voucher) which the customer must sign. A copy is then given to the customer for his or her records.

DID YOU KNOW?

Not all businesses can accept debit cards. This is because their cash registers are not linked to the EFTPOS system. EFTPOS stands for 'electronic funds transfer at point of sale'. For a business to be able to accept debit cards it must be linked to this system.

CREDIT CARDS

The most common credit cards in use today are Access and Visa cards (though you should note that abroad people know Access by the term Mastercard). These cards are accepted by many organisations including garages, shops, restaurants and hotels, and this fact is normally advertised in the window or near the counter.

If businesses are offered a credit card in payment they must check that the card is acceptable and seek authorisation when necessary.

Authorisation by the traditional method

All organisations have a **floor limit**. This is the maximum amount they can accept before they make a special check. The agreed floor limit may be as low as zero or as high as £500.

Above the floor limit a telephone call is made direct to the credit card company who run an immediate check through their computer to ensure the card hasn't been stolen and is not over the credit limit. If there are no problems then they issue an **authorisation code** which is entered onto the voucher. This guarantees the payment.

The new method of authorisation

The advent of new technology has meant considerable changes in the handling of credit cards.

- The card number is keyed into a special terminal linked to the credit card companies.
- The card is swiped through the terminal and information is transmitted 'down the line' and automatically checked by computer.
- If the check runs smoothly then a sales voucher is automatically printed by the terminal. The customer signs this and takes the top copy.
- If the check shows a problem (e.g. that the card is stolen or the customer has exceeded his credit limit) then a referral is made for further information and investigation. The method by which this is carried out may vary depending on the terminal used.

DID YOU KNOW?

Many organisations – especially retail stores – have their own sales vouchers for use with the normal credit cards *as well as* their own store cards. The information from these vouchers is extracted by the store and then transmitted electronically, rather than the vouchers themselves being processed.

Making out a sales voucher

When sales vouchers are not issued automatically by a terminal, the sales vouchers for the appropriate credit card must be made out by hand.

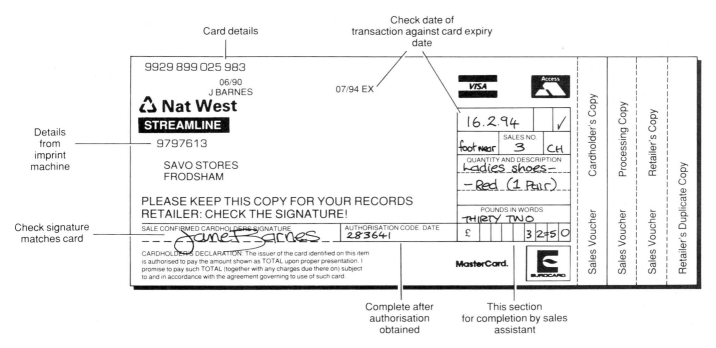

Figure 7.15

The details from the credit card itself are transferred on to the voucher by means of a special imprinting machine.

The voucher is then completed by the sales clerk and the customer is asked to sign it (Figure 7.15). The signature *must* be checked with that on the card and the expiry date on the card must also be checked carefully. If you make a mistake destroy the voucher and start again – don't alter the shop copy because it *must* be identical to the customer's copy.

There are four copies of the sales voucher:

- The top copy is given to the customer.
- The second copy is for the credit card company. This is paid into the bank.
- The third and fourth copies are kept by the retailer (for at least six months).

Within five banking days of making out the vouchers, the company completes a voucher summary form which lists all the vouchers (whether Access or Visa) and takes this and the vouchers to the bank for reimbursement.

However, under the new computerised terminal system there is no need for the retailer to deposit any vouchers at the bank. The top copy issued is given to the customer and the duplicate issued by the terminal is kept by the retailer.

Because the credit card company computer has already checked and logged details of the transaction the money will be credited direct to the retailer's account.

The increasing use of credit cards

It used to be the case that people who couldn't pay immediately for what they bought were considered rather irresponsible. Today, you are as likely to see someone paying by credit card as by any other means. Therefore society has changed its views on people 'buying today and paying tomorrow'.

The major advantage of using a credit card is that *no* interest is charged if the holder pays his or her account in full each month. Depending on the date of purchase, therefore, a customer can gain up to about six weeks *free* credit. However, many credit card companies charge an annual fee for the card, and there is the problem that people may be tempted to spend beyond their means and then have problems paying off their account.

Another advantage of using credit cards is that if the purchaser has any problem in relation to faulty goods, non-delivery or poor service and it seems impossible to get any satisfaction from the store itself, then a claim can be made against the credit card company which provided the finance. For that reason, it is often advisable to pay for items such as holidays by credit card. If, then, the tour operator 'fails to deliver' as promised a claim can be made against the credit card company *as well as* the travel agent.

Activity

Credit card companies *deduct* a percentage from the payment they make to retail organisations as their commission. Following a recommendation from the Monopolies and Mergers Commission, organisations can now charge different prices, if they like, for goods bought by cash and goods bought by credit card. *As a group*, discuss why many organisations are against the idea of introducing such a dual pricing system.

DID YOU KNOW?

It may be the case that you are asked for credit by a customer because:

- he hasn't enough money with him
- he has forgotten his cheque book, debit or credit card
- he knows your boss well or has had credit before.

You should *never* agree to anyone taking goods without paying without specific authorisation from your supervisor – no matter what the customer tells you!

Evidence Collection Point 7.15

1 Write a few sentences explaining each of the following terms used in relation to credit cards:

a authorisation
b authorisation code
c sales voucher.

2 List the advantages and disadvantages of using credit cards from the suppliers' *and* from the customers' points of view.

HIRE PURCHASE AND CREDIT SALES

In both these cases the customer is 'buying now and paying later'. It is usual for a customer to leave a deposit in either case, but sometimes organisations waive this requirement as a type of special offer (e.g. 'Buy now, nothing to pay until June').

However, there are some basic differences between hire purchase and credit sales.

Hire purchase

The customer does not become the legal owner of the goods until he or she has paid the last instalment. If the customer defaults on the payment then the item can be **repossessed** (i.e. taken back). However, two factors are taken into consideration:

- the amount which has already been paid
- whether or not the customer has offered to *try* to meet the payments (e.g. offered a reduced amount per month because of financial problems).

Usually, before a company will allow a customer to buy on hire purchase staff have to check that the **credit rating** of the customer is acceptable. This is done by contacting a credit reference agency which will give information on existing credit and whether the potential customer is known as a good or bad payer. Only if the rating is satisfactory will the agreement be signed.

In some cases (e.g. at large stores) the organisation itself provides the finance, and is therefore the legal owner of the goods until the final payment has been made. In others (e.g. garages) the company has an agreement with a finance company, which provides the finance and then becomes the temporary legal owner.

Credit insurance

It is possible for customers to take out credit payment protection insurance to cover the possibility of their not being able to meet the payments because of illness or unemployment. However, this can be expensive and may have restrictive terms which mean that it is unsuitable for some buyers. For example:

- The buyer must be employed full-time (and have been so for a specified period).
- There is no cover if a previous illness recurs.
- There is an upper age limit.

If a customer enquires about insurance then you should seek expert help from a supervisor.

Credit sales

Many clothes shops and mail order firms offer credit sales (e.g. pay over 20 weeks). In this case the customer becomes the legal owner immediately the first payment has been made. If he or she then defaults the shop can take the customer to court and sue for the amount owing, but cannot repossess the goods.

DID YOU KNOW?

A credit sale is used for goods which would have little value if repossessed. Obviously, no-one wants to repossess second-hand clothes, whereas if a finance company repossessed a second-hand car there would be a resale value. Therefore the company could recoup some of the amount it was owed.

Evidence Collection Point 7.16

It may be considered unethical to try to persuade customers to spend more than you think they can afford. For instance, a customer comes into an organisation planning on spending no more than £400. You know you can tempt him or her to spend a lot more – and as you are on commission this will increase your weekly bonus. What do you do?

Discuss *as a group* whether you consider a *profit-making organisation* will try to persuade a customer to spend the largest amount possible. Write down your own views on this.

DID YOU KNOW?

People who buy on credit are protected by the law in the same way as people who pay cash. Therefore if goods are faulty, the buyer has the right to return the goods and cancel the agreement.

Calculating how much is owed

Calculating the amount which the customer owes, and the amount of the monthly repayments, must obviously be done carefully. The amount will depend on:

- the total sum borrowed
- the interest rate
- the period of the loan
- the administrative charges.

Some organisations have special charts that staff can follow, which – provided you know what you are doing and follow the lines correctly – will give you the information you need. In other organisations you have to calculate it yourself. In this case *make sure* you have your figures checked before you quote anything to a customer.

In addition, your company has a legal obligation to inform the customer about the Annual Percentage Rate of charge (APR) of the loan. This is the true cost of borrowing the money (see below). It is therefore important that you are aware of the law in relation to companies which provide credit facilities to their customers.

The Consumer Credit Act 1974

This Act is the major one relating to consumer credit. It covers a wide range of types of credit agreement and places strict controls upon people who provide credit facilities in the course of their business.

The Act also lays down strict rules governing the form and content of agreements. The object of the rules is to protect the borrower by giving him or her the fullest possible information about rights and obligations.

A credit agreement must be issued to the buyer in a form which complies with the Act. It must contain details such as:

- the names and addresses of the parties
- the APR

- the cash price, deposit and total amount of credit
- the total amount payable
- the repayment dates and amount of each payment
- sums payable on default
- other rights and protections under the Act.

Customers who buy goods may have the right to *cancel* the agreement if they change their mind, provided:

- they have signed the agreement at home or anywhere else *except* on the trader's business premises
- they have bought the goods 'face-to-face' with the dealer.

Goods sold over the telephone are not covered and the customer cannot cancel such an agreement later.

If a customer signs a credit agreement at home, he or she must get a copy immediately. Every copy of a cancellable agreement has a box labelled 'Your right to cancel' which tells the buyer what to do. About a week later a further copy or separate notice of the cancellation rights is sent to the buyer by post. Starting from the day after the buyer receives this second copy he or she has five days in which to give the trader *written* notice of the wish to cancel.

APR – Annual Percentage Rate of charge

This *must* be calculated by all credit companies in a standard way set down by law. Basically all the interest and other charges for giving credit are added together and the total is expressed as an annual percentage rate. This gives the true cost of borrowing, which 'monthly rates' do not.

Therefore, the lower the APR the better for the borrower.

If *you* ever buy something on credit *always* shop around and compare the APRs of different companies. It is often given in adverts, can always be obtained by asking for a written quotation and must be clearly shown in all credit agreements.

Note that the monthly rate of interest is not a good indication at all. A company quoting a *lower* monthly rate than another may have a *higher* APR!

cash might mean that you could buy the goods more cheaply as well. A typical example is a car – virtually all garages will reduce the price if they are offered cash. So you would therefore be saving twice!

Activity

Imagine that a customer calls at in the store where you work and buys a computer priced at £800. You have a special offer on at present for goods bought on credit – nothing to pay for three months then 0% APR. The customer starts to write out a cheque for the computer. Do you give any advice to the customer – and if so, what do you say?

DID YOU KNOW?

The **Consumer Protection Act 1987** (see Chapter 12) also relates to finance, in respect of the *price* of goods:

- The price must not be misleading.
- There must be no 'hidden extras'.
- If the goods are 'double priced' then the lower price applies.
- Prices must include VAT unless they are quoted as VAT *exclusive*.

Evidence Assignment 7D

Below are given four problem situations. In each case state *who* is right and why.

1 A customer has just taken delivery of a new photocopier from your company which you are advertising at £2700 + VAT. He has now telephoned you to point out that his invoice is for £3655 and he has no intention of paying any more than the advertised price.

When you investigate you find that the additional charges are for a variety of extras, including service, maintenance, paper not yet supplied by your company and so on. The customer says that had he known of these he wouldn't have bought the copier.

You insist that as he has taken delivery, and agreed to buy it, he must pay his bill. Are you right?

2 Your friend is upset because her mother listened to a salesman who called at her home and signed an agreement for double glazing. This is a credit agreement which means the double glazing will be paid for over the next three years. Apparently when her mother sat down and read the agreement carefully she suddenly realised the payments were more than she thought and she couldn't afford them.

What would you advise your friend?

3 You walk into your local supermarket one lunchtime with a fellow student. You both want to buy some coffee. You buy identical jars and, whilst waiting in the checkout queue, notice that yours is priced at £1.50 whilst the one your friend is holding is priced at £1.40. Your friend is convinced you will both be charged £1.50 but you think the supermarket will have to charge you the price as marked on the jar.

Who is right – and what price will you each be charged?

4 A young lady has complained to your organisation that the music centre she bought on hire purchase last week is faulty. She says she wants a replacement or the hire purchase contract cancelled immediately and her deposit refunded.

The member of staff she spoke to has informed her that, because the goods have been bought on hire purchase, she has no right to either but must bring in the music centre to be repaired.

Who is right?

Evidence Assignment 7E

You have worked in your local record shop for several weeks each Saturday. Until now you have been helping customers to find the records and CDs they want, dealing with general enquiries and complaints, and looking up information for customers in record catalogues. This week

you are on the electronic cash register for the first time. You have been shown how to use it and don't expect any problems. What would you do, therefore, when each of the following occurs?

1 A female customer – who you know to be a 'regular' – has chosen several items and you have wrapped them up. Then she realises she has left her credit card at home. The value of her purchases exceeds her cheque guarantee card and company rules state that no cheque must be accepted if it exceeds this amount.

2 A young man hands you his credit card. When you swipe it through the terminal you find that it is unacceptable as it has been reported stolen.

3 A young teenager comes to you and asks for change to use the payphone outside your shop.

4 A man comes up to you very annoyed. You dealt with him a few moments ago when he bought a record for cash. He now claims he gave you £20 whilst you only gave him change for a £10 note.

5 A young lady pays for several CDs in cash. You notice there is a mixture of English and Southern Irish bank notes She says that both are perfectly acceptable.

6 A gentleman hands you his debit card. You try to process it through your till but receive the message that the card is unacceptable (probably because there is not enough money in his bank account).

Discuss your answers with your tutor.

PAY SLIPS

You may find some of the documents used in business a bit uninspiring or even boring! The one which you will *always* find interesting, however, is your **pay slip** – sometimes called a **pay advice note**.

This section explains how pay slips are made up. In Chapter 3 you learned about wages, taxation and National Insurance. You may wish to turn to page 65 now, to revise the main points before you continue to read this chapter.

You should know that:

● People are normally paid either weekly or monthly.
● The total amount people earn is known as **gross pay**.

- **Deductions** are made for income tax, National Insurance, pensions, charitable contributions, social clubs, etc.
- The amount of money a person actually receives, after deductions, is known as **net pay**.

A pay slip is either enclosed in a pay packet (for people paid in cash or by cheque) *or* given to people whose money is paid directly into their bank account.

It is important that you can understand your pay slip, otherwise you will be unable to check it and will not be able to see if a mistake has been made.

All pay slips contain the employee's name and usually their personal number. In most organisations employees are given a unique pay reference number which is particularly useful for computer records. Large organisations will also include the name of the department – which may again be shortened to a simple reference number. The pay slip will also state the **pay period** – this may be a month or a week **number**. This is the week in the tax year in which payment is being made.

DID YOU KNOW?

The tax year is also known as the **fiscal year** and runs from 6 April one year to 5 April the following year.

Calculating income tax

Pay slips are made out by the wages department who are also responsible for calculating the income tax and National Insurance payable by each employee. In Section 1 you learned that income tax is not payable on all your earnings – the amount of your taxable income and your free pay (i.e. the amount you can earn before paying tax) will depend on your allowances. The Inland Revenue notifies each person of their PAYE code number on a Notice of Coding and also informs their employer.

The wages department uses the code number to look up the amount of free pay for the employee each week or month by referring to tax tables issued by the Inland Revenue. This amount is then deducted from the total gross pay to date to find the taxable pay. Another set of tables shows how much tax is due on the taxable pay to date, up to certain weekly or monthly limits.

The wages department records the information on a Tax Deduction Card (called a P11) for each employee. If an employee changes jobs during the year the wages clerk prepares a P45 which gives details of the employee's code number, total pay to date, tax due and tax paid to date. This is given to the new employer so that tax can continue to be calculated correctly.

DID YOU KNOW?

1 An employee without a code number is put on **emergency coding** until everything is sorted out. On this code *more* tax is deducted than usual. It is therefore important that anyone on emergency coding completes a coding claim as soon as possible and sends this to the Inland Revenue so that the correct tax code can be allocated.

2 A tax code will change if an employee's circumstances change and these affect the allowances to which he or she is entitled. Because there may be some delay before the tax code is adjusted, this can mean a person receiving a tax rebate in one particular week. This will put things straight if too much tax has been deducted in previous weeks.

Calculating National Insurance

This is also done by referring to a set of tables. Contributions are payable by *both* employees and employers and the tables state the correct amount to be deducted according to the gross pay. There are different tables depending on whether the employee has or has not contracted out of SERPS, the state earnings related pension scheme.

The deductions for National Insurance are also entered on the P11.

The job of the wages department

It is the responsibility of the wages department to prepare:

- the individual deductions working sheet for each employee (P11)

- the individual pay advice slip for each employee
- the payroll for the organisation

In addition they will obtain money for cash payments and notify the bank about pay to be transferred direct to employees' bank accounts under the BACS system (Bankers Automated Clearing System).

Every month the tax and National Insurance collected is sent to the Inland Revenue. Once a year the wages department completes an end of year return for each employee. This gives details of all pay received, tax deductions, NI contributions and statutory sick pay or statutory maternity pay received during the last year. The employee receives a copy – known as the P60.

The P60 is really an alternative version of the final pay slip for the year. This is because, on *each* pay slip, there are details of current earnings *as well as* information on total pay received and total tax paid so far in that tax year.

DID YOU KNOW?

Some employees don't earn enough to be liable for either income tax or National Insurance. This would be the case, for instance, if you did a Saturday job whilst you are a student. In this case you must sign a student exemption form when you start work.

Activity

Employers usually prefer to pay wages direct into staff bank or building society accounts rather than by cheque. Some organisations do not pay any wages in cash at all.

As a group, list as many reasons as you can why this is the case.

Now consider it from the *employee's* point of view. What is the best way to receive wages, and why?

DID YOU KNOW?

Some organisations operate a payroll *giving* scheme. If you join this you can agree to donate a certain amount to charity each week or month and this amount will not be taxed.

Other employees may choose to *save* a regular sum out of their salary by subscribing to a Save As You Earn (SAYE) scheme.

Evidence Assignment 7F

1 Bill Gibson, a driver at Qualprint, is paid on an hourly basis. His standard rate is £5.20 an hour and he receives time and a half for Saturday work (i.e. his hourly rate plus half as much again) and double time for Sunday work.

a Last week he worked 38 hours at standard rate, 4 hours on Saturday and 3 hours on Sunday. What was his gross pay for the week?

b His deductions for the week amounted to £72.50. What was his net pay for the week?

c His tax code is currently 300H. Bill wants to know what the letter 'H' means. Using the tax leaflets you obtained in Section 1 (Chapter 3) for reference, write a paragraph explaining this to him.

d Bill is thinking of arranging for his wage to be paid directly into his bank account in future. Suggest three advantages to him if he does this.

2 Karen Sharples is employed on the stationery counter at Qualprint. She is paid monthly directly into

PAY ADVICE			Pay period	May 199–
Emp no. 15	Employee name KAREN SHARPLES		Dept A1	Tax code 325 L
Pay and allowances			NI no BD 301048C	Method of payment BACS
Hrs	Rate (£)	Amount (£)	Deductions	Total pay to date 1550.00
			Item · Amt (£)	
			Tax · 134.50	Tax to date 274.50
			NI · 32.30	NI to date 64.40
			Social fund · 2.00	Taxable pay to date 1010.00
			SAYE · 10.00	
GROSS PAY	£ 775.00		total deducations £187.70	net pay £ 583.30

Figure 7.16

her bank account, and because this is a fixed amount there are no entries under hours and rate. Her latest pay slip is shown in Figure 7.16. Karen has the following queries – can you help her? (Again, the booklets you obtained in Section 1 will help you.)

a Karen's tax code has recently changed and she has now discovered she is paying less tax than before. Can you suggest what may have happened?

b Karen is thinking of joining the payroll giving scheme and contributing £5 to charity each week. She wants to know if this amount will be taxed.

c Karen has heard that some organisations which operate a monthly scheme pay their employees 12 times a year and others pay them 13 times a year (e.g. every four weeks). Her annual salary is £9300. How many times a year is she paid?

d Karen has noticed that the difference between her total pay to date and her taxable pay to date is over £500. What does this figure represent?

e Karen thinks that the wages department has made a mistake on her payslip when they calculated her net pay. Do you agree? If so, state where they have gone wrong and give the correct figure.

DID YOU KNOW?

Although you may be asked to complete a pay slip from information you have been given, actually calculating income tax and National Insurance is a specialist job for which you need to be trained. In most organisations today computers are used to calculate wages and salaries and the pay slips and payroll are printed automatically.

PETTY CASH VOUCHERS

Businesses normally keep a small amount of cash available to pay for items such as milk bills, taxi fares, etc. The money is kept in a lockable petty cash tin and a receipt is obtained for each payment. In larger businesses someone in authority (e.g. a manager) may have to approve the expenditure to make sure that the system is not abused. The authorisation form – called a **petty cash voucher** (Figure 7.17) – and the receipt are clipped together and kept safely.

In most organisations petty cash is used:

- to pay for small items which would not be paid for by cheque (e.g. magazines for reception, coffee, tea, sugar, etc.)
- to reimburse (pay back) members of staff who have paid for an item out of their own pocket (e.g. a taxi fare)
- to pay service people who prefer their accounts to be settled immediately in cash (e.g. the milkman and the window cleaner)
- to pay for emergency requirements where the goods are not normally kept in stock (e.g. a jiffy bag to protect a special parcel)
- to pay for special items of postage (e.g. the fee for a registered letter).

DID YOU KNOW?

A petty cash voucher is also a form of *receipt* to show how money has been spent. Businesses normally have an upper limit on the amount of money which can be spent on each purchase through the petty cash system (e.g. £10). Anything above this amount must be bought using a purchase order form.

The voucher system

To make sure that only correct amounts are paid out, petty cash vouchers are used to record the money spent. All vouchers are numbered and should be issued in *numerical* order.

- The vouchers are usually issued *before* the money is spent.
- Junior staff must obtain authorisation *before* spending any money on behalf of the company or claiming any money from petty cash. Senior members of staff may spend money first and then present the petty cash voucher for reimbursement.
- An official receipt should be attached to the voucher as proof of the amount of money spent.
- Vouchers for multiple items must be checked to ensure the addition is correct.
- Completed vouchers must be filed safely, in numerical or date order.
- Any claims for unauthorised expenditure or discrepancies should be referred to the petty cashier. No payment should be made until the matter has been sorted out.

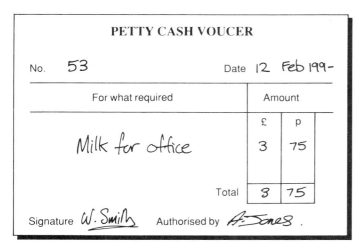

PETTY CASH VOUCER

No. 53   Date 12 Feb 199-

For what required	Amount	
	£	p
Milk for office	3	75
Total	3	75

Signature *W. Smith*   Authorised by *A. Jones* .

Figure 7.17

The job of the petty cashier

There is usually a petty cashier in charge of petty cash. He or she is in charge of ensuring that:

- all expenditure from petty cash is only for authorised payments
- all expenditure is recorded accurately
- there are no discrepancies between recorded expenditure and the amount actually paid out
- security procedures for keeping petty cash are correctly followed
- the petty cash book balances at the end of the month.

At the end of a given period (usually each month) the petty cashier will add up the petty cash expenditure on a special analysis page. This breaks down the expenditure into different categories (e.g. travel, stationery, office sundries, etc.), This enables the manager to see how much is being spent in each area. The total spent *must* be balanced against the total on the vouchers which have been issued.

The money spent is then usually reimbursed by the company cashier, so that the **petty cash float** is back to its original total at the beginning of the next accounting period. This is known as the **imprest system**. The float can vary from as much as £500 to as little as £20, depending upon the size of the company and the type of expenditure allowed under the petty cash system.

DID YOU KNOW?

When a company is VAT registered then any VAT paid on petty cash items *must* be listed separately on the vouchers. This is because the total amount of VAT which has been spent can be reclaimed from HM Customs and Excise at a later date.

Evidence Collection Point 7.17

Complete three petty cash vouchers (using copies of forms at the back of this book) for the following items of expenditure. Number these consecutively starting at 301 and use today's date.

Bear in mind that you must enter the VAT in its own column if this is shown separately.

1 Flowers for reception £13.50

2 Taxi fare £3.50 plus train fare of £12.00

3 Stationery £24.00 + £4.20 VAT = £28.20

Sign the vouchers and ask your tutor to authorise them.

DID YOU KNOW?

Occasionally, because of a large amount withdrawn or a few 'emergencies', the amount of cash in the petty cash box may run low before the imprest is due to be restored. If this occurs then the petty cashier should be notified immediately.

Evidence Collection Point 7.18

1 In each of the following cases, work out how much money should be remaining in the petty cash tin on the date given. Identify any case(s) where the amount remaining is too low and should be reported to the petty cashier.

a 16 November – imprest amount £100. Vouchers paid out to date: £16.50, £4.85, £2.00, 85p, £18.32.

b 12 December – imprest amount £50. Vouchers paid out to date: £6.58, £3.20, 60p, 45p, £14.20, £3.48, 98p.

c 16 January – imprest amount £350. Vouchers paid out to date: £64.20, £22, 75p, £23.20, £16.80, £85.43, £22.97, 56p, £40, £28.30.

2 Paul is in charge of petty cash at Qualprint and has the key to the tin. Mary, who has just started work in the sales department, asks for £15 to buy three ribbons for their computer printer. At Qualprint the petty cash limit is £10. Write down what you think Paul should say to Mary to explain the petty cash system and what Mary should do to get her ribbons.

· RECEIPTS DOCUMENTS ·

Receipts documents confirm that an amount of money has been paid from one person (or organisation) to another. These may take the form of:

- written or printed receipts
- cheques
- bank paying-in slips
- bank statements.

In all these cases the document will state the amount of money which has been paid and the date.

Three of the receipts documents listed above are related to banking transactions. Almost all business organisations use the services of a bank to help them to process their financial transactions. Originally banks were used to store people's money in a secure place. Banks still have large safes and strongrooms for this purpose. In modern times banks provide a wide range of services for both members of the public and businesses. One of the main services is the provision of current accounts.

A **current account** is one where money can be paid in and withdrawn easily. Money in the form of cheques and cash can be paid in. Cheques can be written to pay other people or businesses and cash can be withdrawn. Money can also be transferred from one current account to another by credit transfer (e.g. the BACS system of paying wages).

If you have a current account of your own then you will know that the three main documents used in connection with this account are cheques, paying-in slips and bank statements.

Written or printed receipts

Customers who pay in cash often expect a receipt as proof of payment. Organisations that do not use a till usually make out a receipt on a special form. Customers may specifically request a receipt, particularly if they wish to claim the money back from someone else. Each receipt is numbered for ease of reference.

DID YOU KNOW?

Receipts are always made out in *duplicate* so that the company also has a copy for its own records.

Completing a receipt

Receipts normally have the following items to be completed – and you can easily remember these by noting all the words beginning with a 'w':

- **who** has made the payment (name of payee)
- **when** payment was made (date)
- **what** amount was paid
- **why** the money was paid
- **who** received the money (on behalf of the organisation)

DID YOU KNOW?

A ticket is a form of receipt, because it shows that you have paid to attend an event or travel on a particular form of transport. As you know, it is important that you look after the ticket, particularly if you have paid in advance. You need to be extra careful if your ticket does not include the name of the purchaser as it can be used by someone else very easily.

A special kind of ticket is a raffle ticket. These are used, for instance, by charities to raise money. Again it is important that it is kept safely as it is needed as proof of payment if a prize is to be claimed.

Receipts can also be issued if goods are left at a shop (e.g. if you take clothes to be dry cleaned or a watch to be repaired). The receipt must be produced when you collect the goods to give proof of ownership.

Evidence Collection Point 7.19

1 Study the handwritten receipt shown in Figure 7.18. Write out what information comes under each of the headings given above.

QUALPRINT LTD
22 CARNEI WAY
GLENDALE
NEWSHIRE
FE1 8CA

RECEIPT   No. *147*

RECEIVED FROM   *J. Donovan*

the sum of   *Thirty-two pounds*

                                £32-00

in payment of   *Replacement side window*

Received by   *Katherine Edwards*   Date *15 March 19-*

Figure 7.18

2 Collect at least five receipts yourself. Your sources may include till receipts, tickets, invoices marked 'received with thanks', cash deposit machine print-outs at a bank or handwritten receipts.

3 You have received the following payments in cash. Make out a receipt for each one, starting with receipt number 101. Use copies of the receipt forms at the back of this book. Use today's date and don't forget to sign them.

a	Mr A. McFarlane	£45.00
b	Miss A. Petersen	£125.60
c	Mr H. Reisinger	£204.05
d	Ms V. Nayyar	£74.80

Cheques

You already know quite a lot about cheques from the point of view of completing them. When a cheque is received by a business it must be checked carefully to see that all the information is correct. If anything is wrong then the bank may refuse to accept the cheque and return it to the payee. This will also occur if the drawer (the person who wrote the cheque) does not have enough money in the account to pay the amount and the cheque has not been covered by a cheque guarantee card. A cheque will not be acceptable if:

- the date is more than six months ago or in the future
- the name of the payee is wrong or misspelled
- the amount in words is different from that in figures
- the signature does not match that on the cheque guarantee card
- alterations have been made and not initialled by the drawer.

In addition, a cheque will only be covered by a guarantee card if the card has not expired (check the expiry date) and the bank sort code number is the same as that printed on the cheque.

It is up to the receiver to write the cheque card serial number on the back of the cheque. Most organisations would also expect you to initial the back of the cheque too, and some organisations also ask for the customer's address.

Receipts are not usually sent when cheques are received because the drawer has a record of the payment on the cheque counterfoil. In addition, when you have presented the cheque to the bank and the money has been transferred a record of the transaction will appear on the **bank statement** of both the payee and the drawer. There will also be a record on the **paying-in slip** used by the payee.

DID YOU KNOW?

Modern cash registers usually print all the details on a cheque automatically. All the customer needs to do is to sign the cheque.

Clearing cheques

When a cheque is paid into a bank by the supplier the money is not officially available to go into the account until is has been *cleared*. Clearing means checking that the writer of the cheque has enough money in the account to pay. Only then is the money transferred. This process usually takes about three to five days and it is important that, during this time, the bank account holder does not depend on this money when drawing out cash!

DID YOU KNOW?

A **post-dated cheque** is one which is made out for a later date than the date on which payment is being made. Most companies refuse to accept these.

DID YOU KNOW?

Many banks issue the same card for a variety of purposes (e.g. cash card, cheque card, debit card). The words *cheque guarantee* may therefore *not* appear on the front of the card you are offered, but on the reverse.

Evidence Assignment 7G

Imagine that you are working on the stationery counter at Qualprint today. Write notes on the following.

1 The cheque shown in Figure 7.19 has been handed to you by a girl of about 16. She is obviously not used to writing out cheques. Assuming the amount for which it is made out is correct, what advice would you give her for writing out cheques in future?

2 When you ask her for her guarantee card you notice it is not signed. What would you tell her and why?

Figure 7.19

3 Chris Gaston considers that the amount of £50 on most cheque guarantee cards is too low. He is therefore prepared to accept cheques made out for up to £100 provided that the customer can offer other adequate identification. List three forms of identification which you think would be acceptable and give your reasons in each case.

4 A customer offers you a cheque which is for a 'special savings account'. On the bottom of the cheque are printed the words 'Minimum amount £100'. The customer has made out this cheque for £90 and has no other cheque book or credit cards with her. What would you do?

Paying-in slips

To avoid large sums of money being kept on the premises, takings (money received during the day) should be banked regularly. A very large organisation may employ a security company (e.g. Securicor) to transfer the money. Even a small organisation should bank its takings quickly and use the night safe if the bank has closed by the time it has cashed up (added and checked the takings). Any cash left on the premises must be locked away in the safe.

The counter clerk in the bank will check the amount of money handed over, counting notes and weighing bags of coins. The clerk will tick each entry on the paying-in slip (for details see below). If all is correct he or she will initial both the paying-in slip and the counterfoil (or duplicate) and date-stamp it. The clerk keeps the paying-in slip.

DID YOU KNOW?

Money can now be paid into the bank at automated deposit machines. These are usually situated *inside* the bank and are useful if the counters are very busy. See if you can see one in your local branch and watch it being used – but don't get too close or people might think you are trying to see their personal identification number (known as the PIN).

On the back of each paying-in slip there is space to list the drawers of cheques and the amount of each cheque. The total of this is **carried forward** to the front and added to

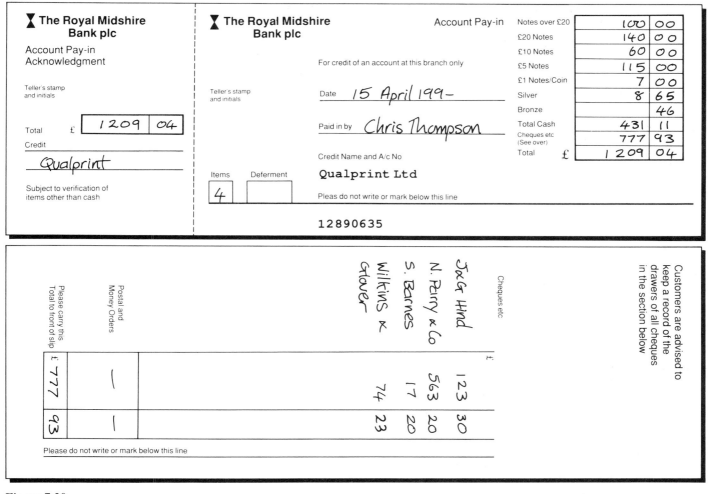

Figure 7.20

the cash total. A *separate* list of all cheques should also be kept by the company in case there are any queries.

The cash must be **analysed** (i.e. divided into different denominations). The example in Figure 7.20 has been completed by a cashier who had the following:

2 × £50 notes	7 × 20p coins
7 × £20 notes	9 × 10p coins
6 × £10 notes	17 × 5p coins
23 × £5 notes	17 × 2p coins
7 × £1 coins	12 × 1p coins
11 × 50p coins	

In addition the cheques have been listed on the reverse and the total carried forward. (Postal orders are also listed with cheques – in exactly the same way.)

Evidence Collection Point 7.20

Complete a paying-in slip for Qualprint and date it today. Use a photocopy of the form at the back of this book. Your takings are:

Three cheques – £185.45 (Mr A. Brand), £63.60 (Mr J. Long) and £1060.00 (Vale Engineering Ltd)

Cash –		
1 × £50 note	17 × 20p coins
15 × £20 notes	6 × 10p coins
5 × £10 notes	15 × 5p coins
16 × £5 notes	13 × 2p coins
13 × £1 coins	3 × 1p coins
22 × 50p coins	

Bank statements

Every so often, typically once a month, a bank sends each of its customers a statement. This lists all the transactions which have taken place since the previous statement. A statement should be checked to make sure that the entries are correct.

Activity

Figure 7.21 shows Qualprint's April statement. Check the items carefully.

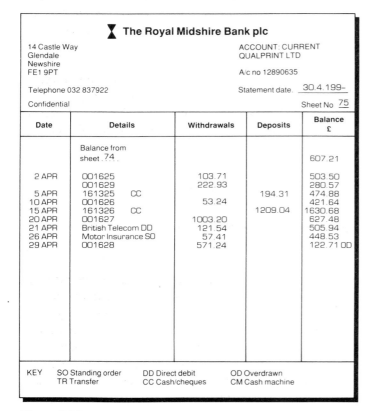

	The Royal Midshire Bank plc			

14 Castle Way
Glendale
Newshire
FE1 9PT

ACCOUNT: CURRENT
QUALPRINT LTD

A/c no 12890635

Telephone 032 837922

Statement date. 30.4.199–

Confidential

Sheet No 75

Date	Details	Withdrawals	Deposits	Balance £
	Balance from sheet .74.			607.21
2 APR	001625	103.71		503.50
	001629	222.93		280.57
5 APR	161325 CC		194.31	474.88
10 APR	001626	53.24		421.64
15 APR	161326 CC		1209.04	1630.68
20 APR	001627	1003.20		627.48
21 APR	British Telecom DD	121.54		505.94
26 APR	Motor Insurance SO	57.41		448.53
29 APR	001628	571.24		122.71 OD

KEY	SO Standing order	DD Direct debit	OD Overdrawn
	TR Transfer	CC Cash/cheques	CM Cash machine

Figure 7.21

Withdrawals

These are mainly cheques which have been written in payment to creditors. The number in the 'Details' column is the serial number of the cheque. 'Date' shows the date

on which the money was transferred out of the account, *not* the date on which the cheque was written.

'Withdrawals' also include standing orders and direct debits. These are both regular payments which are made out of the account. A standing order is where the account holder has an agreement with a company to pay them a fixed amount at regular intervals. A direct debit is more flexible; the agreement allows the organisation being paid to vary the date and the amount of payment, provided the account holder is notified.

Activity

Can you find one standing order and one direct debit on Qualprint's bank statement? What are each of these payments for?

Deposits

The 'Deposits' column shows when money was paid into the account. Compare the sample paying-in slip on page 223 with the statement. Can you find the entry for the deposit? What does the number in the Details column represent?

DID YOU KNOW?

Traditionally, if a bank account holder was overdrawn (i.e. had taken out more money than he had deposited) the bank would print this amount in red. From this comes the expression 'being in the red'. Today bank statements are produced by computer and cannot be printed in red. The letters OD may then appear against any overdrawn amount to draw the account holder's attention to the problem.

Checking a statement

When a business receives a statement, all the entries need to be checked.

● Deposits must be checked against the entries in the

paying-in book. If some deposits have been made just before the statement was printed then they may not appear.

- Withdrawals should be checked against the cheque counterfoils. It is usual to tick each cheque counterfoil to denote the amount has been withdrawn. In some cases people do not pay cheques into their accounts immediately. In this case, there will be outstanding cheques which have not yet been presented.

DID YOU KNOW?

Most companies 'reconcile' their bank statements at the end of each month. This means that they add on any deposits which have not been included on the statement and subtract any withdrawals. In that way they know exactly how much money they have in their account.

Evidence Collection Point 7.21

1 Without looking at the notes, study the sample statement shown as Figure 7.21. For each of the following entries write a couple of sentences explaining each item and why it needs to be included on the statement:

a bank account number
b statement date
c withdrawals
d deposits
e balance
f date of transaction
g cheque number
h paying-in slip number
i the letters 'OD'.

2 Chris Gaston notes that on 30 April he paid £1304.20 into the account but this is not shown on his statement. There are also two outstanding cheques – for £30.26 and £74.18–which have still not been presented for payment.

How much does Qualprint really have in its current account at the end of April?

· SECURITY ·

Security is a vital aspect of financial transactions and a major reason why all financial documents must be completed neatly and accurately. Three main aspects of security are:

- authorisation of orders
- reconciling invoices against orders and GRNs
- authorised cheque signatories.

Authorisation of orders

You should already know that when an order is sent to a supplier, the business sending it is almost committed to accepting the goods and paying for them. Because sending an order is the same as spending money it is very important that an order is sent when it is *definite that the organisation needs the goods*.

Therefore it is also important that someone with the correct authority *authorises* the order. This means that they will probably sign it and are responsible for making sure that it is appropriate for the business. There are two main criteria for deciding who authorises an order:

- the *amount* of money to be spent
- the *type* of goods being purchased.

The amount of money

The general rule is that the larger the amount of money involved, the more senior the person who has to authorise it. The actual amounts will vary between organisations but, generally, managers will be responsible for authorising general expenditure in their own areas. Therefore a training manager could authorise payment for £300 for a video recorder for use on courses. However, the board of directors would have to approve the building of a new training block costing half a million pounds.

People who authorise orders will probably have a **budget** to work to. In other words, they will be allowed to spend up to an agreed limit each month or year (see page 193).

The type of goods

People are normally only allowed to authorise orders for items which are *appropriate for the work for which they are responsible*. For example, a maintenance supervisor could order a spare part for a machine but could not order a new drinks vending machine! The catering manager *would* be allowed to order this type of equipment.

Evidence Assignment 7H

Rachel Williams is the administration manager in a factory. She is allowed to authorise orders up to the value of £250 for any single item. One day the purchasing department receives an order from her for a new carpet to be fitted in her office. The value of the order is £410. The maintenance department is responsible for decorating and maintaining the buildings and this would normally include the purchase and installation of carpets and other fittings.

1 Assume you are the purchasing manager. Write a tactful memo to Rachel in your own name explaining why the order cannot be allowed. Tell her what she should do if she needs a new carpet.

2 Write a short paragraph explaining why the purchasing manager needs to take this action.

Evidence Collection Point 7.22

In Chapter 4, you learned about the different departments of a company. Bearing in mind the work carried out in each department, decide on three items each of the following managers would be allowed to order which is under £500 in value and which would be appropriate for his or her particular area of responsibility.

In addition, think of one item which he or she would *not* be allowed to order because it would be too expensive.

- The design and production manager
- The personnel manager
- The financial manager
- The administration manager
- The sales and marketing manager
- The distribution manager.

Invoices, orders and GRNs

You should already know that:

- An order gives details of goods required from a supplier.
- An invoice is a request for payment for the goods once they have been delivered.
- A goods received note (GRN) is completed by the person receiving and checking the goods when they arrive.

If you are not sure about any of these documents, refresh your memory by looking back at pages 198–202.

Invoices should not be authorised for payment until someone with the appropriate authority has satisfied him or herself that everything is correct. This means that the information on the invoice must be identical with that on the original order *and* with the details entered on the GRN. Once an invoice has been authorised, the finance department will make the payment automatically.

Processing invoices for payment

Ideally a variety of people should be involved in checking the invoice. It should *not* just be the responsibility of one person, especially if it is for a very large amount of money. The procedure for checking invoices was covered on page 201.

Usually the document is stamped with a rubber stamp showing the stages it must pass through (see Figure 7.22). As each person carries out their function they initial the appropriate box.

ACCOUNT VERIFICATION		
Item	Status	Verified by
Goods received		
Invoice details as Order		
Invoice details as GRN		
Invoice correct		
Payment approved _____ (signed)		

Figure 7.22

DID YOU KNOW?

In very large companies it may be uneconomic to employ someone to check every invoice, especially those for very small amounts. In this case invoices over a certain figure (e.g. £100) would be checked and smaller totals would be *batch* checked; i.e. certain invoices would be checked at random.

Types of discrepancy

Here are some reasons why an invoice would not be passed for payment:

- The invoice may have been incorrectly completed (e.g. with the wrong goods, price or quantity).
- Items may have been delivered at different times (in a 'split' order) and so more than one GRN would have to be found and checked.
- The GRN could have been incorrectly completed and contain inaccurate or insufficient information.
- The person receiving the goods may not have checked them properly (e.g. some may have been reported damaged and returned at a later date).
- Invoices are often printed by computer or typed. GRNs are more likely to be completed by hand. If someone's handwriting is illegible it may be impossible to check the GRN against the invoice.

Problem-solving

If you find a mistake or discrepancy on an invoice you must know how to deal with it. The procedure is often different in small and large organisations. In a large organisation the problem would be referred to a supervisor. In a small organisation the clerks in the accounts department may have to sort it out themselves.

- If the discrepancy is small and the organisation is one which is dealt with regularly, then it is normal to telephone them to point out the error. They may issue a replacement invoice but are more likely to send a supplementary invoice or a credit note for the difference.
- If the discrepancy is large it is better to write to the organisation as any correspondence will then be on file and can be referred to later if there is a dispute.

- If there are regular discrepancies from a particular organisation then a more formal letter of complaint may be sent by the manager.

DID YOU KNOW?

A *reputable* company points out errors whether they are being overcharged or undercharged! Most companies would rather keep their reputation than save a few pounds by keeping quiet about a mistake which will probably be discovered by the supplier at a later date.

Paying the account

When the invoice has been authorised for payment then the accounts department will pay the supplier, usually by cheque. However, in many cases the company waits until a **statement** has been received from the supplier showing the balance owing to date. This document is also checked before the cheque is sent. However, if a company can take advantage of cash discount terms by paying more promptly it is more likely that payment will be made before the statement is due.

Evidence Assignment 7 I

1 Study the invoice, order and GRN in Figures 7.23–25 carefully and then write down your answers to the following questions:

a Can payment of the invoice be authorised? If not, list the discrepancies you have found.

b What action should now be taken?

2 Brainstorm other reasons why someone checking invoices against orders and GRNs may not be able to authorise payment. Write a list of the more sensible items and include this in your portfolio.

Cheque signatories

When a person or business opens a bank account which has a cheque facility the bank asks for a sample signature

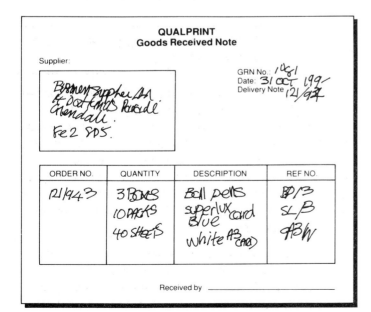

QUALPRINT LTD
22 CARNEI WAY
GLENDALE
NEWSHIRE
FE1 8CA

TEL 032 745612   **ORDER**   VAT REG NO: 680/73842/88

TO.   Business Supplies Ltd   DATE 23rd October 199–
     14 Docklands Parade
     GLENDALE   ORDER No. 121/934
     FE2 8DJ

PLEASE SUPPLY

QUANTITY	DESCRIPTION	Ref No	Unit price
10 Packs	A4 Superlux Card Blue	SL/3	£11
3 Boxes	Blue ball pens	BP/4	£3.20
50 Sheets	A3 Card White	C/A3/W	20p

DELIVERY   As soon as possible

SIGNED   *G. Graston*

Figure 7.23

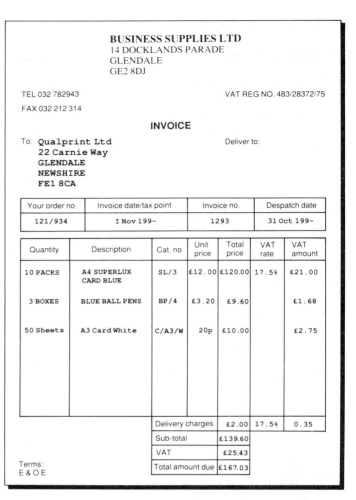

BUSINESS SUPPLIES LTD
14 DOCKLANDS PARADE
GLENDALE
GE2 8DJ

TEL 032 782943   VAT REG NO. 483/28372/75

FAX 032 212 314

INVOICE

To: Qualprint Ltd   Deliver to:
     22 Carnie Way
     GLENDALE
     NEWSHIRE
     FE1 8CA

Your order no.	Invoice date/tax point	Invoice no.	Despatch date
121/934	I Nov 199–	1293	31 Oct 199–

Quantity	Description	Cat. no	Unit price	Total price	VAT rate	VAT amount
10 PACKS	A4 SUPERLUX CARD BLUE	SL/3	£12.00	£120.00	17.5%	£21.00
3 BOXES	BLUE BALL PENS	BP/4	£3.20	£9.60		£1.68
50 Sheets	A3 Card White	C/A3/W	20p	£10.00		£2.75

		Delivery charges		£2.00	17.5%	0.35
		Sub-total		£139.60		
		VAT		£25.43		
Terms: E & O E		Total amount due		£167.03		

Figure 7.25

from everyone who will be allowed to sign cheques. Those people who provide the signatures are those who must sign the cheques which are used to pay suppliers. The reason for this is that a signature is almost impossible to forge. This means that cheques can only be signed by those people who have the correct authority. Each of these people is known as an **authorised cheque signatory**.

The bank keeps the sample signatures and checks them against those on the cheques which are presented for payment if there are any queries. In practice this happens very rarely for small amounts, but if a forged cheque is presented and the bank pays out the money, in law it is responsible and has to stand the loss.

QUALPRINT
Goods Received Note

Supplier:

Business Supplies Ltd
14 Docklands Parade
Glendale.
Fe2 8DS.

GRN No.: 1081
Date: 31 OCT 199–
Delivery Note 121/934

ORDER NO.	QUANTITY	DESCRIPTION	REF NO.
121/943	3 Boxes	Ball pens	BP/3
	10 Packs	Superlux card Blue	SL/B
	40 Sheets	white A3 (card)	A3W

Received by _____

Figure 7.24

Company signatories

A business can nominate who it likes to authorise cheques.

- Some organisations have rules which say how much a particular signatory can authorise. Normally for large amounts of money the cheques are signed by a very senior person, such as the chief executive or managing director.
- Another organisation may insist that cheques need two signatures, especially if they are for large amounts of money (e.g. over £500).
- Some companies nominate three or four signatories with the agreement that any one or any two can sign.

These measures are designed:

- to prevent fraud
- to ensure that money is paid correctly (i.e. the right amount to the right person or business at the right time)
- to protect those people who *are* allowed to sign cheques from allegations or doubt as to their actions (if two people are always involved then each person has another witness as to his or her actions).

DID YOU KNOW?

On most occasions, people who sign cheques don't complete the other details. This is done by someone else or even by computer. It is also common practice to have a pre-printed signature when many similar cheques are to be paid out. These are stored in a cheque signing machine which can automatically process the signing of cheques very rapidly. Needless to say, the machine is locked when not in use. Without one of these the chief accountant of a county council would have a very sore hand each pay day!

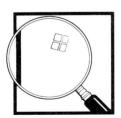

Evidence Assignment 7J

Ray Smith, the accountant at Hightown College, was always very careful to keep the college cheque book locked in the safe. Unfortunately, one day there was an exception. He was sitting at his desk signing cheques when the phone rang. His wife, who was very upset, told him that their young son had been involved in an accident and taken to hospital. Ray was obviously very alarmed and ran straight to his car to go and see his son.

Although his son was not badly hurt, it was a while before Ray remembered the cheque book on his desk. He dashed back to the office to find the cheque book gone, along with some letters he had signed.

1 Write a short report on what could happen to the stolen cheques. Also say what action Ray should take.

2 Ray is later approached by a group of students who want to raise money for charity. They want to open a bank account in which to keep the funds.

 a What are the advantages and disadvantages of the students operating their own account?
 b If they go ahead, what should they do about arranging for cheques to be signed?
 c Are there any security procedures you think they should take in relation to

 - cashing up the money they receive
 - transporting the money to the bank
 - paying it into the account
 - keeping money overnight because the bank has closed
 - keeping records of their financial transactions?

Evidence Collection Point 7.23

Obtain from business organisations as many examples as you can of the different documents discussed in this chapter. Ask around your family and friends and see if you can obtain any when you are on work experience placement (but remember to ask first!). Your tutor may be able to help with examples of invoices, orders etc. from the college or school office. It doesn't matter whether or not they have been completed.

If you are working on a Saturday or have worked during the holidays then you may have an example of a completed pay slip. Unless you know someone very well indeed it is doubtful if you could obtain an example from anywhere else! However, other books may give you an idea of the different styles and you *may* be able to obtain a blank pay slip at your work experience placement.

Note: If anyone gives you an example of a cheque or other document which could be of value then don't be surprised if they write 'cancelled' through it quite clearly first!

1 Collect all your example documents in order to file in your portfolio.

2 Compare those you have collected with those of your fellow students.

3 Write a report on how these examples differ in style and layout from those found at the back of this book. Use clear headings for each type of document you are going to discuss.

DID YOU KNOW?

It may give everyone in your class a boost if you organise a competition around this. Give a limited time for collection (e.g. a month, preferably including your work experience placement), and give a prize for the person who can bring in the greatest number of documents.

Evidence Checkpoint

At this stage check carefully that you have completed all the ECPs and assignments in this chapter and filed your work neatly. It may be an idea to make a list of these and make sure you have completed them all. You may also wish to look through some of your documents and revise how to complete these correctly before you attempt the **Evidence project** which starts on page 231.

Revision Test

True or false?

1 VAT inspectors regularly check the accounts of companies which are VAT registered.

2 A post-dated cheque is one which is made out with the wrong year.

3 Cash discount is given to encourage companies to pay promptly.

4 All cheques must be signed by at least two people.

5 Faulty goods cannot be returned if they have been bought on hire purchase.

Complete the blanks

6 Another name for a financial plan which shows proposed income and expenditure is a ....

7 The two main types of annual accounts are the .... and the ....

8 The amount on a cheque must be written in .... and ....

9 Goods inwards are recorded on a ....

10 The document sent by a company to its customers, which shows all the transactions which have taken place that month, is called a ....

Short answer questions

11 Give four reasons why financial transactions must be recorded.

12 State three problems which occur if financial documents are completed incorrectly or illegibly.

13 Give five items which must be included on a written receipt.

14 State three differences between debit cards and credit cards.

15 State four reasons why an invoice may not be passed for payment.

Write a short paragraph to show you clearly understand each of the following terms:

16 Petty cash system.

17 Authorisation of orders.

18 Paying-in slip.

19 Pay slip.

20 Delivery note.

chapter **8** EVIDENCE PROJECT

Learning Objectives

This project is designed to enable you to put into practice the skills of completing different types of financial documents. Each document is part of a record of a transaction and its purpose has been explained in the previous chapter. You should know:

- **why** the document is needed
- **when** it should be completed
- **who** might complete it and who will receive it.

Before starting this project you are advised to spend some time revising these aspects if you have forgotten them!

• SAMPLE DOCUMENTS •

Throughout this project you will need copies of the blank financial documents included at the end of the book. *Do not mark or complete the original documents in this book – or you will not have enough to work with.* Your tutor will help you to photocopy the quantity you need.

If you start a document and make a mess of it you should start again. In business it would not be acceptable to send out anything which is scruffy, illegible or crossed out and then corrected. If possible try to type the majority of sales and purchases documents you produce (e.g. invoices, orders and statements). You are obviously expected to write those documents which are normally handwritten – cheques, petty cash vouchers and receipts.

• BACKGROUND INFORMATION •

You have recently been employed by Chris Gaston of Qualprint to work as an administrative assistant/accounts clerk. He knows that you have obtained a GNVQ level 2 in Business and therefore expects you to have a good knowledge of the various types of financial documents used by the company.

Qualprint is a small organisation which produces various types of printed material to customers' orders. In addition Qualprint supplies office and stationery goods and has a small retail/trade counter.

The organisation chart for Qualprint is shown in Figure 8.1.

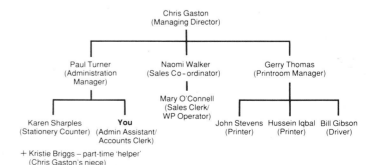

Figure 8.1

The staff in the administration section deal with all aspects of the business, including:

- processing purchase orders and documents
- receiving goods
- processing sales documents
- financial record-keeping
- banking transactions
- attending to the retail counter.

Your job

You start work for Qualprint on 1 June and work for the Administration Manager, Paul Turner. On your first day, Paul explains that he has devised a training programme for you so that, within a month or two, you will be able to do most of the jobs around the office without supervision. However, as you are the newest member of staff it will also be part of your job to make the tea and run any errands!

Paul gives you a copy of the training programme (Figure 8.2). So far as is possible you will follow this programme – unless any other members of staff are absent or an emergency job arises – in which case you may be expected to take on additional duties.

WEEK COMMENCING	DUTIES
1 June	Purchasing – making out orders and GRNs, checking and paying purchase invoices
8 June	Sales – checking orders, making out delivery notes and sales invoices
15 June	Cash handling, receipts, receiving cheques, banking procedures
22 June	Petty cash and pay slips plus any other duties as required

Figure 8.2 *Your training programme*

• WEEK 1 - PURCHASING •

Day 1 – Monday, 1 June

Paul Turner explains to you the system of ordering goods at Qualprint and shows you a blank order form. He emphasises that:

- The name and address of the supplier must be correct – as must all the other details on the order!
- The order numbers after the / are in sequence. The last order number used was 121/937.
- Delivery is normally requested 'as soon as possible'
- All order forms must be passed to him for signing.

Task 1

Several items of office stationery are required for the stationery counter. Karen Sharples has sent a memo (Figure 8.3), detailing what is required and the name of the supplier she usually uses.

Make out the orders required and date them 1 June.

MEMO

TO	Paul Turner
FROM	Karen Sharples
DATE	28 May 199–

Can you please arrange for the following items to be ordered as soon as possible:

1 From Business Supplies Ltd, 14 Docklands Parade, Glendale, FE2 8DJ

   10 boxes of blue ballpoint pens (12 per box) – ref BP/3 – 75p per box

   120 A4 writing pads – ref WP/16. These come in packs of 10 and cost £8 a pack

   10,000 10" × 7" brown envelopes – ref EV7 – £15.50 per 1000

2 From Stationery Stores Ltd, 16–18 Hamilton Road, Glendale, FE7 8MS

   250 wallet folders (assorted colours) – ref 3090 at 15p each

   500 manilla folders ref 2080 at 10p each

We get 10% trade discount from both companies.

Figure 8.3

Task 2

Chris Gaston has chosen an executive chair from the Super Office Ltd catalogue. Order this for him. The address of the company is Shorrock Way, Prespool, Newshire, PR3 1QH. The reference number is EC27 and the price is £170 plus VAT.

Day 2

Several deliveries are due today and Paul wants you to make out goods received notes and to check the stock as it arrives. Any item which is damaged on arrival should be referred to him and *not* listed on the GRN. He stresses that:

- The reference number and description of the goods must be copied carefully. If there are several items of the same type of goods they should be counted.

- Small items (e.g. boxes of pens) are not normally opened and counted – this is reserved for high value items.
- The original order is available against which you can check the deliveries, if required.
- The goods will be accompanied by a delivery note. Check that this matches the actual goods delivered and notify the accounts department of any items which are to follow.
- Goods may be delivered in the stationery shop – in which case Karen Sharples will have signed the delivery note as 'received but not examined'.
- The last GRN number was 1080. Numbers follow on consecutively.

Task 3

At 11 a.m. a delivery is received from R & T Supplies Ltd. The delivery note is attached (Figure 8.4). The goods are correct. Make out the GRN.

R & T SUPPLIES LTD
SAUNDERS INDUSTRIAL ESTATE
HIGHTOWN
H64 7AT

DELIVERY NOTE

To QUALPRINT LTD
    22 CARNEI WAY
    GLENDALE

No: 72364

YOUR ORDER NO	INVOICE DATE/tax point	invoice no	dispatch date
121/928	2 June 199–	KL4862/90	2 June 199–

QUANTITY	DESCRIPTION	REF NO.
10 boxes	Printing ink – black	8634
10 boxes	– red	8635
2 boxes	– green	8636
5	Litre drums – industrial cleaner	2862

Received but not examined K.S.

Received by K.Sharples   DATE 2/6/9–

Figure 8.4

JS COMPONENTS LTD
ABINGDALE ROAD
GLENDALE
FE4 7TF

DELIVERY NOTE

To QUALPRINT LTD   No: A2/458/B
    22 CARNEI WAY
    GLENDALE

YOUR ORDER NO	INVOICE DATE/tax point	invoice no	DISPATCH DATE
121/920	2 June 199–	TJ 48726	2 June 199–

Quantity	Description	Ref No
1	Electric fan heater Model 628*	HT20
10 packs	15 amp fuses	J104
20 packs	60W light bulbs	J150
50 packs	100W light bulbs	J151

Received but not examined K.S.

RECEIVED BY K.Sharples   *1 fan heater to follow

DATE 2/6/9–

Figure 8.5

Task 4

At 1 p.m. a delivery is received from JS Components Ltd. The delivery note (Figure 8.5) shows that only one electric fan heater has been delivered although two were ordered. The second is due to follow shortly. Make out the GRN and type a short memo to the accounts department informing them of the missing item.

Task 5

At 3 p.m. goods are delivered from D & D Packaging (Figure 8.6). The order is complete but the small plastic boxes are in a very bad condition because they were poorly packed. Paul has gone to visit a client.

a Make out the GRN.

b Type a brief memo about the boxes to Paul which you can leave on his desk.

Day 3

Task 6

Paul passes you four invoices (Figures 8.7–8.10) which he wants you to check. Only one relates to goods which have been delivered – and the invoice is correct against the GRN. The other three relate to services which have been provided.

Paul wants you to check the calculations on each invoice. If these are correct then you should make out a cheque for the amount due. Use today's date. These will be passed to Mr Gaston for signing later.

If any invoice is incorrect, note the details in a brief memo to Paul Turner.

D & D PACKAGING
15 WESTON PARK
GLENDALE
FE2 7EG

DELIVERY NOTE

Received but not examined K.S.

To QUALPRINT LTD
22 CARNEI WAY
GLENDALE

No: 1348

YOUR ORDER NO	INVOICE DATE/tax point	invoice no	DISPATCH DATE
121/925	2 June 199–	456753	2 June 199–

Quantity	Description	Ref No
6 rolls	corrugated paper	L825/5
4 rolls	industrial cling film	L216/9
12	plastic packing boxes (small)	K614/2
12	(med)	K614/3
12	(large)	K614/4

RECEIVED BY *K. Sharples.*   DATE *2/6/9–*

Figure 8.6

Thomas Wilcox
Plumbing and Heating Engineer

17 Greenaway Road
GLENDALE
FE2 4RT

Qualprint Ltd
22 Carnei Way
Glendale
Newshire

No **449**   Date: **1 June 199–**

INVOICE

TO

Replacing leaking radiator:

1 600 mm × 2000 mm radiator	£93.25
1 thermostatic radiator valve	8.50
$5\frac{1}{2}$ hours @ £9.50 per hour	£55.25
	————
	£157.00

E & O E

Figure 8.7

Task 15

Paul asks you to make out sales invoices to relate to the delivery notes you have completed. He asks you to pay particular attention to making sure that all the details and all your calculations are correct. He tells you that

- Normal terms are 28 days.
- Glendale Borough Council and Greenbank Engineering receive 10% trade discount and Blades Ice Arena receive 5%.
- There are no delivery charges for any of these customers.
- Invoices should be given the same date as delivery notes.
- The next invoice number is 2876 and invoice numbers run consecutively.

Day 2

Last Friday some special printing orders were delivered in a rush. The delivery notes were made out by another member of staff who has listed the details in Figure 8.18.

NAME	ORDER	DESCRIPTION	PRICE	TERMS
J Tyler Ltd 15 Dell Road Hightown HG4 9DK	38297	2000 A4 4-page leaflets	£1.10 each + VAT	no discount £10 delivery charge
Parr Finance Peters Street Glendale FE3 5KM	6909/65	1000 A5 leaflets 5000 A4 2-page leaflets	30p each + VAT 80p each + VAT	5% discount no delivery charge
Mrs T Ryan 14 Tenby Walk Glendale FE7 2HS	–	100 wedding invitations 200 place cards 200 service sheets	30p each + VAT 5p each + VAT 20p each + VAT	no discount £5 delivery charge
Hightown College Cheyne Walk Hightown HG4 7GX	KM30191	5000 A4 coloured brochures 1000 A3 posters	£1.50 each + VAT 25p each + VAT	10% trade discount 5% cash discount if paid within 10 days no delivery charge

Figure 8.18

Task 16

From the information given make out invoices, noting the terms quoted in each case.

Paul asks you to take particular care over the invoice for Hightown College which quotes cash discount, as this affects the amount of VAT which is included.

Day 3

Task 17

Paul Turner has received a letter from a customer who was overcharged (Figure 8.19). He asks you to check the refund due and, if this is correct, make out the cheque.

He also asks you to draft a letter of apology to Glendale Marketing saying that the error was an oversight on the part of the accounts staff. He will check the letter on Monday.

GLENDALE MARKETING LTD
15 Abbey Walk
Glendale
FE3 9MM

3 June 199–

Qualprint Ltd
22 Carnei Way
Glendale
FE1 8CA

Dear Sirs

Last month you printed 5000 brochures for us, at a price of £1.60 each + VAT, for our new sales campaign. You may remember that at the time the price for these was negotiated you also agreed to allow us 15% trade discount provided we placed the order within 3 days.

According to our calculations, this means that your invoice should have shown a reduction of £1,200 and then VAT added in the sum of £1190, making a total due of £7990. Your invoice, however, showed a total sum owing of £8,000 plus £1,400 for VAT.

Unfortunately your invoice, in the sum of £9,400, was passed for payment by a junior member of staff even though the discount had not yet been allowed. We should therefore be grateful if you could let us have your cheque for the discrepancy, ie £1,410, as soon as possible.

Yours faithfully

John Peters
Accounts Manager

Figure 8.19

Day 4

Again you are accompanied by Kristie, who asks you to explain the work you are doing this week. You tell her that you have been involved with orders received, delivery notes and sales invoices, but that you won't be doing statements of account yet as these are only sent out at the end of the month.

As last week, you agree to type out some notes for her.

Task 18

1 Prepare notes on all the documents listed above *including statements of account*. Explain why each of these is used.

2 Stress the importance of the documents being completed and calculated correctly and explain the problems which can occur if this is not done.

Naomi Walker is thinking of starting to sell computer disks – both $3\frac{1}{2}$" and $5\frac{1}{4}$" sizes. She knows that these can be single, double or high density and single or double sized. She wants further information on the type of disks local suppliers stock and the prices they charge.

Task 19

Either by visiting local shops which sell disks *or* by looking in business supplies or computer supplies catalogues, find out the type of disks which are stocked and their current selling prices. Give a range of at least three prices in each case.

Type a memo to Naomi Walker giving her the information she requires.

Day 5

Task 20

Karen Sharples passes you a list of goods she has sold on credit this week (Figure 8.20) and asks you to send out invoices for each of them. All the goods were collected except for those required by Hightown College. A delivery note is therefore only required for the final order on the list.

She asks you to take details of the reference number and price from a copy of Qualprint's price list.

NAME	ORDER	QUANTITY	DESCRIPTION	TERMS
F W Green Ltd	1829	6	A4 lever arch files	5% trade discount
Perry Place		12 reams	A4 typing paper (white)	
Glendale		12 pkts	Black felt tip pens	
FE4 9IK		12 pkts	Blue felt tip pens	
		4	Flipchart pads – A1 size	
J Moore & Sons	901	2 reams	A4 Bond paper (white)	No discount
16 Monks Road		1000	Printed letterheads	
Glendale		500	Printed compliment slips	
FE1 8TT				
Hightown	KM30191	100 reams	A4 Duplicating paper (white)	terms as usual
College		30 reams	A4 Bond paper (white)	for the College
Cheyne Walk		100 reams	A4 Photocopying paper	No delivery charge
Hightown				
HG4 7GX				

Figure 8.20

Task 21

Paul Turner gives you a copy of an order which has been received from a new customer (Figure 8.21). He has noticed several errors on the order but hasn't had time to check these in detail. He suggests you make a note of any problems and then draft out a fax message to Philips and Drew notifying them of your queries and asking them to clarify their requirements as soon as possible.

A copy of Qualprint's fax message form is included at the end of this book.

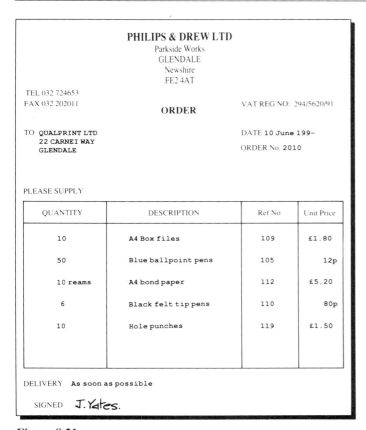

PHILIPS & DREW LTD
Parkside Works
GLENDALE
Newshire
FE2 4AT

TEL 032 724653
FAX 032 202011

ORDER

VAT REG NO: 294/5620/91

TO QUALPRINT LTD
22 CARNEI WAY
GLENDALE

DATE 10 June 199-

ORDER No. 2010

PLEASE SUPPLY

QUANTITY	DESCRIPTION	Ref No	Unit Price
10	A4 Box files	109	£1.80
50	Blue ballpoint pens	105	12p
10 reams	A4 bond paper	112	£5.20
6	Black felt tip pens	110	80p
10	Hole punches	119	£1.50

DELIVERY   As soon as possible

SIGNED   J. Yates.

Figure 8.21

WEEK 3 - CASH HANDLING AND BANKING PROCEDURES

Day 1 – Monday, 15 June

This week you are assigned to help Karen Sharples in the stationery shop. Karen informs you that your tasks will include:

- receiving cash and cheques
- making out receipts
- cashing up at the end of each day
- paying money into the bank.

Each day a £20 float is put into the cash register. This machine prints standard receipts but sometimes customers require a written receipt as well.

Task 22

Karen is worried because Kristie called in on Saturday, when they were busy, and Chris Gaston allowed her to help with stationery sales. Whilst Karen was having her afternoon break, Kristie accepted four

The Royal Midshire Bank plc
Date 13 June 19 9-   16–13–99
Pay Qualprint Ltd   or order
Ten pounds only   £ 10 – 00
                         S HARPER
49287·16...1399:62481021·   S. Harper

The Royal Midshire Bank plc
Date 13 June 19 9-   16–13–99
Pay Qualprint Ltd   or order
Twenty two pounds
57p only   £ 22 ——— 57
                         D AND J. WATSON
20481·16...1399:71482011·

Westchester Bank plc
Date 13 August 19 9-   20–14–81
Pay Qualprint Ltd   or order
Fifty seven pounds 80p   £ 57 ——— 80
                         P. PRICE
10010 201481 62481472   P. Price

Westchester Bank plc
Date 13 June 19 9-
Pay Qualprint Ltd   or order
Five pounds . 20p only   £ 5/——20
                         W. ALLEN
205216 203081 74864100   W. Allen

Figure 8.22

cheques (Figure 8.22) and Karen is worried that some of these were not checked properly.

She asks you to go through them, note any errors and advise her what action she should take in each case. Luckily, Kristie has had the sense to write the customer's name and address on the back of each cheque in addition to the cheque card guarantee number.

Amount tendered	Amount owing	Change given
3 × £20 notes	£54.20	
1 × £10 note and 3 × £5 notes	£21.80	
1 × £5 note	£1.95	
1 × £10 note	£7.13	
7 × £1 coins	£6.40	
2 × £5 notes and 6 × 50p coins	£12.62	
2 × £20 notes	£31.18	
1 × £50 note	£22.85	

Figure 8.23

QUALPRINT LTD – cashing up sheet

Date *15 June 199–*

Notes/coins	No. in till	Amount received
£50	1	£50.00
£20	6	£120.00
£10	8	£80.00
£5	5	
£1	24	
50p	17	
20p	12	
10p	16	
5p	2	
2p	13	
1p	7	
CASH TOTAL		
Cheques		
TOTAL		
Less £20 float		
TOTAL RECEIVED		

Signed _____

Figure 8.24

Task 23

During the afternoon you serve several customers who pay cash. How much change will you have given in each of the cases? Copy out Figure 8.23 and insert the missing figure in each case.

Task 24

By 5.30 p.m. Karen has started to complete the cashing up sheet which is made out each day (Figure 8.24). She says she likes this system as she can cope even if she is interrupted part way through. When it is complete it is sent to the administration section together with the money received. After five minutes Karen is called away urgently. She asks you to complete the sheet and to remember that three cheques have been received that day – for £14.20 from Mr J. Backhouse, £16.00 from Miss S. Caton and £65.30 from Mr F. Patel.

Day 2

Task 25

At 9.30 a.m. Mr P. Scott, a teacher from a local school - Parkway Secondary – arrives in a hurry to buy six clipboards. He needs a receipt so that he can claim back the money from petty cash. Make out a written receipt. Bear in mind that the next receipt number is 1230.

Task 26

The next customer wants to pay by cheque and requires a written receipt. She is a fairly regular customer – Mrs Peters – but her cheque card is for less than the amount of the cheque (Figure 8.25). You know you must ask for additional identification.

a What identification would you be prepared to accept?
b Make sure that her cheque is made out correctly.
c Write out the receipt she requires.

The Royal Midshire Bank plc

Date 16 June 19 9-   16–13–99

Pay *Qualprint Ltd*   or order

Eighty two pounds - 62p   £ 82-62

MARGARET PETERS

205713…1399:1 64182910

Figure 8.25

Task 27

Mrs Ryan calls in to pay the invoice she received last week. Unfortunately she has lost her copy. Look back in your records to see how much she owes.

She offers you 1 × £50 note and 3 × £20 notes. How much change does she require?

Make her out a written receipt for the payment.

Task 28

Complete the cashing up sheet at the end of the day which Karen has started (Figure 8.26). The only cheque received is the one from Mrs Peters.

Day 3

Task 29

Karen passes you a telephone message which has just been received from a Mr J. Tyler. He urgently needs some items of stationery and will collect these in half an hour and pay in cash. She asks you to make up the order and to write a note on top saying how much he must pay. He requires:

QUALPRINT LTD – cashing up sheet		
Date 16 June 199-		
Notes/coins	No. in till	Amount received
£50	2	
£20	3	
£10	4	
£5	17	
£1	16	
50p	25	
20p	12	
10p	15	
5p	7	
2p	22	
1p	1	
CASH TOTAL		
Cheques		
TOTAL		
Less £20 float		
TOTAL RECEIVED		
Signed _____		

Figure 8.26

2 reams A4 bond paper
5 A4 writing pads (200 page size)
6 blue ballpoint pens
1 box pencils
2 A4 box files

Write the note to Mr Tyler, remember to add VAT!

Task 30

Paul Turner wants the money which has been received over the last two days taken to the bank. He asks you to:

1 Get together the cashing up sheets for Monday and Tuesday. Remember that it is the total *received* which must

be banked. It is therefore suggested that you count one £20 note *less* each day into the paying-in slip.

2 Note that all four cheques accepted by Kristie last Saturday are now correct for paying in.

3 Include three cheques received by post that morning:
  a J. Tyler – £2596.75
  b C. Preston – £116.20
  c Meredith Retail Stores – £56.20

4 Make out the paying-in slip required.

Day 4

Task 31

Kristie comes to help you on the retail counter. You are concerned about this as you know what a mess she made accepting cheques last Saturday.

a Type a note for her which states exactly what procedure should be followed when accepting cheque payments.

b Include on the note a brief description of written receipts and bank paying-in slips.

c Explain the importance of the correct completion of both of these documents.

Task 32

You allow Kristie to complete the cashing-up sheet (Figure 8.27) for the day. No cheques have been received. Check her work and make a note of any errors to discuss with her next week.

Day 5

Task 33

You serve several customers who each pay cash. Copy out Figure 8.28 and state how much change you will give in each case.

QUALPRINT LTD – cashing up sheet

Date 18 June 199 –

Notes/coins	No. in till	Amount received
£50	1	£ 50 – 00
£20	8	£ 140 – 00
£10	6	£ 60 – 00
£5	5	25 – 00
£1	17	17 – 00
50p	15	7 – 50
20p	24	4 – 40
10p	5	50
5p	2	10
2p	1	1
1p	6	6
CASH TOTAL		329 – 57
cheques		
TOTAL		329 – 58
Less £20 float		20 – 00
TOTAL RECEIVED		319 – 00

Signed *Kristie Briggs*

Figure 8.27

Amount tendered	Amount owing	Change given
2 × £20 notes	£37.12	
1 × £10 note and 1 × £5 notes	£13.04	
1 × £20 note	£18.80	
1 × £50 note	£38.72	
4 × £1 coins	£3.53	
12 × £1 coins	£11.16	
4 × £10 notes	£32.90	
1 × £5 note	£3.60	

Figure 8.28

The Royal Midshire Bank plc

Date *19 June* 19 *9 –*   16-13-99

Pay *Qualprint plc*   or order

Sixteen pounds + 21p only   £ *16-12p*

MR MRS R PREST

1104810·16...1399:34281619

Judith Prest

Figure 8.29

Task 34

A Mrs Judith Prest buys six plastic rulers, two reams of photocopying paper and two small A4 writing pads.

Examine her cheque (Figure 8.29) to make sure that it is correct. If it is not, explain exactly what you would tell her.

Although she is paying by cheque she also asks for a written receipt. Make this out as requested.

Task 35

Paul Turner asks you to go to the bank again. He knows you have Thursday's cashing up sheet and hands you Wednesday's – which Karen Sharples completed (Figure 8.30). He asks you to add on the following cheques which have been received by post that morning:

Glendale Marketing	£540.60
Hightown College	£1600.84
Mrs P. Bryant	£73.20

Make out the required paying-in slip.

Task 36

Complete a new cashing up sheet for Friday. Karen hasn't been able to make entries today. When you count the coins in the till you set them out as follows:

QUALPRINT LTD – cashing up sheet

Date *17 June 199 –*

Notes/coins	No. in till	Amount received
£50	1	50 - 00
£20	6	120 - 00
£10	4	40 - 00
£5	2	10 - 00
£1	8	8 - 00
50p	11	5 - 50
20p	12	2 - 40
10p	3	30
5p	1	5
2p	6	12
1p	4	4
CASH TOTAL		236 · 41
Cheques		—
TOTAL		236 - 41
Less £20 float		20 - 00
TOTAL RECEIVED		216 - 41

Signed *Karen Sharples*

Figure 8.30

50p coins – 25	£50 notes – 0
10p coins – 13	20p coins – 17
1p coins – 6	£10 notes – 5
£5 notes – 13	£1 coins – 16
2p coins – 14	£20 notes – 11

You have no 5p coins but have received two cheques – one for £16.50 from J. Parker and the other from Mrs Prest. You know you haven't set out your cash in the order Karen normally uses and decide you will follow her system more carefully next week. In the meantime you have to transfer the information quickly to the cashing-up sheet and total this for Paul Turner.

WEEK 4 – PETTY CASH, PAY SLIPS AND OTHER DUTIES

Day 1 Monday, 22 June

Paul Turner asks you to take responsibility for petty cash. An imprest system is used with a float of £150. This is renewed at the end of every month. Vouchers can be presented up to £25 in value provided they have a manager's authorisation. At present the system is in a bit of a mess as no-one has been looking after it very well for the past fortnight.

Task 37

Paul tells you to ignore new vouchers and just to check the old ones stored in the tin against which payment has been made. At present there is £80.35 in the petty cash tin. Bearing in mind the voucher amounts, does it balance? If not, provide a brief list for Paul of what could have gone wrong.

Voucher number	Amount
210	£16.80
211	£6.20
212	£4.34
213	£18.20
214	£8.20
215	£0.70
216	£14.20

Task 38

Make out two vouchers for goods which have recently been purchased by Paul Turner and reimburse him with the money. Remember to keep your voucher numbers consecutive.

Sandwiches for lunchtime meeting £9.60
Jug kettle for use in office   £20.40
(replacement)   + VAT

Task 39

Make out a voucher for Naomi Walker to cover her travel costs. Reimburse her with the money.

Taxi fare to station   £2.60
Train fare   £9.80

Task 40

Assuming Paul Turner has made sure your imprest amount was straight after you 'balanced' your books this morning, how much should you now have left in petty cash?

Day 2

Disaster strikes today – Karen Sharples is away ill. You are asked to cover the retail counter as well as look after administration. Paul Turner warns you that from now on you will be expected to do whatever jobs are necessary!

Task 41

Make out a written receipt for Mr J. Andrews who buys two reams of photocopying paper and two reams of typing paper and pays in cash. Your next receipt number is 1242.

Task 42

Paul Turner asks you to go out and buy some coffee and tea. You buy a 300g jar of instant coffee and 120 teabags. Make out a petty cash voucher for the amount you spent and adjust your balance accordingly. Paul Turner will obviously authorise your expenditure.

Task 43

Make out a purchase order to Business Supplies for ten boxes of black ballpoint pens ref BP/4 at 75p per box and ten thousand 10" × 7" white envelopes – ref EV9 at £40 per 1000.

Task 44

Paul Turner has received the invoice for the Jetforce printer (Figure 8.31). He asks you to check if this has been calculated correctly. If so make out a cheque in payment.

COMPUTER SYSTEMS
15 Highway Walk
Glendale
Newshire
FE3 9OM

INVOICE

To: Qualprint Ltd
     22 Carnei Way
     Glendale

Deliver to:

Your order no.	Invoice date/tax point	Invoice no.	Despatch date
121/941	22 June 199–	72482	15 June 199–

Quantity	Description	Cat. no	Unit price	Total price	VAT rate	VAT amount
1	Jetforce printer	P40	385.00	385.00		
	Less 10% trade discount			38.50		
				346.50	17.5%	60.64
	Delivery charges			10.00		1.75
	Sub-total			356.50		
	VAT			62.39		
	Total amount due			418.89		

Terms: 28 days
E & O E

Figure 8.31

Task 45

Cash up the takings for the day and enter these on a cashing-up sheet. These amount to:

Three cheques – £185.45 (Mr A. Brand), £63.60 (Mr J. Long) and £160.00 (Vale & Peters Ltd)

In cash you have:

1 × £50 note	17 × 20p coins
15 × 20 notes	6 × 10p coins
5 × £10 notes	15 × 5p coins
16 × £5 notes	13 × 2p coins
13 × £1 coins	3 × 1p coins
22 × 50p coins	

Day 3

Task 46

Paul Turner asks you to take yesterday's takings and those for Monday to the bank. He gives you the cashing-up sheet which Karen Sharples made out on Monday evening (Figure 8.32 on page 248). He also asks you to add on a cheque for £783 received from Simon Engineering that morning. Make out the paying-in slip for the bank.

Task 47

Make out cheques to the following organisations. Then give them to Paul Turner who will arrange for them to be signed.

Stoneware Products Ltd	£42.35
J. Sinclair & Sons	£16.10
Peter Norris Ltd	£254.30

QUALPRINT LTD – cashing up sheet

Date __22 June 199–__

Notes/coins	No. in till	Amount received
£50	—	—
£20	4	£80·00
£10	3	£30·00
£5	5	£25·00
£1	8	8·00
50p	15	7·50
20p	30	6·00
10p	10	1·00
5p	1	5
2p	6	12
1p	1	1
CASH TOTAL		157·68
Cheques	—	—
TOTAL		157·68
Less £20 float		20·00
TOTAL RECEIVED		137·68

Signed __Karen Sharples.__

Figure 8.32

Task 48

Several goods are delivered from Stationery Stores Ltd. The delivery note is attached (Figure 8.33) from which you should make out the GRN. When you unpack the goods you find that 100 manilla folders are bent and cannot be resold.

Task 49

Mr J. Watts from Highcliffe Electronics, Whitehead Road, Glendale, telephones you. He urgently requires 100 reams of A4 photocopying paper, 50 reams of A4 bond paper and 2000 white envelopes. He says that their usual supplier has let

STATIONERY STORES LTD
16–18 Hamilton Road
Glendale
FE7 8MS

DELIVERY NOTE

To   Qualprint Ltd
     22 Carnei Way
     Glendale

No: 61859

YOUR ORDER NO	INVOICE DATE/tax point	invoice no	DESPATCH DATE
121/971	23 June 199–	72487	23 June 199–

Quantity	Description	Ref No
300	Manilla folders	2080
100	Plastic rulers	1062
100	Clipboards	1050
50	A4 box files – blue	2014

RECEIVED BY __P. Turner__   DATE __23/6/9–__

Figure 8.33

them down and if you can have the goods ready for collection, with the invoice, in 15 minutes then he will give you their custom from now on. He also asks for discount – and Paul Turner agrees he can receive 5%.

Make out the invoice required. Your next invoice number is 2894.

Day 4

Because it is nearing the end of the month Paul Turner wants to start preparing statements of account. These list all the transactions which have been carried out between Qualprint and its customers during the course of the last month.

He asks you to help by making out statements for the following customers:

Greenbank Engineering
Blades Ice Arena
Glendale Borough Council
Hightown College
Parr Finance

All these companies have outstanding balances at the end of the month.

Paul Turner gives you a sheet (Figure 8.34) which includes transactions you may not know about, and asks you to include your own figures for sales invoices you have made out.

The sheet also includes the outstanding balances at the beginning of the month, where appropriate.

Make out the five statements required.

However, although the computer is working correctly, the printer has jammed and the pay slips will have to be made out manually.

From the information in Figure 8.35, make out pay slips as required. Because Paul Turner knows that you have studied pay slips, he expects you to be able to insert any missing information. Write out the cheque for Mary O'Connell and attach it to her pay slip for signing.

Day 5

Problems occur in a different way today. On the last Friday of the month Paul Turner is responsible for paying the wages at Qualprint. These are calculated by computer.

INVOICES SENT – JUNE 199–

Date	Customer	Invoice No	Amount
8 June	Greenbank Engineering	2876	
8 June	Glendale Borough Council	2877	
8 June	Blades Ice Arena	2878	
9 June	Parr Finance	2880	
9 June	Hightown College	2882	
10 June	Hightown College	2885	
15 June	Glendale Borough Council	2890	£164.20
16 June	Blades Ice Arena	2892	£70.20
18 June	Hightown College	2894	£640.28
24 June	Parr Finance	2900	£540.20
26 June	Greenbank Engineering	2908	£1 890.00

PAYMENTS RECEIVED – JUNE 199–

2 June	Parr Finance	£610.00
4 June	Greenbank Engineering	£405.20
13 June	Blades Ice Arena	£210.50
19 June	Hightown College	£1 600.84

OUTSTANDING BALANCES AS AT 1 JUNE 199–

Parr Finance - £610.00
Blades Ice Arena – £210.50
Hightown College – £2624.80
Glendale Borough Council – £608.45
Greenbank Engineering £405.20

Figure 8.34

PAY SLIP INFORMATION

Pay period – June 199–

Standard information

Emp No	Name	Dept	Tax Code	NI No	Method of Payment
15	Karen Sharples	A1	325L	BD 30 10 48 C	BACS
17	Mary O'Connell	S2	322L	YB 45 60 98 B	Cheque
22	Yourself	A1	300L	DQ 32 57 98 D	BACS

Variable information (this month only)

Emp No	Gross pay	Deductions	Total pay to date	Tax to date	NI to date	Taxable pay to date
15	£775	Tax £132.50 NI £32.20 SAYE £10	£2325.00	£464.50	£96.60	£1575.00
17	£792	Tax £136.00 NI £34.80	£2376.00	£408.00	£104.40	£1626.80
22	£620	Tax £103.00 NI £26.20	£620.00	£103.00	£26.20	£440.10

IMPORTANT NOTE: – All employees at Qualprint pay £2 a month to the social fund.

Figure 8.35

Task 52

You have been reminded that you are still on emergency coding as your code number has not yet been received. This means you are paying more tax than necessary. What must you do to rectify this situation? Make out a reminder note to yourself about what action you should take.

Task 53

Chris Gaston has decided that Kristie should receive some payment for the work she has done that month. He decides to pay her £30. Because she is still a student she is not liable for tax or National Insurance. Paul tells you to list her under the administration department and give her pay reference 28.

a Make out her pay slip and her cheque.

b Because you were too busy to see her yesterday you realise she knows about virtually everything you have done except petty cash. You have a feeling she may think this system doesn't matter because it only relates to small amounts of money – you know differently!

Type out a brief note for her, in the same style as those you have done before. Explain the petty cash system and why accuracy is so important. As a final paragraph you can add that you will explain about pay slips when she has had more experience!

chapter **9** CONSUMER DEMAND

Learning Objectives

This chapter is concerned with the characteristics of consumers and how these affect buyer behaviour. The effects of changing trends in consumer demand are examined in relation to both general trends and particular products, as well as reasons for these changes.

After studying this chapter you should be able to

- identify the main characteristics of consumers
- identify trends in consumer demand for goods and services using relevant information
- explain causes of changes in consumer demand for goods and services.

Activity

Think ahead

For one of the exercises in this chapter you will need to study different newspapers. *As a group*, try to acquire a copy of each of the following: *Times, Guardian, Daily Express, Daily Mirror, Daily Mail, Sun.*

Note that whilst the date doesn't really matter – provided that each is relatively recent – it will certainly help you to compare them if you obtain each one for the *same date*. Then you can see how:

a different items of news are covered
b the reporting of the *same* items is treated differently.

· CONSUMER DEMAND ·

Today there are more outlets for goods and services than ever before and the choice of goods on offer is quite staggering. This is because:

- people have more 'disposable' income to spend (i.e. income remaining after essential living expenses have been paid) – so demand for consumer goods is high
- goods can be quickly and cheaply produced using modern machinery and equipment
- goods can be rapidly transported across countries and even across continents.

You only have to go to your local supermarket with an older member of your family and ask him or her how the range compares with goods on offer in the 1950s to find there is a considerable difference! If you look through your *Yellow Pages* you will find a whole host of service industries, from decorators to plumbers, cleaners to travel agents and hairdressers to taxi firms. Today you can have virtually anything you want, if you have the money to pay for it. If you haven't, then you may find adverts placed by finance companies, banks or building societies to try to tempt you to borrow the money instead (if you are over 18).

DID YOU KNOW?

In 1990 the people of Britain spent about eight times as much *in real terms* on consumer goods as they did in the early 1950s.

In economics the phrase 'in real terms' is often used. This relates to the **real** value of money at a given point in time, allowing for changes in the value of money because of inflation.

Imagine that last year you received £10 a week spending money. This year you receive £11. This will only be a *real* increase if inflation is 10 per cent or less. If inflation is 15 per cent then you will actually be worse off – as you would need £11.50 to buy the same goods which cost you £10 spending money last year.

Evidence Collection Point 9.1

1 Look through the headings in *Yellow Pages* and list ten different *types* of organisations which you consider weren't in existence 20 years ago. Discuss as a group why there is now a demand for the goods and services they offer and write down your conclusions.

2 You have received a letter from your friend Steven who is thinking of borrowing £250 to buy a new computer. You think he is being foolhardy – he is a student and only earns £20 a week doing part-time work. Write a reply to him giving your views and telling him *why* you think borrowing the money would not be wise. Discuss your letter with your tutor. (You may like to refer back to Chapter 7, which gives further information on loans and APR before you do this exercise.)

Identifying customers

All organisations need to know which consumers buy their product or service (and which do not, and why not). In other words they need to know which consumers are their **customers**. We are *all* consumers as everyone buys goods or services or receives them 'free of charge' from the government (e.g. library services or police protection)

1 Please indicate whether you are offering the following courses. Please also supply the names of the teachers of these subjects as well as the pupil numbers and ages.

Course subject	Name of teacher	Position	Pupil numbers	Age range
GCSE Economics				
A level Economics				
GCSE Business Studies				
A level Business Studies				
BTEC/GNVQ Levels 2 and 3:				
Business				
Health & Caring				
Leisure & Tourism				
NVQ Levels 1 & 2 Business Administration				
Shorthand*				
Typing: Stage I				
Stage II				
Stage III				
Word processing:** Stage I				
Stage II				
Stage III				
Desk top publishing				

*Which shorthand system are you teaching? ....

** Which word processing package are you using? ....

2 Do you see the balance of subjects being taught changing in the next couple of years?
  e.g. less A level and more GNVQs
          less Economics and more Business Studies
Please specify ....
....

3 [ ] Please tick this box if you would like to be placed on the mailing list to receive newsletters giving details of The Economics Association **Economics Education 16-19 Project** published by Heinemann. No need to tick if you are already on the mailing list.

Any other comments ....
....
....
....

Please return your completed questionnaire as soon as possible to:
Rosalyn Bass, Heinemann Educational, FREEPOST, Halley Court, Jordan Hill, Oxford OX2 8BR

Thank you very much for your help.

Finding out what the market wants

even though people in employment pay for these through taxation. However, we are only customers if we pay a supplier for a specific product or service. Knowing which consumers are their customers – and how to increase their number – is an important goal for most organisations.

Organisations also need to be able to find out when consumers are changing their buying habits – and why – so that they can adapt their product (or make new ones) to cope with changing demand. There is a variety of methods by which companies can find out this information:

● by sending out questionnaires to existing customers
● by questioning people who are not (yet) customers
● by studying statistics about people that give information on changes which will affect their buying habits

- by finding out about the success (or otherwise) of competitors' products.

It is pointless a company spending large sums of money on developing new products which no-one wants or continuing to produce goods for which there is no longer a demand.

Assessing demand

Finding out about potential and actual demand is undertaken by the **marketing department** of an organisation (see page 121).

Market research is the term given to finding out answers to the following questions:

- *Who* is a customer (in terms of age, gender, income, etc.)?
- Who is *not* a customer (and why not)?
- What trends are taking place which may increase or decrease the potential number of customers?
- What does the typical customer *want* from the product?
- What alternative products are on the market?
- What changes are taking place in consumer attitudes and lifestyles?

Market research is used both for potential products and for existing ones. Either by means of a postal survey, a telephone survey or personal interview, an organisation will try to find out what people think about its own products and those of its competitors.

Postal surveys are cheap but response rates are poor. Personal interviews mean the correct age group and gender of the consumer can be accurately targeted and the interviewees have each question read to them by a professional interviewer – but this method is slow and expensive. Some agencies undertake telephone surveys for their clients. They keep a list of people who have agreed to answer questions. The list shows their name, address and telephone number, age, occupation, number of children and ages etc. This information helps them to target 'users' and 'potential users' more accurately.

Computer databases (see page 450) are used extensively for targeting customers. Specialist agencies record details of people, including their name, age, income, number of children, assets and possessions, and provide address lists to companies on request. These lists can highlight relevant factors. For instance, a company selling cheap motor insurance specially to the over-50s would not want to send mail shots to people in their 30s! Using this system, mail shots can be sent to those people who would be interested in the product.

Activity

A novel form of targeting was carried out by Porsche, the luxury sports car firm. It stopped advertising altogether in 1992 and, instead, sent a glossy video pack on its new £70 000 car to 1000 image conscious top earners in the country.

1 Why do you think Porsche changed its approach?

2 If you had to define a typical Porsche driver, how would you identify this person in terms of:

- age
- taste
- lifestyle?
- gender
- income

Discuss this as a group and write down your ideas before you read further.

· CHARACTERISTICS OF CONSUMERS ·

For the last activity you may have said that the average Porsche driver is male, in his 30s, has a taste for luxury and fast cars, a well-paid job and an active social life. Therefore Porsche marketing will be targeted at this group. There would seem to be little point in sending the information to a 76-year-old female pensioner – although there are exceptions to every rule!

Some goods have a specific market (e.g. sports cars, caravans, nappies), others are bought by nearly everyone at some time. For instance, basic necessities such as food and clothing are required by everyone. However, consumer characteristics are still important as in many cases these still affect buyer behaviour. **Brand names** may be promoted by an organisation to try to sub-divide the market. In this case, the characteristics of people who buy the individual brands are often different.

Evidence Collection Point 9.2

A typical area where brand names are used to sub-divide a market according to consumer characteristics is make-up and beauty products. Whilst cosmetic companies will obviously target their marketing mainly at women, brands do differ in their appeal to different *types* of women – in terms of age, taste, income and lifestyle. And, of course, sometimes the packaging is designed to attract the attention of someone who might be wanting to buy a special present for a friend.

1 Visit a local shop and find out the type of goods produced by Rimmel, Max Factor and Estée Lauder. Write down a sample of their prices and make a note of the design of their packaging.

2 From this information, decide what you think are the characteristics of each of their average customers in terms of age, income and lifestyle.

3 Identify five other well-known manufacturers of beauty products and explain to which type of customers they would appeal. From this you should be able to identify which manufacturers are in direct competition, and which are not!

4 Obtain an example of an advertisement from each of the cosmetic manufacturers mentioned above (and those which you identified). Explain in each case to what extent you think the content and style of the advertisement is aimed at the target market.

For a moment, think about the goods that are bought by yourself and other members of your family. The chances are that you don't buy the same type of goods as your parents, neither do you (or they) buy the same goods as your grandparents. If you have brothers or sisters then, again, the type of goods each of you buys will vary. This is because, in many cases, the type of goods we buy is influenced by our **age** and our **gender** (i.e. whether we are male or female).

Age-groups

Our age often determines the type of products we buy. If you look around your own shopping centre you will see different age-groups in different types of shops. Record and computer games shops will have more young customers, as will fashion boutiques and chain stores such as Next. Marks & Spencer will attract older customers and so will men's tailors and exclusive dress shops. Therefore the range of goods carried by these retail stores and their decor are influenced by the age of the customer they expect to serve. Large companies will have a range of stores, in the same high street, but all appealing to different customers. For example, Burton Group own Debenhams which may appeal to older men and women, Principles which attracts people in their 20s and 30s with fashionable but classic clothes and Dorothy Perkins which caters for younger women who may only just have started work and who do not earn a lot.

Manufacturers make different versions of the same type of product for different age-groups. A good example of this is toiletry products. If you visit a store such as Boots, you will see different age-groups buying different types. Mothers will buy baby powder for infants and Matey bubble bath for young children. You may buy hair gel or fixing spray. All your family may use shower gel – yet your grandparents may think that this is an extravagance, and simply buy soap.

Do bear in mind that as people grow older their buying habits may not keep pace with changing fashion. This may be because:

- they are more set in their ways
- they are less mobile
- they have less money to spend after retirement (especially true if people are totally dependent on their old age pension).

Evidence Collection Point 9.3

1 Walk around your own shopping centre. List six retail outlets which are regularly used by young people and six which are used by older people. State the goods which are sold in each case. Give one example, in each case, of how this has affected the style and decor of the shop.

2 A friend of yours, Matthew Baker, who lives some miles away, belongs to a family in which there are two young children under 10, two teenagers, parents in their early

40s and an elderly grandparent in his 60s. They are visiting your area on a shopping trip and have asked you to suggest where they could have something to eat around mid-day. Where would you suggest if:

a you wanted to please the young children
b you wanted to please the teenagers
c you wanted to suggest somewhere which would appeal to the parents
d you had the grandfather in mind?

Write a letter to your friend (invent the address) giving your suggestions with reasons in each case.

DID YOU KNOW?

Britain is getting older. In the early 1950s there were:

5.6 million people over 65
1.6 million people over 75
234 000 people over 85.

In the early 1990s there were:

9 million people over 65
4 million people over 75
892 000 people over 85.

The same pattern is true for all European countries, mainly because of improvements in diet and health care, which mean that people can expect to live longer.

Saga Holidays Ltd. Leading the way for people in retirement

Demographic trends

The word **demography** relates to the population. Organisations are very interested in population trends as this gives an idea of future demand for their products.

The figures above explain the increasing demand for products and services targeted at older people (e.g. Saga holidays, lower car insurance premiums for the over 50s, old people's homes and sheltered accommodation).

DID YOU KNOW?

It is forecast that in Europe, whereas just under a fifth of its population are already 60 plus, this will rise to over a third by 2020.

The European version of *Social Trends* is called *A Social Portrait of Europe*. However, many tables in *Social Trends* also include an international aspect.

Gender

You have just seen that people are living longer. However, the figures for males and females, in terms of life expectancy, are different. A baby boy born in 1986 can expect to live until he is 71 years and 9 months old. A baby girl can be expected to reach 77 years and 6 months. For this reason, more products and services aimed at the elderly are likely to be bought or used by women than by men.

Whilst there would appear to be some very obvious differences between the products bought by men and women, manufacturers have to be careful. In many cases, items which are *used* by one sex may be bought by the other (e.g. women buying after-shave and ties, men buying perfume). It is therefore pointless for a manufacturer of, say, shaving foam to target all marketing at men if shaving foam is bought by women doing the weekly shopping at the supermarket!

In the car market manufacturers have started to become aware of the influence of women on men's buying behaviour. In the more progressive motor dealers salespeople have been less inclined to dismiss the views of any women present. However, it is still the case that car advertisements for men are likely to emphasise engine performance whilst those for women will emphasise storage space for shopping and economy!

Evidence Collection Point 9.4

1 Obtain six car advertisements from different sources (e.g. Sunday colour supplements and women's magazines). Compare the models advertised and the ways in which the advertisements are worded. Write a summary of the differences between those targeted at men and at women.

2 Identify one other product which is bought by both men and women but which is advertised differently in each case. Obtain examples of advertisements.

3 Obtain a hobby magazine which would be bought by men (e.g. on DIY, darts, snooker, fishing) and examine the type of goods advertised in this. Compare these advertisements with those found in women's magazines and state the differences you find both in terms of products advertised and style of advertisement.

4 The trend today is for fewer people to smoke cigarettes. Tobacco manufacturers promote cigarettes in magazines even though they cannot do so on television. Examine Figure 9.1, which shows the trend in terms of people giving up smoking. State:

a how these figures could be used by tobacco com-panies to influence *where* they advertise in the future

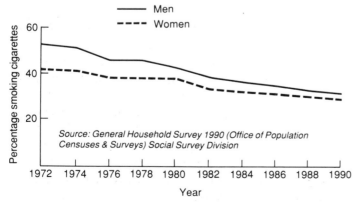

Figure 9.1 *Trends in cigarette smoking in the UK between 1972 and 1990*

b how these figures could be used by the manufacturers of anti-smoking patches to promote *their* products.

5 Enter the information in Figure 9.1 on a spreadsheet. Assuming the current trend continues, what will be the approximate number of male and female cigarette smokers in the year 2000?

DID YOU KNOW?

There is one toy on the market which is identical, in terms of its composition, when it is bought by girls and by boys. Yet the packaging is entirely different. Indeed, if you buy a boy the 'girl's box' or a girl the 'boy's box' as a present, you may find you have a riot on your hands! Can you name the toy? (The answer is given at the end of this chapter.)

Tastes

Imagine a world where we all liked exactly the same things. Everyone would wear identical clothes, have the same hairstyle, drive the same car, read the same books, furnish and decorate their houses in the same way and so on. But we don't. Why do we all prefer different things? Why is it that you prefer one TV programme and your friend prefers another?

The reason is that we all have different **tastes** – in music, clothes, shoes, food and drink, cars, and almost anything else you care to name. Taste relates to our individual preferences and these change with age, fashion and opinions. Tastes also vary between men and women. 'Taste' is the reason why, given two similar products at a similar price, you might choose one brand and your friend might choose the other, or why she may order coffee whilst you always drink tea.

Your taste is influenced in a variety of ways. Imagine you leave home to live in a flat. Initially you buy many of the products that were bought by your parents (e.g. their brand of soap powder, coffee etc.). If you share your flat with a friend you may be influenced by his or her choice of goods and reasons for buying them (and you would also influence your friend's behaviour). You may also be influenced by advertisements you see, articles you read and television programmes you watch. Education often changes our 'tastes' – we may change our minds about what we want and need as we learn more about the world. If you obtain a job which takes you to another country your tastes may change again – they may become more cosmopolitan. In Britain, people's taste for foreign food has increased as they have returned from holidays abroad where they have sampled different types of food.

Evidence Collection Point 9.5

1 You have recently made friends with someone who is very much against using animals to test products. He will only buy toiletries from Body Shop or which are clearly labelled as not being tested on animals and is aghast that you have never considered this issue.

How may his opinions change your buying habits? If more people took this view, how might this change manufacturers' behaviour?

2 As an individual member of your group, write out your own answers to the points below. Then compare your answers. Ask each person in your group to try to say *why* they have made the choices they have. What do their reasons tell you about how people develop different tastes?

a Your top five TV programmes.
b Your top five groups or singers.
c Your two favourite soft drinks.
d Your five favourite foods.

Activity

1 Imagine you have asked six people what they do for a living. From their occupations (given below) put them in order according to who you think would earn the most, the second most and so on, down to the least.

a Head teacher.
b Pensioner.
c Police sergeant.
d Labourer.
e Plumber.
f Hospital consultant.

2 Each of them buys one of the following daily newspapers. Who you think buys which? (Use the papers you were asked to collect at the beginning of this chapter to help you.)

● *Times*
● *Daily Mirror*
● *Guardian*
● *Daily Express*
● *Sun*
● *Daily Mail*

Note: There obviously is no absolute answer to this question – only a *probable* answer. Try to decide before you read on.

Lifestyle

This describes the way in which we live and how we spend our time. Lifestyle may be determined by our job – which dictates our income, the amount of leisure time we have, the people we mix with and their interests. Lifestyles can also be affected by what is fashionable and what is not. Today more people are health conscious, which has reduced tobacco consumption and increased demand for wholefood products and vegetarian meals. There are also more working mothers today, so that the 'lifestyle' of many families has changed, with husbands now helping with the shopping and doing more of the household chores.

Consumers and occupations

One method which organisations use to find out who their potential customers may be is to refer to the UK classification of social class (see Figure 9.2). This ranks people according to their occupations. Whatever we may think about the fairness of this type of grouping, it does give quite a reliable guide to the relationship between a person's job and income. It also gives an indication of different patterns of buying goods. For instance, those in the top income groups are more likely to pay for private health insurance, private education and expensive cars. Those in lower income groups have to spend a higher proportion of their income on necessities such as food, rent and clothing.

Classification/grade		Occupation	Percentage of population
A	Upper/upper middle class	Top managers and professionals	4%
B	Middle class	Senior managers, professionals and administrators	19.5%
C1	Lower middle class	Supervisors, junior managers and clerical staff	21%
C2	Skilled working class	Skilled manual workers	30.5%
D	Working class	Semi-skilled and unskilled manual workers	17%
E	Lowest level of subsistence	State pensioners, disabled, casual workers and unemployed	8%

Figure 9.2 *UK classification of social class*

Key to newspapers

According to statistics, the newspapers most likely to be bought by our readers on the previous page are as follows:

Times – Hospital consultant (A)
Guardian – Head teacher (B)
Daily Express/Daily Mail – Police sergeant (C1) and Plumber (C2)
Daily Mirror/Sun – Labourer/pensioner (D/E)

Of course, if our pensioner is a retired hospital consultant this confuses the picture! Therefore, it is important to remember that the table can only be used as a *guide* – other factors such as lifestyle also have a bearing on buyer behaviour.

Evidence Collection Point 9.6

Assume you work for a travel agent. You have the following brochures to send to potential customers. Which classification would you choose for each brochure?

a A caravanning holiday in Wales.
b An inclusive package holiday to Ibiza.
c Self-catering holidays in French villas.
d Two-week fly-drive holidays to the USA.
e World cruises on the QE2.
f Hotels and boarding houses in Blackpool.

Again there is no definite answer. An unemployed teenager might like the idea of going to Ibiza for two weeks, but it is doubtful whether he or she would have enough money to be able to afford it! You are *likely*, therefore, to be more successful if you target your brochures according to income.

In recent years organisations have paid increasing attention to **lifestyles**. A lifestyle is a behaviour pattern adopted by a particular group. Products and services can be developed and targeted to support a particular lifestyle.

Evidence Collection Point 9.7

1 What type of lifestyle would you associate with each of the following people?

• a company director
• a shop assistant
• a person who is unemployed.

Think in terms of income, leisure time, entertainment and hobbies, goods and services each would buy.

2 In what way do you consider lifestyle changes in relation to:

a age
b income
c the place where people live?

Discuss these issues *as a group* and then summarise your answers.

Local factors

Believe it or not, there is a difference in buyer behaviour in the various regions of the UK. Tastes and preferences are different, as Figure 9.3 shows.

	Regions of England							England	Wales	Scotland	Overall
	North	Yorkshire and Humberside	North West	East Midlands	West Midlands	South West	South East/ East Anglia				
Milk and cream (pt or eq. pt)	3.80	4.05	4.00	4.21	4.01	4.30	3.96	4.02	3.66	4.11	4.01
Cheese	3.58	3.72	4.04	4.24	4.39	4.78	4.31	4.19	3.51	3.98	4.13
Meat and meat products	37.14	37.24	36.98	34.22	40.50	38.84	34.81	36.58	35.29	37.37	36.59
Fish	5.68	6.07	4.66	4.51	4.78	5.02	5.16	5.13	4.45	4.70	5.06
Eggs (number)	3.31	3.00	2.55	2.70	2.42	2.78	2.27	2.58	2.39	3.62	2.67
Fats and oils	10.08	10.06	9.95	9.85	10.62	10.56	9.11	9.80	10.43	10.05	9.86
Sugars and preserves	8.80	8.99	8.44	8.62	9.58	10.65	7.73	8.65	8.20	10.45	8.79
Fruit	27.80	27.18	28.70	27.85	30.88	36.25	37.62	32.61	28.81	27.34	31.92
Vegetables	91.28	83.15	83.14	88.55	85.71	91.71	76.66	82.99	86.07	82.14	83.09
Cereals (incl. bread)	58.83	55.55	54.14	57.67	56.61	53.54	49.88	53.61	52.38	59.79	54.12
Beverages	2.90	2.58	2.76	2.64	2.59	2.75	2.64	2.67	2.70	2.50	2.66

The figures are in *ounces*, except for milk/cream (pints) and eggs (number).
Source: *Household Food Consumption and Expenditure 1988* (MAFF)

Figure 9.3 *Food consumption (per person per week) by region in 1988*

The geographical features of different regions can influence consumer demand. Obviously, regions where there are high numbers of tourists each year will sell more souvenir goods, areas next to the sea or a lake will have a demand for boating equipment, mountainous areas will have camping or mountaineering shops and so on.

In addition, lifestyles in each region may be different. This will depend on a variety of factors, including the number of large towns or cities or, conversely, on whether parts of the region are comparatively isolated.

Evidence Collection Point 9.8

1 Use *Social Trends* to find out how:

- income from employment, and
- household disposable income

varies between all the regions of Great Britain and Northern Ireland.

2 Find three other tables in either *Social Trends or* the *Family Expenditure Survey* which give information by region. State how each of these tables would be useful for a particular manufacturer.

3 Identify three products which are popular in your particular region but may be difficult to find if you travel out of the area. How can you account for their popularity?

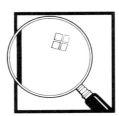

Evidence Assignment 9A

Figure 9.4 below shows an analysis of mid-day meals eaten each week by children aged 5–14 years in 1988. Figure 9.5 shows the trend since 1978. Study these carefully and then answer the questions below.

1 In which region were the least school meals eaten?

2 In which region were the least packed meals taken to school?

3 In which region did most children eat at home?

	Meals not from the household supply		Meals from the household supply	
	School meals	Other meals out	Packed meals	Other
All households	1.95	0.32	1.69	3.04
Analysis by region				
Scotland	1.83	0.29	1.08	3.80
Wales	1.95	0.31	1.67	3.07
England	1.97	0.32	1.76	2.95
North	2.61	0.23	1.11	3.05
Yorkshire & Humberside	2.37	0.28	1.07	3.28
North West	2.13	0.32	1.83	2.72
East Midlands	2.27	0.33	1.05	3.35
West Midlands	2.00	0.31	1.76	2.93
South West	1.49	0.30	2.46	2.75
South East/East Anglia	1.68	0.37	2.05	2.90

Source: *Household Food Consumption and Expenditure 1988* (MAFF)

Figure 9.4 *Average number of mid-day meals per week per child aged 5–14 years in 1988*

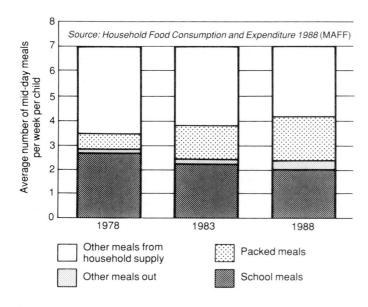

Figure 9.5 *The trend in the number of mid-day meals since 1978*

Legend:
- Other meals from household supply
- Other meals out
- Packed meals
- School meals

4 Generally, people eat out more in the South East than in any other region of the country. Can you offer any reasons for this?

5 Examine carefully the figures for your own region. Can you offer any reasons for the way eating habits where you live differ from those in other places?

6 From Figure 9.5, are more or fewer children eating packed lunches than before? Can you offer any reasons for this?

7 Is the trend towards eating out, in general, or towards eating at home?

8 Other figures show that the number of meals eaten outside the home is highest for households with high incomes and where the mother is either under 25 or between 45 and 54. What reasons can you suggest for this?

9 Design a bar chart which shows the regional figures in Figure 9.4 using the stacked bar chart format shown in Figure 9.5. Instead of the years underneath, your bars will then show regions.

10 Survey the eating habits of the students in your school or college – and the popularity (or otherwise) of your refectory or canteen. Do your findings support those for your region, or not? Can you give reasons for any differences?

DID YOU KNOW?

If a company wants to test market a product it may choose to start selling only in one region to start with. It would therefore choose its region carefully, based on previous patterns of expenditure for that type of product in that area. It would also advertise its product on regional television programmes. From the sales figures the company could assess the success (or otherwise) of the test marketing campaign.

National differences

Consumer demand also varies from one nation to another, sometimes quite considerably. This is because tastes and lifestyles are even more different from one nation to another than they are between regions. In addition, because wealthy nations will spend more on household appliances (known as **consumer durables**), more of these goods will be sold in some countries than in others.

Evidence Collection Point 9.9

Figure 9.6 shows the eating habits of the people in a variety of countries between 1987 and 1989. Figure 9.7 shows the ownership of consumer durables in the same countries. Study these carefully and then answer the questions below.

1 In which country is the most fresh produce sold and in which the least? Can you suggest any reasons for these differences?

2 In which country are the most eggs eaten? Try to talk to someone who has been to that country and find out the different variations available when you order egg dishes which you won't find in Britain!

3 In which country is the most fish consumed? Can you offer any geographical reasons for this?

4 Choose a country you would like to visit. From the comparative figures given for that country and the UK, summarise the differences in eating habits you may expect to find.

	Austria	Belgium	Denmark	France	WGermany	Italy	Netherlands	Spain	Sweden	Switzerland	UK	USA
Fresh produce	232.7	271.1	184.6	246.5	265.1	313.6	218.9	362.6	177.8	209.2	238.2	99.6
of which:												
vegetables	76.9	97.2	66.7	95.0	77.7	173.4	61.0	164.1	44.0	80.3	67.8	35.7
potatoes	61.8	99.1	64.5	77.7	70.6	38.2	85.0	107.0	63.3	62.6	50.2	19.2
fruit	94.0	74.8	53.4	73.8	116.8	102.0	72.9	91.5	70.5	78.7	62.4	44.7
Meat	92.8	103.2	104.3	90.5	104.9	87.5	81.9	95.0	58.5	87.6	77.3	100.6
of which:												
beef & veal	21.9	22.0	19.3	23.6	23.6	26.7	19.3	11.4	16.1	26.1	21.6	34.0
pork	47.8	49.0	71.7	28.5	62.7	30.5	45.0	47.0	31.9	43.2	24.8	26.9
lamb & mutton	0.5	1.8	0.8	3.3	0.9	1.6	0.7	6.1	0.7	1.7	6.6	0.6
poultry	13.7	17.2	11.7	21.3	11.3	19.5	15.0	21.4	5.3	10.9	18.2	77.8
Fish	3.5	10.2	43.0	21.7	7.5	10.3	9.9	17.8	15.8	4.4	3.5	7.0
of which:												
fresh fish	3.4	9.5	40.7	14.8	7.0	9.4	8.0	16.8	6.6	4.1	3.2	4.5*
Cereals	92.2	97.3	93.1	100.4	97.7	157.7	73.7	97.1	78.9	77.4	119.1	85.7
Eggs	14.6	13.1	14.3	14.9	15.4	11.3	11.1	15.7	11.7	12.4	11.6	16.3
Milk (litres)	101.4	62.0	123.0	78.9	54.6	67.9	60.6	95.2	163.9	96.2	119.7	106.9
Bread	51.1	84.6	29.7	63.9	60.8	132.6	60.2	52.8	38.9	22.9	44.4	
Frozen convenience foods	12.9	16.0	36.2	21.1	22.8	6.1	16.3	12.1	27.9	22.1	22.4	
Canned food	12.2	34.6	15.2	37.7	35.0	12.4	16.9	11.7	18.9	15.2	26.8	

*Includes frozen fish.

Source: *Business Comparisons – An Analytical and Statistical Survey of Europe and the USA* (Economist Intelligence Unit)

Figure 9.6 *National eating habits 1987–89 (kg consumption per person)*

	Austria	Belgium	Denmark	France	WGermany	Italy	Netherlands	Spain	Sweden	Switzerland	UK	USA
Television	96	95	94	94	93	94	97	98	90		98	99
Video recorder	6	13	24	10	30	9	32	19	10	14	50	
Radio	95	90	98	98	84	92	97	95	93	99	99	
Record player	27	30	60	65	72	60	81	49	64	65	29	
Vacuum cleaner	97	91	75	88	97	90	99	47	99	98	97	99
Refrigerator	97	94	97	98	91	88	98	94	96	96	98	100
Freezer	61	58	87	40	78	42	47	18	70	68	75	
Washing machine	87	86	65	87	91	91	89	94	60	68	85	73*
Tumble drier	8	21				10	17	2	25	14	39	62*
Dishwasher	27	27	25	28	34	24	9	13	30	32	9	43*
Microwave oven	12	8	9	17	20	10	22	2	25	15	35	61*
Food processor	82	91	83	83	92	48	84	50	77	91	80	

*These are for 1987.

Source: *Business Comparisons – An Analytical and Statistical Survey of Europe and the USA* (Economist Intelligence Unit)

Figure 9.7 *Percentages of households owning consumer durables in 1988*

5 Which household appliance is owned by most people in most countries?

6 Far more households in the USA own dishwashers then in the UK. Can you suggest two reasons for this?

7 From the figures given, if you were to open household appliance shops in Belgium and in Spain, what difference would there be to the type of products you should stock?

The international aspect

Despite national differences in terms of taste, lifestyles and income, there are a great number of similarities. People in the western world dress similarly, so clothes can be sold internationally (think of jeans!). In many cases, people's tastes are actually becoming more similar, especially in areas such as music, films and cars. It is believed that this is because communications and travel between countries are greater than ever before. We are therefore all assimilating the ideas of other people, and our tastes and preferences are changing.

Global marketing

Today more and more companies market their goods across continents. A typical example is the film industry – films made in Hollywood are distributed around the world. Some people claim that this breaks down barriers between nations, but other disagree.

In reality, social customs, traditions and lifestyles affect consumer choice, so that what will sell in one country won't sell in another. As an example, it is only in the last few years that Smarties packets in Britain have contained *blue* Smarties, as the British traditionally don't like blue sweets! The car market is particularly changeable in terms of models, colours and size from one country to another. In America, for instance, the average size of cars is much larger than in Europe. In addition, regulations on pollution and safety are stricter. A company which sells its products worldwide needs to be aware of all these facts.

DID YOU KNOW?

In China a new invention currently being advertised is a high voltage 'self-defence vest' which will overpower attackers by giving them an electric shock! What do you think would be the reaction if these were sold in Britain, and why?

· CONSUMER INFORMATION ·

Market research finds out the views of individual consumers and these can be combined to get an idea of the market as a whole. Sometimes companies don't need to go to so much trouble and expense – as someone else has done the work for them! This is particularly true if the company is trying to obtain specific statistics (as in the tables in this chapter) or to identify major **trends** in society (e.g. are people getting older or younger, richer or poorer? What do they want to spend their money on?).

Sources of information

There are numerous publications which give information on consumer behaviour. If you go to your local school or college library then you should be able to find several, including these:

- *Social Trends* – which gives information on a wide variety of topics, from changes in the population to how much money people borrow.
- *Family Expenditure Survey* – which gives details of how much money people are spending, the goods they are buying and in what quantities.
- *General Household Survey* – which gives information on people (including gender and age), households and families.
- *British Social Attitudes* survey – which gives information on what people think about such issues as religion, how companies should distribute their profits, the environment, sex equality and race relations.
- *Annual Abstract of Statistics* – which gives a variety of facts and figures including consumer expenditure patterns over several years.
- *Monthly Digest of Statistics* which gives up-to-date information on expenditure, prices and wages.
- *Household Food Consumption and Expenditure* – published by the Ministry of Agriculture, Fisheries and Food, this book gives trends and information on the buying of food and drink.

In addition, government departments regularly issue a whole host of statistics from import and export figures to the number of vehicles which carry goods by ferry to Europe!

DID YOU KNOW?

Companies can input current information on computer and, by means of a spreadsheet package, forecast ongoing trends and changes. (See Technology Core Skills, page 452).

Evidence Collection Point 9.10

1 Examine Figure 9.8. From the information given, state:

   a the type of organisations which

Research into consumer attitudes to the environment shows that they do the following regularly:	
Buy environment-friendly aerosols	55%
Buy free-range chicken or eggs	39%
Buy toiletries or cosmetics not tested on animals	33%
Return bottles, tins, newspapers etc. for recycling	32%
Buy environment-friendly washing powders/detergents	31%
Choose to eat less meat	25%
Choose products made of recycled materials	23%
Refuse unnecessary packaging or wrapping	17%
Buy organically-grown fruit and vegetables	8%

Source: *British Social Attitudes*, produced by Social and Community Planning Research

Figure 9.8 *Consumer attitudes and the environment*

would find this information useful

b how this could influence the advertising of their products.

2 Obtain a current copy of *Social Trends*. Find out how many people belong to voluntary environmental organisations and how this has changed over the years. Enter the figures given into a spreadsheet and give your projections for membership in five years' time.

DID YOU KNOW?

Brands of goods which cause least damage to the environment are being awarded 'eco-labels' by the European Community. Manufacturers of goods as diverse as washing machines, dishwashers, light bulbs, hairsprays, toilet paper and tissues can apply but will have to pay to use the label.

Using statistics

A company which manufactures toys needs to know such facts as:

- the birthrate (is this rising or falling?)
- whether more boys than girls are being born.

These two facts reveal whether the total market is increasing or declining. The company may also want more specialised information (e.g. how old parents are today, how much the average parent earns, how much they spend on toys each year – and whether this is likely to increase or decrease).

Evidence Assignment 9B

At a recent toy conference manufacturers and advertisers were discussing how children have changed – both in what they want to buy and in the type of adverts to which they respond. Not only are children more sophisticated (65% of 3–4-year-olds can distinguish between a television commercial and a programme and know what an advert is trying to do) but most prefer watching 'adult' programmes (e.g. Neighbours and EastEnders) to traditional children's programmes.

Boys, rather than girls, favour electronic games and are more apt to follow fashions and crazes. Girls are still keen on traditional toys, such as dolls, but expect these to be more realistic – Barbie now speaks with a modulated not a monotonous voice, thanks to the microchip.

Microchip technology is also being used to target younger children, such as a baby's rattle which makes animal sounds and games which incorporate words and music for pre-school children. The main growth area for older children is likely to be in virtual reality headsets and gloves.

Can parents afford these expensive electronic gadgets? Toy manufacturers are confident that, as more babies are today likely to be born to mothers aged over 35 than ever before, and many of these are either established in careers or likely to return to work, then time to play with their children is going to be a bigger problem than money. Some of the 'guilt' of a busy working mother can therefore be made less by buying expensive toys to occupy her child.

1 Why were advertisers interested in the type of television programmes watched by children?

2 a To what extent do you think the toy market can be divided by gender? Identify two toys which would *only*, in your opinion, be used by boys, two which would *only* be used by girls and two which could be used by *either*. State how these findings would influence the style of your packaging and advertising if you were a manufacturer.

b Does packaging (for example, the picture on an electronic games machine showing a boy playing with it) make boys, rather than girls, want to have one?

3 Find out from *Social Trends*:

- whether the birth rate has been increasing or decreasing over the last ten years
- whether, currently, boys outnumber girls or vice versa
- the total number of boys and girls under 16 years of age.

If you were a toy manufacturer, how would this information affect your forward planning?

4 Your boss is trying to find out:

a how the regions of Britain vary in their birth rate
b which countries of Europe have the highest birth rate.

Again, using *Social Trends*, can you find out this information?

5 What changes in lifestyles have been identified in the above passage which influence parents in their decisions about what to buy for their children? To what extent do you think this affects the type of products produced and their price?

6 Electronic games are referred to a 'solitary playthings'. What do you think this means? Do you think there will be a greater emphasis on this type of toy in the future, and if so, why?

· CONSUMER TRENDS ·

We live in a rapidly changing world. No organisation can ignore this – products which were popular 20, ten or even five years ago may be unsaleable today. Companies that make or sell products or services must stay with the times, or fail. Some trends can be identified as *general*, because they affect a wide range of goods and services. Other trends relate to specific products. In both cases trends relate to *long-term* changes in our patterns of expenditure.

General trends

Long-term changes can be ascribed to various causes, some of which have already been mentioned, including lifestyle and changing tastes. Consumer attitudes and new technology also affect demand. If you look around your home, it is likely that many consumer durables have changed over the past ten years. Televisions now have remote controls, stereo sound and teletext. Video recorders can be programmed using bar codes from magazines. Microwave ovens have pre-programmable settings to defrost or cook different types of food. Even toasters contain a microchip to enable them to toast frozen bread. In addition, many products are getting smaller – computers, telephones and cameras are typical examples.

However, probably the biggest influence on long-term demand are changes in attitudes, tastes and lifestyles:

- Today we are more health conscious. We smoke fewer cigarettes, eat more calorie reduced foods, buy fewer animal fats and drink more fruit juice. More people are becoming vegetarians and less meat is being eaten each year.
- People's lifestyles are changing. An important event in the life of any family occurs if the mother starts work, as this can have a variety of effects. The type of food the family buys and the ways in which they prepare it will change. Today more women work than ever before and there has been a surge in the sales of convenience foods and household appliances (especially microwaves).

- Social attitudes are also changing. More people use credit cards today (30 years ago being in debt was considered to be awful!), and fewer people go to church. More and more people shop on Sundays, and fewer and fewer people think this is wrong.

- People in Britain have more disposable income than ever before and work fewer hours. This has led to an increase in leisure time, which has resulted in increased participation in leisure activities and holidays and increased sales of sports goods, DIY products and magazines and equipment for people pursuing a hobby.

All these changes influence the type of products which people think they need and want.

Evidence Collection Point 9.11

1 Obtain at least *two* sets of statistics from either *Social Trends* or the *Family Expenditure Survey* which confirm the trends listed above.

2 *As a group* hold a brainstorming session. Try to name *at least* 30 products or services which are sold today which weren't available 20 years ago. In each case try to identify whether their introduction can be attributed to advances in technology, changing social attitudes, or fashion and current trends (or a combination of these).

3 Visit a local store which sells pre-packed sandwiches and other take-away foods. Summarise the ways in which changing attitudes to health have influenced the products they sell and the ways in which these are labelled.

4 By referring either to *Social Trends* or the *Family Expenditure Survey*, find three other changes which have occurred to the lifestyles and expenditure of families as a result of more women working.

5 Undertake a survey of the opening hours of supermarkets in your area. To what extent do you think the increase in numbers of working women has affected these hours, and why?

6 *As a group*, survey the types of product stocked in a major supermarket in your area. List *at least 20 items* which are examples of 'convenience' foods.

7 Find out the current situation on Sunday opening in your area. Hold a debate in class both for and against Sunday trading. Research the topic as well as you can (use your library!) and see who wins the debate. Write up your findings using a word-processor.

Evidence Assignment 9C

A company manufacturing disposable nappies has already made the following assumptions:

- Their customers are mainly young mothers (though there may also be some grandmothers and child-minders who buy the product).
- Many new mothers are dependent on their husbands' wages.
- Their customers want a product which is:
  - soft
  - absorbent
  - long-lasting
  - well-fitting
  - easy to dispose of.
- They also consider that they can make the assumption that working mothers are more likely to use disposable nappies, as they have less time to do great quantities of washing.

1 You have to carry out a survey to find out what new mothers think about disposable nappies and which brand they are currently using. Design a short questionnaire for this purpose. (If you are not sure how to do this, refer to the Core Skills section on Application of Number, page 416). Remember that you are trying to assess the strength of the competition as well as the number of potential sales and the importance of *price* to consumers. Check your work with your tutor.

2 If possible, carry out your survey on a minimum of *20* people. Discuss with your tutor beforehand how you intend to identify people you wish to 'target' as your respondents.

3 Analyse both your own results and your group's results and note down the information you receive and the conclusions you reach.

4 Obtain examples of two types of statistics which would help you to ascertain whether the total market for disposable nappies is increasing or declining. What is your conclusion?

5 Environmentalists have argued that terry nappies (made out of towelling), because they can be used for years, are far more environmentally friendly than

disposable nappies. The plastic outer layer on the disposables can take years to break up (most are put into landfill sites). What is your opinion? Should mothers be able to use disposable nappies if they wish, or should they be more environmentally aware? How much notice do you think mothers will take of these opinions and what could manufacturers of disposable nappies do to counter these claims?

DID YOU KNOW?

You should never ask someone, in a survey, how much they earn. Or, if you do, then you will have to be prepared to be told to mind your own business! Instead, market research companies ask people for their *occupation*. This gives a very good idea of someone's earnings.

Particular products

Changes in fashion, attitudes, tastes and lifestyles affect some products more than others. In some cases (e.g. refrigerators) there is little change from one year to another. In others there can be considerable change. This may be because the product itself is at the sharp end of developments in new technology or affected by changes in legislation. However, even with standard items our tastes change. Ten years ago there was only a simple choice between instant coffee and fresh coffee on the market. Today you can buy a whole range of products – decaffeinated, instant, cappuccino, espresso, ground and so on. As we become more sophisticated so the range of products marketed by organisations increases.

DID YOU KNOW?

Changes in government legislation can affect the demand for products. Since the drink-driving laws were introduced fewer people go out to have a drink and more alcohol is consumed in the home. This has increased the sales of alcohol in supermarkets and stores. Another example is reading glasses. Until 1984 registered opticians had virtually a monopoly in dispensing glasses. Today ready-to-wear reading glasses can be bought at a range of

outlets, and sales have increased dramatically. Today the trend is towards contact lenses rather than glasses. In 1991, 2.9 million single lenses were sold compared with 803 000 in 1982.

Evidence Assignment 9D

Record companies are now considering stopping the manufacture of vinyl single records. In 1992 the industry lost around £25 million on singles. Today cassette and compact disc singles are more popular (Figure 9.9).

Statistics show that in 1986 singles were in the charts for an average of six and a half weeks. By 1992 this had dropped to 4.2 weeks. In the 1960s groups were in the charts for as long as 13 weeks or more! In addition the average age of the record buying public has increased. Teenagers buy far fewer records than ever before – the greatest number of sales are to those aged between 24 and 35.

1 How would you account for the decrease in the sale of vinyl single records?

2 Why do you consider teenagers spend less money on records than ever before?

3 From Figure 9.9, can you predict what the situation will be in 1996? Use a spreadsheet to help you.

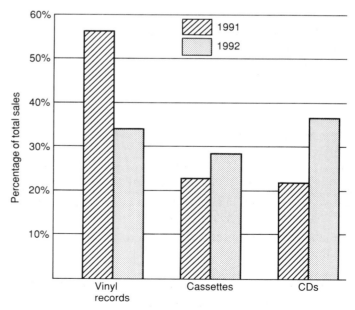

Figure 9.9 *How the market for recorded entertainment is changing*

4 Record shops are now selling other products as well as records, CDs and tapes. Visit at least one shop in your area and investigate what other goods are being sold and why.

• OTHER REASONS FOR CHANGE •

You have already seen why long-term changes occur. However, both short- and long-term changes in demand can occur if people have less money to spend.

Throughout this chapter we have concentrated on various reasons for consumer demand but have never directly mentioned the price of goods! The way in which price influences buyer behaviour is complicated, and depends very much on the type of goods (or service) being provided. As an example, you may try to buy the cheapest can of beans on a shelf but are unlikely to select a foreign holiday by the same method! Equally, the woman who buys Estée Lauder cosmetics (think back to ECP 9.2) and the Porsche driver have not had price in mind when they made their decision to buy. In some cases, a low price can actually have a negative effect on buyer demand. A sweater at £5 may be considered rubbish whereas one at £20 is considered good value for money!

However, in general you can apply two rules to buyer behaviour:

● With most normal goods, the lower the price the more goods are sold.
● The more people earn, the more money they spend (and vice versa).

Disposable income

One of the key considerations in how much you spend is your **income** – not your gross income but your **disposable income**; i.e. the amount you have left to spend after you have paid your tax, National Insurance and all your essential living expenses, such as rent, council tax, fuel and food.

Therefore if you have an increase or decrease in salary this will directly affect not only the quantity of goods you can buy but the type of goods.

The confidence to spend

Interestingly, it is not only *actual* increases or decreases which affect people's behaviour but their *expectations* of the future. If you think you are going to lose your job you will reduce your spending and start to save. Equally if you expect to do well in the next few years then you may be less cautious. In other words you have *confidence* in the future. Your confidence may also be affected by the actions of the government.

Activity

1 Name at least two products which you would buy if either the price was lower or your income was higher.

2 Can you name at least one item which you buy now but which you would *not* buy if your income increased?

DID YOU KNOW?

The government may tax some goods to make them more expensive and directly reduce demand (e.g. excise duties make alcohol and cigarettes more expensive). In addition, the current rates of interest and unemployment affect demand, because if interest rates are high or unemployment is high then people have less to spend.

The cost of living

The cost of living is measured by the Retail Prices Index (RPI). Quite simply, the RPI is calculated by taking a 'basketful of goods' and then, month on month, finding out how much these cost. In January 1987 the RPI stood at 100. In February 1993 it was 138.8. This means that a basketful of goods which cost £100 in 1987 would cost £138.80 in February 1993. In other words, between 1987 and 1993 the inflation rate had been 38.8 per cent, an average of just under 6 per cent a year.

This would have been perfectly acceptable for you if, in those six years, you had received rises in salary which were above the level of inflation. Otherwise you would have had less money to spend *in real terms*. (If you have forgotten what this means, look back to page 252.)

Evidence Assignment 9E

In 1992 holiday bookings went well at the beginning of the year but holidaymakers became nervy once the general election was called. Because of this many holidays were sold at reduced prices. The year before had seen reductions in travel abroad because of the Gulf War. In early 1993 tour operators were worried about bookings.

Tour operators were hoping that new trends for far flung places – the Caribbean, Australia and Canada rather than Majorca – would continue. However, all agreed that in the early months of 1993 it was special offers, rather than consumer confidence, which had helped bookings.

1 What does the above mean when it refers to 'special offers, rather than consumer confidence'?

2 Why do you think customers lost confidence in 1992 when the election was called?

3 What had caused them to lose confidence in 1991, and why?

4 What are the current trends in consumer travel?

5 Refer to a consumer information book and find out the latest figures on foreign travel. Is this increasing or decreasing, and why?

6 Why are holidays one of the first things consumers will sacrifice if their income falls?

DID YOU KNOW?

Economists believe there are two possible reasons for inflation.

- Organisations put up their prices because their costs have risen and they need more revenue to keep their profit margins. In turn, their customer organisations put up prices because they have to pay more to workers who demand large pay increases to cover rising costs, and so on.

- People have too much money to spend on too few goods. In this case, increases in income result in increases in demand for goods. Because producers cannot instantly meet this increased demand the number of goods on the market is insufficient. Suppliers therefore put up the price of those remaining.

DID YOU KNOW?

- Sometimes when people want to compare wage rates between now and a time in the past, they don't just state money earned. They may look at how long someone has to work to earn the money for a Mars Bar. And these days, Big Macs are used for comparison, too.

Evidence Collection Point 9.12

1 The RPI figures for each year from 1987 to 1992 are given below. In which year was inflation the worst and in which year was it the least?

1987	101.9	1990	126.1
1988	106.9	1991	133.5
1989	115.2	1992	138.5

(Source: *Monthly Digest of Statistics*)

2 Look in the *Monthly Digest of Statistics* in your library and obtain the rate of inflation for each year since 1992. Calculate the average rate of inflation between 1987 and the latest year in your table. Input all the rates into a spreadsheet and, assuming the average rate will continue, predict the rates in the year 2000 and 2010.

3 Visit your local shops and list the prices of ten completely different products or services; e.g.

- the train fare to a nearby town
- the entrance fee to a disco or club
- the price of a pair of shoes or haircut
- the price of a season ticket to your local football club.

From the index you compiled in question 2, what price will each product or service be in the year 2000 and 2010?

4 In 1993 the average wage for students who worked on a Saturday was £18. Bearing in mind your findings, how

much will students who work on a Saturday in the year 2000 and 2010 have to earn on a Saturday to have the same standard of living?

5 An elderly couple retired in 1993 with savings of £50 000. From your projections, how much worse off will they be *in real terms* in the year 2010? How is this likely to affect their demand for consumer goods?

Hint: think what interest £50 000 will earn each year in a building society account. What will a bag of potatoes or a pound of mince cost in 2010?

DID YOU KNOW?

In a recession, people:

- stay in more
- spend less on clothes and more on underwear.

Draw your own conclusions!

Recessionary times!

Evidence Project

Identify one product or service which has changed substantially over the last ten years. Prepare a report which covers the following:

1 Classify the typical type of customer for this product (or service).

2 Analyse the demand for the good and the way in which this has changed. Support your arguments with statistics from any of the books listed which give information on consumer demand.

3 Suggest reasons for the changes which have occurred.

To give you some ideas you may like to consider any of the following:

- the growth in foreign holidays
- the greater variety of bread on the market (from French bread to pitta bread)
- changes in cinema attendances and the introduction of the split screen cinema.

Alternatively, by looking through *Social Trends* or other books you may think of a good idea yourself. Your report should be produced on computer and preferably include *at least* one graph or chart which shows the projected trends into the future.

Answer to children's toy (page 256)

The children's toy which is identical for both boys and girls is **Lego**. Only the packaging (and details of what to build) are different!

Evidence Checkpoint

There are quite a number of evidence assignments and collection points in this chapter. Check with your tutor that you have completed all that are necessary and to a suitable standard. Is there anything you could improve upon to gain a better grade?

Revision Test

True or false?

1 Rising inflation increases the cost of living.

2 People in different regions have different preferences for goods.

3 Men live longer than women.

4 People's tastes and preferences change as they get older.

5 The amount of people's income affects the type of goods they buy.

Complete the blanks

6 Two books which give information on consumer demand are .... and ....

7 The letters RPI stand for ....

8 Finding out what customers think about a product is the job of the .... section in an organisation.

9 The amount of income remaining to spend after tax, National Insurance and essential living expenses have been paid is known as .... income.

10 The word demography relates to ....

Short answer questions

11 State three reasons why demand for a product may change.

12 Give four examples of products or services for which there has been greater demand in the last ten years.

13 Give two examples of changes in consumer's lifestyles in the last few years.

14 State three ways in which age can affect buying habits.

15 State five different characteristics of consumers.

Write a short paragraph to show you clearly understand each of the following terms:

16 Consumer demand.

17 Cost of living.

18 Lifestyle.

19 Taste.

20 Confidence to spend.

chapter **10** PROMOTIONAL MATERIALS

Learning Objectives

This chapter is concerned with promotional materials and the ways in which these may be produced. Guidance is given on methods of production. The chapter explains why promotion is carried out and the types of promotion used by business organisations. The potential of different types of media to promote particular products and events is also examined.

After studying this chapter you should be able to:

- identify and explain the objectives of promotional materials

- describe the constraints on the content of promotional materials
- identify different types of promotion
- identify the resources required to produce promotional materials
- investigate the potential of different media to produce promotional materials
- produce and use promotional materials to promote a product or event.

· A CASE STUDY IN PROMOTION ·

In July 1985, Bob Geldof's Live Aid concerts in Philadelphia and London raised £35 million for famine relief. Ten months later, in May 1986, the Sport Aid event, which took place in 277 cities in 78 countries, raised over £67 million for the same cause. In both cases, the money was raised because a tremendous number of people, all over the world, participated in both events. They joined in for two reasons:

- They were committed to the cause; i.e. they wanted to raise money for Ethiopian famine relief.
- They *knew* how they could help.

How did they know? Because both events took place in a blaze of publicity – for weeks beforehand. The purpose of the promotion had been to:

- create public **awareness** of the campaign
- capture people's **attention**
- gain their **interest**
- **change** their **attitude** towards famine
- make them **want** to help
- tell them how they could take **action.**

Bob Geldof used every promotional method he could to further his cause. This included:

- **Advertising** – in the press, through poster campaigns and on TV.
- **Promotions** – a special Christmas record, sponsorship, special events etc.
- **Personal selling** – he regularly gave interviews to the press and appeared on TV programmes.
- **Publicity** – he gained free coverage in the media by attending functions, supporting others who were raising money, visiting Downing Street, etc.

The campaign was a tremendous success in terms of the money it raised at the time. There is no doubt that this could not have been achieved without substantial promotional activity to bring both the famine and the fund-raising to the attention of the public – and to continue to hold this attention over a period of more than a year.

DID YOU KNOW?

The record 'Do They Know It's Christmas' written by Bob Geldof and Midge Ure had the highest sales of any single record in the UK. Approximately 12 million copies have been sold worldwide to raise a total amount of £110 million from sales and royalty fees.

· PROMOTIONS AND ORGANISATIONS ·

All organisations are regularly involved in promotional activities to make sure that customers do not forget about the products they produce or the services they supply. It is easy to think of promotions which are aimed at persuading us to buy different products or services – but promotion is used by a wide variety of organisations with different aims (see Figure 10.1).

The aim and type of promotion will affect the range and style of the promotional materials which are produced. As an example, a university may produce quite formal brochures and booklets with photographs of the campus, facilities and student accommodation. A promotional leaflet from McDonald's is likely to be far more informal with a different style of wording and less formal illustrations.

Objectives of promotional materials

The objectives of promotional materials are the same for virtually all organisations. These are:

To create demand by

- persuading customers that they will benefit from buying the product or service
- giving information about new or 'improved' products or services
- giving information about special offers
- keeping the name of the organisation and/or the product to the forefront of the customer's mind.

Promoter	Aims of promotion
Industry	To sell industrial goods, to persuade retailers and wholesalers to stock goods, to attract investors to buy shares, to recruit staff, to give information about their products.
Retail stores	To promote their store, to inform the public about sales, special offers, product ranges and services, to inform the public of new stores opening
Political party	To win votes, to change attitudes on a specific issue (e.g. unemployment)
Pressure groups (e.g. Greenpeace, Friends of the Earth)	To win support for a cause, to lobby government, to attract donations
Charity	To attract support, raise money, attract volunteers, gain sympathy for their cause
Entertainment and sports industries	To increase attendance, to attract people to the event
Educational establishment	To give information about courses, to give information about the establishment itself, to attract students or pupils
Local government	To give important information on local services and relevant changes (e.g. road closures in the area), to give information on planning applications
Central government	To give information on new laws, to promote health and safety, to discourage antisocial or unlawful behaviour
The media (e.g. radio, television, newspapers, magazines)	To increase their readership or viewing/listening figures, to encourage advertising

Figure 10.1 *The different aims of promotion*

To create sales by

- informing people about where and how they can obtain the product or service
- building up customer loyalty to a brand or organisation
- persuading consumers that this particular product or service is better than those offered by competitors
- creating consumer awareness of a *range* of products.

To influence customer perceptions by

- improving general awareness of the organisation and its policies
- creating a favourable image in the mind of the public

- giving information – about alternative products, matters of public interest or safety or new laws (particularly for motorists).

The image created may simply be to convince consumers that an organisation has good customer relations, is environmentally friendly and produces quality products. The hope is that the public will think highly of this company, and therefore buy its goods.

An organisation will only achieve objectives of creating demand and increasing sales if the promotional materials themselves:

- attract the **attention** of consumers (e.g. by the use of colour, good layout, a 'punchy' headline or slogan and by being used in the right time and in the right place)
- gain their **interest** (e.g. by including a special offer, eye-catching pictures or illustrations or text which makes the reader want to know more)
- create a **desire** to own the product or buy the service (e.g. by persuading the consumers that they will gain pleasure and satisfaction from the purchase)
- explain to the consumers how they can take **action** (e.g. where the goods are on sale, what they must do next).

If you look back to page 271, you will see that these elements featured in the purpose of Bob Geldof's promotion. They are known by the acronym **AIDA** – and apply to every type of promotional campaign.

Evidence Collection Point 10.1

1 Look through about four magazines and newspapers. Select ten advertisements which attract your attention and make you interested enough to read further.

Analyse what it was that caught your eye and made you interested, and the features of the advertisement which have been deliberately included to create desire.

2 Next time you are watching television advertisements, try to see at least one made for a large multinational company (e.g. an oil company, ICI, Coca-Cola). See how many of these are concerned with company image rather than promoting an actual product. (Expect stirring music, scenes of the countryside or wildlife, friendship across nations, etc!)

Write down your comments on at least one advertisement of this type.

Organisational or brand image

The aim of a promotion is not only to communicate an idea or a message to consumers but also to create an image in the mind of the potential customer. The type of image conveyed will depend on the business in which the organisation is involved. This may be one of solid dependability (e.g. for a bank) or a fun place to be (e.g. a theme park). Most organisations attempt to establish a unique image in the mind of the consumer and to promote their goods or service in an original but effective way. The organisation will have researched the characteristics of its potential customers (see Chapter 9) and this will influence the way in which the material is presented.

Once a theme has been established, the organisation will then use this so that eventually consumers recognise simple images and associate them with the organisation itself. This may be done through the use of colour, special lettering, logos or slogans.

The range of promotional materials

These will vary depending upon whether the company manufactures a product or promotes a service.

In both cases the company will have its **stationery** printed in a way that reflects its image. An engineering company or solicitor may have a relatively 'sober' design, a computer company may have a hi-tech design. Blackpool Pleasure Beach has a brightly coloured illustration of the big dipper incorporated into its letter heading and uses the colours yellow, blue and pink to indicate fun and entertainment!

A manufacturer would then have to ensure that the **packaging** of the goods reflected the company image. This would again include a careful choice of colours. If you analyse the use of colour you will find that cool, light colours – such as blue and green – are often used to promote bathroom toiletries. Perfumes may be packaged in containers which include gold or black to give the idea of luxury and natural materials. Bright, primary colours (e.g. blue, yellow and red) are often used to signify being modern and up to date whilst more subtle colours – such as dark green and navy – can be used to indicate quality or sophistication. Masculine products are often packaged in dark colours and may include the use of silver – it would be a mistake to design a container in pale pink to contain after-shave! Natural food products (e.g. muesli) often have brown packaging because the colour itself is associated with nature.

In many cases, even the delivery vans used by the organisation will have the same design or theme as that chosen for the image of the organisation.

A service company may not be interested in packaging but instead may produce brochures and leaflets. Even a small organisation, such as a restaurant, will be concerned about the style of its menu and the design of the interior to reflect its image.

Virtually all organisations advertise. They will be concerned that posters and newspaper, magazine, TV and cinema advertisements reflect their image (or that of the product being promoted). This will therefore be a chief concern for anyone concerned in preparing their promotional materials.

DID YOU KNOW?

Companies sometimes spend many thousands of pounds in choosing a suitable name for their products, and often employ specialists to do this for them. A good name should be easy to remember and may even imply some benefit of using the product, or have a pleasurable association.

There have been some disasters with product names in the past. Henry Ford named a new car Edsel (after his son). It flopped. So did Fiat's car called Rustica (can you think why?!). Part of the problem lies in the fact that names might not translate properly into other languages. A specialist company will check a proposed name in every country where the product may be sold. An alternative is to change the name from one country to another. Vauxhall's Nova was called Corsa in Spain because the word Nova translates into 'No Go' in Spanish. And now that we have the Single European Market, Vauxhall is consolidating its range of products and in the UK the Nova has been replaced by the Corsa!

Evidence Collection Point 10.2

1 Visit a local supermarket or store and select six products where colour has been used effectively for the packaging or container. Write a summary of each one, stating the product and its purpose and why you think the colours used were chosen.

2 Find ten products where the name has been chosen to imply a benefit or association. To help, you may like to think of themes such as freshness or personal cleanliness for bathroom toiletries, speed for household cleansers and romantic or exotic names for chocolates. In each case state the name, the product and why you think that name was chosen.

Evidence Assignment 10A

Chocolate is a highly competitive market. The Big Three manufacturers are Cadbury, Mars and Nestlé/Rowntree. All spend a large amount on advertising – so much that their campaigns are often known in the press by the term 'bar wars'. Cadbury, for instance, has a total marketing budget of about £35 million, and spends about £17 million on media advertising.

In addition, the companies are using the names of their products to move into related markets – ice cream, chocolate desserts and other products. They are having tremendous success. Mars 'invaded' the ice cream market, to the detriment of long-standing brands such as Lyons Maid and Walls.

1 Why do you think the three largest chocolate manufacturers are prepared to spend so much on advertising? As a clue, think of:

- economies of scale (see Chapter 2)
- competition
- companies having to retaliate because of the arguments *against* eating chocolate.

2 Identify four names of chocolate bars which you think are well chosen and easy to remember. State in each case *why* you think that name was chosen.

3 Visit a local supermarket and investigate its range of ice cream and chocolate desserts. How many have identical packaging to chocolate products so that consumers can instantly recognise the product?

4 For a week, log the television adverts you watch which feature chocolate products. Note down their content, their frequency and their 'message'. State which you find the most effective, and why.

. CONSTRAINTS ON PROMOTIONAL . MATERIAL

When you are trying to attract attention and create interest with promotional materials you may be tempted to make wild or exaggerated claims about the benefits of a product! You may not be telling a deliberate lie, but it may be that you have not quite told the whole story – for your own reasons! If this is the case, you could be in trouble. Every organisation which promotes its products or services must be aware of the controls that exist on advertising in Britain. Some of these are **voluntary**, others are **legal**. Voluntary controls may be classed as **ethical** constraints on advertising; i.e. they would be improper or wrong to most right-minded people as they offend or deliberately mislead people.

Evidence Collection Point 10.3

Below are given the themes of six advertisements. In each case the message is unacceptable. Can you say why? Keep your work safely – you will need to refer to it later.

1 An advert on television for expensive chocolates a week before Mother's Day with the message that 'all children who love their mothers will buy these'.

2 An advert in a newspaper for a local slimming club which guarantees you will lose at least 5 lb a week.

3 An advert for beer at the cinema which implies that after a couple of drinks you can cope with anything.

4 An advert for a finance company in a business newspaper which promises you there is no risk if you invest with that company.

5 A television advert which implies that a particular model of car is too sporty to be driven by women drivers.

6 An advert on television for a toy gun and badge which shows a child without these being rejected by other kids in the gang for not owning them.

Voluntary Codes of Practice

In Britain, most advertising is self-regulating. This means that the advertising industry *itself* acts as its own 'policeman'. An organisation which instructed an advertising agency to create an unethical advertisement would be told by the agency that this would be unacceptable. Similarly, a newspaper would refuse to accept an advertisement that might offend its readers.

Codes of Practice are **guidelines** which say what is acceptable and what is not. The relevant codes are:

- The British Code of Advertising Practice
- The British Code of Sales Promotion Practice
- The Independent Television Commission (ITC) and Radio Authority (RA) Codes of Advertising Standards and Practice.

The first two codes apply to printed and cinema advertising. The ITC code covers television advertising (including satellite and cable channels) and the RA code covers advertising on commercial radio.

The codes have been drawn up by people who are in the advertising business (e.g. advertisers, advertising agencies and the media), all of whom have agreed to follow them.

Basic guidelines

The main message of the British Code of Advertising Practice is that all advertisements should be 'legal, decent, honest and truthful'. It particularly covers areas such as:

- testimonials and recommendations by famous personalities
- advertising aimed at children
- advertisements for cigarettes, alcohol, slimming and medical products
- comparative advertising (where one advertiser compares his product with another).

No advertiser is allowed to make a claim which cannot be proved.

The British Code of Sales Promotion Practice regulates promotional offers, such as:

- vouchers, coupons and special offers
- competitions
- reduced-price and free offers
- charity promotions and those involving famous personalities.

DID YOU KNOW?

Advertisers have to be careful when they make claims concerning other products in comparative advertisements. If one manufacturer claims its car is more economical than a rival, it must be able to prove it. A recent cereal advert claims that one spoonful contains fewer calories than a bite from a piece of toast with low fat spread. This is being challenged by the Association of Master Bakers – and much depends on proving the average size of a bite of toast!

The Advertising Standards Authority

This is an independent organisation which investigates complaints from the public about the content of advertisements. In some cases advertisers may send a copy of an advertisement to the ASA for checking before it is put into print.

Each year the ASA receives about 8000 complaints and each month publishes a Case Report which gives details of the complaints investigated and the action taken. If a complaint is upheld then the advertiser will be asked to withdraw or change the advert. The ASA may also ask the media not to accept any more adverts on the same theme.

The Independent Television Commission and the Radio Authority

The ITC is responsible for all advertising on television and the Radio Authority is responsible for that on commercial radio. Certain types of advertising are not allowed on television (e.g. products such as cigarettes and spirits, and services such as betting shops). Every TV commercial and radio script is checked carefully (particularly those involving medical products or aimed at children) and must be approved or 'cleared' before it is broadcast.

Complaints about television advertising are investigated by the ITC. The Broadcasting Standards Council is usually involved if there are claims that an advert shows excessive violence or is indecent.

Other controls

Consumer legislation, which is covered in Chapter 12, also applies to anyone in the business of promotion.

- **The Trade Descriptions Act** makes it an offence for business organisations to make false claims about their products (e.g. to say shoes are made of 'real leather' when they are not). Complaints under this Act are investigated by local Trading Standards Officers. In a recent case, Boots were fined £250 for selling a diet chocolate bar, called Shaper, which actually contains as many calories as ordinary brands of chocolate.
- **The Consumer Protection Act** makes it an offence to claim that goods are being offered at a lower price unless these are genuine reductions.
- **The Food Act** relates to the labelling and advertising of food.
- **The Medicines Act** includes rules about the type of claims which can be made by manufacturers and advertisers of medical products, especially when these are reinforced by the use of doctors and nurses in the advertisement.
- **The Control of Misleading Advertising Regulations** reinforces the voluntary advertising controls included in the codes of practice.

Evidence Collection Point 10.4

1 Write to the Advertising Standards Authority at Brook House, 2–16 Torrington Place, London WC1E 7HN, and ask for literature on their work and a copy of a recent Case Report.

a Find the regulations which apply to advertisements aimed at children. Compare these with the effects adverts have on children you know (or had on yourself when you were young).Write a brief report on how effective you think the controls are.

b Give examples of two products or services in the Case Report where there was a complaint about an advert and the claim was upheld, and two where it was not. State the reasons in each case.

2 Find out the address of the ITC from your local library. Write to them and ask for a copy of their code of practice. Make a list of all the types of goods and services which cannot be advertised on television and give your comments on why you think these have been banned.

3 Find out *why* there are restrictions on the claims which can be made by producers of medical products. Give two examples of claims which cannot be made and give a reason in each case.

4 From the information you have obtained, write a brief comment on which part(s) of the codes were breached by each of the advertisements in Evidence Collection Point 10.3.

· TYPES OF ADVERTISEMENTS ·

The most popular method of promotion is by advertising – in the press, on radio, in the cinema, on television or outdoors (e.g. posters and billboards). There are advantages and disadvantages to using each of these, and the particular features which apply often influence the content and style of the advertisement.

The press

Advantages

- Magazines and business journals are often kept for a few days or weeks, so the advert may be seen several times or by several people. The reader can cut it out for reference if he or she wishes.
- Special-interest magazines and newspaper readership can be categorised by social class (see Chapter 9, page 258). This means that particular readers can be targeted.
- Advertisers can include tear-off coupons so that readers can reply to the advert. By coding these so that they can be identified by the organisation when they are received, it is possible to assess the effectiveness of each particular advert. In the advert in Figure 10.2, can you spot the reference number?
- Newspapers and magazines are frequently read by people other than the buyers (e.g. in waiting rooms, in libraries).
- Colour printing is now possible because of modern technology.

Disadvantages

- The reader may skim through quickly and either miss or ignore the advert.
- The language used must be easy to understand, taking account of the readership of the paper or magazine. This may limit what can be conveyed.

You run your own business.

Suddenly life changes.

You're the boss. You're the one who has to work all hours.

You're the one who'll have to worry if you're ill and unable to work

You're the one who'll have to make sure you have something to show for the sacrifices you're making now

To make life easier, NatWest has created its own range of life assurance, investment and pension plans*

They're easy to understand. They're value for money. They're simple to arrange.

And because starting a business is likely to be one of many changes in your life, why not ask to see a NatWest adviser? It could help you to make the right financial decision at every stage of your life

Call free to arrange an appointment or post the Freepost coupon. If you have a business to run, we're here to make life easier

Personal Financial Services, National Westminster Bank Plc FREEPOST, London EC4B 5JL.

Phone	**0800 255 200**
FREE	Quoting reference 36072 Monday to Friday 8am to 8pm Saturday 9am to 6pm

Please ask a NatWest adviser to contact me to arrange an appointment.
Post to: Personal Financial Services, National Westminster Bank Plc, FREEPOST, London EC4B 5JL.

National Westminster Bank *We're here to make life easier*

Figure 10.2

- An advert for one type of paper or magazine may be unsuitable for another, and have to be rewritten.
- Most daily newspapers are thrown away after being read.
- The clarity of newspaper adverts is quite often poor, especially for those containing photographs.
- Adverts may be grouped together on a page, so that each loses individual impact. It is therefore better if each has 'white space' around the text so that it is easily distinguished from its neighbours.

Television

Advantages

- Television has impact and power. The combination of sound, colour and action means the viewer can identify quickly with the product, and recognise it easily when he or she sees it. The highest recall rates for advertisements are for those seen on television.
- The audience is 'captive'. Viewers watching a programme may accept the adverts almost as another type of programme – particularly if they feature a famous personality, tell a story or are 'serialised' – as in the adverts with the famous Gold Blend couple.
- Advertisements can be repeated time and again to a large audience. Over 20 million people watch some popular programmes.
- Adverts are seen by traders, businessmen and private individuals. Television is therefore suitable for all types of products – from business computers to washing powder.
- Advertisements can be very high quality, especially if professional actors and directors are employed.
- The adverts can be targeted at a specific audience on some channels. For instance, sports channels can be used to advertise sports equipment. Independent television will accept adverts to be shown in certain areas or across the whole network (which is obviously more expensive as this is the same as nationwide). Therefore a relatively small, regional business can take advantage of local rates at off-peak times to advertise on television.

Disadvantages

- The cost is critical – television is too expensive for many organisations. Production costs can be high, and thousands of pounds are charged to screen an advert at peak viewing time.
- People may leave the room to make a cup of tea, 'channel hop' or start to talk whilst the adverts are on.
- Many people use their televisions for other purposes these days (i.e. linked to a personal computer or to watch a film on their video player). In both these cases they wouldn't see any adverts.
- Many people who see an advert will not be interested in the product. Audiences cannot be targeted as selectively as they can in the press.
- The message must be clear, simple and memorable. It is impossible to give any detailed product information in television adverts. The emphasis is therefore on *persuasion* rather than *information*.
- There are a considerable number of restrictions on what can be advertised on television – and when (see pages 275 and 6).

Evidence Collection Point 10.5

1 *As a group*, discuss whether you see more adverts in the press or on television.

2 Your answer is likely to be 'on television'! Now see how many *you* can remember. Each person should write down the *first five adverts which come to mind* (i.e. the products that were advertised).

Now combine your responses, and see how many match. Compile a 'recall league table' to see which adverts are the most memorable in your group's opinion.

3 Finally, try to analyse *why* you remembered the adverts you did. Did they tell a story? Were they funny? Were they repeated so often you knew 'the message' off by heart? Try to identify the aspects of the advert which attracted your interest and kept your attention.

DID YOU KNOW?

Teletext is an alternative (and cheaper) method of advertising on television. Advertisements are usually placed between the 'pages' of information the viewer has called up. The message has to be very short and to the point.

Commercial radio

Advantages

- Radio advertising is much less expensive than either the press or television – both to produce and to put on air. Spot announcements are even cheaper.
- If the signal is strong, quite a large audience may be reached. Many of these can be classed as a 'captive audience' (e.g. car drivers) but many other people put the radio on while they work, in factories, hairdressing salons and in the home.
- The advert can be repeated many times a day to catch different people.
- The voice which delivers the advert can be persuasive, a feature which is impossible with a press advert.

- Radio advertising is ideal for local traders because of its price, and the fact that most commercial radio stations operate on a local network basis.

Disadvantages

- Sound is not as memorable as pictures. Therefore a radio advert will soon be forgotten.
- Country-wide advertising is impossible as the only networked channels are operated by the BBC (which does not accept adverts).
- If the signal quality is poor then the listener may not be able to hear clearly what is said.
- Repetitive adverts on radio (e.g. jingles) may annoy rather than attract the listener.
- The listener may 'station hop' whilst the adverts are on.

The cinema

Advantages

- A cinema audience is the most captive audience in the world. They cannot talk very much (because of the sound levels) or change to another programme!
- Advertising on the cinema screen is cheaper than on television. Adverts can therefore be longer to give more impact.
- The wide screen and (sometimes) very good quality sound gives tremendous impact to a professional advertisement.
- Local traders can show advertisements quite cheaply in their own area.
- Cinema audiences mainly comprise young people. The medium is therefore ideal for the type of products bought by people under 25.
- Advertising can be paid for in a cinema by audience number. In this case the advertisement will be shown until a specific number of people have seen it. This is checked by the tickets at the door. If audiences are poor the advert will therefore be shown over a longer period.

Disadvantages

- People have short memories, and may remember the film but forget the adverts.

- There is no impact because of repeat advertising/ viewing – apart from with regular cinema-goers.
- People may be irritated at the delay in seeing the film they have paid to watch and have a 'negative' reaction to the adverts which cause the delay.
- Audience figures may be very low in bad weather, if the cinema is old or the seating uncomfortable, or if the films on at present are not very good.
- Many people prefer to wait until a film comes out on video and see it in their own home. However, cinema audiences are now increasing after being very low indeed during the 1970s.
- People can still leave the area whilst the adverts are on, or talk to a friend.

Evidence Collection Point 10.6

1 *As a group*, discuss how often you go to the cinema. Research current attendance figures in a journal such as *Social Trends* for your age-group. How typical is your group?

Produce a bar chart, preferably on a computer, which shows the trend in cinema attendance over the last five years. If the trend continues what will be the attendance figures over the *next* five years?

2 What measures have cinema owners taken to help to increase audience figures? Outline the way cinemas have changed over the last ten years.

3 What is your recall of cinema advertisements like – good, bad or indifferent? What *type* of goods did you see adver-tised? (Concentrate on the film type adverts – not the local traders.) Were any products advertised which are not allowed to be advertised on television – if so, which ones?

4 *As a group*, decide which cinema adverts you find the most effective and give your reasons.

Outdoor advertising

Advantages

- A poster can remain in place for a long time to gain the attention of people who pass by.

- Posters can be big, bold and colourful. Many have messages with considerable impact.
- Campaigns can be targeted on specific towns or regions. Conversely a national campaign can be planned with just a few posters in main towns and cities.
- In places where people have nothing to do (e.g. in train stations, on trains and buses, travelling on the underground), some read the adverts for entertainment!
- Bus adverts can be specially targeted for local readers. It is even possible to decorate a whole bus so that it is eye-catching and memorable!
- Electronic adverts can have enormous impact – with both colour and movement. Think of Piccadilly Circus in London.

Disadvantages

- Damage to posters can be done by vandals, or the weather.
- Messages *must* be brief because the travelling public and motorists have little time to read. Any detail is therefore completely out of the question.
- Environmentalists may object to posters as detrimental to the area.
- Posters and billboards can distract drivers.
- If a lot of small posters are concentrated in one area (e.g. on a bus or in an underground station) the impact of each one may be lost, and few (if any) remembered.

Evidence Collection Point 10.7

1 Look around your own area and find examples of four posters or billboards which attract your attention. Look for those with a strong, clever or witty headline or a very eye-catching design.

2 What differences do you find between the type of goods advertised on hoardings and those advertised on buses? Give examples of two bus adverts you have seen recently which have caught your attention.

3 The positioning of posters can be critical. For instance, hoardings and poster sites near supermarkets carry food advertisements, those near a bank may advertise

financial services, those in airports may advertise goods and services related to travel, and so on.

Find three different poster sites in your own area and give examples of the types of goods advertised.

DID YOU KNOW?

Many organisations pay an **advertising agency** to produce the artwork and make all the arrangements necessary for a *combined* media campaign. In this case, adverts on television will be shown at the same time as they appear in the press and posters are placed on hoardings. This means that the public is bombarded with information on a particular product or service over a certain period of time.

. ADVERTISING THEMES . AND CAMPAIGNS

It is useless spending a lot of money promoting a product or service (or giving information) if the message is unclear, ambiguous or too long to be remembered.

Organisations usually employ specialist advertising agencies to design an advertising campaign, think up slogans, produce artwork, etc. The type of campaign – and the message – will depend on:

* the product or service being promoted
* the method of advertising being used
* whether the aim is to *persuade* or *inform* people.

Persuasive advertisements

The idea of a persuasive advert is that it changes consumers' attitudes towards a product or service. This, then, will induce them to buy it. They will be further tempted if:

* the brand name sticks in their mind (so they will remember it next time they are shopping)
* there is a logo or trademark which means they can instantly recognise the company
* benefits are suggested or implied in the message or slogan.

You may notice that many messages are not just those linked with the product! For instance, it is often implied that by buying a particular product the customer will be more attractive to the opposite sex.

Logos are symbols and designs used by a company so that its adverts and products are instantly recognisable. Both logos and **trademarks** are protected by law once they have been registered by a company. No-one else can use or reproduce them without that company's permission.

Slogans are often employed because they are memorable. 'Put a tiger in your tank' was a famous Esso slogan for many years. Nintendo have recently developed the slogan 'Will you ever reach the end?' to promote their software products. The benefit of a short, punchy, slogan is that it is easily remembered, becomes associated with the product (or company) and can be used on posters and billboards – which motorists have to see (and remember) quickly.

Another way of making adverts memorable is to make them humorous. One of the most famous – and successful – campaigns has been the PG Tips and chimpanzee adverts. Gordon's Gin cinema adverts and Heineken adverts are both well-known for their humour.

Evidence Collection Point 10.8

1 Many logos and trademarks are so well known that you can instantly recognise the company. Can you answer the following:

* Which bank has a 'flying horse'?
* Which car has a lion symbol?
* Which driving school has a red map of Britain in a triangular sign?

2 Find out the logo for each of the following:

* British Rail
* Barclays Bank
* Audi cars
* British Telecom
* Lacoste clothes
* Kentucky Fried Chicken.

3 Which companies use the following slogans?
  * Play time

- Everything we do is driven by you
- It's the real thing
- Helps you work, rest and play
- The ultimate driving machine.

4 Collect a minimum of six adverts from newspapers or magazines which you think use either a good slogan, humour or some other device which attracts you. For each one, note down the features you like. Compare your adverts with those your fellow students rated highly. Write down any comments of theirs which you think are relevant, and which you did not think about on your own.

Informational advertisements

The press is the main medium used for informational advertisements. Printed adverts can contain a considerable amount of detail.

The skill of the **copywriter** is to get your attention, so that you will continue to read the advert to the end. To do this he or she will probably use an eye-catching heading, bold print, dramatic pictures or other visual effects and effective use of space.

Informational adverts are typically used for financial investments, cars (to give information about engine size etc.) and computers. They are also used for charity appeals. Note that some adverts *combine* the use of persuasive and informational advertising, as in the BT advert in Figure 10.3.

Figure 10.3

DID YOU KNOW?

1 The basic difference between informational adverts and persuasive adverts is that the first are used when there are definite advantages or features to the product which make it different from its competitors. Persuasion is used when there are not.

2 Ironically the most successful financial advertising campaign during 1992 used persuasion in the form of slogans and adapted these for use on TV, in the press or for outdoor adverts. This was the Prudential's 'Wanna Be' campaign, which used persuasion rather than information to promote its financial services (see Figure 10.4). So there appear to be no hard and fast rules to follow – provided you have a good idea!

Figure 10.4 *Prudential advertisement: a strong message and wide use of all media have proved a winning combination*

Evidence Collection Point 10.9

If you advertise a possession in your local paper you, too, have to give the reader information. However, too much detail will cost you money – as you will probably pay 'per word'. The skill is in keeping to the main selling points and saying these in as few words as possible.

1 Look through your local newspaper to see how other advertisers have achieved this. Make notes of those words and phrases you think would be effective.

2 Choose any one of the following. Invent any details you want and write out an advert to try to sell the item in your local newspaper. Try to keep the number of words you use to fewer than 20.

- A personal stereo.
- A portable compact disc player.
- An expensive tennis racquet.

• OTHER METHODS OF ADVERTISING •

Leaflets and brochures

Many organisations produce leaflets and brochures on their products or services to give additional information to consumers and customers. When you wrote to the ASA (Evidence Collection Point 10.4) you probably received several leaflets on their services. If you visit your local tourist information office or trading standards office you will see other examples. Travel companies are an obvious example of organisations which produce glossy brochures advertising holidays. Your school or college may have a glossy brochure too, which it uses for promotion purposes – though it will probably call this a prospectus. It may also have leaflets available on individual courses.

If the leaflet is mainly informational it is likely to contain text and a few illustrations. Compare this with a travel brochure, which has much less text and more photographs to persuade you to visit the place being advertised.

Mail shots

Direct mail has been growing in importance since the 1970s and is now the third most important method of promotion, after advertising on television and in the press. Mail shots are the materials that arrive unannounced through your door. The mail shot may consist of letters written to you and addressing you by name. This approach is often used by financial organisations (trying to persuade you to borrow money) and charities (trying to persuade you to give them money).

Today these documents are easily produced and individually named by means of a computer or word-processor. Because they are cheap to produce, and many people like receiving and opening mail, mail shots are often a very effective method of promotion. Not only that, but if the company is selective about the addresses to which it sends its mail shots, it cuts down the cost of the promotion.

The message may be just text (e.g. a letter) or include pictures. Charities such as the RSPCA, NSPCC and Help the Aged usually illustrate their appeal literature. They always include a donation form and may even arrange to follow up the mail shot with a telephone call at a later date if no reply has been received.

Alternatives to personalised literature sent by post are the leaflets and booklets that are delivered through your door. The advertiser may use the Post Office's Household Delivery service or the services of a private company. The leaflets may include money-off coupons or trial-size offers. Perfume manufacturers often include a sealed section which has been impregnated with the perfume – to give the potential customer a sample with the mail shot.

With all types of mail shot it is possible to target customers by postcode, by TV area or demographically (so that potential customers are identified by age, address, status, profession, income, etc.).

DID YOU KNOW?

Many organisations with a large computer mailing list (e.g. credit card companies, local authorities) *sell* their mailing list to other companies wishing to set up their own database for direct mail shots.

Evidence Collection Point 10.10

1 Obtain three examples of leaflets or brochures advertising totally different products or services. Analyse these in terms of layout, amount of text and number of illustrations. Compare your analysis with those of other people in your group. Can you find any link with design and the type of product or service which is being promoted?

2 Collect at least two examples of direct mail shots which have been received either by yourself or a friend or relative. Try to obtain one from a private company and one from a charity. Compare these in terms of approach, wording and appeal.

3 You are going on a 20-mile charity walk a week on Sunday to raise money for Shelter – a charity which helps the homeless. You want your friends and relatives to sponsor you. Write a letter on your word-processor, asking for their help. Make this as persuasive as possible. Save your document and then enter the names and addresses of six of your friends or relatives. Use the mail merge function on your word-processor to produce an individual letter for each person.

Sponsorship

Sponsorship is given with the objective of raising awareness. Commercial sponsorship is concentrated mainly in two areas – sports and the arts. About £2 million a year is spent by large companies on sports sponsorship alone. As an example, Coca-Cola has sponsored swimming events, athletics, the Olympic Games and is now spending £3 million a year sponsoring the Football League. The event being sponsored gets money from the promoter and every time that event is mentioned in a sports report, the sponsoring company's name is also mentioned.

An alternative form of sports sponsorship is when a clothing or equipment manufacturer pays a famous personality to wear or use their products (tennis player Agassi is paid large sums to wear Nike clothing and footwear). Sports sponsorship has therefore the highest

profile – which means you will probably know quite a bit about it even before you read this section!

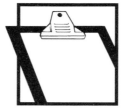

Activity

As a group, answer the following:

1 Which bank sponsors the UK football Premier League?

2 Which insurance company sponsors cricket test matches?

3 Which cigarette company sponsors the World Darts competition?

4 Which brewery sponsors the Rugby League?

5 Which organisation sponsors your local football team?

6 Name two cigarette manufacturers that are involved with motor racing.

DID YOU KNOW?

The latest company to become involved in motor racing is Sega, which has just signed a sponsorship deal with the Canon Williams Formula One team. The cost of this is likely to be more than £2 million. From now on drivers will have the word 'Sonic' on their helmets and the Sega name will be printed on the side of the car!

The advantages of sponsorship

- There is constant promotion of the sponsor's brand or name in relation to:
  - publicity for the event
  - the holding of the event
  - constant association with the sport.

  Bear in mind that audiences are large and that some sports seasons last a long time (e.g. the football season).
- It provides a route by which manufacturers of goods which must not be directly advertised on television can have their name shown on hoardings and posters.
- Television commentators may mention the company as they discuss the sport. A winning team will be associated with their sponsor. This is particularly true in the case of sports such as motor racing and yachting, where different companies sponsor different drivers or crews. A winner at any sport can increase sales – the sales of Puma racquets rose by about $50 million after Boris Becker first won Wimbledon in 1985.
- It may prove more cost-effective for a company to sponsor an event (in terms of publicity, television coverage etc.) than to pay for advertisements. Whitbread (who sponsor the round-the-world yacht race) estimated that for an investment of approximately £8 million the company achieved advertising worth £30 million worldwide.
- The company can take customers to watch the event or even participate in the sport. One organisation involved in sponsoring showjumping at the Barcelona Olympics – Henderson Administration – claimed it was cheaper to charter a plane to Barcelona than it was to take customers for a day out at Wimbledon.
- The company image is promoted and often enhanced with those potential customers to whom it most wants to appeal.

More about company image

The image given to a product or company sponsoring a sport is often one of grace, style, fitness and the ability to meet a challenge. In many cases masculine products are linked to masculine sports.

Other companies use sponsorship to promote a caring image – especially in a related area. For example, Mothercare sponsors research at Great Ormond Street Children's Hospital. This is also the case for organisations which sponsor a charity event.

You should note that a company will only sponsor an event which matches the image it is trying to project and/or one to which its customers (and potential customers) are likely to go. For instance, the *Financial Times* might sponsor an opera, ballet or play, but would be extremely unlikely to sponsor a pop concert or a wrestling match! The *Sun* newspaper might make exactly the opposite decisions.

The Opera Factory at Glyndebourne have a novel approach to sponsorship. They recently persuaded Haagen-Daz to provide ice cream to be eaten during the banquet scene of Don Giovanni. For an opera about two shepherds they were asking for sponsorship from the International Wool Secretariat, the Sheep Shop in London and the Nationwide Building Society (because the latter includes sheep in its adverts)!

DID YOU KNOW?

Because of the importance of 'company image', companies will not sponsor famous personalities whom they consider may bring them into disrepute. Pepsi withdrew its offer to sponsor Madonna's tour in 1989 when she released what they considered to be an 'unsuitable' record.

Evidence Assignment 10B

You and five of your friends have decided to form an Enterprise group linked to your Business Studies course. Your idea is to clean and valet cars parked in and around the town whilst the owners are shopping. You obviously need hot running water to do this so you may be limited by the type of car parks you can use (e.g. supermarket ones rather than multi-storey). You would obviously need the permission of the owners of the car parks before approaching their customers.

Your aim is to charge a reasonable rate and give 80 per cent of the proceeds to a charity (of your choice). The remaining 20 per cent is to meet your costs. However, you have calculated that if you could obtain sponsorship for your venture, you may be able to give all the money you raise to charity.

1 Assess your local area and make out a list of possible car parks which would be suitable – if the owners agree.

2 Which supermarkets and other car park owners would you approach to support your scheme? List the *additional* help you could ask for if they were willing to sponsor your idea.

3 Note down any other possible sponsors in the area. These could include companies you know well or companies linked to the materials you will be using to clean the cars, or the suppliers of these materials. Try to think of some novel ideas – as the Opera Factory did!

4 Note down how you would approach these companies to 'sell' your scheme, and what you would ask for. Do bear in mind that sponsors want some return for their support. What would your sponsors have to gain from being involved with you?

5 Assume that you now have several sponsors. *As a group*, hold a brainstorming session to decide the ways in which you could promote your scheme so that the general public knows about it. Make a list of the best ideas.

Competitions

Most people, at some time in their lives, have entered a competition. This may have been a promotion by a manufacturer or by a publisher (e.g. in a magazine or newspaper). Sometimes, to be able to enter, it is necessary to buy the product several times – either because clues are given over a period of time or because tokens have to be collected to be able to enter. The aim in both cases is to turn the occasional customer into a regular buyer of the product.

To be legal, the competition has to require an element of skill so that there is an outright winner. For this reason, most competitions have a tie-breaker, where a slogan or reason for entering has to be written. Results must be published so that anyone who entered can see who were the winners.

The success of competitions can vary enormously

depending upon the prize. Most people prefer cash (or a car) rather than other goods (which they may already have) or a holiday (which might be difficult to take).

The public sector can use people's liking for competitions to raise money. Today Premium Bonds are advertised as 'Win £250 000 or your money back'. The proposed government lottery will be run on the same basis – except that those who are unlucky will not be able to claim a refund! The aim is to raise additional money for public sector spending without increasing taxes or government borrowing.

DID YOU KNOW?

Some competitions can be too successful. Cadbury's ran a treasure hunt to find 12 'gold' eggs worth £10 000 each (as a promotion for their Cream Eggs). Over 100 000 people wrote to the company to obtain the storybook which contained the clues. When some people became so enthusiastic they started digging up an archaeological site in Cornwall, Cadbury had to cancel the hunt for that particular egg.

Evidence assignment 10C

The current computer games rage is for Nintendo and Sega, and a fast growing market at the moment is in computer magazines. In the next year or two the number of magazines on the market is likely to increase substantially.

Imagine that you work for a small publishing company which is thinking of producing a computer magazine to meet the increasing demand. The company have asked you to work as a member of a small group to undertake research, and to present your findings to the management team in two weeks' time. In addition you should prepare a brief report which includes a section on each area of investigation.

As a group you have been asked to carry out the following tasks.

1 Visit two local newsagents which stock a range of these magazines (preferably a large stockist such as WH Smith). Assess how many are currently being sold and note their titles and prices.

2 Note down any types of promotional offers you can find that are used to tempt someone to buy one magazine rather than another – (e.g. free gifts, special offers). Make sure you know exactly what is being offered in each case.

3 Think of a name for the new magazine. Bear in mind that the name must be different from all existing magazines.

4 At what price do you think it should be sold? Justify your decision.

5 What advertising and promotional methods would you use to build up consumer knowledge and demand *before* the magazine was launched? Be as precise as you can (e.g. for the press, specify *which* newspapers or magazines you would use for your advertisements). In addition, if you decide a special offer would be appropriate, state what you would offer and why.

6 Invent a competition which you could run in the first few editions to promote the magazine. Bear in mind the 'skill' element! Decide what you would offer for prizes.

7 Prepare a ten-minute presentation, with visual aids, to inform the management team of your findings. At the presentation give them a copy of your report, preferably produced using a computer.

▪ RESOURCES REQUIRED FOR ▪ PROMOTIONS

In several Evidence Assignments and ECPs in this chapter you have actually started to create promotional materials and to think about methods of promotion. You may have found some of these easy and some difficult. How will you cope if you have to design and create a range of promotional materials to sell an actual product or event? It

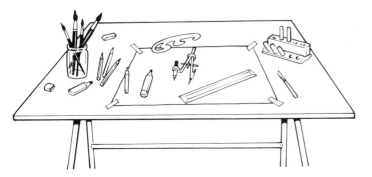

is one thing calling in specialists to design the campaign for you, and quite another to do it yourself! What resources are you likely to need and how can you go about obtaining them?

The time factor

A promotional campaign normally has four distinct stages:

● the **planning** stage
● the **production** stage
● the **post-event** stage
● the **evaluation** stage.

The amount of time you can allocate to each stage will depend on the total amount of time between getting your 'brief' – or instructions – and the deadline for the product launch or event.

Planning

This is a key part of any campaign and should never be skimped. A good plan is the bedrock upon which you build your campaign. If you hurry this stage then nobody – including you – will have a clear idea about what they are doing!

Your plan should include the following:

● what you aim to achieve
● the methods you will use
● the people who will be involved
● the timing of each part of the campaign
● the materials and resources you will need and how these will be acquired
● the theme of your campaign
● how the tasks should be allocated between members of the team.

Production

This is when the real work begins – creating posters, writing to people to obtain sponsorship, taking photographs, printing leaflets, making films.

You must allow time for people to be creative, to correct mistakes, to reply to letters and to edit films.

It is always a good idea to end a promotional campaign with something of importance, rather than let it fade out like a damp squib. If you are running a competition then it is a good idea to make a presentation to the winner. If you are publicising an event then the date of the event is critical, and you will want to arrange publicity coverage on the day.

Post-event

Usually after the main day, you can follow up to obtain post-event publicity (e.g. films of the actual event, presentation or launch or articles about it in the press or staff magazines). It is important that this is done promptly – before everyone forgets what actually happened and it becomes history rather than news!

Evaluation

This is when the production team meets together afterwards to evaluate the success of the campaign. What went well and what did not? What could be improved upon next time? Again the meeting should take place fairly quickly after the campaign has ended, while people still have it in mind and are still talking about it!

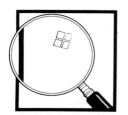

Evidence Assignment 10D

Your school or college is holding a Christmas Fayre on the second Saturday before Christmas. All proceeds will go to a local children's charity. You have been asked to help promote the event to parents and local organisations.

1 What methods of promotion will you use to advertise this event?

2 Assuming you are a member of a team of four, draft out a plan of action which shows the dates on which you aim to start planning your campaign, the timescale for planning and producing your materials, and the date on which you want to start advertising for maximum impact. (Bear in mind that if this is too early it will lose impact, if it is too late people won't be able to make arrangements to come.)

3 What methods will you use to evaluate the success (or otherwise) of your campaign?

Human resources

Human resources simply mean *people*. If you are involved in promotional activities then you will probably be expected to work as a member of a team. Each person on the team will have different strengths and weaknesses and possess a variety of skills. A good team uses these to its advantage. The type of skills required for a promotional team will include:

- the ability to deal with people
- the ability to listen to other people's points of view
- the ability to write good, clear 'copy'
- graphic design skills
- the ability to sell the idea and persuade other people to help (e.g. by placing an advertisement in their shop or becoming a sponsor)
- the ability to use different media and equipment (e.g. cameras, camcorders, computers and reprographic equipment).

In addition, *all* members of the group should support one another and show consideration when things aren't going too well. A sense of humour (at the right time) can be an invaluable asset.

Copywriting skills

Copywriting is the skill of writing a message which will sell a product or event. Even if the copy will be supported by illustrations the wording is critical. The copywriter must work closely with anyone involved in visual aspects of the work so that the two parts join together and don't clash and the size and weight of the text is correct.

Here are some important rules to remember:

- People tend not to *read* advertisements – they 'scan' them. The message must therefore use the minimum number of words.
- Every word must be easily understood, so the language used must be simple and appropriate.
- Buzz words attract (e.g. free, new, now).
- Action words hold the reader's attention (e.g. try, watch, come, enjoy, take, buy, do, remember, consider, explore).
- Adjectives create an image in the reader's mind (e.g. wonderful, beautiful, super, exciting, amazing, time-saving, mouth-watering, economical).

- Alliteration or rhyme makes a phrase memorable. An alliterative sentence is one in which the sound is repeated several times (e.g. Cuddles – the complete caring cat food). Examples of alliteration and rhyme from actual advertisements include:

  We're going well, we're going Shell
  A Mars a day helps you work, rest and play
  Don't be vague, ask for Haig
  Nissan – hot hatch of the year
  The Cannon copier gives copies round the clock.

- Think of a bold headline which attracts attention. (Remember the ones you found on posters?) Look through magazines for examples.
- Many adverts appeal to people's emotions. A burglar alarm advertisement would appeal to the need for security, a dating agency for the need for companionship and love, a health product for the need for self-preservation. Find examples of charity adverts which appeal to the emotions in a range of different ways.
- Make sure all the key information is included so that the reader knows what to do next (e.g. the date, time and place where an event will be held). If you omit anything there is very little point doing an advert in the first place.

Evidence Assignment 10E

Your organisation, Taylor & Watts Ltd, produces a weekly staff newsletter on A4 paper. Your boss, Michaela Andrews, is the Personnel Officer and has recently made arrangements for the Blood Transfusion Service to visit the company two weeks on Thursday at 2 p.m. Blood is urgently needed and she is hoping employees will respond -especially as they can give blood during working hours.

She has asked you to design an advertisement to be placed in the newsletter which will give information about the visit and persuade as many people as possible to attend. Donors should be told to go to the works canteen.

Graphic design

You may find graphic design skills rather lacking in your team. After all, if you were all potential designers you would presumably be taking a GNVQ in Art and Design! Some basic hints and tips, however, may be useful.

1 The average focal point (for most people) on a poster is one-third from the top of the page – not half way down. You will therefore often achieve a better effect by dividing a poster or advert into thirds, as in Figure 10.5.

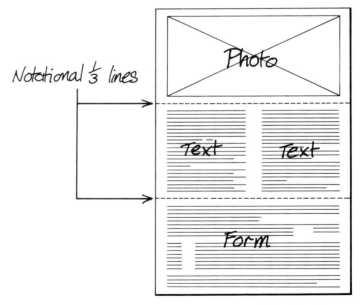

Figure 10.5 *Imagine the depth divided into thirds for best effect*

2 A headline can be positioned in a variety of ways, not just across the top, left to right! Its size can also vary (see Figure 10.6 for examples). Don't be scared to think big! Generally, it is better not to use a mixture of colours in one headline because this is apt to look childish.

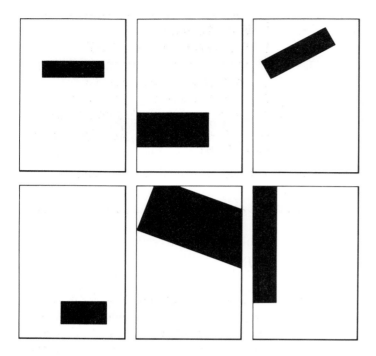

Figure 10.6 *Where to place the headline?*

3 Position illustrations and text in unusual ways and unusual places for different effects. Keeping plenty of empty space means the poster or advert has more impact and is easier to read (see Figure 10.7).

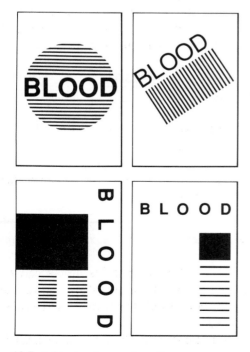

Figure 10.7 *Achieving interesting effects*

4 Remember that you do not have to show 'all' of something to indicate it is there – part of an illustration will often be enough, especially if it is enlarged (see Figure 10.8).

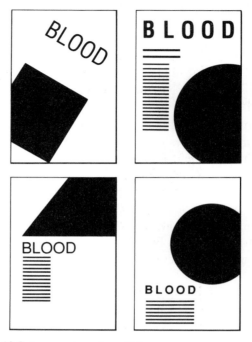

Figure 10.8 *Images dropping off the page*

5 Combinations of lines and shapes can give dramatic effects (see Figure 10.9).

Figure 10.9 *Combinations of lines and shapes*

6 Use colour to indicate mood. Yellow and blue give the impression of a bright sunny day (look at travel posters), black is dramatic, and so on. Think in terms of buying paper or card with a coloured background – but make sure the colour of text you choose shows up well.

7 Choose a typeface (text size or shape) which is appropriate for the kind of poster you are designing. You are safer keeping to the same one throughout (see Figure 10.10).

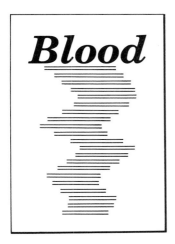

Figure 10.10 *Choosing an appropriate typeface*

8 Be *very* careful about using a border – sometimes it spoils your work. Whatever you do, *never* use a fancy one!

You may find it is useful to start by drawing up a thumbnail sketch, similar to most of the illustrations shown here. You can practise your skills by cutting text and illustrations in different shapes and sizes out of a newspaper and moving these around an A4 page. Vary the layout and see what effects you can achieve!

DID YOU KNOW?

If you use a Spraymount adhesive (available from art shops) you can move and reposition items before you finally press them into place.

Evidence Assignment 10F

Your school or college social committee are holding a Halloween Disco on Friday 31 October. It will be held in a local club – Barney's Place – and run from 8 p.m. until 1 p.m. Tickets are £4 each.

Design a poster which is eye-catching and original to advertise the event.

Physical resources

To carry out the assignments given in the last few pages you have already required several physical resources – a room in which to work, a desk or table on which you can set out your work, coloured paper or card, felt-tip pens and mounting spray.

The range of physical resources at your disposal will determine the type of work you can produce. In a professional studio you would find adjustable drawing boards and a visualiser (which enlarges illustrations). Special copying and printing machines would be available. It is doubtful whether you have these resources at your disposal. However, we shall outline a range of physical resources which are useful for promotional work.

Basic essentials

- Cutting equipment – knives, scissors, a guillotine and/or a rotary trimmer
- An eraser!
- A pencil sharpener. The softer the pencil you use the more you will need to sharpen it.

Pencils and markers

- Black pencils with different leads. Use a soft lead to sketch ideas you will want to erase later. B pencils are soft (9B are the softest) and H pencils are hard (10H being the hardest).
- Coloured pencils, felt-tips and/or wax crayons. Each achieves a different effect.

- Marker pens – of different thicknesses (fine line and thick line). If you use marker pens bear in mind that water-based markers can be 'layered' for different effects. Marker pens dry up quickly so keep the caps on when they are not in use.

Paint and brushes

- Paint. Acrylic paints are very popular today and can be used on almost any surface. Another alternative is gouache. If you use the latter and want to cover a large area, mix it with Chinese white to make your life easier. Watercolours are available in two standards – artists' quality and students' quality. Choose the latter – they are cheaper and quite adequate to practise with.
- Brushes are hard or soft and are sold in different shapes and sizes. They can be flat, round or oval-shaped. Sizes start at 00 (very small) and go to about size 14 (quite large). Brushes must be washed after use and stored dry, either standing with the bristles upwards or lying flat and kept in the fresh air.

Materials

- Paper and board. Many different types of papers are available. Layout paper is the cheapest and gives you the chance to try out your ideas without spending much money. Tracing paper is useful if you want to copy a design or illustration. Cartridge paper is heavier weight and often used for drawing. Board is simply high-quality drawing paper put on to a stiff backing board. Different weights of board are available and many graphic design shops will cut these to the required size. Both paper and board are available in a variety of colours.
- TV layout pads are packs of pre-printed paper with TV screen-shaped masks. They are ideal if you are preparing a storyboard prior to making a video (see page 294).
- Film or acetate transparencies are needed if you are preparing a promotion which will involve the use of an overhead projector.
- Masking film – to cover up areas you don't want to paint. You can make a mask of letters for your headline, paint or spray around it and when you peel the film away your headline will be the only area not covered and will therefore stand out.
- Dry transfers (e.g. Letraset). These give instant lettering in a variety of typefaces but are expensive!

Equipment

- A copying machine – either a photocopier or offset litho machine. The former is easier to use. If you have a colour photocopier then you may have to produce your artwork in stages and this will need great care.
- A computer and laser printer. This enables you to produce a variety of graphics and typefaces with ease (see pages 297, 456, 457).
- A camera or, even better, a Polaroid. This means that you can remedy any disasters immediately without having to wait until your film is developed.
- A camcorder to produce your own videos (see page 294), and a video machine on which to play them. (Plus video tape!)

Evidence Collection Point 10.11

Go through the list above carefully with the rest of your group and your tutor. Identify how many items:

- you can provide
- other members of your group can provide
- your school or college can provide.

Remember that in acquiring resources you have sometimes to be resourceful yourself! If your father has a Stanley knife then this is ideal for cutting board. Someone you know may be prepared to lend you a camera if you don't own one yourself. You may be able to beg or borrow items from a student in the art department, and so on.

Bearing this in mind, *as a group*, how many ideas can you come up with for acquiring the resources which you don't own at the moment?

Financial resources

You may find that no matter how hard you try, you still have certain items missing. You now have two choices – you either manage without them or find the money to pay for them! It may also be the case that, if you are organising a special promotion, you need items which *can't* be produced in-house. As an example, many charity campaigns incorporate the use of printed stick-on badges (or even proper printed badges) and you would need a professional to make these for you.

You may find that there are resources in your school or college (e.g. through the petty cash system) which will pay for small requirements such as paper, board or marker pens. If you want to aim higher you may have to raise the money yourself. Rather than starting 'blind' it is sensible to cost out what you need and then use this cost as a target.

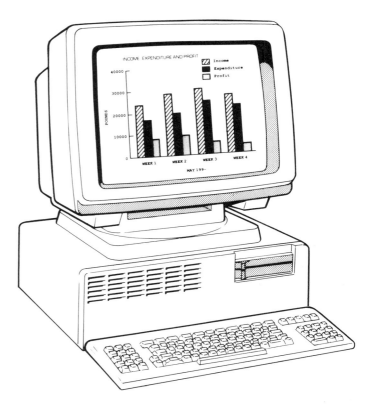

DID YOU KNOW?

You actively save money if you look after the equipment and materials you use. This means they need replacing less often and there is more money available for other things to be bought! Try to find a lockable cupboard you can use as a group.

Evidence Collection Point 10.12

1 Visit a local art shop and cost the following materials:

- two good-quality paint brushes
- a large piece of coloured board, size A1
- Spraymount adhesive
- six dry markers in different colours and widths.

2 If your group wasted the equivalent of the above material four times a year, how much would that cost your school or college?

3 You have a friend who is careless and untidy. He spends a fortune on stationery each year. Write down four hints or tips to help him save money.

• PROMOTIONAL MATERIALS •

When producing promotional materials you have basically a choice between:

- paper-based materials (e.g. leaflets, brochures, posters, advertisements)
- lens-based materials (e.g. photographs or video film)
- computer-based materials (e.g. graphics packages, 'clip-art' or desktop publishing packages).

You can use a mixture of these. A simple example is designing a poster which incorporates photographs. In a professional studio you would find that computers are used for a wide range of graphics and for producing video films.

However, different types of material are more suitable for certain types of products, services or events. You wouldn't produce a video to tell people about a fireworks party at your school or college any more than Heinz would sell tomato ketchup by giving out a newsletter.

The following section should give you some idea of the potential of different approaches. It is up to you then to decide which would be the most appropriate in different circumstances.

DID YOU KNOW?

A **digitiser** converts an image on a drawing, photograph or video still into a series of digital impulses which produce the image on a computer screen. This enables sophisticated graphics to be created and printed. You may have observed one in operation if you have seen designs on T-shirts being produced from people's photographs.

Paper-based materials

These have been discussed in the previous sections and hints and tips given on their production. Turn back a few pages and revise what was mentioned if you have forgotten about them!

Lens-based materials

Cameras

Today most cameras have automatic focus and you don't have to make special adjustments for light. The most basic camera will probably be quite adequate if you follow a few simple rules. A zoom facility is useful, so is a wide angle lens (if you need a panoramic view). You can achieve special effects if you buy a slow film – but will need to use your camera on a tripod (otherwise the wobble will show). As an experiment, try setting up a camera to take a photograph of a relatively busy road at night on slow film. The subsequent patterns made with the headlamps and tail-lights of cars is quite something!

Here are some tips for taking suitable pictures:

1 Black and white photographs can be *very* effective. If you are taking photographs for a black and white leaflet or for an advert in a newspaper then there is little point in using colour film at all.
2 Make sure you check the distance between people's heads and the top of your picture (see Figure 10.11). This is important both for still photographs *and* when making video films.

Too little headroom   Too much headroom   Just right

Figure 10.11 *Getting the right amount of headroom*

3 Don't ignore what's happening in the background. A tree in the wrong place can look as though it is growing out through the top of somebody's head! The less cluttered the background the better.
4 Try unusual angles (e.g. photographing something from *above*).
5 Close-ups can be effective – but be careful you don't get so near that the automatic focus doesn't work.
6 If you are taking a picture of something at low level (e.g. an animal or child) then get down to their level. Don't point the camera down at them.
7 Take a picture at an unusual time of day to get interesting effects of light and shadow.
8 Action shots are a million times more interesting than posed pictures.
9 Don't be afraid to experiment!

Producing a video

The usual stages for this are:

- deciding on the storyline
- producing the storyboard
- writing the script
- rehearsing the action
- shooting the film
- editing the film.

You will only be able to do the latter if your school or college has editing facilities (see page 297). Otherwise you will have to shoot the film in the order it will be screened. Depending on your camcorder you may be able to edit your film 'in camera'.

Bear in mind that producing videos professionally is a skill which can take years to learn. This section therefore only contains brief hints and tips about what you can do. You can learn more if you go to your school or college library and do a little research before you begin – or ask the help of someone who has done it before!

The storyline

This will depend totally on your subject matter. Some of the most effective storylines for adverts are the simplest. Watch several adverts on television and jot down the main storyline. Starting out with something too complicated can put you off making videos for ever – and spoil it for the viewers.

As an example, a simple storyline for an advert for a computer could be:

Harassed employee with stacks of work to do visits a friend that evening. Uses her computer and gets everything done quickly and professionally. Following day gives work to boss and recommends company buys a computer. They do.

The storyboard

This is simply the storyline in pictures. It doesn't matter if you can't draw – *very* basic sketches will do. The idea is that you know the key shots for each part of your video. This is very important if you are going to make your film continuously. Even if you are going to edit the film later you will need to shoot action shots together. This saves you going to the local park for one set of shots and then having to return the following day because you didn't remember what came next.

A storyboard for the storyline above could vary tremendously. You could just follow the employee about, which would be very boring. A more interesting sequence of shots would be:

1 Employee surrounded by mountain of work – looks very fraught.
2 Stuffs it into briefcase to take home.
3 Looks at watch, remembers she has to call at friend's house.
4 With friend – who is using computer. Is asked to stay – refuses because of work.
5 Now using computer – friend has insisted she tries it.
6 Leaves friend's house with work done – smiling.
7 Shows boss work – she is pleased.
8 Van delivering computers to company.

From this you will see that you don't have to show every minute of the sequence to imply things have happened. For instance, the time between starting to use the computer and finishing the work is signified by the pile of completed work.

Writing the script

Remember your audience! The film above would have a different script depending on who would see the film. It would depend on:

- their age
- previous knowledge of computers
- whether the emphasis is on the computer itself or the type of work which can be done
- the amount of detail required
- if dialogue will be used or there will be a 'voice-over' explaining what is happening (i.e. telling the story).

The length of the film is also important. You are *far* better making something short and punchy than something which drags on and bores everyone! Do bear in mind that videos are *visual* – the viewer is watching what is happening and therefore does not need a detailed explanation at the same time.

Make sure the script is typed, and includes indications of 'feelings' as well as words. On the script you should also give an indication of where the action will be taking place and the camera shots at each point (Figure 10.12).

FADE IN

1 INSIDE OFFICE – DAY
   LONG SHOT OF WOMAN AT DESK

   Woman looks upset and harassed. Large piles of work in front of her. She turns over some papers, stares at one and looks puzzled.

2 ZOOM TO WAIST SHOT

   WOMAN:
   I don't believe it. How can I possible be expected to get through this lot by tomorrow morning (*shuffles through papers*). This is the second time this week I've had to take everything home and start again. I might as well move my bed in here.

   Woman starts to pack papers into briefcase.

3 LONG SHOT AS SHE GETS UP AND MOVES TO DOOR

Figure 10.12 *Part of a single camera shooting script*

DID YOU KNOW?

Professional actors and actresses often do 'voice-overs' for commercials – see if you can spot them. A middle-aged male is always used if an 'authoritative message' is being delivered. Therefore, a promotional film about new tyre laws, for instance, would be unlikely to have a young female doing the voice-over.

Activity

As a group, designate different people to watch television adverts on different nights. Find out how many have voice-overs and how many have dialogue. Watch for the 'cuts' between shots which indicate time has elapsed. Time the adverts – and see how short some of them are!

Try to spot the difference between a long-shot, a close-up and a waist-high shot. Remember to put what you have learned into action yourself.

Rehearsing the action

This is when you begin to find out if your ideas are workable – and how bad/good the people are who will appear in your video. Sometimes you may have to make a tough decision and drop someone because they simply cannot get it right. (Be kind and offer them a job 'backstage' to compensate!)

Check your planned camera shots, so that you can see what the *viewer* will see. You may find some of your original thoughts don't work at all, in which case it's 'back to the drawing board'. Make any notes of alterations on your copy of the script. If the script has been typed on a word-processor it can be amended before you start to film.

If you are shooting short pieces of film and then editing afterwards, you may rehearse then shoot each individual part immediately afterwards. If you are shooting continuously for several minutes you may need several rehearsals to check everyone knows exactly what they are doing before you start to film.

Shooting the film

If you have never used a video camera before then you could do with a little expert tuition first. This is especially

Figure 10.13 *Brace yourself to take steady shots!*

necessary for you to become used to the equipment. Basic things to note are:

1 Cameras which wobble about make awful films! Either use a tripod (preferably one on wheels) *or* rest your arm on something rigid (e.g. a wall or the floor). Figure 10.13 shows some examples.
2 Shots where the subject is central are balanced but become boring. Try to balance shots in different ways for variety (Figure 10.14).

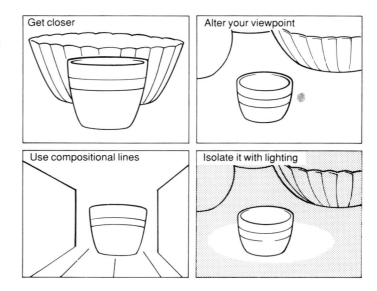

Figure 10.14 *Use a variety of shots*

3 Find out where your zoom is – but go for a waist-high shot rather than a real close-up unless you want the audience to start examining your subject's face in detail! You can then pull back for more interest.
4 Learn how to darken shots to cut between one piece of action and the next.
5 Find out how to focus – or everything will be in a fog.
6 Use focus to pick up different types of action. If someone turns to an open door then bring the *door* into focus as a person starts to enter (Figure 10.15).

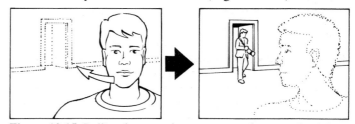

Figure 10.15 *Pulling focus: as he turns, you refocus on the visitor*

7 Be careful of the background. Bright white and other strong colours can be distracting (Figure 10.16). So too is a lot of clutter and poor camera angles which cut off part of the subject or show it from a view which is unrecognisable!

Avoid clutter

Do not cut off parts of subjects

Don't show an unfamiliar view of subject

Figure 10.16 *Some things to be avoided!*

Have contrasting background tones

Avoid shadowing the subject

8 Get a speaker to move rather than move your camera about. Try to stop him or her fidgeting!

9 Music can be useful for the opening sequence (to gain attention). Fade the music as someone starts to speak. Bring up the music at the end to signify to the audience the film is ending. Remember the *type* of music you choose can be critical as it sets the mood!

DID YOU KNOW?

In the film world the gaffer is the electrician – who, amongst other things, organises the lighting. The continuity person makes sure that when there is a gap in shooting nothing has changed – objects are in the same place, people are wearing the same clothing (and hair styles) etc. You may get by without a gaffer but, unless you are going to shoot your film in one session, you are advised to nominate someone to be in charge of continuity!

Editing the film

Much will depend on the equipment you have available. Editing means playing through your tape, cutting out bits which are boring or too long, removing errors (and inserting retakes), adjusting the length and – if you wish – putting your shots into a different order.

Some cameras enable you to edit as you film. In other cases you may have access to editing equipment you can use after shooting (but you will need help to use this). If neither of these is available then you will have to shoot 'live' – and in sequence – and keep your fingers crossed!

Evidence Collection Point 10.13

1 Find out what type of video equipment you would be able to use if you made a film, and the amount of expert help you would receive as a group. This will probably determine the type of project you are capable of undertaking.

2 If possible borrow a camera (to take still shots) or a video camera and practise taking some shots. Then critically analyse them afterwards. (Do bear in mind that if you are using film then you must check first if the money is available for processing it!)

Write a short report on the main areas where you went wrong and what you would do next time to avoid these problems.

3 Think of an idea for a short film to promote a product of your own choice. Draw a storyboard to show your ideas.

Computer-based materials

Today computers are used for a wide range of graphic material and promotional literature. In professional studios computer illustration is becoming a specialisation in itself.

Graphic packages offer the artist the choice between drawing and painting modes. The most sophisticated package of all is Quantell Paintbox and the most popular choice of computer with artists and designers is the Apple Mac.

There are various benefits in using computer graphics:

- Each stage of the illustration can be stored and recalled as necessary.
- Illustrations can be manipulated through various degrees, or copied at the touch of a key.
- Special effects are relatively easy to obtain.
- Animations can be achieved by running illustrations together.
- 'Clip art' is available for amateurs. This is pre-drawn art, stored on disk, which can be selected and included in other documents.

Videos and computers

Computers can be linked with video recorders to enable:

- titles to be produced and incorporated on video film
- graphics to be included in the film
- photographs and other illustrations to be included
- animations to be included (e.g. a moving logo!)
- background colours to be changed
- sound-effects to be incorporated.

However, you will be very lucky indeed to have such facilities in your school or college – and if you do you will probably need professional help to use them. Far more likely is that you will be able to produce paper-based promotional materials on computer – usually by means of a desktop publishing package.

Desktop publishing

This enables you to bring text and graphics together in a document. The document could be a poster, newsletter or advert. Text is keyed in using a compatible word-processing package. Graphics are usually 'scanned' in using a hand scanner or a document scanner. The package enables you to:

- choose different fonts, or typefaces, for your text
- position your text where you wish (in columns if you are producing a newsletter)

- create headings of different sizes
- move, cut, trim, enlarge or reduce your graphics to fit your page
- draw different borders around illustrations by varying the type of box you use (e.g. square or rounded corners), and the line thickness.

You really need a laser printer to get the best from a desktop publishing package. If this is a *Postscript* printer, which stores the fonts in memory, then you will have a wider range of typefaces from which to choose. Check with your tutor what type of printer you will be using.

A DTP package is ideal for designing the title page of your projects. Simply draw two or three boxes on your page and insert the main text (Figure 10.17). Keep the design simple until you know what you are doing!

Figure 10.17 *Produce professional looking titles for your reports*

Evidence Collection Point 10.14

Either

1 Watch someone at work using a computer graphics package or desktop publishing package and write a brief summary on what they did.

or

2 Use a desktop publishing package to produce a short promotional page on a topic of your own choosing. This could be a favourite hobby, a place you like to visit or a type of office equipment. If possible include an illustration.

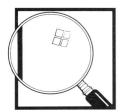

Evidence Checkpoint

At this stage you should have obtained a considerable amount of evidence on producing promotional materials. Check with your tutor that your work is complete for this element.

Evidence Project

Undertake *one* of the following four projects *as a group*. After it is completed write a report of approximately two A4 pages in length which explains:

● how the project was planned
● the process followed (i.e. the stages in which it was created)
● your own contribution and that of other members of your group.

Project 1

Part A

You have been asked to produce paper-based materials for a promotional campaign on behalf of the Royal Mail. For this you will work in a group of between three and five people. You will require a range of materials including:

● pencils, erasers, knife and sharpeners
● information on Royal Mail services
● stickers, counterfoils and forms for Royal Mail services
● a large piece of medium-weight board, either white or coloured, *approximately* 1 metre across by 800 cm down
● felt-tip pens and marker pens in different colours and thicknesses
● possibly some paint and brushes (if anyone in your group is artistically inclined)
● brown wrapping paper and some hessian (for some groups only) with which to make small parcels and 'sacks'
● dry transfers (if you can afford them) or a lettering pen.

1 Identify the items which are either free or will be provided free of charge by your school or college.

2 Identify the items which can be contributed by yourself or other members of your group.

3 Cost out the missing items and work out how much money you need to buy them.

4 Either put in a plea to your tutor, contribute a proportion of the cost each, raise the money to pay for them or decide how you are going to manage without them!

Part B

Your group has been asked by the Royal Mail service to make a large display which can be used at educational exhibitions for schools and colleges.

You have a choice of subjects:

● **mail services overseas** (i.e. airmail, swiftair, surface mail, international business reply, airstream)
● **safe and secure mail services** (i.e. registered mail, recorded delivery, certificate of posting, advice of delivery, compensation fee parcels)
● **speedy services** (i.e. special delivery, swiftair, datapost, international datapost)

- **parcel services** (i.e. Parcelforce 24, 48 and standard, datapost, small packets service, compensation fee parcels, cash on delivery, postage forward parcel service, parcels abroad)
- **business services** (i.e. freepost, business reply, mailsort, Admail, household delivery, Printed Postage Impressions).

Your instructions are to design an eye-catching and original poster which preferably incorporates some of the coloured Post Office stickers which are used for the different services.

1 Visit your main post office and obtain leaflets to research the various services on your subject list.

2 Obtain as many stickers and other visual aids as you can.

3 Design your poster (this is best if you work around a theme). If possible, include photographs you have taken yourself.

(See if your tutor wants to judge between the different posters submitted by your class or will ask an outside visitor to do this – e.g. a Royal Mail liaison officer.)

Project 2

You have been approached by McDonald's to make a new informational video about their products. If you want to try to shoot inside your local McDonald's then do remember you will need permission.

Some basic facts about McDonald's are given below. You can probably obtain more from one of their leaflets. You can also add to the information yourself if you wish.

Make a short video (maximum 45 seconds) on their products or restaurants.

Facts you may find useful

- The first UK McDonald's opened in Woolwich, London, in October 1974. Nobody went in all day.
- In September 1990 McDonald's sold its 80 billionth burger and today serves 23 million people every day.
- Restaurants in the UK increase by 40 every year. At present there are 472. Worldwide there are 13 090 restaurants.
- In 1992 UK customers ate 32 000 tons of fries and 275

million buns. They drank 4.5 million gallons of milk.
- Sales in 1992 were £578 million.
- Every second McDonald's sells 100 burgers somewhere in the world.
- Burgers have no additives, fillers, binders or flavour enhancers.
- In Britain the average customer spends £2.75 each time he or she goes to McDonald's.
- Staff in McDonald's in the Strand, London, serve 1300 customers an hour in summer.
- Altogether McDonald's employs 31 373 staff in the UK.

Project 3

You have been asked to make a promotional film about your school/college to show to prospective students next year. Your film should last no more than five minutes. You have been asked to concentrate on the facilities available and the type of courses students can take.

Project 4

You have formed a student committee with the other students in your class to produce a student newsletter.

1 Decide a suitable title and design a logo.

2 Write several articles which will be of interest to other students and input these to a computer using a word-processing package. Save them on disk.

3 Decide on other items you could include (e.g. a competition, quizzes etc.) which would help to 'sell' your newsletter.

4 Decide on suitable graphics or cartoons you could include and draw these.

5 Create a student newsletter, using a desktop publishing package. Scan your graphics to include them where appropriate. The newsletter should have two or three columns and *preferably* be on two pages.

6 Reproduce the newsletter on a photocopier and distribute it to students. If you want, you could charge a small price for the newsletter to pay for the materials. If your school or college has paid, perhaps you could donate your proceeds to charity.

Revision Test

True or false?

1 Spirits cannot be advertised on television.

2 The ASA is the Advertising Standards Association.

3 Competitions must contain some element of skill to be legal.

4 Computers can be used with videos to obtain special effects.

5 Planning is usually the most important stage in a promotional campaign.

Complete the blanks

6 There are two types of adverts – .... and ....

7 Television advertising is controlled by the ....

8 Drawing the key shots for a video is done using a ....

9 Newsletters, adverts and posters can be produced on computer using a .... package.

10 A machine which converts pictures into digital images which can be shown on a computer screen is called a ....

Short answer questions

11 State the six different stages of video production.

12 Write down six tips on effective poster design.

13 State three advantages to an organisation of sponsoring an event.

14 Give four disadvantages of advertising on television.

15 State three objectives of producing promotional materials.

Write a short paragraph to show you clearly understand each of the following terms:

16 Computer-based materials.

17 Lens-based materials.

18 Ethical constraints on advertising.

19 Physical resources.

20 Sponsorship.

chapter **11** PROVIDING CUSTOMER SERVICES

Learning Objectives

This chapter is concerned with the needs of customers, the reasons why organisations try to meet these needs and the methods by which this is achieved. We look at different types of communications, how queries and complaints are handled, differences in customers and the legal requirements which underpin all customer relationships.

After studying this chapter you should be able to:

- identify customer needs

- explain the reasons for meeting customer needs

- give examples of polite communications which would meet customers' needs

- provide prompt service to a range of different customers

- refer customer queries to the correct person

- deal with customer complaints according to agreed procedures

- explain the ways in which service to customers must meet legal requirements.

▪ CUSTOMER NEEDS ▪

Customers contact an organisation for a variety of reasons:

- to obtain information on its goods and/or services
- to place an order
- to enquire about progress of their order
- to clarify details
- to query details
- to query their accounts
- to complain, if they are dissatisfied with the service they have received or the product they have purchased
- to ask if they can return goods, or have them repaired.

Whether they call in personally or telephone the organisation, customers need one or more of the following:

1 **Information** (e.g. on the range of goods you stock, prices and delivery times)

2 **Help or assistance** (e.g. to find a product which suits their needs, to answer a query about their account)
3 **After sales service** (e.g. to obtain a refund or replacement)
4 **Care and attention** – There is nothing more annoying than to feel that neither an organisation nor its staff care one jot whether you buy something or not.

There is a variety of jobs where you may have to deal with customers on a daily basis. These range from members of the public (if you work in a bank, the local town hall or a shop) to foreign visitors or specialist industrial buyers (if you work for a manufacturing company). In the first case you would probably be expected to know enough about the products or services your organisation provides to assist the customer yourself. In the second, you would have to act professionally in your dealings with customers and clients, even if it was not your job to assist them specifically.

First impressions

Have you ever noticed how you remember 'firsts'–like the first day you went to secondary school or the first time you visited somewhere or met someone? For some reason, these occasions often assume more importance than subsequent visits or meetings. We have all heard people give their opinions of someone after only one meeting. This can be unwise, because we may have met someone on a bad day, or in a situation where they were none too happy. In this case, if we get to know them well we may have to change our opinion. In business, unfortunately, a poor first impression is likely to lead to losing a customer. There may never be an opportunity to repair the damage, as a customer who forms this view of an organisation is unlikely to return to give it a second chance.

For this reason, how you greet people who visit your organisation is critical, especially as many of them may be calling for the first time. Although it may not seem fair, if you are the first person they meet, *you* are the person who will influence their opinion of the whole company. What you say, and what you do, can therefore be critical.

Basic facts and information

What do you need to know before you can start to help someone? Ideally you should know all the following:

- Your company structure – who deals with what type of queries.
- The products/services your company offers – not just a broad appreciation but details of what you can and can't offer. The expertise you can gain in this area will depend very much on the type of company you work for.
  - **a** In a *retail organisation* sales assistants should know their stock well, its uses, the range, what can be ordered and so on.
  - **b** In a *service industry* (e.g. an insurance company), staff should know the full range of services offered and who to contact in the organisation for further information if required.
  - **c** In a *manufacturing industry* the technical details of some products may be too intricate to be known by anyone other than the technical specialists. In this case you should have a good knowledge of the range of products manufactured and know who to contact in relation to the particular query you are asked.
- Which goods have guarantees and warranties and for how long – and whether special insurance can be taken out to prolong cover.
- Your company procedures and the main methods of communication between and within departments in the company.
- Basic facts about the law in relation to your organisation and its customers (e.g. the Sale of Goods Act and the Trades Description Act).
- What literature is available (e.g. brochures, leaflets, price lists, reference books).
- Company policy on refunds and replacements of goods.
- The after-sales service offered by your organisations.
- The correct procedure for dealing with customer complaints
- Where to go for more information, help or advice.

- look at the products sold (if possible)
- listen to (and watch) experienced colleagues
- ask questions
- **remember the answers!**

Evidence Collection Point 11.1

1 Discuss as a group the occasions when:
- you have contacted a shop or other organisation and received very poor service
- you have asked about products or services but the person you spoke to didn't know (or care!) enough to help you.

Write down your comments and how this affected your opinion of these organisations.

2 Have you, or any other member of your group, ever worked for an organisation (full-time or part-time) where you have received specific training on customer service? Did the company have any type of merit system for service (e.g. the McDonald's 'star' badge system)? Compare your notes and write a brief report.

3 Think of several things that have happened to you in shops and stores (and ask your parents or friends for examples as well) which have annoyed you or put you off returning. List as many things as you can.

General enquiries

At a basic level, people may approach you with a general query either about the goods that you stock or the services you provide. On many occasions you might not know the answer, but you can still appear helpful, if necessary by finding another member of staff who *could* help them. Over time, you can store up the answers to the general enquiries you receive and within a short space of time become a mine of information! You will know you are succeeding if, as time passes, you find you are able to answer more and more queries on your own.

Use the chart in Figure 11.1 to see how you should handle general enquiries. Make sure you know or find out the following:

1 *Where* to get the information you need and *what* type of information is available – leaflets, catalogues, brochures etc. Don't forget that people will always want to know about the price, and the ways in which they can pay (e.g. by cheque, credit card, instalments).

2 *Who* to ask for help or further information, if that is required. Don't 'overstep' your area of responsibility by promising anything to a customer which is outside your area of authority.

3 *Enough* about the customer to be able to recommend the right product or service for him or her. You should not be so keen to recommend a product or service that you 'land' customers with something that will not suit them, because:

- they will probably come back to complain later, and/or
- they will go elsewhere next time
- in some financial service industries this is actually illegal!

4 *How* to follow up the enquiry. This means taking full details of the enquiry and making any special notes which will be useful or relevant to your colleagues who may have to follow it up. Most organisations have standard procedures for dealing with enquiries and standard forms to fill in. If there are any *additional* details which do not seem to 'fit' anywhere on the form, then write these out neatly and clip your notes *securely* to the form. Make sure you process the enquiry on to its 'next stage' without undue delay.

5 *How to keep the customer informed!* Tell the customer the procedure that is to be followed, how long it will take, what delays (if any) may be expected – and why. Promise to keep him or her informed if the situation changes in any way. This type of assurance would be essential, of course, if your company is out of stock of the product required and it has to be ordered. It is far more professional to tell customers that *you* will inform *them* when it is available, rather than asking them to ring you.

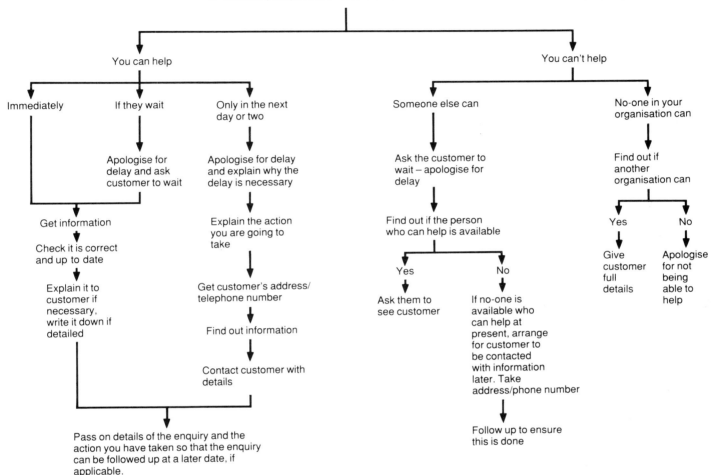

* Greet the customer with a smile and a greeting such as 'May I help you?'
* If you know their name, use it.
* Listen whilst you ascertain what their enquiry is about.
* If it is long or complicated, write down the details.
* Check anything you are not sure about.

You can help

Immediately | If they wait | Only in the next day or two

Apologise for delay and ask customer to wait

Apologise for delay and explain why the delay is necessary

Get information

Check it is correct and up to date

Explain the action you are going to take

Explain it to customer if necessary, write it down if detailed

Get customer's address/ telephone number

Find out information

Contact customer with details

Pass on details of the enquiry and the action you have taken so that the enquiry can be followed up at a later date, if applicable.

You can't help

Someone else can | No-one in your organisation can

Ask the customer to wait – apologise for delay

Find out if another organisation can

Find out if the person who can help is available

Yes | No

Yes | No

Ask them to see customer

If no-one is available who can help at present, arrange for customer to be contacted with information later. Take address/phone number

Give customer full details

Apologise for not being able to help

Follow up to ensure this is done

Figure 11.1 *Answering general calls and enquiries*

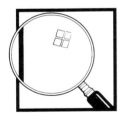

Evidence Assignment 11A

Imagine that you have worked in a local bookshop each Saturday for several months. A new Saturday assistant has just been employed and, for the first few weeks, you have been asked to keep your eye on her. The first morning you are very busy unpacking some new stock. When you come out of the stockroom you are horrified to see a queue of customers forming at the sales desk and the new employee standing at one end of the shop, obviously chatting to a friend who has called in.

When you have a word with her she says she couldn't help anyone as she doesn't know where anything is and no-one has shown her how the till works.

1 Was the new employee correct in saying that she couldn't help anyone? What do you think she *should* have done in this situation?

2 To what extent were you and the other bookshop staff at fault that morning?

3 If your boss now decides to spend the first hour with new staff on basic training, what items do you think should be included, and why?

DID YOU KNOW?

If you are getting together literature to give to a customer you should *never* take the last copy without making sure that either:

- you have ordered some more, or
- you get some more from stock to replace what you have taken.

There is nothing more infuriating for other staff than to find that they have run out of essential information because someone keeps using the last copy without telling anyone!

- *Read* about the product from the literature available. Note down the main features and selling points.
- *Ask* your supervisor to clarify any points which you do not understand.
- *Practise* explaining how the product functions (and how to demonstrate it in operation, if this is applicable).
- *Find out* the price.
- *Think about* any questions you may be asked.
- *Be prepared* to compare one make of product with others in a range (e.g. one make of calculator with another).

Evidence Collection Point 11.2

In the case of each of these enquiries, discuss as a group and then write down:

- the type of procedures which would be followed
- the type of forms which would be completed
- what could go wrong through staff inefficiency.

1 An order for a book not in stock at a bookshop.

2 An application to open a bank account.

3 An enquiry to replace existing window frames with plastic PVC frames.

4 An application from a potential student to attend a college course.

Evidence Assignment 11B

Choose *either* an item of equipment you have at home which you could easily bring to class (e.g. a personal stereo or calculator) *or* a suitable item of equipment in school or college (e.g. a photocopier).

Follow the instructions above to familiarise yourself with how it works and its main features. Then prepare a short demonstration to the rest of your group – one of whom should play the role of the customer and ask you questions (just as they would if they were thinking of purchasing the product).

Record your demonstration on tape and then write up a commentary on your own performance, and the areas in which you think you still need to improve.

Information on goods and products

In some organisations your main role will be to ensure that customers are put in touch with an appropriate sales person who can give them detailed information. In some cases, a representative may visit a potential customer at home to talk about their requirements in more detail. In others, there may be sales people who specialise in particular types of products – in this case you need to know who knows about what.

However, there are times when *you* will be expected to know enough about products to describe them properly to customers and give them basic technical information. To do this you should:

DID YOU KNOW?

'Product' knowledge is still important if you work in the tertiary sector or services industry, because the services you sell are your 'products', whether these are banking facilities or types of insurance.

In many cases, in these industries, a good knowledge of the 'product' range is vital. You know this yourself – if you visit your local travel agent and are thinking of spending your carefully saved money on the holiday of a lifetime, you want sound, professional advice – not someone simply waving an arm towards a stack of brochures.

Related services

Customers don't just want to know about the products they can buy. Your organisation may also be judged on the additional services it provides; for example:

- free delivery
- extended warranties or guarantees
- special offers
- free help desk or phone line for customers
- ordering goods which are currently out of stock.

If you forget to mention any of these then you may lose a sale for your company. Bear in mind also that you need to keep up to date – in particular on special offers as these may change regularly.

Refunds and replacements

Most organisations have a policy on what staff should do if a customer returns goods, either because they are faulty or because the customer has changed his or her mind. How to cope with faulty goods is dealt with in full in Chapter 12, as this involves knowing about consumer legislation – though in most cases you would be expected to get a supervisor's second opinion. Customers who bring back faulty goods they have purchased have a *legal right* to a refund; they do not have to accept a credit note.

The policy on exchanging goods is more varied. Large stores such as Bhs and Marks & Spencer have a policy whereby goods can be exchanged at any branch if the customer later changes his or her mind. If you find the novel you bought at Books etc is boring, the company will refund your money so long as the book is in good condition. However, this is not standard practice with all organisations.

After-sales service

This is probably one of the most important factors for a consumer in deciding whether or not to either buy a particular make again, or visit the same shop again. After-sales service relates to the help and assistance that is given to customers later, after the sale has been completed, and normally concerns the repairs of goods which develop a fault in use.

A typical example is household appliances. These are all sold with specific guarantees or warranties. Most customers are then given the option of extending this period by taking out special insurance. This may mean that the cost of labour and spare parts will be free if the appliance breaks down, or the policy may cover labour charges only.

▪ REASONS TO MEET CUSTOMER NEEDS ▪

An organisation which makes a specific effort to meet its customers' needs will benefit in several ways.

1 **a** It will retain existing customers.
   b Word will get around, and new customers will be attracted.

   These factors will improve company performance as sales will increase and, therefore, so will profitability.

2 Service will be improved as the company (and staff) will learn from mistakes made in the past and put the best of their 'good practice' into everyday use.

3 It will improve the morale of staff and customers. If you *know* that you will be encouraged to give good service to customers then this will improve your own morale. We all get a 'buzz' out of helping people. Equally the person you help will also be grateful, and think well both of you and the company.

Activity

Imagine that you work in a hotel. A couple arrive in reception complaining that although they ordered a room with a bath they have been given a room with a shower. You tell them you will see what you can do. Five minutes later another couple appear in reception. They have been given a room with a bath when they ordered a room with a shower. You decide the obvious solution is to switch them around. When you do so, both are delighted and thank you profusely.

How would you feel at this stage? Would this give you a 'buzz' or would you be unaffected? Discuss your reactions as a group.

DID YOU KNOW?

Companies which concentrate on giving excellent customer service can often rely on word of mouth to boost the number of customers, rather than advertising. Marks & Spencer is a good example. You will rarely see an M & S advert in the press or on television, so their advertising costs are relatively low. Instead they rely on their good name and promote this by good customer service and by helping the community and local charities.

Evidence Collection Point 11.3

1 Visit three large stores in your own area. Assess customer service in relation to:

a speed of assistance
b staff appearance
c staff knowledge of goods and products
d attitude of staff
e policy on refunds.

2 Find at least one example of a store which has its 'customer service pledge' in a prominent position. Copy out the main points of this and comment on how these would help the customers.

3 Some organisations show a list of staff and give their titles. How do you think this might assist the customer?

· COMMUNICATIONS ·

When you communicate with a customer you give an impression, not just of yourself but of the organisation you represent. This is the case whether you speak face to face or over the telephone. For the customer you *are* the organisation.

There are actually two ways in which you communicate with customers – verbally and non-verbally. Non-verbal communication is often called 'body language' and relates to our facial expressions, gestures and posture.

DID YOU KNOW?

It is useless saying or doing the right thing if your body language says the opposite! If you *look* bored and are slouching then the words you say are irrelevant – customers will form their impression of you from the way you look. Therefore your body language *must* match your words. Stand up straight and look interested – even if you aren't!

Verbal communications

You speak to people every day – your parents, relatives, friends and even total strangers. How many of them find you 'easy to talk to', how many of them understand you easily? Or do you create confusion and irritation as people try to work out what you mean?

A good verbal communicator:

- has a clear speaking voice
- speaks at the right 'pace' (too slowly and you bore people, too fast and they may not follow what you say)
- is a good listener
- chooses the correct words and 'tone' for the situation
- puts people at their ease
- has the confidence to talk to strangers
- understands how non-verbal communication gestures can affect people.

What do you sound like?

Many people are horrified the first time they hear their voice on a tape recorder. It is a nasty shock to find that you don't sound the same to other people as you sound to yourself!

There are two aspects to your voice which affect what you sound like. The first is **timbre** – or quality of sound – and the second is your **accent** and the way you pronounce words.

If you think your voice is squeaky or sharp then try to lower the pitch just a little. Try not to get excited or rush too much as this can make you sound harsh.

Regional accents and dialects can be very attractive, but if you have a *very* broad regional accent you must remember that this may be almost unintelligible to someone from another part of the country or from abroad. The situation will be even worse if you use regional or slang expressions as well!

Activity

As a group make a list of words you use which may not be easily understood by a listener from another part of the country *or* of another age-group. Your list should include regional words and slang expressions which are in vogue at the moment.

Make a second list of slang expressions which just don't sound good when you are involved in a business discussion. 'OK' is the most obvious!

Evidence Collection Point 11.4

1 Prepare a talk of 3–5 minutes on your favourite interest or hobby or a place you know well. *Tape* your talk, preferably without reading from your notes.

2 Play back the tape and write down your own criticisms of it from the point of view of how you *sounded* (rather than what you said). You should lose a mark every time you said 'er' or 'um' and when you used words or expressions that would not be understood by someone else (either because they are slang or jargon). Check the pace of your speech. Was it gabbled or hesitant and slow? Did

you say the words clearly, and pronounce the *ends* of words? Was the volume too low, too loud or just right?

3 Now tape your talk again, and see if you can improve on your first attempt.

Listening skills

Most people are actually poor listeners. They listen to the first part of a conversation, then think of a reply and wait impatiently for the speaker to be quiet so that they can start their own response. During this time they are not listening to a word being said!

'If only he'd stop talking I could make a really good point'.

You should try to concentrate on:

● listening until someone has *finished* speaking
● not interrupting them in mid-sentence!

Remember that if *you* go on speaking for too long, people will have stopped listening to you, too!

Tone

'Tone' is a skill which is important for all types of communications. It is so important that it should be one of the main factors which determines the words and phrases you choose. The 'tone' of what you are saying will make it acceptable or unacceptable to the receiver.

Evidence Assignment 11C

You take a telephone message for a colleague to say that a dental appointment, originally made for tomorrow at 2 p.m., has had to be cancelled as the dentist is ill. The patient should ring next week to make another appointment.

Write down, or record on cassette what you would say if you were passing this message to:

a the managing director of the company for which you work, Mr Sharpe
b your colleague in customer services, Mrs Browne, who is ten years older than you
c your best friend.

Analyse the difference in tone in each message.

Non-verbal communication

Non-verbal communication (NVC) can be divided into four separate areas:

- facial expressions – especially the use of the eyes
- gestures
- touching and spatial relationships (the distance between people)
- posture.

Knowing something about non-verbal communication means that you can:

- realise how people read *your* NVC
- improve your communication skills
- 'read' other people's NVC better, and change your reactions accordingly.

Activity

You have just received some wonderful news you want to share with a friend. When you find him he is sitting in a chair, with his elbows on the desk, holding his head in his hands.

1 Would you still bounce in and give him your good news?
2 If not, why not?
3 What greeting would now be more appropriate?

Facial expressions

These are usually the main 'give-away' on how we are feeling. However, most people are aware of this and sometimes take action to 'cover up' their feelings. For instance, if you receive a present which was a total

disappointment you may try not to show this to the giver, and alter your expression accordingly.

Facial expressions should tell you how the content of the message is being received – i.e. if the listener understands and approves or disapproves of what you are saying.

Expressions are also an indication of people's attitudes towards each other. If someone wants approval they often smile and nod their head more than someone who isn't bothered about what the other person thinks.

Finally, expressions indicate how seriously a remark should be taken. You can usually tell if someone is joking because of the expression on their face.

Eyes are very important. Usually you look at someone between 25 per cent and 75 per cent of the time – more when you are listening than speaking. The fact that someone looks *away* from us usually gives us the signal they have nearly finished speaking and it is now 'our turn'. We *expect* **eye contact** – if someone doesn't look at us at all we think they are 'shifty' or have something to hide. If you have a close relationship with someone then the amount of eye contact you have increases considerably.

DID YOU KNOW?

 You use twice the number of muscles in your face to frown as you do to smile – so there's no excuse for looking glum!

Gestures

The smart, well-dressed young man who looks supremely confident may give away his inner nervousness by continually touching or adjusting his cuffs.

Gestures often give away our feelings. A man who drums his fingers on the desk or taps his foot is signalling impatience – usually the faster he 'drums' the more impatient he is becoming!

We use gestures to:

- communicate to someone a distance away
- accentuate what we are saying
- (subconsciously) echo what we are feeling.

Touching and spatial relationships

We subconsciously try to maintain a certain distance between ourselves and other people, though the 'gap' we try to keep will depend on:

- how well we know (or would like to know) the person next to us
- the type of event (e.g. business meeting or party)
- the country in which we have been born or brought up.

We are always more wary of people being in front of us than behind us. In a crowded lift you will be more concerned about someone in front of you than someone behind you, and will do your utmost to avoid eye or body contact.

The distance we find 'comfortable' varies from one nationality to another. British people on holiday in an Arab or Latin country can find themselves moving backwards almost constantly to try to maintain a distance their host considers almost anti-social.

If you are with someone you know very well, or like very much, then you usually stand or sit much closer to them – often within 'touching' distance.

Posture

Posture can give various hints about feelings.

- You stand upright if you are interested or confident.
- You stand with your shoulders hunched if you are miserable, depressed or bored.
- You unconsciously 'mirror' the position of someone you agree with.
- You point your feet and body towards the things that interest you. If you are only marginally interested in someone passing by then, if they speak to you, you will turn your head towards them but leave your body in the same position. This is the signal to keep the communication short! If you are in a group you 'welcome' a newcomer by 'opening a gap' and angling your body towards them.

Evidence Collection Point 11.5

1 How would you interpret the following gestures?

- someone shrugging their shoulders

- the 'thumbs up' sign
- someone licking their lips
- a man straightening his tie and then touching his hair before moving towards a girl he has seen across the room.

2 In which girl is the man on the settee interested? How can you tell?

3 Try to maintain an excessive gap between you and a friend. Start to speak to him or her *further away* than you normally would (when you are both standing). Then keep still. If he or she moves towards you then move backwards. Record what happens.

4 Observe *yourself* over the next few days. Write down an example of when you find yourself:

- 'mirroring' someone's stance or movements
- avoiding eye contact
- using gestures

- turning your head towards someone but leaving your body pointing away from them.

5 Observe other people. Go into a large store and watch an assistant who gives you the impression of being polite, charming and efficient. Write down *why* you have reached this opinion. Now find someone who gives you the opposite impression and analyse what brought you to that conclusion.

Face-to-face communications

This means that the person you are talking to is actually in front of you. In this case you have all the clues of his or her voice to tell you how they feel *and* non-verbal communications as well.

Regular customers

Unless you work in a very large store, most organisations have their 'regular' customers. Although all customers are important to an organisation, regular customers are *vital*. It can take years, and a considerable amount of hard work (and money spent on advertising), to build up a good customer relationship. Yet this can be ruined in minutes with poor service or back-up or surly staff.

A **golden rule** is always to greet regular customers *by name*. We all react favourably to this type of treatment as it makes us feel important. If you *should* know someone's name but have forgotten it then don't bluff. Admit, at the outset, that you don't know (e.g. 'I'm sorry, I know I should remember your name but ...') – if you pause at the right moment you will find that the customer will happily give you the information you want. The trick to remembering someone's name is to repeat it several times within the next few minutes during your conversation with them. At the same time, try to memorise what they look like – the experts on memory tests suggest that you should look for some feature you can link to the name (e.g. Mr Brown has brown hair), but this isn't always as easy as it sounds.

In addition to their names, you will always be more effective if you can remember some details about your 'regulars' (e.g. their likes and dislikes). This will enable you to give them a far more personal service which will be noticed and appreciated. If nothing else, try to remember the last time you dealt with them and what it was about.

New customers and casual callers

Virtually all organisations train staff to welcome customers with a smile and a greeting (e.g. 'Good morning, may I help you?'). Do try to make the customers feel that you are there if you are needed but will not harass them (for instance, if they are just looking around). Casual callers may prefer to be left alone for a while and you should respect their wishes. You can judge if this is the case by watching for their first reaction. Do they mirror your smile or look hesitant and avert their eyes?

The type of organisation for which you work will affect the number of casual callers you are expected to deal with. Casual callers are far more likely to call in a retail establishment than in any other type of organisation.

Discussing business

Even if you are not able to give a customer specific information, you can still help them effectively. To do this you need to be able to convince him or her that, after contact with you, progress has been made in the area of concern. Customers should feel that by seeing you they have achieved something. If you leave customers feeling that they have made little, if any, progress then they will probably take their business elsewhere in future. At the very least, they will be annoyed that their time has been wasted as nothing has been achieved. Golden rules to remember include:

- Remain polite and helpful throughout the conversation.
- *Never* do anything which will annoy the customer and distract them from the conversation (e.g. chew, sniff or scratch!).
- If you know it, use the customer's name at frequent intervals.
- Don't try to be clever or witty – it doesn't work.
- If you take a message for someone then make sure you pass it on promptly.
- Say 'goodbye' to someone *properly*.

Activity

Practise your social skills *either* by role playing with another member of your group *or* (even better) acting as a guide next time your school or college hosts a Parents' Evening, Open Evening or similar event when visitors are invited.

DID YOU KNOW?

In a new job most people don't like answering the telephone in case they won't be able to cope with the call. In fact it is perfectly possible to sound competent and efficient *and* give a good impression *without* being able to give someone specific help.

Using the telephone

The main difference between face-to-face communication and using a telephone is that now you have no non-verbal clues to help you. In addition, you may only be used to using a telephone at home, and speaking to your friends. Now, the tone – and the words you use – must be different.

DID YOU KNOW?

If you smile as you speak on the phone, your good mood will transmit itself to the person you are speaking to. It will make all the difference to your telephone conversations. Try it and see!

Activity

As a group discuss:

- how you first greet a telephone caller on your own phone
- how you end a telephone call
- the type of slang words and expressions you use
- what should be different in a business call!

Hints and tips

1 *Never* answer a telephone without a pen or pencil in your hand and a piece of paper (or preferably a message pad) nearby.
2 Answer *promptly* (the caller can't see how busy you are!).
3 *Never* eat or drink when using the telephone.
4 *Always* sound pleasant and helpful.
5 If the call is for someone who is available:

   - ask who is calling
   - ask the caller to hold the line a moment (*please*!). *don't* say 'hang on'
   - tell the person being called they are wanted and give them the name of the caller.

6 If the call is for someone who is not available:

   - ask if he or she would like to speak to someone else
   - see if you can help
   - suggest the caller rings back later or suggest the person they want to speak to rings them back later – this may depend on the policy of your organisation.
   - offer to take a message.

7 If the caller wants information which will take you a while to find, *don't* keep them holding on. Offer to ring back when you have it to hand.
8 *Never* promise to ring someone back and then let them down.
9 *Always* check with your supervisor if you are being asked for information which you think may be confidential.
10 Be aware that a receiver left lying on a desk picks up the general office conversation and casual remarks!
11 Treat important information you receive over the telephone as confidential.

DID YOU KNOW?

Sometimes callers with an enquiry need to be transferred to another extension. It is important that all employees know how to do this correctly on their telephone system so that they don't cut anyone off by mistake. You should also know how to divert your calls to another extension if you are going to leave your telephone unattended.

The professional touch

People who sound really effective on the telephone usually know one or two things that other people don't:

- Using a person's name during a conversation makes them feel important.
- Concluding a call by saying 'thank you for calling' has the same effect.
- If you are cut off in the middle of a conversation then the person who made the call should attempt the reconnection.
- Figures said in *pairs* are always easier to understand; e.g. '45' ... '62' ... '34' *not* '456' ... '234'.
- It is always better (if possible) to let the person who made the call conclude it.
- A 'smile' in the voice is identified as being friendly on the other end of a telephone.
- There is nothing wrong in asking people to repeat a name or a figure to check you have written it correctly. People with an unusual name are quite used to having to spell it out over the telephone, and you should *always* read back a telephone number to make sure it is correct.
- It is far better to check all the details *before* ringing off rather than to have to ring back later.
- If you are making a call then make sure you have all the relevant facts and figures before you ring. If you prepare well you sound more efficient.

Evidence Assignment 11D

You have obtained a part-time job in your local video rental shop and work there one evening a week and all day Saturday. The shop is open from 9.30 a.m. to 9.30 p.m. each day. Films must be returned by 8 p.m. the following day or a daily fine is levied. Customers must be members and a list of these is kept on a computer database, together with the membership number. The database also gives the date of hire of each film and any fines not paid. Customers who owe more than £5 are not allowed to rent any more films unless the manager, Mrs Karen Robbins, gives her permission. Films can be ordered over the telephone and will be saved for up to three hours.

1 Today you are working on the counter and answering the telephone. You receive the following telephone calls. Either role play these and record your

conversations (which is better) *or* write down what you would say in each case. Then discuss your responses with your tutor and state how these could be improved (or role play them again).

a A call from a Mr Benson who wants to reserve the film *Rough Justice*. When you look on the shelf you see there are three copies in stock. He quotes his membership number as 3160.

b A call from a Miss Paula Saunders. She wants to hire two films for that evening. When you check the database record you find that she owes £10 in fines and still has one film out on hire.

c A call from a Mr Zaheer Ahmed. He has just borrowed the film *Cape Fear*. When he started to watch it he found it was totally blank. You have no more copies of this film in stock.

d A young child telephones and asks if he can reserve a cartoon film.

e The regional manager telephones and asks to speak to Mrs Robbins about a confidential matter. You know that she has gone to a nearby shop for a minute to buy a birthday card for her son.

f A young man phones and asks if he can reserve a film which is for over-18s only. From his voice, you are fairly sure that he is only about 13 or 14.

g A Mr Samuels telephones. He is very upset. He has just returned from three-weeks' holiday and found a video film which he thought had been returned to you. When you check your database you find that the fines have amounted to £28. He says he will not pay as he has been a customer for years and never been a day late returning a film. He thinks you should let him off on this occasion.

h You receive a call from a regular, elderly customer, Miss Threlfall. She gives you the title of quite an old film she wants to hire. You *think* you might have a copy upstairs, where some old stock is kept, but it will take you some time to find out if you are right.

2 On your day off you want to telephone the shop yourself. Mrs Robbins has asked if you can work an extra evening for the next two weeks. You can't manage next week as you have already made arrangements to go out that night. You can, however, work the following week. Write down, or record on cassette, what you would say to Mrs Robbins.

3 Design a database record card which could be used for recording customer information at the shop. Include all the sections which would be useful for staff.

4 How do you think having a database of customers improves customer service in the shop? How might this, in turn, affect business performance?

5 The manager notices that several customers have overdue films but are not bringing them back – presumably because they are frightened about having to pay large fines. What could the shop do to try to get the films returned? If possible, the manager does not want to take legal action against anybody as the size of the fines would not warrant the cost.

· DIFFERENT TYPES OF CUSTOMERS ·

Customers are different in age, temperament and personality. Some will be obliging and patient, others ill-tempered or impatient. Some are confident and know what they want, others are uncertain or even shy and tongue-tied. Therefore you have two aspects to consider:

- the type of person you are dealing with
- their wants or needs.

It is impossible to give specific advice on every combination you are likely to meet. It is, however, relatively easy for all staff to acquire some basic skills and knowledge which they can then *adapt* according to the person and the situation.

Children

Whether you have to deal with children or not will depend very much upon where you work. If you are in a sweet shop then you will have them as customers all the time. If you work for a furniture company then this is less likely!

Children who are accompanied by an adult are usually less of a problem (unless they are misbehaving and their parents are ignoring the fact). Unaccompanied children may have arrived on their own *or* may even be lost – in which case you should offer help.

- Bear in mind that most children will not know exactly what they want – you'll have to give them help.
- Their vocabulary will vary with their age. So will their level of understanding *and* the number of things they can remember at once!
- They may need help sorting out their money. A grubby

hand offering an assortment of coins may be irritating in a busy shop, but you should take the opportunity to explain which coins you are taking – and why.

- If you get to know a child well then address him or her by name, just as you would an adult. Remember, if you *did* own a sweet shop you'd want their custom – and you never know, they may grow up to be a regular, rich customer!
- If a child is misbehaving then first of all check if his or her parents are around, and re-unite them! Otherwise speak firmly – there's no need to shout.
- If a child is lost then find out his or her name and age. Most children know both these facts at a very early age. If your organisation has a public address system you can then give out the details and the location where the parent should go. *Don't* take the child off the premises, or you could be in trouble yourself.

DID YOU KNOW?

Some organisations which deal with large numbers of children (e.g. theme and amusement parks) have special points for 'lost children'. As well as details of a child's name and age, the clothes they are wearing are also often described over the public address system – in case there is more than one child lost with the same name!

Individuals with special needs

The handicapped

If you deal with people regularly then you will obviously meet people who are handicapped in one way or another. Many people feel awkward if they have to deal with handicapped customers. Whilst this may be understandable – especially if you have no experience of dealing with handicapped people – there really is no need to see this as a problem. The important thing to remember is *not* to be patronising or treat people as if they are less

intelligent just because they have a physical handicap. Remember that they are used to coping with their disability and don't feel embarrassed.

- **The deaf** – Bear in mind that you won't know that someone is deaf (unless they tell you) as there are no visible signs. If you think this might be the case make sure you *look* at the person when you speak to them (in case they lip-read) and speak *relatively* slowly and clearly. *Don't* shout!

- **The blind or partially sighted** – Speak as you approach them, to avoid startling them. Your voice will also guide them towards you. Someone who is completely blind may have a white stick and/or a guide dog. Companies usually have special rules for guide dogs on the premises. If you want a blind person to follow you then *find out* if they wish you to lead them – don't just grab hold of them. If you approach any steps then say whether these are *up* or *down* and how many there are.

- **The disabled** – Life will be much easier for any disabled customers if there are ramps, rather than steps, in your building (especially if they are confined to a wheelchair). Be ready to open doors if necessary. *Don't* try to rush them or appear impatient. Apart from being attentive and thoughtful and prepared to offer help when necessary, concentrate on the *person* rather than the disability.

- **The mentally handicapped** – People with a mental handicap may have difficulty in saying what they want or making you understand them as their vocabulary may be limited. Be patient. They normally know what they want but just need *time* to cope with the situation.

Foreign visitors

Another caller with a special need is the customer who does not speak English very well. In this case you might struggle to find out what it is he or she really wants.

Listen carefully	**Don't** speak quickly
Use simple English	**Don't** use long sentences
Repeat carefully what you think is meant to check you are right	**Don't** shout!
Ask for help if you cannot understand the customer at all	**Don't** become impatient

Shy and nervous customers

These customers can be of either sex and of any age. You may be able to identify them because their non-verbal communication will show that they are hesitant or ill at ease. They may try to avoid eye contact if they do speak to you. They may move backwards as you approach them.

Make sure you appear friendly without over-whelming them

Don't be pushy or impatient

Offer to help and speak gently, calmly and deliberately (nervous people don't 'take things in' quickly)

Don't try to rush them or finish off sentences for them

If they want to take their time then agree and keep a watchful eye on them

Don't neglect them or forget all about them

Confidential matters

Another type of caller with a special need is one whose requirements are very personal or confidential. In this case you can hardly expect them to give you heaps of information because the person they want to see is not available. Equally you should realise that any information *you* have should be given out with care. If you called in to the bank to ask for information on the balance of your account, you would not expect the cashier to shout this information to you so that everyone else can hear! For this reason, it is important that you are sensitive to the type of enquiries where the content is such that it should not be discussed in a public area. For example:

- **financial** discussions on loans, income, expenditure, payment difficulties, etc.
- **medical** discussions about personal health or the health of close family, serious illnesses, etc.
- **personal** discussions when information is relevant to past/future behaviour, criminal records, marital relations, etc.

All organisations that have these types of discussions with customers will have private offices where interviews can be held. Every company will have a room where clients and customers can be taken if they need to pass on restricted information or discuss a particular problem.

The standard procedures and forms will still be completed with the relevant details, and often full, separate details of the visit are summarised for the benefit of other staff dealing with the customer later. Any such documents are usually kept in a customer file, marked **confidential**, and should *never* be the topic of open discussions with other staff *or* discussed outside the company.

Evidence Collection Point 11.6

1 Discuss *with your group* and your tutor the type of enquiries and occasions when your school or college might need to see parents in private and keep information confidential. (Bear in mind that for an educational establishment the parents and students are the customers!) Write down your ideas.

2 Identify which of the following discussions should be held in private and why. In *each* of the cases you identify note down *why* you think it is important that a record of the discussion is kept in the relevant file.

   a Travel agent – discussion with client regarding a holiday in Malta.
   b Building Society – discussion about extending a mortgage repayment period.
   c Estate agent – discussion with client about buying a property.
   d Accountant – discussion regarding tax payable on additional earnings.

3 Assess your school or college for access and facilities provided for customers with special needs and compare it with three other public buildings or shops in your town.

   a What features do architects and builders incorporate into buildings to help people with special needs?
   b How does your building score in relation to the others you have assessed?
   c What additional help can organisations offer to customers with special needs?

Satisfied and dissatisfied customers

Satisfied customers are usually easy to deal with. They are pleased with the service they have received and will probably call again when they want something else.

Dissatisfied customers are different. They may be dissatisfied because:

- they want a service you cannot provide
- they consider the service they have received to date is unsatisfactory and want to make a complaint
- they have a query which no-one seems to be able to answer
- they are annoyed at something you have told them (e.g. they cannot have credit)
- a product they bought is faulty.

'… but this parrot is dead!'

Basically, whether you have to deal with a difficult customer face to face or over the telephone, the way to handle the situation is the same (see below).

Some organisations have standard procedures for dealing with complaints. In others you may be on your own! It is, however, usual for complaints which can't be solved quickly and easily to be referred to a supervisor or manager. In this way he or she can keep a watchful eye on the way the business is run, and take steps to rectify problem areas.

Dealing with complaints

You may be the 'first stage' of someone making a complaint, even though you are not the last. The way in which people will make a complaint will vary depending upon their personality and how well they know their consumer rights (see Chapter 12). They may be hesitant and apologetic or angry. The way you respond can make all the difference to their reaction.

Listen sympathetically	**Don't** interrupt in the early stages of the conversation
Take down all the facts	**Don't** give vague excuses
Check you have these down correctly by checking them with the customer	**Don't** put the blame on anyone
Remain polite, patient and reasonable	**Don't** get annoyed yourself
Refer the problem to your supervisor if you cannot solve the problem or if the customer is very rude or aggressive	**Don't** try to pretend the problem doesn't exist

If necessary, explain that the problem will be investigated and give the customer a specific time when he or she will hear from your company.

Don't make promises outside your control

Evidence Assignment 11E

Imagine that you work for a large company which manufacturers household appliances that are sold through a range of retail outlets. All machines are covered by a one-year guarantee and the company operates its own regional service centres for faulty appliances – whatever their age. Therefore, when an appliance is faulty the customer telephones the regional service centre, not the manufacturer or retailer.

In the last few weeks your office has received several complaints on the service it gives, including:

- telephone line constantly engaged
- telephone line not answered during working hours
- unhelpful staff (e.g. won't book a service call unless the caller knows everything about the machine, including the model number)
- restricted hours of repair staff which are incompatible with customers who go out to work all day
- long delays between calls being received and the visit of the repairman
- few parts carried by repairers (often a second call has to be booked when the part is available, which may be several days later).

1 Write down how you consider a customer will react to this situation, both immediately and in the long term.

2 List your suggestions to correct *each* problem.

3 Conduct a role play, with yourself in the role of an employee at the service centre and one of your fellow students in the role of a householder whose washing machine has broken. The customer is annoyed because no-one has called although she first telephoned your organisation four days ago. Record your conversation and write a brief report on your performance.

· LEGAL REQUIREMENTS ·

All customers have a legal right to be protected from:

- dangerous goods
- faulty and damaged goods
- professional negligence
- accidents occurring through the negligence of employees
- being deliberately misled by company staff
- being quoted a misleading price.

In other words they have a legal right in relation to **health and safety** and **honesty**.

Consumer legislation is covered in full in Chapter 12. This chapter concentrates on health and safety and the *general* honesty of employees in relation to the ethics and standards of the organisation.

Consumer requirements and expectations

As a consumer yourself you know that when you buy a product or service – or even when you use a seemingly 'free' service you have certain requirements and expectations. For instance, you do not expect your local library to contain very few, tatty old books and to have a grumpy librarian who can't find anything without an hour's notice. If that was the case, no doubt you would want to complain to the chief librarian or, if that failed, to your local authority (which finances the library service).

However, if you paid a considerable amount of money for something which turned out to be absolutely useless then you would probably do more than complain. You would insist on your money back, or want to know what to do next if the manager of the shop was unco-operative.

As a consumer you have certain legal rights. You also have the right to redress (or compensation) in law if the company which supplied you with the product or service is at fault.

However, it is important to note that in some cases a customer may be dissatisfied and yet not be able to get compensation in law. This is because basic customer requirements are covered by consumer protection laws, but some aspects of service (e.g. polite and friendly staff) are not.

Health and safety

As you saw in Chapter 5, the Health and Safety at Work Act covers employees. But what about customers or visitors to a company? What could you do if you slipped and broke your ankle because a cleaner had mopped the floor and forgotten to put up any warning signs?

Any organisation which deals with or admits members of the public on to its premises can find it is liable to claims in law. Examples are:

- if a customer (or workman) is injured, through negligence on the part of an employee, unsafe premises or fittings, etc.
- if a customer is injured because a product is faulty
- if a customer suffers personal financial loss or distress through professional negligence, faulty workmanship, etc.

For this reason most firms take out insurance to cover themselves against such claims. Typical policies include:

- **public liability insurance.** This is a legal requirement for some businesses such as builders and hairdressers. It covers the business against claims because of personal injury caused by negligence, defects on the premises, etc.
- **product liability insurance.** This covers claims for injury caused by faulty goods.
- **professional indemnity.** This covers claims for damages caused by professional negligence. This type of policy is usually taken out by architects, accountants, solicitors, etc.

Most **trade associations** offer policies for their members. Trade associations are bodies associated with specific trades (e.g. the Building Employers Federation,

the Association of British Travel Agents). They provide advice, assistance and information to their members and frequently have a voluntary code of practice to which their members agree to adhere. A code of practice is a guide to all members on how customers should be treated and complaints should be handled. Trade associations will also deal with complaints from members of the public about companies in their industry, though they obviously have more influence over companies who are members, rather than those who are not.

DID YOU KNOW?

Many insurance policies have a condition attached that the insurance company will defend any claim on behalf of the insured. They also insist that the company shall not make any admission of liability to the person who has been injured.

Evidence Collection Point 11.7

1 Discuss as a group the different types of public liability claims which might be received by:

- a dentist
- a hotel
- a builder.

2 How do you think staff in an organisation will be affected in their dealings with a customer who has been injured on the premises, bearing in mind the condition made by insurance companies that they must not make any admission of liability to the injured person? Discuss your answer with your tutor.

DID YOU KNOW?

All companies must *by law* insure their employees against accidents at work. This type of insurance is called Employer's Liability Insurance and it covers employees against bodily injury or diseases contracted as a result of their work.

Evidence Assignment 11F

You visit the local hairdresser to have your hair coloured and permed. The person who runs the shop is ill and you are asked if a trainee can do your hair. You agree. The end result is a disaster and your scalp is badly burned because some solution was left on too long. You decide to claim a refund plus compensation for the pain and discomfort you suffered.

1 Does the hairdresser have a *legal* responsibility to take care of you as a customer?

2 Legally, should you win your claim?

3 The hairdresser has taken out insurance for protection against claims such as yours. What is the name of this type of insurance?

4 Could you take out a claim if you had done your own hair at home and not used the product according to the instructions?

5 Would it make any difference if you *had* followed the instructions? If so, who would you claim against?

6 During your visit the owner also told you that:

   • the trainee was in her third year of training, when she was really in her first
   • she had done this work before, when she hadn't
   • it was impossible to arrange your appointment for a week later as the shop would be closed.

   a Which of these statements would be likely to *help* your claim, and why?
   b Which would not?

Honesty

There is a difference between giving inaccurate information which is really irrelevant to a transaction and deliberately misleading a customer. If you tell someone that on Wednesdays you close at 5 p.m. when, in reality, it is 5.30 p.m. then you may have lost a customer but you haven't done anything illegal.

However, if you deliberately mislead a customer about the capabilities of an item or its price then you are probably acting illegally.

This aspect is covered more fully in Chapter 12.

Activity

Look back at Chapter 10. Which Acts make it an offence for organisations to:

a make a false claim about their product?
b claim the goods are offered with a price reduction when they are not?
c label food incorrectly?

DID YOU KNOW?

The **Property Misdescriptions Act** now makes it an offence for estate agents to give misleading or dishonest descriptions of properties. No longer can they write:

• 'interesting town view' (when it is really over the gas works)
• 'small compact garden' (for a 1 metre square plot of land)
• 'interesting original features' (when it means nothing has been done to the house for 50 years!)

Even casual remarks by junior members of staff can mean the agent is liable under the Act. In future, estate agents may have to be rather more careful with adjectives such as 'quiet', 'pleasant' and 'rural'.

Evidence Checkpoint

You should now have completed all the Evidence Assignments and ECPs in this chapter, had these marked and filed them neatly in your portfolio. Check that nothing is missing and nothing can be redone to gain you a higher grade!

Evidence Project

1 You are working on the front desk of Bryant & Walker, a large car distributor in your town. You deal with both face-to-face callers and telephone calls. Your job is on a 'job share' basis with another person – you do mornings, she does afternoons. An organisation chart for the company is shown in Figure 11.2.

In each of the following situations state clearly what you would do. *If you would refer a problem or enquiry to someone else, state who this would be.* Bear in mind that Tom Hill is not available in the morning and Trevor Stevens has an appointment 50 miles away at 12 noon.

a 9.10 a.m. A telephone call from a young man wanting to know if there are any vacancies for mechanics.

b 9.15 a.m. A call from the mother of one of the young mechanics saying he is off ill.

c 9.30 a.m. An urgent call from a customer who bought a new car four days ago and has broken down 30 miles away. She is furious. All your internal extensions are engaged.

d 9.45 a.m. A visit from the VAT inspector who has come to inspect the accounts.

e 10 a.m. A driver arrives who is delivering spare parts for the stores.

f 10.10 a.m. A man and his wife call in – they are interested in buying a new car. They are in a rush and don't want to see a salesman – they just want some basic information about the models you have.

g 10.30 a.m. A child wanders in from the street – lost.

h 10.40 a.m. A telephone call from the bank – it is confidential and concerns the company's bank account.

i 10.55 a.m. An unexpected visit from the regional director.

j 11.10 a.m. A customer brings his car in for a routine service.

k 11.30 a.m. All sales staff are occupied. A young family are looking around the showroom. You notice their little girl is wandering around the cars and stroking them. She has been eating chocolate and is making a mess of everything she touches!

l 11.40 a.m. A foreign gentleman calls. You can't work out what he is saying. You *think* he just wants some leaflets.

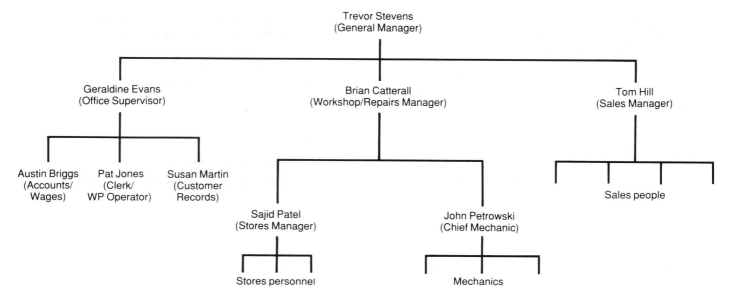

Figure 11.2 *Organisation chart for Bryant & Walker*

322

m 11.50 a.m. A young lady calls with her father who is obviously blind. She leaves him for a few minutes. You think you should offer him somewhere to sit . . .

n 11.55 a.m. A young man telephones. He is complaining that your sales person told him that your organisation sold the latest model more cheaply than any other dealer for miles. He has found four other distributors in the area which have quoted him a lower price.

o 12 noon You receive a telephone call to say your replacement won't be in that afternoon . . .

2 The following day Trevor Stevens sends for you and tells you that a new member of staff will be starting soon and working on reception. He has decided it would be useful if you could produce a simple handbook for the new employee which states:

- how to deal with callers
- how to deal with people over the telephone
- problems you may encounter – and how to deal with these.

Bearing in mind what you have learned so far, and your experiences from yesterday, produce the handbook he requires. If possible incorporate some illustrations which will make it easier to read.

Revision Test

True or false?

1 It is impossible to sound efficient over the telephone unless you can give a caller specific help.

2 Product knowledge is unnecessary if you work for an organisation which provides a service.

3 You should ignore a child who is misbehaving if he or she is accompanied by an adult.

4 If someone is annoyed, make sure you state your own point of view immediately.

5 Organisations have a legal responsibility to provide a safe environment for customers.

Complete the blanks

6 Figures said in .... are always easier to remember.

7 Three types of enquiries which should be dealt with in private involve ...., ... and .... matters.

8 Body language is known as ....

9 If a product is faulty, then the customer has a legal right to be given a ....

10 If you have telephoned a customer and then been cut off, you should ....

Short answer questions

11 State three benefits to an organisation of meeting customers' needs.

12 State two types of handicapped customers and how you would deal with them.

13 Give five characteristics of a good verbal communicator.

14 State the four main types of non-verbal communication and give examples of each.

15 State six ways in which a telephone user can sound more professional.

Write a short paragraph to show you clearly understand each of the following terms:

16 Special needs of customers.

17 Improved business performance.

18 Customer service.

19 After-sales service.

20 Non-verbal communication.

chapter **12** INVESTIGATING CUSTOMER SERVICES

Learning Objectives

This chapter is concerned with the types of customer services provided by business organisations in both the private and the public sectors. It examines how these affect customers and how they can be monitored and improved. It also includes the forms of protection available for customers.

After studying this chapter you should be able to:

- describe the range of customer services provided by business organisations

- investigate ways to monitor customer satisfaction with services

- suggest improvements to customer services

- describe forms of protection for customers

- propose ways to communicate customer protection.

· WHAT ARE CUSTOMER SERVICES? ·

If a member of staff in a large store stopped you suddenly and asked for your opinion of the customer services, what would you say? You might, wrongly, jump to the conclusion that they were merely referring to their customer services desk, where people called with queries and complaints. You might not think of these other aspects of service:

- whether the staff were polite and knew the company's products and services well
- how long you had to wait to be served
- the company policy in relation to faulty goods, 'returned' goods and repairs
- the quality of goods sold, and whether this could be trusted
- the type of response you might receive if you telephoned them about a problem
- their methods of dealing with and investigating problems and complaints.

All these areas are key aspects of customer services for all organisations. Today many businesses are keenly aware that the *quality* of their service not only attracts a customer in the first place (word gets around!) but *keeps* customers coming back again and again. This factor can make the critical difference between success and failure when times get hard.

Some of these factors were covered in the preceding chapter – particularly those that involve communication with customers and dealing with queries and complaints. In this chapter you will see how customer satisfaction can be monitored and the type of protection which exists for customers.

The importance of the customer

In the last ten years, more and more businesses have become 'consumer-led'. In other words, they have produced their goods or offered a service primarily with the customer in mind. Their aim is to:

- increase their market share over their competitors
- obtain new customers
- keep their existing customers.

This is true of organisations in both the private and the public sectors.

The private sector

Quite obviously, for organisations in the private sector, customers are essential for their survival. Such organisations are in business to make a profit and the more customers they have the more goods (or the more of their service) they will sell. The more they sell the more revenue they will receive and, normally, the more profit they will make.

Seeing the customer as the most important person means the company has a **marketing** approach to its business. The difference between a company which concentrates on marketing, and one which simply sells its goods or service, can be expressed like this:

- A company which is market-led will try to find out what the customer wants and do everything they can to provide this – not just during the sale but both before and afterwards. It will also take account of changes – in consumer tastes, fashion, social attitudes and technology (as you saw in Chapter 9).
- The company which is product-led will make its goods, then go out to try to sell them.

I much prefer to talk to this machine about my overdraft ......

- NatWest Bank is transforming its branches so that customers will have more space than the staff (currently staff have 80 per cent and customers 20 per cent). Banks will be open-plan with more automatic cash machines and new sophisticated communications systems to deal with problems and enquiries.

Evidence Assignment 12A

Bill and Ben had been friends for several years. When the local factory closed down and both were made redundant they met to discuss what to do next. Both decided that, as they were good drivers with clean driving licences, they could do well if they set up as licensed taxi drivers in the town. During the next few weeks each of them contacted the local authority, obtained a licence, and started to operate a taxi service.

Bill enjoyed working for himself. He kept his car spotless and regularly serviced and charged a competitive rate. Because he was friendly, polite and punctual people liked using him. He spent some money on having business cards printed, which he gave to customers, so that they could contact him again when they needed him. He bought

DID YOU KNOW?

Companies frequently change their image to keep up to date. This can mean altering the design of their premises or the packaging of their products or the style of their advertising.

- Our Price music stores were redesigned with modernised cash counters which made it easier for customers to sign documents in more places around the store. This was to meet the increased use of credit cards where vouchers have to be signed when goods are purchased.

a car phone so that he could keep in touch with his home and arranged for his wife to accept bookings over the telephone and then contact him when these were received. He didn't mind the long and irregular hours – rather he enjoyed his independence and seeing his income increase. His business boomed. He was so busy that within six months he had bought two more cars and now paid other drivers to work for him.

Ben didn't enjoy his work at all. He objected to the long and unsocial hours, especially over weekends when he used to go out with his friends. After a late night he often slept in the following day, and although he often meant to clean the car or arrange for it to be serviced he very rarely did either. After a good week he would often take several days off – until he needed to earn some money again. Ben preferred to stay on a taxi rank waiting for casual business rather than take bookings in advance. For one thing he could read a newspaper whilst he waited for customers; for another he often forgot arrangements which had been made in advance, and there had been one nasty argument with a customer who had been 'forgotten' which Ben had no desire to repeat. Ben considered that no matter how he ran his business he was bound to be on to a winner – people would always need taxis, no matter what he did. Eventually, though, he found his earnings had dropped so low that he couldn't live on them.

1 List all the features of Bill's business that made it a success and all the features of Ben's that made it a failure.

2 Which of your features for Bill illustrate that he was 'customer-led'?

3 If you use a taxi service what do you consider are the *essential* features for you, as a consumer? What features would be an added bonus?

4 If Bill wanted to expand his business still further how do you think he could do this?

5 If Bill received a complaint that one of his drivers had refused to take three young men in his taxi, all of whom appeared to be the worse for drink, how do you think he should respond?

Do you think the driver was justified in his actions?

Comment on any other occasions when a driver may refuse to take a fare.

The public sector

For organisations in the public sector the reason to be market-led and to put the customer first may be less clear, until you consider the following:

● Many public sector organisations have competitors in the private sector (e.g. an NHS hospital and a private hospital).
● Many organisations in the public sector also depend on people using their services to survive (e.g. your local college can only exist whilst people enrol on courses).
● Because we all pay for the operation of the public sector through our taxes (e.g. income tax and VAT), we can argue that we have just the same right to a courteous and efficient service as if we are dealing with a commercial organisation.
● Complaints against public sector organisations are usually dealt with by 'watchdog' organisations (e.g. Oftel, which oversees British Telecom and Ofgas, which oversees British Gas) or by senior civil servants. Too many complaints may result in regulations being introduced by central government to control the way in which they operate.

Since 1980 the government has introduced a variety of measures to put pressure on public sector organisations to be more responsive to their customers and clients. This was one reason for the privatisation of many organisations (see Chapter 1).

However, privatisation – and having to compete – has not been restricted just to public sector organisations which operated on a commercial basis. Health, education and welfare services have been changed to become more consumer orientated.

Policies in this area are discussed further on page 341.

Customer service sections

If you go into any large retail store you are likely to find a Customer Help Desk or Customer Services Desk where staff are employed purely to deal with customers. Staff are there to:

● give information and help
● process refunds
● give advice on after-sales service

generally prove that the organisation is caring and considerate to all its customers.

Having a customer service desk means that specialisation can take place. Certain staff can be specially trained in both product knowledge and aspects of consumer legislation. They can then assist customers who have either specific or general queries, and there will not be any delay to customers wishing to make a quick purchase at the sales counters. In some large stores (e.g. Harrods in London) there is a section where staff give specialist advice, such as helping foreign tourists to claim back the VAT on goods purchased in the UK.

Some companies have special customer service sections where staff can access a list of customers on a computer database. This is the case in organisations as different as video rental shops, garages and manufacturers of appliances where after-sales service is frequently required (e.g. washing machines, freezers, tumbler driers). When a customer phones to report a fault, the operator can quickly key in that person's name and see the type of appliance, model number, date of sale and other details at a glance. This helps him or her to pass on the correct information to the service engineer.

Customer service sections can also exist in other organisations where people often need help and advice – although you may find them called by another name. A large hospital may have a special desk where visitors can enquire about patients (e.g. their location or visiting hours). A college may have a special section where potential students can enquire about courses (often under the title of 'Student Services'). Your local town hall is likely to have a general information area where you can find out facts about your town or city. This is especially helpful to visitors or newcomers to the area.

Finally, companies may have a code of practice for dealing with customers, which all staff must follow. This may include items such as:

- answering the telephone promptly
- calling all regular customers by their name
- passing on all reported complaints to a supervisor or senior member of staff
- replying to all letters within three days
- writing company literature so that it is jargon-free and designed and printed in the approved company style
- dealing with all customers in a courteous and polite manner.

If an organisation does everything it can to ensure that all staff follow the code of practice – including instigating staff training and establishing systems for them to follow – it can then be more certain of the **quality** of its service to customers. Quality signifies that the same type of service is given by all staff to all customers, under all circumstances.

DID YOU KNOW?

Crystal Mark

Clarity approved by Plain English Campaign

The Crystal Mark is a special mark which can be placed on literature whose clarity is approved by the Plain English Campaign. This means that the text is easy to follow and understand, and doesn't contain jargon or specialist words the average person wouldn't know about.

Evidence Assignment 12B

Your friend, Paul, works for a computer shop which sells both game machines and software. He has been employed *not* to deal with customers from behind a counter and process sales, but to give help and advice to customers when they enter the shop. The shop has three different games machines switched on at all times so that potential buyers can test a game before buying.

Paul not only has a very good knowledge of the hardware he sells but also has his own computer system for which he buys games.

1 How effective do you think Paul is likely to be in giving help, good service and accurate information to customers? Do you think his opinions may be apt to be biased in any way? What can he do to guard against this?

2 What type of after-sales service would you, as a customer, expect to find if you bought a computer from the shop? What type of guarantee or warranty would you expect to operate?

3 Some people return games to the shop after a few days, saying they are faulty. On some occasions the games still load on the shop machines. What do you think the manager should do in this situation? Do you think there is any danger for a computer shop in freely exchanging 'faulty' software – or do you think this should be part of the service?

4 During Paul's lunch hour he is replaced in his duties by another member of staff, Nicole. She is unsure about the machines and often gives customers the wrong information. Several times Paul has had to cope with customers who have returned to the shop to complain, after being served by Nicole. Yesterday he told her in no uncertain terms that if she couldn't do the job properly then she should stay behind the till where she belonged. Nicole flounced off and was later found crying in a back room.

   a What is your opinion of Paul's actions?

   b What action would you recommend should be taken to solve this problem?

5 What active measures do you think the shop can take to tempt 'first-time buyers' to become regular customers? In what way does the computer industry help them to do this?

· MONITORING CUSTOMER · SATISFACTION

How does an organisation know if its customers are satisfied with the service they receive? There are several methods they can use, some of which are more obvious than others.

Monitoring sales performance

If sales increase steadily then either the company has several new customers or their existing customers are buying more from them.

Sales will therefore increase in these circumstances:

- **The number of enquiries which are converted into sales increases**. Some companies keep a record of all the enquiries they receive (perhaps in response to an advertising campaign). They may, for instance, log the names of enquirers into a computer database. They will then record how many of these turn into firm orders, and try to find out why the others have not.
- **Customers make repeat purchases**. The number of repeat purchases each customer makes is easier to track for companies supplying industrial customers than for retail outlets. An industrial customer would expect to buy the goods **on credit** (i.e. buy now and pay after receiving the invoice). Each customer would therefore have his or her own account which would show the number (and value) of transactions in each accounting year.

Obtaining feedback

There are various ways in which this can be done. The method used may depend on the type of organisation and the business it carries out.

- **On-the-spot questions from staff**. The simplest examples are a waiter coming up to you in a restaurant and checking that you are satisfied that everything is all right, or a sales representative giving feedback from customers he or she has talked to.
- **Under-cover customers**. An unknown executive or rep from head office visits a branch as a make-believe customer and rates the branch on the service they receive. Vauxhall do this regularly by sending out their

'mystery buyers' to their dealers. Each dealer then receives a feedback report.

- **Consumer panels**. Members of staff and the public meet regularly to discuss products, service, new ideas etc. Boots plc has operated this for some time in all its stores.

Market research

The role of marketing was discussed in Chapter 4 of this book and market research was also covered in Chapter 9. Market research departments are frequently involved in finding out what customers think of existing products and carrying out surveys on spending patterns. They are also very concerned with customer opinions of the company as a whole.

They will often compile a questionnaire which customers or users of a service can complete which gives their views. As an example, if you go on holiday with a package holiday company you will probably find that on your return you will be asked to complete a questionnaire which asks if certain aspects of the flight, the hotel facilities and services of the representative were excellent, very good, good, satisfactory or poor. The responses are analysed and the company will take action about those areas that can be improved.

DID YOU KNOW?

Organisations will often attempt to find out the names and addresses of their customers by means of special offers. Every customer who fills in a request has to enter their name and address and these details can be recorded on a computer database. The company can then contact them to ask them to complete questionnaires, or send them details of future special offers and new products.

Monitoring complaints

Most organisations record the complaints they have received and the action that was taken in each case. If many complaints are received about one particular aspect of the business then this is likely to be investigated thoroughly.

In addition the company may keep a record of **returned goods**. Returned goods not only indicate that the goods being sold are not up to standard (see pages 307 and 336) but also that at least one customer has been inconvenienced and will be dissatisfied with the company. If the goods have been purchased from one particular supplier then this supplier may be cautioned or even stopped from supplying any more goods.

DID YOU KNOW?

Some companies offer 'inducements' to customers who complain or return goods. This is done as a gesture of goodwill and to try to prevent the customers thinking badly of them in the future. For example, a fast food chain may offer a free meal to anyone who has to wait more than 20 minutes to be served.

Evidence Collection Point 12.1

Compile a questionnaire to find out which of your local retail stores is the most customer-friendly to shoppers with young children – especially if they have prams or pushchairs. As a start you may like to include such factors as:

- whether there are automatic doors or not
- whether there are lifts between floors
- whether or not sweets are placed low down near cash points (so that children can grab them easily!).

As a group think of as many relevant questions as possible (and check these with your tutor). Design your questionnaire and then go out and score each store in your area. If you want to be even more objective, you should obtain the views of some of the parents of small children who you see entering or leaving the store.

Finally, evaluate your answers. Draw up a list of recommendations which the worst store on your list could implement if it wants to improve its sales!

• IMPROVEMENTS AND •
RECOMMENDATIONS

Many organisations already have policies which define their views of customer service. These are publicly stated commitments that can be read in their reports and handbooks. They are often termed as **mission statements**. Here are some examples:

- 'ASDA's mission is to become the UK's leading value for money grocer with an exceptional range of fresh foods together with those clothing, home and leisure products that meet the everyday needs of our target customers.' (ASDA Group plc)
- 'We are a fabrics and furniture group committed to quality, design and first class service to our customers, coupled with the highest standard of integrity in everything we do.' (Cornwell Parker Group)
- 'We are here to make high quality products for our customers. This will be achieved by manufacturing to the required specification, by being vigilant about quality and by careful control of costs and budgets. ... It is important that *all* employees recognise the common objective of working in a safe and hygienic factory *and* producing the final product in order to satisfy our customers' requirements.' (McVitie's Biscuits)
- 'Coca-Cola & Schweppes Beverages Limited is dedicated to building for the future by providing our customers with the best brands, the best equipment and the best service.' (Coca-Cola & Schweppes Beverages Ltd)

All the examples given are policy statements issued by companies in the private sector – companies who must stay competitive and give good customer service to survive. Today, the same type of considerations apply to the public sector (see page 326).

Evidence Collection Point 12.2 – Part A

A branch of Marks & Spencer had a conflict between security, food hygiene, storage capacity and the requirements of its customers. Its food section was situated at the rear of the store with one exit, which led to a nearby car park. The store operated a 'collect-by-car' service so that customers who bought large amounts of foods could walk from the store to the car park, drive their car to the service door (also at the rear of the building) and collect their purchases. Over the Christmas period several things went wrong with this system.

a People were buying goods and not collecting them until hours later. Some food was frozen, and was therefore defrosting during the waiting period.

b The number of bags waiting to be collected rapidly outgrew the space available.

c Some of the temporary Christmas staff became confused because of the large quantity of bags – and gave the people the wrong ones. Sometimes these weren't returned, with the result that other people found their bags had disappeared and complained. The store had to replace the goods that had been in these free of charge.

d On several occasions shoplifters would fill a bag with goods and then use the back exit door for a quick escape.

1 Assume you are the manager of the store. You know that if you stop the 'collect by car' service or restrict it in any way you will receive complaints. What measures would you take to solve the problem? Decide as a group what you would do and then write out your answer.

2 Compare your answer with what actually happened (given in Part B of this Evidence Collection Point on page 331).

You may like to bear in mind that whatever you decide you won't be able to please everyone, and no answer will be totally right or totally wrong!

Recommending improvements

To be able to do this effectively you need to keep in mind the type of service which you would wish to receive yourself, as a consumer.

Do bear in mind that no-one is perfect, and this includes even the best staff in the best companies. People make mistakes, and sometimes these can have unfortunate consequences. Apologising to a customer *on behalf of your organisation* is nothing to be ashamed of – neither does it mean you are admitting responsibility. In truth, you are actually apologising for the inconvenience which the customer has been caused.

Occasionally, difficulties arise not because of staff problems, but because the systems and procedures used by the company aren't working. In some cases this may be because the organisation has grown in size rapidly, and what worked when they were small is no longer successful.

However, whereas it is relatively easy to redesign a procedure it can be more difficult to tell staff when they are wrong. Good training is essential plus praise when people get it right. An alternative is to make sure that those members of staff who are the best at dealing with people are 'on the front line' and those who are good at administration, but poor at dealing with people, are not put in a position where they will find it difficult to cope.

DID YOU KNOW?

Many companies offer awards to sales people who generate the highest number of sales in a year. These can range from a cash bonus to a holiday abroad! However, more companies are offering inducements to all the staff by involving them in profit-sharing schemes. By this means, if profits increase then everyone earns more. This is one way of tempting *all* staff to look after their customers.

Evidence Assignment 12C

Imagine that each Saturday you work in a local record shop which sells tapes, records and CDs for all music in the charts plus a wide range of classical, popular, jazz and blues

music. Your shop does not find it economic to stock less popular titles but will order these if requested. The prices at which the records are sold are competitive with other record shops in the town.

The manager wants to increase his customer base and has asked all staff for their opinions of how to do this.

1 Bearing in mind factors such as layout of the shop and speed of service, what recommendations can you make to reduce the amount of time people spend hunting for a particular record and then getting served?

2 You have found that older people (who usually spend more) are often 'put off' buying records because of the number of young people around the counter. Can you make any suggestions to prevent this?

3 Frequently the counter is 'clogged up' with people enquiring about records and titles. Is there anything that can be done about this?

4 Some customers complain at having to order records they want. Can this be avoided? If not, what can be done to make this service more 'customer friendly'?

5 The manager is constantly receiving complaints about a new member of staff. She looks untidy, chats to other members of staff when customers are waiting to be served and rarely smiles. What training would you recommend, and why?

Evidence Collection Point 12.2 – Part B

To solve the problem the manager introduced a new system from 1 January. He locked the back exit door to try to eliminate the theft problem. He also made a condition that anybody using the collect-by-car service must collect their goods within 20 minutes of purchase. Customers were issued with a numbered ticket saying how many bags they had left and this was clipped to the till receipt. A duplicate ticket was clipped to the bags themselves. All customers had to produce their tickets and till receipt on collection.

1 What complaints do you think were received from customers over the next few weeks?

2 How do you think the store dealt with these?

3 How would you cope with a very distressed woman who claims she has lost her ticket and till receipt when she calls to collect her shopping? Consider whether it would make any difference if you didn't know her or if she was a regular customer you know very well.

Type out your answers neatly, and put them with your answers to part A.

• CUSTOMER PROTECTION •

Consumers are protected in a variety of ways from inferior or dangerous products, poor or inadequate service and from being deliberately misled by those who are out to make a quick profit. The aim is that all consumers can turn to either the law or a specialist organisation for help if they have a problem. The best source of help will depend upon:

- the type of goods or services they have bought
- who was the provider
- the nature of their complaint.

The contract of sale

When you buy goods or a service then you become a 'party to a contract'. A contract is a legal agreement between the seller and the buyer and has two parts:

1 the customer's offer to buy the goods at a given price
2 the supplier's acceptance of the order and/or agreement to sell the goods.

When both parts have been completed there is a **binding contract** and neither side can simply change their mind or alter the terms of the contract. Therefore the customer cannot suddenly return the goods without good reason and expect his or her money back, and the supplier cannot raise the price or make other changes to the agreement. If you are involved in making a contract you are advised to read the small print carefully. It is also useful to know when and how you can cancel a contract if necessary.

DID YOU KNOW?

A supplier has no legal obligation to accept an offer to buy from a customer, so long as his refusal is not on grounds of race or sex.

What is a contract of sale?

Imagine you are walking past a shop window and see a jacket you like. You read the price label and think you can afford to buy it. You go into the shop, try on the jacket, like it and buy it. You hand over your money, the assistant wraps up the jacket and you walk out of the shop with it. This is a perfect example of a **contract of sale**.

There are three main parts to a contract:

- **The offer** – you *offer* to buy the jacket from the assistant.

- **The acceptance** – the assistant *accepts* your offer.

- **The consideration** – you *pay* the assistant. (The idea of the consideration does not apply in Scotland.)

DID YOU KNOW?

To become a party to the contract you must *intend* to enter into the agreement. If you are very young (or very drunk) when you make an agreement the court may hold that you did not intend to make it and the agreement will therefore be held to be **invalid**. This means the agreement cannot be enforced. In the same way, if someone forced you to enter into an agreement (e.g. by threatening you) again you will not be held to it.

The offer

The offer you make must be **certain**. Saying 'I may be interested in a jacket' is not a specific offer.

The offer you make must also be **communicated to the person to whom the offer is intended to be made.** You are not making a specific offer if you advertise in a newspaper to buy a jacket, because you don't specify the person to whom you are making the offer. Neither are you making a specific offer if the offer isn't received by the person to whom you intend to make it (e.g. if you write a letter but it is lost in the post).

DID YOU KNOW?

If you see the phrase **invitation to treat** used, remember that this is *not* the same thing as an offer. An invitation to treat is a statement which is intended to persuade *someone else* to make *you* an offer. In the case of the jacket the invitation to treat is the price label put on by the shop. If the assistant tells you the price is wrong and the real price is much higher, there is nothing you can do. In that case, your offer (in response to the original price) has been rejected – though in some circumstances you may be protected by consumer protection legislation.

The acceptance

Acceptance of an offer can take place in one of several ways:

- **by verbal or written statement** (e.g. if the sales assistant says 'I agree to sell you the jacket')
- **by conduct** (e.g. if the assistant wraps up the jacket, hands it to you and puts your money in the till).

DID YOU KNOW?

Difficulties can arise if you are making or accepting an offer by post. If you see an advert for a jacket in a newspaper and write, offering to buy it, your offer isn't complete until the letter has been received. Acceptance is complete as soon as the person posts you a reply agreeing to accept your offer.

Contents of the acceptance

The acceptance must be **unqualified**. This means it must correspond in every detail with the offer.

It must not **introduce new terms**. If you offer to buy the jacket for £40 and the assistant says the price is £60 there is not complete acceptance. The assistant has introduced a new term and has therefore made a **counter offer**.

Neither must the acceptance of the offer be **uncertain**. If the assistant agrees to think seriously about your offer or says that it will *probably* be acceptable, then the acceptance is not complete.

Activity

Decide *as a group* whether there has been genuine offer and acceptance in the following cases.

1 Your friend offers to buy your car for £2000. You agree to sell it to him.

2 Your friend offers to buy your car for £2000. You agree to sell it but want £2500 for it.

3 You offer to buy a car from your next door neighbour. He hands you the car keys.

Termination of the offer

An offer does not last indefinitely. It lapses:

- if either the person making the offer or the person to whom it is made dies
- if it is not accepted either within a specified time or, if no time is specified, within a reasonable time
- if there is not a valid acceptance (e.g. if it is incomplete or a counter offer is made)
- if it is subject to the fulfilment of a condition and that condition is not fulfilled.

If, for instance, you notice that there is a small tear in the lining of the jacket, but offer to buy the jacket provided the tear is mended, your offer will lapse if the assistant fails to have the repair carried out.

Note that an offer can also be **revoked** (i.e. withdrawn at any time) *before* it has been accepted.

Consideration

A contract must involve some kind of payment or other consideration (but not in Scotland). The courts will not look too closely at the **adequacy** of the consideration. Therefore if you agree to buy the jacket for £1000, although it is really worth only between £50 and £100, that is your decision. If the assistant agrees to sell it to you for 10p, again it is a matter for agreement between the two of you. However, if the consideration is extremely inadequate the courts may look at the situation to see if there has been any undue pressure placed by one party to the contract upon the other.

Capacity

There are certain restrictions placed on some people relating to their capacity to make a contract.

If a person is suffering from a mental disorder listed in the Mental Health Act 1983, then any contract he or she makes is invalid if it can be proved that he or she is so mentally disordered that:

- he or she did not understand what the contract was about
- the other party knew about his or her disorder.

The same principles may be applied to someone who was drunk at the time the contract was made.

A person under 18 is called a **minor** and there are restrictions on the type of contract that is binding upon him or her. If, for instance, you are under 18 you can enter a binding contract for **necessaries** – essential goods and services such as food and clothing. However, when a young man ordered a large number of fancy waistcoats these were not held to be necessaries!

Terms of the contract

The terms can be **express** or **implied**.

Express terms are specifically stated either orally or in writing. Although a contract need not be in written form, it is obviously advisable to have written proof of business contracts or contracts that involve a considerable amount of money.

Terms are **implied** when the agreement does not contain an express term but the courts are prepared to imply a

term into it. This is to give effect to what are *clear,* but unexpressed, intentions of the parties to the contract. If, therefore, you agree to buy a jacket and no price at all is mentioned, the court may hold that there is an implied term in the contract that you will pay a reasonable price for it. However, the court will always look *first* at the express terms and not usually imply a term which contradicts an express term. Therefore, if you have agreed a price, however unreasonable it might be, you will probably be held to it.

Not all terms in a contract are of equal importance. They are therefore divided into **conditions** and **warranties** – of which the first is the more important. For instance, you may find that you have bought a car which has no heated rear window even though that was part of the contract. You may find, however, that the car has no engine! There has been a breach of contract on both occasions but in the first instance the breach relates to a less important term (a warranty) whereas in the second instance the breach has occurred in respect of a very important term (a condition).

DID YOU KNOW?

You can deliberately make a term of the contract an express condition. For instance, if you order the jacket in a particular size, and need it by a particular date, you must state this clearly (and preferably put it in writing). The correct phrase to use is 'time is of the essence in this contract'.

Activity

Decide which of the following contractual terms are likely to be regarded as warranties and which are likely to be conditions.

Contract to buy a box of orange drinks
a fit for human consumption
b specific brand name
c screw tops
d sold in cartons of six.

Contract to buy a jug kettle
a safe to use
b water gets hot when switched on

c holds 1.7 litres of water

d automatically switches off when water is boiling.

The ending of the contract

There are three main methods by which a contract comes to an end:

- **by performance** – you buy a jacket, pay for it and walk out of the shop with it
- **by agreement between both parties** – when you return goods to a shop, these are accepted and your money is refunded
- **by breach** – if one party does not carry out his or her part of the agreement.

If the breach is a breach of warranty (remember, this is a less important term) then you may be able to claim damages (i.e. money). If, on the other hand, the breach is of a condition (an important term of the contract) then you may be able to choose whether you want to claim damages or to end the contract altogether.

DID YOU KNOW?

Note that only someone who is a party to a contract can make a claim. If, therefore, you are given the jacket as a present and discover it is faulty (e.g. a seam is split) then you cannot take it back and ask for a refund (as you were not a party to the contract). In this instance, the contract is between the *buyer* and the *seller*. The person who bought you the jacket must therefore go back to complain.

Evidence Collection Point 12.3

Obtain a copy of a travel brochure from a major tour operator. Assume yourself and four friends have booked a fortnight's holiday with them in summer. You have received an invoice from the company giving information about the holiday and your contract with the company commenced on that date.

1 Read the booking conditions carefully. State what would happen if:

a You wanted to cancel the holiday six weeks before you were due to leave because you had an argument with your friends.

b The *company* cancelled your holiday a week before you were due to leave because of terrorism in the area.

c One of your friends dropped out and you wanted to transfer his booking to someone else.

d The company wanted to increase the price of your holiday at the last moment because of an increase in the price of aircraft fuel.

2 Can you take action for breach of contract if any of the following occur?

a One of your party has far too much to drink in the duty free lounge. He is refused permission to board the aircraft.

b When you arrive at your resort the company has not booked the hotel you requested. You are taken to another resort 30 miles away with none of the facilities you asked for.

c The plane is delayed for three hours because it has a fault which must be checked before it can leave.

d You find out that some friends who have booked the same holiday at the last minute have obtained a 30 per cent reduction on the price you paid.

DID YOU KNOW?

ALL ARTICLES ARE LEFT AT THE OWNER'S RISK

Some organisations may try to evade their responsibility by using exclusion clauses or disclaimers on their premises, tickets, contracts or booking forms (e.g. 'all articles are left at the owner's risk').

Under the **Unfair Contract Terms Act 1977** none of these disclaimers is valid unless the organisation can prove that their terms are fair and reasonable. Therefore, if they lose or damage an article through their own negligence then the owner is probably entitled to compensation. This will not be the case if the organisation can prove they took reasonable care of the goods and could not be held responsible for what occurred.

Notices and disclaimers can *never* absolve an organisation from its liability to either staff or customers if personal injury or death is caused through their negligence.

▪ CONSUMER LEGISLATION ▪

You have already met some examples of consumer legislation. The Unfair Contract Terms Act (above) is one example. So too is the Trades Description Act you read about in Chapter 10. The aim of consumer legislation is to protect people who buy goods and services from inferior or even dangerous goods and from being deliberately misled by those people anxious to make a sale.

Evidence Assignment 12D – Part A

You have been saving up for months to buy a computer. You want it to be able to play games *and* run basic business packages (word-processing, database and spreadsheet). A friend recommends a new shop which has just opened and from them you buy the model recommended by the salesman, plus a couple of computer games.

As a group, hold a brainstorming session to think of all the things that could go wrong with your purchase, and all the different types of problems which could occur under the following headings:

● health and safety
● quality
● value for money
● fitness for the purpose for which you bought it.

You should have a list of at least six items before you read any further.

BUYING GOODS

As a consumer you have certain requirements which are both basic and reasonable. You may also have others which are more optimistic, and it is a bonus if these are met. Others may simply be wishful thinking! For instance, if you buy a car you can reasonably expect it to be capable of taking you from one place to another and to have an engine under the bonnet. Those are fairly basic requirements. You might hope that, as it is a standard model, it is economical to run. That is also reasonable but rather more optimistic – to a certain degree it would depend on your driving. However, you cannot reasonably expect it to go from 0 to 60 mph in 2 seconds, keep going for miles without needing fuel or take you through snow drifts 10 feet deep.

Virtually all our basic requirements are covered in law. This means that if something is wrong you can take action to have it corrected. When you bought your computer you could reasonably expect that:

● it works!
● it runs both games and business packages (because you specified this)
● all the leads and manuals are included
● it has the same size memory and VDU as advertised
● there are no 'hidden extras' on the bill
● there is a guarantee or warranty to protect you if it breaks down within 12 months of purchase
● you were not misled by the seller as to what it can and cannot do
● the computer is safe to use!

If any of these problems occur, then you are covered by consumer legislation.

You may also hope that you do not find your computer on sale somewhere else at half price two days later! However, if this occurs, apart from complaining bitterly to the shop, there is little you can do.

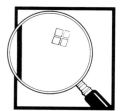

Evidence Assignment 12D – Part B

Let's assume that when you bought your computer you had a bad day. When you arrive home you find that:

a the VDU is half the size of the one illustrated in the brochure
b when you touch the screen you get a nasty shock
c the disk drive won't work
d the computer is not suitable as a games machine.

1 Read the information on consumer legislation which follows. Then decide under which Act you have a claim for *each* of the faults (a) to (d) above.

2 When you go back to the shop the salesman refuses to refund your money. What should you do?

There is a wealth of consumer legislation to cover buying and selling. The laws which apply to goods include:

- Sale of Goods Act 1979
- Trades Description Act 1968
- Consumer Protection Act 1987.

DID YOU KNOW

The above Acts all apply to England and Wales. The situation in Scotland and Northern Ireland is broadly similar though some Acts have different names and dates. The Office of Fair Trading issue special leaflets on consumer rights in Scotland and Northern Ireland and these can be obtained by writing to the OFT, Field House, Bream Building, London EC4A 1PR.

Sale of Goods Act 1979

This is probably the most important piece of legislation as far as the customer and his supplier are concerned. Under this Act, goods for sale must be:

- as described
- of merchantable quality
- fit for the purpose for which they are intended.

'As described'

Where there is a contract for the sale of goods there is an implied condition that the goods will correspond with the description. If you bought some scissors labelled 'stainless steel' and then found out they weren't you could claim your money back.

The Trades Description Act deals even more fully with the question of description (see page 338).

'Of merchantable quality'

This means the goods must work and includes goods sold at sale prices. However, various points should be noted.

- If a defect is specifically drawn to the buyer's attention before the sale is completed then this is acceptable.
- If the buyer examines the goods before the sale and should have been able to see the defect easily (e.g. a scratch on the paintwork of a car) this is also acceptable.
- The seller must be a business seller – private sales are exempt.
- The seller can be a manufacturer, wholesaler or retailer.
- A person cannot reasonably expect the same standard of quality and durability from cheap goods as from expensive goods, although if the goods were bought in a sale the price would probably not be relevant.
- Goods described as 'shop soiled', 'seconds' and 'manufacturers' rejects' cannot be expected to be of the same quality as a new or perfect product.

'Fit for the purpose for which they are intended'

Most goods have an implicit purpose for which they are intended. For example, a hole punch should punch holes in paper. If it will not then the seller is contravening the Sale of Goods Act.

Consumers often place considerable reliance on the advice and experience of the seller or sales representative. If he or she indicates that the goods will do a particular task and they fail that purpose then the seller will be liable.

If the goods do not conform with any one of these three criteria then the buyer is entitled to a **refund**.

- If the buyer *prefers* he or she can accept a replacement or repair but the seller is not obliged to offer anything except cash compensation.
- The buyer does *not* have to accept a credit note. A buyer who does may have difficulty getting money back later if he or she finds nothing else he or she likes.
- Notices such as 'No money refunded' are illegal and should be reported to the local Trading Standards Officer.
- Secondhand goods are also covered by this Act but the buyer's right to compensation will depend on many factors (e.g. price paid, age of the article, how it was described).

- Sale items are also covered by this Act, but if the price is reduced *because* the item is damaged the buyer cannot complain later about that particular fault.
- There is no legal obligation on the buyer to produce a receipt, and so signs such as 'No refunds without a receipt' have no legal standing. However, the buyer can be asked for proof of purchase (e.g. cheque counterfoil, credit card copy sales voucher).

DID YOU KNOW?

The buyer is *not* entitled to anything if he or she:

- changes his or her mind
- decides that something does not fit
- damages the item him or herself
- was aware of the fault or should have seen it
- did not purchase the item him or herself (e.g. received it as a gift).

Trades Description Act 1968

The principal offence under this Act relates to **false description of goods**. Any seller who gives a false trade description of goods or supplies or offers to supply goods which are falsely described is guilty of an offence. This includes:

- selling goods that are wrongly described by the manufacturer
- implied descriptions (e.g. a picture or illustration giving a false impression)
- other aspects of the goods, including quantity, size, composition, method of manufacture, etc.

Usually the spoken word of the seller overrides the written description of the goods, because the buyer is entitled to rely on the expertise of the salesman.

DID YOU KNOW?

Usually, subjective comments are not covered by the Act (e.g. the salesperson telling the buyer how much a garment suits him or her).

'... maybe just a little tuck in the back ... then it's perfect'

Consumer Protection Act 1987

This Act introduced two new areas to consumer protection in general.

Firstly, a person is guilty of an offence if he or she gives consumers an indication that is misleading as to the price at which any goods, services, accommodation or facilities are available. Examples are:

- false comparisons with recommended prices (e.g. saying the goods are being offered at £20 less than the recommended price when they are not)
- indications that the price is less than the real price (e.g. where hidden extras are added to the advertised price, or VAT has been deliberately omitted)
- false comparisons with a previous price (e.g. a false statement that the goods were £50 and are now £25)
- where the stated method of determining the price is different from the method actually used.

Secondly, the 1987 Act creates a new offence – of supplying consumer goods that are not reasonably safe. An offence is also committed by offering or agreeing to supply unsafe goods or possessing them for supply.

Evidence Assignment 12E

You are employed by Townend Electronics in their general office. One of your jobs is to order stationery as it is required and to check that this is correct when it is delivered. How do you think you should react in each of the following situations?

1 You have taken delivery of 12 staplers. When you test these you find that the staples crumple as they are ejected and will not fasten the paper properly. When you notify the suppliers they argue that you must be using them incorrectly. You insist they must take them back. Who is right?

2 You order a large quantity of lever arch files from a local supplier. They arrive packed in flimsy boxes and the front of each file is either bent or badly scratched. Can you insist that these are returned?

3 When you check an order you discover that highlighter pens have been delivered instead of marker pens because you transposed two figures of the catalogue reference number on your order form. Your company doesn't use highlighter pens. Can you insist the supplier takes them back?

4 You buy a disk box, described in a catalogue as holding 50 disks. When it arrives you find that it will hold only 35 at the most. Can you return it and insist on a refund?

5 You buy a large quantity of floppy disks from a local computer shop during a sale. When staff try to use them they find none will format on their computers. The firm argue that you cannot expect the disks to be of the normal quality because they were sale goods. Are they right?

6 You contact a new supplier in the district to order stationery. He refuses to deal with you because he has heard bad reports about your organisation. Can he do this?

7 A representative persuades you to place a large order for photocopying paper with his company. You point out that your photocopier is rather temperamental and will only take good quality paper. He assures you that his paper will suit your machine. When staff try to use it they find it jams in the machine. Can you insist the paper is returned?

8 One of the two new electric staplers you have received has a damaged flex with bare wires showing. When you contact the suppliers they tell you that as the fault is in the wiring of the machine you must take up your complaint with the manufacturer of the equipment. Are they correct?

BUYING A SERVICE

In addition to buying goods, you are also a 'consumer' of various services. If you use a hairdresser or a dry cleaner, have a car serviced or your shoes repaired, or if you arrange for a bricklayer to build a new wall – then in each case a *service* is involved.

In the same way as consumers are protected from faulty goods, they are also protected from poor service – although different Acts apply.

Supply of Goods and Services Act 1982

This Act is in two parts, the first broadly concerned with goods and the second with services.

Part 1 – Goods

This extends the protection for consumers provided by the Sale of Goods Act to include goods supplied as part of a service, on hire or in part exchange. These, too, must be as described, of merchantable quality and fit for the purpose made known to the supplier. Therefore if a garage fits rear seat belts to a car, someone hires a carpet cleaning machine (and specially asks if it can cope with long-pile rugs) and a couple trade in their old gas fire for a new one at the gas showrooms, these 'goods' are all covered under the Act.

Part 2 – Services

This part deals with the standard of services provided by builders, plumbers, TV repairers, hairdressers, garages, etc. It protects the buyer against shoddy workmanship, delays and exorbitant charges. The Act states that all services should be carried out:

- for a reasonable charge
- within a reasonable time
- with reasonable care and skill.

Evidence Assignment 12F

You are about to have another bad day!

1 You visit the hairdresser to have your hair cut. She persuades you to have blonde streaks in your hair but uses the wrong mixture. Your hair turns green.

2 You go to the jewellers' to collect the ring you left there last week for re-sizing. Although they locked it in their safe and have an expensive burglar alarm fitted, the premises were broken into last night and everything was stolen. A large sign behind the desk says that all items are left at the customer's own risk.

3 You next call to collect your shoes – for the fifth time – and they still aren't ready. It's over a month now since you left them for repair and you specifically stated that you needed them back quickly.

4 You go home and your parents are going wild. The car cost twice as much to service as they expected because the garage found lots of other things wrong. And the wall the bricklayer put up last week has just collapsed.

You know the law – so what do you do? Review the Acts you have already covered. Write down your informed opinion of which law is being broken in each case, if any.

Guarantees and warranties

A guarantee or a warranty is an agreement by the manufacturer of a product to repair or replace any parts which are defective free of charge within an agreed time limit. No guarantee can overrule your rights under consumer legislation. A guarantee can only *add* to them in terms of an additional benefit. Standard guarantees may state the following terms:

- The product will be repaired free of charge or replaced if it stops operating because of faulty materials or workmanship within 12 months from the date of purchase.
- Proof of purchase must be given. This is usually a till receipt, but other forms of proof are equally valid (e.g. a credit card voucher).
- Only the manufacturer's own service centres or agreed repairers may be used.
- Any breakdowns because of negligence are not covered.
- An additional warranty period may be purchased to cover the machine or equipment for longer periods.

In many cases you are asked to complete a proof-of-purchase document and send this to the manufacturer when you buy the product so that it can be 'registered' in case of claims. Even if you do not do this, you can still claim under the guarantee. In many cases companies use such 'registrations' to add to their mailing lists more than anything else!

In some cases retailers have their own system of offering warranties or a repair service. In this case you may be offered additional *insurance* to cover the goods being repaired for a longer period than stated in the basic guarantee.

DID YOU KNOW?

A **service contract** is an agreement between a manufacturer or supplier and the purchaser to maintain a piece of equipment at a certain cost over a specified period of time. This may be for household appliances (e.g. a washing machine) or for business machines (e.g. a photocopier). Often the older the machine, the greater the cost of the contract.

Evidence Collection Point 12.4

1 Ask your friends or relatives to lend you three guarantees or warranties which relate to domestic appliances. Compare them for their terms and conditions and list the main differences.

2 Obtain information about a service contract which is held by your family *or* for equipment used by your school or college.

a Find out the type of faults that are *not* covered, and why.

b Why do you think service contracts for machines are more expensive the longer the equipment is used?

3 Survey six different stores in your town and find out if they have their own policy on faulty goods exchange and repair and if there are documents explaining these. Try to obtain examples. Compare how customers buying from stores offering these services will benefit in relation to those who shop elsewhere.

· THE CITIZEN'S CHARTER ·

The **Citizen's Charter**, introduced by the government in 1991, focuses on consumer rights in areas such as health, education, transport and welfare, plus the privatised gas, water, electricity and telecommunications industries and the courts, the tax office and Her Majesty's Customs and Excise officials (i.e. customs officers).

All organisations have to offer a certain standard of service to the public. Those who can prove they do this consistently can use a new 'chartermark'.

In addition, local authorities are now issuing a Charter of Rights which can be obtained by all citizens. This states the function of each department and gives 'promises' to local people of the service they have the right to expect.

The aim of these Charters is to make organisations in the public sector, particularly those which provide a service, more aware of the role of the customer *and* to make consumers of these services more aware of their rights.

The government believes that competition is beneficial for consumers because they have more choice. There have been a variety of measures introduced to increase competition in various areas.

Health

- Hospitals can now 'opt out' of regional management (by becoming 'trusts') and run their own budget.
- GPs now have their own practice budget and 'buy' hospital services for their patients. They can 'shop around' between NHS and private hospitals
- Hospitals have to offer competitively priced services (and short waiting lists) or GPs will buy from elsewhere.
- If a hospital has a poor reputation then patients could ask their GP to send them elsewhere.
- Hospitals now issue a Patients' Charter which states the minimum standards of care and attention which patients can expect.
- Many family doctors are printing booklets for their patients detailing their services and telling patients what to do if they are dissatisfied with the service they have received.

Education

- Schools can 'opt out' to run their own budget and not be accountable to their local authority.
- The government has initiated the publication of examination 'league tables' so that parents can see which schools have the highest number of examination successes.
- Opted-out state schools compete with private and local authority schools for pupils (the more pupils they have, the bigger their budget).
- Further education colleges receive their money on the basis of the number of students they have, their examination results and the quality of their service. Again the idea is that a good college will be 'rewarded' by getting more money for resources than poor colleges.

DID YOU KNOW?

The government is planning to introduce a cheap telephone service called Charterline which people can ring to find out who to complain to if they are annoyed about any public service – from refuse collection to motorway cones.

Evidence Collection Point 12.5

1 Find out about the Citizen's Charter. *As a group*, divide the following tasks so that you have a file containing:

- the Citizen's Charter itself (phone free on 0800 100 101)
- your family doctor's booklet on services
- your local hospital's booklet on the Patients' Charter
- your local authority's Charter of Rights
- a copy of the Travellers' Charter from your local Customs and Excise office
- the mission statement of your school or college.

Note: *You* should already have a copy of the Taxpayers' Charter, from your local Inland Revenue office, from the work you did in Chapter 3.

2 Read *at least* one of the documents in detail and, on a word-processor, prepare a summary of how you think consumers will benefit from this approach.

3 Those in favour of the changes have argued that the public sector will now have to give a better service to their 'clients'. Those *against* the changes have used arguments such as:

- **Health** – GPs will not consult patients about the hospital they will use, but will simply use the cheapest. If this is far away it will create problems for patients and their families visiting them. Hospitals will have to cut costs to be competitive. In expensive areas such as London this will lead to the closure of many famous hospitals.
- **Education** – School league tables only show examination results. They do not include other factors (e.g. whether pupils like the school, whether the school is good for sports).

Do you consider that consumers gain or lose under the new arrangements? Hold a debate both for and against these measures. Remember that many people consider that the motives of providing a 'service to the community' do not co-exist easily with the 'profit' motive as these may conflict in many areas (e.g. in providing unprofitable but socially necessary services).

On a word-processor, prepare a summary of your views. Bear in mind the type of information contained in the Citizen's Charter.

· OMBUDSMEN ·

Originally there was only one Ombudsman. The full title is Parliamentary Commissioner for Administration and the post was created in 1967. The job is to check that central government departments are fair in their dealings with the general public and business organisations and to investigate any claims of injustice.

Cases are usually referred to the Ombudsman via an MP, who has received a complaint from a constituents. Investigations into the complaint are conducted in private and the Ombudsman has the power to call for information from the government department concerned. If injustice or poor administration has taken place then the department is asked to correct the situation. If it refuses the Ombudsman can prepare a special report to Parliament and send a copy both to the department concerned and the MP.

DID YOU KNOW?

In 1992 the Parliamentary Ombudsman carried out 100 investigations between March and August. Of these, 62 were upheld in full and others only partially. The main department against which people complained was the Department of Social Security and 29 cases were upheld out of 46 complaints. Another department which received several complaints was the Inland Revenue!

The growth of the Ombudsman scheme

Today there are several Ombudsmen, all with the same type of role. They provide an independent and objective method of resolving problems and complaints that arise between an organisation and a customer. Today there are Ombudsmen covering:

- local government – to investigate complaints against local councils
- insurance – to investigate claims about the small print of insurance documents, poor communication and inefficient service (compensation can be awarded)
- legal services – to investigate complaints against barristers and solicitors

Stephen Edell, the Building Societies Ombudsman

- health service – to investigate complaints by both patients and staff
- investment – to investigate complaints in this area (compensation can be awarded)
- estate agents – to investigate complaints of gazumping (e.g. artificially increasing the price), misleading descriptions and even downright lies
- banking – to investigate complaints about bank charges, interest rates, poor service, etc.
- building societies – to investigate cases involving complaints about surveys carried out on properties by building society valuers, and fraudulent withdrawal of money from building society accounts
- pensions – for people who are not happy with personal, state or company pensions.

All Ombudsmen will investigate complaints without any charge. In the future there are plans to appoint an Ombudsman to investigate complaints against the prison service.

Evidence Collection Point 12.6

1 Find out the addresses of the main Ombudsmen schemes from a reference book such as Whitaker's Almanack. Write to at least one and ask for details of the scheme.

2 Find out the names of at least three current Ombudsmen.

3 In the Lothian region of Scotland there is a children's Ombudsman. All children in the area have the right to receive stipulated levels of service, be listened to and have their complaints taken seriously. A Children's Charter is in force which has been received by over 95 000 children.

As a group, debate the issue for and against an Ombudsman for *education.* Decide what type of issues he or she could investigate and whether this would be of benefit to students or may be misused. Type out a summary of your discussions.

. CONSUMER ASSOCIATIONS AND . TRADE ASSOCIATIONS

Today a considerable amount of consumer protection is achieved simply because organisations do not want bad publicity. No doubt you have watched television programmes which highlight faulty products, unfair practices and shady dealings. Reputable companies are very concerned about this type of coverage as it can ruin their reputation in minutes. There is little point in spending millions of pounds in advertising if all that publicity is wrecked by one television programme or press report!

Consumer associations

Consumer associations exist at both local and national level.

Local assistance

Citizen's Advice Bureaux. Your local CAB will give you free advice and assistance and may help you negotiate with a trader if you have a problem.

Trading standards officers. Your local authority will employ several such officers. It is their job to investigate consumer complaints in relation to alleged legal offences (e.g. misleading statements or offers, unfair prices).

Environmental health officers. Again these officers are employed by your local authority. Under the Food Safety Act 1990 all premises which serve food must be registered with the local authority. It is the job of environmental health officers to ensure that these premises comply with food hygiene laws and to investigate any complaints of food poisoning.

National assistance

The Office of Fair Trading (OFT). This is a government body which is concerned with three main areas:

- proposing and promoting changes in law and practice where the interests of consumers are being harmed
- taking legal action (if possible) against businesses that cause problems for consumers
- giving consumers the information and advice they need so that they are fully aware of their rights as consumers.

The OFT is also concerned with anti-competitive practices, monopolies and mergers (see page 44).

The Consumers' Association. This association tests and examines goods and services which are offered to the public. It is completely independent and will not even accept advertising from manufacturers as this could appear to influence its views. The results of the tests are published every month in *Which?* magazine. As a consumer you would be sensible to look up the latest *Which?* report on a product before you make a purchase.

The National Consumer Council. This operates a liaison service between the consumer and the government, the public sector and private businesses.

Public sector 'watchdogs'. These are bodies which represent consumers in relation to public sector organisations (e.g. the Post Office) and privatised companies which *used* to be in the public sector. For instance, Ofgas is the regulatory body for British Gas and Oftel is the regulatory body for British Telecom.

The British Standards Institution. The BSI is an independent national organisation financed through subscriptions and by government grants. It is concerned with setting *standards* with which manufacturers will comply and which consumers can recognise as a sign of quality or safety. There is the special **Kitemark** which is awarded to goods that have been tested to British Standards, and the **Firm Mark** which is used for a company that has been assessed to show that it is reliable.

Evidence Assignment 12G

It is suggested that this assignment is undertaken in small groups, with each group researching a different topic.

You work for a large store in your town which has decided to form a consumers' panel, comprising both staff and customers. The panel will meet once a month to discuss:

- customer service
- consumer rights
- store layout
- range of goods on sale
- customer suggestions.

The manager of the store, Paula Stone, feels that it is essential that members of the panel are familiar with consumer legislation and the work of consumer organisations before they take up their duties. The first meeting will take place in two weeks' time and Ms Stone wants you to research, plan and organise a ten-minute presentation on *one* of the following topics:

- The work of the OFT
- Understanding BSI labels
- Local assistance to consumers
- The Consumers' Association and *Which?* magazine.

Your presentation should include suitable visual aids (e.g. brochures and booklets issued by the organisation(s) on which you are talking).

You have been advised to write to or visit the organisation of your choice. The address of the OFT is given on page

337. BSI Education can be contacted at Linford Wood, Milton Keynes, MK14 6LE (tel 0908 220022).

Your local library should stock back copies of *Which?* magazine and you can, of course, visit your local CAB, Environmental Health and Trading Standards Offices for information.

Trade associations

Trade associations are bodies associated with specific trades (e.g. the Building Employers Federation, the Association of British Travel Agents). They provide advice, assistance and information to their members and frequently have a voluntary code of practice to which their members subscribe. (See page 320.)

Evidence Assignment 12H

You have had a jacket dry-cleaned at the local laundry. When you handed it in for cleaning you pointed out a small stain on the front and asked if they could remove it for you.

When the jacket is returned you notice that a wide area around the stain has been bleached white and has completely ruined the jacket.

You complain to the laundry staff who say there is nothing they can do – they treated the stain as best they could and this was the result. They also point out their disclaimer notice – 'all items left at owner's risk'.

1 Are the staff correct, in law, in what they are telling you? If not, what are your rights?

2 You decide to contact the trade association which covers laundries and dry cleaners. Visit the local library and find out its correct title and address.

3 Draft a letter outlining your complaint, and your rights as a consumer, and asking for the help of the trade association.

Evidence Assignment 12 I

The media (advertising hoardings, television, newpapers etc.) affect all of us, whether we want them to or not, so there are various bodies which protect us from them.

Consider an advertising hoarding – if you find an advert distasteful you can't avoid it, so what do you do?

Many people disliked a series of Benetton ads, one of which showed a person dying from AIDS. Other people have been offended by TV advertisements for sanitary towels.

Many people have complaints about TV programmes – sometimes it might just be a general complaint about too much sex, violence or bad language; sometimes it is a specific complaint, for instance a particularly brutal act shown on a Six o'clock News bulletin or recently, during a comedy show, a resident in an old people's home being physically abused by a member of staff.

What happens if a newspaper prints a false story about you, or invades your privacy by printing a story that is true but that you think people shouldn't know about, or a reporter is intrusive at a time of personal stress?

In each of these cases there is an industry watchdog which will look into the complaints of consumers.

1 Find out about *either* advertising *or* television *or* newpaper watchdogs. How does it operate? Can you give recent examples of how it has helped the public?

2 Prepare a five-minute talk for your group using any visual aids you think appropriate.

3 Listen carefully to the talks given by other members of your group. Make neat notes on the two bodies you did not research; file these notes away carefully.

4 If anyone has found out information which you did not know about the watchdog you researched, add this to the material you already have.

• COMMUNICATING CUSTOMER • PROTECTION

Some business organisations inform customers of their rights and this practice is becoming more common. In this chapter and the previous one you have investigated codes of practice and customer policies which have been drawn up by organisations. In many cases this is voluntary, in others it is becoming a legal requirement.

Public sector organisations

Many public sector organisations issue a Charter of Rights. You should have already obtained examples of these and seen how they give details of the type of service and assistance consumers can expect (whether paying or non-paying).

Private sector organisations

Many private sector organisations issue their own Code of Practice which covers their services and their charges (e.g. banks and British Telecom). Alternatively, trade associations can provide information. Many organisations which provide a professional service (e.g. solicitors and estate agents) will explain the conditions carefully to a client and then follow this with written details. Alternatively, the terms and conditions may be printed on the reverse of the invoice or receipt.

However, there are exceptions. Small traders (especially those who provide a service) are unlikely to have written information and much may depend on the contract which is agreed between the buyer and the seller.

DID YOU KNOW?

If you buy something at an auction then you may not be able to exchange it if it is faulty.

The terms and conditions under which you buy will usually be printed in the brochure or written on a sign.

Evidence Collection Point 12.7

Obtain at least five different examples of organisational documents or literature which explain terms and conditions and what consumers should do in the event of a complaint. Examples of sources include:

- brochures from banks and building societies
- catalogues and mail order books
- codes of practice from trade associations or large companies
- copies of contracts or agreements which have the terms and conditions printed on the reverse
- holiday brochures
- guarantees
- insurance policies
- membership application forms.

• AVOIDING PROBLEMS •

Even though consumers are protected when they buy faulty goods or poor service, it is still a nuisance having to pursue a claim. The wise customer will therefore take sensible precautions when making the purchase and will know what measures to take to ensure that any complaint will be handled properly.

DID YOU KNOW?

If you ask for a **quotation** then you will be told the exact amount you will have to pay. If you ask for an **estimate** then you are only asking for a rough guess – the real price could be more.

A ten-point plan for wise buying

1 Start by shopping around, comparing prices. Read a consumer magazine, such as *Which?*, to find out what might be the 'best buy'.

2 If you are buying a service then ask for a quotation and agree on a fixed price at the start. If possible, get this in writing.

3   Don't pay in advance and don't let the supplier include any unexpected extras on the account. Remember that you don't have to pay for anything you didn't agree to.

4   Check the goods or the work that has been done – carefully. Don't pay unless you are satisfied. If the company insists on payment, then write on the bill that you are paying 'without prejudice to my legal rights'.

5   Ask for a receipt which shows the firm's name and address and keep this safely.

6   If a problem occurs, contact the manager of the shop or the company and state your case clearly (but not aggressively). Make a note of the time and date and what was said.

7   Remember that if you have bought goods which are faulty then you have the right to get your money back or have a replacement item or free repair (if you both agree). If a service is poor then the company should undertake to put right the problem free of charge.

8   If you don't receive any satisfaction then write to the company and keep a copy of your letter. Only send a photocopy of the receipt – keep the original in a safe place.

9   If you have no response then see if the company has a head office to which you can complain. Either ask the branch office for the address or look up the address in your local library. If possible find out the name of one of their executives (e.g. the managing director or the sales manager) and write to him or her personally. If you are still unlucky, then contact the appropriate authority (e.g. the trading standards officer) or the firm's trade association or the appropriate watchdog (for a privatised organisation).

10   As a last resort you can sue the company through the county court. For small claims under £1000 the system is very simple. Alteratively some trade associations have their own low-cost arbitration scheme for settling disputes which you can use instead.

DID YOU KNOW?

If you pay for something which costs £100 or more through a credit card company or finance company then you have extra protection. The company which provided you with the finance is also liable! This is particularly useful if you are having difficulties claiming anything from the supplier, or if it has gone out of business altogether.

Public services

If consumers have a complaint against a public service industry (e.g. gas, electric, water, the Post Office, British Rail or British Telecom) then they should start by trying to solve it with their local office. If they have no success, then it is possible to find out the address of their consumer council from the Citizen's Advice Bureau or from the organisation itself.

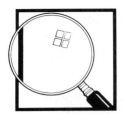

Evidence Assignment 12J

You work for Carter & Moore Ltd in the Customer Service Department. You are hoping to be promoted soon to take on the position of Customer Liaison Officer.

Your manager, Philip Browne, is concerned that anyone who holds this position *must* be able to deal tactfully with a variety of difficult situations and, to see how you would cope, he has given you the following questions to answer. Write your responses on a separate sheet. Label them carefully so that he can see to which question you are referring.

1 A young woman was given two identical toasters as wedding presents and has brought one back to ask for a refund. She understands from her aunt, who gave her the toaster she is returning, that it was bought from your store two months ago, but she has no receipt. She wants your help as she has been told by another assistant on electrical goods that she is not entitled to a refund.

2 An assistant in the store tells you that whenever she demonstrates one of the new batch of electric food processors that has been delivered this week she notices sparks coming from the back of the motor. She has another four of the same model on display and wants to know what to do. (Note – none has been sold so far.)

3 A caller bought an expensive book from you last week for a present but now wants to exchange it as she has found out that the person she was going to give it to already has a copy. She has lost her receipt but has brought her cheque counterfoil with her showing that she paid by cheque and wants to know if this will be acceptable. All your signs clearly state 'no refunds or exchanges without proof of purchase'.

4 A junior assistant from another branch telephones to say that a customer is returning an article she bought at your store. The junior has offered the customer a credit note but she is insisting on the return of her money as the article is faulty.

5 A customer called in at lunchtime yesterday and left her watch to be fitted with a new strap. After she had gone, and while the assistant was putting away the selection of leather straps she had been showing the customer, the watch was stolen from the counter. The woman has called back today to collect her watch and is horrified to discover it has been stolen. She is even more annoyed that the assistant on the jewellery counter has told her that your organisation is not responsible, in keeping with your displayed sign that 'all goods are left at the owner's risk'.

6 A customer calls at your desk. She ordered a carpet four weeks ago on condition that it would be fitted by the end of last week. There is still no sign of it and she insists on cancelling the order. She wanted the carpet laid before her daughter's 21st birthday party and she now wants her deposit returned so that she can obtain the same carpet from another shop which has supplies in stock. The customer has been told by the assistant in the carpet section that she cannot have her deposit returned as the carpet has been specially ordered on her behalf and should arrive 'any time now'.

7 A lady calls at your desk to complain. She brought her elderly mother into the store for lunch and, after they had finished their meal, her mother slipped on the step leading down out of the restaurant and broke her ankle. She complained to the restaurant manager that because the step was carpeted it was difficult to see, and that they would consult their solicitor about suing the store for negligence. The restaurant manager replied that as there is a warning notice about the step shown at the exit to the restaurant your company isn't liable.

8 A young man calls at the counter. He bought his mother a jug kettle in your recent sale. At the time it was labelled 'shop soiled' as it had a slight scratch on one side, but he thought this wouldn't matter. However, his mother feels it would show, and the scratch makes the kettle look a mess. He is now asking for his money back.

9 A customer approaches the desk. She bought a sweater in the sale last week. When she examined it thoroughly at home she found there were three small holes in one sleeve. She had not noticed these when she bought it, neither had they been pointed out to her by the assistant. She has just returned it to the knitwear counter and produced her receipt, but the assistant has informed her that no refunds (or exchanges) can be made for sale goods.

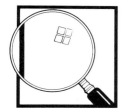

Evidence Checkpoint

You should now have completed all the Evidence Assignments and ECPs in this chapter to a satisfactory standard and filed these in your portfolio. If you are up to date, and have studied these chapters in order, then you may have completed most of the work for this unit of your course.

Check that everything is complete and filed neatly. Then make sure your projects are completed and you know enough to pass your external test!

Evidence Project

Select two different types of business organisations from the following categories:

- A public sector service organisation (e.g. a hospital, town hall or government department or your own school or college).
- An organisation in the private sector which supplies goods (either a manufacturer or a retailer).
- An organisation in the private sector which provides a public service (e.g. British Telecom or British Gas).
- An organisation in the private sector which provides a private service (e.g. a builder, solicitor or accountant).

1 Investigate the two types of organisations you have chosen and find out:

   a the requirements of their customers
   b the ways in which these organisations inform customers of their rights.

2 Assume that despite these measures both are still receiving a high level of consumer complaints. In addition, very few people who contact them are aware of their rights. (How much did *you* know about your rights before you started on this course?)

   a Outline six courses of action that could be taken *in each case* which would improve customer service and reduce the number of complaints.

   b Suggest ways in which consumers or users of the service could be informed of their rights. In each case bear in mind the characteristics of a 'typical' consumer.

Type a report, using appropriate headings, and include any examples of literature you have obtained. Design a suitable front cover, preferably using a graphics or desktop publishing package.

Revision Test

True or false?

1 Providers of public services aren't interested in customer services.

2 Questionnaires assessing consumer opinion are usually designed by the market research section.

3 If a company has a sign which says 'all goods are left at the owner's risk' then it is never liable for claims.

4 The provision of both goods and services is covered by consumer legislation.

5 A very young person cannot enter into a legally binding contract.

Complete the blanks

6 The letters OFT stand for the ....

7 The document introduced by the government in 1991 to give consumers more information is called the ....

8 A term which is stated in writing in a contract is known as an .... term.

9 Kitemarks are awarded by the ....

10 *Which?* reports are published by the ....

Short answer questions

11 State four types of problems which might be dealt with by staff working in customer services.

12 State three ways in which an organisation can monitor customer satisfaction.

13 State two ways in which organisations communicate customer protection.

14 State the three ways in which a contract of sale may be ended.

15 State the three conditions which apply to goods under the Sale of Goods Act 1979.

Write a short paragraph to show you clearly understand each of the following terms:

16 Contract of sale.

17 Customer feedback.

18 Consumer legislation.

19 Guarantees.

20 Ombudsman.

chapter **13** COMMUNICATION

Introduction

No matter what sort of a career you choose you will find that a large part of your day is taken up with *communicating* with other people. During a typical day in an office, for instance, you may find that by the time work officially starts you have talked to the receptionist in the entrance foyer, to the office cleaner, to the security guard and to the other people in the office. Within five minutes of starting work you may have answered or made a couple of telephone calls. You may then talk to your boss either to give him or her some information or to receive some instructions. Throughout the course of the day you may have to write a few letters or memos, prepare some notices for the office noticeboard and even gather together some information for a report. You might also be asked to prepare some charts or graphs. Your finished results are going to be seen or read by a number of people and should, of course, be well presented and free from grammatical, punctuation and spelling mistakes.

If therefore you do have difficulty in communicating with other people – either orally (i.e. by speech) or in writing – you're not really going to enjoy your work.

This chapter tries to help you both to grasp the basic skills and to improve those you already have. There are sections on:

- speaking to people
- delivering a presentation to an audience
- writing to people
- using illustrations.

There is also a section which gives you the basic rules of grammar, punctuation and spelling together with some practical exercises for you to try.

At the end of the chapter is a handy **reference guide** which contains a brief summary of the rules relating to various types of communication and which you can use as a memory aid.

· SPEAKING TO OTHER PEOPLE ·

One of the first things you learn to do is to speak. Your mother will remember the first words you spoke and probably embarrass you by repeating all the mistakes you made when you first tried to get your tongue round awkward words. At that age mistakes didn't matter – you were looked on as sweet rather than as dim.

In adult life, however, the way in which you speak is very important. Not many concessions are made if you cannot be bothered to make yourself understood, or if you make it clear you are bored or irritated by what others are saying to you. Your voice is one of your most powerful weapons. You can inform, persuade, coax, instruct, demand – and you can gain all sorts of advantages if you do these things well.

As with all skills, however, some people are more naturally gifted than others. If you don't think that speaking to people (other than your close friends or family) is one of your best assets don't despair. Like most other things you only need to grasp some basic points, practise a few skills and you'll feel your confidence grow as you see yourself beginning to improve.

By that stage you should be able to see why it is better sometimes to *say* something rather than write it down.

- Speaking is direct, unlike the use of a letter or other form of written document.
- It is quick.
- It is normally much more informal than other forms of communication.
- There is instant feedback – you normally get an immediate response.
- It can be the most persuasive means of communication.

We shall now look at some tips as to what you should be thinking about when you do talk to people. There are some practical exercises to be carried out either individually or in a group.

Accuracy

Although you are speaking to someone rather than writing to them, you should still try to 'think through' what you are saying before you say it. Obviously if you are talking to friends on an informal basis you will be able to correct yourself if you realise you have made a mistake (or someone may point it out to you pretty quickly). Even if you don't realise at the time that you have given incorrect information it may not matter – you can telephone your friends later to say that you have given the wrong time of the start of the football match.

However, if you are talking to someone more formally – at work, in a bank, in a doctor's surgery etc. – you may not be able to correct yourself so easily, and the consequences may be more serious. In other words, put your brain into gear before you put your tongue into operation!

Activity

Work in pairs if possible. Think of two recent events you have attended – a party, a film, a pop concert, a sports event etc. Alternatively, select two television programmes you have watched recently.

1 Without any preparation at all describe to your partner what happened at the first event. Let your partner do the same.

2 Then spend two minutes *mentally* working out what you are going to say about the second event. Don't write anything down. Repeat the exercise. You should feel that you have given a more accurate (and more complete) account of the second than the first event.

Ambiguous or incomplete information

Remember that speech is instantaneous. You can re-read something you have written and alter any obvious errors without anyone but you knowing anything about it. You can't do the same thing when you are speaking, so try to avoid saying something which could be interpreted more than one way (i.e. something which is ambiguous or something which is incomplete and therefore equally confusing). For example:

- Can you come on the 2nd? (the 2nd of what?)
- Can you come on Monday? (which Monday?)
- I want you to bring along the documents relating to the Robinson contract (suppose there are two clients named Robinson?)

Activity

Discuss with your tutor how the following sentences might be misinterpreted. Rewrite them to make them clearer.

- Would you ask Miss Lee whether Mrs Parkinson has finished with her file?
- Ask the caretaker about the radiator because it's cold.
- Please complete that application form in black ink.
- The group of students are not all there.

- If you've nothing on, why not come out with me?
- She watched the experiment taking down notes.
- The members of the meeting are listed on the notice board.
- If you let us know we shall arrange for you to look round the house as quickly as possible.
- This is the very last thing I want to do.
- The work needs doing badly.

Body language

Body language is often referred to as 'non-verbal communication' (NVC) and is normally divided into four areas:

- facial expressions
- eye contact
- gestures
- 'personal space'.

One of the advantages of talking to people direct rather than writing to them is that you can see immediately their reactions to what you are saying. What is also important to note, of course, is that they are forming an impression of how you are reacting to what *they* are saying.

Someone who smiles at you and nods would appear to like what you are saying. Someone who shrugs, stares out of the window or pointedly keeps looking at a watch may seem to be less impressed. Someone who keeps edging away from you might give you the same impression. Be careful, however, to avoid making too many assumptions based on first impressions. The person who enters your 'personal space' by standing very close to you might be indicating that he or she is interested in what you are saying and relaxed in your company; the person who does not might be indicating the opposite. What may also be the case, however, is that the second person is very shy and therefore ill at ease with anyone in that situation – although still agreeing with what you are saying. The same is the case with someone who fails to make eye contact with you – don't necessarily assume that he or she is a shifty character!

An important point to remember is that we tend to 'mirror' what the other person is doing if we agree with

what they are saying. If you look around a group of people at a party you will often find that if one person of a pair has crossed his or her legs the other will also have done so. If one person is leaning against the bar, so is the other and so on. If you want to make use of body language for your own advantage and to use it to create a particular impression – nonchalance, earnestness etc. – think about how you look as well as what you are going to say.

Note: This topic is also covered in Section 4, Chapter 11 in relation to dealing with customers.

Activity

Discuss as a group the body language you might use to show:

- confidence
- amusement
- agreement
- displeasure
- encouragement.

Clarity

When speaking to someone it obviously helps if he or she can hear you properly, and does not constantly have to be asking you to repeat what you have said. Here are some pitfalls to avoid:

- Do not speak too quietly. No-one wants to listen to someone who shouts, but it can be just as difficult to follow someone who mumbles.
- Do not speak too quickly. Often someone who is nervous tends to speak quickly, so if you are in a situation which is new to you or in which you are slightly uncomfortable make a conscious effort to *slow down.*
- Do not be too hesitant. Saying 'er' might give you a bit of thinking time but it can irritate your listener.
- Avoid using abbreviations or jargon all the time. You know what you mean but your listener may not, and may not be bothered to find out.

DID YOU KNOW?

Research has shown that at best people can only take in about 70 per cent of what they hear. Don't reduce that percentage by giving them too much information in too short a space of time.

Activity

1 Spot the deliberate errors in the following conversation.

2 What *should* the clerk have said?

Caller: Good morning. Could you let me me know whether I can speak to Mr Friedrich please.

Clerk: LMF?

Caller: Sorry?

Clerk: Do you want to ..... (inaudible)

Caller: I'm sorry but I just can't hear you.

Clerk: (screams) I said, do you want to speak to LMF?

Caller: Is LMF Mr Friedrich?

Clerk: Yes.

Caller: Well that's the person I want.

Clerk: Well, er, that's a bit, well um, it may be a bit ...

Caller: Sorry?

Clerk: (very quickly) I'll have to check with the R & D section to see if LMF is in an Ops management meeting or whether he has stopped off at Comp services to look at the new MIS system.

Caller: Well, perhaps I'll call back later.

Listening

When speaking to someone it is often easy to make the *wrong* assumption about what is being said – and what is being understood.

Activity

1 How many of the following have you either said (or secretly thought)?

● I can tell whether or not someone is going to be worth listening to as soon as he or she comes through the door.

● He looked such a mess I couldn't be bothered listening to him.

● Sometimes I'm so busy that I have to listen to someone talking to me whilst I'm doing other things. It's OK – I'm used to doing two things at once.

● I'm frightened of looking a fool if I stop someone too often to ask them to explain what they mean.

● I can tell what most people are going to say almost immediately. In fact I often race ahead of them and finish off their sentences for them.

● Sometimes I pretend to listen when actually I'm miles away. No-one notices.

● When I listen to many people I'm amazed at my own cleverness. I often have to interrupt them to correct them on a few points.

● If I think someone is talking nonsense, I've no hesitation in telling them so.

2 Discuss with your tutor why it might be dangerous to believe such statements. (See item on *body language* for some assistance if required.)

Barriers to good communication

Communication is a two-way process and learning how to listen to someone is just as important as learning how to talk to that person. Assuming that you *want* to know what the other person is saying, remember the following points:

● Try to make certain that you are in surroundings which allow you to listen and to concentrate. It *is* possible to carry out a conversation at an airport, in a pub or in a busy office with people shouting to one another across the room, but it isn't easy. The more important the conversation, the more important it is that your surroundings are quiet and free from any distractions.

● Try not to interrupt (no matter how boring you find the conversation). The person who is talking will not become less boring and may possibly take even longer to come to the point.

● Don't pass the time by fiddling with paper clips on the desk, looking out of the window, looking up a telephone number or trying to sort out a few papers. You may miss an important point and you will probably irritate the speaker.

● Remember to assess how you are feeling. It's not always possible to postpone an important conversation because you have a lot on your mind or are too tired to concentrate. But where it is possible, do so. Otherwise simply be aware of your feelings and try to take them into account.

● Remember, too, that sometimes it is more difficult to 'hear' and understand information you don't really want to hear than information which you do. You might be much readier to listen to and to understand your tutor when he or she says that you can have a longer lunch hour than if you are asked to stay an extra hour at the end of the afternoon! If, therefore, you are telling someone some unwanted information you have to be doubly careful that you make it clear.

Activity

Can you repeat a message accurately? Read a passage from a newspaper once to your partner. Get him or her to repeat a summary of what you said to a second person and then the second to a third (conducting all these conversations out of the earshot of the others, of course). Compare the summary at the beginning and at the end of the proceedings.

Tone

'It's not what you say but the way that you say it ...'.

Even if you have something very important or interesting to say you might find you are not listened to if you are saying it in the wrong way. For example, asking a favour from someone in a very abrupt manner is less likely to be successful than if you make the request pleasantly.

Also, it is important to bear in mind to whom you are speaking. Some tones of voice are rarely acceptable – nobody appreciates being bullied or ridiculed or made the subject of a series of sarcastic remarks. You may have to distinguish between talking to a nervous office junior who wants everything explained in detail and to the managing director of a firm who wants some information passed on quickly and efficiently. You may also want to use a slightly different tone of voice to a persistent and unwanted salesman from that you would use to a valued client!

Activity

Discuss as a group what tone of voice you think is likely to be used in the following situations:

● when a mother is trying to prevent her child running into a road
● when a car salesman is trying to sell a car to a customer
● when a member of the Samaritans is taking a telephone call from a frightened and confused caller
● when a DJ is talking to an audience
● when a building society manager is talking to a first-time home buyer about a mortgage.

Telephoning

When you speak to a person over a telephone you are still *speaking* to them. There are, however, certain differences in the techniques you can use.

The use of body language or facial expressions becomes less important – although many telephone technique handbooks do tell you to smile when answering the telephone because that does have an effect on your voice. Some books also advise you to remain standing when making a difficult call, or if you know you have a tendency to talk too long (sheer weariness will make you put down the receiver!).

Because, however, you can't make your body language work for you as effectively over the telephone, your tone of voice and what you actually say become even more important.

Remember:

● Where possible be prepared. You have the initial advantage when making a telephone call that you know what you want to say and, unlike most face-to-face conversations, you are able to write down a brief summary of your opening remarks at least.
● It is even more important in the case of a telephone conversation that you check that your listener *really* understands what you are saying. You won't be able to see an approving nod of the head or a puzzled expression.

Making and receiving telephone calls is dealt with in more detail in Section 4, Chapter 11.

Activity

Discuss with your tutor the ways in which you can check that what you have said has been understood by a person at the other end of a telephone line.

Evidence Assignment 13A

Imagine that you work in a small firm of interior designers which offers a service to the general public by:

- giving advice on all types of house decor
- recommending what types of fabrics, wallpapers and furnishings to use
- supplying the names and addresses of firms of suppliers.

There are four partners in the organisation together with a receptionist/telephonist, an office manager and a part-time clerk. There is also a cleaner.

Decide *as a group* who is to take the part of the customer, the receptionist, the office manager, the part-time clerk, the four partners, the cleaner. Then *act out* the following situations. Discuss with your tutor your performance after each role-playing exercise.

If you are brave enough, *as a group* award first, second and third prizes to your best performers!

Scene 1

Cast The customer
The receptionist

A very good customer comes into the reception area and tells the receptionist that the chairs which he or she has recently had re-upholstered are already showing wear and tear. The receptionist tries not to upset the customer but has just received a phone call from the upholsterers who say that the damage has been caused by the customer's cats. Bear in mind that you do not accept any liability for any recommendation of a supplier – but, obviously, if you do recommend anybody and your advice is acted upon, you will lose a lot of business if that supplier turns out to be unsatisfactory.

Scene 2

Cast The office manager
The part-time clerk

The office manager has to speak to the part-time clerk who, for the past two weeks, has been coming in late. The clerk explains that this has been because his or her bus has either arrived late each day or not turned up at all.

Scene 3

Cast The part-time clerk
The receptionist

The part-time clerk is thinking about applying for a full-time job and discusses with the receptionist the advantages and disadvantages of doing so. (See page 60 for information on part-time employment if you need any help.)

Scene 4

Cast The four partners
The cleaner

There is a meeting of the partners to discuss:

a Whether or not to purchase a new database for keeping customer and supplier records (some partners are in favour, others think it too expensive).

b The bad debt situation. There are three outstanding accounts, one for £150, one for £300 and one for £3000. The first two customers are new, the third has always paid his bills before. Various partners have different ideas as to what to do.

At the end of the meeting the cleaner comes in and demands a wage rise.

• MAKING A PRESENTATION •

On many occasions, you may be expected to stand up in front of a group of people and to talk to them. You may want to give them some information, to sell them something or to persuade them to do something for you. In order to do this you have to sell *yourself* first of all.

You won't sell yourself if you:

- don't know your subject matter
- can't remember what you are going to say
- repeat the same thing over and over again
- speak so quietly that no-one can hear you or so quickly that no-one can understand you
- use confusing technical jargon
- give a mass of confusing and complicated facts
- can't answer questions
- look awful.

Before you start to make a presentation remember that you are not unusual if you feel nervous. Almost everyone, is at the beginning. Look at the comments made below and decide whether or not you feel the same!

- 'I'm far too frightened to stand up in public and say anything at all – even my name!'
- 'I'll make a complete fool of myself – I just know it.'
- 'What if my mind goes blank?'
- 'Suppose everyone laughs at me!'

What you are suffering from here is fear of the unknown. All you need to do is to make one very small, very simple presentation and you'll realise that it's not as bad as you think. As with most other things, however, you need to be prepared. The better prepared you are, the more successful you will be and the more willing to progress to something more complicated. So, you have three major steps to take when making a presentation:

1 You have to *prepare* it.
2 You have to make sure that it is *organised*.
3 You have to be able to *deliver* it well.

Preparation

Bearing in mind that most presentations you will have to make at first will involve a group of people, find out who is going to be in your group and try to get to know them – if you don't know them already. There is nearly always a mixture of personalities in a group so make use of it. The person with the outgoing personality can be the leader of the presentation, the quiet thorough one can take charge of the research, etc. – although be sure that *everyone* takes part in the actual presentation.

Read the instructions carefully. Don't start to research for a topic before you know *exactly* what you want. (Look at pages 371–2 for some ideas on where to find information.)

Find out how long your presentation is expected to be. It will normally be between five and ten minutes. If you are not given a definite time try to make it as brief as possible. After 15 minutes most people in an audience are beginning to fidget, and after half an hour their concentration has almost completely disappeared.

Find out about your audience. Do they know quite a bit about your topic? If so, you have to be very well prepared. Do they know nothing at all? If so, you will have to keep your presentation simple and not confuse them with too much complicated information, too much jargon or too many abbreviations.

This might seem a nuisance, but in the early days at least you should write down *every word* of what you want to say at the presentation. You can then either learn it off by heart (but still have your notes with you as a back-up) or be sufficiently rehearsed to remember all the facts and the order in which you want to give them even if you are not word perfect. Remember that if you are asked to give a presentation as part of your course assessment you will gain marks if you don't merely stand there and read your notes.

Whatever else you do, memorise your introduction and your conclusion!

You may find, however, that you feel awkward clutching several sheets of paper and that you prefer to use small cards instead on which you have written 'key phrases' as memory aids. Suppose, for instance, you were preparing a presentation on 'the making of a presentation'. Your key phrases would include *Preparation*, *Organisation* and *Delivery* (each followed by a short list of points).

Remember also that, however dynamic you may think you are, people will get bored with just sitting and listening to you. Try to think of ways to illustrate your presentation – posters, charts, overhead projection transparencies etc.

Organisation of your material

Speaking is the same as writing in many respects. You don't (or shouldn't) write down the first thing that comes into your head and then keep going. You plan an opening paragraph, the main body of the document and then a suitable closing paragraph. The same is the case when you are making a presentation. *Plan* your talk around the following steps:

1 Introduce yourself and your team.
2 Introduce what you are going to say.
3 Expand on it. Make one point at a time, and illustrate each point with a visual aid or give an example. Make sure your audience knows when you are about to move on to the next point.
4 Summarise what you have said – put emphasis on the points you particularly want your audience to remember.
5 Know when to hand over to the next member of the team.

We shall look at an example. Imagine that you are asked to make a presentation to your group on the problems which have arisen over the student common room in your school or college. Your initial plan could look something like this:

Introduction

The problem – there have been complaints that the student common room is dirty and that there are not sufficient facilities for students.

Main points

1   Cleanliness

By 3 p.m. each afternoon every table in the common room is littered with empty coffee cups and cans and there are empty crisp packets, food containers etc. thrown all over the floor. Ash trays are overflowing.

2   Facilities

There are ten tables and 40 chairs – the chairs are dirty and tables are stained. There is a drinks machine which is always breaking down. There are few bins. The carpet is torn in one area. There are no lockers. The room looks unpleasant – there are no pictures or plants. No-one seems responsible for the upkeep.

Possible solutions

1 The Head could be approached to see whether or not:
   ● a cleaner could be employed for an extra two hours each afternoon to check on cleanliness

   ● the chairs could be cleaned and the tables repolished
   ● more bins could be provided
   ● the drinks machine could be replaced with a newer version – or at least that regular servicing of the existing machine could take place
   ● new lockers could be provided
   ● the carpet could be cleaned and repaired.
2 The student committee could be involved to:
   ● oversee the general cleanliness – through the efforts of the student representatives and by the mounting of a publicity campaign
   ● check on the use of the lockers and possibly be responsible for the issuing and return of locker keys
   ● try to raise some money for plants, posters etc. to brighten up the room.

Conclusion

There are two possibilities. (1) A group representative could speak to the Head about the suggestions made. (2) A meeting of the student committee could be called to discuss the matter further.

Activity

1 Write out the presentation in full.
2 Make crib cards of the key phrases you will use when making the presentation.
3 Discuss as a group what visual aids or illustrations you could use during the presentation. Prepare at least one of them.
4 Ask for two volunteers to make the presentation to the rest of the group.

Organisation of yourself and your surroundings

Preparing your material is of major importance. However, preparing yourself is also important.

Remember also to prepare your surroundings.

Activity

Read the following case study and list what Shaheda has done wrong. Prepare a check list of what she should have done.

Shaheda has to give a presentation to her tutors on the introduction of a new stock control system into a firm. She misses the bus and rushes in to college a few minutes before the presentation is to take place.

She has prepared her notes and crib cards but they are somewhere at the bottom of her bag and she keeps her tutors waiting as she searches for them. She has prepared an overhead projector transparency but, when she switches on the projector, she finds that the bulb has gone. She has forgotten the Blu-tack for the poster she wishes to display. She hasn't given a thought to what she looks like and has turned up wearing a sweat shirt and jeans. She hasn't had time to comb her hair.

Just as she is about to start her presentation she notices that one of the tutors is still standing up and that there are not enough chairs in the room. She also discovers that there is nowhere for her to prop up her notes.

She is so panic stricken that she forgets to take two or three deep breaths to calm herself and launches straight into her presentation. It's a disaster!

Delivery

If you are well prepared, that's half the battle won. The audience doesn't expect you to be a stand up comic, although a bit of humour does help. Remember a few basic rules:

- Smile at the audience. Try to look confident even if you are anything but – but don't worry too much if you know you look nervous. Many people in your audience will sympathise and be on your side.
- If you have not been introduced, introduce yourself (and the rest of your group). Give your name and the subject of your presentation.
- Make a deliberate effort to speak slowly. Nervous people tend to speak far too quickly and the audience loses track of what is being said.

- Make eye contact with your audience. Look at them rather than at the floor or ceiling. But don't fix one particular person with a glassy stare and talk to him or her alone.
- Remember also body language (see pages 310 and 353 for details). Try to avoid using irritating mannerisms. If you are not sure whether or not you have any, ask a trusted friend for an honest opinion.
- Use short words and short sentences. Try to use sentence constructions such as 'I think that this approach will benefit you' rather than 'It is possible that this approach will be beneficial'. Keep it simple.
- Try to show some enthusiasm – that always looks attractive.
- If you dry up, don't panic. Pause, and don't worry that there is a silence. Look at your notes and start again. Sometimes someone in the audience will help out with a question or a comment.
- Remember the value of a pause particularly when you are moving from one point to another. Remember also to tell your audience that you are moving on to a new point.

Activity

You will probably have listened to a number of people who bored or irritated you. You will probably also have half-listened to a number of people who couldn't manage to hold your interest after the first few minutes.

Colin is one of these people. He is a sales representative for a firm of office suppliers. He has come to give a presentation on the latest photocopier. List the points where you think he went wrong and why he failed to make a sale!

Colin: 'Right, I want to talk to you this morning about our new photocopier – well the point is that we have sold over 1000 of them since last year, 25 per cent up on our normal sales, 50 per cent up over our rivals, best photocopier I've ever sold, 30 per cent better than any other photocopier...' (long pause). 'Er let me see – I seem to have lost my place....' (mutters something).

Manager: 'I'm sorry but I can't hear you – can you speak up please'.

Colin:	(Scratches his head) 'The point is – well what I mean to say is – this photocopier is worth buying'.
Manager:	Why?
Colin:	(Mutters something at his feet – scratches his head) 'Well the point is – it's the best on the market' (mutters again).
Manager:	'I'm sorry but I can't seem to hear the end of what you are saying'.
Colin:	'Er ... Do you want to look at some of the ... er ... brochures?'
Manager:	'Perhaps that would be as well. Have you any price leaflets?'
Colin:	'Er ... well the point is ... no, I've forgotten them – but I'll send them on to you'.

Answering questions

Either during or at the end of a presentation you may be expected to answer questions.

If you know your topic well this should not be too much of a problem. If you are having difficulty in answering a question, however, consider one (or more) of the following hints:

- Ask the person to repeat it to gain thinking time.
- If you don't understand the question, say so and ask for it to be re-phrased (e.g 'I'm sorry but I don't know what you mean.').
- Admit you don't know the answer and say you will find out.
- Ask for someone in your team to help. Remember also to help out another member of your team if he or she seems to be struggling, but be careful not to interrupt too soon.
- Throw it open for general discussion.

DID YOU KNOW?

Remember that body language shows how you feel. Check that you and your team are not standing so far apart that the audience think you are not on speaking terms – or that you are huddled in such a tight little group that the audience think you are too frightened to operate as individuals!

Types of question

What you might also find useful is to know the type of question you may be asked (and the purpose for asking it). Look at the following questions.

'Won't this photocopier be very expensive to run?'

That sort of question is what is known as a *concealed objection* question (i.e. where the person asking the question may not be on your side). All you can do at this stage is to be factual and to remain pleasant. If the photocopier is going to be more expensive to run, say so, but try to point out the other *advantages* it may have – better quality, quicker turn round, etc.

'Can this photocopier do double sided pages, collate and staple?'

This might be a *test* question, and the questioner may have some knowledge of the topic. If you don't know the answer, don't bluff. Say that you will find out whether or not it can and that you will get back to the questioner as quickly as possible.

'Can you tell me if this type of photocopier is as good as the photocopier I saw at a recent exhibition I attended in New York?'

This is known as a *display* question (i.e. the person asking the question is merely wanting to show off his knowledge or to let everyone know how important he is). Flatter him by being impressed with what he has to say.

'What makes you think that we need a new photocopier?'

The questioner here might be asking a *defensive* question. For example, he may have chosen the last photocopier and be worried in case you criticise that choice. Be careful not to do so.

Evidence
Assignment 13B

Work in pairs. Research and prepare a short talk on a topic agreed with your tutor.

Topics you might like to consider include:

- New developments in information technology

Pitch

Pitch is the height or depth of your voice. Do you speak too loudly or too gently? Do you lower your voice at the end of each sentence which may make it more difficult for the audience to hear you?

Pace

Pace is the rate at which you speak. Are you speaking too quickly? Does your subject matter affect you (e.g. if you are angry do you speak more quickly than if you are not)? Do nerves or embarrassment make you speak too quickly?

Pause

Are you pausing at the right places? Remember not to confuse pausing with hesitating!

Tone

Do you speak in a monotone (i.e. on one note) or do you vary the tone? Remember that varying your tone does help to keep your audience interested in what you are saying.

Emphasis

If you have a particularly important piece of information to give, do you place sufficient emphasis on it in order to attract the audience's attention?

Figure 13.1 *Guidelines to the way you speak*

Name of presenter   ....

Topic   ....

1   Delivery
Appearance/dress
Confidence
Mannerisms
Eye contact/body language
Pace/enthusiasm

2   Introduction
Did it create interest?
Was it clear?

3   Presentation
Was it clear?
Was it organised?
Was it suitable for the audience?
Was it the right length?

4   Illustrations/aids
Were notes used well?
Were the visual aids good?

5   Questions
Were the questions handled well?

6   Team work
Did the first person introduce the group?
Did each person hand over properly to the next person?
Did the team support each other –
    verbally?
    non-verbally?

Figure 13.2 *Assessment of a presentation*

- A piece of modern office equipment
- Health and safety at work
- Customer care
- The rights of the consumer

Time it to last for four minutes – two minutes each.

1 Record your part of the talk on a cassette. Play it back and try to assess whether or not you need to improve any of the areas listed in Figure 13.1. Write a paragraph about your conclusions.

2   Deliver the talk to each other. You talk for two minutes whilst your partner listens and then you listen to your partner. *Assess* each other by using the presentation assessment sheet in Figure 13.2. Try to be honest but not brutal!

3 Deliver the same (or another) talk to the group as a whole. Ask them (or your tutor) to assess you on the same form and see if you get a better rating.

· WRITING TO PEOPLE ·

Even with the increased use of the telephone there are still going to be many occasions on which you have to write down some information. If you are writing a note to a friend to remind him or her where to meet up on Saturday night, it may not be so important that you are writing clearly and grammatically and that your spelling and punctuation are good. In a business situation it does matter. It also matters that you know in what form the information should be given – a letter, a memorandum, a report, a notice.

In this section, therefore, we deal with the most common forms of written communications and the ways in which they should be presented. In each case:

- an example is given (including an illustration to show the correct layout)
- a 'how to do it' section is included
- there are some practical exercises.

There is also a 'using words in the right way' section which gives you some hints on basic spelling, punctuation, grammar and vocabulary.

LETTERS

Letters are normally sent to people outside your organisation and therefore you should take particular care that they are well presented and organised.

Example

Look at Figure 13.3 for an example of letter layout.

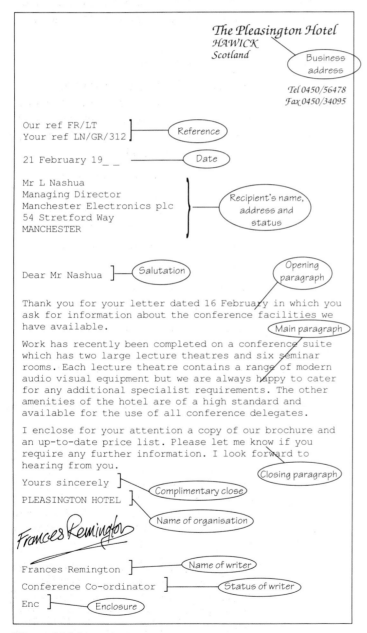

Figure 13.3 *Letter layout*

How to do it

- The 'complimentary close' must match the salutation. 'Dear Sir' or 'Madam' at the beginning requires 'Yours faithfully' at the end. 'Dear Mr/Mrs/Miss/Ms' at the beginning requires 'Yours sincerely' at the end.
- The opening paragraph should refer to any previous correspondence, by date if possible. Otherwise it should state the purpose of the letter.
- The second paragraph – if required – should give a fuller explanation.
- The closing paragraph can be in a number of different forms; e.g.

  'I look forward to hearing from you.'

  'Please let me know if you require any further information.'

  BUT – it must be in the form of a complete sentence. Do not use 'Looking forward to hearing from you' or 'Assuring you of our best attention'. (See page 375 for the difference between a sentence and a phrase or note if you are not sure.)

Beginnings

If you have particular difficulty in starting a letter, try to follow some of the examples below.

- If you are replying to someone, always start by saying 'Thank you for your letter of (date).'
- If you have talked to someone on the telephone you could use as your opening sentence 'Further to our recent conversation' – and then complete the sentence.
- If you are making an enquiry start with a sentence such as 'I should be grateful if you would let me know ...' or 'Could you send me the following information ...' etc.
- If you want to complain you can use wording such as 'I must complain about the ...' or 'I should like to bring to your attention a problem I experienced ...' etc.

Don't use such expressions as 'Referring to your letter...' or 'I am writing this letter...'

Activity

Mr Nashua gives you the following notes.

'This hotel looks quite nice from what I can tell from the brochure but I need a little more information. Can you write back to the Conference Co-ordinator and ask her what is the maximum number of delegates the hotel can accommodate at one time. Ask her to provide sample menus. Check also whether a booking could be made for either 14–16 May or 20–22 June.'

Compose a suitable reply for him to be sent to the Conference Co-ordinator.

DID YOU KNOW?

The most frequent occasions on which a letter is sent include:

- selling or advertising a product
- making or answering an enquiry
- asking for details of goods, products or services
- making or answering a complaint
- asking for payment of an account
- making interview arrangements
- applying for jobs
- giving references
- giving thanks
- giving sympathy
- offering congratulations
- issuing or replying to invitations.

Evidence Assignment 13C

Work in pairs. In each of the following cases one of you should write the letter and one the reply (although it may be better to swap round each time). Make up suitable names and addresses. Discuss with each other what you are going to write and check each other's answer afterwards. *Remember to write clearly and legibly!* Ask your tutor to do an overall check.

Making and answering an enquiry

a You are on a business studies course at college and want to know whether or not the Tudor Suite at the local Civic Centre is available from 9 p.m. to 2 a.m. on Friday 15 June for an end-of-term student disco. You want to book it provisionally for at least 200 people and would like to know how much it costs.

b You are the Bookings Manager of the Civic Centre and send a reply indicating that the suite is available on that evening and that a provisional booking could be made on payment of a deposit of £50. The total cost will be £300.

Making and answering a complaint

a After the disco you send a letter to the Bookings Manager complaining about the facilities – the hall was too warm, the air conditioning was faulty and one part of the floor was cordoned off because it was in the process of being re-carpeted. You want a refund.

b As Bookings Manager, you reply to the student agreeing that the air conditioning was not working properly. You agree also that part of the floor was cordoned off but say that it did not have any effect on the dance or bar area. You are unwilling to give a refund.

Issuing and replying to an invitation

a You, as organiser of the event, send an invitation to the College Principal asking her if she would like to be the guest of honour.

b You, as the Principal, write a letter accepting the invitation.

DID YOU KNOW?

On some occasions you may have to write or reply to a **formal** invitation which is laid out in a different form from that of an **informal** invitation. Look at the example of a formal invitation and a formal reply given in Figure 13.4.

- The language is formal. Instead of saying 'We should like to invite you to Rachel's 18th birthday party' you have to give the names of the people issuing the invitation and the name of the person receiving the invitation.

- There is nearly always a request for a reply. RSVP means *répondez s'il vous plaît* – a French phrase meaning 'please reply'.
- The date is normally given at the bottom of the invitation.

```
25 Riddings Drive
NESTON
Lincolnshire

25th May 19..

Mr & Mrs F Abraham have pleasure in inviting Mr James
Roland to the 18th birthday party of their daughter
Rachel, to be held at 8 p.m. on Saturday 5th June.

RSVP
```

```
56 Harrow Grove
NESTON
Lincolnshire

1st June 19..

Mr James Roland thanks Mr & Mrs F Abraham for their kind
invitation to the 18th birthday party of their daughter
Rachel, and has much pleasure in accepting.
```

Figure 13.4 *A formal invitation and reply*

Activity

Rewrite the invitation to the Principal, and her reply, in formal terms.

MEMOS

Memos are used for internal correspondence and therefore are generally less formal – although a memo to the managing director or senior personnel officer might need the same amount of care and preparation that you would give to a letter to an important client! Note that in formal language a memo = a memorandum, and memos = memoranda.

Example

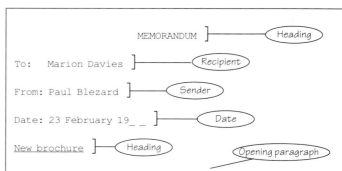

```
                        MEMORANDUM        Heading

To:   Marion Davies        Recipient

From: Paul Blezard        Sender

Date: 23 February 19_ _        Date

New brochure    Heading        Opening paragraph

Thank you for letting me have the first draft of the
proposed layout of the new brochure. I give below my
first reactions:

1  The overall presentation is excellent but the type
   size seems much smaller than in the original
   document. Is this intentional?

2  Is the hotel logo going to appear on all pages or
   merely on the front cover?        Main body

3  Would a personal welcome from the manager, Mr
   Campbell, in the form of a brief introduction at the
   beginning of the brochure, give it more of a personal
   touch?
                                      Closing paragraph
Perhaps we could meet some time next week to discuss the
matter in more detail. Please let me know if you are
free any time next Thursday.

PB        Initials
```

Figure 13.5 *Memo layout*

How to do it

- Remember to use a subject heading.
- A memo is normally shorter than a letter and should deal with one topic only (although this doesn't always happen).
- If you do want to make several points, number each one individually.
- If you are replying to a memo make sure that you cover all points made.
- A memo is normally initialled rather than signed. The full name of the sender is always at the top of the memo anyway and people can always refer back to that.

Activity

Look at the following memo which is a reply to the one given on page 364. Spot the obvious mistakes and re-write it in the correct form. Check also that all the information requested has been given. If it has not, make up a suitable reply.

```
                        MEMORANDUM

To:      Paul Blezard
From:    Marion

Thanks for your memo. The type size of the brochure is
smaller. Is that a problem?

The hotel logo is going to appear on the front cover only.
I'm free all day on Wednesday next week if you want to see
me.

Marion Davies
```

Evidence Assignment 13D

1 You are the Refectory Manager of Manchester Electronics plc and are faced with the task of informing staff that from Monday of next week all prices will rise by 10 per cent. Write a memo to them informing them of this increase. Let them know that you have kept the increase as low as possible and remind them that this has been the first price rise in 18 months.

2 You are the Chief Security Officer with the same organisation and have noticed that members of staff in the Purchasing Department have a tendency to leave their computer terminals switched on at the end of the working day. The cleaners have reported this on four occasions and you therefore feel that you must send a memo to the Purchasing Manager to let him know what has happened and to ask for his co-operation in persuading his staff to be more careful in future.

NOTICES

A notice is a very quick and easy way of sending information to a large number of people – particularly if you want to send it to an unknown audience (e.g. if you want to sell your old car).

Note that an electronic mail system can be used for this purpose and can be used instead of a noticeboard. However, since not all organisations have that facility, be prepared to use a paper-based system if you have to.

DID YOU KNOW?

Notices are used:

- to convey the same information to a large number of people
- to relay informal as well as formal information (e.g. an organisation's noticeboard can contain a wide variety of information ranging from a change in the car parking procedures to arrangements for an inter-departmental trivia quiz competition).

Example

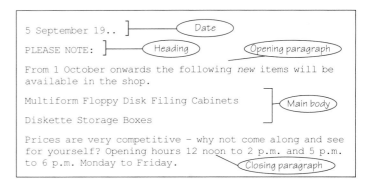

Figure 13.6 *Notice layout*

DID YOU KNOW?

If you can use a desktop publishing package you will find that you can make a notice look very eye-catching by the use of different fonts. But don't go over the top and use too many, because you will merely confuse the reader.

How to do it

- Write the notice so that *everyone* can understand it. You are not sending the information to one person, but to a whole group of people, many of whom you won't know.
- Use clear and simple language. 'ATTENTION PLEASE' is better than 'I should like to draw your attention to ...'.
- Make it short. People won't stand for hours reading a notice on a noticeboard, particularly if they are reading it over somebody's shoulder.
- Use colour if you think it helps, but keep to one or two colours only because too many gives a childish effect.
- Always date it – so that you (or the person responsible for the noticeboard) know how long it has been displayed and when its 'shelf life' is over.

Evidence Assignment 13E

Trevor is a new trainee in the general office of a building firm. One of his jobs is to look after the departmental noticeboard which he is expected to update each week. Last week the following items of information were left on his desk ready for him to sort out and put on the board. Put the information into a suitable form for the noticeboard. If you can use a word-processor or desktop publishing package, try to make use of some of its functions – bold, italics etc.

15th November

Trevor – can you let staff know about the car park. Resurfacing will start next Monday and staff will have to use the temporary car park at the back of the annexe until it is finished. I'm not sure how long it will take – probably at least a week.

Frances

16th November

Trev – I'm desperate for some help for the children's Christmas party. As usual everyone is trying to back out at the last minute and I'm very short of volunteers. Can you try to 'persuade' one or two to help? If anyone is interested you can ask them to contact me direct. My new extension number is 5632.

Eileen

18th November

I'm the proud father of a new baby girl – and I want everyone to know about it! She's called Tamara, she has blonde hair – and she's great!

Cliff Derbyshire

18th November

Share Option Scheme – completed forms to Personnel by Friday, latest, for anyone who wants to participate.

Tamsin

REPORTS

You may be asked to write a short report to be sent either to another member of the organisation or to an outside client or customer. There are several report formats which can be used depending on the level of formality which is required, but most reports contain certain common elements.

DID YOU KNOW?

Reports are used:

- to present some information on a particular topic (a research report)
- to give an account of work carried out during a given period together with an indication of future plans (a work report)
- to give an account of a road accident etc. (an eye witness report).

Example of a research report

Figure 13.7 shows you an example of the finished product.

REPORT

Terms of reference

Report on the Conference Facilities offered by the
Pleasington Hotel

Procedure

1 I wrote to the hotel to obtain information about the
   facilities available and the range of prices.

2 I contacted Mr Timothy Brazier, the Personnel Director
   of Banks Ltd., to see what he thought about the hotel.

3 I visited the hotel to speak to the Conference Co-
   ordinator and to see the facilities.

Findings

1 The hotel brochure was very detailed and the price
   range compared well with those of other hotels I
   contacted.

2 Mr Brazier had been a delegate at a weekend conference
   held at the hotel and said he was impressed with the
   surroundings and the help the hotel staff had given
   him.

3 I liked the attitude of the Conference Co-ordinator
   and the conference facilities I saw.

Conclusion

The facilities provided by the Pleasington Hotel are of
a high quality and the prices charged seem reasonable.

Recommendations

I therefore recommend that serious consideration be
given to holding our next senior managers' conference
there.

Signature

Verity Lamley
Training Manager   Status
3rd May 19..
                    Date

Figure 13.7 *Report layout*

How to do it

- Your *terms of reference* are simply a statement of what you have been asked to do – or what you want to tell the recipient. Sometimes a heading is sufficient.
- It is sometimes necessary to say how you have gathered your information together (i.e. *procedure*) – to prevent someone from asking you whether or not you have thought of a particular approach.
- Your *findings* are statements of fact – not opinions at this stage. (If you are not sure about the difference try working through the activity which follows).
- Your *conclusion* is general.
- Your *recommendations* are based on your conclusions,

are normally more detailed – and state your own opinion.

Activity

As a group, decide which of the following sentences (**a** or **b**) are statements of fact and which statements of opinion.

Example

Fact   The refectory is on the ground floor.
Opinion The refectory seems to be in the wrong place.

1a She has black hair and brown eyes.
1b She is the best looking girl I have ever seen.

2a Liverpool football players wear a red strip.
2b Liverpool is the best football team in the country.

3a The price range is the same as that of the other supplier.
3b The quality of their goods looks much better.

4a Two members of staff expressed dissatisfaction about the new office layout.
4b Staff seem unhappy with the new office layout.

Numbering systems

In many reports you may find it helpful to use a **numbering system** and to keep to that system throughout the report. One method is to use a combination of numbers and letters.

Example

1 MEANS OF TRAVEL IN THE UK

   a Air travel

      i The shuttle service

OR

A MEANS OF TRAVEL IN THE UK

   1 Air travel

      a The shuttle service

Another approach is to used the **decimal** system of

numbering. Numbers are allocated from 1 to 10:

1
2
3 etc.

They can then be sub-divided by adding a decimal point and then 1 – 10 again:

1.1
1.2 etc.

2.1
2.2 etc.

If you want to sub-divide even further, you can repeat the same procedure:

1.1.1
1.1.2 etc.

2.1.1
2.1.2 etc.

Example

1 MEANS OF TRAVEL IN THE UK

  1.1 Air travel

    1.1.1   The shuttle service

2 MEANS OF TRAVEL ABROAD

  2.1 Air travel

    2.1.1   The scheduled flights

The second method is more complicated to understand at first but it does let you divide your material into as many sub-sections as you wish.

Evidence Assignment 13F

You have been asked by the Chief Librarian of your local public library to carry out a survey on what people expect from the library.

You drafted out a short questionnaire and obtained permission from the Chief Librarian to ask a number of people who visited the library over the period of one week to complete it for you. In addition you interviewed the Chief Librarian and two of his assistants. You also visited several other larger libraries in the area.

You found that most library users thought:

- the library was understaffed
- the opening hours should be extended.

You also found that the library staff felt the magazine section was not being used sufficiently, and thought the reason was that the seating area in that section was too small.

You noted from your visits to the other libraries that refreshment areas had been established which were well used and brought in some additional income.

Write a short report outlining your findings and making any recommendations. Try to use the decimal system of numbering.

FORMS

You may be surprised to find how many forms you are expected to fill in both at work and at home. Think, for instance, of a driving licence form, a job application form, a form from the insurance company if you have had a car accident, etc. What you should remember is that you may not get a second chance to fill in a form correctly (particularly if it is an application form for a job) so you have to be particularly careful to be accurate first time round.

How to do it

- Read the form through first.
- Sometimes it is a good idea to take a photocopy of the blank form so that you can have a practice run. You might, for instance, find that you have written your address and postal code all on one line when there is a separate space for the postal code.
- Check that you have all the information you need.
- Check to see *how* you have to complete the form. Is it to be completed in black ink, in block capitals, etc?
- Use a pen which is blotch free.
- Write clearly. This might be more difficult than it sounds – particularly if you normally use a word-processor.
- Try not to leave any blanks. If you really do not have anything to write under a particular heading write N/A

(not applicable) to show the reader that you have at least read the question.

- If you have to write out a full paragraph, practise beforehand to check that you can fit it into the space provided.
- Check the form afterwards and do not forget to sign and date it if required.

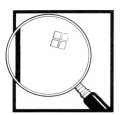

Evidence Assignment 13G

You want to apply for a job as a trainee accounts clerk. Complete the form which you will find at the back of the book, a copy of which you see in Figure 13.8, and ask your tutor to check it.

SUMMARIES

Occasionally you may be asked to summarise (i.e. make shorter) some information for your boss, possibly to save him or her from the trouble of reading a long and complicated document from beginning to end.

DID YOU KNOW?

Examples of the type of information you may have to summarise include:

- an article from a newspaper for inclusion in a report or speech
- some information for use in a sales presentation
- a complicated set of facts and figures for a client, government official, etc.
- some information for the press.

Example

Main passage: Ramblers' Associations in Berkshire, Buckinghamshire, Cheshire, Clwyd, Cornwall, Cumbria, Derbyshire, Hampshire, Hertfordshire, Kent, Lancashire, Leicestershire, Lothian,

---

LANDSHIRE COUNTY COUNCIL

FORM ESC/3

JOB APPLICATION FORM

Application for the post of ....

....

Please use block capitals for Sections 1, 4 and 8

1 Surname ....

   First name(s) ....

2 Date of birth ....

3 Address ....

   ....

   ....

4 Present post ....

   ....

5 Previous posts ....

   ....

   ....

6 Education

   (Please give details of secondary school/college/university attended – together with starting and leaving dates)

   ....

   ....

   ....

7 Qualifications

   (Please include dates, subjects and grades)

   ....

   ....

   ....

   ....

8 Referees

   (Please give the names and addresses of two persons to whom reference can be made)

   ....

   ....

   ....

   ....

   ....

9 Signature ....

   Date ....

Figure 13.8

Northamptonshire, North Yorkshire, Nottinghamshire, Oxfordshire, Somerset, Suffolk and Warwickshire are all co-operating in protesting against the wilful blocking of tens of thousands of miles of Britain's footpaths and bridleways. In England and Wales, according to the Countryside Commission, the Government's countryside advisers, almost one fifth of the 140 000 mile network is impassable.

Final version: Ramblers' Associations in many parts of the country are protesting about the blocking of many of Britain's footpaths and bridleways, 28 000 miles of which are now impassable according to the Countryside Commission.

How to do it

- Skim read the document – don't try to take everything in at once.
- Then read it more thoroughly. What you can do at this stage is to cross out (or underline) unwanted words. Where possible, write over the top of deleted words just one word (or a reduced number) in place of several. For example, instead of the list of individual counties you could write 'in many parts of the country' or 'in most counties of the UK'.
- Next list the main points in note form. Remember that you can leave out examples.
- At this stage your notes might read:

  Ramblers' Associations in a large number of counties protesting about the deliberate blocking of many of Britain's footpaths and bridleways. According to Countryside Commission almost 28 000 miles of network impassable.

- What you should then do is to check your notes against the main document to make sure you haven't left out anything important.
- Your final job is to draft your summary from your notes. Make sure this time that (unless otherwise agreed) you are writing in sentence and not note form (see 'Using words in the right way' on page 375 for the difference if you are not sure).

DID YOU KNOW?

Unless you want always to write in short sentences (and in many cases this is better than long and confused sentences) you may want to think of using 'joining' words such as 'and', 'but', 'although' or 'because' to make what you have written read more smoothly. It is also very useful if you are asked to summarise a passage.

You may have written the following series of sentences:

Simply Red is protesting about the reduced royalty rates they are going to receive. Other groups are also protesting. The recording companies will not negotiate with them.

Although the passage is perfectly understandable, the use of one or two joining words will improve it. So:

Although Simply Red and other groups are protesting about the reduced royalty rate they are going to receive, the recording companies will not negotiate with them.

Activity

Try to make the following passage read better by the use of some 'joining' words – but don't try to turn it into one gigantic sentence!

Many children under five come from homes where English is not spoken. They do have some language skills. They probably have a well developed first language. It could be Mandarin Chinese, Urdu or Bengali. It could be one of the many other languages used in the UK today.

Evidence Assignment 13H

1   Summarise the following paragraphs into about a quarter of their length:

The business world is made up of all sorts of firms which either produce a variety of goods such as food, clothes, cars etc. or give a service such as catering, entertainment, education, distribution, etc.

At regular intervals, everybody who has a bank account – no matter how young or old, rich or poor – will receive a bank statement from the bank. This statement shows how much money is in the account on a particular date. It lists all payments made and money received. There may be a charge made by the bank for this service and such a charge will also appear in the bank statement.

2 Summarise the following passage into about half its length:

<u>Staff Appraisal</u>

When you start work you may find that at the end of each year your supervisor will discuss with you your performance. This is known as staff appraisal. The objectives of staff appraisal are:

- *to assess what you have done during the period in question – and how well you have done it*
- *to help you to improve in any areas where you are having difficulty*
- *to find out what additional training needs you may have.*

If this appraisal is to be successful, however, certain elements must be present. Both you and your supervisor must look at it positively with a view to identifying what benefits can be gained from the exercise. The appraisal must therefore be designed to highlight what successes you have achieved rather than to concentrate on your failures.

▪ PROJECT WRITING ▪

If you are on a business studies course at school or college you may find that you are asked to write up a *project*. The secret here is to allow yourself plenty of time to *think*. Don't ever try to write a project at the last minute – it won't work.

We shall now look at the **main stages in preparing a project**.

Making the right preparations

- Check to see when your project has to be completed. Do you have two weeks, a term, the whole year? Allow at

least 20 per cent of the time to choose the right topic.
- Check to see how long the project has to be. Make sure that you know roughly how many pages of handwriting or typing that is.
- In many cases you will be given some assistance with what headings to use. For example, if you are asked to write a project on *stock control* you may be given as a guide the headings:
- Stock control systems
- Stock control procedures
- Stock reconciliation
- Care and storage of stock
- Health and safety issues.

If you are, don't ignore them. Start looking for material under each of the relevant headings.

Keep to the point. It is a good idea occasionally to refer back to the title of the project to make sure that you are not 'waffling'. Don't try to fool your tutor by finding an article in a magazine or newspaper and copying it out word for word!

Try to 'balance' the material you collect together. If, for instance, you are asked to write a project on stock control and you find out a lot of material on care and storage of stock and very little on stock reconciliation, you may be tempted to pay too much attention to the first item and not very much to the second. Remember, however, that not all the areas you are asked to write about will require the same amount of information (e.g. you should expect to write more about stock procedures than about health and safety issues). It is a good idea to decide beforehand which areas are the most important.

Using the library

When you visit a library remember to take with you a pen or pencil and some paper so that you can make notes. Remember also to have some money with you in case you want to photocopy anything. This is particularly important if you want to use some information which is in a book or magazine marked *for reference only* and cannot therefore be taken out of the library.

Don't struggle on your own. The library staff are there to help you in a number of ways – particularly if you ask them *nicely*. They will certainly be able to direct you to the books and magazines in the library which contain relevant information, and to show you how the indexing system works. They may also do a *literature search* (i.e. collect together a list of books and magazines about this particular topic).

If the book or magazine you want is not on the shelves, find out about how to place a *reservation* for it. Most libraries allow users only a short period of time to borrow a book before asking for its return, so make sure you are next in line for it.

In some cases, the book you want may only be available on what is known as an *inter-library loan* (i.e. your library will ask another library if it can borrow a particular copy).

Evidence Assignment 13I

Work in pairs or small groups. Visit your school, college or local library to check on the sources of reference there.

- In most libraries there will be a standard indexing system known as the *Dewey Decimal System* which classifies books and other material into different categories by means of a numbering system. Check under numbers 650 to 659 to see what selection of books there are relating to commerce and list at least one title under each number. (Note – they will be sub-divided into 650.1, 650.2 etc.).
- Check also to see what *bibliographies* (i.e. lists of books) or *encylopædias* your library has and list at least three of them.
- Your library may be able to access a *computer database* and to carry out what is known as an *on-line search* for you to check on what other information is available on your particular topic. Such a search might merely list titles of articles in magazines or might give you an *abstract* (i.e. a brief summary of what the article says). (Look at Chapter 9 for details of the different sources of reference you can use.)

Prepare a brief summary of what the library can offer. Attach to it any lists or written information the library staff may have given you. Nowadays many libraries have handouts on this.

Using other sources of information

Remember that your library is not your only source of information. Quite often you will be expected to get information from other places. One of your main sources is your course tutor. Others include:

Your friends and family
Local council/town hall
Department of Social Security
Department of Trade and Industry
Department of Employment
British Telecom
Citizen's Advice Bureau
Chamber of Commerce
Consumers' Association
Tourist Information Offices
English Tourist Board
Trade Associations (See *Whitaker's Almanack* for full list)
AA or RAC
Foreign embassies
Insurance companies
Banks
Solicitors, accountants, estate agents, etc.
Office equipment suppliers
Inland Revenue
Local radio station
Local newspaper
Post Office
VAT Office
Public relations departments of large firms
Her Majesty's Stationery Office (HMSO)
The Commission of European Communities

Recording your sources of information

You may be asked to list where you found your information. Make certain, therefore, that when you find some information which you want to use in your project, you write down the author, the book or magazine title, the date of the publication and the page or pages on which you found the information. If you wanted to use the information on this page you would write down: Carysforth, C., Rawlinson, M., Neild, M. (Heinemann, 1993), 'Business Level 2', p. 372.

Writing up the project

Check that you have all the information you want before you start to prepare the document.

Try to arrange the information logically (i.e. in order). Divide it, if you can, into:

- an *opening paragraph* (including a heading if necessary)
- the *main body of the project* which can be any length – you may want to separate the information into numbered points (see page 367 for the different numbering systems you can use)
- a *closing paragraph.*

Remember always to use the headings given and, if possible, to sub-divide into main and sub-headings; e.g:

Main heading *STOCK CONTROL*
Sub-heading *Stock control systems*

Draft (i.e. write out in rough) the document (a word-processor is very useful here). Remember to number the pages.

Read through and check for any errors. If you know you can't spell very well or have difficulty in deciding how to punctuate properly, read through the section on 'Using words in the right way' on page 374. Ask a friend to read your project as a double check.

Allow yourself enough time to have second thoughts and to alter your material where necessary.

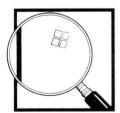

Evidence Assignment 13J

Work in pairs and write a project about *the structure of your school/ college library*. Include the following items:

- Staffing
- The different resources – books, computer facilities, databases, microfilm/fiche, etc.
- The layout – the type of furniture, the surroundings, etc.
- The indexing systems
- Any future developments
- A comparison with another library (e.g. your local library).

Discuss with your tutor beforehand:

a the length of the project
b how much time you have to prepare it.

Evidence Assignment 13K

Imagine that you work as an assistant to the general manager, Imran Hussein, of a small department store, Greenwoods Ltd, Mansfield. During the course of one week you are asked to carry out the following tasks.

1 A customer has complained that an assistant in the electrical goods department has been very rude to her – see the letter in Figure 13.9. The assistant denies this and says that the customer was determined to be awkward and stormed off before he could do anything. You are asked to compose a reply to the customer on behalf of your manager. You are also asked to draft a memo to the assistant reminding him that, however difficult a customer may be, he or she must always be treated with consideration.

2 The January sale has just ended and you are asked to send a memo to all staff thanking them for their efforts and telling them how successful the sale was.

3 There is increasing friction in the administration department between the smokers and the non-smokers. You are asked by your manager to look into the matter. You begin by obtaining the views of each member of staff in the department. Six are very anti-smoking; four do not smoke but do not particularly object to others smoking; five smoke. The smokers suggest that they sit in one area of the department which can be screened off from the rest of the department. Three of the non-smokers agree with this, the other three do not. You have a word with the departmental trade union representative who is also the safety representative. She tells you that it is the union's policy to promote a no smoking environment but to ensure that there is some area which is designated a smoking area and which is the only area in which smoking can take place. She also gives you some information about courses which are available to smokers to help them give up the habit. You decide to

write a report to your employer detailing your findings and making some recommendations.

4 The Secretary of the 'Friends of Wycliffe Hospital' contacts your manager to ask for some staff to take part in the local hospital radio programmes. They will be asked to spend between two and four hours a week there and will receive some training. You are asked to prepare a notice for the staff noticeboard asking for volunteers. Anyone interested should contact you.

5 Greenwoods is trying to improve its image and wants to become an organisation noted for its staff welfare and training. It has therefore applied to join a scheme called *Investors in People*. From the information leaflet given below, write a short summary (of about half its length) of what the scheme is all about, so that details can be put into the staff newsletter. Remember to date it and to use an eye-catching title.

Investors in People

'Every organisation, whether it be a service or production industry or in the public or private sector, relies for its success on the people who work there.

People who are flexible and adaptable, who are willing to learn and enthusiastic about the business and about their work are very valuable assets to any organisation.

What the *Investors in People* scheme therefore aims to do is to improve the skills, knowledge, motivation, commitment, confidence and job satisfaction of all employees. It does so by encouraging activities such as

induction programmes
improved channels of communication
the setting of agreed targets
better training opportunities
better promotion opportunities.

Organisations who achieve the standards laid down in the scheme will be awarded the 'National Standard for Effective Investment in People'.

```
                                    43 Redford Crescent
                                    MANSFIELD
                                    NG19 8QA


                                    28th January 199—

The General Manager
Greenwoods Ltd
Jarrod Street
MANSFIELD
NG17 7DH

Dear Sir,

I have been a customer at your store for many years and,
up until now, I have been very satisfied with the service
given. However, I feel I must now complain very strongly
indeed about an incident which occurred in your store
last week.

Just before Christmas I bought an electric kettle from
your electrical goods department. After only a month's
use it began to leak. I therefore went back to the
department and explained to the assistant what was
wrong.

He could hardly be bothered to listen to me and when I
had finished explaining, asked me what I expected him to
do about it. I asked him to give me a replacement. He
said that he couldn't do that and that I would have to
speak to the manager. I asked him where the manager was
and he merely shrugged his shoulders in reply. I told
him I didn't like his attitude and he merely shrugged
again. When I turned to leave I distinctly heard him
mutter a rude remark. I noted from his identity badge
that his name was Mark Scott.

I trust you will look into this matter and look forward
to hearing from you shortly.

Yours faithfully,

Linda Fairbrother

Linda Fairbrother
```

Figure 13.9 *Letter of complaint*

· USING WORDS IN THE RIGHT WAY ·

It's little use trying to manufacture a car if you don't know how to put all the parts together. The same is the case when you write to someone. Moreover, if you don't know what word to use or how to spell it, or you have difficulty in writing a well put together sentence, your image as an ambitious young executive will slip! Treat this section as a reference section. You or your tutor will know if you have any particular difficulties, but if you are in any doubt try the short exercise at the beginning of each item.

GRAMMATICAL RULES

Activity

Spot the genuine mistake in each sentence. Give yourself two points for each correct answer.

1 Sending you the items today.

2 Details of the new product is to be found on page 2.

3 I think you and me should have a meeting.

4 What reason do you want this information for?

5 Neither the manager or his assistant had heard about the change in plans.

6 He promised to urgently deal with the matter.

Check page 467 for the correct answers. If you have them all right, you can skip the next few pages. If not – read on!

The difference between a sentence and a phrase

A sentence has a verb. If you're not sure what a verb is at this stage it may be better for you to 'copy' the style from another document. You'll probably find that eventually you are writing sentences automatically.

Thinking of you	= note form
I am thinking of you	= sentence form
Raining outside	= note form
It is raining outside	= sentence form
Wish you were here	= note form
I wish you were here	= sentence form

Matching up singular and plural words

Remember the sentence given in the last Activity:

Details of the new product is to be found on page 2.

What should have been written is:

Details of the new product *are* to be found on page 2.

What you are really trying to say in the above sentence is that *details* (which is a plural word) are to be found on page 2, not the *product* (which is a singular word). Therefore the verb must be plural (are) and not singular (is).

If you do have difficulty, try crossing out the words in between the words you want to match up. For example:

The girl, who was with some friends, ... late.

Is it 'was' or 'were'? If you cross out 'who was with some friends' you are left with 'the girl ... late', so you would choose to put 'was'.

Pairs of words

Always put *neither* and *nor* together. Do the same with *either* and *or*:

Neither the girl nor her friend was aware of the problem.

Either we go to the cinema or to the football match.

Do not use *shall* with *should* or *will* with *would*. Use the same word throughout:

I shall be pleased to come with you and shall get ready at once.

He will be able to do the job this morning and will let you have the finished results this afternoon.

Note that if you want to use a combination of the words you must use 'shall' with 'will' and 'should' with 'would':

I should be grateful if you would call in to see me.

Remember also that you would normally use 'shall' or 'should' after 'I' or 'we', and 'will' or 'would' after 'you', 'he', 'she' or 'they'.

It is easy to mix up *who* and *whom* and the grammatical rule is rather complicated. If you are unsure find a way round it. For example, if you want to write:

This is the person who/whom has been selected for the job

and don't know that the correct word in this case is 'who', why not say instead:

This person has been selected for the job.

The use of 'I' or 'me'

If sometimes you have difficulty in deciding whether to say 'you and I' or 'you and me' try changing it over to 'we' or 'us'. For example:

You and I (i.e. we) must go to see the manager.

The manager wants to see you and me (i.e. us) after lunch.

'Split' words

Try not to separate 'to' from other words (e.g. to go, to find, to decide) by putting another word in between:

The manager had *to* decide *quickly* what to do

is better than:

The manager had *to quickly* decide what to do.

Sentence endings

Do not end a sentence with 'to', 'of', 'with', 'about' or 'for'. *Don't* say:

She is the person I gave the information to.

Say instead:

She is the person to whom I gave the information.

Again if you find this difficult, think of a way around it:

I gave the information to her.

'Er' and 'est' words

If you are comparing *two* things then add 'er'. If you are comparing more than two things add 'est'. For example:

Frances walks faster than Bridget.

He is the tallest of them all.

Note that in some cases you cannot use 'er' or 'est' and must use instead 'more' (for two things) and 'most' (for more than two):

He is more handsome than his brother.

She is the most attractive girl in the room.

Double negative words

Remember not to write:

I'm not doing nothing. (If you're not doing *nothing* you must be doing *something*!)

Other common mistakes include:

I can't hear nothing.

I'm not going nowhere.

Activity

Re-test yourself by re-writing the following sentences and scoring two points for each correct answer. Your score should be better! However, just in case you may have made a slight error, the answers are on page 467.

1 He wants to see you and I.
2 The trainee forgot to carefully read the instructions.
3 She is someone I have always had difficulty with.
4 He never has no time for us.
5 Confirming our recent telephone conversation.
6 I shall be pleased if you would provide the information I need.

EASILY CONFUSED WORDS

Some words are very easy to confuse. For instance, it is a common error to mix up 'weather' (e.g. 'What's the weather like today?') with 'whether' (e.g. 'I don't know whether I shall be able to come.'). Where you *know* that you are unsure try to find another way of writing the sentence. For instance, you may want to say that you agree with all the points made in a report except/accept? for one. The word you should use is 'except' but if you are any doubt you can always say instead 'I disagree with only one item in the report'.

It may be useful for you to know some of the more commonly confused words by working through the following exercise.

Activity

Complete the following sentences with the correct word:

To/too/two

('Two' = one + one; 'too' = above a certain standard, e.g. too much, too big)

I have ... see you immediately.
There are ... immediate improvements which can be made.
It is far ... warm in here.

There/their

(Remember that 'their' = ownership, e.g. their hats, their opinions)

Put the shopping over ....
... is no reason for the delay.
Where have they put ... belongings?

Past/passed

(Remember pass is converted into passed)

He ... me in the corridor without speaking to me.
In the ... he has been very helpful.
He ... his examination and gained a distinction.

Of/off

(If you are in doubt say the words out loud. Of sounds like o**v**, off like o**ff**)

He is a man ... few words.
Please keep ... the grass.

Remember, however, not to confuse 'of' with 'have':

I like to *have* a run every day. *NOT*
I like to *of* a run

Whose/who's

(Remember that whose = ownership, who's = who is)

... waving at you?
... coat have you borrowed?

Affect/effect

(Effect = a noun, e.g. the effect of the noise, the effects of the recession; affect = a verb, e.g. He affects me by his bad temper)

What ... will these figures have on the overall position?
Will it ... you at all?

Personal/personnel

('Personal' = about you; 'personnel' = people who work in an organisation)

The ... manager was concerned about the changes made to the staff training programme.
My ... view is that it is too risky.

Principle/principal

('Principle' = standard; 'principal' = main or major, or the head of a school or college)

The ... talked to members of the students' union about the new identity card.
I think the ... item on the agenda should be the possible redundancies in the warehouse.
I agree with it in ... but need some more information before I can act.

Practice/practise

(Practice = noun, e.g. the practice; practise = verb, e.g. to practise)

I think he must learn to ... what he preaches.
The ... of using Ms rather than Mrs or Miss has increased over the past few years.

Check on page 467 to see whether you have answered correctly.

DID YOU KNOW?

Some words are commonly misused. Remember:

- all right NOT alright
- thank you NOT thankyou

Note also that a common mistake is to confuse e.g. (= for example), which refers to general examples, and i.e. (= that is), which refers to a specific instance. Compare the following two sentences:

He talked about many different types of sales techniques (e.g. direct sales, telephone sales, newspaper advertising).

> He made particular reference to what he thought was the most successful method (i.e. telephone sales).

STYLE

The type of language or words you use when writing to someone depends on:

- the subject matter
- the person to whom it is addressed.

If you are writing a postcard to a friend to tell him about your holiday you can use *informal* language. If you are sending a business letter to an important client, you have to be more *formal*. Your friend would be rather surprised if you wrote, 'I hope you will be interested in the following details about the holiday I have just spent in France. Please let me know if you require any further information.' The client would be even more surprised if you wrote, 'Lots to tell you about your recent order. You're going to laugh when you hear it's going to be July before you get it!'

Not only is the **tone** wrong in each case, so too is the use of **vocabulary**.

Although your vocabulary will increase with experience, you may find some of the following exercises useful – particularly if you are aware that you tend to use the wrong word at the wrong time, or if you know that you use the same words over and over again.

Activity

1 Give a less formal alternative for each of the following words (use a dictionary if necessary).

manufactured   commencement
terminate   ascend
emancipate

2 Re-write the following sentences replacing the words in italics with a single word from the list given (again, use a dictionary, if necessary).

incompetent   obsolete
reversed   momentary

maintenance   estimate
incessant

- She asked for an *idea of how much the work would cost*.
- The car *went backwards* into the wall.
- The noise from the engine was *going on all the time*.
- The relief from the pain was only *for a brief space of time*.
- I can't get spare parts for your television as it is now *out of production*.
- The supervisor found that the new employee was *not able or qualified to do the job*.
- The *care and upkeep* of the machinery is essential in our business.

3 Re-write the following sentences using more *formal* vocabulary:

- Count me in when you're fixing up the trip to the match.
- If you can hang on for a week or two I'll be able to give you the info then.
- Thanks a lot for your help. You saved my life!

4 Re-write the following extract from a police report in more understandable language:

'At the commencement of the evening I was proceeding along the thoroughfare when I observed a vagrant attempting to gain access to a stationary automobile. I enquired as to the reason for his actions and he struck me across my countenance with considerable force.'

See pages 467–8 for suggested answers.

It is a good idea to practise using a dictionary. If, for instance, you pick up a dictionary and open it half way, you will probably find that you are looking at the section of words beginning with 'l'. If, therefore, you want to find a word beginning with 's' you would open the dictionary past the half way mark; if you were looking for a word beginning with 'd' you would look for it well before the half way mark, and so on.

Activity

1 Look up the following words as quickly as possible and write down their meanings:

damask	pedestal	truism
collage	impresario	ruminate

2 Look up the following words and – as well as writing down their meanings – try to work out how to pronounce them. Check with your tutor that you are able to pronounce each word correctly.

debris	epoch	grimace
hyacinth	league	myopia

3 Using a dictionary or thesaurus give a synonym for each of the following words:

minion	slaughter	intersect
apex	frivolous	notorious

PUNCTUATION

Activity

Re-write the following passage using the correct punctuation and putting in capital letters where necessary. Check your answer on page 468. Any more than two mistakes and you might be wise to read the following pages dealing with the rules of punctuation.

When we were little and had visitors to the house grandma didnt read to us instead we talked to the visitors and tried to make them play games like hide and seek with us one visitor uncle bernard was particularly good at this although sometimes he got bored and shouted im here the game then ended

The most important punctuation marks are

● the full stop
● the comma
● the apostrophe.

More infrequently, you may have to use:

● a question mark
● an exclamation mark
● a hyphen
● a dash.

You will also have to know where to put capital letters.

The easiest way for you to check whether or not you should use a full stop or a comma is to read the passage out loud. A slight pause normally indicates a comma; a longer pause, a full stop.

Uses of the full stop

● To end a sentence.
● After abbreviations (e.g. B.A. – although nowadays abbreviations are often written without full stops, eg BA).

Note the use of the question mark:

Why are you here?

and the exclamation mark:

He actually agreed!

Activity

Read the following passage out loud and then rewrite it, adding full stops where necessary.

You may remember that I raised the matter of an exchange visit with colleagues working in a college in San Diego I have now received a request from them to send details of anyone interested in taking part in this exchange it may be necessary to have a meeting to discuss the matter further give me a ring if you are interested

See page 468 for a suggested answer.

Uses of the comma

- To separate words or phrases in a list:

  I bought some apples, pears and bananas. (Note that you need not use a comma before an 'and' in such a list.)

  Mohammed Naize, the Chief Purchasing Officer, gave the first presentation.

- To indicate that someone is being addressed: Miss Franks, will you give the panel some further information?

Activity

Using the same procedure as for full stops, read out loud the following sentences and then rewrite them, adding commas where needed.
Check your answers with those on page 468.

- I got up late had no breakfast and ran all the way to the bus stop.
- I sent him to the shop to buy paint wallpaper and brushes.
- Fatima please answer the telephone.
- James and Richard the two best tennis players met in the final.

Uses of the apostrophe

- To show where a letter is missing:

  you'll   = you will
  won't   = will not
  I've   = I have

- To show ownership:

  the student's book = the book of (belonging to) the student

It is this second use which normally causes the problems. Try to remember the following steps:

1 Write down the name of the owner: the student (or the students).
2 Add an apostrophe at the end: the student'(or the students').
3 Add an extra 's' if there is only *one* owner: the student's book (i.e. the book belonging to *one* student). Do not add an extra 's' if the book belongs to more than one student (the students' book).

Note that a few 'ownership' words never need an apostrophe:

his	ours	its
yours	theirs	mine
theirs	hers	

Some words *sound* alike but have different meanings:

its	= belonging to (e.g. its shape, its height)
it's	= it is
their	= belonging to (e.g. their books)
they're	= they are
your	= belonging to (e.g. your eyes)
you're	= you are

Remember also the difference between whose (belonging to) and who's (who is).

Activity

Insert apostrophes where necessary. Check your answer with that on page 468.

Dont worry, I know shell be here before long. In the meantime, can you try to borrow Franks calculator. Yours is not working. Johns not in because hes gone to collect the Managing Directors car. Its also important for you to make certain that all the typists desks conform to the health and safety standards.

Uses of the inverted comma or quotation mark

- For direct speech – the actual words someone has said (e.g. She said, 'I like your hair').

- For a quotation (e.g. He wrote, 'I do like to be beside the seaside').
- For slang (e.g. The speaker admitted he wasn't 'with it' that morning as he had just returned from an overnight trip to London.).

Activity

Rewrite the following sentences putting in inverted commas where necessary. Check your answers with those on page 468.

- The chairman said, I welcome you to this meeting.
- Which television personality uses the catch phrase, Nice to see you, to see you, nice?
- I had never heard of the expression It's not over until the fat lady sings.

Uses of capital letters

- At the beginning of sentences.
- For 'proper' nouns (e.g. Shelagh, Dundee).

Remember not to use too many capital letters on other occasions e.g. company, business, manager, government – Today, these words are usually written without an initial capital.

Activity

Add capital letters to the following sentences. Check your answers with those on page 468.

- there are many colleges in Britain.
- she wants to attend bristol university.
- mary and danny went to nottingham to visit the firm and to see the personnel manager.

SPELLING

Activity

Rewrite the following paragraph correcting all the spelling mistakes. Check your answer with that on page 468.

In buisness you must be good at accounts. You should be able to cheque figures accuratley and also to calcullate the correct amount each time. It is helpfull if you can remember to right clearly and to seperate one line of figures from another. Only competant mannagers are promoted.

Spelling 'tips'

Again, if you are a good speller you can forget about this section. If, on the other hand, you sometimes have difficulty, don't give up! You can't learn every word in the dictionary – that's one reason for buying one – but you can increase the bank of words that you do know how to spell.

Try, however, to remember these hints:

- If you *know* you have trouble remembering how to spell a particular word, use the old trick of making each letter into a word and the words into a sentence. For example, if you always have difficulty with the word 'definite' you could remember it as:

Did **E**ric **f**ind **i**ce **n**ear **I**rene's **t**oy **e**ngine.

The sillier, the better!

- Another method is to use the 'word within a word' technique, e.g:

believe   be **lie** ve
accustomed   ac **custom** ed

- If all else fails use another word. You may not remember how to spell the word 'conscientious'. What you can do instead is to use 'hard working'.

Activity

Think of silly sentences for the following commonly misspelled words:

separate   address
competent   occur

Some spelling rules

a In most words you would put 'i' before 'e':
    e.g. rel<u>ie</u>f
except after 'c':
    e.g. rec<u>ei</u>ve

Exceptions: s<u>ei</u>ze, n<u>ei</u>ther, <u>ei</u>ther, financ<u>ie</u>r, w<u>ei</u>rd, spec<u>ie</u>s, l<u>ei</u>sure.

b When a word ends in 'y' you should drop the 'y' and change it to 'i' if you want to add anything to it:

  e.g. duty becomes dut i ful
     beauty becomes beaut i ful
     copy becomes cop i ed

c If you add 'ing' to words ending in 'e' in many cases you drop the 'e':

  e.g. cease becomes ceas ing
     make becomes mak ing

d When 'full' is added to a word you do not need the second 'l':

  e.g. awful, plentiful

e In most cases you can use either 'ise' or 'ize' at the end of a word – but don't mix them up in the same piece of work:

  e.g. I didn't recognize him. In fact, no-one recognized him. *not* I didn't recognize him. In fact, no-one recognised him.

Activity

Complete the following exercises by referring to Figure 13.10 which contains a list of commonly misspelled words.

Commonly misspelled words

A – D

accommodation	accustomed	acknowledge
actually	advertisement	advisers
already	apparently	arrangement
arrival	assistance	attention
attitude	awkward	because
behaviour	believe	busily
business	careers	colleague
college	coming	conscientious
decision	definite	disappointing

E – I

earnest	embarrassing	emergency
envelope	excited	exercised
exhausted	experience	extraordinary
extremely	families	favourite
February	finally	finished
foreign	forty	frightened
government	honestly	immediately
immensely	information	intentions
interesting	interests	interrupted

J – Q

jealous	limit	liaison
loose	lose	luxury
meant	memories	mortgage
necessary	neighbour	nephew
niece	occasion	occasional
occasionally	opinion	opportunity
organisation	Parliament	patience
preferred	priority	priorities
probably	quality	quiet

R – Y

really	reassurance	receive
recognise	recommend	refer
reference	referred	regret
regrettable	restaurant	routine
scarcely	scheme	separate
similar	stationary	stationery
succeeded	successful	surprise
unconscious	unreasonably	unsuccessful
volunteered	whether	wondered

Figure 13.10

1 Correct the mistakes in the following sentences:

- Please make arrangments for the visit of the carreers officers who are very consientious and are looking forward to comming to the colledge.
- The forein students are dissappointed because they are not going to have an end of term party.
- I must reccomend you to try the new stationary – particularly the new envellopes.
- In my opinnion the goverment have behaved unnreasonably.
- Please list your prioritys when you have the opportunnity.
- He wandered whether or not to say that he was

suprised about the regretable incident.

2 *Work in pairs.* Make up one sentence using at least one word from each of the three columns in each section (e.g. one from A–D, one from E–I and so on). You can use as many other words as you want. For example:

Section A–D

The <u>accommodation</u> mentioned in the <u>advertisement</u> was <u>disappointing</u>.

Still in pairs, dictate the sentences to each other and check your answers.

Evidence Assignment 13L

Imagine that you work in the general office of a college. You are asked to look after a work experience trainee who can keyboard and who is very keen to help but whose grammar, punctuation and spelling are poor. You realise therefore that you will have to check anything he does before it leaves the office. One afternoon you are called into a meeting. When you get back to the office you find that the trainee has, on your instructions, completed the following piece of typing from an audio tape.

1 Read through it and make the necessary corrections

DRAUGHT
Information about the colege to be sent to job aplicants.

Their are ten departments in the colege each one of them provides a wide range of courses. In the Busness Studies department there are flurishing fowndation, intermediate and high level business and finnance courses with a wide variety of options there are also degree courses in business administration and law. The principle management courses are the diploma in management studies the certificate in management studies and the diploma in supervisery studies. Other courses cover marketing purchasing accountancey and personal management.

The departments examination results are good. It's general average has been over 85% and in many cases above 90%. Its' staff are well qualified and motivated and student welfare is regarded as of the utmost importance.

The sennior staff of the department include the head, the deputies, and the divisional heads.

2 You note that the trainee seems to be very unsure about when to use commas and apostrophes. Write or type out a short list of the rules relating to the use of each so that the trainee can keep it beside him as a reminder when he next types out a document.

HOW TO DISPLAY INFORMATION ▪ IN DIFFERENT WAYS USING ▪ VISUAL AIDS

There's an old saying that one picture is worth a thousand words. In many cases this is true.

Which of the following do you find more effective?

<u>A Pig</u>
A wild or domesticated animal with broad snout and stout bristly body

<u>A Pig</u>

Even in business some information is better displayed visually than in written form and you should therefore be aware of the following different methods of display:

- tables
- pie charts
- pictograms
- line graphs
- bar charts.

TABLES

Compare the following two sets of information:

a The Annual Office Furniture Exhibition was held in the Haymarket Centre from 14th to 16th January. An official estimate of the number of visitors to the exhibition was 250 on Monday morning and 280 on Monday afternoon; 180 on Tuesday morning and 210 on Tuesday afternoon; 300 on Wednesday morning and 315 on Wednesday afternoon.

b Number of visitors to Office FurnitureExhibition, Haymarket Centre, 14th – 16th January 19..

Monday		Tuesday		Wednesday	
a.m.	p.m.	a.m.	p.m.	a.m.	p.m.
250	280	180	210	300	315

The second version is obviously easier to read.

Activity

You work in the office of Blackhurst School. One of your jobs is to sort out class timetables from information given to you by the Deputy Head. One note reads:

'Year 1 Blue Group. Monday's timetable. 9 – 10 English; 10 – 11 French; 11 – 12 Computer Studies; 12 – 1.30 Lunch; 1.30 – 2.30 Sports; 2.30 – 3.30 Careers.

Year 1 Green Group. Monday's timetable. 9 – 10 French; 10 – 11 Computer Studies; 11 – 12 English; 12 – 1.30 Lunch; 1.30 – 2.30 Careers; 2.30 – 3.30 Sports.'

Display this information in the form of a table.

PIE CHARTS

A pie chart is always drawn in a circle with each wedge showing the portion of the whole it represents. If, for instance, you want to show the percentage of students of different ages on one year of a business studies course you could display the information in pie chart form. See Figure 13.11.

How to do it

- Use this type of chart to give general information only. It is of little use in the case of detailed information.
- As a start, mark your circle into quarters (each representing 25 per cent or one quarter) and adjust the wedges from there.
- Remember that the total of the percentages must equal 100 per cent.

Number of students	Age range	Percentage
100	16 – 18	50%
60	19 – 21	30%
40	21+	20%

The information could be presented as:

16–18

19–21

21+

or for additional effect (if you want to show one segment separated from the rest):

Note that you need a key.

Figure 13.11 *A pie chart*

Activity

You have been asked to undertake a project on the media and have decided to analyse the time allocated to various television programmes during the course of one evening. Display the following information you have gathered together in the form of a pie chart.

<u>Monday evening</u> BBC 1 5 p.m. – 10 p.m.

Comedy shows	25%
Chat show	15%
News	5%
Football	25%
Documentary	15%
Hospital drama	15%

PICTOGRAMS

Information can be displayed by means of pictures or diagrams called pictograms. Again the information can only be displayed in general form and pictograms are therefore used only for illustrative purposes in sales presentations, promotional material etc. See Figure 13.12 for an example.

Information about the gradual increase in numbers of children attending crèches over the past 30 years could be displayed as a pictogram *either* by using one illustration and increasing it in size:

The increase in the number of children attending the company crèche between 1972 and 1992

1972   1982   1992

or by using an increasing number of illustrations:

The increase in the number of children attending the company crèche between 1972 and 1992

1972   1982   1992

Figure 13.12 *Pictograms*

Activity

You work in a supermarket, Bestbuys, and have been asked to draw a pictogram to show the increase in sales of tinned cat food over the past four years. In 1991, 10 000 tins were sold; in 1992, 15 000; in 1993, 20 000; and in 1994, 25 000.

LINE GRAPHS

Line graphs are used to display more detailed information and to indicate trends. They may be composed of either a single line or more than one line, in which case they are known as multiline graphs.

They are used for many kinds of statistical information, including:

- purchasing and sales figures
- price increases or decreases

- import and export figures.

See Figure 13.13 for an example.

How to do it

- The horizontal axis (line) is known as the *x*-axis. The vertical axis is known as the *y*-axis. Both must be *labelled*.
- Normally amounts are shown on the vertical axis and times on the horizontal axis.
- It is also usual to have the lowest number at the foot of the vertical axis and to move upwards.
- Decide on the amounts you are going to use (10s, 20s, 100s, 1000s etc). Decide also on the times (days, weeks, months, years).
- Decide on what colours or different types of line you are going to use for a multiline graph.
- Put in each dot in pencil and then join up the lines.
- In the case of multiline graphs, include a key to indicate what each line represents.

Sales of deckchairs from January to July

Number

200
150
100
50
0
J F M A M Ju Jul

A comparison of sales of deckchairs and loungers from January to July

Numbers

Multiline graph

200
150
100
50
0
J F M A M Ju Jul

- - - Loungers
—— Deckchairs

Figure 13.13 *Line graphs*

Activity

You work for a firm of opticians. As a publicity measure, you are asked to construct a line graph to indicate the general increase in sales of contact lenses over the past six months.

In July, 30 people purchased them; in August, 50; in September, 60; in October, 55; in November, 65; and in December, 70.

You are also asked to prepare a multiline graph to indicate the difference in the sales of contact lenses and of conventional glasses.

Sales of glasses were – July, 40; August, 40; September, 50; October, 60; November, 65; December, 75.

BAR CHARTS

An alternative to a line graph is a bar chart. In this case, however, bars are used instead of continuous lines.

The bars can be single, or multiple (or compound) if you want to make comparisons (as in the case of a single line and multiline graph). The bars are normally vertical but can be horizontal. The rules for the construction are the same as those for line graphs. See Figure 13.14 for an example.

Activity

Your boss, the manager of Selectarecord, wants you to construct a bar chart to show the way in which the sales of compact discs have increased in comparison with a decrease in cassettes.

- In 1989 sales of cassettes were 2500 and sales of compact discs 1500.
- In 1990 sales of cassettes were 1750 and sales of compact discs 1850.
- In 1992 sales of compact discs were 1650 and sales of compact discs 2000.

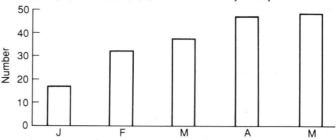

The number of enquiries made for information about the 'Adopt an animal' scheme at the local zoo from January to May

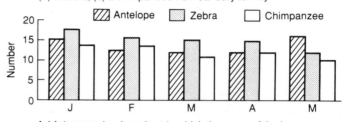

The number of applications received to adopt (a) an antelope, (b) a zebra, (c) a chimpanzee from January to May

A **histogram** is a bar-chart in which the areas of the bars represent the quantities

Figure 13.14 *Bar charts*

DID YOU KNOW?

With the exception of pictograms, charts and graphs can now be created by computer by using a spreadsheet package.

DIAGRAMS, SKETCHES AND PHOTOGRAPHS

If you look through a magazine or newspaper article or pick up a glossy brochure in a car salesroom or the reception area of a firm, you will probably be more tempted to read what is written if the information given is illustrated by means of a diagram, a sketch or a photograph. This is particularly true if you want either to 'sell' something or to make something absolutely clear which is difficult to do by using words alone.

At work you don't have to be a gifted artist to be able to make a rough sketch or diagram to illustrate something you have written, as you will generally be able to hand over your outline to another member of staff who is specifically trained to do any artwork. However, if you need to sketch out something for another purpose (e.g. when making a claim to an insurance company), you may have to rely solely on your own efforts.

Activity

You are driving back from a college disco one evening at about 11 p.m. and stop at a set of traffic lights ready to turn right from a side street, Ruskin Avenue, on to the main road, Brownside Street. Both streets are well lit. The traffic lights change and you move out. As you do so, however, a car on the main road comes through the lights at red (at least you think it was red – the other driver says it was amber) and hits your car. You were moving very slowly and not much damage was done to your car although the other car was badly damaged. No-one was hurt. A woman, Mrs Ellen Parker, waiting to cross the side street on your side of the road, has witnessed the accident and is prepared to say that the other driver did come through on the red light. The other driver is Antony Williams. His car is a red Sierra 1990 registration; yours is a blue Fiesta 1987 registration.

You have to explain to your insurance company what happened. Write a paragraph giving your account of the incident and draw a sketch showing the position of both cars and also where any relevant witnesses were standing. Give any other details you think may be relevant.

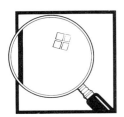

Evidence Assignment 13M

You are a college student on a business studies course. You are particularly interested in marketing and are therefore pleased when you are offered a part-time job in the college marketing department during the summer holidays.

One of the jobs the marketing department has been asked to undertake is to prepare a number of charts to be used in an audio visual presentation about college developments. The presentation will be made to the governors of the college.

You job is to draw up the initial charts and graphs before they are re-presented in their final form.

a Prepare a vertical bar chart to show the projected trends in the number of school leavers in the district from 1993 to 1996:

1993–4	1768
1994–5	1733
1995–6	1910
1996–7	2076

b Draw a pie chart to illustrate the destinations of students who have left the college in 1993–4:

35% went into employment
20% went into higher education
25% continued in further education
15% were unemployed
5% destination unknown.

c Draw a line graph to show the numbers of students attending the college during the past 12 months:

September	8 900
October	11 000
November	10 900
December	10 500
January	12 000
February	11 590
March	11 580
April	11 000
May	10 800
June	9 800

The Principal knows that he is likely to be asked questions about the increase and decrease in the number of students attending the college over the year. The marketing team therefore examine the figures and try to come up with reasons for:

- the rise from September to October
- the slight decrease in December
- another increase in January
- a decrease in June.

Write down what your explanation would be.

· QUICK REFERENCE SECTION ·

How to lay out a letter, memo, notice, report

Letters
(page 362)

Business address
Reference
Date
Recipient's name, status, address
Salutation (Dear ....)
Subject heading

Opening paragraph
Main body of letter
Closing paragraph

Complimentary close (Yours ...)
Name of organisation

Name of sender
Status

Enclosures

Memos
(page 364)

Memo heading

Name of recipient
Name of sender
Date

Subject heading

Opening paragraph
Main body of memo
Closing paragraph

Initials of sender

Notices
(page 365)

Date

Subject heading

Opening paragraph
Main body
Closing paragraph

Reports
(page 366)

Terms of reference

Procedure

Findings

Conclusions

Recommendations

Signature and status of writer
Date

How to write a summary

(page 369)
- Skim read the document.
- Read it more thoroughly.
- Cross out or underline unwanted words.
- Write over the top one word or a reduced number in place of several.
- List the main points in note form.
- Check the list against the main passage.
- Draft the summary from the notes.
- Check grammar, punctuation, spelling.

How to prepare a project

(page 371)
- Check the title of the project and the sections in which it is to be divided.
- Check to see when the project is to be completed.
- Check to see how long it should be.
- Gather together your information from (a) the library and (b) other sources.
- Record your sources-if asked to do so.
- Check to see you have all the information you require before starting to write the project.
- Arrange your information logically, with:

  an opening paragraph
  the main body of the project
  a closing paragraph.

- Remember to use the headings given.
- Check your numbering system.
- Draft out the project.
- Check it or ask a friend or tutor to check it.
- Allow time for second thoughts.

How to write grammatically

(pages 374–6)
- The difference between a sentence and a note.
- How to match up singular and plural words.
- When to use 'neither/nor' and 'either/or'.
- When to use 'shall/should' and 'will/would'.
- When to use 'who/whom'.
- The use of 'you and I' or 'you and me'.
- When not to split 'to' from another word.

- How to avoid ending a sentence with 'to', 'of', 'with', 'about', 'for'.
- When to end a word with 'er' and when with 'est'.
- How to avoid using a double negative.

How to choose the right word

(page 377)
Check on the difference between:

- to/too/two
- there/their
- past/passed
- of/off
- whose/who's
- affect/effect
- personal/personnel
- principle/principal
- practice/practise
- e.g./i.e.

How to punctuate

(pages 379–381)
- The full stop
- The comma
- The apostrophe
- The inverted comma
- Capital letters

How to use visual aids

(pages 383–7)
- Tables
- Pie charts
- Pictograms
- Line graphs
- Bar charts
- Diagrams
- Sketches/photographs

chapter **14** THE APPLICATION OF NUMBER

Introduction

People in all jobs in business organisations work with numbers at some time during the day. They could not do their work without them. At the very least everyone has to check their pay slip to see if the money they have received is correct.

- The personnel manager needs to calculate the cost of a settlement in pay negotiations.
- The production manager has to work out how long it will take his unit to produce a special order.
- The marketing manager checks the number of items sold, against his target.
- The accountant spends most of his working day on budgets, cash flow calculations and many other types of analysis.

This chapter explains the ways in which numbers are used in business. It starts by helping you to find out the types of calculations you can do already without help and those where you might have problems. New types of calculations are introduced with:

a an explanation of when these are used in business
b a worked example section which explains how to do them (if this is appropriate)
c some practice exercises
d business applications exercises.

At the end of the chapter is a handy reference guide. This contains a brief summary of how to do all the different types of calculations contained in this chapter in addition to those you should already know. You can use it at any time for quick and easy reference.

CALCULATIONS YOU SHOULD BE ABLE TO DO NOW

You should be able to do all these calculations in your head. Try them – then check your answers on a calculator.

1	$22 + 10 =$	**9**	$31 + 62 =$
2	$14 + 28 =$	**10**	$71 + 19 =$
3	$52 - 21 =$	**11**	$65 - 8 =$
4	$94 - 56 =$	**12**	$82 - 11 =$
5	$7 \times 10 =$	**13**	$8 \times 5 =$
6	$6 \times 9 =$	**14**	$2 \times 6 =$
7	$30 \div 5 =$	**15**	$49 \div 7 =$
8	$81 \div 9 =$	**16**	$92 \div 2 =$

17	$11 + 5 =$	**21**	$3 \times 9 =$
18	$18 + 53 =$	**22**	$5 \times 4 =$
19	$37 - 15 =$	**23**	$18 \div 3 =$
20	$42 - 31 =$	**24**	$56 \div 8 =$

If you have any problems, either practise more or have a word with your tutor.

DID YOU KNOW?

1 Sometimes special words are used when working with numbers.

- To find the **difference** between two numbers subtract the smaller from the larger.
- To find the **product** of two numbers multiply one by the other.
- The **square** of a number is the result when you multiply a number by itself. 2 squared is written as 2^2 and is 2×2 (= 4), 5 squared is written as 5^2 and is 5×5 (= 25) and so on.

2 When you are adding or subtracting numbers on paper, make sure you line up the numbers – hundreds under hundreds, tens under tens, units under units. Decimal points must *always* be aligned one under the other. You can fill in any blank spaces on the right of the decimal point with a nought if this helps you.

$$261.2$$
$$\underline{324.0}$$
$$\underline{585.2}$$

3 Don't get confused if you are writing a long number which needs noughts inserting in the middle (e.g. three million four hundred and twelve). Think about how many digits are required. If the word 'million' is used you have at least *seven* digits to write and some of these may be noughts (e.g. if no 'thousands' are mentioned). The figure above has three noughts and is written as 3 000 412.

4 Figures which no one can read are no use to anyone! *Make sure you write clearly!*

Activity

What else should you be able to do now?

Calculators are very useful for working out more difficult calculations. However, it is important that you are able to do some calculations either in your head or on paper. Try the following and see how you get on. Use a pen and paper if you want to.

If you have any problems, refer to the reference guide at the end of this chapter to see where you went wrong.

1 State which of the following divides exactly by 3: 9, 18, 20, 32, 66, 94

2 Add 314.32, 60, 4038.220 and 172.

3 Write down the answer to $64 \div 2$.

4 What do you multiply by 7 to make 49?

5 Write eighteen thousand and three in figures.

6 What is the difference between 4×8 and 40?

7 What is 6^2?

8 Calculate 182.32×62.90.

9 Divide £189.20 by 215.

10 Solve $1624 \div 29$.

11 Calculate $3 + 10 - 7$.

12 Solve $22 \div 5$ and give your answer as a decimal.

• DATA IN BUSINESS •

Data refers to facts and figures in their raw state, which have still to be processed. If you carry out a survey to count the number of cars and vans which pass your house each day, the numbers you write down are data. You need to **process** this data to turn it into useful **information**. Therefore, if you discover that Wednesday and Friday are the two busiest days, this is useful information you have obtained by using the data you acquired.

In business you will know the context you are working in. In this situation:

- numerical data is gathered and processed
- situations are represented or problems are tackled
- the resulting information is interpreted and presented.

Evidence Assignment 14A

Rachel Collinge works in the production control office. She is asked to find out why deadlines are not being met which means that customers do not receive the goods on time. The production supervisor says that the main problem is an increase in machine breakdowns.

She checks the records for each machine over the last two months and finds that most of the breakdowns occur on three machines. She counts the number of times each machine stopped and for how long. She also notes the reasons. Finally she summarises the data on a chart and shows it to the maintenance supervisor. She explains that three machines are causing most of the problems.

1 In the situation above when was Rachel:

    a gathering data

    b processing data

    c tackling a problem

    d representing a situation

    e interpreting data

    f presenting data?

2 What events could take place in each of the following situations which would involve activities (a) – (f) above?

- investigating accident statistics
- checking bad debtors
- identifying how many orders each customer places.

In each case assume that a senior manager has asked for an investigation.

FRACTIONS, DECIMALS, PERCENTAGES AND RATIOS

All of these types of number are used to describe or analyse business situations. Quite often the same situation can be described using any one of these four methods. For example:

100 g of baked beans contains 5 g of protein.
This can be written in different ways:

- $\frac{1}{20}$ th of a tin of baked beans is protein.
- Every gram of baked beans contains 0.05 g of protein.
- 5% (or 5 per cent) of baked beans is protein.
- The *ratio* of protein to other ingredients in baked beans is 1:19.

Sometimes one way of describing a situation is better than another. For example, which do you think sounds better?

    'We've captured 50% of the market'   or
    'We've captured $\frac{1}{2}$ of the market'.

Most people would think the first option was correct and certainly it is the most commonly used. You need to know *all* the different methods so you can use the most appropriate in each situation and convert from one to another if necessary.

FRACTIONS

In the business world fractions are not often used. For example, you would be very unlikely to say that $\frac{460}{1720}$ of the workforce is male (even if it is!). Normally a decimal figure or a percentage would be used since these are easier to understand at a glance (unless the fraction is a very common one, e.g. a half or a quarter). A further advantage is that decimal numbers can be entered on a calculator if you have to carry out another calculation, whereas fractions cannot. It therefore helps if you know how to convert a fraction into a decimal in the first place.

Converting fractions to decimals

In fractions, the number on top is called the **numerator** and the one underneath the **denominator**:

$$\frac{2}{5} \quad \begin{array}{l} \text{numerator} \\ \text{denominator} \end{array}$$

To convert from a fraction to a decimal all you have to do is to divide the denominator into the numerator. Therefore $\frac{2}{5}$ as a decimal is:

$$\frac{2}{5} = 2 \div 5 = 0.4$$

The next step could be to convert from decimal figures into percentages (see page 426).

Activity

Convert the following fractions into decimals:

1	$\frac{3}{4}$	**3**	$\frac{25}{7}$	**5**	$\frac{8}{3}$
2	$\frac{7}{8}$	**4**	$\frac{13}{2}$	**6**	$\frac{4}{8}$

DID YOU KNOW?

If the numerator and the denominator of a fraction will both divide by the same number, then the fraction will 'cancel down' to make it easier to work with. For example $\frac{80}{100}$ is really $\frac{4}{5}$ (both numbers divide by 20).

Working with fractions

Adding and subtracting

You can only add or subtract fractions if their denominators are the same. You should already know this. If you don't know what to do refer to the quick reference section on page 425.

Multiplying and dividing

You should already know how to multiply by a fraction. To divide by a fraction you simply turn it upside down and multiply. (See quick reference section, page 425.)

DID YOU KNOW?

If you are working with a whole number and fractions together you should put the whole number over '1' to make it easy to work with:

$$20 \times \frac{6}{7} = \frac{20}{1} \times \frac{6}{7} = \frac{120}{7}$$

You can tell if you answer is greater than 1 because the numerator will be larger than the denominator, as in the example above. Convert this by dividing the denominator into the numerator and writing any remainder as a fraction:

$$\frac{120}{7} = 17\frac{1}{7}$$

Activity

Work out the following. Make sure you always check your answer to see if the fraction can be cancelled down.

1 $\frac{2}{3} + \frac{1}{2} =$

2 $\frac{7}{8} - \frac{3}{8} =$

3 $1\frac{5}{6} + 2\frac{8}{9} + 3\frac{2}{3} =$

4 $\frac{4}{5} - \frac{1}{4} =$

5 $10\frac{1}{2} + 1\frac{1}{3} - 2\frac{1}{4} =$

6 $\frac{1}{2} \times \frac{2}{3} \times \frac{3}{4} =$

7 $\frac{7}{20} - \frac{3}{10} =$

8 $2\frac{5}{8} - 3\frac{1}{2} =$

DID YOU KNOW?

1 The word 'of' means 'multiply'. If you are asked to find $\frac{1}{2}$ of 240 then your 'sum' is:

$$\frac{1}{2} \times \frac{240}{1} = \frac{240}{2} = 120$$

2 *Time* can be expressed as a fraction (e.g. $5\frac{1}{2}$ hours). In this case you must be careful to remember that you are dealing with a fraction of *60*; i.e. $5\frac{1}{2}$ = 5 hours 30 minutes.

Activity

Business application exercises

1 At inspection on a production line, 105 products are checked and 15 found to be faulty. What fraction of products is faulty?

2 A bank employee joins a pension scheme. He is told that his final pension will be $\frac{1}{60}$ th of his best year's salary multiplied by the number of years he works for the bank. If he works there for 30 years, and his final year's salary is £40 000, what will his pension be?

3 A mechanic for a photocopying company is paid a basic wage of £3.60 an hour. He is paid time and a third for week-day overtime and time and a half for working on a Saturday. Last week he worked his basic 38 hour week, six hours overtime mid-week and four hours on Saturday. What was his wage?

4 Your boss is ordering new carpet for his office which is $7\frac{1}{2}$ metres long and $6\frac{1}{4}$ metres wide. How much carpet does he require? (Note: area = length × width)

5 A computer shop is reducing the prices of all printers by a third for a limited period. How much would you pay for a printer normally priced at £314.20?

6 Your boss is driving on the Continent next week. He knows that a kilometre is $\frac{5}{8}$ of a mile. He works out his journey on the map and it totals 2336 kilometres. How far is this in miles?

7 A businessman travelled from his office in London to an office in New York on business. The total journey took him $10\frac{1}{2}$ hours. He spent $\frac{3}{4}$ of the time on the plane, $\frac{1}{8}$ of the time travelling by road and the remaining time waiting at airports.

a For how long was he on the plane?
b For how long was he travelling by road?
c What fraction of his journey was spent waiting at airports?

8 A businessman is told by his accountant that his van will depreciate (i.e. go down in value) by one quarter in the first year and a further one fifth *of the original price* for each of the next three years. The van costs £12 000 and the businessman keeps it for $2\frac{1}{2}$ years. How much is it worth when he sells it?

DID YOU KNOW?

Sometimes fractions are used to give approximate information. For example if, out of £10 100 worth of stock in a food store, £957's worth is found to be past the sell-by date, someone could say 'One tenth of the stock will have to be thrown away.' In other words, $\frac{957}{10\,100}$ is near enough to $\frac{1000}{10000}$ o be able to call this $\frac{1}{10}$.

Sometimes people working in business only need to know approximate information. If someone asked you how long it would take you to finish a task they wouldn't expect you to say $\frac{1}{11}$ minutes and 20 seconds! It would be quite enough if you said 'about 10 minutes'.

On other occasions complete accuracy is vital. Invoices must be calculated accurately or the business will lose money and/or upset its customers. You will naturally expect your pay to have been calculated accurately!

DECIMALS

There are two main uses for decimal figures. First of all, many things which need to be measured can't be described in whole numbers. For example, the length of a room would probably not be a whole number of metres. Equally the weight of potatoes pre-packed in a bag is unlikely to be exactly 5 kg – it may be 5.02 kg or 5.03 kg.

The second main use of decimals in business is for money. Two pounds and twenty pence is written as £2.20, five pounds and three pence as £5.03 and so on. In each case the amount in pence is a decimal.

Rounding decimals

Quite often a calculation will give an answer which has several numbers after the decimal point. For example, £21.22 shared among five people is:

£21.22 ÷ 5 = £4.244 each.

For most uses, two figures after the decimal point is accurate enough. In the above example you can't give someone 0.4 pence. Changing a number with several figures after the decimal point is called **rounding.**

The rule for rounding is as follows:

.5 and above - round *up*
.4 and below - round *down*
e.g. £3.48 ÷ 5 = 0.696 = 0.70 (rounded up)

If your answer contains several more decimal places than you need, then always use the figure to the right of the number you need:

£72.34_7_1 = £72.35 (rounded to two decimal places)

DID YOU KNOW?

When you deal with large amounts of money in business it is usual to omit the pence (i.e. to drop the decimals and round *up*). On VAT forms, for instance, the total amounts of purchases and sales are only entered in whole numbers (e.g. £12 542 *not* £12 541.83). In some cases figures might even be rounded to the nearest hundred or thousand. A company would not say it had sales of £253 251.60. What would it say?

Activity

Round the following to two decimal places:

1 74.892 **2** 18.977 **3** 16.6558

Calculate the following and round your answers to two decimal places:

4 £142.68 ÷ 15 **5** £63.70 ÷ 4 **6** £27.42 ÷ 4

Activity

Business applications exercises

1 Your office buys 8 reams of paper at £4.26 a ream, 10 folders at 25p each and 1 dozen pens at 11p each. What is the total cost of the stationery order?

2 Your boss is visiting America on business and wishes to change £200 into dollars. The exchange rate is currently $1.55 to the pound. How many dollars will he receive?

3 A solicitor is drawing up a will for a client who wants his total assets to be divided among his five children. His house is worth £115 000, he has £15 000 in a building society savings account and £38 000 worth of shares. His remaining assets are valued at £28 000. If the value of his shares remains unchanged, how much will each of his children receive?

4 A town hall employee is allowed to claim 38.4p a mile if he uses his own car for business. In one week he covers 240 miles. What will be his claim?

5 Carpet tiles cost £12.54 each and 143 are required to cover the floor in reception. How much is the total cost of covering the reception area?

6 You know that an inch = 2.54 centimetres. What is the size in centimetres of:

a a $3\frac{1}{2}$ " computer disk
b a $5\frac{1}{4}$ " computer disk?

7 A company charges 2.5p per copy for photocopying. What is the cost of making 542 copies?

8 A paint company produces paint at the rate of 840.48 litres an hour. How much will be produced:

a in a single shift of 8 hours
b in three days, if the company works two shifts a day
c each week from Monday to Friday? Note there is only one shift on a Friday.

PERCENTAGES

If the amount of income you spend on clothes is £23 out of every £100, you could say that you spend 23% of your money on clothes. Percentages are used to compare one number with another. For example, if a small shop makes a profit of £20 000 in one year on sales of £100 000 then the profit on sales is 20%. A supermarket selling a similar range of goods could make a profit of £1 000 000 on sales of £10 000 000. This would be a profit of 10%. In this sense the small shop makes twice as much profit on sales as the supermarket.

DID YOU KNOW?

The situation described above is not unusual! However, before you start thinking all small shopkeepers must be millionaires – remember which shop makes the most actual profit!

The percentage of a number

You may be asked to carry out a percentage calculation where you are given the percentage and asked to find the number; e.g. find 12% of 340 or find 15% of £60.

The easy way to do this is to remember that 12% means 12 in every hundred (which is the same as $\frac{12}{100}$):

$$12\% \text{ of } 340 = \frac{12}{100} \times 340 = \frac{4080}{100} = 40.8$$

$$15\% \text{ of } £60 = \frac{15}{100} \times £60 = £9$$

On a calculator you can press the % key. Simply enter the two numbers as a multiplication and press the % key. If you don't have a % key, multiply the two numbers together and divide by 100.

DID YOU KNOW?

If you have a fraction which will cancel down – such as that in the calculation above – it is always easier to do this *first*. Then you are working with smaller numbers.

Activity

Calculate the following to two decimal places:

1 16% of 25   **2** 112% of 80

3	22% of 1830	**7**	168% of £426
4	30% of 180	**8**	16% of £93.24
5	62% of £98.50	**9**	74% of 2354 kg
6	$12\frac{1}{2}$% of 110 kg	**10**	81% of £12.30

A quantity as a percentage

On other occasions you may be given two numbers and asked to find what percentage one is of the other, e.g. what is 24 as a percentage of 400? This is done by showing the two numbers as a fraction and then converting them to a percentage by multiplying by 100%:

$$\frac{24}{400} \times 100\% = 6\%$$

On a calculator you would enter the top number (24), press ÷, then enter the bottom number (400) and press %.

Activity

Express the following as percentages. Round to two decimal places where necessary.

1 18 as a percentage of 60.
2 40p as a percentage of £3.20.
3 0.134 as a percentage of 5.
4 135 as a percentage of 400.
5 90 kg as a percentage of 2500 kg.
6 £85 as a percentage of £50.
7 950 as a percentage of 500.
8 106 as a percentage of 108.
9 12.5 as a percentage of 20.25.
10 £36.40 as a percentage of £108.20.

DID YOU KNOW?

The phrase 'per cent' originates from the fact that another way of saying one hundred is to say a century (as with runs in cricket, years etc.) or centum. Originally the phrase 23 per centum was used – now shortened to 23 per cent or 23%.

Interest rates

When we invest money in a bank or building society we are paid **interest**. Similarly, if we borrow money we are charged interest. Knowing about percentages enables you to calculate the interest you will receive (or will be charged).

There are two types of interest – simple interest and compound interest. In this section we deal only with simple interest.

Imagine you have invested £500 in a building society and the current interest rate is 12%. How much interest are you owed? You can calculate this as follows:

Interest paid = 12% of £500

$$\frac{12}{100} \times 500 = £60$$

DID YOU KNOW?

Interest charged on loans by companies has to be clearly stated to the borrower. This is done by stating the Annual Percentage Rate (APR) charged on the loan. It is calculated by adding together the interest due on the outstanding loan and administrative charges.

The lower the APR, the cheaper the loan. Always make sure you look for the APR and ignore the monthly rate (which looks much cheaper) when calculating how much interest you would pay.

Activity

Business application exercises

1 There are 350 employees working in the offices of your company. 12% work in purchasing, 24% in office administration, 20% in sales, 14% in personnel, 18% in accounts, 2% in transport and 10% in production. From these figures calculate the number of employees in each department.

2 A company gives discounts of 5%, 8% and 12% to grade A, B and C customers respectively. How much discount will each of the following be allowed?

- C. Jones – grade A – order £126
- J. Roberts – grade B – order £230.10
- B. Clements – grade C – order £414.50

3 A survey in your office regarding a proposed vending machine has shown that out of 80 people in the office, 33 want it to provide coffee, 21 prefer tea, 11 like orange juice and eight consider hot chocolate their favourite. Five people don't mind and two said they wouldn't use it anyway as they dislike vending machines. Express all the preferences as percentages and round these to the nearest whole number so that you total 100%.

4 Your friend has £650 in the bank. How much would she receive in interest if the rate was:

a 8% **c** 12.75%

b 11.5% **d** 13.75%?

5 You need to borrow £250. The following are the APR figures for the sources from which you could borrow. How much interest would you repay in one year in each case?

a Company A – APR 41.5%
b Company B – APR 35%
c Company C – APR 29.8%
d Company D – APR 24.65%

Value Added Tax (VAT)

Being able to calculate percentages is obviously essential to calculate VAT.

DID YOU KNOW?

To calculate VAT quickly *without* a calculator (e.g. 17.5% of £60) you should:

- find 10% (divide by 10)   = £6
- halve your answer (= 5%)   = £3
- halve your answer again (= 2.5%) = £1.50
- add your answers together (= 17.5%) = £10.50

Obviously an organisation will send an account for the total *plus* VAT. Under normal circumstances you would calculate the amount of VAT and then add it on. To find VAT on a calculator you would enter the original amount,

press the × key and then enter the VAT rate followed by the percentage key. Then add the original amount:

£60 × 17.5% = £10.50
£60 + £10.50 = £70.50.

DID YOU KNOW

1 If you want to calculate the total quickly on some calculators, then instead of pressing the × key, press the + key; e.g. the plus VAT price of £60 is:

60 + 17.5% = £70.50.

Test if this works on your calculator!

2 If it does, then the same short-cut can also be used for finding an amount *less* a percentage. Simply press the − key instead; e.g.

£30 − 10% = £27.

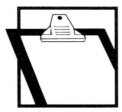

Activity

Business application exercises

1 *Quickly* work out what the VAT is on the following amounts *without* using a calculator.

a £10 **c** £42
b £180 **d** £28

2 How much VAT would an organisation add on to each of the following amounts?

a £420.40 **d** £25.58
b £18.80 **e** £610
c £116.80 **f** £85.25

3 Re-enter the figures above and calculate the total amount of each account.

VAT inclusive accounts

In some cases the amount paid on an account is *inclusive* of VAT (e.g. petrol). If a petty cash voucher is submitted for a VAT-inclusive item then the amount of VAT has to be calculated so that it can be recorded separately on the analysis sheet (see Section 3, Financial Transactions, page 218).

Calculating VAT on inclusive accounts – worked example

Work this out by using the following formula:

$$\frac{\text{rate of VAT}}{\text{VAT rate} + 100} \times \text{amount spent}$$

To see how this works, imagine a representative has spent £88 on petrol. VAT is 17.5%.

$$\frac{17.5}{17.5 + 100} \times £88 = \frac{17.5}{117.5} \times £88 = £13.106 = £13.11$$

Calculating the exclusive price – worked example

This is worked out *either* by subtracting the amount of VAT you have just calculated from the total paid (£88 – £13.11 = £74.89) *or* by using the following formula:

$$\frac{100}{\text{VAT rate} + 100} = \frac{100}{117.5} = \frac{40}{47} \times \text{amount paid}$$

This is a better system as it gives you a double check on your first figure, as obviously the VAT + the exclusive price must equal the total amount.

Changing VAT rates

The formula will operate even if VAT rates change. All you need to do is to substitute the new figures. For example, if VAT went up to 20% the formula to calculate the VAT would be:

$$\frac{20}{\text{VAT rate} + 100} = \frac{20}{20 + 100} = \frac{20}{120} = \frac{1}{6}$$

2 Calculate the cancelled down formulae if VAT was lowered to:

a 5% **b** 10% **c** 15%

RATIOS

In the example given earlier, where the small shop was twice as profitable as the supermarket, it could be said that the profitability ratio was 2:1. If you were diluting concentrated orange squash a ratio of 1 part squash to 5 parts water could be used – a ratio of 1:5. Usually ratios are whole numbers, but not always. You may, for instance, see the ratio 1.5 to 1 (which could also be expressed as 3:2).

DID YOU KNOW?

1 You can cancel down ratios in the same way that you cancel down fractions. Rather than say 24:12 it would be better to say 2:1.

2 Fractions, ratios and percentages are very similar. For example, if $\frac{3}{4}$ of the population drink mostly coffee and $\frac{1}{4}$ drink tea, this could also be written as

coffee drinkers:total population = 3:4,
or $\frac{3}{4} \times 100\%$ of the population drink coffee
$\Rightarrow$ 75% of the population drink coffee.

Activity

Business application exercises

1 Calculate the VAT and the exclusive price on each of these VAT inclusive amounts (to two decimal places):

a £65.55   **d** £17.63
b £97.75   **e** £64.50
c £35.65   **f** £22.60

Activity

1 Convert $\frac{1}{5}$ into a ratio and a percentage.

2 25% of a class drink Pepsi, the rest drink Coke.

a What is the ratio of Coke to Pepsi drinkers?
b What fraction of the class drinks Pepsi?

3 The ratio of men to women attending a football match is 9:1. Express this both as a fraction *and* a percentage.

Activity

Business application exercises

1 A dye is made up in the ratio of 2:3:1 of white, navy blue and yellow. If 600 litres of dye are required, what quantity of each colour will be used?

2 Your company employs 72 men and 48 women. What is the ratio of men to women?

3 The ratio of the time taken to key in graphics on a computer and to print them out is 17:2. If it takes 2 hours 16 minutes to key in the data, how long will it take to print?

4 In a single day, 361 people visit a fast food restaurant but 215 arrive during the busy period between 5 p.m. and 7 p.m. Work this out as a ratio to two decimal places. Then express it as a percentage and as a fraction using an appropriate approximation.

Evidence Assignment 14B

You work for J. Marlor plc, a company which manufactures and distributes cosmetics. You are employed as an assistant in the administration department and your work entails a considerable amount of number work. You have been given the following tasks to undertake by Jean Miller, your supervisor.

a Calculate your answers carefully and check you are correct.

b Write a memo to Jean Miller giving her the information she requires. Set this out as numbered points to match the questions below.

c Retype the price list with the amended figures in numerical order with the information displayed attractively.

1 A new photocopier was installed recently. The cost per copy is 1.1p. Last month the administration department made 6294 copies. How much is your department's account?

2 Two reps have submitted petty cash claims for petrol. In both cases VAT is *inclusive*. Jeremy Barnes spent £42 on petrol last month and Claire Stevens spent £68. Calculate the VAT in each case.

3 The price list in Figure 14.1 needs amending as Marlor's are offering a special discount to all agents next month. All goods which have codes starting with the figure 1 will be reduced by 5%, those with the figure 3 will be reduced by 7.5% and those with the figure 5 will be reduced by 12.5%. Adjust the prices and type out an updated version of the list *in numerical order*.

COSMETICS PRICE LIST OF J. MARLOR PLC		
Code	*Item*	*Price*
1098	Eye shadow	£3.50
3029	Concealer	£5.50
5090	Professional brushes	£6.50
1030	Lipstick and lip gloss	£6.75
5229	Lip brush	£5.00
3997	Blusher	£3.95
3109	Face powder	£5.70
3581	Foundation	£6.95
1779	Mascara	£5.80
1610	Eye pencils	£3.95
5003	Skin care products	£7.50
5813	Cosmetic sponge	£1.20

Figure 14.1

4 Jean Miller is having her office redecorated and has decided on carpet tiles for the floor. She cannot make up her mind between two types of tile. Type A cost £12 each + VAT and are 1 m². Type B cost £17 each + VAT and are $1\frac{1}{2}$ m². Her office is 6 metres long and $8\frac{1}{4}$ metres wide. Calculate the cost of using both types of carpet tile.

5 Jean Miller is assessing the popularity of the vending machine. Out of 500 employees she has assessed that:

- 250 prefer coffee
- 100 regularly drink tea
- 75 prefer cold drinks
- 50 like hot chocolate
- the rest are non-users
- the ratio of men to women users is 2:1

a How many men use the machine?
b How many women use the machine?
c Calculate the usage of the machine both as fractions *and* as percentages.
d What is the ratio of coffee drinkers to tea drinkers?
e What is the ratio of coffee drinkers to hot chocolate drinkers?

f Last month 1800 cups of coffee were sold.

   i What would you expect the sales of *all* the other drinks to be?

   ii If all hot drinks cost 25p and all cold drinks cost 20p, how much would have been spent in total?

   iii How much would the company have to pay the vending machine company in VAT?

FORMULAE, EQUATIONS, DIAGRAMS AND PROBABILITIES

FORMULAE

A formula (plural is formulae but sometimes you may see it as formulas) is a set of words, figures or symbols that gives a rule or statement that can be used again and again in similar situations.

One of the most simple formulae was given to you on page 393 – area = length × breadth (or width). This formula applies to finding the area of both squares and rectangles. It is written as follows:

$$A = l \times b \text{ or } A = lb$$

You use a formula by substituting numbers for the letters. The one above can always be used to calculate area. If a piece of paper measures 6 cm × 9 cm then, by substituting the numbers in the formula, you find the answer:

$$A = l \times b \qquad A = 6 \times 9 \qquad \text{Area} = 54 \text{ cm}^2$$

DID YOU KNOW?

If two letters are placed immediately next to each other then this means *multiply*. There is therefore no need to keep writing $A = l \times b$ because $A = lb$ means the same thing!

Constructing a formula

You can make your own formula to help you when you are doing conversions. You should already know that

1 inch ≈ 2.54 cm from work you have done at school. You could represent this in a formula by

- representing inches by the letter x
- representing centimetres by the letter y

Your formula would be $2.54 \times x = y$, therefore $y = 2.54x$.

Worked example

A marketing department calculated the total cost of producing a booklet by adding together the cost of the copywriter at £25 per hour, a graphic designer who charged £50 per hour, and a printer who charged £40 an hour. They could:

- represent the copywriter by the letter x
- represent the designer by the letter y
- represent the printer by the letter z
- represent the total cost by the letter C

to construct the following formula:

$$C = 25x + 50y + 40z.$$

If the booklet took 4 hours to write, 3 hours to illustrate and half an hour to print, the total cost would be calculated by the using the formula as follows:

$$C = 25 \times 4 + 50 \times 3 + 40 \times 0.5$$
$$= 100 + 150 + 20 = £270$$

Transposing formulae

A formula can be transposed (rearranged) to be used in a different way. The formula for area was given as $A = lb$. In this form, A is the **subject** of the formula, i.e. the quantity which will be found by using the formula. If you transpose the formula you can make another quantity the subject of the formula. For example, from $A = lb$ you can get:

$$l = \frac{A}{b}$$

If you know that the area of a room is 30 m² and the breath is 6 m, you can use the formula to calculate the length:

$$l = \frac{30}{6}$$

Therefore $l = 5$ metres

Activity

Practise your skills

1 a Transpose the formula for area to make breadth the subject.

b Use your formula to calculate the breadth of a rectangular field which has an area of 5400 m² and is 90 metres long.

2 a Volume of boxes and cubes is calculated by multiplying length × breadth × height. Write this as a formula.

b Use your formula to calculate the volume of a cupboard which measures 1.2 metres in length, 0.7 metres in breadth and is 1.9 metres high.

Activity

Business application exercises

1 A photocopier uses toner (a powder form of ink) at the rate of 3 grams for every 1000 copies. Express this as a formula and then calculate the amount of toner required to make 15 000 copies.

2 a The cost of decorating a room is calculated by adding together the number of tins of paint used, the number of rolls of wallpaper and the time spent by the decorator. Paint costs £5 a tin, wallpaper is £14 a roll and the decorator's time is charged at £30 an hour. Write a formula to represent these charges.

b Use your formula to calculate the cost of decorating a room where three tins of paint are used, eight rolls of wallpaper and it takes 12 hours to complete.

3 The formula for calculating simple interest is

$$I = \frac{PRT}{100}$$

where P = the principal (i.e. amount borrowed)
R = rate per cent
T = time in years

a Use the formula to calculate the interest if £5000 is borrowed at a rate of 12% over 5 years.

b Transpose the formula to make T the subject.

EQUATIONS

A statement which shows that one quantity is equal to another is called an **equation**. You have already met some examples; e.g.

1 inch = 2.54 cm
$A = lb$

There is very little difference between a formula and an equation. Usually equations are used to help you find an 'unknown' figure. In an equation, it is usual to call your unknown figures by a letter, usually 'x', 'y' or 'z' (or a, b, c). You can then use the rules which apply to equations to find your answer.

If you are given the equation $4x = 20$, then from this you can calculate that $x = 5$ by making x the subject of your equation:

$$4x = 20$$

$$x = \frac{20}{4} = 5.$$

Rules of equations

1 If a quantity is connected to one side or the other by a plus or minus sign it can change to the *other side* provided you remember to **change the sign**. Therefore a plus becomes a minus and a minus a plus.

Suppose you were asked to solve the equation $x + 5 = 12$. To find the value of x you need it to be the only quantity in front of the equals sign. For x to stand alone you *must* take off 5. What you do to one side of an equation you must do to the other:

$$x + 5 \,(-5) = 12 \,(-5)$$
$$x = 12 - 5 = 7$$

In short – you have moved the 5 to the other side of the equals sign and changed its sign.

2 In an equation such as $3x = 4y + 2$ to get x on its own, you need to divide the right-hand side by 3 to get $x = \frac{1}{3}(4y + 2)$. Similarly for an equation such as $\frac{x}{y} = z + 2$ you need to multiply the right-hand side by y to get $x = y(z + 2)$.

3 Equations can be simplified by adding together or subtracting **like terms**. For instance, $6x + 5x + 3x$ can be simplified to $14x$.

4 Unlike terms cannot be simplified. You cannot add $3y$ to $4x$!

Activity

1 Simplify $10x + 6x + 9x - 2x$.
2 Simplify $x + 4 + 8 = 2y$.
3 Simplify $y \times y \times y = x \times x$.
4 Solve $\frac{x}{4} = 12$.

5 Solve $2x + 1 = 7$

6 If $x = 2$, $y = 2$ and $z = 4$, solve

a $x + y + z$
b $5x - 3y$
c $\frac{xz}{y}$

Activity

Business application exercises

1 A company deposits £x in the bank each week for a year. The second year it increases its deposits to £y per week.

a Write an equation to show the amount of money in the bank after 2 years (ignoring interest).
b If $x = 80$ and $y = 100$, how much has the company saved in 2 years?

2 a A business sells £x per month and spends £y per week. Write an equation to show the amount of profit in one year.
b If $x = 4400$ and $y = 600$, how much profit will have been made?

Activity

Try this with a friend. Ask him or her to think of a number between one and five and then follow these steps:

multiply it by 2
add on 4
take away the number first thought of
add on 3
take away 6
take away the number first thought of
add on 5
divide by 2.

Now the number in your friend's head should be 3!

Does this work for any number? Suppose your friend just started with x ... do this as a sum on paper.

Can you now improve on this fun sum and make it even more complicated?

DIAGRAMS AND CHARTS

'A picture is worth a thousand words.' This saying neatly gives the reason why information in the form of numbers can be easier to take in at a glance if a diagram can be used. Diagrams can include

- line graphs
- bar charts
- pie charts
- pictograms
- flow charts.

All these are covered in the Core Skills chapter on Communications (pages 351–389).

Go back to Evidence Assignment 14B and choose an appropriate visual format to display the information about the vending machine. (Ignore the ratio of men to women users.)

PROBABILITIES

In many situations in business, people have to estimate what may happen in the future. The marketing manager has to forecast sales, the production manager assesses the risk of a machine breaking down when accepting an urgent order. In other words, future situations often have an element of risk involved. People have to assess the risk using numbers and this is known as **probability**.

An obvious example of probability is when someone tosses a coin. The chances of heads or tails is even, and this would be a probability of 0.5 heads, 0.5 tails on each occasion when a coin is tossed.

Using probabilities

Probability is expressed as a number between 0 and 1. The first, 0, is the certainty that something will *not* happen. The second, 1, is the certainty that something *will* happen.

Assessing probabilities

In business, probabilities are **assessed** or **estimate**d. For example, the production manager referred to earlier may think that the probability of a machine breaking down is 0.1. In other words there is a one in ten chance that it will happen. He or she will make this assessment based on a knowledge of the machine and its maintenance history.

Worked examples

The following are examples of events where probabilities are known.

1 A machine producing CDs is faulty and out of 1000 CDs in a particular batch, 150 have faults resulting in poor sound quality.

The probability of one CD taken at random from the batch being faulty is therefore:

$$\frac{150}{1000} = 0.15.$$

2 Records show that a certain photocopier breaks down once in every 20 working days. The probability of it breaking down on any particular day is:

$$\frac{1}{20} = 0.05.$$

Combined probabilities

The main point with probabilities is to identify where two events are *independent* of each other. For example, think back to the case of the batch of 1000 CDs containing 150 faulty ones. Say some of these left the factory and were distributed to the retailers by mistake. It is likely that only *some* customers (say half) would notice and complain. It may be that some people aren't too fussy about sound quality. The important point is that the proportion of faulty CDs which exists, and the taste of customers are not connected, so these two situations are called **exclusive** events.

The rule is that the probability of *both* events happening is found by multiplying the probabilities together. In the case of the CDs this is worked out as follows:

probability of a CD being faulty = 0.15
probability of a customer noticing = 0.5

therefore the probability of a customer complaining is $0.15 \times 0.5 = 0.075$.

Worked examples

1 An office worker is regularly late once every two weeks (i.e. 1 in 10 times) and another once a week (i.e. 1 in 5 times). The probability of them both being late on the same day is:

$$0.1 \times 0.2 = 0.02.$$

2 A marketing manager estimates that two new products, launched into different markets, have probabilities of 0.5 and 0.8 of being successful (i.e. making a profit). The probability of them *both* succeeding is:

$$0.6 \times 0.8 = 0.48$$

Activity

1 You have a faulty alarm clock which fails to wake you on time one morning in every ten. What is the probability of your being late for your first class?

2 You are going on holiday for two weeks in March to a place where there is a 1 in 5 chance that there will be no sunshine at all. Your friend is going away at the same time to a place where there is a 1 in 2 chance of no sun. What is the probability:

a that you will return with a suntan?
b that she will return with a suntan?
c that you *both* will return with a tan?

3 You and your friend have each bought a ticket for a raffle for which 2000 tickets have been sold and there are 20 prizes.

a What is the probability that you will win a prize?
b What is the probability that you *both* will win prizes?

Evidence Assignment 14C

You work for Eastern Insurance Brokers as a clerk in the general office. The manager, Tim Clark, has asked you to undertake several calculations for him and, in each case, to give him your answers in a short, typed memo.

1 Tim Clark has been looking at the types of insurance sold by the brokers for inclusion in an advertising brochure. He has calculated that:

35% is car insurance
27% is household contents insurance
23% is house buildings insurance
10% is travel insurance
5% is for miscellaneous insurance cover.

He has asked you to design a pie chart, either by hand or on computer, to illustrate these figures. Make sure you have a clear key.

2 The brochure will be produced by an advertising company who charge £30 an hour for copywriting, £60 an hour for artwork, £35 an hour for printing and £35 an hour for consultancy fees.

a Construct a formula to show this.
b Tim Clark has the choice of two styles of brochure. The first will have more text and fewer graphics and the second will be the reverse.

Type 1 will take six hours to write, two hours to illustrate, one hour to print. There will be three hours spent on consultancy.

Type 2 will take 4 hours to write, $3\frac{1}{4}$ hours to illustrate, $1\frac{1}{2}$ hours to print and $2\frac{3}{4}$ hours consultancy will be required.

Use your formula to calculate the cost of each brochure.

3 Tim Clark regularly travels to London by train but grumbles because the train is often late. He has worked out that on the last 120 journeys the train has been late 45 times! He has been asked to attend a very important meeting next Monday and can't work out whether to travel down that morning or go the day before and stay overnight – which will cost him more. He knows that only if the train is punctual can he arrive at the meeting on time.

a What is the probability of his being punctual?
b What would you advise him to do?

4 On checking the files, Tim Clark has discovered that out of 251 drivers of high performance cars in the age-group 18–25 years, 172 have at least one accident claim in a year. He has asked you to estimate the probability of a single driver putting in a claim.

UNITS OF MEASUREMENT – CONVERSION

Have you noticed that some petrol stations give the price of petrol in gallons and some give it in litres? As time goes by fewer and fewer will quote the price in gallons. At present some quote the price both ways to help people who are more familiar with the traditional 'gallons' of petrol than they are with litres.

In the same way, some people buy a bag of potatoes which they think of as being 5 lb in weight whereas it may be marked as 2.27 kg. Equally, most cars driven in Britain show the speedometer markings both in miles per hour and kilometres per hour.

Why do we have different systems of measurement? The answer is that they were developed in different countries before international trading began. There was therefore no need for them to have the same system. Out of all the systems which existed the main two which have survived are **metric** and **imperial**.

The metric system uses metres (length), grams (weight) and litres (volume). The imperial system uses yards (length), pounds (weight) and gallons (volume). The metric system came from France, the imperial system developed in Britain.

In the metric system measurement is in multiples of 10, 100 or 1000 on the basic unit; e.g.
1 kilometre = 1000 metres;
1 millilitre = one thousandth of a litre;
1 kilogram = 1000 grams.

In the imperial system there are different ratios between different units. For example, 12 inches in 1 foot, 14 lb (pounds) in one stone etc. This is very hard to remember.

Because of this the metric system is gradually becoming standard throughout the world, but the change in this country is very slow. So in business, you will find that *both* systems of measurement are used and it is important to be able to convert between the two.

When people have to convert from metric units to imperial units at work, they usually use a set of conversion tables. Have you got some or can you find them in the library?

DID YOU KNOW?

The metre is one ten millionth (what a fraction!) of the distance between the North Pole and the equator on a line which travels through Paris.

Activity

See if you can find out the connection between a metre and a krypton 86 atom!

LENGTH AND DISTANCE

You should already know that in the **metric system:**

10 millimetres (mm)	= 1 centimetre (cm)
100 cm	= 1 metre (m)
1000 m	= 1 kilometre (km)

In the **imperial** system:

12 inches (in)	= 1 foot (ft)
3 ft	= 1 yard (yd)
1760 yd	= 1 mile

Conversions

To be able to convert imperial to metric and vice versa you need to know equivalents. To two decimal places these are:

1 cm = 0.39 in	and	1 in = 2.54 cm
1 m = 1.09 yd	and	1 yd = 0.91 m
1 km = 0.62 miles	and	1 mile = 1.61 km

Worked examples

1 The length of a corridor is known to be 25.20 yards. A carpet firm supplies in metric length. How many metres of carpet are needed?

1 yd = 0.91 m
25.20 yd = 25.20 × 0.91 m = 22.93 m

2 A sales representative has to drive from Paris to Nice. On his map it shows this is a journey of 934 km. He has no 'feel' for the journey as he is used to miles. He also knows that he can average 55 mph. Tell him how far he

has to drive and how long the journey is likely to take him.

1 km = 0.62 miles
934 km = 934 × 0.62 = 579.08 = 580 miles
$\frac{580}{55}$ = 10 hours 54 minutes

Activity

Convert the following:
1   18 in to centimetres
2   15.20 km to miles
3   2 ft 6 in to millimetres
4   240 cm to yards and also to feet.

WEIGHT

You should know that in the **metric** system:

1000 grams (g) = 1 kilogram (kg – sometimes called 'kilo')
1000 kg   = 1 metric tonne (don't confuse this with 'ton' as used in the imperial system)

In the **imperial** system:

16 ounces (oz)	=	1 pound (lb)
14 lb	=	1 stone
8 stones	=	1 hundredweight (cwt)
20 cwt	=	1 ton

(Note that stones are rarely used for measurement of weight these days although older people may weigh themselves in stones and pounds.)

Conversions

1 g = 0.035 oz	and	1 oz = 28.35 g
1 kg = 2.21 lb	and	1 lb = 0.45 kg
1 tonne = 0.98 tons	and	1 ton = 1016.00 tonnes

Worked examples

1 An old machine is to be moved and the removal firm needs to know the weight in kilograms. A label on the machine gives its weight as 265 lb.

1 lb = 0.45 kg
265 lb = 265 × 0.45 kg = 119.25 kg.

2 Convert 5.5 ounces to grams.

1 oz = 28.35 g
5.5 oz = 5.5 × 28.35 g = 155.92 g.

The answer to question 1 above is probably far more precise than the information required by the removal firm. What figure would have been near enough?

Activity

Convert the following:
1   280 g to pounds
2   5 tons to tonnes
3   7 lb to kilograms
4   2.20 oz to grams.

VOLUME

You should know that in the **metric** system:

1000 millilitres (ml) = 1 litre (l)

In the **imperial** system:

20 fluid ounces (fl oz) = 1 pint
8 pints = 1 gallon

Conversions

1 ml = 0.09 fl oz	and	1 fl oz = 10.99 ml
1 litre = 0.22 gallons	and	1 gallon = 4.55 litres
1 litre = 1.76 pints	and	1 pint = 0.57 litres

Worked examples

1 The instruction manual for a machine says that it needs filling with oil and that its capacity is 2.3 gallons. The oil is sold in litres. How many litres does it need?

1 gallon = 4.55 litres
2.3 gallons = 2.3 × 4.55 = 10.46 litres.

2 Convert 10.74 ml to fluid ounces.

1 ml = 0.09 fl oz
10.74 ml = 0.09 × 10.74 = 0.97 fl oz.

Activity

Convert the following:

1 4.72 gallons to litres
2 21 litres to gallons
3 5.4 fl oz to ml
4 2.75 litres to fluid ounces
5 9 pints to litres.

Activity

Business application exercises

1 You have been asked to take a parcel which weighs 25 lb to the post office. You know the post office charts for postage rates are given in kilograms. How many kilograms does your parcel weigh?

2 A businessman is driving from Brussels to Frankfurt, a distance of 401 km. He wants to know the distance in miles.

3 You have to send a fax to your office in Rome. The manager there is visiting the UK in two weeks and will be driving from London to your Scottish office in Aberdeen. You know this is 543 miles. He wants the distance in kilometres.

• ESTIMATING •

When using measurements of length, weight and volume it is often not necessary to be very precise. For instance if a decorator is giving a price to a householder for painting a room he or she will only need to know *approximately* how many square metres need to be painted.

Worked examples

1 A painter is told that a wall is 6.82 metres long by 3.2 metres high. He estimates this by multiplying 7 metres by 3 metres to give 21 square metres. In both cases the figures of 7 and 3 are near enough to give him his answer. The accuracy of this calculation can be checked by working it out with the exact figures: $6.82 \text{ m} \times 3.2 \text{ m} = 21.82 \text{ m}^2$.

2 A person who is responsible for purchasing in a company which owns a fleet of lorries needs to give an estimate of the total fuel bill per month at a meeting. The figures in his file show that the number of gallons of diesel fuel used is 2964 a month and that the price paid is £1.98 per gallon. The estimate he could give is $3000 \times £2 = £6000$. The actual figure is $2964 \times £1.98 = £5868.72$.

Activity

1 Best steak costs £7.89 per pound. Approximately how much do you think 7 oz will cost?

2 A man calls at a DIY shop and sees that the price of paint is £3.80 per tin and brushes are £2.20 each. He needs four tins of paint and one brush and he has £20. Can he afford them?

3 You are meeting your friend in half an hour. You still have to wash your hair (5 minutes), dry it (8 minutes), get changed (10 minutes) and get there (5 minutes). The phone rings in the middle and you spend 5 minutes talking. *Quickly* – can you still get there on time?

4 You are on the phone to your friend one afternoon for 19 minutes. Local calls cost 3p a minute at that time. You offer your mother 50p for the call. Is it enough?

Activity

Work out estimates for the following situations in your head and then check your answers using a calculator.

1 A supermarket manager is given a price of £3216 for a new checkout station. He needs 19 and he has a budget of £70 000 to spend on them. Can he afford them?

2 A production supervisor knows that a machine produces 72.5 litres of fluid per hour. One Friday the machine will be shut down early and it will only operate for 4 hours and 10 minutes. How many litres will it produce?

3 A computer department works a 5-day week for 49 weeks of the year. Each day 250 invoices are produced. Estimate the number produced each year.

4 Estimate the cost of 1542 pencils at 9p each and 189 files at £2.05 each.

DID YOU KNOW?

When carrying out different types of calculation it is useful to estimate the result as a check. If you bought a chocolate bar for 19p and a drink for 29p the total is *about* 50p (20p + 30p). If you gave a £1 coin you should receive *approximately* 50p change.

Estimating conversions

Sometimes it is useful to estimate a conversion between metric and imperial units. Some of these estimates are easier than others. A tonne is *almost exactly* the same as a ton (see page 406). A yard is only slightly less than a metre.

Worked example

An office manager is told that the cost of cleaning carpets is 20p (£0.20) per square yard. He knows that the total floor area of his office is 420 square metres. He quickly calculates that cleaning would cost him 4.20 × 0.2 = £168.

Since a metre is slightly less than a yard he estimates the cost at £150.

Activity

Calculate the *exact* cost of the cleaning operation and work out the difference between this and the estimated figure given above.

Evidence Collection Point 14.1

You already know that one tonne is approximately the same as 1 ton and that 1 metre is similar to 1 yard. Think of handy conversion factors you could use for:

a metres to miles   **e** millilitres to fluid ounces
b kilometres to miles   **f** litres to gallons
c grams to ounces   **g** litres to pints.
d kilograms to pounds

If you have a problem with this exercise discuss it with your tutor. When you have worked out your answers, test them by using them to do the following calculations. Then check your answers for accuracy using the correct conversions shown earlier in this chapter.

1 Convert 12 yards to metres.
2 Convert 2 metres to inches.
3 Convert 10 kilometres to miles.
4 Convert 5 ounces to grams.
5 Convert 8 pounds to kilograms.
6 Convert 2 fluid ounces to millilitres.
7 Convert 4 gallons to litres.
8 Convert 5 litres to pints.

CONVERSIONS USING TABLES, GRAPHS AND SCALES

Tables can be used to convert between metric and imperial units accurately. Graphs and scales can be used to obtain *reasonably* accurate results.

Tables

A conversion table gives a list of conversions from one type of system to another. For example:

Inches		Millimetres
0.04	1	25.40
0.08	2	50.80
0.12	3	76.20
0.16	4	101.60

This may look complicated at first but when you study it you will find that:

1 mm = 0.04 inch
3 inches = 76.20 mm.

An easy way to use the table is to remember that you move vertically downwards and then horizontally across.

DID YOU KNOW?

Tables are not very useful since they only convert from whole numbers. If you wanted to know what 3.5 mm was in inches you would have to *estimate*.

Graphs

Graphs can be used for conversions by reading off the number on one axis with the number on the other axis.

Worked example

Figure 14.2 shows an example of how a graph can be used to convert from gallons to litres. Using the figure we can estimate how many litres are in 6.5 gallons.

This is done by finding 6.5 on the horizontal scale, following the vertical line (see arrows) to the point where it meets the diagonal line. This is identified by point A. Then follow the horizontal line, again shown by arrows, to point B on the vertical scale (marked in litres). Read the vertical scale at this intersection. The answer is approximately 29.5.

DID YOU KNOW?

If the number you are looking for is not on the graph then you have to estimate. For example, 4.8 gallons on the scale in Figure 14.2 would be at about the point marked C.

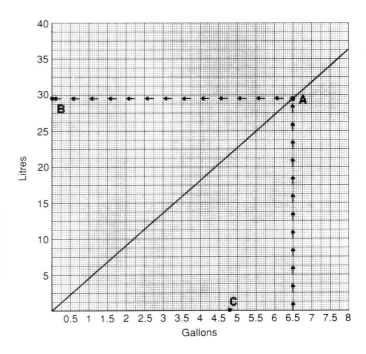

Figure 14.2   *Converting gallons into litres*

Activity

Using Figure 14.2, convert the following:

1 4.5 gallons to litres
2 38 litres to gallons
3 7.8 gallons to litres
4 42 litres to gallons.

You can check the accuracy of your answers using the conversion figures on page 406.

Scales

A scale can be used for conversions in a similar way to a graph. See Figure 14.3 for an example of a scale.

Worked example

To find out what 5 inches is in millimetres, look for 5 on the inches scale on the left-hand side of the vertical line. This is shown by point A. Then look for the reading on the right-hand scale which is in millimetres. The answer is approximately 12.7.

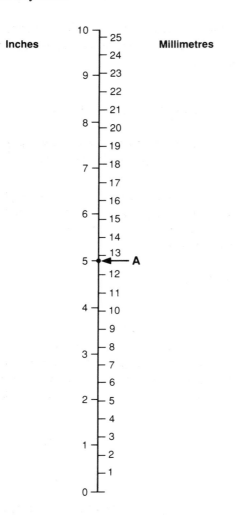

Figure 14.3

Activity

Use Figure 14.3 to convert the following:

1 7 inches to millimetres
2 15 millimetres to inches
3 8.5 inches to millimetres
4 11.5 millimetres to inches.

You can check your answers using the conversion figures on page 405.

Evidence Assignment 14D

Imagine that work for a publishing company. Your boss, Sarah Taylor, is responsible for obtaining ideas for new books, liaising with authors and updating books which have been out for some time. She has asked you to undertake the following tasks and let her have your reply in a memo.

1 Sarah Taylor is visiting the Continent next week. She will be driving from Calais to Paris, then to Basle and Brussels before returning to Calais. Distances are as follows:

  Calais to Paris – 276 km
  Paris to Basle – 484 km
  Basle to Brussels – 543 km
  Brussels to Calais – 236 km

  a Sarah isn't used to kilometres and is too busy to work out how far she has to go. What is the total distance she will be covering *in miles?*
  b If she drives at an average speed of 40 mph, how long will it take her to do each stage of her journey?
  c Petrol claims are allowed at 35.5p a mile. How much will her claim be for the total trip, assuming that in addition to the above she also drives 150 miles to Dover and back from your office?
  d Sarah Taylor wants some French francs to take with her. At present the exchange rate is 8.04 francs to the pound. If you take £150 to the bank, how many francs do you estimate she will receive if the bank deducts £5 for changing the currency?

2 Sarah is updating an old recipe book and wants to show quantities in both the imperial and metric systems. Below is given the recipe for damson jam. Convert all the quantities to metric quantities.

  4 lb damsons
  4 $\frac{1}{2}$ lb granulated sugar
  half pint of water

3 A new book is priced to retail at £9.95. Sarah wants to cover production costs of £2 a book, distribution costs of 50p a book and has to allow for retailers to make 100% profit. She also has to pay her authors 10% in royalties on the published price.

a She estimates the book will sell 10 000 copies. How much do you *estimate* the company will gain in revenue?

b What do you *estimate* the book will sell at to the *retailers*?

c What are her *estimated* production, distribution and royalty costs when you add them together?

d How much profit do you *estimate* the company will make?

TWO- AND THREE-DIMENSIONAL OBJECTS

You should already know:

● A **two-dimensional object** is one which is flat. An example would be the floor area of an office. It has two dimensions – width and length.

● A **three-dimensional object** is one which has length, width and height – for example an office desk.

These are often referred to as **2-D** and **3-D objects**.

DID YOU KNOW?

When people refer to the 'fourth dimension' they are referring to **time**.

In reality all objects have three dimensions. A piece of paper resting on a flat desk has the two dimensions of length and width *but* it also has thickness, which is the third dimension. However, it is sometimes useful to think of things in terms of two of their three dimensions. A company which manufactures glass for windows would probably measure output per machine as so many square metres per hour with a *standard* thickness (i.e. one which does not vary).

TWO-DIMENSIONAL OBJECTS

Areas and perimeters

Sometimes it is necessary to find the area of a two-dimensional shape. For example, a company which cuts grass on playing fields needs to know how many square

metres there are in a particular field. Then they can estimate how long it will take to cut it.

In business, most shapes for which areas are needed are either **rectangular** (where the corners are 90° or right angles) or **circular**.

DID YOU KNOW?

A square is a special type of rectangle where all four sides have the same length.

The **area** A of a rectangle is found by multiplying the length by the width. The **perimeter** P of a rectangle is found by adding up the lengths of the four sides. Expressed as formulae these are:

$A = lb$ and $P = 2l + 2b$
where l = length and b = breadth.

The **area** of a circle is found by the formula $A = \pi r^2$ where r is the radius. The radius is the distance from the centre to the outside of the circle. The **perimeter** or circumference, C of a circle is found by the formula $C = 2\pi r$. π or 'pi' is a fixed number which, to two decimal places, is 3.14.

DID YOU KNOW?

Pi is a number which never ends. To 7 decimal places it is 3.1415927. Mathematicians have checked it using computers. The numbers after the decimal point go on endlessly without any pattern.

A useful approximation to π is $\frac{22}{7}$. Try working it out to see how close it is.

Worked examples

1 An office is 22.1 m long by 18.6 m wide and the manager needs to know the area and the perimeter.

Area = length × width = 22.1 × 18.6
$\qquad\qquad$ = 411.06 *square* metres

Perimeter = 2 × length + 2 × width = 2 × 22.1 + 2 × 18.6
$\qquad\qquad$ = 44.2 + 37.2 = 81.4 metres

2 An advertising agency wishes to produce a large metal disc, trimmed with blue ribbon around the edge, for a promotional display. The radius of the disc is 2.8 m. What area of sheet metal will they need and what length of ribbon?

Area $= \pi r^2 = 3.14 \times 2.8^2 = 3.14 \times 7.84$
$= 2.462$ square metres

Perimeter (for ribbon) $= 2\pi r = 2 \times 3.14 \times 2.8$
$= 17.58$ metres

3 A kitchen is shaped as shown in Figure 14.4. What is the floor area and the perimeter?

To work out the area, you need to divide the kitchen into rectangles, as shown by the dotted line. Then find the area of the two sections and add them together.

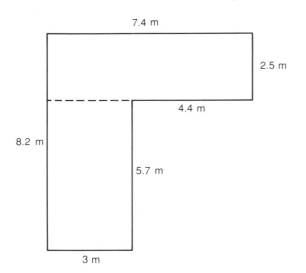

Figure 14.4

Area $= 5.7 \times 3 + 7.4 \times 2.5 = 17.1 + 18.5$
$= 35.6$ square metres

The perimeter is
7.4m + 2.5m + 4.4m + 5.7m + 3m + 8.2m = 31.2m

DID YOU KNOW

Another way to solve question 3 above is:

$7.4 \times 8.2 - 5.7 \times 4.4 = 60.68 - 20.58$
$= 35.6$ square metres

How has this been done? Check with your tutor if you don't understand this.

Activity

Work out the area and perimeter of the following shapes. Write out the formula first, then fill in the numbers and complete the calculations.

1 A rectangle 15.2 cm by 13.8 cm.

2 A square with sides of 2.9 m.

3 A circle with diameter of 2.3 m.

4 A kitchen worktop with the shape shown in Figure 14.5(a).

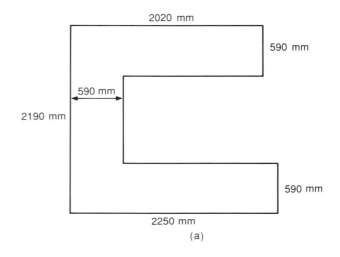

(a)

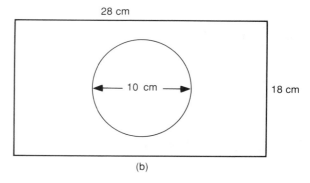

(b)

Figure 14.5 (a) (b)

5 A wall clock surround has the shape shown in Figure 14.5(b), with a circular hole in the centre. Calculate the area of wood it contains.

THREE-DIMENSIONAL OBJECTS

It is sometimes useful to sketch a 3-D object. Place a paperback book on a table and look at it from above with one corner nearer to you. You can't see some of the edges but they *can* be drawn in using dotted lines (see Figure 14.6).

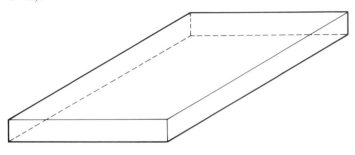

Figure 14.6

Activity

Try sketching a rectangular box for yourself – say a packet of breakfast cereal. Hint – if you use paper with lines on you can use the printed lines for the horizontal lines of your sketch.

DID YOU KNOW?

Because you are sketching on a flat piece of paper, you are working in *two dimensions*. You have therefore made a *two-dimensional representation of a three-dimensional object*.

Drawings and sketches

A sketch is a rough, incomplete or rapid drawing. It may be the first stage towards a finished drawing. The graphic designers who produced the artwork for this book started with sketches, but these would not have been satisfactory as the 'finished product'. You can make a quick sketch when you are short of time, when you only need a *rough* idea of what something looks like or when you want to convey this idea to someone else quickly.

DID YOU KNOW?

If you have ever played a game like Pictionary, when you have to convey an idea in pictures quickly, then you will know all about the difference between sketches and drawings! This topic is also covered in Core Skills, Chapter 13 on Communication.

Working to scale

Another difference between a drawing and a sketch may be that some drawings are *to scale*. You may have seen scale models of cars in toy shops. Working to scale means that the length of each line of the drawing is in the same proportion to the actual object. For example, if a box is 300 mm high, 400 mm long and 200 mm wide, it could be shown by a drawing which is 30 mm by 40 mm by 20 mm (see Figure 14.7).

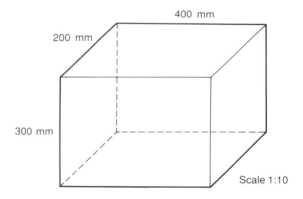

Figure 14.7

There are two other points to note. Firstly the actual lengths of the box dimensions are shown on the diagram, *not* the scaled down lengths. Also the 'scale 1:10' means that the actual lengths of the horizontal and vertical lines of the drawing are all one tenth of the dimensions of the box itself.

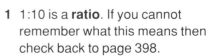

Activity

1 1:10 is a **ratio**. If you cannot remember what this means then check back to page 398.

2 Find a box, such as a pack of breakfast cereal, measure its dimensions and draw it to a scale of 1:10. Show your finished drawing to your tutor.

Activity

Business application exercise

You work for a company which is ordering a desk, tables and chairs for a new reception area. Your reception area measures 9 metres by 10 metres and is shown in Figure 14.8. Draw this area to scale on a piece of graph paper.

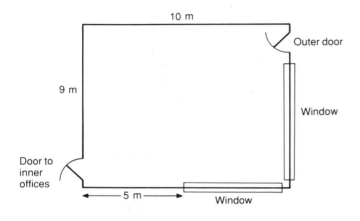

Figure 14.8

From an office furniture catalogue select some suitable furniture. Cut out some cardboard shapes, to scale, to represent the reception desk and the tables and chairs. Arrange these so that there is the maximum amount of seating without making the area congested.

Volume

Volume is the amount of space taken up by a 3-D object. For rectangular or cubic objects the volume is found by multiplying length (l) by height (h) by breadth (b). The formula for volume is therefore:

$$V = l \times h \times b$$

The **surface area** of a 3-D rectangular object is the sum of the area of the 6 surfaces. The formula is therefore:

$$a = 2h \times l + 2h \times b + 2b \times l$$

Worked example

An engineer is responsible for installing an air-conditioning system of a large room. Once the system has been installed the room will be known as a 'clean' room because it will have filtered air blown into it at a constant temperature. He has to calculate the volume of the room so that he can work out the size of air-conditioning plant to install. The room floor is shaped as in Figure 14.9 and the height of the room is 2.9 m.

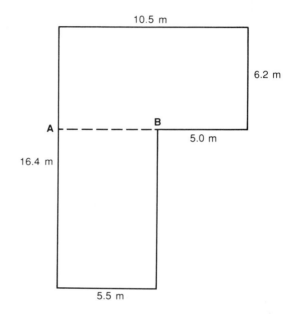

Figure 14.9

1 Divide the floor area into two sections by drawing a line from A to B. This gives two rectangles, 10.5 m × 6.2 m and 10.2 m × 5.5m

2 Use the formula given above to calculate the volume of each:

$V_1 = 10.5 \times 6.2 \times 2.9 = 188.79$ m^3 (cubic metres)
$V_2 = 10.2 \times 5.5 \times 2.9 = 162.69$ m^3

3 Add the two amounts together to find the total volume:

$188.79 + 162.69 = 514.17$ m^3

Note that the engineer would not need such a precise figure and would probably use the figure of 500 m^3 when working out his other calculations.

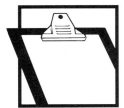

Activity

1 A man wishes to lay concrete on his drive. It is shaped as in Figure 14.10.

a He wishes to make the concrete 140 mm thick. How many cubic metres of concrete does he need?

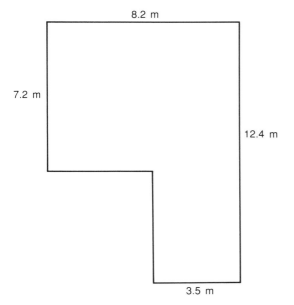

Figure 14.10

b If the readymix concrete supplier will only deliver in quantities of half a cubic metre, how much should he order?

Activity

Business application exercises

1 A washing powder manufacturer supplies washing powder in boxes which are 12 cm wide, 26 cm long and 37 cm high. The average contents of a box takes up 10 484 cm³ (cubic centimetres). What is the volume of space left at the top?

2 A rectangular heating oil storage tank for a company has the following internal dimensions – length 3.1 m, width 2.5 m and height 2.7 m. What volume of oil is in the tank when it is half full?

2-D representations of 3-D objects

Another way of showing 3-D objects on paper is to show **elevations**. An elevation is a picture of what an object looks like if you look at it from the front, side or above. These are known as the **front, side** and **plan** elevations. For example, the box in Figure 14.11(a) can be represented as three elevations as shown in Figure 14.11(b).

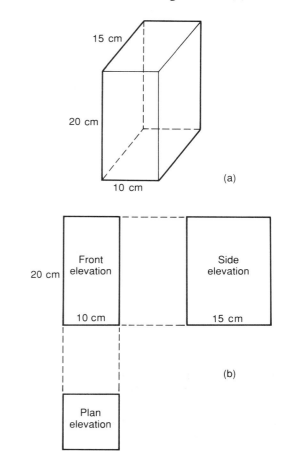

Figure 14.11

Activity

1 The elevations in Figure 14.11(b) have all been drawn to scale. Can you work out what the scale is?

2 *Sketch* the three elevations of a table.

3 *Draw* the three elevations of a paperback book to scale.

Activity

Business application exercise

For the reception area you created before, you created a **plan** elevation to make sure you had enough space for the furniture. Your boss wants to have an idea what the area would look like from the front and the side so that he can decide how to decorate the area, hang pictures. In other words, he wants to view the area from the customer's point of view. Sketch the reception area you designed from both of these elevations.

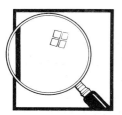

Evidence Assignment 14E

You work for a local hospital which has opted out of district management and undertakes a number of fund-raising activities to raise money to finance expansion, new equipment and facilities for children and their parents who stay with them. Your boss is Tom O'Brien who is the Appeals Director. The hospital has a spare area, off a main corridor on the ground floor, which has been allocated for use as a gift shop. The hospital joiners will construct your counter and the display stands will be purchased from a local supplier. Figure 14.12 gives an outline of the area together with the measurements.

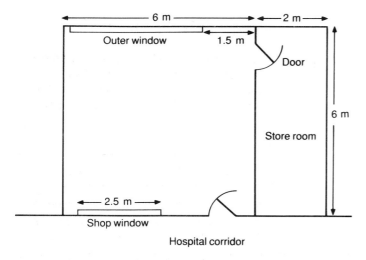

Figure 14.12

1 Decide where you will put the main counter and display stands. Measure the amount of room you have available for the counter and, in a memo to Mr Marsh, the chief joiner, tell him:

   a the measurements of the counter
   b the volume of space it will occupy.

2 Obtain information on a range of display stands from a local supplier. Sketch the area of the shop *to scale* using a plan elevation to make sure there is enough room for the fixtures you want.

3 The window of the shop is rectangular and measures $2\frac{1}{2}$ metres across and 2 metres in depth. Tom O'Brien wants a special window display for the opening which will feature red ribbon around the window and coloured circles, to represent balloons, across the top.

   a How much red ribbon will you need to buy to cover the perimeter of the window?
   b If each circle has a radius of 150 centimetres how many circles will you need to go across the window?
   c What will be the total area of the window covered by all the circles?

4 It has been decided that the shop should sell books, magazines, sweets, drinks, tapes, T-shirts and fluffy toys. Tom O'Brien wants a display stand near the window which features most, if not all, of these items so that people can easily see the goods which are sold even when the shop is closed. He has asked you to make a sketch of the stand to show him how you think it should be set out. Note that this particular stand has four shelves but the heights of these are adjustable.

. SURVEYS, QUESTIONNAIRES AND STATISTICS .

Have you ever wondered how the music industry decides which record is top of the charts each week? The chart is based on the number of records sold in the shops but how are the numbers of sales found out? There are thousands of shops in the country and it would be very difficult to get the information from each one.

The answer is that only a *selection* of shops is asked. This is called a **survey** and the selection is called a **sample**. It is important that the sample is *representative*. In other words, the shops chosen must be in different parts of the country and in small towns as well as cities.

The way in which the record chart is produced is an example of the use of **statistics**. Statistics involve:

- **collecting** data (collecting figures of record sales from selected shops)
- **analysing** the data to produce useful information (producing a list of best selling records)
- **displaying** the results in the form of tables, diagrams, graphs or charts.

Activity

You have been asked to find out how many people eat meals in your school or college each day during a week. Discuss with your fellow students and your tutor how this information could be:
a collected
b analysed
c displayed.

DID YOU KNOW?

Surveys are often carried out to obtain information about people's attitudes or behaviour.

- Why do people prefer a certain brand of canned drink?
- Why is one nightclub more popular than another?
- What kind of facilities would people like in a new sports centre?

It is easier to obtain this information in the form of numerical date (i.e. as numbers). This way the results are easier to analyse.

Questionnaires are used to obtain descriptive information. They can also be used to collect numerical data as well.

In this section we will first look at how data is collected. Later on methods of analysis and display will be described.

Surveys

The first step of conducting a survey is to decide exactly *what* you want to know. A supermarket manager may want to know how many customers use his shop at different times in the week. He can then plan when he will need extra part-time staff for busy periods at the check-outs.

The next step is to decide *how* the data could be collected. In the case of the supermarket the manager could have someone standing at the entrance making a note as people walk in. The data is collected on a specially designed **observation sheet**.

Worked example

A sewing machine which is used to produce jeans occasionally develops a fault. There are two types of fault. Sometimes the thread breaks and sometimes the needle falls out. The production supervisor asks the machine operator to record how often it happens so that she has information to give to the maintenance section. She produces the following observation sheet:

SEWING MACHINE FAULT RECORD	
Date	
Thread break	
Needle falling out	

DID YOU KNOW?

When carrying out this type of survey, a simple 'tally' system is often used. The first four occasions are recorded as 'IIII'. When the fifth occurs it is recorded as ⳾. The sixth starts a new set - ⳾ I.

Activity

Design an observation sheet to count the number of vehicles which pass in either direction on a road in an hour. You wish to distinguish between goods vehicles and private cars. Use your sheet and add up the results. It might be interesting if two or three of you carried out the survey independently at the same time. Are your results the same? If not, can you find out why?

Questionnaires

Have you ever seen someone standing in a shopping centre with a clipboard, talking to passers-by? They could be using a questionnaire to find out what people think about something. For example, they may be trying to find out people's reactions to a new product or which way they intend to vote in a forthcoming election.

The rules for designing questionnaires are:

1 Think carefully about what you need to know. For instance, do you want facts or opinions?

2 Word your questions carefully. There are two types of question.

- A **closed** question asks for a 'yes' or 'no' answer; e.g. 'Do you watch pop music programmes on television?'
- An **open** question asks for more general information; e.g. 'What do you think about sport on television?'

Questions can give either **quantitative** information (i.e. a numerical answer) or **qualitative** information (i.e. an opinion). Quantitative information is much easier to analyse – in many cases computers are used (see also point 8 below).

3 Be careful, too, how you phrase your questions so that you don't cause offence. For instance, don't ask people questions which they would prefer not to answer or would find embarrassing (e.g. about their earnings, weight, medical history or personal relationships).

4 A common mistake is to make the questionnaire too long. Keep to the *essential* points you *must* know about.

5 Carry out a **pilot** survey by getting a small number of people to fill in the questionnaire. Then check that they understand the questions. If some questions were ambiguous then you may need to reword them.

6 Decide how many people you wish to get information from (i.e. the *size* of your survey). If the organiser of a music festival wished to know people's opinions on various events, he or she would probably find out what was needed by asking 100 people *at random*. Different

types of people would need to be questioned (e.g. different ages, sex, etc.) to make sure that the results were not biased (slanted to give a false outcome).

7 Decide where you need to be to carry out your survey. There is little point in standing in a bus station to do a survey on cars! You may also want to consider the best time to do it. For instance, if you wanted to survey mothers with young children, you would be better in a shopping centre during mid-morning or afternoon, rather than during the lunchtime or late in the day when people are passing through on their way to or from work.

8 Analyse your questionnaires when they are returned. Draw a statistical diagram to analyse your result (see pages 383–386).

DID YOU KNOW?

Questionnaires can be sent through the post or given to people to complete and return in their own time. This can be cheaper as more people can be surveyed more quickly. The problem is that usually only a low percentage of them are returned.

An alternative method is the telephone survey. This is being more frequently used by many market research companies.

Activity

As a group, decide where you would go and at what time, and the type of people you would ask if you were carrying out a survey on each of the following:

1 The success of a new type of games console.

2 What people think of your local cinema.

3 What people think of a new brand of paint.

4 The popularity of your local post office.

5 The average amount of spending money given to youngsters in your area.

6 whether a new perfume fragrance would be popular.

Worked example

The owner of a computer shop which sells games notices that many people who come into the shop leave without buying anything. She wonders if they intended to buy anything in the first place, were just curious to know what was the latest game on the market, or whether they simply wanted to play on some of the computers. Perhaps they had been prepared to buy something but were unable to find what they wanted. She is aware that she does not stock a complete range of games for all machines. She also wonders whether she should hire games out as well as sell them.

She designs the questionnaire shown in Figure 14.13:

COMPUTER GAMES – CUSTOMER QUESTIONNAIRE

We are carrying out a survey to find out the kind of computer games people prefer. We would be grateful if you would help us by answering a few simple questions.

1 Do you own a computer games machine?   Yes ☐
    No ☐

2 If so, what make is it? _ _ _ _ _ _ _ _ _ _ _ _ _ _ _ _ _

3 Do you buy games?   Yes ☐
    No ☐

4 Do you rent games?   Yes ☐
    No ☐

5 When looking at the games in this shop, do you find what you need?
   Always ☐   Sometimes ☐   Never ☐

6 If you have looked for something recently, and been unable to find it, please state the item(s) you were looking for:
   ----

7 Is there anything you think we could do to improve our service?

Figure 14.13

Activity

In the survey above, which questions are asking for quantitative information and which ones are asking for qualitative information? Which are open and which are closed questions?

Using the questionnaire

At first the owner leaves the questionnaires next to the door for people to fill in and place in a box. After the first day she is disappointed with the number returned and several have been filled in incorrectly or are unreadable. She then decides to ask one of the assistants to stand by the door, ask people the questions and fill them in herself. This works much better and about 70% of people co-operate.

When she analyses the completed questionnaires she discovers that:

1 83% of people coming into the shop own games machines.

2 A games machine recently introduced on the market is not popular. The market leaders are Sega and Nintendo.

3 92% of people buy games.

4 Only 22% rent games (although some of these also buy games as well).

5 Only 23% always find the game they want, 54% sometimes find it and 11% say they never do.

6 Three or four games seem to be popular – none of which she stocks.

7 Quite a few people think the shop is too cluttered with not enough space between the racks. Also people have to queue too long at the pay point.

Activity

Overall the owner has received information which will help her to run the shop better if she takes note of the comments. She wonders about the 30% of people who didn't answer the questionnaire and why some answered 'never' to question 5 but didn't answer question 6 at all.

1 What changes do you think she should make to the shop from now on?

2 Why do you think some people refused to answer the questionnaire?

3 What explanation(s) can you offer that some answered 'never' to question 5 and then ignored question 6?

Evidence Collection Point 14.2

1 *With a small group of fellow students*, design and use a questionnaire for people in your class. The aim is to discover:

- what make of jeans people prefer
- how much they spend when they buy them
- how many pairs of jeans they own
- how many they buy each year
- what style they prefer (e.g. tight/flared, dark or pre-washed denim, zip or buttons, etc.).

If possible, you also want to know the *reasons* for their preferences. Try the questionnaire out on a small group. Compare the design of your questionnaire with other groups and decide which is the best and why.

2 Make out a neat version of the best questionnaire (or combine your best efforts) and photocopy or duplicate this. Now carry out your survey amongst fellow students within your school or college. Decide how large you want your survey to be and where/when you will carry it out to get the best results.

3 Analyse your results. If you were a jeans manufacturer whose sales have fallen recently, what information have you obtained and how could you use it to improve sales?

Using statistics

When information from surveys or questionnaires is obtained, the next step is to analyse it and perhaps show the results in the form of a diagram. This section concentrates on histograms, but bar charts, pie charts and pictograms can also be used.

Mean and range

When a set of numbers needs to be analysed, the **mean** (or **arithmetic mean** to give it its full name) and the **range** are usually the two most important things which need to be found out.

Calculating the mean is also known as working out the average. Three people aged 6, 9 and 21 have an average

age of 12 (i.e. the mean is 12). All we have done is add the figures together and divide by the number of people.

The formula for finding the mean is:

$$\overline{x} = \frac{s}{n}$$

$\overline{x}$ is the **mean**. A bar over any letter represents the mean of a set of data.
s is the **sum** of the items
n is the **number** of items.

So in the case above, the formula is $x = \frac{36}{3} = 12$.

The **range** of a set of numbers is the difference between the highest and lowest values. In the question above, the range is from 21 to 6, which is 15.

Activity

There are ten people working in the sales office of a large company. The number of months each has worked for the company is given below:

85, 60, 18, 142, 56, 32, 128, 6, 4, 134

1 What is the mean or average time worked for the firm? Give your answer in years and months.

2 What is the range?

3 Mean and range are both examples of *summarising* numbers. This means that they give some important information about a set of numbers. How useful do you think the above information would be to the personnel department, and why?

4 Why do you think the figures for analysis were given in months and not in years and months? Can you think of any other occasions when you may have to convert figures in this way?

Statistical diagrams

If a set of numbers can be converted into a picture the information is more interesting and people can interpret it (and remember it!) more easily. A common form of statistical diagram is a **histogram**. This is similar to a bar chart except that the areas of the bars represent the data (compare Figure 14.14 with the bar chart in the Core Skills chapter on Communication, page 386).

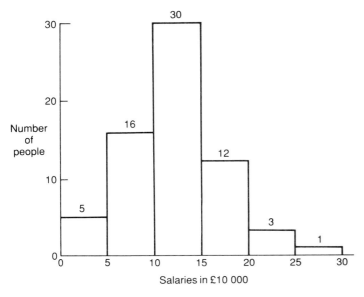

Figure 14.14

This is the picture which might emerge if the salaries of 35 people working in a business were placed in bands of £5000. Guess which band the Managing Director comes in!

The 'y' axis (the 'number of people' scale) is called the **frequency** and the 'x' axis (the bands of £5000) is divided into **class intervals**.

Evidence Assignment 14F

1 Draw a histogram to represent the information you were given on page 420 about the length of time ten people had worked for a company.

2 The owner of a shopfitting company is worried that he is receiving so many orders that he cannot complete work to customers' deadlines and is losing orders. He analyses the orders received over the last 12 months and discovers that the monthly workload in man-hours is:

Jan	1682	July	1208
Feb	1428	August	1640
March	2039	September	1750
April	1938	October	2060
May	1518	November	1510
June	1200	December	1027

a Calculate the mean and the range.

b Draw a histogram to represent the information.

c The average number of hours worked by full-time employees is 40 and by part-time employees is 25.

● If the owner wanted to employ *only* full-time workers *and* to have enough employees on the staff all year to cover the busiest times, how many people would he employ?

● If he paid each full-time employee an average of £300 a week, what would be his total wage bill each week? What would he pay in wages each year?

● Many employees can be hired on a casual basis (i.e. hired only when they are needed to work on a part-time basis). The average part-time rate is £150 per week. If you owned the business, what would be your ratio of full-time to part-time employees *each month*? (Bear in mind that you will want some full-time workers at all times because they are more committed to work hard for the company.)

● On the figures you calculated above, what would be your total wage bill for the year? How much have you saved by using your staff more efficiently?

▪ QUICK REFERENCE SECTION ▪

This section contains a list in alphabetical order of all the calculations you should be able to do for GNVQ level 2. It is designed to:

● help you, if you have any problems working out the calculations at the start of the chapter

● act as a quick reference if you forget how to carry out the calculations you learned when you worked through the chapter.

If you are asked to do a calculation in other sections of this book, and have some difficulty, try looking here. If you are still struggling, ask your tutor for help.

All measurements are given in the metric system. Use the conversion tables (under C in this section) if you need to convert to the imperial system.

Area

Area is the amount of space covered by a flat object and is measured in the number of centimetre squares or metre squares it takes up. This space is in **two dimensions**.

Rectangle – multiply the length by the width:

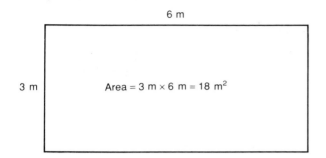

Square – even easier, as length and width are the same:

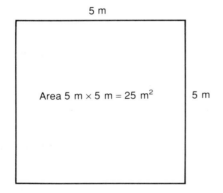

Circle - use the formula $A = \pi r^2$ where r is the radius (the distance between the centre and the circumference). π is very close to $\frac{22}{7}$, so if a circle has a radius of 7 metres, its area is:

$7 \times 7 \times \frac{22}{7} = 154 \text{ m}^2$.

If you use a calculator you can enter $7 \times 7 \times 3.14$ instead – and you will get the answer 153.86 m^2.

Average

This is also known as the **mean**. It is found by adding together a set of figures and dividing by the number of figures there are in the set. If a bus was late on five consecutive days by 1, 3, 7, 4 and 0 minutes then the average time it is late is

$$\frac{1+3+7+4+0}{5} = \frac{15}{5} = 3 \text{ minutes}$$

Calculators

If you have a calculator then it is worthwhile learning how to use it properly. A business calculator is easier to use than a scientific calculator for most of the calculations you need to carry out in business – and there are fewer functions to learn. However, only a scientific calculator will include π – though you can easily substitute the decimal figure 3.14.

A desktop calculator enables you to print out your calculations, which is useful for checking none has been missed or entered wrongly. The list can also be kept as a permanent record. These calculators normally have a date key which can also be used to enter the operator's number at the top of the printout.

Check that on your calculator you know the following (if not, refer to the manual).

a The difference between the CE key and the C key. CE = clear last entry only, C = clear all the current calculation. On some pocket machines this is the same key. Pressing it once = CE and pressing it *twice* = C.

b You should always start a new calculation by pressing Clear first. This ensures that any previous calculations are no longer stored and will not affect your current work.

c On a desktop calculator, always end a calculation printout by turning up the paper a short distance, so you can tear off the printout without cutting off the last few lines.

d There is no need to enter zeros after a decimal point – therefore enter 48.50 as 48.5.

e If you are using a desktop calculator and carrying out calculations involving money – check that you are operating with two decimal places before you start.

f If you are entering money calculations in pence only, always start with the point.

g Learn how to use the memory function. It saves time entering and re-entering figures. On a calculator there are usually three or four memory keys:

M+	add to memory	MR	recall memory
M-	subtract from memory	MC	clear memory

If your machine only has three memory keys it is likely one is marked MRC and does the work of both MR and MC.

Use M+ when you are entering columns of figures and want to add the *totals* of each column as well. Enter the column and then enter the total into memory by pressing M+. Press CE (C on some machines) so that the screen clears but the memory signal still shows. Enter the next column and press M+ when you have reached the total and so on. At the end press MR to see the total of all the figures you have entered into memory. Then press MC to clear the memory.

Use M– if you want to *subtract* the total of one column from the total of another. Press M+ after the first column total (as above) and then M– after the second column.

Use the memory whenever you want to carry out any numeric operation and keep the total for later use; e.g.

47 small widgets @ £20 each + VAT	......
62 large widgets @ £42 each + VAT	......
	____
Sub-total	......
Less 10% discount	......
	____
TOTAL	____

A good test of whether you can use memory properly is whether you can input the exercise above with each line entered as one process and no figure having to be entered twice!

Circles

See *Area* and *Perimeter*

Conversion tables

Length and distance

In the **metric** system:

10 millimetres (mm)	= 1 centimetre (cm)
100 cm	= 1 metre (m)
1000 m	= 1 kilometre (km)

In the **imperial** system:

12 inches (in)	= 1 foot (ft)
3 ft	= 1 yard (yd)
1760 yd	= 1 mile

Equivalents

1 cm = 0.39 in	and	1 in = 2.54 cm
1 m = 1.09 yd	and	1 yd = 0.91 m
1 km = 0.62 miles	and	1 mile = 1.61 km

Weight

In the **metric** system:

1000 grams (g)	=	1 kilogram (kg)
1000 kg	=	1 metric tonne

In the **imperial** system:

16 ounces (oz)	=	1 pound (lb)
14 lb	=	1 stone
8 stones	=	1 hundredweight (cwt)
20 cwt	=	1 ton

Equivalents

1 g = 0.035 oz	and	1 oz = 28.35 g
1 kg = 2.21 lb	and	1 lb = 0.45 kg
1 tonne = 0.98 tons	and	1 ton = 1016.00 tonnes

Volume

In the **metric** system:

1000 millilitres (ml) = 1 litre (l)

In the **imperial** system

20 fluid ounces (fl oz) = 1 pint
8 pints = 1 gallon

Equivalents

1 ml = 0.09 fl oz	and	1 fl oz = 10.99 ml
1 l = 0.22 gallons	and	1 gallon = 4.55 l
1 l = 1.76 pints	and	1 pint = 0.57 l

Cubes and cube roots

One meaning of the word 'cube' is a 3-dimensional object where the length of each side is the same:

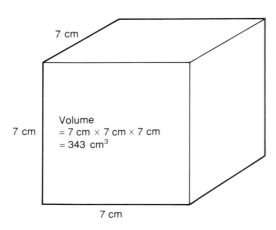

The **volume** of a cube is found by multiplying the length × breadth × height. Therefore the answer is given in cubic metres or centimetres.

The word **cubed** is used for any number which is multiplied by itself three times. Therefore 5 cubed is $5 \times 5 \times 5$ and is written as 5^3.

The **cube root** of a number is the number which needs to be multiplied by itself three times to give the first number. For example, the cube root of 8 is 2 because $2 \times 2 \times 2$ (or 2^3) = 8.

Decimals

A decimal is a way of writing a number which is not a whole number. For example, if your class lasts for 1 hour then this is a whole number. If it lasts for $1\frac{1}{2}$ hours then this can be written as 1.5 which is a decimal. The decimal point, ·, separates the whole numbers from the decimal fractions. The first number to the right of the decimal is in tenths, the next in hundredths and so on. So 1.642 means:

$$1 + \frac{6}{10} + \frac{4}{100} + \frac{2}{1000}$$

For most business uses figures are **rounded** to two decimal places (see page 394).

Decimals are easier to use than fractions when adding and subtracting. To multiply and divide calculations where *both* numbers are decimals, most people use a calculator. Otherwise carry out the calculation as you would with a whole number, but:

- remember to include the decimal point (write a nought before it if necessary to help you remember)
- always make sure your decimal points are written under each other.

Remember that money is usually written in decimal form.

Converting decimals to percentages

Convert decimals to percentages by multiplying by 100; e.g. 0.342 as a percentage = $0.342 \times 100 = 34.2\%$.

Equations and formulae

Equations and formulae are very similar.

a In an equation letters are used to represent numbers to help you find the value of an 'unknown' figure.

b A formula is set of words or symbols which can be applied many times in similar situations.

As an example, $A = l \times b$ or $A = lb$ is an equation and a formula. Letters are used to represent the area, length and breadth and, as a formula, it can be applied to find the area of a rectangle of any size.

- **Construct a formula** by substituting the items given by letters.
- **Transpose** a formula (or equation) to make a different quantity the subject. Remember to change the sign if you move a quantity to the other side of the equals sign (plus to minus, minus to plus). For example:

1 Find the value of y if $x + 3 = y$

If $x + 3 = y$ then $x = y - 3$

2 If $26x = 3y$, find the value of x and y

$x = \frac{3y}{26}$ and $y = \frac{26x}{3}$

- **Simplify** a formula (or equation) by adding or subtracting **like terms** (e.g. all the '*x*s' or all the '*y*s'). Remember you cannot simplify **unlike terms**. For example:

Simplify $3x + 5y = 4x + 2y$
$5y - 2y = 4x - 3x$
$\therefore 3y = x$

Fractions

Fractions, like decimals, are used when a number is less than a whole number. They are written as follows: $\frac{1}{2}, \frac{1}{4}, \frac{1}{3}$. Common fractions, such as these, we use in everyday speech – such as 'just half a cup of coffee please'. Sometimes fractions are more complicated, e.g. $\frac{1}{7}$ or $\frac{2}{9}$. At other times whole numbers and fractions go together, e.g. $2\frac{1}{8}$ or $5\frac{2}{3}$.

Adding fractions

If there are whole numbers do these first. Then make sure all the fractions have the same **denominator** at the bottom. Do this by finding the lowest number into which all the denominators will go (i.e. the **lowest common denominator**). Then multiply the numerator (top number) by the same number:

Example $8\frac{1}{6} + 1\frac{3}{4} =$

1 Whole numbers first: $8 + 1 = 9$

2 Find the lowest number both denominators will go into – answer = 12.

3 How many times does each numerator go into this figure? Answer: 6 goes into 12 twice and 4 goes into 12 three times.

4 Multiply each numerator by this figure:

$$\frac{1 \times 2}{12} + \frac{3 \times 3}{12}$$

5 Write this as one sum and work it out:

$$\frac{2 + 9}{12} = \frac{11}{12}$$

6 Count back in any whole numbers. Final answer:

$$9\frac{11}{12}.$$

Subtracting fractions

1 If the second fraction of the two is smaller than the first one, then do in the same way as addition; i.e.

- calculate whole numbers first
- find the lowest common denominator
- multiply the numerators
- carry out the subtraction
- cancel down your answer, if possible, e.g.

$$4\frac{2}{3} - 1\frac{1}{6} = 3\frac{4-1}{6} = 3\frac{3}{6} = 3\frac{1}{2}$$

2 If the second fraction is larger than the first then you need to change the fractions into **improper** fractions. In this case the numerator is greater than the denominator and the value is more than 1. After carrying out the subtraction you convert your answer back to whole numbers and fractions. For example:

$$5\frac{1}{2} - 3\frac{3}{4} =$$

$$\frac{11}{2} - \frac{15}{4} = \frac{22 - 15}{4} = \frac{7}{4} = 1\frac{3}{4}$$

Multiplication and division of fractions

1 Multiply fractions by multiplying the numerators together and then multiplying the denominators together. Then cancel down your answer (if possible). For example:

$$\frac{5}{9} \times \frac{3}{8} \times \frac{3}{10} = \frac{45}{720} = \frac{5}{80} = \frac{1}{16}$$

2 Divide by turning one of the fractions upside down and multiplying. For example:

$$\frac{2}{3} \div \frac{7}{9} = \frac{2}{3} \times \frac{9}{7} = \frac{18}{21} = \frac{6}{7}$$

Remember - you can make life easier for yourself by cancelling down before you carry out the calculation; e.g.

$$\frac{2}{3} \times \frac{9}{7} = \frac{2}{1} \times \frac{3}{7} = \frac{6}{7}$$

Converting fractions to decimals

Divide the numerator by the denominator; e.g. $\frac{3}{4} = 3 \div 4 = 0.75$.

Converting fractions to percentages

Multiply by 100; e.g. $\frac{1}{2} \times 100 = \frac{100}{2} = 50\%$

Mean

See under *Average* (page 422).

Percentages

A percentage represents the number of parts out of one hundred. If 8 faulty components were found in every batch of 100 components then this could be written as 8%.

Converting fractions and decimals to percentages

Multiply by 100; e.g. $\frac{1}{4} \times \frac{100}{1} = 25\%$

$$0.20 \times 100 = 20\%.$$

Converting percentages to decimals and fractions

Simply divide by 100; e.g. 70% as a fraction is

$$\frac{70}{100} = \frac{7}{10}$$

53% as a decimal is $\frac{53}{100} = 0.53$.

Finding the percentage of a number

Multiply the number by the percentage and divide by 100. 25% of £6 is therefore:

$$\frac{25 \times 6}{100} = \frac{6}{4} = £1.50.$$

Showing a quantity as a percentage

The relationship between two numbers, with one as a percentage of the other, is done by first showing the relationship as a fraction and then multiplying by 100. 30 as a percentage of 150 is therefore:

$$\frac{30 \times 100}{150} = 20\%$$

Increasing and decreasing by percentages

Increase by firstly turning the number into a decimal (i.e. 15% = 0.15) then *adding* 1. Therefore 1 + 0.15 = 1.15. Then multiply. If the price of an article is £12 without VAT and VAT is 17.5%, the price including VAT is:

$$£12 \times 1.175 = £14.10.$$

Decrease by turning the number into a decimal and *subtracting* from 1. For example, if a company offers 10% discount on a price of £56 then:

$$10\% = 0.10 \text{ and } 1 - 0.10 = 0.9$$
$$£56 \times 0.9 = £50.40.$$

Perimeter

The perimeter is the distance round a shape.

The perimeter of a **rectangle** is found by adding up the length of the four sides:

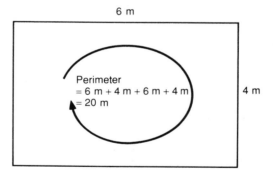

The perimeter or circumference C of a **circle** is found by using the formula $C = 2\pi r$. Remember that $\pi = 3.14$ or 22/7.

Therefore a circle with a radius (r) of 5 cm would have a perimeter of $2 \times 3.14 \times 5 = 31.4$ cm.

Remember that the perimeter of a circle is more *usually* called its **circumference**.

Ratios

A ratio is the proportion of one figure in relation to another. If there are 10 girls in a class and 15 boys then the ratio of girls to boys is 10:15 or 2:3.

Squares and square roots

The **square** of a number is the result when you multiply a number by itself. Therefore 4 squared is $4 \times 4 = 16$. This is written as 4^2.

The **square root** of a number is the opposite of a square. In other words, a number's square root is the one which, multiplied by itself, gives the original number. The square root of 16 is therefore 4. This is usually written as $\sqrt{16} = 4$.

Volume

This is the space which something takes up in three dimensions. The volume of a **rectangular** shape is found by multiplying length × breadth × height:

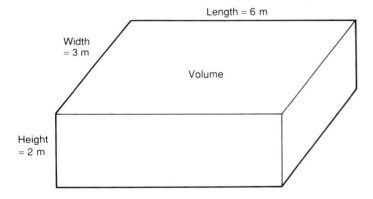

Length = 6 m
Width = 3 m
Volume
Height = 2 m

Therefore the volume of the rectangle above is
$6\,\text{m} \times 2\,\text{m} \times 3\,\text{m} = 36$ cubic metres, written as $36\,\text{m}^3$.

(See also **cubes**, pages 424).

chapter **15** INFORMATION TECHNOLOGY

Introduction

Information technology has transformed our lives over the past few years. If you own a digital watch or automatic camera, play video games or an electronic keyboard, or use your TV set to display teletext then you are involved in IT in its widest sense – as all these devices incorporate microchip technology. When you are away from home you are also involved with IT. The shop you visit will process your purchases by means of a bar-code reader at an EPOS cash register (EPOS = electronic point of sale), your bank can give you an automatic printout of the balance of your account from any cash point, and the car in which you travel may have a digital voice telling you to fasten your seatbelt!

The same type of transformation has taken place in factories and offices. Today many products are designed using CAD – computer-aided design techniques. Both in the factory and in the office, equipment may be controlled by microchips – examples are photocopiers, telephone switchboards and fax machines. Above all, computers are used to process, store and communicate a vast amount of information every hour of the working day. By the year 2000 it is forecast that the IT industry will comprise 10 per cent of world economic activity and will be able to produce machines that can recognise and understand human speech and reasoning. In the future, developments in IT are likely to get more, rather than less, intense.

It is therefore impossible for you to work effectively in any organisation if you have no idea what a computer is or what it does. However, a very basic knowledge will only make you a very average employee. To be *really* effective you need to know enough to be able to think for yourself, set your own (high!) standards and use your own initiative when you come up against a problem.

The aim of this chapter is not only to give you the basic information you require but also to help you develop the skills you need to become a valuable employee.

DID YOU KNOW?

It is estimated that by the year 2000, personal computers will use 10 per cent of the world's power supply (let alone the world's paper supply!). New developments in computers include the facility to switch off both themselves and any linked terminals when they have not been used for a while – just to save electricity.

The basics

As a first step, you need to be familiar with

- computer equipment or **hardware**
- business application packages or **software**
- health and safety and IT
- security systems.

The skills

To be an effective operator you need to:

- know how to use properly the software available to you
- appreciate the need for confidentiality and security and take precautions to protect information as necessary
- follow recognised and standard procedures for producing documents, storing information and making back-up copies
- format documents so that they look attractive
- follow specific instructions **or** make sensible decisions on your own
- know the quickest and most efficient way of carrying out a specific routine
- operate within normal office time constraints
- produce high quality documents consistently
- understand the terms used in relation to IT equipment and software.

At the end of this chapter is a **Quick Reference Section** which gives an alphabetical list of all the main terms used, together with a brief definition. Use this if someone refers to something and you've forgotten what it means!

▪ COMPUTER HARDWARE ▪

The hardware of a computer system consists of

- **input devices** – used to put the information into the system
- **the CPU (central processing unit)** – the 'brains' of the system which carries out all the instructions received (either from the operator or from the program)
- **storage devices** – used to save both data and programs
- **output devices** – used to display the end result.

The links between these can be seen in Figure 15.1.

Types of computer system

The exact type of equipment you will find in an office will depend on whether the organisation has stand-alone microcomputers, a networked system or a mainframe computer.

Stand-alone system

In this case your equipment (see Figure 15.2) will consist of:

- a keyboard
- a screen (called a visual display unit – VDU)
- a central processing unit (CPU)
- a disk drive
- a printer.

The term 'stand-alone' is used because the system is self-contained and is not dependent on any other piece of equipment to operate. You may find such a system referred to as a **workstation.** One advantage of a stand-alone system is that it is easily transportable and can therefore be used in a different place (especially if it is only small, such as a laptop or notebook computer).

Although the system is 'stand-alone', there may be a telecommunications link between a workstation and other central computing facilities.

A networked system

In a network all the microcomputers in an organisation are linked together, so that they all have access to the same information. This may be in the form of:

- software programmes, which are available on all or some machines
- information which is useful to most or all of the staff (e.g. a customer address list).

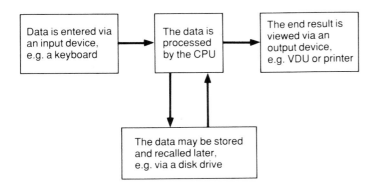

Figure 15.1 *The links between input and output devices*

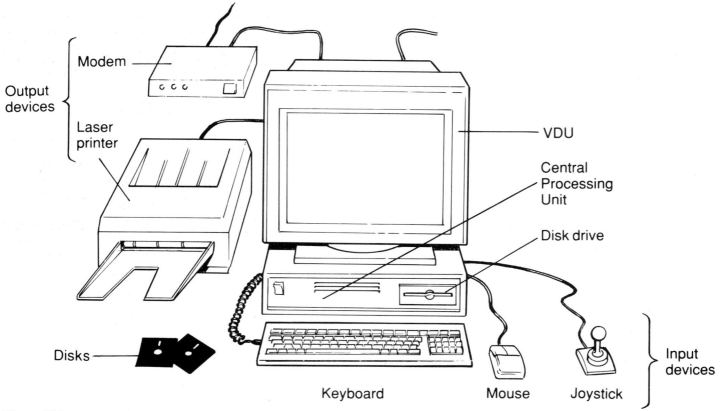

Figure 15.2 *A stand-alone system*

If an organisation links its computers over a small (geographical) area then this is known as a **LAN (local area network)**. If the system is over a greater area this is referred to as a **WAN (wide area network)**.

Users have to **log on** to a network by means of their own user code and a personal password. On most networks users must change their password regularly as a security precaution. Some users may have access to 'higher level' (i.e. more confidential) information than others (see also page 461).

You should note that on some of the more sophisticated networks more than computers are linked. A wide variety of office equipment can be incorporated into a network (e.g. fax machines, photocopiers and telex machines).

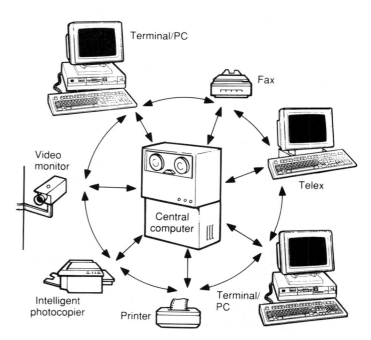

Figure 15.3 *An ideal set-up, where everything is interconnected and compatible*

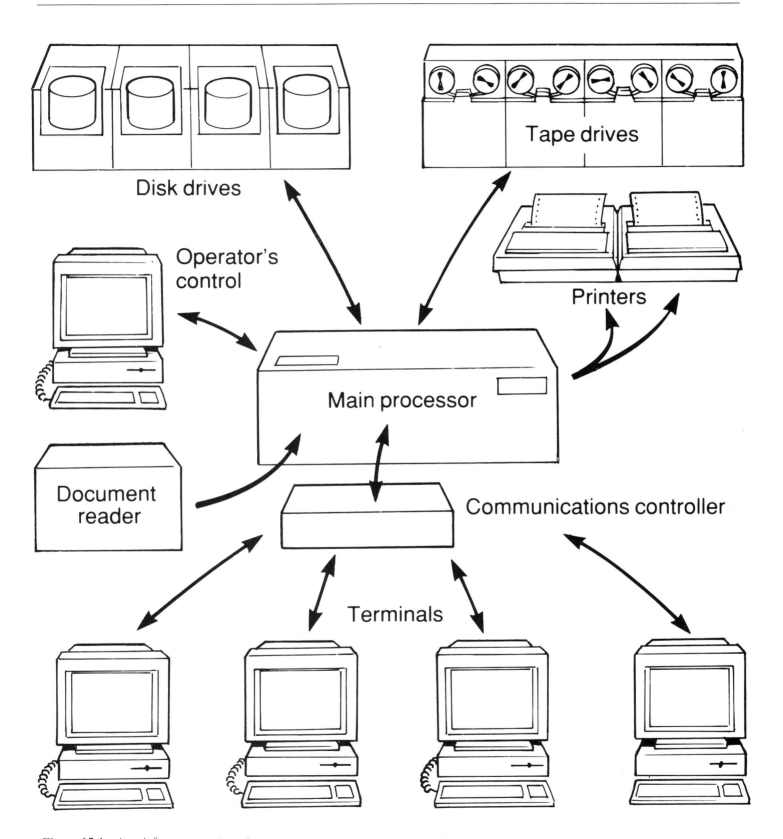

Figure 15.4 *A mainframe computer set-up*

Using a networked computer

As mentioned above, each user of a network has to log on to gain entry to the system. When the user has finished working on the machine he or she must **log out** so that access has been officially ended. Computer staff can keep a record of the number of users and this can be useful for several reasons – including determining the main periods of use, whether the system is becoming overloaded and so on. It is important that, as a user, you use the correct procedure for logging in and *never* switch off the computer without logging out of the system properly.

There will again be a security system in operation so that confidential information is available only to specified staff.

A large mainframe computer will have a very large memory and a high processing speed. Despite this, much of the routine work (e.g. processing invoices) is done overnight so that the computer is not overloaded during the daytime. For this reason, many companies with a mainframe computer operate a shift system so that computer staff are on duty 24 hours a day.

Note: Further information on micro and mainframe computers is contained in Section 1, Chapter 3.

DID YOU KNOW?

If you leave *any* computer switched on for a long period, with text or graphics showing on the VDU, then this can create 'screen burn'. This means that the image will be 'burned on' to the screen and can be seen even when the computer is switched off. For this reason many computers are designed to blank the screen automatically after a few minutes of non-use. Pressing any key on the keyboard restores the 'picture' to the screen.

DID YOU KNOW?

Executives who travel can take their computers with them if they own a **laptop** or **notebook** computer. Both of these machines are small, portable, self-contained units which incorporate a keyboard, floppy or hard disk drives and a screen. The laptop (Figure 15.5) is the slightly larger version (but small enough to be used on the operator's lap). The notebook is as small as its name suggests. The latest computers are known as **palm top** or **pen computers**. Palm tops can be held in the hand and the latest measures only 18 cm × 10 cm.

Mainframe computers

A **mainframe computer** is a computer which is capable of handling and processing a vast amount of information. These machines are leased or rented by large companies who have special computer departments and employ their own programmers and operators. Because these machines can be used by a number of people simultaneously, staff will each have a **terminal** on their desk – usually just a keyboard and a VDU – which is linked to the mainframe (see Figure 15.4).

The software may have been individually written for the company by their own programmers and will probably include payroll, stock control and invoicing. In addition there may be some bought-in packages (e.g. spreadsheets and word-processing).

Figure 15.5 *A laptop computer*

It is possible to communicate with the office via a portable computer and both send and receive information. This is done via a telephone line and a modem, which may be built in to the machine. (For details of modems see page 89.)

Activity

For virtually all organisations it would be disastrous if a fire destroyed the company's computer system. Discuss *as a group*:

1 the **costs** involved if such an event occurred (and try to think beyond the costs of the equipment!)
2 the precautions a company could take to prevent this type of occurrence.

DID YOU KNOW?

Computers vary in the speed at which they can process an instruction. The faster they operate the more powerful they are and so the more they cost usually. Faster computers are required for complex programs such as graphics, CAD and CAM (computer aided manufacturing) packages. For character-based software, such as word-processing, databases and spreadsheets, the processing speed is less important. However, if you use an applications package which is linked to a graphics operating system (e.g. Windows), then you will find it much easier if you are operating a computer with a high-speed processor.

Memory

The amount of data which can be processed by a computer at any one time is determined by the size of its **memory**. The memory size is measured by the number of characters or **bytes** which the computer can store at any one time.

The memory capacity of microcomputers is measured in Kilobytes (K = 1024). Therefore a small games computer with a 64K memory can handle approximately 64 000 characters at once.

Most business microcomputers have a base memory size of 640K with optional extended memory of up to a further 1024K.

The memory capacity of mainframe computers is measured in:

● megabytes (mega = 1 million), and
● gigabytes (giga = 1000 million).

RAM

The proper term for a computer's 'working' memory is **RAM – random access memory**. You can access any part of this set of data as you are working and replace anything with something new if you want to.

RAM only operates on a temporary basis. When the computer is switched off any data held in RAM is lost. For this reason you need a **backing store** – usually a hard disk (see below) – so that data can be saved until it is next required.

ROM

Computers also have a **ROM** – a **read only memory**. In this part of the memory you can read the information but cannot change it. A typical example is **DOS** – the **disk operating system** of the computer (an alternative version in common use now is **Windows**). When you switch on the computer it already knows how to operate because a systems program telling it how to do this is already stored in ROM. You can therefore use this information, but cannot change or delete it.

Storage devices

Hard disks

Many computers today have hard disks installed. A hard disk is an unremovable disk positioned inside the

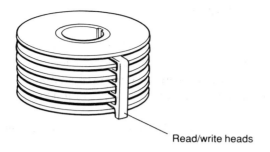

Read/write heads

Figure 15.6 *A stack of hard disks*

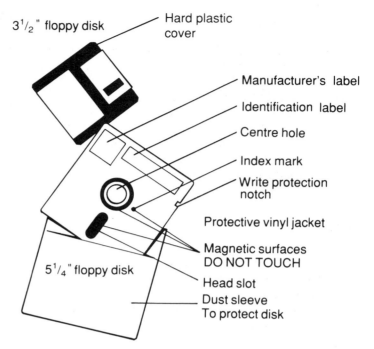

$3\frac{1}{2}$" floppy disk — Hard plastic cover

Manufacturer's label
Identification label
Centre hole
Index mark
Write protection notch
Protective vinyl jacket
Magnetic surfaces DO NOT TOUCH
Head slot
Dust sleeve To protect disk

$5\frac{1}{4}$" floppy disk

Figure 15.7 *Typical floppy disks*

computer which can hold a large number of programs and a large amount of data (see Figure 15.6).

Before a hard disk computer can be moved, special 'heads' must be parked to secure the disk to avoid damage. This is usually either an option on the menu when you are exiting the system or else it occurs automatically.

Floppy disks

These are available in two sizes – $5\frac{1}{4}$ inch and $3\frac{1}{2}$ inch. The amount that can be stored on them depends on whether the disk is single- or double-sided and whether the density is single, double or high. The type of disk you use will depend on the type of data you need to store. For instance, graphics take up much more disk space than text, so if you were regularly storing computer graphics you would be sensible to use double-sided, high density disks.

The $3\frac{1}{2}$ inch smaller disks have a hard plastic case with a metal cover which slides back when the disk is placed into the disk drive (see Figure 15.7).

All floppy disks have the ability to be read/write protected, which means that no further information can be added to or deleted from the disk. This can protect your work and prevent anyone else from overwriting something important by accident. On a $5\frac{1}{4}$ inch disk you must cover the read/write protect notch with a small piece of paper (provided with the disk). On a $3\frac{1}{2}$ inch disk there is a small plastic clip which can be slid into position.

Before you can use a floppy disk you must **format** it so that it is configured for use on your particular computer system. Remember that a disk formatted for one system will not work on another unless you reformat it – in which case you will lose all the documents you have saved.

Care of floppy disks

1　Handle these with care and respect at all times, or you may lose all the work you have so carefully saved!
2　Write the label for a disk *before* sticking it on. Never press on the disk itself with a pen.
3　Always keep a disk in its dust jacket when not in use.
4　Always store disks carefully in a special, purpose-made disk box.
5　Never overfill a disk box so that the disks rub against each other.
6　Keep the disks away from anything magnetic.
7　Keep the disks away from direct heat (e.g. radiators or sunlight).
8　Don't touch the exposed recording surface.

Optical disks

These are similar to music CDs and are gaining in popularity as they can store a vast amount of information, are less apt to be damaged than magnetic disks and data can be retrieved more quickly than from floppy disks. Different types of optical disks are used for different purposes:

- CD-ROM disks are used for large databases. The user can access the information but cannot erase or replace it.
- CD-WORM disks enable the user to write information to the disks but again it cannot be erased. They are mainly used with electronic filing systems. (Note – WORM stands for Write Once, Read Many Times.)
- Erasable optical disks can be used as ordinary disks – the user can store and erase data as often as he or she wishes. These are very expensive at present but as prices are falling they will probably become the 'floppy disk' of the future.

Care of hardware

1 Never switch a computer quickly off and on again.
2 Never move a computer without permission and without parking the heads on the hard disk first.
3 Never switch off a computer without logging out properly.
4 Never try to take out a disk while the disk drive light is on.
5 Never leave a computer or a printer switched on when you have finished using it.
6 Never put food, drink or other liquids near a computer.
7 If your machine shows an unknown error message, check with your supervisor, tutor or user manual before pressing any keys – or you may make the problem worse.
8 The machines and the screens should be cleaned regularly but **only** by using the special products made for the job.

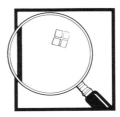

Evidence Assignment 15A

1 Obtain a copy of a computer supplies catalogue.

   a Compare the prices of double-sided low-density disks and

double-sided high-density disks.

b Find out the price of a lockable disk box.

c List the types of products used for cleaning computers and their prices.

2 You are operating a stand-alone microcomputer which has a base memory of 640K and an extended memory of 1024K. You are told it has a 40Mb hard disk.

a How many characters can be stored simultaneously in its base memory?

b How many in its extended memory?

c How many characters will the hard disk hold before it is full?

3 Either from advertisements for microcomputers *or* from a computer catalogue, compile a list of four different machines, in each case stating the price, processing speed and memory size.

Can you find any correlation between this information which would help you to choose the 'best buy' of the four machines you have listed?

Peripherals

This term is used to describe any item of equipment which is attached to or controlled by the computer – and, strictly speaking, includes the disk drive. However, it is more usually used to describe the range of input and output devices which may be used by a computer operator, as well as communications devices (e.g. a modem – see page 89).

Input devices

In offices the main method of inputting data is by keyboard. However, in some organisations alternative methods may be preferred:

- **A bar-code reader** is used to read the bar-code on goods to input sales information into computerised electronic cash registers.
- **touch sensitive screens** are used by personnel who are not trained typists, to input data. The operator simply touches the VDU screen at the required option. They are found in organisations such as banks and hospitals.
- **A mouse** is a small box moved around on the workstation to change the position of the cursor on the screen. It is often used by non-typists and with graphics programs.
- **A light pen** (Figure 15.8) is used to wipe over bar-codes or, more often, to produce graphics on screen by 'drawing' as with a normal pen to create pictures and designs. It is often used with CAD programs.
- **A graphics tablet** (Figure 15.8) is used extensively in CAD as shapes can be drawn with a light pen. The

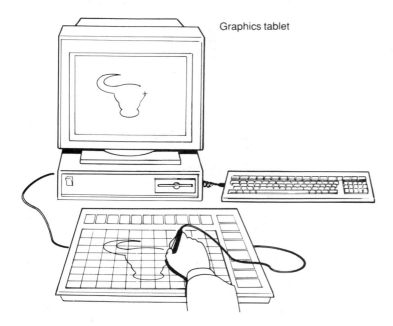

Graphics tablet

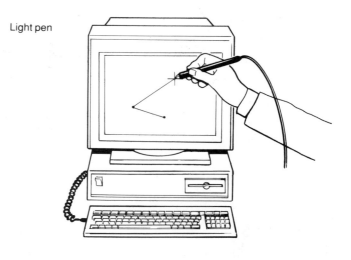

Light pen

Figure 15.8 *Input devices*

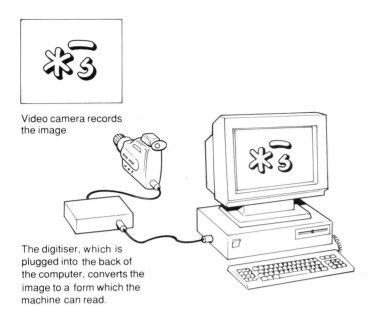

Video camera records the image

The digitiser, which is plugged into the back of the computer, converts the image to a form which the machine can read.

Figure 15.9

operator can also undertake other functions automatically, such as changing the angle of a drawing.

- **A digitiser** is used to create sophisticated graphics on computer by converting drawings, photographs and video stills to a series of digital impulses which are displayed on the VDU screen and stored on disk (Figure 15.9).
- **A document reader or scanner** is a device which automatically reads text or graphics and puts this into a computer. This may be a machine into which is fed a sheet of paper or a hand-held device which is 'rolled' over the required information.
- **Magnetic ink character readers** are used by banks to identify cheques automatically by the numbers on them which are printed with special magnetic ink.

Activity

Look at a cheque and identify the three sets of numbers which are printed in magnetic ink. Try to find out what each number represents.

Output devices

The main output device is the printer. There are two main types of printer (see Figure 15.10):

- **impact** printers (e.g. dot matrix, where direct contact is made with the paper)
- **non-impact** (e.g. ink jet or laser, where ink is placed on the paper without any contact being made).

Other output devices include:

- **VDU screen**
- **plotter** – used to produce graphs, charts and a variety of other graphics. Colour can be used (although the

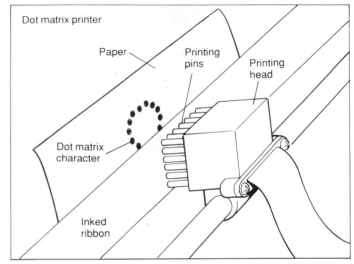

Dot matrix printer

Paper
Printing pins
Printing head
Dot matrix character
Inked ribbon

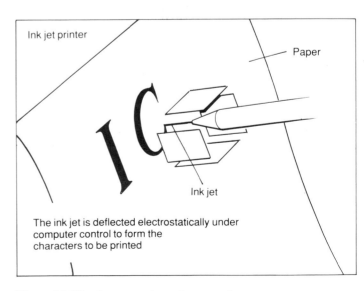

Ink jet printer

Paper

Ink jet

The ink jet is deflected electrostatically under computer control to form the characters to be printed

Figure 15.10 *Impact and non-impact printers*

number of colours is limited except on very expensive machines) and some can produce two-dimensional drawings.

- **COM** – Computer output to microfilm. On a mainframe system the output is automatically produced as microfiche so that large amounts of information can be stored in a small area.

Computer printers

The type of printer which is used in an office will depend on the type of output being produced. In-house documents such as payroll listings and account transactions need not be high quality and yet need to be produced quickly. A cheaper printer will therefore be quite suitable for this purpose.

Letters, memos and other business documents need to be printed on a good quality printer so that customers gain a good impression of the organisation. Graphics and desktop publishing packages need a high quality printer, especially if sophisticated shading or special text effects are required.

Dot matrix are the cheapest type of printer. The image is formed by a series of dots placed on the paper. Quality is only fair but the printing is quite rapid. Quality can be improved by using the NLQ (near letter quality) function which means the printer goes over each character twice to improve the density.

Daisywheel printers are most commonly used with word-processing packages as the quality is good. Some printers are bi-directional (i.e. the print wheel moves in one direction and then in the other) which speeds up printing. The daisywheel is a small wheel in the machine consisting of 'petals' which fan outwards. At the end of each petal is a character. Different daisywheels can be used with a variety of type styles and special characters (e.g. for foreign language work). Daisywheel printers are quite expensive and are declining in popularity as the daisywheels are fragile and expensive to replace, and other printers (see below) are more versatile and falling in price.

Ink-jet or bubble jet printers spray tiny droplets of ink onto virtually any surface – paper, glass, plastic or metal. The quality is excellent and they are equally good for graphics and text. Desktop models are reasonably priced

although the cost of replacing the ink cartridge can be quite high. They are relatively slow and the range of graphics and text sizes is limited.

Laser printers use laser beams to transfer the original image to a drum which then transfers it to paper. Desktop models are now quite common in most offices even though they are quite expensive. The copy quality is excellent both for text and graphics. A Postscript laser printer is one which stores a range of fonts (typestyles) in its memory digitally. Such a machine is ideal for desktop publishing work although it may be expensive.

Massive 'smart' laser printers cost many thousands of pounds and are used mainly by computer centres and by newspaper publishers. Forms and headings can be memorised by the printer and printing is so rapid that hundreds of copies can be produced each minute.

Care of printers

1 First of all – and very important – find out how to stop the printer quickly if there is a problem. This usually means typing in a command on the computer, *not* just pressing the 'off' switch! Remember that your command will vary from one computer program to another.
2 Make sure that your paper is properly loaded into the machine and correctly aligned. Continuous stationery should be positioned with the sprocket holes placed over the sprockets to keep it in position. Single sheet paper should be fanned first. Make sure it is correctly aligned with the paper guides on your printer.
3 Use only the recommended paper for your printer. This is particularly important for laser printers where the quality and weight of the paper can be vital.
4 *Never* block the area where your printout emerges. Otherwise you may find you have reams of continuous stationery 'backing' into the printer and jamming it.
5 Use the TOF (top of form) or FF (form feed) button to turn up the paper automatically.
6 Remember that your printer *must* be **on line** before it will print. This is the first thing to check if, for any reason, nothing is happening.
7 Read your printer manual to find out
   - how to rectify *simple* faults (e.g. a paper jam)
   - how to change the ribbon, ink cartridge or laser cartridge.

8 *Never* tamper with the printer if you are not sure what you are doing. Ask your tutor for help.

DID YOU KNOW?

An alternative form of output is to send your message to someone else's computer by electronic mail. If you are linked by a network then it is likely an Email system will be in use. Each user has a mailbox which can only be accessed if he or she types in his or her user ID and password. This is to prevent any unauthorised person gaining access to what is, in effect, a private mailbox. Messages are stored in the mailbox to be read, replied to, sent on to someone else, saved or deleted. The system is quick and easy to use.

A business which wants to communicate with its customers or suppliers by Email may subscribe to Telecom Gold or Prestel and obtain a company mailbox. This can be accessed from any part of the world – given a computer, a modem and a telephone line.

Evidence Assignment 15B

Obtain as much information as you can from manufacturers of computer printers about their products. You can do this either by looking through computer magazines or by finding advertisements for printers (look in the national press) and sending off for literature.

Obtain information on at least three makes of dot matrix, ink jet and laser printers. Then copy out the headings on the chart below and complete it with the information you have found. If possible, produce a printed version using a word-processing package.

COMPUTER PRINTERS – COMPARISON CHART			
Make	Type of printer	Cost	Main features

• THE ROLE OF THE OPERATOR •

A computer is simply a device which enables you to process information quickly and easily. It has no in-built intelligence but simply follows your instructions. It is therefore impossible for it to 'go wrong' on its own – if an error occurs it is because you made it! If you think of it as a rather clever slave, rather than having a life force of its own, you will be more likely to take responsibility for your own actions!

To be able to operate one efficiently you need to know how to use the equipment correctly *and* understand how the software is meant to operate and the functions it can carry out. Failure to understand the first can result in expensive and time-consuming problems, if you inadvertently damage part of the system. Ignorance of the second can mean you waste hours of everyone's time, including your own. To be really effective you also need to take a pride in your work, so that the documents you produce are of consistently high quality and you gain a reputation for reliability and conscientiousness.

This usually pays dividends as you will be rewarded with progressively more difficult and challenging tasks – which will make your job more interesting and varied, as well as preparing you for a more senior position with more responsibility.

Using a keyboard

Keyboards vary from one computer to another although most have the standard QWERTY keyboard together with the following special keys. Find out where these are and learn how they work with *each* of the programs you use.

Function keys	Usually up to 12, these will be either above or to the left of your character keys. Each will have a special use for each program you use.
Backspace	Deletes the character to the left of the cursor
Delete	Deletes the character at the same position as the cursor.
Cursor keys	These are the four arrow keys which move the cursor up, down, to the left or right.

Page Up/ Down	Normally programmed by the software to move you forwards or backwards one page at a time.
Home key	This will either move your cursor to the beginning of the document or to the left of your screen.
End key	Will either move your cursor to the end of the document or the right of your screen.
Esc key	Usually enables you to escape from the option you have just chosen (useful if you choose the wrong one!).
Alt and Ctrl keys	Usually have specific functions for the program you are using. You may like to note that holding down both Control and Alt together and pressing the Delete key will normally reset your computer. This can be useful to know if your screen 'freezes' for any reason.

Using a mouse

If possible, use this on a special mouse mat which prevents dust and fluff being picked up from the desk and transferred to the rubber ball underneath. Roll it over the surface of the mat smoothly. If you are about to fall off the edge of the desk then remember that you can lift up the mouse to reposition it without moving your cursor on screen.

A mouse usually has two buttons (see Figure 15.11) and clicking these will enable you to:

• select an option from a list on screen
• draw lines and shapes.

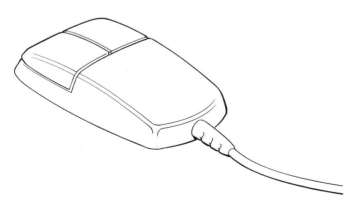

Figure 15.11

If you point to a specific option and then hold your button down you may find you can **drag** an image or icon from one part of your page to another.

Two rules to note:

1 Make sure you know which button does what on the program you are using.
2 Clean your mouse regularly by removing the detachable plate underneath and cleaning the little rubber ball.

DID YOU KNOW?

Many programs which require a mouse will only work if the mouse is connected *before you load the program*. If, therefore, nothing seems to work once you have switched on, switch off again, check your mouse is connected properly and then try again.

Using a scanner

The first rule is – make sure the document you are scanning is clean. Otherwise the scanner will interpret every dirty mark as a character, and you will have the job of erasing them all on screen! You will also have a much clearer, higher definition image if you make sure your original is black and white, rather than colour (if necessary, photocopy it first).

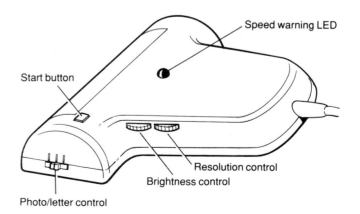

Figure 15.12

A full-size document scanner usually takes a sheet of A4 paper and, provided you insert it so that it is straight, there is little that can go wrong. A hand-held scanner (see Figure 15.12) is more tricky – it needs to be moved slowly and steadily down the image you are scanning. Do remember that you can easily erase the image on screen and start again if you make a mess of it – the answer is plenty of practice!

DID YOU KNOW?

Scanners are now being used in systems known as **document management**. This means scanning all documents and filing them *electronically* rather than in filing cabinets. The documents are kept on optical disk, so thousands can be held on a very small area. The aim is to reduce the amount of paper, and the cost of the storage space it occupies.

· COMPUTER SOFTWARE ·

Software refers to the programs which are loaded into the computer to tell it what to do. Two types of program are used with microcomputers.

Systems program

This is the program which controls the computer's operation and instructs it how to function. Whilst the most common is **DOS** (Disk operating system), the latest innovation is called **Windows 3**. Not only is this more powerful than DOS, enabling the user to work on several tasks at once, it is also more user-friendly as it relies on a system of **icons** (small pictures) and drop-down menus rather than keyed-in commands.

Applications programs

These are the actual business programs which can be loaded so that the computer can be used for a variety of business applications. An applications program is usually sold as a **package** comprising the software, a user manual and, sometimes, a tutorial disk or booklet.

DID YOU KNOW?

1 The small block on your screen where the colours are reversed and often flashing is called your **cursor**. The cursor must be at the point at which you want to do something – whether this means choosing an option or changing some text.
2 Most packages are cleverly designed so that all the prompts are given to you on screen. Unfortunately, many people don't bother reading these so all this effort by the programmer is lost! If you're stuck, before you try to find help, *always read your screen*. It is very likely that the answer to your problem is staring right back at you!

· BUSINESS APPLICATION PACKAGES ·

In business a wide variety of software is used, all of which has different uses and functions.

- **Word-processing** packages are used for creating documents such as memos, letters and reports.
- **Database** packages are used for keeping records of customers and suppliers.
- **Spreadsheet** packages are used for carrying out calculations mainly based on future plans (e.g. what will happen to our profit if we give all the staff a pay rise?).
- **Graphics** packages may be used to create artwork for posters and adverts.
- **Desktop publishing** packages are used to create posters, newsletters and advertising material.
- **Payroll** packages do just that – they automatically calculate wages and print pay slips and the other statutory returns required by companies.
- **Accounts** packages are used for general book-keeping, producing invoices, calculating VAT returns and printing end-of-year financial documents.

At some time in your future career you may be asked to use any of these types of software. If you work in a manufacturing organisation you may also see **CAD** (computer aided design) or **CAM** (computer aided manufacturing) in operation. At this stage in your career it is likely that you may be asked to *use* word-processing, database and spreadsheet packages together with some basic DTP or graphic packages.

Activity

Packages can be divided into three types – textual, graphical and numerical. From the descriptions given above, which software types do you consider are classified under each type of package?

DID YOU KNOW?

Today many packages are **integrated**. This means they are compatible so that, for instance, a spreadsheet from one package can be 'imported' into a word-processed document.

User-friendly packages

Some programs are advertised as 'user-friendly' – because they are supposed to be easy to learn and use. This usually means that they will incorporate either **menus** or **windows**. A menu simply gives you a list of choices and you move the cursor to the option you want (or key in the letter to identify this option). A window operates on a similar basis: a range of options is shown across the top of your screen and when you select the one you want a menu drops down under this option, giving you a range of choices.

DID YOU KNOW?

On *any* package you *must* press your 'Enter' key (or click the correct mouse button) to select the option you want. The computer cannot know which choice you have made until you do this!

If you make the wrong choice by mistake, then pressing Esc (on most packages) will take you back to where you were before (or select this option with your mouse).

Common features

Features which are common to many different types of package include:

Status line(s) Gives information on the piece of work you are creating.

Prompt line Gives information on what you can do next.

Entry line Usually identified by >. You enter your command immediately after this symbol.

Help feature Most packages utilise a special Help key on your computer. This will give you the assistance the programmer thought you might need if you are stuck at this part of the program.

Commands These vary considerably from one package to another. Learn the ones you need to use on a regular basis (make a note of them to start with on a quick reminder sheet). You can look up the more obscure commands as and when you need them. The main commands you need to know are:

- **retrieve** – how to recall information already stored on disk
- **save** – how to save information you have created on to disk
- **print** – how to print a hard copy of your work
- **quit** – how to close down the package when you have finished.

DID YOU KNOW?

To use software or disks on a particular computer they must be **compatible** with the system you are using. You cannot take a disk which you have used on an Apple machine and suddenly use it on an IBM machine. In a similar way, you must make sure that any software you buy is compatible with the hardware system you are using.

Document formats

Don't get this term confused with formatting a disk (see page 436)! **Document format** is the term used when you decide what your document will look like. This means you will choose:

- the paper size
- whether your text or graphics will be printed portrait or landscape (see Figure 15.13)
- the size of your margins (left, right, top and bottom) and your page length
- line spacing
- whether or not to **justify** your right-hand margin
- the type of characters to use and their size
- the number of columns you will use and the size of these
- the layout of documents such as letters, memos and reports
- the design of any tables or diagrams you are including.

Many organisations have standard settings for certain documents which you need to check carefully.

Portrait: paper
short side at top

Landscape: paper
long side at top

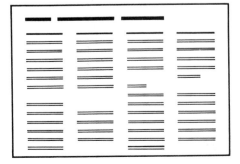

Figure 15.13 *The differences between portrait and landscape presentation*

The problems may start when you are left to your own devices and expected to set out a professional document.

It has been said that anyone creating a document should be something of an artist. By this it is meant that any work you produce in printed form should be visually pleasing and well balanced. In addition, if you want to be considered reliable and responsible it *must* be accurate in every detail (see proof-reading below).

DID YOU KNOW?

If you want to set a format command which will apply *throughout* the document (e.g. margin width or justification) then you usually need to have your cursor at the **beginning** of the document when you make the command. Otherwise you will find that only the text *after* the cursor position has been affected!

Hints and tips

1 Most office documents are printed on A4 paper (and many printers can only cope with this size of paper). You can always enlarge or reduce it later on a photocopier. However, in some cases you may have a wider printer – for instance if you are operating with large spreadsheets which will not fit on A4 paper.
2 It should be relatively easy to decide whether landscape or portrait paper is the most suitable. Again, your printer may make the decision for you because only certain types (e.g. ink jet and laser) will print out in landscape format. Use your common sense! If you are creating a table or poster which is wide but not deep then go for landscape, if it is deep and narrow then stick to portrait.
3 A good guide for left-hand and right-hand margins is 4 cm each side. A document always looks better if the margins are equal. If, however, this would mean a small amount of text being carried to another page then change the margins. The wonderful thing about computers is that you can change your margins several times and keep looking at the different effects.

4 The top and bottom margins determine the page length. Again they usually look better when they are equal. If you only have a small amount of text on a page then you could go for wide top and bottom margins and double line spacing to make it look more effective.

5 On virtually all packages your text or figures at the left side of the page will automatically be justified (i.e. start at the same point). Word-processed documents look much more professional if you also choose right justification as well – so that they look more like a printed page. The same applies if you are creating documents on a desktop publishing package. On a spreadsheet you can choose whether you want information in cells to be left or right justified – experiment to see which looks best.

6 A character set is a particular group of characters. Your keyboard holds one character set (usually ASCII codes – pronounced 'askey'). On some packages you have the opportunity to use other sets which will include graphics or symbols not held on the standard set; for instance:

- other languages, e.g. Greek (β), Indian   , Cyrillic (Π)
- mathematical and scientific signs, e.g. ÷, ≡ and ∴
- other symbols not normally found on your keyboard, e.g. ‰, ☞, § or ✈.

The important thing is whether your printer will be able to print these out, even if you can select them in your program!

7 Fonts relate to different typefaces and styles. You can choose different fonts in some word-processing packages and in all desktop publishing packages. However, for a wide range of fonts you need a Postscript laser printer (see page 440). Examples of fonts are shown in Figure 15.14.

8 The size of your characters will also be determined by your printer. Again if you have a Postscript laser printer you can vary these more. Size is given in *points* (see Figure 15.14 for some examples.)

9 On *some* word-processing packages and all desktop publishing packages you can produce work in columns. This means your finished document looks something like a newspaper. From two to four columns is the best (three is often ideal). More than four means your text width is too narrow

This is an example of Times typeface

This is an example of Courier typeface

This is an example of Helvetica typeface

This is an example of Palatino typeface

This is 8 point

This is 12 point

This is 24 point

This is 36 point

Figure 15.14 *Examples of typefaces and sizes*

to be read easily. Drawing vertical lines between columns (only possible on a DTP package) makes your finished work look more professional. As a general rule it is best to stick to equal columns with equal spaces between them. Most packages have *pre-set* column widths which are standard size. Stick to these until you know what you are doing.

10 Document layout is dealt with in full in Core Skills, Chapter 13 on Communication. Bear in mind that you should be able to use both block and indented paragraphs and should *always* use headings if you are typing a long piece of continuous prose as this makes your document much easier to read.

Using numbered points and indenting your text so that it is aligned throughout will also make your work look more attractive.

11 Producing tables and diagrams is much easier if you are working with a package which does these almost automatically.

On some word-processing packages the 'outline' of a table can be produced automatically. You then simply readjust the column widths to fit in with your text; e.g.

MACHINE OUTPUT – LEEDS			
	January	February	March
Machine 1	29 738	48 379	19 728
Machine 2	20 389	22 038	19 361
TOTAL	50 127	70 417	39 089

Note that in the table above:

- the main heading has been typed in capitals, centred and emboldened for effect
- the headings and total lines have been emboldened to make them easier to read
- a space has been left after the 'thousands' column in the figures – to make the numbers clearer.

These effects are known as **text enhancement** and are achievable on most types of packages (see page 446).

Any tables or diagrams you produce should be:

- well-balanced
- easy to read
- clearly labelled
- well positioned
- pleasing to the eye.

Proof-reading

No matter what package you are using it is important that you check your work carefully. There is little point in knowing your program backwards and being a whizz-kid at formatting if your work is full of mistakes! On word-processing packages you may find you have a spell-check facility to help you – but this won't pick up keying-in errors if the word you have typed is still recognisable (see page 449).

You need to remember that:

- Proof-reading from a screen is a *skill* which must be developed.
- Generally people find it harder to read 'word by word' from a screen than from a piece of paper.
- Proof-reading on a computer may mean having to scroll backwards and forwards to check that you have spelled a word the same way every time.
- The process is even more difficult – and more important – when figures are involved. The reader will *know* when the word you have typed is wrong, because the sense of the sentence will give it away. No-one can tell if a figure is wrong just by reading a document, and yet this kind of mistake could be disastrous.

If you have problems then *always* take a hard (paper) copy of your work and proof-read this, with someone else as 'reader'. If necessary, you can then make any corrections before taking a final printout.

▪ WORD-PROCESSING PACKAGES ▪

Word-processing packages are used to produce letters, memos, reports and other business documents. They have removed much of the drudgery and repetitive work this used to involve. A variety of packages are on the market, including WordPerfect, Word, Wordstar, etc. If there is a number after the name of the program then the *highest* number indicates the most up-to-date version of the software.

You may be pleased to know that whereas the packages are not identical, the type of features to be found on a word-processing package are always the same. It may be only the commands and the layout of your screen that are different. Therefore if you know one package well, this should help you to learn others quickly.

Figure 15.15 shows how a short document might appear on the screen.

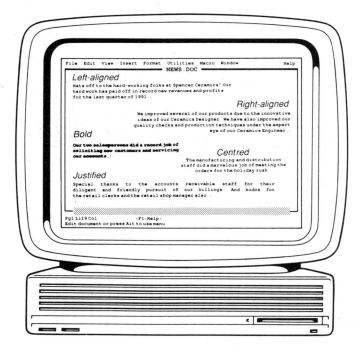

Figure 15.15

Main features

Editing	Text can easily be inserted, deleted or amended in a document. There is never any need to retype pages just because some alterations must be made.
Text enhancement	Text can be enhanced by using bold, underline or other options (see above). Some packages enable you to produce text in special fonts – very large or very small, italic or other forms of typeface, such as a shadow effect. How these come out will depend very much on the printer you use.
Blocks	Blocks are chunks of text with which you want to do something. You may want to move, copy, delete or enhance a block. The first step is to define your block by identifying where it starts and finishes. You then give the command for the operation you require.
Reformatting	Any aspect of the layout of a document can be changed at any time. You can alter the margins, change the style of your headings (e.g. from left to centred), justify the right-hand margin, change paragraphs and number the pages. You can change the design when you have seen what the finished document will look like, to improve the final appearance.
Search (and replace)	You can search for a particular word or phrase throughout any size of document. If you wish you can replace this with another word or phase either by choice (as you look through) or automatically.

Mail merge
Mail merge is the way to produce personalised letters quickly and easily. You type in the letter and store it under one file name and then type in your 'variables' and store these under a different file name. Variables are those parts of the letter which are different for each recipient (e.g. name, address and possibly special details in the body of the letter, such as an interview time). When you give the computer instructions it will 'merge' the two files in such a way that personalised letters are produced.

Printing
Your print screen menu will usually give a variety of options, such as choice of line spacing, margin settings, justification and so on. You may also be able to print out selected pages only or multiple copies, as required.

DID YOU KNOW?

All WP systems have a directory which shows all the documents stored on a particular disk. Systems vary in the way in which you can name documents for later identification. On some of the best systems you can do a 'search' for a specific document if you know any part of its title or the date on which it was produced.

Good directory management is essential if you are using a hard disk, because hundreds of documents could be held on this at any one time. Two basic rules should be followed:

1 Don't keep documents on disk longer than necessary. Erase them.
2 Set up a system of main directories and sub-directories. You may have a main directory (sometimes called the root directory); e.g. WPLETTERS for all the letters you type. In this you could have six sub-directories, for instance, if you produce work for six different people. These could be labelled by their surnames (e.g. WPLETKING, WPLETBROWN and so on). The directories would then hold a smaller number of documents and each would be easier to find.

DID YOU KNOW?

This type of electronic filing is often known as 'tree and branch filing'. Think of the main or root directory as the 'tree' and the sub-directories as separate 'branches' off the main 'tree'. Each branch can have further divisions if you wish (see Figure 15.16). In this case your 'tree' is your filing cabinet, your branches are the drawers and so on.

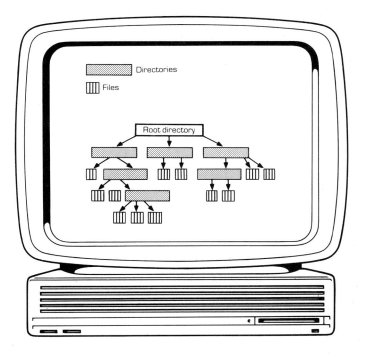

Figure 15.16

Activity

Bearing in mind the directory system above, what would you do about naming directories for memos and reports you also produce for these people?

Additional features

Headers and footers These commands put a space (and text if you want) at the top and bottom of documents automatically. If, for instance, you wanted to put the name of your organisation at the top of one or more pages then you would create a header with this information. If you wanted to put a special note at the bottom you would create a footer.

Pagination This refers to inserting page numbers automatically. Page numbering is an essential feature of a long document in case someone drops it on the floor and needs to sort it out again!

Spell checks Some packages will automatically check your spelling by comparing the words you have typed with those in their electronic dictionary. Highly technical words and proper nouns (e.g. place names) will probably not be in the dictionary but can be added if you want. Do bear in mind that words you have spelled wrongly but which still make a 'proper' word will be ignored by your spellcheck (e.g. form/from, now/know, kind/king, work/word etc). So you still need to proof-read!

Thesaurus An electronic thesaurus will give you a list of words similar to the one currently at your cursor position. This can be useful to improve the vocabulary of a document or by replacing 'repetitive' words. If you use a thesaurus do make sure you know the difference between a noun and a verb – otherwise you could replace a word with one which doesn't have the same meaning at all! For instance,

object (noun) is 'an article, a commodity or a thing', object (verb) means 'to protest or dispute'. So be careful!

Word count This may be included with your spell check. It can be useful if you have to complete a report or project of a certain length. You can check the length as you go and add or delete words as required.

Graphics This can mean actual graphics or, more usually in this context, tables and/or boxes (see page 444).

Footnotes This option automatically numbers and places footnotes for you at any point in the text where they are required.

Switch screens This option means you can work on two documents at once and simply 'toggle' between them, moving text as you wish.

Using a word-processing package

The only way you can become expert at word-processing is to practise regularly. However, some basic pointers right at the beginning will help you to do well more quickly.

1 *Don't* 'hunt and peck' around the keyboard! *Really* try to learn keyboarding properly at the outset – it saves hours later.
2 Learn how to move around your screen easily and quickly (using a combination of the arrow keys and special commands for larger jumps).
3 *Never* delete lots of text and retype it when all it needs is a quick deletion or insertion at a specific point!
4 Learn the commands you need to use regularly. These will usually include:
   - **text commands** – bold, underscore
   - **format commands** – changing margins, centring text, typing to a flush right margin, justification, inset/indented paragraphs, choosing size of paper.
   - **editing commands** – insert, delete, move/delete/copy blocks of text, search and replace, spell check and thesaurus.
   - **print commands** – number of copies, size of paper, line spacing, specific pages only.
5 Learn the functions you need for the job you do. For instance, if you regularly have to produce personalised

letters, then learn how to use your mail merge facility. If you have to type and store standard paragraphs then learn how to do this properly.

6 Develop a *sensible* and *logical* system for saving your documents, so that you can access them easily (see page 447).

7 Set up directories for different types of documents (see page 447), rather as you might store different types of files in a filing cabinet.

8 File your printouts in the same way using folders and files which are correctly labelled with the same names as your directories.

9 Learn the correct layout for business documents (see Core Skills, Chapter 13, on Communication). Then, when you go to work, check the layout you are required to use by your employer. Make sure that the documents you produce are correct and professionally produced so that they won't need altering by anyone else before they can be used.

10 Use your common sense and initiative. Don't expect to be told:
- to proof-read your typing
- to check your spelling
- to use the correct layout (or set it out as clearly and attractively as you can)
- to save an important document
- to save the original document
- to keep confidential information to yourself
- to print out the correct number of copies.

You should do all this *automatically*!

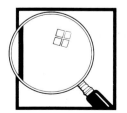

Evidence Assignment 15C

Imagine that you have recently started work for a local charity. Money is scarce and you notice that they have several old typewriters. The manager, Mrs Thornhill, is 'anti-computer'. She thinks that:

- they are expensive
- they are limited – envelopes are still difficult to produce on a computer printer
- word-processors are useless for filling in forms
- they are useless if there is a power cut.

Your boss, Mark Sharp, doesn't agree and is desperate to buy a fairly cheap word-processing system. He thinks the work could be done twice as quickly and the money would therefore be well spent.

He has asked for your help in trying to persuade Mrs Thornhill to buy a word-processor.

1 List the advantages of using a word-processor for standard documents such as letters, memos and reports.

2 Investigate at least two reasonably priced word-processing systems and printers and compare their main features. Write a paragraph stating which system you recommend and give your reasons.

3 Examine Mrs Thornhill's arguments carefully. Try to suggest a solution which will keep both Mrs Thornhill and Mr Sharp happy!

4 Produce a brief report for Mr Sharp which summarises all your investigations. Use a word-processor to produce this and use text enhancement features so that your document(s) are themselves a good advertisement for using a word-processor!

• DATABASE PACKAGES •

A database is an **electronic filing system** which not only stores and recalls information quickly and easily but can also sort it in various ways to suit the needs of the user.

You can keep a database on *anything* which you might record on ordinary paper records:

- a list of customers – names, addresses, telephone numbers, credit allowed, etc.
- a list of cars in a fleet (e.g. for a hire car company) with model, year, registration number, date last serviced, etc.

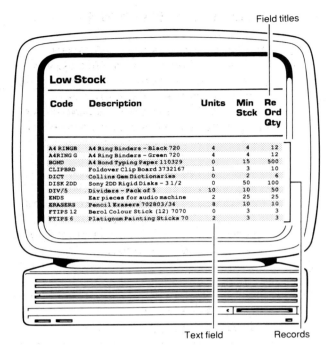

Figure 15.17

- a list of books in a library with title, author, publisher, index number, year of publication, etc.
- a list of students in a college or school with name, address, course attended, work experience placements, etc.

The problem with manual filing is not in entering or keeping the records but in *rearranging* them to find specific information. If your college or school kept student records on a card index system it would be very time-consuming to sort through them all to find a specific student, or to sort through them to make lists under different criteria, e.g.

- all students aged under 18
- all students who live more than five miles away
- all female (or male) students
- all students who did not complete their course.

On a database system this can be done at the press of a key (or two!).

Main features

Form This is the 'card' on screen (similar to a paper record card) which will contain the information (see Figure 15.17).

Field These are the areas for completion with specific information.

Data The information to be entered in each field.

Record The name given to a completed form.

Editing The ability to change information in each field.

File The name of a specific system. In the system described above the file name would probably be 'students'. When the database is completed the file will hold all the student records.

Additional features

Report A report can be designed and printed to reorder the information and display it in a number of different ways.

Search This command will enable you to find a record very quickly. You simply key in a relevant piece of information and press the Enter key. The record you require will then be shown on screen in a matter of seconds.

Formulae Can be entered to calculate amounts at certain points (see also under spreadsheets). For instance, if each college student can claim bus fares for every day attended then the record may have three fields:

Name   Amount of fares   Days attended

A formula could be entered to multiply the amount by the number of days attended and only the result would appear on the report.

Essential data On many systems you can specify whether data must be entered in a field or not. On a student record the 'name' field would be 'essential data' but details of work experience would not.

Using a database

1 Learn all your basic commands (e.g. load, save and print). Find out how to start to design a blank form.
2 Think about the type of file you are going to create, the design of the records and decide what fields you need.
3 Choose field title names which cannot be misinterpreted by other users and decide the length of information which will need inserting after each field name. This determines the lengths of your fields.
4 Create a record card on screen. Learn how to change and rearrange field names and field lengths and print out a copy of the blank form for reference.
5 Practise keying in data on several records. Learn how to edit your records in case you make an error, and how to **resave** your latest version on disk.
6 Practise moving quickly from one record to another using the search command.
7 If you are operating an easy package you may be taught how to design a simple report. Think about the type of information users may want and specify reports to give them this.
8 Print out reports and check that the layout is 'user-friendly'.

DID YOU KNOW?

1 Many database records are subject to the provisions of the Data Protection Act (see page 461) and it is therefore usual to have a security system in operation so that the records cannot be accessed by unauthorised personnel (see page 460).
2 Computerised stock records are simply another version of a database. The cards have been specially designed to give details of stock held.

Activity

Discuss as a group the type of reports you would wish to see if you were operating a computerised stock record system.

DID YOU KNOW?

An *on-line* database is one to which users subscribe to obtain information. Teletext, which you can access on your television, is an example. Another well-known example is Prestel. This is an *interactive* database as users can both request and transmit information. Your school or college library may have access to

specialist databases – often known as databanks – e.g. LEXIS which gives legal information and DIALOG which gives details of publications. Or you may have access to Campus 2000, an on-line database especially aimed at schools and colleges.

Evidence Assignment 15D

Your organisation has many visitors from other parts of the UK and from abroad who are frequently entertained by the company's executives. It has been decided to create a database file on restaurants in your area.

1 Plan a suitable record card with field names and fields for information you think would be useful.

2 Decide on what criteria you would want to sort the cards to produce different reports. Produce a list for your computer technician.

3 Use your local *Yellow Pages* to make a list of 12 restaurants you think should be included.

4 *If possible,* produce a printout of at least one report for inclusion in your portfolio.

• SPREADSHEET PACKAGES •

Spreadsheet packages are used by company accountants or financial managers to assess how well the company is performing and/or how proposed changes will affect its performance. They may also be used by sales, production and personnel staff if they are involved in making calculations or predictions based on numerical information.

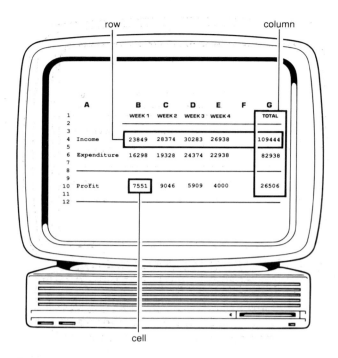

Figure 15.18

A large sheet of paper (which gives the spreadsheet its name) is ruled off into **columns** and **rows**. Headings can be given to both the columns and the rows. Figures can then be added to show income, expenditure, sales, profit etc., either on a weekly or monthly basis (see Figure 15.18).

Spreadsheets are particularly useful for 'what if' calculations. If you are involved in manual calculations you will know that problems occur when alterations have to be made to past figures, or when you want to try to predict the results of possible changes in the future. For instance, if you obtained a part-time job which paid you an extra £25 a week but your spending increased to an average of £16 per week, can you say immediately how much more money you would have at the end of the year? And whether you would be able to afford to go abroad on holiday? If you had a spreadsheet you could enter the new figures and know the answer in seconds!

Main features

Columns	These always go *down* a spreadsheet and are identified by a letter – A, B, C etc.
Rows	These always go *across* a spreadsheet and have an identifying number – 1, 2, 3 etc.
Cells	Each square or box on the spreadsheet is a cell. The cell you are working on is called the **active cell**. Cells are always referred to by using the column letter first (e.g. A1, B5, W49).
Entry line	This is immediately underneath or above your spreadsheet. It is the line on which you enter text, figures, formulae or commands. Pressing the Enter key moves the data into the cell on which your cursor is positioned.
Figures	These are entered by simply keying them in on the entry line and pressing Enter. Figures can be entered either in whole numbers (called **integers**) or to a specified number of decimal places (two decimal places if you are dealing in money).
Text	On some packages this must be prefaced with a special sign so that the computer knows you are entering, say, a heading and not a set of figures for a calculation.
Formulae	A mathematical formula has to be entered at each point where a calculation has to take place. Normally these aren't visible on the spreadsheet.

DID YOU KNOW?

? The spreadsheet on which you are working is usually known as a **worksheet**. You can design this so that it is more user-friendly by using effects such as underline to separate headings from data underneath and to differentiate totals clearly.

DID YOU KNOW?

? Because a spreadsheet is so large only a small part is shown on your screen at any time. Therefore if you jump from cell A1 to cell W58 you are moving to a totally different part of the spreadsheet. There is usually a command to enable you to jump from one cell to another and it is well worth finding this!

Activity

Bearing in mind that some spreadsheets can have literally hundreds of columns and/or rows, as a group can you suggest how columns are identified after the letter 'Z' has been reached?

Additional features

Format	This can include the type of numbers you are displaying (e.g. integer or decimal), column width, right or left justified text. You have the choice between whether to change the format of all the cells of a spreadsheet (i.e. a **global** command) or just one specific cell, row or column.
Erase	Blanking a cell to remove the existing information.
Delete	Removing a row or column.
Copy	Copying an entry from one cell to another.
Insert	Inserting a new row or column.
Protect	Protecting specific cells and formulae against erasure.
Locking	Locking title cells in place (e.g. January, February, etc.) so that they continue to show on screen as the spreadsheet scrolls.
Graphics	Spreadsheet packages are designed to enable you to print out your finished results in graphic form (e.g. by producing a bar chart, line graph or pie chart).
Recalc-ulating	Spreadsheet packages recalculate the answer in every column or row automatically when you make an alteration to a figure. Whilst this is useful it can be time-consuming if you have to wait for a large spreadsheet to be recalculated each time you make an entry. Therefore you have the option to turn recalculate 'off' whilst you make several entries. However, you must remember to turn it back on again

The spreadsheet on screen shows:

	A	B	C	D	E	F	G
1		WEEK 1	WEEK 2	WEEK 3	WEEK 4		TOTAL
2							
3							
4	Income	23849	28374	30283	26938		SUM (B4:E4)
5							
6	Expenditure	16298	19328	24374	22938		SUM (B6:E6)
7							
8							
9							
10	Profit	B4-B6	C4-C6	D4-D6	E4-E6		G4-G6
11							
12							

Figure 15.19

	afterwards or all your work will have been wasted!
Replic-ating	Once you have decided on your formula (see below) it would be time-consuming to enter it dozens of times. For instance, if you are trying to find the sum of 50 columns you wouldn't want to enter a 'sum' formula 50 times. If you use the replicate command this copies your command across all the other columns you specify.

Using a spreadsheet

1 Learn your basic commands (blank, edit and format) and how to enter figures and text.

2 Make sure you are aware of how to **load** a spreadsheet (from disk), **save** (to disk) and **print**. Learn how to clear your screen (which may be the command to **zap** the spreadsheet). If you are printing out a large spreadsheet on A4 paper you will need to know how to specify condensed (smaller) print.

3 Make sure you understand how to insert formulae. Simple formulae include add, subtract, multiply and divide. Bear in mind:

- The answer will always be shown in the cell where your cursor is positioned
- You can identify cells for inclusion in the formula *or* specify numbers (e.g. A1+C7 *or* A1+18).

4 Understand the signs used for inserting formulae:

- You can add by simply specifying cell names with a plus sign in between (e.g. A1+C3). However, this would be impractical for a large number of cells so you need to find out how to enter a **sum** command for your package. This means the figures in any number of cells will be added together.
- A subtraction is done by identifying the cells and inserting a subtraction sign (e.g. A1-B1).
- Multiply is entered using the symbol * (e.g. B3*D7).
- Divide is entered using the symbol /. Therefore D48/4 means divide the figure in cell D48 by 4.

DID YOU KNOW?

When professional users insert the replicate command they never specify a basic range of cells but always add one on. Then if they need to insert an extra figure later the formula doesn't need to be altered!

Graphics

Most spreadsheet packages will create a variety of graphics and charts (e.g. line graphs, bar charts and pie charts). The commands for creating these will vary from one package to another. Here are some tips:

1 Decide on the type of graph or chart you want to produce.

2 Work out the **headings** and **labels** that must be included. Each heading must appear somewhere in your spreadsheet. If it doesn't then insert it in a blank cell – preferably one some distance from your main working area.

3 Identify the cells which you want to illustrate.

4 If you are creating a line graph or bar chart you need to know that the **vertical** axis is the **y-axis** and the **horizontal** axis is the **x-axis**, so that you can label each axis correctly.

5 Information which will be shown on the graph or chart consists of **variables**. For instance, a bar chart with savings and expenditure has *two* variables, a bar chart for income, expenditure and profit has *three* variables and so on. A pie chart can only have one variable or you would need more than one circle! You will need to know the range of cells in which each variable (set of information) is contained.

6 **Time labels** are used only on line graphs and bar charts. They refer to the time period the graph or chart is covering (see Figure 15.20).

7 **Variable labels** are used to give a bar chart or line graph its *key* – otherwise no-one will understand what the lines or bars represent.

8 **Point labels** refer to the labels on a pie chart.

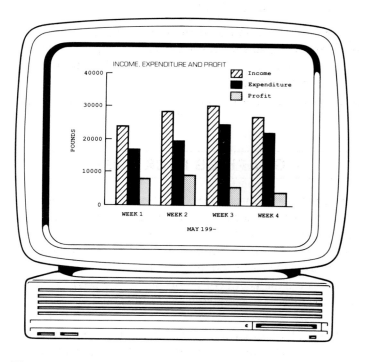

Figure 15.20

Evidence Assignment 15E

Imagine that you work for a company which has branches in various parts of the country. You have been asked to enter the monthly sales figures for January to May and find the totals for each region and each month.

Adjust column widths as necessary and rule off appropriately.

SALES BY REGION

	Jan	Feb	Mar	Apr	May	Total
South	8300	8966	9031	6890	7801	
Midlands	3898	4890	4881	3989	3991	
North	5897	5887	4789	5992	4118	
Scotland	3778	4283	4576	7503	3990	
Wales	5008	5882	5940	3082	4801	
N Ireland	3900	4800	5700	2890	4893	

If possible, ask your tutor to help you enter a formula which will check that the total of the sales (horizontally) agrees with the total for each region when added together.

If you are able to produce graphs and charts on your package, use the data to produce:

- a line graph, showing the performance of each region
- a bar chart, showing the sales per region per month
- a pie chart just for one month, showing the percentage of sales per region.

· GRAPHICS PACKAGES ·

Computer graphics can be used in business to create drawings, graphs and charts (see Figure 15.21). These can be printed on paper, overhead transparencies or slides. Some packages are extremely sophisticated and can be used to create animation and even paintings – though an (expensive) colour printer would be required for the latter.

Virtually all require the use of a **mouse** to operate them. An alternative is to use a **graphics tablet** where the artist draws on a small area with an 'electronic pen'. Pointing

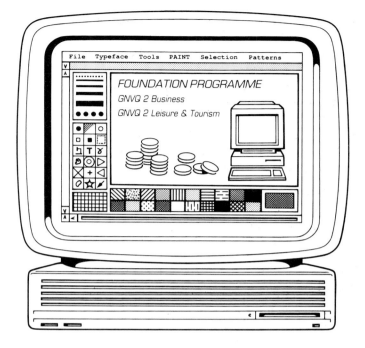

Figure 15.21

to different options enables him or her to obtain different thicknesses of line, brush strokes, special effects etc.

Main features

Pencil	This is used to draw ordinary lines.
Eraser	To rub out mistakes!
Spraycan	To create a paint spray effect.
Delete	To remove lines or parts of an object.
Copy	Will replicate a drawing somewhere else.
Move	Allows you to change the position of anything you have drawn.
Gridlock	Enables you to position items precisely by aligning them to a predetermined set of points.
Toolbox	May include different items (e.g. to enable you to cut out parts of your drawing).
Text	Enables you to type small amounts of text.

Additional features

Rotate	Allows you to rotate a drawing to see it from different angles.

Zoom	Enables you to focus on a particular part of the drawing and make very precise changes.
Shapes	Gives you a wide variety of shapes (e.g. squares, rectangles, circles).
Patterns	Enables you to fill in shapes with different patterns, or create some of your own.

situation being portrayed. A headset contains stereo earphones for sound and the user either sits in a specially designed console or puts on a 'datasuit' so that all the movements of the body are electronically sensed and transmitted.

Virtual reality systems are used for flight test simulators, robot control in environments where humans cannot exist (e.g. space stations) and in computer arcade games.

DID YOU KNOW?

1 Most of the graphics you see on television are today produced on computer using sophisticated graphics packages. These are then animated to produce many of the effects you see on screen.
2 A **pixel** is the name given to a small block on a drawing. The higher the resolution of your VDU the smaller (and more) pixels you have. You can therefore obtain better effects on a graphics package. If you zoom into a picture you normally see part of it pixel by pixel and you can change each one of these separately if you wish.

USING A GRAPHICS PACKAGE

1 Learn how to use the mouse – without it you're lost!
2 Find out how to load the program (and any files on disk), save and quit before you do anything else.
3 Play with the items in the toolbox or paintbox – see what effects you create. Don't be frightened to experiment because this is one case where you truly 'learn by doing'. Don't forget, you can always erase disasters and if you select the wrong option then pressing 'Esc' (escape) will usually put you back to the beginning.
4 Learn how to print out your work. The quality will be far higher if you have access to a laser printer.

DID YOU KNOW?

Virtual reality is the name given to the latest types of animated graphics which are so realistic that the user acts as if he or she is in the

· DESKTOP PUBLISHING PACKAGES ·

A desktop publishing package is neither a graphics package nor a word-processing package. It is one which enables you to put together text and graphics to produce a variety of documents (e.g. notices, posters, reports, presentations and newspapers). However, DTP packages can also be used to design simple graphics, such as shaded boxes for title pages of projects. Apart from the basic graphics and simple lines of text, other graphics and text are created using other types of software and then 'imported' into the DTP package where they are merged into one document, usually referred to as a **publication** (see Figure 15.22).

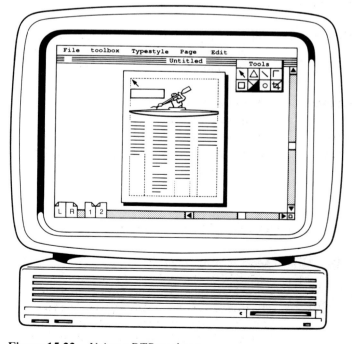

Figure 15.22 *Using a DTP package*

Main features

Text   This is usually input on a compatible word-processing package and then imported into the publication.

Fonts   This refers to the size and shape of the text. The variations you can achieve will depend on your printer but there are several typefaces and sizes from which you can choose.

Graphics   These are usually input via a document scanner which may be a full scanner or a small one which is held in the hand. All graphics should be 'clean' before they are scanned, because it is time-consuming removing all the dirty marks which have also been scanned in.

Toolbox   This will enable you to draw lines and shapes, shade them and resize, cut or trim any graphics on your document.

Lines   These can be drawn to any length, to a variety of thicknesses and horizontally or vertically.

Shades   Can range from white through grey to black.

Columns   You can design your page to have columns if you wish (like a newspaper).

Additional features

Rulers   These are guide lines which show on screen but not on your finished document. They enable you to align your text properly.

Guides   These will enable you to position text and graphics more precisely.

Text wrap   This will automatically wrap text around any drawings or graphics you import into your publication

DID YOU KNOW?

Clip-art is the name given to pre-drawn shapes and designs which have been produced already. You can buy disks of these and use them as you wish by importing them into your own document. You can resize them if you wish. At the back of this book are some examples of clip-art which you can scan into your own computer, if you have a scanner, and use them to enhance your own designs.

Using a desktop publishing package

1 Learn how to load the package, start a new publication and/or load a saved publication.
2 Again, being able to use a mouse is essential.
3 Find out how to design your page (e.g. if you want columns of a certain number or width).
4 Find out how to import text you have produced on a word-processing package and how to adjust this to fit your columns.
5 Experiment with the different fonts and typefaces you have available to find out which you can use with your printer and which give the best effects.
6 Find out how to import or scan in graphics and how to size these. It is important that you keep these in proportion or the results can be disastrous. You can easily make someone or something extremely fat or thin if you alter the width but not the height!
7 Learn some of the basic rules about design: leaving white space for effect, not putting too much information on one page, using margins effectively etc. (see Chapter 10).
8 Don't be frightened to experiment. Some DTP packages are quite difficult to get used to, keep your ideas simple and straightforward to start with and you are more likely to be successful!

DID YOU KNOW?

Hypermedia packages are now available that will store, retrieve and manipulate information in the form of text, graphics and **sound**. Today computers are commonplace in recording studios. They are linked to electronic instruments with a MIDI (musical instrument digital interface) socket (e.g. a MIDI keyboard) and the 'sound' is then transferred to the computer. Other effects can be added (e.g. rhythms via a drum machine) and laid down on separate tracks. A **sequencer** program is used to coordinate all the instruments and create the final product. Perhaps the day of the musician is over?

· PAYROLL PACKAGES ·

These packages are very popular in many companies because they save hours of work calculating and producing wages documentation.

The package itself is actually a very sophisticated form of database which has been programmed with the latest National Insurance and income tax rates. If these change during the year the suppliers of the package send an updated disk to their customers containing the new information. This is then loaded into the computer and the rates are automatically revised.

Main features

Constant (i.e. unchanging) information on the company and the employees is entered. It is, of course, possible that *some* 'constant' details may change (e.g. an employee may move home) but generally the following items will remain unchanged:

- **company details** – name of the organisation, tax office reference, bank details, pay rates, etc.
- **employee details** – name and number of each employee, address, date of birth, NI number, tax code, rate of pay, bank details, union information, etc.

Variable data is information which changes from one week or month to the next. It includes hours worked, overtime, holiday pay, sick pay and deductions (see Figure 15.23). In a large organisation this may be entered on a daily basis.

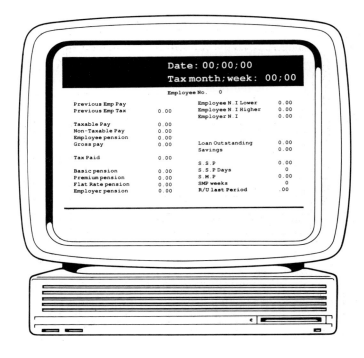

Figure 15.23 *Using a payroll package*

Additional features

Payroll processing	The system will automatically calculate the gross pay, deductions and net pay of each employee and print out the pay slip.
Cheque payments	The package may print a list of cheques required or even print the actual cheques.
Credit transfers	This is a list of all personnel who will be paid direct through the banking system. This list can then be taken directly to the bank.
Year end process	The package will produce P60s and P45s as required as well as providing a complete listing for the Inland Revenue.

· ACCOUNTS PACKAGES ·

There is a variety of accounts packages on the market today, (see Figure 15.24) many aimed at small businesses. A good accounts package will not only keep a record of all purchases, sales and cash/credit transactions but will also undertake all the book-keeping required for the business.

Main features

Customer/ supplier records	The package usually includes a basic database for entering all customers and suppliers, together with their address, telephone number and discounts allowed.
Cash/credit transactions	The package divides transactions into two types – those payments which are immediate and those which are deferred (e.g. where the customer is given several weeks to pay).
VAT calculations	If the organisation is registered for VAT then this is automatically calculated on each document and recorded in a separate VAT account.
Month-end reports	These can be generated at the end of each month to print out the 'accounts' for the company.

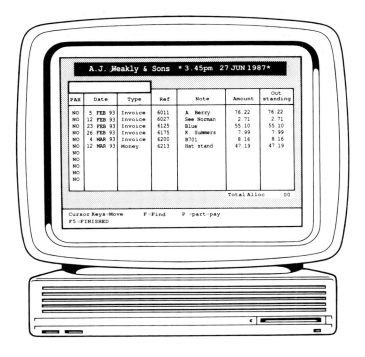

Figure 15.24 *Using a an accounts package*

| Year-end reports | The package will automatically produce the profit and loss account and balance sheet at the end of each year. |

Additional features

| Lists and reports | These can include details of money outstanding, money which must be paid, a list of all transactions to date, details of cash received or paid and lists of customers or suppliers. |

DID YOU KNOW?

Some accounts packages can be integrated with payroll packages so that the wages totals are automatically transferred to the wages account and the company's bank account automatically credited with the total amount paid.

Stock control packages can also be integrated so that the value of stock each month, and the amount spent on stock, is also transferred to the accounts section of the package so that all the figures agree.

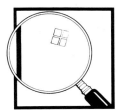

Evidence Assignment 15F

Your brother owns a small retail business. He is a good salesman but a useless accountant! He employs two part-time staff and every week he moans about having to calculate their wages and keep his accounts. He has just found out that he will now have to register for VAT as his sales figures have gone above the minimum level for registration. This means even more accounts work and he is looking desperate. Write him a letter telling him of the advantages of using a computer to do most of this work for him. If possible, obtain details of at least two low-cost packages which he could use. List their main features and the cost of *both* the hardware and the software.

· HEALTH AND SAFETY AND IT ·

People who are asked to work on computers for the first time may be concerned about health and safety implications. This does not mean they are worried that when they plug in or use a computer they will get an electric shock! The main concerns are over:

- backache
- eye strain
- headaches and migraine
- RSI
- using VDUs when pregnant.

Backache is usually caused through poor seating, bad posture or sitting for hours on end at a computer. Eye strain can be caused by flickering screens, poor lighting, sunshine reflecting on a screen or by staring at a VDU for a long time. Headaches and migraine often follow on from eye strain.

RSI stands for **repetitive strain injury** and is caused by making repetitive or awkward movements over and over again. A common form of this is tenosynovitis, which occurs when the tendon sheaths in the hand, wrist or arm become inflamed as a result of constantly hitting the keys to input data. The initial symptoms are aching, tenderness or numbness, but as the swelling increases movements become more restricted and painful and some people lose the ability to grip altogether. By then the pain may have spread to the neck and shoulders. Left untreated, tenosynovitis may cause irreversible damage and permanent disability.

Some pregnant women are concerned that radiation or other emissions from VDUs may harm their unborn child. Special shields can be attached to VDUs to protect them but, as yet, there is no evidence that VDUs give off rays in enough quantity to be harmful.

Health and safety legislation

Directives issued by the European Community on IT and health and safety are now law. These lay down certain standards on equipment, seating and lighting.

- **Seating** – All chairs must be capable of swivelling up and down and be on a movable base (i.e. castors). The chair should be comfortable and have an adjustable back rest to give the support which is required.
- **VDU desks** must not reflect light, must be 68 cm high and be large enough to hold all the equipment plus any paperwork.
- **Keyboards** must be separate from VDUs and adjustable to lie flat or slope upwards at an angle of between 10 and 15 degrees. The keys should have a matt finish. Good keyboard design is essential to reduce or prevent the chance of RSI. Keys should be concave to reduce the risk of fingers slipping off them *and* to reduce the shock on the fingertips, fingers, wrists and arms.
- **VDU screens** must be adjustable in terms of the angle at which they are positioned and the brightness and contrast of the screen. The screen should be non-reflective and flicker-free.

In addition the directives include the right for VDU operators to:

- have a free eye test prior to VDU work and regularly thereafter
- have regular rest breaks
- be involved in the evaluation of workstations.

Evidence Assignment 15G

Imagine you are employed as an assistant in the Personnel Department of Quantum Electronics. The Personnel Manager is Ms Margery Stevens. The company employs several staff as VDU operators and has recently changed its policy in line with the EC directives. In future all operators will:

- receive a free eye test at regular periods
- have regular rest breaks away from their machines.

In addition the main office areas where VDUs are sited have been redecorated and new lighting and new workstations have been installed.

To make sure that all employees know why these measures have been taken, and other important aspects of working with VDUs and health and safety, Ms Stevens has decided to hold a short training session for all VDU staff tomorrow afternoon. She has asked you and your colleagues to:

a Carry out your own research on this subject, both from the information provided and from that available in the library. She has suggested that you might like to obtain additional information by contacting your local HSE (Health and Safety Executive) office. The address is in your phone book.

b Prepare a short (ten-minute) presentation to highlight the main points. Use visual aids such as overhead transparencies to make your main points.

c Prepare a simple booklet which will summarise the main points and which can be given to all staff who attend the training session. If possible, create this on a desktop publishing package or integrated word-processing and graphics package so that you can include illustrations where these would be appropriate.

· SECURITY SYSTEMS ·

You have already learned that security systems exist to:

- prevent the accidental erasure of information on a disk (page 434)

- prevent the accidental erasure of formulae within a spreadsheet (see page 453)
- prevent unauthorised people from using a computer network (see page 429).

In some computer installations very elaborate security procedures exist to prevent access by unauthorised individuals to certain areas. These may include locked doors which will only respond to a key code, a swipe card or even a voice or hand print!

However, most organisations have a system of user identification (**IDs**) and **passwords** to prevent or restrict access to important or confidential information, such as bank account information, staff wages and salaries, customer accounts, and the contents of electronic mailboxes. Each user will have his or her own ID. Against this the computer department will have a set of authorities for that particular person. This may restrict or prevent access to certain files. For instance:

- Category A files may be unobtainable
- Category B files may be read only
- Category C files may be available to be read and amended.

A director of the company may have full access to all files. A junior employee may be able to view category C files. A supervisor may be able to view some files and have full access to others, and so on.

In addition, each user will have his or her own password. This has to be used in conjunction with the ID and enables the computer to check whether the person logging on is the genuine user. Needless to say, no-one is expected to tell someone else his or her password. All passwords should be:

- changed frequently
- remembered – not written down
- original words rather than obvious ones (e.g. using the password 'Xmas' in the middle of December and 'holiday' in the middle of July!).

A final precaution may be to make certain files inaccessible unless a specific password is known. This may only be given to high ranking people in the organisation or those in charge of, say, computer maintenance who may need to be able to access system or operating files not available to anyone else.

DID YOU KNOW?

1 When you type in a password it *doesn't* show on screen. If it did, anybody standing near you would be able to read it and use it themselves later!
2 A 'hacker' is a person who illegally gains entry into a computer system by working out the password. Many films and television programmes have been made about hackers and you may find reports of their activities in the newspapers.

Computers and the law

Data kept in a computer is covered by the **Data Protection Act 1984**, which gives legal rights to individuals regarding personal data held about them on computer.

- Companies who hold data on people on computer *must* register as data users with the Data Protection Registrar.
- Any information held on computer must have been acquired legally.
- Personal data must not be disclosed to others for any reason which is not compatible with the purpose for which it is held.
- The data must be accurate and kept up to date and not excessive for the purpose for which it is required.
- Proper security measures must be taken against unauthorised access to the data or alteration, disclosure, loss or destruction of the information held.
- Personal records should not be kept longer than is necessary.

Under the provisions of the Act a person can find out the information which is held on him or her by:

- referring to the Data Protection Register (a copy is held in all major libraries) which lists all holders of data
- writing to the holder and asking for a copy of the data held.

A holder *cannot* refuse to give the information unless the data is held for national security. In addition, information on criminal, tax and social work records may also be withheld.

However, finding out information is not necessarily free! It can cost over £10 a time to find what data is being held.

You should note that the Data Protection Act covers information *only* about 'people' held on computer – with the exception of an organisation's own payroll. Exemptions include:

- information on companies or other topics (e.g. a book or car list)
- all manual systems
- information held on personal computer systems for household use only.

DID YOU KNOW?

One of the biggest headaches for computer maintenance staff is not hackers or unauthorised access to information, but **viruses**. A virus is a rogue program which is introduced into a computer system and which can create untold damage. This may include blanking screens, blanking hard disks or even making the whole system inoperable. Floppy disks 'carry' the virus – if a floppy disk becomes 'infected' then it will pass on the virus to every other computer in which it is used.

Floppy disks which are suspected of carrying the virus are 'swept'. This checks if the virus is present. If it is then the only solution is to wipe the disk clean. This not only gets rid of the virus but also any other information on the disk. For that reason it is sensible to keep back-up copies of all your work – and the content of your hard disk – safely locked away. Otherwise you could lose important and irretrievable information for ever.

Evidence Assignment 15H

Imagine that your school or college has a networked system for computer users. Most students are regular users of the electronic mail system and also use the computer for IT assignments. All students have their own disks which they take from room to room. In recent weeks there have been several problems with security:

- Insulting messages have been sent to some students on the electronic mail system.
- Several students have been printing out information from the student database and giving out other people's addresses and telephone numbers.
- Computers have been left on overnight which has resulted in 'screen burn' to several machines.
- Last week a virus was found in one of the IT rooms. All the disks had to be swept and several students lost page after page of a project they had been working on for months.

The head of IT wants to make some changes.

1 Produce a report on a word-processor giving your solutions for improving security to either minimise or prevent these problems from occurring.

2 Prepare a poster on a desk-top publishing or graphics package which states the main rules that students should follow and which can be put up in every computer room.

· QUICK REFERENCE SECTION ·

The following are all IT terms you should know. Read them once through and then check that *you* could write a definition for each one which closely resembles that given below. Note that words and phrases that are **highlighted** are those for which a separate definition is to be found elsewhere in the list.

Applications package	A package containing a program designed to carry out a specific task for the benefit of the user (e.g. an accounts package or a word-processing package, plus all the instructions and manuals for the program).
Backing store	A device for storing programs and data in memory (e.g. a disk drive).
Back-up copies	Copying data on to floppy disks for use if the first disk or hard disk fails to work.
Bar-code	A pattern of bars and spaces which can be read by a computer scanner.

Bubble jet printer   See **Ink jet**.

Buffer   The part of memory which stores data temporarily. For instance, documents may be held in a printer buffer until the printer is free to print them.

Bug   An error in a program which causes it to fail or not to operate properly.

Byte   The amount of computer memory required to store one character of data. A byte contains eight bits. Computer memory is measured in bytes (e.g. **kilobytes** and **megabytes**).

CAD (computer aided design)   Using computers to create drawings and designs which may be 2-dimensional, 3-dimensional or even animated.

CAM (computer aided manufacture)   Using computers to help in the production of goods (e.g. by controlling robots or machines).

CD-ROM   A compact disk with a **read only memory**. The disk is manufactured with the data in place and this cannot be changed by the user.

CPU (central processing unit)   The 'brain' of the computer which processes information, carries out instructions and controls the **peripherals**.

Character set   A set of symbols which can be recognised and used by the computer.

COM   Producing microfilm on a mainframe computer.

Cursor   The symbol which shows the position where the next character will appear. It is usually a small flashing block which may appear in reverse mode.

Daisywheel printer   A printer which has a small plastic or metal disk with many spokes – called petals. Each petal contains a character. The disk rotates and strikes against a ribbon to print text but not graphics.

Database   A program which enables the user to reorganise and re-sort data to give particular types of information.

Data communications   The sending or receiving of data and information by telephone, fax or computer (e.g. electronic mail).

Data protection   Safeguards for individuals to ensure that information about them which is held on computer is used only for specified purposes.

Data security   Measures which are taken to prevent data being lost or misused (e.g. user IDs, passwords and write-protect mechanisms on floppy disks).

Desktop publishing   Packages which bring together text and graphics to produce newsletters, posters and other types of advertising material.

Digitiser   A device which enables a video signal to be displayed on a computer.

Directory   A list of file names under specific headings.

Disk   A backing store for data.

Document reader   An input device which recognises characters on preprinted documents.

DOS (disk operating system)   The most common type of operating system for micro-computers.

Dot matrix printer   A printer which produces characters by making a pattern of small dots. The final result is not of a high quality but suitable for internal documents (e.g. payroll and accounts listings).

EPOS (electronic point of sale)   Electronic cash registers which read bar-codes via a scanner and automatically print itemised till receipts and adjust stock levels.

Email   Electronic mail – messages are sent

from one user to another and stored in the user's personal mailbox.

File A collection of data in a computer's memory.

File access The ability to read or amend the data in a particular file.

Floppy disk A flexible and removable disk on which data is stored.

Font The printing design of a set of characters.

Format The layout and design of a document.

Gigabyte Generally used to represent 1000 **megabytes**. More precisely is equal to 1024 megabytes.

Graphical user interface (GUI) The way in which a user communicates with the computer (i.e. by using a menu or clicking on an icon). The latter method involves the use of a **mouse**.

Graphics programs Programs which enable the creation of drawings and paintings on a computer.

Graphics tablet A device which enables drawings to be input into a computer by moving a stylus over a special pad.

Hacking Illegal access to a computer.

Hard disk A non-removable disk which can contain large amounts of data.

Hardware The physical components of a computer system.

Hypermedia Software in which text, pictures and music may be linked to create a presentation.

Icon A small picture which represents the function a user may wish to use.

Impact printer A printer which creates characters by hitting an inked ribbon which transfers the image to the paper beneath.

Ink jet printer A printer which creates graphics and text by spraying fine jets of ink onto paper.

Input device A device for entering data into a computer.

Joystick A vertical control stick which operates as an input device for computer games.

Justification The alignment of text to the left or right of a page.

Kilobyte A unit of computer memory which equals 1024 bytes.

Laptop computer A portable microcomputer.

Laser printer A printer in which a high quality image is formed by laser beams.

Light pen An input device which can indicate certain locations on a computer screen.

LAN (local area network) A system which links computers over a small geographical area (e.g. between certain rooms or buildings).

Log off The process by which a network user exits the system.

Log on The process by which a network user identifies himself or herself to the system.

Mainframe computer A powerful computer with a large memory capacity.

Megabyte Memory equal to 1024 **kilobytes** (sometimes used for 1 million bytes).

Memory The storage of data or programs on a temporary or permanent basis.

Menu A list of options for the user to choose.

MIDI (musical instrument digital interface) An interface which enables electronic musical instruments to be linked to a computer.

Modem A device which enables computer data to be transmitted over a telephone line.

Mouse An input device which is used to manipulate objects and select options on a computer screen.

Multimedia See **Hypermedia**.

Network A series of connected computers which share the same data and programs.

Notebook computer A small, portable computer.

OCR (optical character recognition) The means by which text can be recognised and input into a computer via a scanner.

Optical disks Laser disks which can store vast amounts of information.

Output device A device for displaying computer data and information.

Palmtop computer A tiny computer which can be held in the palm of the hand.

Password A secret word which confirms the authenticity of the user.

Peripheral A device which is linked to or controlled by a computer.

Pixel A single dot on a computer screen.

Plotter An output device which draws pictures or diagrams, often in colour.

Prestel The viewdata service provided by British Telecom.

Publication A document produced on a desktop publishing system.

RAM (random access memory) Memory which can be read and changed by the computer but which is lost when the computer is switched off.

ROM (read only memory) Memory which can only be read but cannot be changed (e.g. the operating system of the computer).

Root directory The top directory in a 'tree-and-branch' filing system.

Scanner A device which produces a digital image of a document for inputting and storing in a computer.

Scrolling Moving data on a VDU screen upwards or downwards to view lines at the top or bottom of the document.

Search A specific request for information by the user of a database.

Smart card A plastic card which stores data (e.g. bank account details or an ID number) and which can be used to gain or display information or obtain access.

Software Computer programs.

Speech synthesis Computer generated speech (e.g. directory enquiries).

Spreadsheet A program which enables calculations to be input and analysed.

Systems program A program designed to enable the computer to operate.

Teletext A form of on-line database for television users. Ceefax is available on BBC; Oracle on ITV and Channel 4.

Touch screen A screen which enables the user to input data by touching certain parts of the screen.

Tree-and-branch filing A system where files are stored in directories. Main directories may be sub-divided into smaller directories and so on.

User documentation Instructions and manuals provided with a computer program.

User ID The special name input to identify a certain user.

Virtual reality Computer simulation where the participant perceives himself or herself as part of an simulated environment.

VDU (visual display unit) The screen on which computer data **is** displayed.

Virus — Rogue program which can transfer itself from one computer to another via floppy disk and which can damage or destroy data.

Voice output — See **Speech synthesis**.

WAN (wide area network) — A network which connects computers over a wide geographical area.

Word-processor — A program which allows for the manipulation, storage and retrieval of text.

Worksheet — A spreadsheet currently being worked on.

WORM (write once read many times) — Similar to a CD-ROM. Once the disk contains data it cannot be erased or replaced.

WYSIWYG (what you see is what you get) — A program which prints documents in the same format as that shown on screen.

ANSWERS

Answers to Activity on page 375

1 I am sending you the items today.
2 Details of the new product are to be found on page 2.
3 I think you and I should have a meeting.
4 For what reason do you want this information? (*or* Why do you want this information?)
5 Neither the manager not his assistant had heard about the change in plans.
6 He promised to deal urgently with the matter.

Answers to Activity on page 376

1 He wants to see you and me.
2 The trainee forgot to read carefully the instructions (*or* to read the instructions carefully).
3 She is someone with whom I have always had difficulty (*or* - if you are stuck – I always find her difficult).
4 He never has any time for us.
5 I confirm our recent telephone conversation.
6 I should be pleased if you would provide the information I need (*or* I shall be pleased if you will provide the information I need).

Answers to Activity on page 377

a To/too/two
● I have to see you immediately.
● There are two immediate improvements which can be made.
● It is far too warm in here.

b There/their
● Put the shopping over there.
● There is no reason for the delay.
● Where have they put their belongings?

c Past/passed
● He passed me in the corridor without speaking to me.
● In the past he has been very helpful.
● He passed his examination and gained a distinction.

d Of/off
● He is a man of few words.
● Please keep off the grass.

e Whose/who's
● Who's waving at you?
● Whose coat have you borrowed?

f Affect/effect
● What effect will these figures have on the overall position?
● Will it affect you at all?

g Personal/personnel
● The personnel manager was concerned about the changes made to the staff training programme.
● My personal view is that it is too risky.

h Principle/principal
● The principal talked to members of the students' union about the new identity card.
● I think the principal item on the agenda should be the possible redundancies in the warehouse.
● I agree with it in principle but need some more information before I can act.

i Practice/practise
● I think he must learn to practise what he preaches.
● The practice of using Ms rather than Mrs or Miss has increased over the past few years.

Answers to Activity on page 378

(Note that you may have slightly different answers to questions 3 and 4. Check with your tutor whether your answer is still correct.)

1	
manufactured	made
terminate	end
emancipate	free
commencement	beginning
ascend	climb

2 ● She asked for an estimate.
   ● The car reversed into the wall

- The noise from the engine was incessant
- The relief from the pain was only momentary.
- I can't get spare parts for your television as it is now obsolete.
- The supervisor found that the new employee was incompetent.
- The maintenance of the machinery is essential in our business.

3 - Can you include me when you are making arrangements for the trip to the match?
- If you can wait for a week or two I shall be able to give you the information then.
- Thank you for your help. It was most useful.

4 - 'At the beginning of the evening I was walking along the road when I saw a tramp trying to break in to a parked car. I asked him what he was doing and he struck me hard across my face.'

Answer to second Activity on page 379

When we were little and had visitors to the house, grandma didn't read to us. Instead we talked to the visitors and tried to make them play games like 'hide and seek' with us. One visitor, Uncle Bernard, was particularly good at this although sometimes he got bored and shouted, 'I'm here'. The game then ended.

Answer to third Activity on page 379

You may remember that I raised the matter of an exchange visit with colleagues working in a college in San Diego. I have now received a request from them to send details of anyone interested in taking part in this exchange. It may be necessary to have a meeting to discuss the matter further. Give me a ring if you are interested.

Answers to first Activity on page 380

- I got up late, had no breakfast and ran all the way to the bus stop.

- I sent him to the shop to buy paint, wallpaper and brushes.
- Fatima, please answer the telephone.
- James and Richard, the two best tennis players, met in the final.

Answers to second Activity on page 380

Don't worry, I know she'll be here before long. In the meantime, can you try to borrow Frank's calculator. Yours is not working. John's not in because he's gone to collect the Managing Director's car. Its also important for you to make certain that all the typists' desks conform to the health and safety standards.

Answers to first Activity on page 381

- The chairman said, 'I welcome you to this meeting'.
- Which television personality uses the catch phrase, 'Nice to see you, to see you, nice'?
- I had never heard of the expression 'It's not over until the fat lady sings'.

Answers to second Activity on page 381

- There are many colleges in Britain.
- She wants to attend Bristol University.
- Mary and Danny went to Nottingham to visit the firm and to see the Personnel Manager. To write personnel manager is also correct.

Answer to third Activity on page 381

In business you must be good at accounts. You should be able to check figures accurately and also to calculate the correct amount each time. It is helpful if you can remember to write clearly and to separate one line of figures from another. Only competent managers are promoted.

QUALPRINT LTD
22 CARNEI WAY
GLENDALE
NEWSHIRE
FE1 8CA

Tel: 032 745612

ORDER

VAT Reg. No. 680/73842/88

To:

Date:

Order No.:

Please supply:

QUANTITY	DESCRIPTION	REF. NO.	UNIT PRICE

Delivery:

Signed:

QUALPRINT
Goods Received Note

Supplier:

GRN No.:
Date:
Delivery Note No.:

ORDER NO.	QUANTITY	DESCRIPTION	REF NO.

Received by _____

QUALPRINT LTD
22 CARNEI WAY
GLENDALE
NEWSHIRE
FE1 8CA

DELIVERY NOTE

To:

VAT REG NO 680/73842/88

YOUR ORDER NO.	INVOICE DATE/tax point	INVOICE NO.	DISPATCH DATE

QUANTITY	DESCRIPTION	CAT NO.

Received by _____   Date

QUALPRINT LTD
22 CARNEI WAY
GLENDALE
NEWSHIRE
FE1 8CA

TEL 032 745612

VAT REG NO 680/73842/88

INVOICE

To:

Deliver to:

Your order no.	Invoice date/tax point	Invoice no.	Despatch date

Quantity	Description	Cat. no	Unit price	Total price	VAT rate	VAT amount
			Delivery charges			
			Sub-total			
			VAT			
			Total amount due			

Terms:
E & O E

QUALPRINT LTD
22 CARNIE WAY
GLENDALE
NEWSHIRE
FE1 8CA

Tel: 032 745612

Fax: 032 849783

VAT REG NO 680/73842/88

STATEMENT

To:

Date: Account no.

Date	Details	Debit	Credit	Balance

FAX MESSAGE

FROM: Qualprint Ltd
        22 Carnei Way
        Glendale

FAX No: 032 849783

TO:

DATE:

Date _____

▼ The Royal Midshire Bank plc

Date _____ 19 __   16–13–99

_____

_____

Pay _____   or order

_____

£ _____

£ _____

265540

..·265540·16...1399:1 2890635...·

Date _____

▼ The Royal Midshire Bank plc

Date _____ 19 __   16–13–99

_____

_____

Pay _____   or order

_____

£ _____

£ _____

265541

..·265541·16...1399:1 2890635...·

▼ The Royal Midshire Bank plc

Account Pay-in
Acknowledgment

Teller's stamp
and initials

Total   £

Credit

Subject to verification of
items other than cash

▼ The Royal Midshire Bank plc

Account Pay-in

For credit of an account at this branch only

Teller's stamp
and initials

Date _____

Paid in by _____

Credit Name and A/c No

Items   Deferment

Qualprint Ltd

Pleas do not write or mark below this line

12890635

Notes over £20		
£20 Notes		
£10 Notes		
£5 Notes		
£1 Notes/Coin		
Silver		
Bronze		
Total Cash		
Cheques etc (See over)		
Total £		

Customers are advised to keep a record of the drawers of all cheques in the section below

Please carry this Total to front of slip

Postal and Money Orders

Cheques etc

£

£

Please do not write or mark below this line

QUALPRINT LTD – cashing up sheet

Date _____

Notes/coins	No. in till	Amount received
£50		
£20		
£10		
£5		
£1		
50p		
20p		
10p		
5p		
2p		
1p		
CASH TOTAL		
Cheques		
TOTAL		
Less £20 float		
TOTAL RECEIVED		

Signed _____

QUALPRINT LTD
22 Carnei Way
Glendale
Newshire
FE1 8CA

RECEIPT

No _____

RECEIVED FROM _____

the sum of _____

in payment of _____

£ _____

Received by _____

Date _____

PETTY CASH VOUCHER   No. _____   Date _____

Name:

Purpose (attach all receipts & invoices)	TOTAL (incl VAT)	VAT	Net (excl VAT)
	£	£	£

The sum of (in words as far to the left as possible)

Approved by: _____   date _____

Received by: _____   date _____

PETTY CASH VOUCHER   No: _____   Date _____

Name: Dept

Purpose (attach all receipts & invoices)	TOTAL (incl VAT)	VAT	Net (excl VAT)
	£	£	£

The sum of (in words as far to the left as possible)

Approved by: _____   date _____

Received by: _____   date _____

PAY ADVICE

Emp no	Employee name		Dept	Pay period

		NI no	Method of payment	Tax code

Pay and allowances

Hrs	Rate (£)	Amount (£)	Deductions	
			Item	Amt (£)

		Total pay to date
		Tax to date
		NI to date
	Total deductions	Taxable pay to date
GROSS PAY £	£	NET PAY £

LANDSHIRE COUNTY COUNCIL

FORM ESC/3

JOB APPLICATION FORM

Application for the post of ....

....

Please use block capitals for Sections 1, 4 and 8

1 Surname .... *First name(s)* ....

....

2 Date of birth ....

3 Address ....

....

....

4 Present post ....

5 Previous posts ....

....

6 Education

   (Please give details of secondary school/college/university attended – together with starting and leaving dates)

....

....

7 Qualifications

   (Please include dates, subjects and grades)

....

....

8 Referees

   (Please give the names and addresses of two persons to whom reference can be made)

....

....

9 Signature ....

   Date ....